Contents

PART III JACQUES DERRIDA *1984–2004*

Derrida

Derrida
A Biography

Benoît Peeters

Translated by
Andrew Brown

polity

First published in French as *Derrida* © Flammarion, 2010

This English edition © Polity Press, 2013

Reprinted 2021

Polity Press
65 Bridge Street
Cambridge CB2 1UR, UK

Polity Press
350 Main Street
Malden, MA 02148, USA

ISBN-13: 978-0-7456-5615-1
ISBN-13: 978-0-7456-5616-8

A catalogue record for this book is available from the British Library.

Typeset in 10.5 on 11.5 pt Times New Roman MT
by Servis Filmsetting Ltd, Stockport, Cheshire
Printed and bound in Great Britain by TJ Books Limited, Padstow, Cornwall

The publisher has used its best endeavours to ensure that the URLs for external websites referred to in this book are correct and active at the time of going to press. However, the publisher has no responsibility for the websites and can make no guarantee that a site will remain live or that the content is or will remain appropriate.

Every effort has been made to trace all copyright holders, but if any have been inadvertently overlooked the publisher will be pleased to include any necessary credits in any subsequent reprint or edition.

For further information on Polity, visit our website: www.politybooks.com

Acknowledgements

I can never thank Marguerite Derrida enough for placing her confidence in me, without which the present work would have been unimaginable. She gave me free access to the archives and answered my countless questions with patience and precision. I am also extremely grateful to Pierre and Jean, the sons of Marguerite and Jacques Derrida, as well as to René and Évelyne Derrida, Janine and Pierrot Meskel, Martine Meskel, and Micheline Lévy.

Many of Derrida's archives are kept at IMEC, the Institut Mémoires de l'Édition Contemporaine, at the Abbaye d'Ardenne. It was a particular pleasure to work there. Thanks are due to the whole of the team, in particular to Olivier Corpet, the general director, to Nathalie Léger, deputy director, to Albert Dichy, literary director, and to José Ruiz-Funes and Mélina Reynaud, who are in charge of the Derrida collection and his correspondence. Their friendly assistance and their competence have been of the greatest value to me. I must also thank Claire Paulhan, who suggested more than one fruitful path for me to follow.

The other part of Jacques Derrida's public archives is preserved in the 'Special Collections' of the University of California, Irvine. Thanks to Jackie Dooley, Steve McLeod, and their whole team for their great efficiency.

Particular thanks must also go to Patricia de Man, Jacqueline Laporte, Dominne and Hélène Milliex, Christophe Bident, Éric Hoppenot, Michael Levinas, Avital Ronell, Ginette Michaud, Michel Monory, Jean-Luc Nancy and Jean Philippe, as well as to Marianne Cayatte (archives of the Lycée Louis-le-Grand), André Vivet (Association des Anciens Élèves du Lycée Montesquieu in Le Mans), Françoise Fournié (archives of Gérard Granel), Myriam Watthee-Delmotte (Henry Bauchau collection in Louvain-la-Neuve), Catherine Goldenstein (Paul Ricoeur collection in Paris), Bruno Roy (archives of Roger Laporte), Claire Nancy (archives of Philippe Lacoue-Labarthe), and to all those who have enabled me to find rare letters or documents.

A huge thank you to those who have helped me, with their advice, their remarks, or their encouragements: to Valérie Lévy-Soussan, first and foremost, for lending me her ear, her advice, and her support every day, but also to Marie-Françoise Plissart, Sandrine Willems, Marc Avelot, Jan Baetens, Jean-Christophe Cambier, Luc Dellisse, Archibald and Vladimir Peeters, Hadrien and Gabriel Pelissier. Thanks also to Sophie Dufour, who transcribed several quotations, with both care and enthusiasm. And particular thanks to Christian Rullier: he knows why.

To Sophie Berlin, director of the Human Sciences department at Flammarion, I am immensely indebted. Without her, I would never have had the idea of embarking on this project, nor the energy to bring it to completion.

Translator's Acknowledgements

Thanks to Benoît Peeters for replying so readily to my questions and generously providing me with original source materials. Thanks also to Jean-Pacal Pouzet, Chloé Szebrat, and Jane Horton for help and advice. And thanks, most of all, to Justin Dyer for his scrupulous copy-editing and ability to track down the most recalcitrant translations of Derrida and company into English. All mistakes are my own (*toutes les erreurs me sont propres*). A few further reflections on Derrida and biography can be found at *http://benequildatuit.blogspot.co.uk*.

No one will ever know the secret from which I write and the fact that I say it changes nothing.

Jacques Derrida, 'Circumfession'

Introduction

Does a philosopher have a life? Can you write a philosopher's biography? This was the question raised, in October 1996, at a conference organized by New York University. In an improvised statement, Jacques Derrida began by saying:

> As you know, traditional philosophy excludes biography, it considers biography as something external to philosophy. You'll remember Heidegger's reference to Aristotle: 'What was Aristotle's life?' Well, the answer lay in a single sentence: 'He was born, he thought, he died.' And all the rest is pure anecdote.[1]

However, this was not Derrida's position. Already, in a 1976 paper on Nietzsche, he had written:

> We no longer consider the biography of a 'philosopher' as a corpus of empirical accidents that leaves both a name and a signature outside a system which would itself be offered up to an immanent philosophical reading – the only kind of reading held to be philosophically legitimate [. . .].[2]

Whereupon Derrida called for the invention of 'a new problematic of the biographical in general and of the biography of philosophers in particular', a rethinking of the borderline between 'corpus and body [*corps*]'. This preoccupation never left him. In a late interview, he again insisted that 'the question of "biography"' did not cause him any worries – indeed, one might say that it was of great interest to him:

> I am among those few people who have constantly drawn attention to this: you must (and you must do it *well*) put philosophers' biographies back in the picture, and the commitments, particularly political commitments, that they sign in their own names, whether in relation to Heidegger or equally to Hegel, Freud, Nietzsche, Sartre, or Blanchot, and so on.[3]

Within his own works, Derrida himself was not averse, when discussing Walter Benjamin, Paul de Man, and several others, to bringing in biographical material. In *Glas*, for example, he frequently quotes Hegel's correspondence, referring to his family and his financial worries, without considering these texts to be minor or extraneous to his philosophical work.

In one of the last sequences of the film on Derrida made by Kirby Dick and Amy Ziering Kofman, Derrida went even further, replying provocatively to the question of what he would like to discover from a documentary about Kant, Hegel, or Heidegger:

> I'd like to hear them talk about their sexual lives. What was the sexual life of Hegel or Heidegger? [. . .] Because it's something they don't talk about. I'd like to hear them discuss something they don't talk about. Why do philosophers present themselves in their works as asexual beings? Why have they effaced their private lives from their work? Why do they never talk about personal things? I'm not saying someone should make a porn film about Hegel or Heidegger. I want to hear them talking about the part love plays in their lives.

Even more significantly, autobiography – that of others, Rousseau and Nietzsche mainly, but his own too – was for Derrida a fully fledged philosophical object: both the principles underlying it and the details contained in it were worthy of consideration. In his view, autobiographical writing was even *the* genre, the one which had first given him a hankering to write, and never ceased to haunt him. Ever since his teens, he had been dreaming of a sort of immense journal of his life and thought, of an uninterrupted, polymorphous text – one that would be, so to speak, absolute:

> Memoirs, in a form that does not correspond to what are generally called memoirs, are the general form of everything that interests me – the wild desire to preserve everything, to gather everything together in its idiom. And philosophy, or academic philosophy at any rate, for me has always been at the service of this autobiographical design of memory.[4]

Derrida gave us these Memoirs that are not Memoirs by disseminating them across many of his works. 'Circumfession', *The Post Card*, *Monolingualism of the Other*, *Veils*, *Memoirs of the Blind*, *Counterpath*,[*] and many other texts, including many late interviews,

---

* In most cases, especially for his first works, Derrida preferred to go against common use and avoid capital letters in the French titles of his books. 'I agree – *L'écriture et la différence* [*Writing and difference*]', Philippe Sollers wrote to him in a

as well as the two films about him, add up to an autobiography that is fragmentary but rich in concrete and sometimes quite intimate details: what he on occasion referred to as an '*autobiothanatoheterographical opus*'. I have drawn a great deal on these invaluable notes and sketches, comparing them with other sources whenever possible.

In this book, I will not be seeking to provide an introduction to the philosophy of Jacques Derrida, let alone a new interpretation of a work whose breadth and richness will continue to defy commentators for years to come. But I would like to present the biography of a philosophy at least as much as the story of an individual. So I will mainly focus on readings and influences, the genesis of the principal works, their turbulent reception, the struggles in which Derrida was engaged, and the institutions he founded. However, this will not be an *intellectual biography*. I find this label irritating for several reasons; mainly the exclusions it seems to involve: childhood, family, love, material life. For Derrida himself – as he explained in his interviews with Maurizio Ferraris – 'the expression "intellectual biography"' was in any case deeply problematic. Even more so, a century after the birth of psychoanalysis, was the phrase 'conscious intellectual life'. And the boundary between public life and private life seemed just as fragile and wavering to him:

> At a certain moment in the life and career of a public man, of what is called – following pretty hazy criteria – a public man, any private archive, supposing that this isn't a contradiction in terms, is destined to become a public archive if it isn't immediately burned (and even then, on condition that, once burned, it does not leave behind it the speaking and burning ash of various symptoms archivable by interpretation or public rumour).[5]

So this biography has refused to exclude anything. Writing the life of Jacques Derrida means writing the story of a Jewish boy from Algiers, excluded from school at the age of twelve, who became the French philosopher whose works have been the most widely translated throughout the world; the story of a fragile and tormented man who, to the end of his life, continued to see himself as 'rejected' by the French university system. It means bringing back to life such different worlds as pre-independence Algeria, the microcosm of the École Normale Supérieure, the structuralist period, and the turbulent events of 1968 and afterwards. It means describing an

1967 pre-publication letter. [Sollers' point is that the French title would more usually be *L'Écriture et la différence*. Derrida's – inconsistent – practice cannot always be followed in the English translations, nor of course, *a fortiori*, in German. – Tr.]

exceptional series of friendships with major writers and philosophers, from Louis Althusser to Maurice Blanchot, and from Jean
Genet to Hélène Cixous, by way of Emmanuel Levinas and Jean-
Luc Nancy. It means going over a no less long series of polemics,
waged over serious issues but often brutal in tone, with thinkers
such as Claude Lévi-Strauss, Michel Foucault, Jacques Lacan, John
R. Searle, and Jürgen Habermas, as well as several controversies
that spilled over from academic circles into a wider audience, the
most celebrated of them concerning Heidegger and Paul de Man.
It means retracing a series of courageous political commitments in
support of Nelson Mandela, illegal immigrants, and gay marriage.
It means relating the fortune of a concept – deconstruction – and
its extraordinary influence that went far beyond the philosophical world, affecting literary studies, architecture, law, theology,
feminism, queer studies, and postcolonial studies.

In order to carry out this project, I have of course embarked on as
complete as possible a reading or rereading of an oeuvre which is, as
everyone knows, very prolific: eighty published works and innumerable uncollected texts and interviews. I have explored the secondary
literature as much as possible. But I have relied mainly on the considerable archives that Derrida has left us, as well as on meetings
with a hundred or so witnesses.

The archive was, for the author of *Paper Machine*, a real passion
and a constant theme for reflection. But it was also a very concrete
reality. As he stated on one of his last public appearances: 'I've
never lost or destroyed anything. Not even the little notes [. . .]
that Bourdieu or Balibar used to stick on my door [. . .] I've got
everything. The most important things and the most apparently
insignificant things.'[6] Derrida wanted these documents to be openly
accessible. He went so far as to explain:

> The great fantasy [. . .] is that all these papers, books or texts,
> or floppy disks, are already living after me. They are already
> witnesses. I'm always thinking about it – about those who will
> come after my death and have a look at, for example, such and
> such a book I read in 1953 and will ask: 'Why did he put a tick
> by that, or an arrow there?' I'm obsessed by the structure of
> survival [*la structure survivante*] of each of these bits of paper,
> these traces.[7]

The major part of these personal archives is gathered in two collections, which I have methodically explored: the Special Collection of
the Langson Library at the University of California, Irvine; and the
Derrida collection at the IMEC – the Institut Mémoires de l'Édition
Contemporaine – at the Abbaye d'Ardenne, near Caen. I've gradu-

ally familiarized myself with a handwriting that all of Derrida's friends knew was difficult to decipher, and I was lucky enough to be the first person to be able to measure the incredible sum of documents accumulated by Derrida throughout his life: school work, personal notebooks, manuscript versions of books, unpublished classes and seminars, the transcriptions of interviews and debates, press articles, and, of course, his correspondence.

While he scrupulously preserved the least little letter that he was sent – and was still regretting, a few months before he died, the only correspondence that he had destroyed* –, Derrida only rarely made drafts or copies of his own letters. So considerable research has been necessary to track down and consult the most significant of these exchanges: for example, those with Louis Althusser, Paul Ricoeur, Maurice Blanchot, Michel Foucault, Emmanuel Levinas, Gabriel Bounoure, Philippe Sollers, Paul de Man, Roger Laporte, Jean-Luc Nancy, Philippe Lacoue-Labarthe, and Sarah Kofman. Even more valuable are certain letters sent to friends of Derrida's youth, such as Michel Monory and Lucien Bianco, during his formative years. Many others cannot be located or have been lost, such as the great number of letters sent by Derrida to his parents.

One far from negligible detail is that I embarked on this biography in the immediate aftermath of Derrida's death, just when we had barely started to enter into 'the return of Jacques Derrida', to quote a phrase of Bernard Stiegler. Begun in 2007, it was published in 2010, the year when he would have been eighty. So it would have been absurd to draw only on written material when most of the philosopher's associates were potentially accessible.

The trust placed in me by Marguerite Derrida has been exceptional. She has allowed me access to the full set of archives, but has also granted me several interviews. Meetings, often long and sometimes repeated, with witnesses from every period have been essential. I have been lucky enough to talk to Derrida's brother, sister, and favourite cousin, as well as many fellow-students and companions of his youth, who shed light on what he once described as a thirty-two-year-long adolescence. I was able to question a hundred or so of his associates: friends, colleagues, publishers, students, and even some of his detractors. But I have not, of course, managed to make contact with all the potential witnesses, and some did not wish to meet with me. A biography is also constructed from obstacles and refusals, or, if you prefer, resistances.

---

* 'I once destroyed a correspondence. With grim determination: I crushed it – it didn't work; burned it – it didn't work . . . I destroyed a correspondence that I should not have destroyed and I will regret it all my life' (*Rue Descartes* no. 52, 2006, p. 96). There are several indications that this destruction occurred at the end of the 1960s or the beginning of the 1970s.

More than once, I have felt giddy at the extent and difficulty of the task on which I had embarked. It probably needed a certain naïvety, or at least ingenuousness, to get such a project off the ground. After all, Geoffrey Bennington, one of the best commentators on Derrida's work, had sternly dismissed the possibility of a biography worthy of the name:

> It is of course to be expected that Derrida will some day be the subject of biographical writing, and there is nothing to prevent this being of the most traditional kind [. . .]. But this type of complacent and recuperative writing would at some point have to encounter the fact that Derrida's work should at least have disturbed its presuppositions. I would hazard a guess that one of the last genres of academic or quasi-academic writing to be affected by deconstruction is the genre of biography. [. . .] Is it possible to conceive of a multiple, layered but not hierarchised, *fractal* biography which would escape the totalising and tele-ological commitments which inhabit the genre from the start?[8]

Without denying the interest of such an approach, I have sought, in the final analysis, to write not so much a Derridean biography as a biography of Derrida. Mimicry, in this respect as in many others, does not seem the best way of serving him today.

The faithfulness that counted for me was of another kind. Derrida had accompanied me, beneath the surface, ever since I first read *Of Grammatology*, in 1974. I got to know him a little, ten years later, when he wrote a generous piece on *Right of Inspection*, a photo album that I produced with Marie-Françoise Plissart. We exchanged letters and books. I never stopped reading him. And now, for three years, he has occupied the best part of my time and has even slipped into my dreams, in a sort of collaboration *in absentia*.[*]

Writing a biography means living through an intimate and some-times intimidating adventure. Whatever happens, Jacques Derrida will now be part of my own life, like a sort of posthumous friend. A strange, one-way friendship that he would not have failed to ques-tion. I am convinced of one thing: there are biographies only of the dead. So every biography is lacking its supreme reader: the one who is no longer there. If there is an ethics of biographers, it can perhaps be located here: would they dare to stand, book in hand, in front of their *subject*?

---

* Readers curious to know more about how this book was written, and the prob-lems the author encountered, can refer to *Trois ans avec Derrida: les carnets d'un biographe* (Paris: Flammarion, 2010).

PART I
Jackie
1930–1962

1

The Negus

1930–1942

For a long time, Derrida's readers knew nothing of his childhood or youth. At most, they might be aware of the year he was born, 1930, and the place, El Biar, on the outskirts of Algiers. Admittedly, there are several autobiographical allusions in *Glas* and even more in *The Post Card*, but they are so woven into various textual games that they remain uncertain and, as it were, undecidable.

Only in 1983, in an interview with Catherine David for *Le Nouvel Observateur*, did Derrida finally agree to proffer a few factual details. He did so in an ironic, vaguely tetchy way, somewhat telegraphic in style, as if in a hurry to get shot of these impossible questions:

> *You mentioned Algeria just now. That is where it all began for you.*
>
> Ah, you want me to say things like 'I-was-born-in-El Biar-on-the-outskirts-of-Algiers-in-a-petty-bourgeois-family-of-assimi-lated-Jews-but . . .' Is that really necessary? I can't do it. You'll have to help me . . .
>
> *What was your father's name?*
>
> Ok, here we go. He had five names, all the names of the family are encrypted, along with a few others, in *The Post Card*, sometimes unreadable even for those who bear these names; often they're not capitalized, as one might do for 'aimé' or 'rené' . . .*
>
> *How old were you when you left Algeria?*
>
> You really are persistent. I came to France at the age of nine-teen. I had never left El Biar before. The 1940 war in Algeria, in other words the first underground rumblings of the Algerian war.[1]

---

* As we discover in the following pages, 'Aimé' and 'René' (with capitals) were the proper names of members of Derrida's family, but when used in lower case are adjectives ('beloved' and 'reborn'). – Tr.

In 1986, in a dialogue with Didier Cahen broadcast on France-Culture ('Le bon plaisir de Jacques Derrida'), he restated his previous objections, while acknowledging that writing would doubtless enable him to tackle these questions:

> I wish that a narration were possible. Right now, it's not. I dream, not of managing, one day, to recount this legacy, this past experience, this history, but at least of giving a narrative account of it among other possible accounts. But, in order to get there, I'd have to undertake a particular kind of work, I'd have to set out on an adventure that up until now I've not managed. To invent, to invent a language, to invent modes of anamnesis . . . .[2]

Derrida's references to his childhood gradually became less reluctant. In *Ulysses Gramophone* (first French edition published in 1987), he mentioned his secret forename, Élie,* the name that was given to him on the seventh day of his life; in *Memoirs of the Blind*, three years later, he described his 'wounded jealousy' of the talent for drawing that his family recognized in his brother René.

The year 1991 was a turning-point, with the volume *Jacques Derrida* coming out in the series 'Les Contemporains', published by Éditions du Seuil: not only was Jacques Derrida's contribution, 'Circumfession', autobiographical from beginning to end, but in the 'Curriculum vitae' that followed Geoffrey Bennington's analysis, the philosopher agreed to submit to what he called 'the law of genre', even if he did so with an enthusiasm that his co-author described, delicately, as 'uneven'.[3] But childhood and youth were by far the most heavily emphasized parts of his life, at least as regards any personal reflections.

Thereafter, autobiographical references in Derrida's written work became increasingly frequent. As he acknowledged in 1998: 'Over the last couple of decades [. . .], in a way that is both fictitious and not fictitious, first-person texts have become more common: personal records, confessions, reflections on the possibility or impossibility of confession.'[4] As soon as we start to fit these fragments together, they provide us with a remarkably precise narrative, albeit one that is both repetitive and full of gaps. They constitute a priceless source – the main source for that period, and the only source that enables us to describe Derrida's childhood empathetically, as if from within. But these first-person narratives, of course, need to be read, first and foremost, as texts. They should be approached as cautiously as the *Confessions* of Saint Augustine or Rousseau. And in any case,

---

* The French equivalent of English 'Elijah' (and also 'Elias'). – Tr.

as Derrida acknowledges, they are belated reconstructions, both fragile and uncertain: 'I try to recall, through documented facts and subjective pointers, what I might have thought or felt at that time, but, more often than not, these attempts fail.'[5]

The material traces that can be added to, and compared with, this wealth of autobiographical material are, unfortunately, few and far between. Many of the family papers seem to have disappeared in 1962, when Derrida's parents left El Biar in some haste. I have not found a single letter from the Algerian period. And, in spite of my efforts, I have not been able to locate even the least document from the schools that Derrida attended. But I have been lucky enough to have access to four valuable witnesses from those distant years: René and Janine Derrida – Jackie's older brother and his sister – and his cousin Micheline Lévy, as well as Fernand Acharrok, one of his closest friends from that period.

In 1930, the year of Derrida's birth, Algeria celebrated in great pomp the centenary of its conquest by the French. During his visit there, French President Gaston Doumergue made a point of lauding 'the admirable work of colonization and civilization' that had been carried out over the previous century. This was seen, by many people, as the high point of French Algeria. The following year, in the Bois de Vincennes, the Colonial Exhibition received thirty-three million visitors, whereas the anti-colonial exhibition organized by the Surrealists met with the most modest of successes.

With its 300,000 inhabitants, its cathedral, its museum, and its broad avenues, Algiers, the 'white city' ('Alger la Blanche'), was a kind of display window for France in Africa. Everything in it was deliberately reminiscent of the cities of metropolitan France, starting with the street names: there was the avenue Georges-Clemenceau, the boulevard Gallieni, the rue Michelet, the place Jean-Mermoz, and so on. The 'Muslims' or 'natives' – as the Arabs were generally called – were slightly outnumbered by the 'Europeans'. The Algeria in which Jackie would grow up was a profoundly unequal society, as regards both political rights and standards of living. Communities coexisted but barely mingled – in particular, there were few mixed marriages.

Like many Jewish families, the Derridas had come over from Spain long before the French conquest of Algeria. Right from the start of colonization, the Jews had been considered by the French forces of occupation as useful people, potential allies – and this distanced them from the Muslims with whom they had hitherto lived. Another event separated them even more markedly: on 24 October 1870, French minister Adolphe Crémieux gave his name to the decree granting French citizenship, en bloc, to the 35,000 Jews living in Algeria. This did not stop anti-Semitism from breaking out in Algeria after 1897. The following year, Édouard Drumont, the notorious author of *Jewish France*, was elected as *député* for Algiers.[6]

One of the consequences of the Crémieux Decree was an increase in the level of assimilation of Jews into French life. Of course, Jewish religious traditions were maintained, but in a purely private space. Jewish forenames were Gallicized or, as in the Derrida family, relegated to a discreet second place. People referred to the 'temple' rather than the 'synagogue', to 'communion' rather than 'bar-mitzvah'. Derrida himself, much more attentive to historical questions than is often thought, was keenly aware of this change:

> I was part of an extraordinary transformation of French Judaism in Algeria: my great grandparents were still very close to the Arabs in language and customs. At the end of the nine-teenth century, in the years following the Crémieux decree of 1870, the next generation became more bourgeois: though my [maternal] grandmother had to be married almost clandestinely in the back courtyard of a town hall in Algiers because of the pogroms (this was right in the middle of the Dreyfus Affair), she was already raising her daughters like bourgeois Parisian girls (16th Arrondissement good manners, piano lessons, and so on). Then came my parents' generation: few intellectuals, mostly shopkeepers, some of modest means and some not, some who were already exploiting a colonial situation by becoming the exclusive representatives of major metropolitan brands.[7]

Derrida's father, Haïm Aaron Prosper Charles, was called Aimé; he was born in Algiers on 26 September 1896. When he was twelve, he was apprenticed to the wine and spirits company Tachet; he was to work there all his life, as had his own father, Abraham Derrida, and as Albert Camus's father had done – he too was employed in a wine-shipping business in Algiers harbour. Between the wars, wine was the main source of revenue for Algeria, and its vineyards were the fourth biggest in the world.

On 31 October 1923, Aimé married Georgette Sultana Esther Safar, born on 23 July 1901, the daughter of Moïse Safar (1870–1943) and Fortunée Temime (1880–1961). Their first child, René Abraham, was born in 1925. A second son, Paul Moïse, died when he was three months old, on 4 September 1929, less than a year before the birth of Jacques Derrida. This would make of him, he later wrote in 'Circumfession', 'a precious but so vulnerable intruder, one mortal too many, Élie loved [*aimé*] in the place of another'.[8]

Jackie was born at daybreak, on 15 July 1930, at El Biar, in the hilly suburbs of Algiers, in a holiday home. Right up until the last minute, his mother refused to break off a poker game: poker would remain her lifelong passion. The boy's main forename was probably chosen because of Jackie Coogan, who had the star role in *The Kid*. When he was circumcised, he was given a second forename, Élie, which was not entered on his birth certificate, unlike the equivalent names of his brother and sister.

Until 1934, the family lived in town, except during the summer months. They lived in the rue Saint-Augustin, which might seem like too much of a coincidence given the importance that the saintly author of the *Confessions* would have in Derrida's work. He later retained only the vaguest images of this first home, where his parents lived for nine years: 'a dark hallway, a grocer's down from the house'.[9]

Shortly before the birth of a new child, the Derridas moved to El Biar – in Arabic, 'the well' – quite an affluent suburb where the children could breathe more freely. The parents plunged themselves into debt for many years when they bought their modest villa, 13, rue d'Aurelle-de-Paladines. It was located 'on the edge of an Arab district and a Catholic cemetery, at the end of the chemin du Repos', and came with a garden that Derrida would refer to later as the Orchard, the *Pardes* or PaRDeS, as he liked to write it, an image of Paradise and of the Day of Atonement ('*Grand Pardon*'), and an essential place in kabbalistic tradition.

The birth of Derrida's sister Janine gave rise to an anecdote that was constantly being retold in the family, the 'first words' of his that have come down to us. When his grandparents beckoned him into the bedroom, they showed him a travelling bag that probably contained the basic implements used in deliveries in those days, and told him that his little sister had just come out of it. Jackie went up to the cot and stared at the baby before declaring, 'I want her to be put back in her bag.'

At the age of five or six, Jackie was a very charming lad. With a little boater on his head, he would sing Maurice Chevalier songs at family parties; he was often nicknamed 'the Negus' as his skin was so dark. Throughout his early childhood, the relation between Jackie and his mother was particularly intense. Georgette, who had been left with a childminder until she was three, was neither very affectionate nor very demonstrative towards her children. This did not stop Jackie from completely worshipping her, almost like the young Narrator of *À la Recherche du temps perdu*. Derrida later described himself as 'the child whom the grown-ups amused themselves by making cry for nothing', the child 'who up until puberty cried out "Mummy I'm scared" every night until they let him sleep on a divan near his parents'.[10] When he was sent to school, he stood in the schoolyard in tears, his face pressed against the railings.

> I vividly remember being really upset, upset at being separated
> from my family, from my mother, my tears, my yells at nursery
> school, I can still see the teacher telling me, 'Your mother's
> coming to fetch you,' and I'd ask, 'Where is she?' and she'd
> tell me, 'She's doing the cooking,' and I imagined that in this
> nursery school [. . .], there was a place where my mother was
> doing the cooking. I can remember crying and yelling when I
> went in, and laughing when I came out. [. . .] I went so far as
> to make up illnesses to get me off school, I kept asking them to
> take my temperature.[11]

The future author of 'Tympan' and *The Ear of the Other* mainly
suffered from repeated attacks of earache, which aroused considerable anxiety in his family. He was taken from one doctor to another.
Treatment at the time was aggressive: rubber syringes filled with
warm water that pierced the eardrum. On one occasion, there was
even talk of removing his mastoid bone, a very painful but in those
days quite common operation.

A much more serious and dramatic event occurred during this
period: Derrida's cousin Jean-Pierre, who was a year older, was run
over by a car and killed, outside his home in Saint-Raphaël. The
shock was made even worse by the fact that, at school, Jackie was
at first wrongly told that it was his brother René who had just died.
He would always be scarred by this first bereavement. One day, he
would tell his cousin Micheline Lévy that it had taken him years to
understand why he had wanted to call his two sons Pierre and Jean.

At primary school, Jackie was a very good pupil, except when it
came to his handwriting, which was deemed impossible to read, and
would remain so. 'At break, the teacher, who knew that I was top
of the class, would tell me, "Go back and rewrite this, it's illegible;
when you go to the *lycée* you'll be able to get away with writing like
this; but it's not acceptable now."'[12]

In this school, doubtless like many others in Algeria, racial problems were already very much to the fore: there was a great deal of
brutality among the pupils. Still very timid, Jackie viewed school
as hell – he felt so exposed there. Every day, he was afraid that the
fights would get worse. 'There was racist, racial violence, which
spread out all over the place, anti-Arab racism, anti-Semitic, anti-
Italian, anti-Spanish racism . . . All sorts! All forms of racism could
be encountered . . . .'[13]

There were many 'native' youngsters at primary school, but they
tended to disappear when it was time to enter the *lycée*. Derrida
would describe the situation in *Monolingualism of the Other*; Arabic
was considered to be a foreign language, and while it was possible
to learn it, this was never encouraged. As for the reality of life in

Algeria, it was kept completely out of the picture: the history of France taught to pupils was 'an incredible discipline, a fable and a bible, yet a doctrine of indoctrination almost ineffaceable'. Not a word was said about Algeria, nothing about its history or its geography, whereas the children were required to be able to 'draw the coast of Brittany and the Gironde estuary with our eyes closed' and to recite by heart 'the names of all the major towns of all the French departments'.[14]

However, with '*Le Métropole*', as France had officially to be called, pupils had a relationship that was ambivalent at best. A few of the privileged ones went there on holiday, often to spa towns such as Évian, Vittel, or Contrexéville. For all the rest, including the Derrida children, France – at once close and faraway, on the other shore of a sea too deep and wide ever to be crossed – appeared like a dream country. It was 'the model of good speech and good writing'. It appeared less as a native country than as an 'Elsewhere', both 'a strong fortress and an entirely other place'. As for Algeria, they felt they knew it 'by way of an obscure but certain form of knowledge'; it was something other than one province among others. 'Right from childhood, Algeria was, for us, also a country [. . .].'[15]

The Jewish religion played a rather low-key part in the Derridas' family life. On high days and holidays, the children were taken to the synagogue in Algiers; Jackie was particularly affected by Sephardic music and singing, a taste that would stay with him throughout his life. In one of his last texts, he would also remember the rites involving light in El Biar, starting on a Friday evening. 'I see again the moment when, all care having been taken, my mother having lit the lamp, *la veilleuse*, whose small flame floated on the surface of a cup of oil, one was suddenly no longer allowed to touch fire, to strike matches, especially to smoke, or even to let one's finger touch a light switch.' He would also remember joyful images of Purim with the 'candles planted into tangerines, almond *guénégueletes*, white flatcakes full of holes and covered with icing sugar after having been dipped in syrup then hung like laundry over a cord'.[16]

In the family, it was Moïse Safar, the maternal grandfather, who, although not a rabbi, incarnated the religious consciousness: 'a venerable righteousness placed him above the priest'.[17] Austere in manners, and very observant, he would stay seated in his armchair, absorbed for hour after hour in his prayer book. It was he who, shortly before his death, at Jackie's bar-mitzvah, gave him the pure white tallith that he would evoke at length in *Veils* – the prayer shawl that he later said he liked to 'touch' or 'caress' every day.[18]

The maternal grandmother, Fortunée Safar, outlived her husband by many years. She was the dominant figure in the family: no decision of any importance could be taken without her being consulted; she stayed for long periods in the rue d'Aurelle-de-Paladines with the Derridas. On Sundays, and during the summer months, the house was filled to overflowing with people. It was the rallying-point for the five Safar daughters. Georgette, Jackie's mother, was the third: she was famed for her bursts of uncontrollable laughter and for her flirtatiousness. And even more for her passion for poker. Most of the time, she kept a kitty with her mother, which enabled them to balance out losses and gains. Jackie himself later told how he had been able to play poker long before he learned to read; he was capable at an early age of dealing the cards with the dexterity of a casino croupier. He liked nothing better than to stay sitting among his aunts, delighting in their silly gossip before passing it on to his male and female cousins.

Georgette loved having guests, and she could also occasionally whip up a delicious couscous with herbs, but she did not much bother her head over everyday practicalities. During the week, the shopping was delivered from the nearby grocer's. And on Sunday mornings, it was Georgette's husband whose job it was to go to the market, sometimes in the company of Janine or Jackie. Aimé Derrida was a rather taciturn man, without much authority, who hardly ever protested against the power of the matriarchs. 'It's Hotel Patch here,' he would sometimes say, mysteriously, when the women dolled themselves up a bit too much for his taste. What he liked doing was to attend the horse races on certain Sunday after-noons, while the family would go down to one of the beautiful fine sandy beaches – often the one at Saint-Eugène called the Plage de la Poudrière.[19]

War had been declared, though as yet without much impact on Algerian territory, when tragedy struck the Derrida family. Jackie's young brother Norbert, who had just turned two, was laid low by tubercular meningitis. Aimé did everything in his power to save him, consulting several doctors, but the child died on 26 March 1940. For Jackie, then nine years old, this was the 'source of an unflag-ging astonishment' in the face of what he would never be able to understand or accept: 'to continue or resume living after the death of a loved one'. 'I remember the day I saw my father, in 1940, in the garden, lighting a cigarette one week after the death of my little brother Norbert: "But how can he still do that? Only a week ago he was sobbing!" I never got over it.'[20]

For several years, anti-Semitism had flourished in Algeria more than in any region in metropolitan France. The extreme right campaigned for the Crémieux Decree to be abolished, while the headlines in the *Petit Oranais* repeated day after day: 'We need to subject the synagogues and Jewish schools to sulphur, pitch, and if possible the fires of hell, to destroy the Jews' houses, seize their capital and drive them out into the fields like rabid dogs.'[21] And so, shortly after the crushing defeat of the French Army by the Germans, the 'National Revolution' called for by Marshal Pétain found more than favourable ground in Algeria. In the absence of any German occupation, local leaders showed considerable zeal: to satisfy anti-Jewish sentiment, anti-Semitic measures were applied more quickly and thoroughly than in metropolitan France.

The law of 3 October 1940 forbade Jews from practising a certain number of jobs, especially in public service. A *numerus clausus* of 2 per cent was established for the liberal professions; the following year, this measure would be made even stricter. On 7 October, the Minister of the Interior, Peyrouton, repealed the Crémieux Decree. For this entire population, which had been French for seventy years, the measures passed by the Vichy Government constituted 'a terrible surprise, an unexpected catastrophe'. 'It was an "inner" exile, expulsion from French citizenship, a drama that turned the daily lives of the Jews of Algeria upside down.'[22]

Even though he was only ten, Jackie too suffered the consequences of these hateful measures:

I was a good pupil at primary school, more often than not top of the class, which allowed me to note the changes that resulted from the Occupation and the rise to power of Marshal Pétain. In the schools of Algeria, where there were no Germans, they started getting us to send letters to Marshal Pétain, to chant 'Marshal, here we are!', etc., to raise the flag every morning at the start of class, and they always asked the top of the class to raise the flag, but when it was my turn, they replaced me by someone else. [. . .] I can't make out, now, whether I was hurt by this intensely, dimly, or vaguely.[23]

Anti-Semitic insults were henceforth authorized, if not encouraged, and they erupted at every moment, especially among the children.

As for the word *Jew*, I do not believe I heard it first in my family [. . .]. I believe I heard it at school in El Biar, already charged with what, in Latin, one would call an insult [*injure*], *injuria*, in English, *injury*, both an insult, a wound, and an injustice [. . .]. Before understanding any of it, I received this word like a blow, a denunciation, a de-legitimation prior to any legality.[24]

The situation rapidly deteriorated. On 30 September 1941, following the visit to Algeria of Xavier Vallat, the General Commissioner for Jewish Affairs, a new law established a *numerus clausus* of 14 per cent for Jewish children in primary and secondary education, a measure that had no equivalent in metropolitan France. In

November 1941, the name of Jacques's brother René appeared on the list of excluded pupils: he would lose out on two years of study, and thought he might stop going to school for good, as did several of his friends. His sister Janine, aged just seven, was also expelled from her school.

As for Jackie, he entered the first form of the *lycée* at Ben Aknoun, a former monastery very close to El Biar. Here he met Fernand Acharrok and Jean Taousson, who would be the main friends of his teenage years. But if this first year at high school was important, this was above all because it coincided for Jackie with a real discovery: that of literature. He had grown up in a house where there were few books, and had already exhausted the modest resources of the family library. That year, his French teacher was a certain M. Lefèvre.* He was a young, red-headed man who had just arrived from France. He talked to his pupils with an enthusiasm that sometimes made them smile. But one day, he started singing the praises of being in love, and mentioned *The Fruits of the Earth* by André Gide. Jackie immediately got hold of a copy of this work and was soon ecstatically immersed in it. He would read and re-read it for years on end.

> I would have learned this book by heart if I could have. No doubt, like every adolescent, I admired its fervour, the lyricism of its declarations of war on religion and families [. . .]. For me it was a manifesto or a Bible [. . .] sensualist, immoralist, and especially very Algerian. [. . .] I remember the hymn to the Sahel, to Blida, and to the fruits of the Jardin d'Essai.[25]

A few months later, it was another – and altogether less desirable – face of France that he would be forced to confront.

---

* According to Fernand Acharrok, this teacher's name was actually M. Verdier.

2

Under the Sun of Algiers

1942–1949

Entry into adolescence happened all of a sudden, one October morning in 1942. On the first day of the new school year, the *surveillant général* of the Lycée Ben Aknoun called Jackie into his office and told him: 'You are going to go home, my little friend, your parents will get a note.'[1] The percentage of Jews admitted into Algerian classes had just been lowered from 14 per cent to 7 per cent: yet again, the authorities had outstripped Vichy in their zeal.[2]

As Derrida would often say, this exclusion was 'one of the earthquakes' in his life:

> I wasn't expecting it in the least and I just couldn't understand it. I am striving to remember what must have been going through me at the time, but in vain. It has to be said that, even in my family, nobody explained to me why this was the situation. I think it remained incomprehensible for many Jews in Algeria, especially as there weren't any Germans; these initiatives came from French policy in Algeria, which was more severe than in France: all the Jewish teachers in Algeria were expelled from their schools. For this Jewish community, things remained enigmatic, perhaps not accepted, but suffered like a natural catastrophe for which there is no explanation.[3]

Even if he refused to exaggerate the seriousness of the experience, which would be 'offensive' given the persecutions suffered by European Jews, Derrida acknowledged that this trauma left its mark on him at the deepest level, and contributed to making him the person he was. He wished to erase nothing from his memory, so how could he have forgotten that morning in 1942 when 'a little black and very Arab Jew'[4] was expelled from the Lycée Ben Aknoun?

> Beyond any anonymous 'administrative' measure, which I didn't understand at all and which no one explained to me, the wound was of another order, and it never healed: the daily

insults from the children, my classmates, the kids in the street, and sometimes threats or blows aimed at the 'dirty Jew,' which, I might say, I came to see in myself.[5]

In the weeks immediately following this hardening of anti-Semitic measures, the war took a major turn in Algeria. On the night of 7–8 November 1942, American troops landed in North Africa. In Algiers, fierce fighting broke out between the Vichy forces, who did not hesitate to shoot at the Allies, and groups of resistance fighters led by José Aboulker, a twenty-two-year-old medical student. Derrida gave a detailed account of that day to Hélène Cixous:

> At dawn, we started to hear gunfire. There was an official resistance on the French side, there were French gendarmes, French soldiers who pretended to be going off to fight the English and Americans coming in from Sidi Ferruch. [. . .] And then, in the afternoon, we saw soldiers deploying outside our house [. . .] with helmets like we'd never seen. They weren't French helmets. We said to ourselves: they're Germans. And they were Americans. We'd never seen American helmets, either. And that same evening, the Americans arrived in force, as always handing out cigarettes, chewing gum, chocolates [. . .]. This first disembarkation was like a *caesura*, a break in life, a new point of arrival and departure.[6]

This was also a turning point in the Second World War. In metropolitan France, the southern, so-called 'free' zone was invaded on 11 November by the Wehrmacht and became an 'operational' zone. As for the city of Algiers, which had hitherto been preserved from the direct effects of war, it was subjected to over a hundred bombing raids, which caused many deaths. The view from the hills of El Biar was terrifying: the sea and the city were lit up by the guns of the navy, while the sky was crisscrossed by searchlights and ack-ack fire. For several months, the sirens wailed and there was a stampede to the shelters almost every day. Jackie would never forget the panic that seized him one evening when, as so often, the family had taken shelter in a neighbour's home: 'I was exactly twelve, my knees started to tremble uncontrollably.'[7]

Shortly after being expelled from the Lycée Ben Aknoun, Jackie was enrolled at the Lycée Maïmonide, also known as Émile-Maupas, from the name of the street on which it was located, on the edge of the Casbah. This improvised *lycée* had been opened the previous spring by Jewish teachers driven out of their jobs in state education. While his exclusion from Ben Aknoun had deeply wounded Jackie, he balked almost as much at what he perceived as a 'group identification'. He hated this Jewish school right from the start, and 'skived off' as often as he could. The general chaos and the difficulties of everyday life were so great that his parents seem never to have been informed of his absences. Of the few days he did actually spend at Émile-Maupas, Derrida kept a memory that he described in his dialogues with Élisabeth Roudinesco:

> It was there, I believe, that I began to recognize – if not to contract – this ill, this malaise, the ill-being that, throughout my life, rendered me inapt for 'communitarian' experience, incapable of enjoying any kind of membership in a group. [. . .] On the one hand, I was deeply wounded by anti-Semitism. And this wound has never completely healed. At the same time, paradoxically, I could not tolerate being 'integrated' into this Jewish school, this homogeneous milieu that reproduced and in a certain way countersigned – in a reactive and vaguely specular fashion, at once forced (by the outside threat) and compulsive – the terrible violence that had been done to it. This reactive self-defence was certainly natural and legitimate, even irreproachable. But I must have sensed that it was a drive [*pulsion*], a gregarious *compulsion* that responded too symmetrically, that *corresponded* in truth to an *expulsion*.[8]

As Jackie was coming up to his thirteenth birthday, he needed to prepare for the exams he had to take for his bar-mitzvah – or 'communion', as it had long been known among Algerian Jews. But his apprenticeship amounted to very little. Jackie pretended to study a little basic Hebrew with a rabbi from the rue d'Islay, without showing the slightest enthusiasm for the task. The rites, which had fascinated him since his earliest years, now greatly irritated him. All he saw in them was an empty formality imbued with mercantilism.

> I started resisting religion as a young adolescent, not in the name of atheism, but because I found religion as it was practiced within my family to be fraught with misunderstanding. It struck me as thoughtless, just blind repetitions, and there was one thing in particular I found unacceptable: that was the way honors were dispersed. The honor of carrying and reading the Torah was auctioned off in the synagogue, and I found that terrible.[9]

Instead of going to the Consistory school, Jackie spent his days with his cousin Guy Temime who worked in a little watch-maker's shop right next to the Casbah and just opposite one of the biggest brothels in Algiers, Le Sphinx. Half-amused, half-fascinated, the two boys never wearied of observing the soldiers queuing up outside the establishment.

Another favourite pastime was the cinema, as soon as they had enough money to buy a ticket. In Jackie's eyes, this was real time out, an essential emancipation from his family, but also a sort of erotic initiation. He would remember all his life an adaptation of *Tom Sawyer*, especially the scene where Tom is trapped in a cave with a small girl.[10]

The political and military situation developed rapidly during 1943. The Allies wanted to embark on their reconquest of France from Algeria. Algiers, which had been the heart of colonial Vichyism, soon became the new capital of Free France. According to Benjamin Stora, the Jewish populace greeted the American soldiers with particular enthusiasm and 'passionately followed the progress of the Allied armies on maps pinned to their dining room walls'.[11] For Jackie, it was 'a first amazing encounter' with foreigners from a faraway land. The 'Yankees' ('*Amerloques*'), as he and his friends called them, brought in quite an abundance of foodstuffs and introduced them to hitherto unknown products. 'Before I ever went to America, America took over my "home",' he later said.[12] His family struck up a friendship with a GI, welcoming him into their home on several occasions and even continuing to exchange letters with him after his return to the United States.

For the Jews of Algeria, however, it was some time before life returned to normal. For over six months, during the period of power-sharing between General Giraud and General de Gaulle, the race laws remained in force. As Derrida told Hélène Cixous, 'Giraud's only plan was to renew and extend the Vichy decrees and ensure that Algerian Jews were still seen as "native Jews". He didn't want them to be citizens again. And only when de Gaulle ousted Giraud, using those cunning manoeuvres for which he had such a genius, were the Vichy laws abolished.'[13] The discriminatory anti-Semitic measures that had been brought in were abolished on 14 March 1943, but only at the end of October did the French Committee of National Liberation, with de Gaulle at its head, reinstate the Crémieux Decree. The Jews of Algeria could finally reassume a nationality of which they had for two years been deprived.

In April 1943, Jackie was allowed to go back to the Lycée Ben Aknoun, at the end of the *cinquième*. So his absence had lasted less than a year. But the return to proper education happened in a haphazard and rather unenthusiastic way: 'I was taken back into the French school system. This was not something one could take for granted. I was very unhappy about this return: not only my expulsion, but my return too was quite painful and upsetting.'[14] The *lycée* buildings had been transformed by the British into a military hospital and a POW camp for Italians. Lessons took place in extremely rickety barracks, and since the men teachers had almost all been called up, retired teachers and women teachers were brought in.

For Jackie, something had broken as a result of his exclusion. He had been an excellent pupil up until then, but had now acquired a taste for a freer life which the surrounding chaos made easier. Over the next four years, he took a far greater interest in the war and in football than in the subjects he was taught. He continued to bunk off whenever he could and, together with his schoolmates, indulged in ragging that could be violent and sometimes cruel. As a result of this very hit-and-miss education, he would have serious gaps in his knowledge.

Throughout his teenage years, sport would play a major role. This was probably the easiest way of ensuring he was accepted by the group and his chums, in a non-Jewish milieu that he did his utmost to make his own.

My passion for sport in general and football in particular dates back to the time when going to school meant heading off with a pair of football boots in your satchel. I had a real fetish [*culte*] for those boots, I waxed them and took better care of them than of my exercise books. Football, running, baseball (taught us by the Americans), matches against the Italian POWs, this is what kept us busy; our education was much less important.[15]

On his return to the *lycée*, Jackie chummed up again with the boys who would remain his closest friends until he left for mainland France: Fernand Acharrok, nicknamed 'Poupon' ('Baby'), and Jean Taousson, nicknamed 'Denden', who, like Jackie, lived in the Mont D'Or district and was one of the rising stars of the RUA, the Racing Universitaire Algérois.* The three would often continue to play late into the night on the Ben Rouilah stadium near the Lycée Ben Aknoun. There is a legend, fostered by Derrida himself, that during those years he dreamed of becoming a professional footballer. One thing is certain: football was at that time the dominant sport for all the communities of Algeria – practically a religion.

Fernand Acharrok remembers: 'Like Albert Camus before him, Jackie was determined to be a brilliant footballer.' But there were

---

* At the age of twenty, Jean Taousson became a journalist at *L'Écho d'Alger* before becoming close to the OAS and then following a career as a lead reporter for *Paris-Match*; he also joined the circle around Charles Pasqua. [The OAS, or Organisation Armée Sécrete, was dedicated to retaining French control of Algeria. – Tr.] In the 1980s or 1990s, Derrida spent an evening with Jean Taousson. Despite being saddened by the way his old friend's politics had evolved, he was always keen to meet up with him again, as also with Fernand Acharrok.

closer models: René, his older brother, was also an excellent, passionate player; as goalie for Red Star, he played competitive football several times.

> Jackie liked to imitate the defence of the goalie in this club's first team, kicking his heels up. [. . .] In football, like everywhere else, he liked to hear the opinion of competent people. After one game that our team had lost, he walked all the way from the stadium in Saint-Eugène, a suburb of Algiers, to hear what a well-known player had to say. It was a pretty long way to walk! But the next day, he was really rather proud at being able to explain it all to us.[16]

On more than one occasion, Derrida described his adolescence as that of a little 'rogue' [*voyou*], a word he liked and that he would use as the title of one of his last works. According to Fernand Acharrok, the term would be really rather exaggerated to describe the things they got up to at the time. 'We were no angels in our little gang. We sometimes did some dumb things, but we weren't rogues, no . . . .' To his wife Marguerite, however, Derrida later recounted various car trips made after drinking heavily, and plans to blow up the prefabricated buildings in the *lycée* with some explosives they had picked up. It is difficult to form any precise idea of their misdeeds, but these seem in the main to have remained mere fantasies. Jackie and his friends were probably among those 'Clarks' mentioned by Camus – 'agreeable adolescents who take the greatest pains to look like gangsters' and try and seduce the 'Marlènes'.[17]

One thing is certain: within the Derrida family, relations that year were very strained, especially between Jackie and René, his older brother by five years. Jackie felt that his brother was valued more highly than he was, when it came to both sporting and academic achievements. He could not stand René's wish to exert authority over him since their opinions on most subjects were at odds, especially when it came to politics: René tended to espouse right-wing positions, whereas Jackie took every opportunity to declare that he was on the left.

From this time onward, Derrida's main weapon was silence. He was capable of not uttering a word throughout an entire meal. In one of his last texts, he admitted that he had an unusual capacity for refusing to reply. 'I've been able, ever since childhood, as my parents knew only too well, to keep up an obstinate silence, one that no torture could overcome, in the face of anyone who does not seem worth replying to. Silence is my most sublime, my most peaceable, but my most undeniable declaration of war or contempt.'[18]

Unlike what one might expect from a reading of 'Circumfession', Derrida's relations with his mother were very tense all through adolescence. He had the impression that her life was easy, while his father was a martyr to work, exploited by his family as much as by his employer.

> My compassion for my father was infinite. Hardly had he begun school when, at the age of twelve, he had to begin working for the Tachet business where his own father had been a modest employee. After being a sort of apprentice until the age of adulthood, my father became a commercial representative: he was always behind the wheel of his car.[19]

Jackie found this profession both exhausting and humiliating. In his 'poor father' he saw 'a sacrificial victim of the modern age', and in his ceaseless trips driving down bumpy roads 'an intolerable strain'. Four days a week, Aimé Derrida would leave the house early, at 5 a.m., in his blue Citroën equipped with a primitive gas producer since the beginning of the war. He would return in the evening, 'shattered'. From his rounds in the hinterland he brought back supplies of groceries that at least enabled his family to suffer less from their poverty than did many other people. At daybreak, before heading off, he needed to tot up the receipts from the day before on the kitchen table. And when the figures did not balance, it was a real disaster. He kept heaving a sigh, complained about his exhausting schedule, but remained grateful to his bosses for not sacking him when anti-Semitic measures were brought in, as they might have done. These demonstrations of gratitude wounded Jackie particularly.

> There was the boss and the employee, the rich and the poor, and even within the family I saw my father as the victim of a sombre ritual. Obscure, cruel, and fatal. The word 'sacrifice' came up constantly: 'He is sacrificing himself for us.' Sometimes he said it himself. During my entire adolescence, I suffered with him, I accused the rest of the family of not recognizing how much he was doing for us. That was the experience of the 'humiliated father': a man of duty above all, bending beneath his obligations. Stooped. And he was stooped; his bearing, his silhouette, the line and movement of his body, it was as though they all bore this signature. The word 'stooped' [*voûté*] imposes itself on me all the more in that I have never been able to dissociate it from his destiny: my father worked in an area whose name was nothing other than 'the vaults [*les voûtes*],' at the port of Algiers.[20]

As soon as he had learned to drive, Jackie regularly went with Aimé on his rounds. This was an opportunity to have a private talk with a man who, he often said, opened up to him more easily, and who called on him to 'witness the lack of understanding or the indifference of other people'. But these trips were also an opportunity for Jackie to make his first discovery of the dazzling Algerian landscape, especially Kabylia:

> No name can ever be inscribed for me in the same series as these Berber names [. . .]: Tizi Ouzou, Tigzirt, Djidjelli, Port Gueydon – that was the itinerary our tour took – and then Yakouren Forest. [. . .] I enjoyed so much driving on those winding roads, but I was especially determined to help my father, to demonstrate a sort of 'political solidarity' with him, to share my concern for this 'wretched of the earth'.[21]

The family did, however, show another face at times – that of an extended and merry tribe of cousins male and female with whom Jackie and his sister Janine enjoyed spending whole days on the Plage de la Poudrière, travelling down to the beach in small groups by bus, tram, or trolley bus. Micheline Lévy, who would remain Derrida's favourite girl cousin, still has a poignant memory of those times that helped them to forget the war.

> We had a code to arrange a meeting: you would let the phone ring twice to let everyone know it was time to head off. We'd go down to the beach in small groups, taking eggs and pastries as a picnic. Jackie was very greedy; he was particularly fond of almond cigars. He was a very strong swimmer, too; he'd venture right out to sea. At one time we managed to rustle up enough money to buy ourselves a yellow dinghy that we all just loved. [. . .] When he was a teenager, Jackie didn't much like dancing; he preferred staying out on the beach until late in the evening. We'd go for long walks together as night fell. With most people he was reluctant to say more than the minimum, but he was a bit chattier with me. Anyway, I managed to winkle out a lot of his secrets and I told him all of mine. He was in love with my best friend Lucienne, a very pretty girl. She was his first love, but as far as I know their relationship remained platonic.[22]

In the evenings, on the way back up to El Biar, the little gang would often stop off to see a film. Many years later, Jackie would nostalgically recite the names of the cinemas in Algiers: the Vox, the Caméo, the Midi-Minuit, and the Olympia, not forgetting the Majestic, the biggest cinema in North Africa . . . Jackie was an avid movie-goer, and did not mind what films he saw or where they came from:

For a young *Algérois* like me, cinema still represented an extraordinary form of travel. You could travel a lot with the cinema. Not to mention the American films, absolutely exotic and at the same time close to us, there were the French films that spoke in a very individual voice, moved along with recognizable bodies, showed landscapes and interiors that really impressed a young teenager like me who'd never crossed the Mediterranean. Books didn't give me the same thing: this direct, immediate transport into a France that was unknown to me. Going to the cinema was going on a journey where everything was laid on from the start [*un voyage organisé*]).[23]

Reading was still Jackie's favourite activity. His love of literature had continued to grow ever since he had started the *lycée*, with M. Lefèvre's fervent praise of Gide. This was a passion that he nourished by himself, ever more freely and independently of his academic obligations. At home, his parents had divided the veranda in two so that Jackie could have a room of his own. He would shut himself away there to read for hours at a time. Above his bed he set up a little set of bookshelves with the books he worshipped. The small amount of pocket money that he received went straightaway on books.

I grew up in a world where there were few books, a few bad novels, that I read, Paul Bourget . . ., and that was it. I bought my first books in Algiers with my weekly pocket-money. So I totally fetishized them.[24]

After Gide's *The Fruits of the Earth*, he enthusiastically read *The Immoralist, Strait is the Gate, Paludes*, and the *Journal*. 'For me, he wasn't a novelist, but a moralist who told us how to live,' he explained later.[25] Jackie probably knew that Gide was living in Algiers at the very same time as he was discovering his works with such enthusiasm. The writer arrived in the city on 27 May 1943 and a month later dined in El Biar, in the villa occupied by General de Gaulle. Over the following months, now settled in the home of his friend Jacques Heurgon in rue Michelet, Gide would sometimes play a game of chess with Saint-Exupéry. Jackie could quite easily have crossed the path of the very man he was reading with such passion.

But he was soon fascinated by other authors. Rousseau, whom he had discovered at school, very soon became one of his favourites; he read and re-read *The Confessions* and *The Reveries of a Solitary Walker*. At the age of thirteen or fourteen, as if following advice from Gide, he also immersed himself in *Thus Spake Zarathustra*, then other works of Nietzsche's, and this contributed to his moving

even further away from the Judaism of his childhood. He loved
Nietzsche as much as Rousseau, however dissimilar they might be:
'I remember this debate inside myself very clearly, I tried to recon-
cile them, I admired them both equally, I knew that Nietzsche was
a merciless critic of Rousseau, and I kept wondering how one could
be a Nietzschean and a Rousseauist at once.'[26]

Jackie did read very widely, but he took very little interest in
classic novels. He had only a superficial acquaintance with authors
such as Dumas, Balzac, Stendhal, or Zola. On the other hand, he was
fascinated by Paul Valéry, both as poet and as essayist. And even
though he quoted him less frequently, he also liked Albert Camus:
as in Gide's *The Fruits of the Earth* and *The Immoralist*, he found in
Camus's *Nuptials* and *The Stranger*, which latter had recently come
out, an almost miraculous encounter between French literature, 'the
experience of a world without any tangible continuity with the one
in which we lived',[27] and his own concrete environment.*

Among the most formative readings of Derrida's adolescence, we
should not forget Antonin Artaud, even though few of his texts were
accessible.

> If I try to remember the first time Artaud's name made an
> impact on me, it was probably through reading Blanchot, who
> referred to Artaud's *Correspondence with Jacques Rivière*. So I
> read those Artaud letters and, in a movement of identificatory
> projection, I found myself in sympathy with that man who said
> that he had nothing to say, that nothing was being *dictated*
> to him, as it were, while at the same time he was inhabited by
> the passion and the drive to write, and probably also to create
> drama. [. . .]
> So why did I, as a young man, identify with Artaud in this
> way? I began in my adolescence (it lasted until I was thirty-
> two . . .) writing passionately, without writing, with this sense
> of emptiness: I know that I must write, that I want to write,
> that I have to write, but basically I don't have anything that
> doesn't begin resembling what's already been said. When I
> was fifteen–sixteen, I remember, I had this sense of being *pro-
> téiforme* [protean] – this is a word I came across in Gide, and
> it really took my fancy. I could assume any form, write in any

---

* In those years, Jackie communicated his love of literature to his cousin Micheline
Lévy, who had to leave school at a very early age. He encouraged her to join a
library and advised her about what to read. Thanks to him, she became an ardent
reader, very keen on Gide, Camus, Chateaubriand, and Dostoevsky. Later on, she
would be the only family member to follow Derrida's publications closely, sometimes attending his conferences or his seminars and ritually having lunch with him
once a year.

tone knowing that it was never really mine; I was responding to what was expected of me or I was finding myself in the
mirror held out to me by the other. I said to myself: I can write
everything and so I can't write anything.[28]

Like many teenagers, Jackie kept a diary, filling his school exercise books with private autobiographical notes and reflections on
his readings. He also liked to write directly on the pink paper sheet
covering his table, before cutting out the fragments that he liked.
While he was less tempted by the novel form, this did not stop him,
at the age of fifteen, dreaming up a plot based on the theft of a
newspaper, and an act of blackmail.

At that period, Jackie took a great interest in literary life. He
devoutly read the literary reviews and supplements, sometimes out
loud. Actually, Algiers had become a sort of second French cultural
capital at the end of the war and the start of the postwar period.
At the end of 1942, Edmond Charlot, who published Camus's first
works, set up the series 'Les Livres de la France en guerre' ('The
books of France at war'); in it he reissued Vercors's *The Silence of
the Sea*, before publishing Gide's *Interviews imaginaires*, Kessel's
Army of Shadows, and works by Jules Roy, Max-Pol Fouchet, and
several others. The review *L'Arche*, edited by the Kabylian poet
Jean Amrouche, set out to rival the *Nouvelle Revue Française*, which
was compromised by its part in collaboration. In 1947, Emmanuel
Roblès founded *Forge*, soon a home for writers such as Mohamed
Dib and Kateb Yacine.[29]

Derrida wrote poems at this period; he later said he hated them,
and forced himself to get rid of them, with the exception of one
line of verse, quoted in *Glas*: 'Glu de l'étang lait de ma mort noyée'
['Glue of the pool milk of my death drowned'].[30] But at the time,
he sent them to several reviews. In March 1947, Claude Bernady,
who ran *Périples, revue de la Méditerranée*, assured him that he
had taken '*real* pleasure' in reading his poetry: 'You possess very
fine qualities and you owe it to yourself to cultivate them.'[31] He
promised to publish one of the poems in the next issue of the review,
but *Périples* ceased publication before this could actually happen.
Although other texts do seem to have been published in those years,
these were in little reviews that I have been unable to find.

While Jackie's reading was exceptionally wide and deep for his
age, this did not make him a good pupil. Ever since he had been
expelled from the *lycée*, in his second year there, he had been
casual about his high school studies and was still poor at certain
basic subjects. He was really not strong in mathematics or Latin,
or in modern languages, though he was not particularly bothered
by this. But when, in June 1947, he failed the first part of his

baccalaureate, he was really upset. He worked hard all summer, and got into the habit of rising very early, so that he passed the exams in September. 'All of a sudden, he changed completely,' his brother René remembers.

Thereupon, Jackie left the Lycée Ben Aknoun to enter the Lycée Émile-Félix-Gautier, a respected institution in the centre of Algiers. His philosopher teacher, Jean Choski, was particularly famous for his 'unforgettable voice, dragging out the final syllables of words and adding shovelfuls of grave and circumflex accents to the vowels', as well as for the big black umbrella from which, according to some people, he was never separated. 'If anyone asks you why you have come to Émile-Félix-Gautier, you'll say that it's to do philosophy with Choski!' he announced in his first class. In the view of one of his ex-pupils, he was a 'real character, unpredictable, alluring, eccentric, a poser at times, sometimes even a real pain, but an educator, powerfully original, sparkling with intelligence, and gifted with thoughts that were at once clear, elegant, and precise. And at times he could be dazzling: what flights of eloquence (especially on Kant)! A real philosopher, a great one'[32] We have no information about any precise influence this teacher had on Derrida. We merely know that, among the books Derrida read, the works of Bergson and Sartre were those that left the deepest impression.

It was during his final year at school that Jackie's mother, who had long been suffering from attacks of renal colic, underwent major surgery. The stone was so big that she had to have a whole kidney removed. In his personal notes for 1976, Derrida returned elliptically but very significantly to the importance of this event in his relationship with his mother, marking as it did the end of a long period of tension.

> My mother's operation.
> I date my 'reconciliation' with her back to that time. Describe it in very concrete detail. The frequent visits to the clinic. Fear during the operation. She was surprised and touched by my solicitude. Mine too. End of a war. Report transformed into 'studies', etc. etc.[33]

At the time he took his baccalaureate, Jackie had only a rather vague idea of what he wanted to do next. Ever since he had been fourteen or fifteen, he had felt sure he would have to write – literature, if possible. But since he did not for a moment imagine that anyone could earn a living that way, becoming a teacher in the humanities had long seemed to him to be 'the only possible, if not desirable, job'.[34] With the discovery of philosophy, the project developed somewhat:

It was in my final year that I really started reading philosophy; and since this was when I discovered that, not having studied Greek at the *lycée*, I wouldn't be able to try for the *agrégation de lettres*, I thought to myself basically: why not unite the two and become a philosophy teacher? The great models of the day, such as Sartre, were people who did both literature and philosophy. And so, gradually, without giving up on literary writing, I decided that philosophy was, professionally speaking, a better bet.[35]

In a fascinating interview from 1989, 'This strange institution called literature', Derrida explained even more clearly the hesitations he had felt at that period:

No doubt I hesitated between philosophy and literature, giving up neither, perhaps seeking obscurely a place from which the history of this frontier could be thought or even displaced – in writing itself and not only by theoretical or historical reflection. And since what interests me today is not strictly called either literature or philosophy, I'm amused by the idea that my adolescent desire – let's call it that – should have directed me toward something in writing which was neither the one nor the other.[36]

This tangle of wishes would find a classic solution. A few days after the results of the baccalaureate came out, Jackie happened to catch a broadcast on Radio Algiers offering careers guidance. A humanities teacher spoke very highly of the *hypokhâgne*, a broad and varied training that meant you did not have to specialize too early; in particular, he related that Albert Camus had been his pupil, in 1932–3. Derrida, who had never heard of the École Normale Supérieure, went to see this teacher the very next day and registered for the *hypokhâgne* class at the Lycée Bugeaud, a highly regarded class with pupils from all over Algeria. It was here that he would meet Jean-Claude Pariente and Jean Domerc, with whom he soon became friends. They would leave for Paris at the same time as he did.

'There were quite a few people from the Oran district in Bugeaud's *hypokhâgne*,' remembers Pariente.

There was also a contingent from Constantine. But one of the things that partly distinguished it was the fact that it was a mixed class, at a time when boys and girls went to different establishments. Generally, pupils went there to study so they could meet the demands of higher education, and continued in the arts department at the University of Algiers. There weren't many of us who wanted to try for Normale Sup. The presence of girls changed the atmosphere in class: relationships between us were more polite than in the classes we'd been in before, and the pupils in the other classes of the *lycée* were pretty jealous of us. But overall, this wasn't of any great significance. Even if he was comfortable around girls, I don't remember Derrida having a girlfriend in that class.[37]

Although he was an excellent pupil, Pariente was then starting on his second *hypokhâgne*. Bugeaud offered a complete cycle of *classes préparatoires* in the sciences, but there was still no *khâgne* in Algeria at that time. Pariente wanted to take the competitive exam for the École Normale Supérieure in Algiers, rather than in Paris itself, at the end of that year. The plan did not seem absurd, as you could get some rather high-quality teaching in that class. Paul Mathieu, the teacher whom Derrida had heard on the radio, was an old-style humanist. He was a former *normalien*, and continued to venerate the École Normale Supérieure, encouraging his best students to do their utmost to get a place there. But his lessons were based on literary history in the style of Lanson, and were too old-fashioned for Derrida. He also provided a thorough grounding in Latin, a discipline in which Derrida really did not shine. In history, Lucien Bessières, who had been deeply affected by the war, from which he returned with a fine array of decorations, gave classes that were very precise, but too slow for the taste of most pupils.

The philosophy teacher, Jan Czarnecki, was a progressive Protestant who would later be one of the courageous signatories of the 'Manifesto of the 121'.* He was a pupil of Le Senne and Nabert, a follower of the tradition of French idealism and spiritualism, but he was very open to questions of epistemology as well as to other philosophical trends. He taught a very rationalist philosophy, rather dry in tone, but Derrida, whose own ideas were starting to become clearer, rather liked him. 'I had a quite remarkable teacher in *hypokhâgne*,' he later told Dominique Janicaud. 'He gave us some very cursory and precise lessons on the history of philosophy: he went over everything from the Presocratics to modernity.' Indeed, among the documents preserved in the Special Collection of the University of California, Irvine, there are several traces of the classes that Derrida attended that year.

It was from Czarnecki's lips that Jackie first heard the name of Martin Heidegger. As soon as he could, he got hold of the only work of his that was then available in French, *What is Metaphysics?*, a selection of texts translated by Henri Corbin. 'The question

---

* This manifesto, published in September 1960, was signed by 121 intellectuals denouncing the attitude of the French Government to Algerian demands for independence. – Tr.

of anguish, of the experience of nothingness prior to negation, suited my personal sense of pathos much more than did the frigid Husserlian discipline to which I came only later. I was in tune with that pathos, so widely felt at the time, just after the war.' [38] Thanks to Czarnecki, Derrida also started reading Kierkegaard, one of the philosophers who would fascinate him most, and one to whom he would remain faithful throughout his life.

However, the most decisive influence that year was Sartre's. He was then at the apogee of his fame, and Jackie started to read him in his final year at the *lycée*; but it was in *hypokhâgne* that he really immersed himself in Sartre's works. While preparing a long paper on 'Sartre, psychology – phenomenology', he read *Being and Nothingness* in the library at Algiers, but also took an interest in earlier works such as *The Imagination, The Imaginary*, and *Sketch of a Theory of Emotions*. In his essay, Derrida emphasized the influence of Husserl on Sartre, even though he still had only an indirect acquaintance with the great German phenomenologist.

In tandem with *Being and Nothingness*, Derrida read *Nausea* 'in a certain ecstatic bedazzlement', 'sitting on a bench in Laferrière Square, sometimes raising my eyes toward the roots, the bushes of flowers or the luxuriant plants, as if to verify the too-much of existence, but also with intense moments of "literary" identification'.[39] Many years later, he still admired this 'literary fiction based on a philosophical "emotion"'. His passion for Sartre extended to *No Exit*, a performance of which he saw on stage, the review *Les Temps modernes*, and the first two volumes of *Situations*.

Even though Derrida subsequently deemed his influence 'baleful' and even 'catastrophic', the author of *What is Literature?* was at that time, for him as for many others, an essential author.

> I recognize my debt, the filiation, the huge influence, the huge presence of Sartre in my formative years. I have never striven to evade it. [. . .] when I was in the philosophy class in *hypokhâgne* or *khâgne*, not only the thought of Sartre, but the figure of Sartre, the character Sartre who allied philosophical desire with literary desire, were for me what is rather vacuously called a model, a reference point.[40]

It was also thanks to Sartre that Derrida discovered several writers who would become essential for him. He made no bones about the fact: 'The first time that I saw the name of Blanchot, the name of Ponge, the name of Bataille [. . .], was in *Situations*. [. . .] I started by reading Sartre's articles on those people, before reading them.' As far as *Being and Nothingness* is concerned, the work would strike him as 'philosophically weak' once he had embarked on his reading of the three big 'H's – Hegel, Husserl, and Heidegger. In Derrida's view, Sartre's work was not great literature either, *Nausea* apart, but it remained 'unrivalled' for its impact on his own personal history as on that of his whole generation.

Sartre's view of commitment also corresponded to Derrida's first real politicization. We must of course avoid any anachronism: even if the terrible Sétif massacres in May 1945 appeared in retrospect to mark the beginning of the Algerian War, Jackie's positions at that time were not anti-colonialist, but traditionally reformist, as indeed were those of the French Communist Party:

> When I was in *hypokhâgne* in Algiers, I was starting to belong to 'left-wing' *Algérois* groups. There was Mandouze at that time, in the years 47–48–49. [. . .] I belonged to groups that took up positions, I was politically more enlightened. Without being in favour of Algerian independence, we were against the hard-line policies of France. We were militating for a decolonization via the transformation of the status which Algerians had been allotted.[41]

In many respects, *hypokhâgne* seems to have been a happy year. Surrounded by a group of young men and women, many of whom shared the same interests as he did, Jackie was not subjected to the pressures of the least exam. But his results overall were good, and in philosophy he came second out of seventy. His friend Jean-Claude Pariente, the most brilliant boy in the class, took the exam for the rue d'Ulm, but failed – badly. This convinced Derrida not to try to do the same thing. If he was to have any serious chance of getting into Normale Sup, he would need to be in metropolitan France, he told himself. Like Pariente and Domerc, he gained a place at Louis-le-Grand, the most prestigious of Paris *lycées*, the one which had been attended by Victor Hugo and Charles Baudelaire, Alain-Fournier and Paul Claudel, Jean-Paul Sartre and Maurice Merleau-Ponty. Even though these studies imposed a great financial sacrifice on Jackie's parents, they were ready to support the brilliant student that he had become since his final year in *lycée*. Of course, there was no question of his renting a room in Paris; he would be a boarder at Louis-le-Grand. Not for a moment did Jackie imagine what that could mean.

3

The Walls of Louis-le-Grand

1949–1952

At the end of September 1949 came the feared and longed-for moment of departure for Paris. This was Jackie's first real trip: the first time he had left his parents, the first time he had taken the boat, the first time he had travelled by train.

The crossing, on the *Ville d'Alger*, was hellish, with a terrible seasickness and twenty hours of almost uninterrupted vomiting. Jackie saw nothing of Marseilles and left almost immediately for Paris. After a long day in the train, his arrival in the capital, which so many books and films had led him to dream about, was a cruel disappointment, an 'instant degradation'.[1] Everything struck him as grey and gloomy, in a Paris that was rainy and dirty. 'From Algiers, the white city, I arrived in Paris, the black city, since Malraux had not yet come along to re-surface the façades.'[2] But the most dismal thing of all was 123, rue Saint-Jacques: the Lycée Louis-le-Grand, whose doors he entered for the first time on 1 October.

Derrida – boarder no. 424 – was, like all boarders, obliged to wear a grey smock from sunrise to sunset. Discipline was strict and the timetable draconian. In the huge dormitory there was not the least privacy, not even a curtain to separate the beds. Hygiene was reduced to a strict minimum: students had to wash in cold water, even in midwinter. As for the meals served in the canteen, they were unappetizing and the portions were small – the privations of the postwar period were still in evidence. Jackie felt like a prisoner. His old childhood horror of school came back to him in those few days of solitude before the start of term: 'a week of distress and a child's tears in the sinister boarding house of the "Baz'Grand"',[3] as the *lycée* was nicknamed.

The letter that Fernand Acharrok sent his friend Jackie shortly after term began must have made a weird impression on him. 'Dolly' hoped that his old friend had already seen the sights of Paris; he thought he was 'bloody lucky' to be living there. Had he seen 'the famous Saint-German-des-Prés district' and the 'Royal Saint-German, where Jean-Paul Sartre [was] supposed to have his HQ'?

Had he been to the Club Saint-Germain and the Vieux Colombier? True, all those more or less mythical hotspots in existentialist Paris were near the rue Saint-Jacques, where Louis-le-Grand was situated, but the boarders were allowed out only under strict regulations. In any case, in Algiers, Acharrok continued, everyone's thoughts were occupied with other things: the death of the boxer Marcel Cerdan* has 'appalled the whole city, including the non-sporty'.[4]

That left the classes, from which Jackie was expecting a great deal. He was, after all, in the most prestigious *lycée* in France, where the success rate for passing the exam to the École Normale Supérieure was far and away the highest. But in this respect too, Louis-le-Grand would be something of a disappointment to him. Solid work was preferred to brilliance, and the approach in most subjects was still quite academic.

If Derrida had been a pupil at the Lycée Henri-IV, the neighbour and rival of Louis-le-Grand, his philosophy teacher would have been Jean Beaufret, one of the main writers to introduce Heidegger into France, and the addressee of the latter's 'Letter on humanism'. But the teacher whose classes he attended for six hours a week, together with all the pupils in *khâgne* no. 2, was Étienne Borne – distinctly less charismatic. He was an ex-student of Alain, an admirer of Emmanuel Mounier and Gabriel Marcel, and a pillar of the MRP – the Mouvement Républicain Populaire.† He was a Catholic, and published work frequently in *La Croix* and *Esprit*, with the result that he was sometimes called 'the hack of the bishopric'. In his physical appearance and movements, there was something farcical about Borne: he was as thin as a rake, and rocked from leg to leg while fiddling with his watch. Having to speak seemed such torment for him that his students expected 'to see him drop dead at the end of each sentence'. He would wave 'his arms around like a maniac' and, as he gesticulated, belch out 'the first syllables of certain words to put them into italics'.[5] None of this stopped him being a good teacher, who enabled students to master the art of the essay and to knock off a good bit of 'blah', i.e. a twenty-minute piece on any subject whatever.

Borne was soon appreciating the philosophical qualities of Derrida's first exercises: 'careful analysis, good focus on problems, nice turn of phrase'. Derrida's marks went from 12.5 to 14/20 – pretty satisfactory in the context. But Borne's comments were often harsh. Derrida referred frequently to Heidegger in his essays, and this tended to annoy Borne: 'you use an existentialist language that needs explaining', 'don't imitate existentialist language too slav-

---

* Cerdan was a boxing world champion from a *pied noir* background in French Algeria: he was killed in a plane crash on 28 October 1949. – Tr.
† This was a centre-right French political party, of Christian Democrat tendencies, that existed from 1944 until 1967. – Tr.

ishly', he noted in the margins of several of Derrida's essays, and mercilessly crossed out anything that struck him as beside the point.

At the start of this academic year, Jackie talked a lot with Jean-Claude Pariente, who had arrived from Algiers at the same time as him. As Pariente recalls,

> Our shared enthusiasm for philosophy had brought us together, while also arousing a certain rivalry between us, one that remained purely intellectual. My interest for questions of epistemology surprised him, and his references to existentialists (Kierkegaard) or phenomenologists (he was already talking about Husserl and Heidegger) meant nothing to me. I remember one argument, the subject of which I've forgotten now, but it was definitely ambitious, as happens when you're at the start of your career, and he concluded it by saying to me, basically: 'I can't understand in what way thinking about the sciences can shed any light on philosophical questions.' The distance between us at the time didn't get in the way of a real friendship. I could sense in him a true profundity of thought, but it expressed itself in forms that remained foreign to me.[6]

At the Lycée Louis-le-Grand, in those days, there was a real barrier between the boarders and the rest. There were very many *khâgne* classes, and in them two completely distinct groups formed, united by one thing alone: disdain for students on the other side of the rue Saint-Jacques, at the Sorbonne, far removed from the holy of holies of French higher education comprised by the *grandes écoles*.

Derrida had little opportunity to meet any of the non-boarding students: they generally went home for lunch and left the *lycée* in the afternoons, as soon as classes were over. Pierre Nora, Michel Deguy, and Dominique Fernandez were among these Parisians from good families, well dressed and well fed. The boarders, such as Michel Serres, Jean Bellemin-Noël, and Pierre Bourdieu, were provincial boys from often modest backgrounds. The grey smock which they wore all the time meant you could distinguish them at a glance: in many respects, they were the proles of the *khâgne*.

In comparison with this rigid social barrier, the fact that one came from Algeria appeared a mere detail. Such a more far-flung origin even meant you enjoyed a certain exotic prestige, especially as the three students who had come over from Algiers in the autumn of 1949 – Pariente, Domerc, and Derrida – were more self-assured than most of the provincial boys. As Jean-Claude Pariente remembers, they amused their schoolfriends on more than one occasion by improvising little sketches about Algiers for them: 'Jackie, who had a very olive skin and a very stocky physique, could speak fluent "*pataouète*", the language of the working classes in Algiers, especially the harbour fishermen. His father's office was right on the harbour, on one of the ramps leading down to it, and he must have gone down that way many times.' Being Jewish was no particular problem, either: in a milieu such as Louis-le-Grand, in the immediate postwar years, it was a source of neither awkwardness nor of prestige. Some pupils could flaunt anti-Semitic opinions, but their comments were vague and general, as if they did not in the least apply to fellow pupils whom they knew to be Jewish.

As all ex-pupils acknowledge, living conditions for boarders were unpleasant.

> In 1949, the standard of living in France was still not very high, and we were in an old-style boarding school: we slept in a huge dormitory, with a little cupboard at the head of the bed, and a few washbasins near the entrance. Lights out was at 9:30 p.m. The food was so awful and the menus so repetitive that we went on hunger strike several times in protest. Derrida suffered even more than most of the rest of us from this lifestyle, from the constant proximity of our fellow pupils, not to mention the fact that he had health problems that made the diet there particularly bad for him.[7]

As for the discipline to which the boarders were subjected, it was both strict and infantilizing. The *surveillant général* kept an eye on all their comings and goings, even if it was just to buy a demi-baguette at the baker's on the corner of the rue Saint-Jacques and the rue Soufflot to try to stave off the pangs of hunger. More than once, Derrida and his friends were put in detention for being a bit late or going out without permission. As a result, they were filled with fierce hatred of the '*pions*', sometimes of the same age as themselves, who tended to exert their petty powers too energetically.

The enforced cohabitation and the harshness of living conditions meant that boarders got to know each other quickly. When it was time for an afternoon snack, the private study room smelled like a cheap restaurant: provincial boys who received food parcels shared them with their friends. After a few weeks, Jackie started to strike up a friendship with several pupils, including Robert Abirached, who had just arrived from Lebanon. As he recalls,

> Derrida and I were both from the Mediterranean, with a sense of humour a bit different from the others. And we were rather chatty, which brought us together. Also, we each had an uncle in Paris and, by an amusing coincidence, these two uncles were practically neighbours. They lived in the rue Félix-Ziem, right near the Montmartre cemetery. We'd often go to theirs for

lunch on Sundays, so as to get a good meal, even if we had to put up with some rather dull conversation. On the way back, we always had lots of funny stories to tell each other.[8]

At the home of aunt and uncle 'Ziem', as he nicknamed them, Jackie sometimes met his brother René, who had been in Paris since 1947: he was doing a basic training course in medicine so as to finish his studies to become a chemist. The first time he saw Jackie coming out of Louis-le-Grand, with his long grey smock, René could not conceal his surprise: the rebellious adolescent and the eager reader of literary reviews now had the face and bearing of a prisoner.

Another close friend that year was Jean Bellemin-Noël, who had come from Aix-les-Bains. As he relates,

> I probably reassured Jackie, since unlike him I had an easy-going temperament. I slept well and I could digest pretty much anything. We'd often have ourselves woken up at 5 in the morning by the night guard, so we could get a good two hours' work in before classes started. We'd place our towels on the bedrail and the guard would give us a tap on the feet. Sometimes, I'd put Jackie's towel in position myself, to make him work. He'd never done any Greek, but he knew he'd need it later on; I gave him beginner's lessons two or three times a week. In return, he acted as my dictionary of philosophy. The secondary school I'd attended had been a religious school, so I'd never heard of Hegel or Schopenhauer, nor, *a fortiori*, of Nietzsche or Husserl. Most of the time, Jackie was able to answer my questions very precisely. But he sometimes stalled on a subject, just dried up completely. He had a very unsociable side to him and could suddenly withdraw into himself.[9]

Their friendship did not depend on work alone. Between the end of classes and the start of private study, they sometimes organized poker games. They both played an excellent game. 'We found a method for winning a bit of money from a few better-off boys who lived at home, such as André Tubeuf, Dominique Fernandez, and Michel Deguy. We'd agreed to bid higher than each other. This gave us a bit of pocket money for when we went out.'

But they went out quite rarely. On Thursdays, the boarders had three hours' free time. They generally used this to see a film at the Champo cinema, at the corner of the rue des Écoles and the rue Champollion; the seats were very cheap. As Derrida would relate, much later: 'Cinema followed me throughout my student life, which was difficult, depressing. In this sense, it often acted on me as a drug, a pick-me-up, a world to escape to.'[10] As when he lived in Algiers, the films he saw were almost always American films, as entertaining as possible and almost immediately forgotten – quite the opposite of what your usual cinephile would watch.

When they could obtain permission, Bellemin-Noël and Derrida would go out together on a Saturday evening, though they had to make sure they were back by 11 p.m. They walked along the *quais*, trying to dig up a few cheap books: it was here that they found, in particular, their first volumes of Freud. As for cafés, there were two that they liked to drop into: the Mahieu and the Capoulade, at the corner of the boulevard Saint-Michel and the rue Soufflot, just opposite the Luxembourg Gardens. 'We'd talk about literature and philosophy, but also about sport and girls,' Bellemin-Noël recalls.

> What brought us together was mainly the fact we'd both lost our innocence sexually, which was rare in student milieus in those days, and even rarer in the *classes préparatoires*. In a school where most young men were virgins when they arrived, neither he nor I was: I had grown up in a spa town, which provided opportunities, and he had the brothels of Algiers. Jackie felt superior because of this experience. On the Boul'Mich, you'd see a lot of young women: secretaries, sales girls, some of them a bit more sociable than the girl students. Jackie could already turn on the charm . . . All this coexisted in him with bursts of mysticism and religiosity, a thirst for the absolute that was evident in the personal writings that he sometimes gave me to read. I remember one poem that began like something by Valéry and ended almost in the hymn-like forms of Claudel. Only the first two or three stanzas were regular, then the constraints became looser and looser. It was already impossible for him to comply with any norm whatsoever.

At this time, Derrida was already a close enough friend of Bellemin-Noël for the latter to invite him to stay with his family for the Easter holidays: so Aix-les-Bains was the first French town he discovered after Paris. Another experience brought the two young men together during this first year of *khâgne*. The theatre group at Louis-le-Grand, which had quite a good reputation, decided to put on Schiller's *Don Carlos*. Since the rehearsals were held in the '*thurne de musique*',* a pleasant music room that was heated better than the rest of the building, Bellemin-Noël and Derrida offered their services as halberdiers. To their minds, the preparations for the performance were mainly a good excuse for prolonging their evenings.

It was during the rehearsals that Derrida first noticed Gérard Granel, whose path he would often cross subsequently. Granel, a

---

* *Thurne*: student slang for a room. – Tr.

brilliant student considered by some to be 'a prince of philosophy', had been admitted to Normale Sup the previous year and was returning to the *lycée* simply to play the title role in the play. Both fascinated and annoyed by the insolence and the cavalier manners of the young actor, Derrida would never forget this 'primal scene' which marked the start of their relationship:

> It wasn't even a 'first meeting'. At the time, he didn't see me [. . .]. This dissymmetry that left me in the shade [. . .] says something about the later destiny of our friendship. [. . .] In *Don Carlos*, I had a walk-on part as an obscure and silent 'Spanish grandee' with a beard as black as my velvet-embroidered doublet. And from the anonymous background to which I was relegated, he was glory in person and everything radiated out from him, even when he was on his knees in the light.[11]

Towards the end of the year, Jackie moved away somewhat from Bellemin-Noël and grew closer to Pierre Foucher, and especially Michel Monory, who, for nearly ten years, would be his closest friend. Monory had already been a boarder at Louis-le-Grand for two years; he had been a *hypokhâgne* pupil there, before a primary infection obliged him to abandon his first *khâgne*. Shy and sentimental, he played the organ, liked theatre, read and re-read *Le Grand Meaulnes*; he was also one of the '*talas*', the school's nickname for those who '*vont-à-la-messe*' (go to mass). The relationship between him and Jackie started to intensify one evening at the Lysimaque, a Greek restaurant behind the Gibert bookshop. From then on they enjoyed long, often rapt conversations or silent walks down the boulevard Saint-Michel or along the *quais*. Jackie gave Michel *Gravity and Grace* by Simone Weil, which had just been published; Michel reciprocated with a little *Van Gogh* illustrated in colour. He was often impressed by his friend: it seemed to him as if Jackie had been born having already read everything, even the complete works of Plato.[12]

It was true that Derrida's marks in philosophy were good enough to inspire jealousy. In the first term, he had the best results in the class, with an average of 14 and a more than positive evaluation from Étienne Borne: 'Cultivated. Gifted. Thoughtful. Good results.' In the second term, he came second, probably behind Pariente, but with an average mark of 14.5 and a congratulatory note: 'First-class philosophical qualities.' Unfortunately for him, philosophy was far from being the only subject that counted. At that time, there was no specialization in the competitive exam for entry to Normale Sup. And selection was so stringent that you could not afford the least slip in any subject. Derrida's marks in history-geography and French were good – 'valuable qualities which he needs to bring out more' –, English was 'not yet up to the standard required', and 'needs to make more effort' was the comment for German.[13] As for Latin, he was poor at unseen translation and very weak in prose, where he scored just 2.5. If he was to have any chance of passing the exam, he would absolutely need to take 'remedial Latin' – in other words, take additional lessons from some friends who were better at this subject.

Despite these uneven results, Jackie was, at least during that year, convinced that he would sooner or later pass the exam, and pretty confident in his own lucky star. One day when he was out strolling with Bellemin-Noël, they passed in front of the buildings of the École Normale Supérieure in the rue d'Ulm, and he assured his friend that they would both get in – a prediction which turned out to be quite correct. On another occasion, on the place du Panthéon, he halted for a moment in front of the façade of the Hôtel des Grands Hommes, celebrated by André Breton in *Nadja*, and uttered the words: ' I really should spend a night there sometime.'

As he waited for these happy events to come to pass, he was preparing for the exams by swallowing great quantities of Maxiton, an amphetamine that could then be purchased over the counter (Sartre himself was a great consumer), though it disturbed his already fragile sleep. Jackie turned up for the exam in a feverish state: it was held in the halls of the rue de l'Abbé-de-l'Épee and he fell half-asleep over several of his papers. His marks in the written exam were too low for him to go on to take the orals. In any case, his hopes had not been high: it was considered normal to fail the exam when you took it at the end of your first *khâgne*. Only a few passed first time. For most people, this first attempt was a kind of dress rehearsal – one more reason for going to listen to the oral exams being taken by those of his fellow pupils who had reached this stage. In philosophy, the oral examiners were Vladimir Jankélévitch and Maurice Merleau-Ponty: this would be the one time in his life that Derrida would set eyes on the latter, the author of *Phenomenology of Perception*.

Throughout the summer, which he spent in El Biar, Derrida exchanged a constant stream of letters with Michel Monory. Their year as boarders had weighed heavily on both of them, but the return to the family hearth was a far from joyous occasion. Jackie found it very hard to rediscover his previous close bonds with his teenage friends and now felt himself to be a 'corrupted Algerian':

> For me too, the holidays are a real drag, terribly monotonous. I really can't wait to get back, if not to work and active life, at least to winter in Paris, away from the family, near you and the others. Here, the weather leaves me exhausted and the only relationships I have with people are either distant and awkward, or natural and animalistic. In fact, this doesn't even bother me very often, and this shows how dull things are.[14]

Whenever he could, Jackie went with his father on his rounds, especially to Kabylia, an area he was particularly fond of. 'These are the most tiring but also the most interesting days in the week.' Apart from that, he felt 'more liverish and neurasthenic than ever. [. . .] I indulge in the least demanding pleasures; I also play bridge, poker, I go for a drive, I go for a train ride, and I enjoy the company of people whom I know – in the abstract – to be of no interest.' The over-rich food he was given at home quickly put back the pounds he had lost in Paris. But he really did not like his new paunch and wrote on the back of the photo he sent to Michel: 'Look at the huge thing I've turned into. I don't have anything in common with "myself" and that also fills me with gloom.'

Many of the letters the two boys sent each other over the summer were devoted to comments on their respective readings. Derrida could not get into Julien Green's *Journal*, recommended to him by Monory:

> You'll have to forgive me if I sound pretentious when I tell you that the genre of the 'Diary' is a genre that's always tempted me too strongly, and from which I personally *abstain* too much to be indulgent towards the weaknesses and facile writing that it brings out in other people.
>
> For instance, I've been re-reading Gide's *Journal* in the Pléiade edition and I have to *explain* Gide through an infinite network of determinations, i.e. I have to *cancel* him, if I am not to view him as a monument of stupidity, of bland innocence, if not of intellectual rottenness; and Gide was the writer I really admired a few years ago.[15]

Derrida did all the same re-read *Strait is the Gate*, and was again thrilled by it. And he discovered Maurice Sachs, whom he thought was remarkable.

As was traditional, Jackie changed class when he repeated his year at school, from K2 to K1. But most of his friends stayed with him; it was the teachers who were new. In philosophy, this made a considerable difference: the Christian Democrat Étienne Borne was succeeded by Maurice Savin, a disciple of Alain. He had come from the Lycée Fénelon: allegedly, he had been transferred because he was a little too fond of the girls, though some of them continued to find an excuse, any excuse, to meet him as he was leaving Louis-le-Grand. Savin was a literary man, mad about theatre: he regularly published in *Les Temps modernes*, *Le Mercure de France*, and *La Table ronde*. In his classes, he would sometimes mention Proust and Ravel, Bachelard and Freud, while advising his students not to refer to them in their exams.

In spite of these somewhat modernist tendencies, Maurice seems to have appreciated Derrida's style less than Borne had. His first essay earned him just 12.5 out of 20, an okay mark but nothing more in the context of Louis-le-Grand. His teacher's remarks were severe but astute:

> There is undeniably a philosopher lurking somewhere in this writer. If I think of the whole historical part, I have to say that there is much too much philosophy in these pages. Because potted summaries of philosophy don't add up to much. So the whole beginning of your essay left me uncertain and even unhappy. But when you start to analyse things, despite your over-'specialized', hermetic language, your text becomes really interesting and has several good qualities.

In the margins of one paragraph that is indeed rather contorted, Savin noted: 'I confess I find this really difficult to follow. Remember the reader . . .' In a thoroughly non-academic way, Derrida had ended his work with two and a half pages of 'Marginalia'. These were a series of short paragraphs, composed almost like aphorisms and completely detached from the overall movement of the essay. The final remark occupies just one line and bears but a distant relationship to the subject supposedly under discussion: 'Love: to yield to the incommensurable; to madness.' 'Interesting, but irrelevant', Savin soberly noted.*

As for madness, Jackie sometimes felt he was on the verge of succumbing to it as he started his second year in *khâgne*. Discipline in the boarding school weighed on him even more heavily than it had the previous year. The cold, the lack of hygiene, the horrible food, and the absence of any privacy had become intolerable. Some evenings he fell into a crying jag and was unable to work or even talk to his friends. Only his ever-more intense friendship with Michel Monory enabled him to keep going. Working together in the *thurne de musique* – Michel had special permission to keep the key to it –, they wrote sketches for short stories and poems that they nervously submitted to each other. But as the weeks went by, Jackie complained more and more of a 'malady' as serious as it was ill defined. He was constantly on the edge of a nervous

---

* This essay, like many others, was preserved by Derrida to the day he died and can now be found in the Special Collection at the University of California, Irvine. The habit of adding a long postscript to certain texts would stay with him: such is the case with the contribution he wrote for the fiftieth anniversary of *Les Temps modernes*: ' "Dead man running": Salut, salut', published in English in *Negotiations: Interventions and Interviews, 1971–2001*, ed. and tr. by Elizabeth Rottenberg (Stanford, Calif.: Stanford University Press, 2002), pp. 257–92.

collapse: he suffered from insomnia, loss of appetite, and frequent nausea.

In December 1950, Derrida's morale had sunk to a new low. For reasons that remain unclear, he did not go back home for the Christmas vacation, but remained alone in Paris – probably at the home of his uncle, since the boarding school was closed. In prey to a vague attack of melancholia, he moped around far from his friends. In a letter to Michel, the beginning of which has unfortunately been lost, Jackie tried to explain his confused feelings. For some time, he had felt as if he were going around 'in regions too difficult, if not to explore, at least to show even to one's dearest friend'. The lack of any letter from Michel for several days did not help matters. More depressed than ever, Jackie may have contemplated suicide. But now, the worst of the crisis seemed to be behind him:

So, now that the storm has passed, since the worst thing about the storm is the fact that it passes, I've decided, or almost, to go back to Algiers for this term, if I can swing things with the 'Strass' [student slang for the administration]. Your letter first made me waver in my decision and then confirmed it. But I'll be seeing you on Wednesday. I can't hold a pen and it's always going to be too difficult for me.[16]

The two friends met up briefly in Paris, just before Jackie returned to El Biar to get some rest with his family. In fact, he stayed there for the whole of the second term, at the risk of wasting his year or even having to leave Louis-le-Grand. For a while, he was unable to write and *a fortiori* to work. Then began an almost daily correspondence with Michel – a remarkable set of letters that ought to be published in full one day: it is perhaps as important in Derrida's development as the young Freud's correspondence with Wilhelm Fliess. Jackie, vulnerable and lacking anyone he could really talk to in Algeria, confided fully in Michel in a way he would never do subsequently. As for Michel, he may have been perplexed by the mysterious malady from which his friend was suffering, but he showed an unstinting goodwill: 'You keep telling me about this illness that in my great ignorance and my lack of perspicacity I can see only hazily.' He advised him to work, and sent him Latin prose exercises. For the time being, Jackie was not up to doing them. Writing a letter to his dearest friend was already a test of his strength:

Here, I'm leading a very gloomy, impossible life; I'll give you the details one day. All I can say in writing, all that I could ever say, would never be enough to express this terrible experience. [. . .] I can't see any *natural* way out. Oh, if only you were here! [. . .]

I'm not able to produce anything other than tears. [. . .]
Weeping over the world, weeping for God. [. . .] I'm almost at
the end of my tether, Michel, pray for me.

I'm in a very bad way, Michel, and I'm still not strong
enough to accept the distance that now lies between us. So I've
given up trying to cross it even a little.[17]

Gradually, the violence of the crisis started to fade, giving way
to 'a subdued, calm sadness'. It was three weeks since Jackie had
left Paris. He was working and reading a little, 'waiting for the two
months of penitence to go by'. To avoid a relapse, he wanted at
all costs to live outside the school after the Easter holidays. More
immediately, he begged Michel to write to him 'often, really often'.
He wanted him to inquire about the conditions required for him
to be admitted to the restaurant run by health and social services,
as the food there would definitely suit him better than the canteen
at Louis-le-Grand. Jackie also wanted to be sent the programmes
for the certificates in Latin, French, and history of philosophy that
he would need to obtain at the Sorbonne, as well as that for the
Normale Sup entrance exam. In spite of these requests, it was not
all one-way traffic: as Michel was struggling with his philosophy,
Jackie sent him 'a few notes on the Beautiful' to provide material for
his forthcoming essay, while claiming that he was not satisfied with
them. These fifty pages intensified the admiration his friend felt for
him; they earned him his best mark of the year.

In spite of the constraints on his own life as a boarder, Michel
did his best to prepare for Jackie's return. He set off in search of a
rented room that his impecunious friend would be able to afford. He
also went to see someone he knew vaguely, an inspector of school
hygiene, who promised to write a letter giving him permission to
have his meals in the medico-social restaurant. And he sent him a
few exercises, even though he thought it must be really difficult to
write Latin prose in Algeria: 'You need these black walls and these
incomplete dictionaries, this sour smell of dust and old tobacco, and
the hum of the cooking pots.'[18]

Jackie's letters were still as sentimental, but they became a little
less sombre:

Just six weeks to wait; then we'll go out, we'll go for walks
together again, we'll think and feel together; together we will
keep silence, too, between long, long private discussions; for
then we will tell each other what letters cannot say. Will we
have any moments of peaceable, trusting joy, Michel? I almost
feel I am no longer capable of this without you, but will I be so
with you? [. . .] Your friend who will never abandon you and
who forbids you to think of such a thing.[19]

Jean Bellemin-Noël also got onto the case, sending the programmes for the *licence*, as well as the dates of the written exams
for Normale Sup. Meanwhile, Jean Domerc managed to find a very
cheap attic room belonging to a certain Mme Bérard, a friend of his
family. The room was at 17, rue Lagrange, very close to Louis-le-
Grand, without heating or running water but wonderfully light and
with its own staircase. Anyway, the opportunity was better than he
could have hoped for and Jackie pounced on it. Even though he still
felt fragile, he did not conceal how much he longed to get away from
El Biar, since he found this return to family life almost as bad as life
at boarding school:

> I'm really at the end of my tether here. I could tolerate this
> condition at the beginning of term, thinking it would help me
> do some good work, that my health would improve notably;
> in particular, I'd only just left you, you were still present and
> letters merely justified this feeling; now, I feel far, far away.
> [. . .] Michel, don't forget me, I have only your friendship.[20]

Unfortunately, just as Jackie was about to return to Paris, Michel
was at home with his family in Châtellerault for the whole of the
Easter break. In one last letter, Derrida referred to his recent rereading of *Nausea*. After the tribulations he had just endured, the
book had taken on a new resonance for him:

> I have only ever laboured to make the world seem strange to
> me, to make all things arise around me as if by miracle; I no
> longer know what nature – or the natural – is, I am painfully
> amazed by everything. As for the words I use, the attitudes
> I strike, my gestures, my thoughts, they bear a strange and
> increasing resemblance to those of the Roquentin of *Nausea*,
> who went through an experience that I thought until now I had
> understood, assimilated and moved beyond. Well, I was far
> from doing so. [. . .] The difference is that Roquentin had no
> friend and didn't want one. I am different: I have you to hope
> in, Michel.[21]

Once he was finally back in Paris, Jackie lived out of the school
from 2 April onwards. This was an enormous burden off his shoulders. Now he was free to organize his work and his life the way he
wanted, once classes were over. But he continued to behave like an
invalid, going to bed early and eating only the meals served at the
special restaurant in Port-Royal. He worked as hard as he could,
but it was not enough to make up for all the time he had lost. After
such a long absence, the results of this second *khâgne* were disastrous, except in philosophy, where Maurice Savin considered Jackie

to be a 'reliable, hard-working pupil', in whom one could place 'some hope'. In French, despite his 'good attitude', his marks were 'no better than middling'. In other subjects, they were frankly poor and Derrida failed to hand in a great deal of work.[22]

On 28 May 1951, Jackie sat down to take the written part of the entrance exams in an altogether deplorable physical and psychological state. He had been through a series of sleepless nights and stuffed himself with amphetamines followed by sleeping pills, and was yet again on the verge of nervous collapse. Stress did the rest. Unable to write, he handed in a blank sheet of paper at the first test and had no choice but to abandon the exam. A few days later, he was in despair; he confided his distress to his old friend Fernand Acharrok. Jackie feared that Louis-le-Grand would not take him back for a third *khâgne* after such a disastrous year. But returning to Algeria would not just be humiliating; it would force him to give up any hope of a university career and to become a schoolteacher instead.

In one last surge of hope, Derrida went to see his French teacher, Roger Pons. In many ways, he was an old-style schoolmaster, more straightforward than some other teachers at Louis-le-Grand. But he probably showed himself more attentive to Jackie's situation. At all events, this meeting was to be decisive, at least psychologically, as Derrida wrote a year later in a letter to Pons, after passing the entrance exam:

> My gratitude also reminds me, among many memories, of that morning in June 1951 when, still downcast by an event that I thought was irreparable [. . .], I came to you for advice and, above all, encouragement. I left you feeling much calmer, determined to continue in spite of my disappointment, which I really thought I would never recover from. Can I confess to you that I would have never gone on with my studies in *khâgne*, or perhaps anywhere else, if I had not paid you a visit that morning?[23]

At the Sorbonne, on the other side of the rue Saint-Jacques, certain teachers showed themselves to be decidedly less impressed by Derrida's personality. He had to take several papers for the *licence*: in the general history of philosophy exam, for an answer on Malebranche, he was awarded a stinging 5/20. The comments of examiner Henri Gouhier are quite farcical, and must have stung him deeply.

> These answers are brilliant in the very same way that they are obscure. [. . .] An exercise in virtuosity, with undeniable intelligence, but with no particular relation to the history of philosophy. Has studied Descartes. Can't make his mind up

about Malebranche. Can come back when he is prepared to accept the rules and not *invent* where he needs to be better *informed.* If we fail him, we will be doing this candidate a favour.

'Accept the rules and not *invent*': an entire programme for a future philosopher. While this haughty tone and espousal of conformism were typical of the mandarins of the 1950s and 1960s, they were a foretaste of the attitude that the French university system would long assume towards Derrida. Judgements like these were of a kind that none of his later successes would ever allow him to forget.

At the beginning of July, Jackie left for Algiers. Most of the time, he would make the trip by boat, but sometimes he would travel more cheaply, 'often semi-clandestinely, in any case not according to regulations, on board small cargo planes that didn't look very reassuring'. These flights were uncomfortable and rather scary, 'seated on a bench in the middle of cases full of vegetables'.[24]

On his arrival, he wrote to his dear friend Michel, who had also failed the entrance exam to Normale Sup and was starting to lose heart. In Jackie's view, success required an impossible and complicated mixture of intelligence and dumbness: 'it's a miracle in the basest sense of the term'. He knew that his friend was playing with the idea of leaving Louis-le-Grand and starting at the Sorbonne, even if his father still opposed the idea. The prospect of no longer being able to see Michel almost every day worried Jackie as much as it saddened him.

As in the previous year, Jackie felt that summer in Algiers was a numbing experience on the intellectual level:

> I read very little; I am trying to write, but I abandon the attempt every time. My ambitions are huge and my means tiny. Thinking will never be a creative activity for those who lack genius. Damn!
> And then exhaustion overpowers me with this heat; real exhaustion, the same as that I suffered when I took the exam.[25]

He thought he was forever doomed to a nervous exhaustion that the doctors could not cure, or even understand. So 'it's a hideous sloth, of the kind that doesn't even have the strength to worry about itself or barely so, sloth which nothing can affect and which mocks everything. At odd moments, it's a respite for breathless readings or exultations.' These readings were highly eclectic, and extended from the Bible to Sartre, via Jane Austen, Laurence Sterne, Kierkegaard, Thierry Maulnier, Émile Bréhier, and Jean Wahl. 'Don't be alarmed at this variety: I haven't read more than seven to eight pages of each of them. That's the only way I can read.'[26] He would, however, remain faithful to some of the authors he mentioned. He read Plato patiently: 'If I had the strength, I'd wax enthusiastic about him.' And he was really excited to rediscover Francis Ponge: 'Never has anyone surprised me . . . so little. And that's why I find him so marvellous. I'll bring *Proèmes* for you.'[27]

The sun and the sea gradually reassumed their rights. Jackie renewed his friendship with Taousson and Acharrok, the companions of his teens, but this filled him with a kind of remorse:

> For the past few days, I've allowed myself to be distracted a bit by a gang of friends who've been taking me out, pretty much everywhere, unwillingly – and with my car. It was mindless fun: the sea, dance halls, alcohol, life in the fast lane, etc. And having tasted anew these things of my youth (don't laugh: I did have another youth, different from the Parisian, student exist-ence of Louis-le-Grand) I have now definitively lost any taste for them; and in any case, my health won't allow me the least misdemeanour.[28]

Over the weeks, the letters started to dry up, on both sides, and Derrida found this worrying. If Michel were to withdraw his affec-tion and trust, Jackie was sure he would soon become 'a nasty little earthworm, pretentious, narrow-minded, and shapeless'. More than ever, he needed the support of his friend:

> Here, I am faced by countless challenges that have left me exhausted. Never, even in the worst hours of my collapse, have I known such a state. I can't sleep any more: I sometimes get up in the middle of the night to slip barefoot through the house and try to get a little peace or confidence from hearing the breathing of my sleeping family. Pray for us, Michel . . .[29]

Monory was still a practising Catholic and at this period went on retreat in an abbey. This was an opportunity for Derrida to describe his own religious convictions, or rather his own anxieties:

> As so often, I wish I could do the same as you. But I can't. Firstly because a certain religious 'condition' prevents me; secondly, and above all, because I would still be too weak, if I am not too anxious, not to transform prayer, silence, achieved peace, hope, and meditation into spiritual comfort; and even if this comfort would be the end (the conclusion and the goal) of a dreadful torment, I don't feel and will probably never feel that I have the right – if prophecy isn't stupidity in a case like this – to accept it.[30]

At the beginning of October 1952, Jackie finally returned to Paris. Before embarking on a third *khâgne* at Louis-le-Grand, he needed to take exams for the *licence*: he had hardly done any preparation for them and was very scared. He was relieved to pass them, even if his results were no better than middling. Then it was back to Louis-le-Grand, which he now knew like the back of his hand. At the beginning of the year, he struck up a friendship with one of the youngest pupils in the class, Michel Aucouturier, who would never forget the first times they met: 'Derrida – or rather the Der's, as we called him at the time – was one of the brains in *khâgne*. He really intimidated me, even if he was always affable and almost protective towards me. He sometimes told me that, being a blond, I reminded him of his little brother Norbert who'd died at the age of two.' Aucouturier was sufficiently impressed by Jackie's talents to tell his sister Marguerite one day, showing her the class photo: 'Try to spot the philosopher of genius!' Aucouturier passed the entrance exam at his first attempt, at the same time as Jackie, and they would become even closer friends at the École Normale Supérieure.[31]

As for Michel Monory, he stayed at Louis-le-Grand for only the first two months of the year. Having finally obtained his father's agreement, at the November half-term break, he left the *khâgne*, where he felt out of place. He found a job as 'au pair housemaster' at the Lycée Chaptal, while finishing his *licence* in classics at the Sorbonne and writing a *mémoire de diplôme* on 'Aloysius Bertrand and the birth of the prose poem'. This did not stop the two friends from remaining close. They would arrange to meet in the little room on the rue Lagrange or outside the Lycée Chaptal, right next to the Gare Saint-Lazare. Sometimes, Michel would drag Jackie along to the Théâtre de l'Athénée or the Théâtre Hébertot. Even though he was much better than the previous year, Jackie was still of a sombre and melancholy temperament. In his 'secret and chaotic' letters he asked forgiveness for his silences, his periods of depression, and the times when he could be harsh. Michel Monory sometimes felt as if he were disintegrating under Derrida's gaze, as if he were 'just something small, empty and ridiculous'. 'You force me through your friendship to be very humble,' he wrote to his friend.[32]

During this third *khâgne*, Derrida grew closer to Pierre Foucher. He too now lived outside the school, and rented a room in the same district as Jackie, in the rue Quatrefage, near the Jardin des Plantes. With Foucher, Derrida had a less sentimental friendship than with Monory, and more rooted in the everyday.

It was during this third year of *khâgne* that we were closest. We met up in the morning and cycled to the *lycée*. For lunch and dinner, we went together to the special restaurant at Port-Royal. It was a distinct improvement on the canteen at

Louis-le-Grand: the food was better, healthier, and the atmosphere was pleasanter. Generally speaking, we weren't a very
happy lot of young people – a question of generation, probably. We'd only just emerged from the war with its privations,
we hadn't any career planned out and we didn't imagine our
future was going to be very rosy. Still, our lives were noticeably less hard now that we weren't subject to the discipline
imposed on boarders. We often went to the cinema. Sometimes
we played bridge, a game he liked almost as much as poker . . .
I also remember that on 1 May 1952, Jackie turned up at my
place with a bunch of lily of the valley.* This was really unusual
between two boys and I was touched.[33]

The main thing was still getting ready for the entrance exam. In
spite of the temptations available to Jackie now that he lived outside
the school – including, according to some people, an affair with
a married woman –, he spent this year working assiduously and
methodically, without skipping a single subject. 'We spent most of
our evenings together,' Pierre Foucher remembers.

It's largely thanks to him that I really started to work. I helped
him with his Latin, as I was better than him; he helped me in
English, where he was very good. I was also poor at philosophy, since I'd had a lousy teacher in my last year at high school.
One Sunday evening, as I was unable to finish my essay, I asked
Jackie to help me out, and he dictated the whole final section to
me. When Borne handed our work back to us, his verdict was
trenchant: the work was second-rate, apart from the last two
pages, which were remarkable!

As the years went by, however, Derrida was getting less and
less out of the philosophy classes given at Louis-le-Grand. For
instance, neither Borne nor Savin felt any affinity with Heidegger,
whom he had started to read assiduously. Generally speaking,
pupils in *khâgne* were not really encouraged to confront the great
texts; instead, they were taught to use summaries and to master the
rhetoric of the essay. So it was on his own initiative that Derrida
approached Heidegger's oeuvre. But few of his works were available
in French at the beginning of the 1950s. Only 'What is metaphysics?',
Kant and the Problem of Metaphysics, and a few chapters of *Being
and Time* had been translated, but in versions already acknowledged
to be quite inadequate. Derrida would later describe as 'monstrous
[. . .] in many respects' the translation of the concept of 'Dasein'

---

* A typical gift on 1 May in France. – Tr.

as 'human-reality' suggested by Henry Corbin in 1938 and later popularized by Sartre in *Being and Nothingness*.[34] Unfortunately, at that period, Derrida's knowledge of the German language was too limited for him to read the original texts by himself.

As the written exams approached, in spring 1952, he was a little less anxious than in the two previous years. His marks for this year were very satisfactory and neither his teachers nor his fellow pupils had any doubts about his success. If his Latin was still 'uneven', 'decisive progress' had been made in the second term. In English, he was viewed as 'very hardworking', despite the frequent absences owing to his still uncertain health. In French, this 'very good pupil' was simply advised to abstain from a 'tendency to complication' and to '*superior verbalism*'.

In philosophy, where his results had always been good, Derrida was really starting to shine. When handing essays back to his students, Borne, who rarely complimented anyone, often made very flattering remarks about Derrida's work. In the first term, he only came third, but his average mark was 14.5 ('excellent in every respect; very fine philosophical qualities'). In the second term, he came top, with a 16/20 that was exceptional for Louis-le-Grand ('reliably brilliant results; a definite philosophical personality'). The day before the exam, Borne got Jackie to write one last essay, whose subject had obviously been concocted with him in mind: 'Do you have a philosophical mind? Do you think, if you look into yourself, that there is an incompatibility between the literary mind and the philosophical mind?' Borne did not give a mark for this piece of work, simply appending this flattering judgement: 'Coherent and *thought through*. You *must* succeed.'

None of this ruled out anxiety, since Derrida knew that he might crack up at the last minute. This time, it would be a real drama: if he failed again, the doors of the École Normale Supérieure would be closed to him once and for all. Even if the temptation to reach for the Maxiton was great, he tried not to overdo it. The night before the first exam, unable to get off to sleep, he woke up the two old ladies from whom he rented his room and with whom he had become friendly over the past few months. He drank several tisanes as he talked with them, and eventually went back to bed.

The written exams went by without too many snags. Over the next few weeks, Derrida prepared for the orals, which he dreaded even more, as he feared losing all his self-confidence. Even if you were gifted and worked really hard, a place at Normale Sup was never guaranteed. In Jackie's class, only Serres, Lamy, Bellemin-Noël, Carrive, and Aucouturier would pass at the same time as he did. Pupils as brilliant as Michel Deguy and Pierre Nora would flunk the exam, and they bore the scars for the rest of their lives.

We still have the detailed account of the exam that Derrida finally passed, as he related it to Roger Pons, his French teacher. The big surprise is to discover what a remarkable narrator he could be, even though he would later claim that he was unable to tell a story:

> My exams were perfectly normal. The only thing that marked them out was an oral result so poor it set me back ten places. I was actually 6th in the written exams, 4.5 points behind the top pupil – this was in spite of a very disappointing mark in philosophy. [. . .]
> In the orals, I fell back in German and ancient history. These went disastrously – I thought I'd almost scored a duck. In French, where I was given a generous 12, I took a dislike to everything: the jury, whose appearance at least took away any desire I might have to share with them the joys of *explication*. M. Castex put on the airs of an inspired prophet to utter a few commonplace, summary, and superficial judgements. The other examiner, to whom I spoke more, was more rigorous, more anxious, but there still hung around him and his thoughts that subtle dust which imbues official papers, the documents of notaries, and even the school booklets for the baccalaureate.

In this exam, Derrida had been given a page of Diderot taken from the *Encyclopédie*, 'a rather unalluring piece overall, where everything was displayed on the surface, underlined and explicit'. And he had tackled this text by doing a Derrida *avant la lettre*, as if the main lines of his method were already drawn up:

> I decided that this text was a trap, that the intention of a certain Diderot, mistrustful and cautious, was being deployed between the lines, that everything about it, in its form, was ambiguous, implied, indirect, convoluted, complicated, suggested, murmured . . . I deployed all my resources to uncover a range of meanings fanning out from each sentence, each word. I invented a Diderot who was a virtuoso of litotes, a maverick of literature, a resistance fighter from the word go.

But dialogue with the jury seems to have been difficult, with one of the examiners, M. Schérer, objecting to the candidate:

> 'Look, this text is quite simple; you've simply made it more complicated and laden with meaning by adding ideas of your own. In this sentence, for example, only this bit is explicit . . .'
> 'Explicitly, this text doesn't exist; in my view, it has no literary interest . . .'

Castex smiled sadly, raising his eyes to the ceiling; Schérer pointed at his paper, saying:

'There was nothing to stop you saying so right at the start.'

In the final analysis, whether one came first or lower down was of no importance. The main thing was to have passed. Derrida claimed that he was mainly glad of the material security which the École could now offer him – he would be paid the salary of a teacher starting his first job – and the relief this would mean for his family. Sending him to Paris had been a considerable material sacrifice for his parents, and this had caused him a great deal of worry over the last three years.

With elegance and kindness, Derrida wrote a long letter to thank Roger Pons for all that he had gained from his teaching, despite a certain lack of polish – or indeed because of it:

I have the immense and inexcusable pretention to believe that, apart from yourself and Monsieur Borne, no teacher in *khâgne* taught me anything I did not know already or that I would not have been able to learn for myself. What I mean is that the others merely taught me, when they taught me anything, a métier, a technique, a corpus of objective and useful know-ledge. I feel that I have learned, in your class, from you, that which of course is part of a métier, but also that which is, within the métier, more than the métier: intellectual honesty and modesty, the taste for rigour and a sense of rigour, the desire to reach – simply, and without allowing oneself to be led astray by pseudo-profundity or specious qualities – assured judgements in which the greatest empathy is combined with the greatest lucidity. From the first work I submitted to you, I learned some very hard lessons in style and intellectual rigour. The chaotic and overblown pseudo-lyricism in which I then blindly placed my trust and which I still have a tendency to indulge in suf-fered a great deal from these lessons – fortunately. However scathing some of your remarks may have been, why did I never feel humiliated, offended by them? That was the effect of your presence.[35]

Winning a place at Normale Sup did not protect one from every-thing. It was just after the oral exams that a revealing incident happened. Another pupil at Louis-le-Grand, and a great lover of poetry, Claude Bonnefoy, invited Jackie to the family château in Plessis, near Tours. Derrida probably did not know how right-wing was the milieu in which he found himself. René Bonnefoy, Claude's father, had been general secretary in the Ministry of Information, in Pierre Laval's government; he was sentenced to death after the war,

but this was commuted in 1946 to lifelong national disgrace, plus
the confiscation of his property. At one dinner, where there were
many former members of Vichy present, one of the women guests
said: 'Oh, the Jews, personally I can smell them a mile off, Monsieur
. . .' 'Really?' replied Derrida in a loud voice. 'Well I, Madame, am
Jewish.' Which caused quite a chill around the table.

A few days later, Jackie wrote a long letter to his friend. In a tone
both firm and calm, he explained that he had no right to conceal his
Jewishness, even if this question struck him as 'artificial'. His 'condition as a Jew' did not define him more than anything else. He never
made much of it, however, except when he was confronted with any
display of anti-Semitism: this was a position close to that developed
by Sartre in his *Reflections on the Jewish Question* published in 1946.
Derrida used the incident to compare the French situation with that
he had experienced in Algeria:

> A few years ago, I was very 'sensitized' to this topic and any
> allusion of an anti-Jewish type would have made me furious. At
> that time I was capable of reacting violently. [. . .] All this has
> calmed down in me somewhat. In France I have known people
> who remained quite untouched by any trace of anti-Semitism. I
> learned that in this area, intelligence and decency were possible,
> and that this saying (unfortunately common in Jewish circles)
> – 'everything that is not Jewish is anti-Jewish' – was not true.
> It has become less of a burning issue for me, it has retreated
> into the background. Other non-Jewish friends have taught me
> to link anti-Semitism to a whole set of defining factors. [. . .]
> Anti-Semitism in Algeria seems more immovable, more con-
> crete, more terrible. In France, anti-Semitism is part, or claims
> to be part, of a doctrine, of a set of abstract ideas. It remains
> dangerous, like everything which is abstract, but less tangible in
> human relationships. Basically speaking, French anti-Semites
> are anti-Semitic only with Jews they do not know.[36]

Derrida claimed that he was convinced that 'when an anti-Semite
is intelligent, he does not believe in his anti-Semitism'. He would
like, he said, to have had an opportunity to discuss the incident
again with his friend and the latter's parents. In his reply, Claude
Bonnefoy seemed not to measure the full extent of what had happened: 'So here in the château we are all overcome by remorse over
a few words [. . .] doubtless frequently uttered as a cliché.' Mulling
over the situation, he insisted on the difficulty his parents now faced,
being 'officially damned, excluded from society'. And as if to get
Jackie to forget the unfortunate phrase, he suggested that the latter
participate, in the form of articles or short pieces, in the journal *La
Parisienne* that the writer Jacques Laurent (a friend of his parents

from the same collaborationist milieu) was about to set up. Derrida had no intention of doing so. But the incident seems not to have affected his relations with Claude Bonnefoy in the slightest.

After the exhausting exams and a trip back to Algiers that was both long and uncomfortable, Jackie allowed himself, not without a sense of guilt, to fall back into his 'natural tendency towards concrete existence':

> Right now I'm completely stupefied by exhaustion, the heat, my family. I'm unable to read or write. The only things I enjoy are undemanding pastimes, absurd games, the sun and the sea . . . I have a strong feeling that I'm not going to do anything during this vacation. I'm dull and dried up; will I ever recover?[37]

He would really have liked Michel Monory to come to Algiers for part of the summer, but this was impossible, and it was Pierre Foucher and his neighbour Pierre Sarrazin who joined him for a few weeks. 'The Jackie we found when we arrived was very different from the Louis-le-Grand student,' Pierre Foucher remembers.

> He'd put on his costume as an Algerian Jew, while still remaining on our wavelength. His family, dominated by his maternal grandmother and his mother, was very numerous and close-knit, while also being very welcoming. On Sundays, we would go for big picnics on the beaches at Zeralda, Sable d'Or, etc. I admired this harmony and understanding, this very tolerant style of family life. On weekdays, we'd often head out to Kabylia, accompanying his father on his rounds. It was always Jackie who drove the Simca Aronde, very fast and with a great deal of enjoyment, like the young men from that milieu.* He had a kind of self-assurance, almost superiority.[38]

That summer, Jackie, accompanied by his two companions, discovered several Algerian towns and regions that were new to him. In the evenings, they went out to the cinema or the casino, or played long games of poker. But in less than two weeks he was tired of this restlessness and the continual squabbling of the two Pierres: 'I don't have the strength to take them out all the time. I need immobility and inactivity.'[39] So great was his desire for solitude that he eventually sent them to stay for a few days with one of his uncles. And,

---

* Derrida's lack of caution at the wheel meant his licence was withdrawn for ten days, as notified on 1 October 1952 by the El Biar police station.

as each time that he was overwhelmed with melancholy, it was to
Michel Monory that he turned:

> If only you knew how deflated, disorientated, and desiccated
> I feel. I don't know where to look for any new zest in spirit or
> soul, anything that even distantly resembles enjoyment, ardour,
> a hint of inner lyricism, a faint desire to talk to someone or to
> myself. Nothing, nothing, nothing . . . Lethargy, anaesthesia,
> psychasthenia, neurasthenia, iron in the soul.[40]

He had no desire to read, even less to work. Perhaps it was the ambiance of Algeria that prevented him. Without altogether daring to, he
would like to have let himself sink into that state of immanence so
eloquently described by Camus in *Nuptials*. 'In one sense, but only
in one sense, life here is too good for anyone to think of reading,
perhaps even too good for anyone to think.'
    That Algeria would soon be no more than a memory.

4

The École Normale Supérieure

1952–1956

Arriving at the École Normale Supérieure in October 1952 was a real liberation after all the years of trammelled life in *khâgne*. Even though Jackie had to leave the rue Lagrange to share a room with three other students, it marked a turning-point in his life. Finally, he was 'there'; finally, he 'belonged'.

Founded in 1794 under the Convention, the École Normale Supérieure has been located at 45, rue d'Ulm, since 1847. It is just a few hundred metres away from the Lycée Louis-le-Grand. It awards no degrees itself: its particular feature resides in the way it takes in students in sciences and humanities in roughly equal proportions, even if the two worlds remain quite separate. The ENS is, above all, an extraordinary breeding ground for talent. It is impossible to list all the famous *normaliens*. Henri Bergson, Jean Jaurès, Émile Durkheim, Charles Péguy, Léon Blum, Jean-Paul Sartre, Raymond Aron, and a host of others had, over several generations, ensured the celebrity of this institution by the time it was Derrida's turn to enter it.

This little world, at that time exclusively populated by young men – even though young women had no difficulty in visiting it – was known as the 'cloister on the rue d'Ulm', and it generated its own mythology and rituals, hymned by authors such as Romain Rolland and Jules Romains. Students study there for four years, with the third year generally being devoted to preparing for the *agrégation* and the last year to starting work on a dissertation. The students have the status of trainee civil servants and commit themselves to working for the state for at least ten years after they enter.

Since the beginning of the twentieth century, students at the École have used their own jargon to refer to particular local features. A '*turne*' or '*thurne*' is the room of a boarder, and '*thurnage*' is the complex procedure in which *thurnes* are allotted to students from their second year onwards. The student who comes top in the entrance exam is called a '*cacique*'. An '*archicube*' is a former student, and the directory of former students is called the '*archicubier*'. In the middle of the square courtyard there is a pond with a fountain, and goldfish called 'Ernests' (from ENS): '*ernestisation*' involves throwing a student into the pond. The '*aquarium*' is the main entrance hall on the ground floor. '*Pot*' designates the École's restaurant, where meals are served in the morning, at noon, and in the evening. By extension, '*pot*' refers to pretty much everything related, in whatever way, to food. The cleaning women and more generally all the service technicians are called '*sioux*'.[1]

Even though this *normalien* mentality would irritate Derrida more and more as the years went by, he initially accepted it gladly, and did not grumble at taking part in a bit of good-natured ragging which involved students prising off street signs with the names of former pupils on them, or causing consternation among the clientele of the 'Rumpelmayer' tea room by uttering some incongruous remark. Jackie did not fail to attend either the École ball, which takes place every winter and where a tuxedo is *de rigueur*, or the much more relaxed garden party at the beginning of June. And he got plenty of laughs in the annual review, with a highly polished number as a *pied noir* gangster, with his hat pulled down over his face.[2]

In a half-serious, half-parodic fashion, he also drew up a motion on the so-called 'special diet' table, before getting several other students to sign it, including Emmanuel Le Roy-Ladurie. In these two pages of typescript, he highlighted the main causes of frustration, including the way meat had systematically been replaced by ham, while *pâté de tête*, sausage, and mushy peas were too prominent on the menu. Above all, the quantities of every kind of food except soup were inadequate:

> The starters have been stopped. Why? Perhaps we may take the liberty of stimulating the chef's imagination by suggesting that he choose from those vulgar fruits, tomatoes and olives, and that inexpensive root: carrots, either grated or raw. [. . .]
>
> Among the scraps used to feed us, we find, this evening, a camembert. It was, a considerable time ago, cut into slices that are approaching the consistency of brick. You be the judge: allow us to present you with this piece of evidence. [. . .]
>
> It is necessary to dispel the idea that the patients we are (to our regret) are privileged beings who demand a richer, better food than ordinary, while we would in fact be happy with a different kind of food, so long as it is good for us.[3]

Initially, Jackie continued to go, whenever he could, to the dietary restaurant at Port-Royal. But after a few months, his health had improved sufficiently for him no longer to need to eat at the special food table, at Normale Sup or anywhere else. Now that he had a bit of money, he could more easily take advantage of the local restaurants, especially the handful of cafés patronized by the students of the École. Even though they still frequented the Mahieu and the Capoulade, they were more often to be found in the aptly named Normal'bar just opposite the rue d'Ulm, on the corner of the rue des Feuillantines and the rue Gay-Lussac, whose table football they enjoyed. They also liked Chez Guimard, commonly known as Le Guim's, on the small square in front of the church of Saint-Jacques-du-Haut-Pas, right next to the rue Saint-Jacques, which provided them with a quiet place for a leisurely talk.[4]

For most students, the first year at Normale Sup came as a deliverance after the harsh discipline of the years in *khâgne*. Admittedly, there were a few *licence* exams to be taken at the Sorbonne before the summer, but they did not have to prepare for any competitive exam or write a dissertation. It was the long-awaited moment to enjoy life and make the most of the Latin Quarter. Now that he had much more money at his disposal than in previous years, Derrida could finally afford to buy books and go out whenever he wished. He often went to the cinema, especially with Robert Abirached, announcing in solemn tones, as if it were some piece of scientific research, 'We're going to do some applied filmology'.

Politics played a major part in *normaliens'* everyday life. The quarrel between Sartre and Camus had flared up the previous spring, but it continued to fuel debate. In 1952, it was an article by Francis Jeanson, 'Albert Camus, or the rebel soul', which had opened up hostilities. Disdaining to go via the author, Camus replied directly to Sartre in his 'Letter to the Editor of *Les Temps modernes*':

What we find in your article [. . .] is silence or derision vis-à-vis any non-Marxist revolutionary tradition. [. . .] I'm starting to get a bit tired about seeing myself, and especially seeing old militants who have never refused to take part in any of the struggles of their time, having to put up with endless lessons in effectiveness from censorious folk who have only ever placed their armchairs to face the way history is going, I won't insist on the sort of objective complicity that a similar attitude in turn presupposes.[5]

Sartre replied in the same issue, even more brutally:

But tell me, Camus, for what mysterious reason can't anyone argue with your works without depriving mankind of its reasons for living? [. . .] What if your book were simply evidence of your philosophical incompetence? What if it were made up of hastily acquired, second-hand knowledge? . . . Are you so scared of being contradicted? [. . .] Our friendship wasn't easy, but I'll

miss it. If you're breaking it off today, it was probably bound to
happen. There were many things drawing us together, and few
that separated us. But that little was still too much: friendship,
too, tends to become totalitarian.[6]

The article 'The Communists and peace', in which Sartre stated
his support for the USSR and posed as a fellow traveller of the
French Communist Party (PCF), led, a few months later, to a more
painful break with Maurice Merleau-Ponty. The two men had met
at the École Normale in 1927; they were allies in various quarrels
before founding *Les Temps modernes* together. In politics, Merleau-
Ponty was often ahead of Sartre, even acting as a 'guide', but the
author of *Dirty Hands* now accused him of neglecting the political
questions of the moment and turning to an overly detached philosophy of the world. Above all, he could not forgive him for having
criticized the USSR at the height of the Cold War. In his eyes, there
was no salvation outside the 'Party'. 'An anti-Communist is a dog,
I can't see any way out of that one and I never will,' he was even to
write a few years later.

These two conflicts, which split the intellectual world of the
time from top to bottom, were particularly important for Derrida
since, each time, he felt, 'like Sartre himself, no doubt, [. . .] in
contradiction and on both sides at once'.[7]

In any case, at the rue d'Ulm, it was impossible to ignore the
Communist question: the Party had dominated the École ever since
the Liberation. There were a lot of peculiar rituals to many aspects
of this. Every morning, straight after breakfast, the members of the
École's 'cell' would gather in the *'aquarium'* to read *L'Humanité*
and wave the best pages around. During this period, a few rebels
who felt closer to the Italian Communist Party would ostentatiously
immerse themselves in *L'Unità*. On the day of Stalin's death, 5
March 1953, the Communists – many of whom could not dry their
tears – forced the École to observe a minute's silence, while trying
to find out to whom in the USSR they could address a telegram of
condolence. But the militants – the most active at this time being
Emmanuel Le Roy-Ladurie, Jean-Claude Passeron, Pierre Juquin,
Paul Veyne, and Gérard Genette – put pressure on other people in
an often intensely annoying way. They would keep turning up in
your *thurne* to summon you to meetings, noisily flog *L'Humanité*,
and endlessly present you with petitions to sign.

Like his friends Lucien Bianco and Pierre Bourdieu, Derrida tried
to keep to a difficult line, refusing to oppose the Communist Party
head-on, but even less inclined to be dragooned into it. The militants
soon came to classify him as one of those whom they could not hope
to bring into the Party, even though such people were admittedly on
the Left, and might in some circumstances be useful allies. On good

days, they were considered as 'decent guys', in other words considerably less than 'fellow travellers'; on bad days, they were denounced as 'social traitors'. In a late homage to the great Sinologist Lucien Bianco, Derrida would remember this period:

> All around us, in the school in the rue d'Ulm, among our closest friends, the most dogmatic form of 'Stalinism' was then living through its last days. But it did so as if it had the whole of the future still ahead of it. Both of us were then politically active, in a more or less predictable and conventional way, in groups on the Left or non-Communist extreme Left. We attended every meeting, at La Mutualité and elsewhere, we sealed envelopes for I forget which committee of anti-Fascist intellectuals (against colonial repression, torture, French actions in Tunisia or Madagascar, etc.).[8]

To the great fury of the Communists, the little group soon founded a section of the 'Intellectuals' Action Committee in Defence of Liberties', which brought together the Left and the non-Communist extreme Left, and managed to attract many students. They would spend hours discussing the political questions of the moment, after reading *Le Monde*, *L'Observateur*, or *L'Express*.

Jackie almost became a full collaborator on the weekly *L'Express*, as we find from a letter sent by Jean-Jacques Servan-Schreiber to Derrida dated 15 May 1953, the day before the first issue came out. The two men had met a few weeks beforehand, and discussed the possibility of Derrida contributing to the magazine's editorial team. Right now, Servan-Schreiber wrote, he could not see exactly what he might ask of the young philosopher, and confessed he was still groping around to find the right formula for his weekly. But if an opportunity arose, he promised that he would not forget to call on Derrida. A collaboration of this kind would not have been in the least demeaning: shortly afterwards, it was in *L'Express* that Roland Barthes published his *Mythologies* and Alain Robbe-Grillet several of his manifestoes for the New Novel.

At the École Normale Supérieure, out of an intake of some thirty students, only four chose philosophy that year. Two came from Louis-le-Grand (Michel Serres and Derrida); two from Henri-IV (Pierre Hassner and Alain Pons). But they were far from comprising a real group: neither Serres nor Hassner lived in the rue d'Ulm and they were not often seen there. So it was often in the company of Alain Pons that Derrida would go to the Sorbonne, sporadically attending lectures given by Henri Gouhier, Maurice de Gandillac, Ferdinand Alquié, and Vladimir Jankélévitch. But from the teachers at the École itself, he met two who would turn out to be decisive.

On his very first day, he was given an appointment to see Louis Althusser, who was in charge of students heading for a course in philosophy. When Derrida met him, Althusser was thirty-four; he had still published nothing and was completely unknown. Only a dozen or so years later would he become a legendary figure. Like Derrida, Althusser had been born in the surroundings of Algiers. He grew up in a Catholic environment and passed the entrance exam to the rue d'Ulm in 1939. He was immediately called up into the army, and soon taken prisoner; he spent five years in a stalag and was able to return to the École only at the end of the war. He could not take the *agrégation* until 1948, when he was thirty; the same year, he picked up his membership card for the PCF. He was immediately appointed '*caïman*' in philosophy, in other words the professor responsible for preparing students for the *agrégation*; he would keep this post for over thirty years. From 1950, he was also secretary of the École Littéraire – a vaguely defined position that seems to have been invented specially for him. 'Le Thuss', as he was often called, occupied a very dark office on the ground floor, to the right of the '*aquarium*'. But he was mainly concerned with looking after the students as they prepared for the *agrégation*. During this first year at the École, Jackie met him only occasionally.[9]

A few weeks after the start of the academic year, however, Derrida started attending the course on experimental psychology that a certain Michel Foucault (another unknown figure) had been giving since the previous autumn. Like the other members of the audience in the classes he gave on Monday evenings, in the little Cavaillès room, Derrida was struck by the charisma of this professor, who was only four years older than himself: 'His eloquence, authority and brilliance were impressive.' Sometimes, Foucault would take a few students to the Saint-Anne hospital, where one of his psychiatric friends had a practice. This direct experience with madness was something that Derrida would never forget. 'A patient was brought in and a young doctor questioned and examined him. We were present for that. It was really upsetting.'[10] The doctor would then retire and, after drawing up his observations, he would come and give a kind of lecture in front of Georges Daumezon, who was in charge of the practice. Foucault and Derrida soon struck up a friendship; this was made easier by the fact that, although he had been appointed to a junior lectureship at Lille, Foucault at this period still lived in the École.

Another, even more decisive meeting occurred in February 1953. Michel Aucouturier, whose father had given him a car as a reward for passing the entrance exam, took three friends, Michel Serres, Élie Carrive, and Jackie, on a week's holiday in the ski resort of Carroz-d'Arâches, in Haute-Savoie. But if this break is worth mentioning here, it is less for the young skiers' tumbles in the snow than

for Jackie's first encounter with Marguerite, Michel's elder sister –
an encounter that they would allude to, in veiled terms, in the film
Derrida. The young woman, a beautiful blonde of just twenty, was
suffering from tuberculosis, like many students of her generation.
She had been hospitalized for several months in the sanatorium at
Plateau d'Assy, and her state of health was still uncertain, with good
and bad test results alternating. Right from this first meeting, Jackie
took an interest in Marguerite, but he did not have any opportunity
to see her in private. As far as she was concerned, he was still just
one of the boys in the group. Only a year and a half later, when
Marguerite returned to Paris, did their relations become more
personal.

As the months went by, Derrida allowed himself to be dragged into
a sort of pleasant whirlwind. As he wrote to his cousin Micheline,
'the life we lead here calls for long, calm, silent, solitary holidays.
You can't imagine how much we jump around, run everywhere,
spread ourselves thin. At the end of a day, you're horrified to look
back on how you've spent your time.'[11] But, as if to catch up, Jackie
spent much of the summer of 1953 in El Biar immersed in reading a
book that would be of fundamental importance for him, the *Ideas
Pertaining to a Pure Phenomenology and to a Phenomenological
Philosophy* by Edmund Husserl, a work better known under the title
Ideen I. It had been translated into French, with an introduction
and commentary, by Paul Ricoeur. 'So it was this great reader of
Husserl who, more rigorously than Sartre and even Merleau-Ponty,
first taught me to read "phenomenology" and who, to a certain
extent, acted as my guide thereafter,' Derrida would acknowledge in
a late homage to Ricoeur.[12]
    In other respects, August and September went by, yet again,
in a mixture of indolence and melancholy. 'I bless the end of the
vacation,' Jackie wrote to Michel Serres. 'I've finally yielded to the
cowardly desire to flee my family completely. This is what happens
when you love too much.'[13] Apart from Husserl, he hardly did any
work, barely preparing for the certificate in ethnology that he had to
take at the Sorbonne, since it was this discipline that he had chosen
as the scientific subject for his *licence*.
    Jackie was dismayed by one thing in particular: the distance that
had grown between himself and Michel Monory since his entry into
Normale Sup. He had not found the same degree of intimacy with
any other of the students at the École. And it was in nostalgic tones
that he wrote to his friend:

Why don't we even have the strength to write to each other any
more? You know that, on my side, I haven't forgotten you.
It's not my friendship that has died or lost its 'salt', but rather

something inside me. I'd need to tell myself – as well as you –, I'd need to 'recite' the things that have happened over the past two or three years, up to more recent events, to shed some light on it all.

And then I don't want to write any more, I can't. This is all the more distressing since I'm sure that I could save myself – here below, of course – only if I wrote constantly, at least for myself.[14]

At the start of the academic year in the autumn of 1953, the *licence* exams at the Sorbonne put Jackie in a bad mood. As he would tell people later, when he received the Légion d'Honneur in one of the lecture halls in which he suffered at that time,

> *khâgne* and the École Normale Supérieure conferred on some of us a puerile sense of hauteur, of being part of an elite, which did not exempt us, for all our condescension, from coming down to this very place and registering properly at the Sorbonne for our exams. And it did not exempt me, as one of their number, from exams . . . that I failed quite a few times.[15]

At the end of October, not having had 'time to draw and measure bones', Derrida flunked the practicals in ethnology, despite having passed the written exams. So right at the start of a year which he would like to have devoted entirely to working on his *diplôme*, he found himself faced with what he described as a 'ridiculous chore'.[16] Luckily, he passed in psychology.

Another piece of good news was that he shared a comfortable *thurne* with his friend Lucien Bianco – 'Coco', as he was then called – in the new buildings of the École. He wrote to his cousin: 'Working conditions here are ideal and I don't think we've ever done better. We're freed of any material worries, and if we were really selfish, really carefree, we'd soon doze off to sleep in this sort of Artificial Paradise, the École.'[17] Together, Jackie and Lucien bought an old car, a 1930 Citroën C4 that they nicknamed 'T'chi t'cheu'. Admittedly, it was pretty clapped out, and they regularly had to move it from one side of the road to the other to avoid a series of parking tickets, but it still enabled them to go for a spin now and again. And above all, this car – the first to be owned by *normaliens* – attracted the admiration of their fellow students. It was in 'T'chi t'cheu', driven by Derrida in a, shall we say, rather audacious way, that he would go to the Musée de l'Homme with Alain Pons to follow the ethnology classes that he still had to attend.[18] Here he learned, in particular, to distinguish the skulls and bones of human beings from those of anthropoid apes.

Bianco, as 'well-behaved, studious' companion, decided to

specialize in the history of modern China and started to learn Chinese. ('T'chi t'cheu' actually means 'car' in Chinese, at least in an approximate French transcription.*) Jackie, working at the next table, followed his progress with admiration. Later on, he would marvel at the way his friend could speak the language fluently, in a Chinese restaurant near the Gare de Lyon. And he would recall the discussions he had at this time with Bianco when he referred to the phono-ideographic model of writing of Chinese writing in *Of Grammatology*.

Meanwhile, Jackie was mainly thinking of the subject of his *diplôme d'études supérieures*, equivalent, these days, to a dissertation for a Master's. At the end of November, he decided to work on *The Problem of Genesis in Husserl's Philosophy*, under the supervision of Maurice de Gandillac – an old fellow student of Sartre at the École, and Professor of Philosophy at the Sorbonne since 1946. Derrida would often explain that, though Husserl had not been his first love in philosophy, he had left a lasting influence on his work, as a 'discipline of incomparable rigour'. At that time, the beginning of the 1950s, he was not alone in his interest: Husserl's phenomenology had still made few inroads into French universities, but it appeared indispensable to many young philosophers. Before turning to sociology, Pierre Bourdieu himself had thought of devoting his thesis to Husserl.

Derrida wished to replace 'French-style' phenomenology, as developed by Sartre and Merleau-Ponty, with 'a phenomenology more turned to the sciences'. In his view, this represented almost as much of a political project as a philosophical necessity. Impressed by a recent book by the Marxist Tran-Duc-Thao, he too wanted to link phenomenology to certain aspects of dialectical materialism. The word 'dialectical' cropped up insistently in his *diplôme* piece; he would soon abandon it.

Like many others, Derrida was fascinated by Husserl's unpublished manuscripts – especially on temporality, 'passive genesis', and the 'alter ego' – all texts which could be consulted only in the Husserl Archives in Louvain. In January 1954, Maurice de Gandillac sent a letter of recommendation and obtained the assurance of Fr Herman Van Breda that he would grant access to these precious documents.

Derrida set off for Louvain in March and spent several weeks there. This was the first time he had left French territory. In the attic of the Institute of Philosophy, where a vast number of the 40,000 pages of unpublished work left by Husserl had been preserved since 1939, Jackie worked assiduously. In spite of his only average understanding of German, he deciphered and carefully copied out several passages, even though he eventually derived a rather small

---

* In pinyin, *qìchē* – Tr.

proportion of his *diplôme* study from this work. He seems not to have taken a liking to the Belgians he met. Luckily, he struck up a friendship with Rudolf Boehm, a young German philosopher who was collaborating on editing Husserl's manuscripts. Every day, as they walked through the town's streets and parks, they held long philosophical discussions together, on Husserl, of course, but also on Sartre and Merleau-Ponty. As soon as he could, Derrida would bring the conversation round to Heidegger, whose work was becoming increasingly important to him – Boehm, a former student of Hans-Georg Gadamer, had an excellent knowledge of it.[19]

It was during this stay that Derrida discovered *The Origin of Geometry*, one of Husserl's late texts, which had only just been published in Germany. It would hold a great importance for him over the following years.[20] This did not, however, stop him feeling rather glad to get back to Paris, with his *thurne* and his friends waiting for him. Over the next few months, he worked intensely, writing a text of some three hundred pages, on old bureaucratic forms and pieces of headed notepaper for Mercier and Mumm champagne, piles of which he had picked up at his father's. Lucien Bianco would remember that Derrida sometimes read him passages of what he had just written; but since he had never heard of Husserl before, he did not understand much of it.

This is not the place to discuss such a technical work as *The Problem of Genesis in Husserl's Philosophy*. But one of the most striking things about what is presented as a mere dissertation is Derrida's self-confidence. He goes through all of Husserl's work and is not afraid of questioning it. At the risk of committing an anachronism, one might even say that he is starting to 'deconstruct' Husserl's work. At the end of the introduction, he does not hesitate to write:

> In spite of the immense philosophical revolution that Husserl undertook, he remains the prisoner of a great classical tradition: the one that reduces human finitude to an accident of history, to an 'essence of man' that understands temporality against the background of a possible or actual eternity in which it has or could have participated. Discovering the *a priori* synthesis of being and of time as foundation of any genesis and every meaning, Husserl, to save the rigor and purity of 'phenomenological idealism', did not open up the transcendental reduction and did not adjust his method. To this extent, his philosophy cries out to be overtaken in a way that will only be a prolongation or, inversely, for a radical explicitation that will be a veritable conversion.[21]

In spite of supervising the dissertation in a way described as 'benevolent and vigilant', the *diplôme*'s sole official reader, Maurice

Patronnier de Gandillac – sometimes nicknamed 'Glandouiller de Patronage' ('Layabout Supervisor') –, merely looked through it. This was because he could immediately perceive the quality of the work, he would later say; but mainly it was because he was not at all a Husserl specialist. Be this as it may, Derrida was very disappointed at this absence of reaction to his first work of any scope. He had been hoping for a real philosophical dialogue, a dialogue he had embarked on with Rudolf Boehm, but not been able to pursue with any of his friends. 'My *diplôme* work would be interesting in other conditions and for other readers,' as Jackie confided to Michel Monory. Neither Althusser nor Foucault seems to have offered to read it. Only Jean Hyppolite would do so, a year later, when he encouraged Jackie to get it published. But Jackie was by then in the middle of preparing for the *agrégation*, and did not follow up this idea.

The Problem of Genesis in Husserl's Philosophy is much more than a simple *diplôme* piece. Many fundamental elements of Derrida's work are already in place in it and, when the work was eventually published, thirty-seven years later, Derrida would be disturbed at how he 'recognized without recognizing [. . .] a way of speaking that has, perhaps, hardly changed, the old and almost *fateful* position of a voice, or rather of tone'. He was even more disturbed to find in it a sort of law whose stability would strike him as 'all the more astonishing in that, *even in its literal formulation*, it will not have ceased to determine, ever since', everything he had written. From this early time onwards, what counted for him was 'an originary complication of the origin, [. . .] an initial contamination of the simple'.[22] When Jean-Luc Nancy discovered this text, he would write to Derrida: 'The incredible thing about this book is that you can't find the young Derrida in it, the one you'd like to catch out committing some youthful error. The genesis of Derrida, yes, but not the young Derrida. He's already completely there, fully armed and helmeted like Athena. However, it's evident what he lacks – a certain youth, with its playfulness.'[23]

In spite of his excellent relationship with Lucien Bianco, Derrida would still miss his friendship with Michel Monory. The 'frigid hubbub' of the École left him feeling numbed, and he longed 'for those long silent solitudes of the rue Lagrange during which, and emerging from which, you are really most yourself'.[24] Michel had passed the written exam for the CAPES* in *lettres* the year before, and was a probationary teacher in two *lycées* in Nancy. This made it difficult to meet up: when the two managed to do so, their encounters were generally too short to be other than disappointing. Jackie

---

* The CAPES (Certificat d'Aptitude au Professorat de l'Enseignement du Second Degré) is a competitive exam used to select schoolteachers. – Tr.

felt he was closing in on himself, becoming harsh and selfish. In April 1954, succumbing to a new attack of gloom, he implored his friend to stay for at least a whole weekend in Paris:

> Try to see me before the vacation, when you're the only friend left to me; nobody, nothing, nobody. When people talk to me here, even when they show friendship towards me, they are addressing a ghost. And a person soon becomes a shadow in his own eyes when this happens. [. . .] I want to see you, as I always have.
>
> The life I'm leading is glum, depressing, and anxious. [. . .] I don't know why this is, but even my glumness is changing shape; it is starting to be permanent, dry or acidic. I think it used to draw sustenance from *another* joy or another hope, truer than it was itself.[25]

Michel missed his friend too, and 'those fulfilling times' of their life in Paris: breakfast together at the corner of the rue Gay-Lussac, 'those trips to Sceaux, on the banks of the Seine at night, to Orly in the old boneshaker, that page of *Don Quixote* that you read to me in your room at the École, laughing like a child'. In his letters, he expressed his 'tender feelings' for his dear friend Jackie over and over again. But he was often worried that Jackie was drifting away: 'Perhaps, for you, I'm lost in the mist, a pale shadow of a friend, awkward? [. . .] I don't know if I deserve your friendship, or if my friendship for you is strong enough.' [26]

Jackie's relations with women at this time are still rather mysterious. At the Sorbonne, he met Geneviève Bollème, a student in *lettres*, a Flaubert devotee who was already frequenting literary circles. Apparently the young woman roused Derrida's interest, but she herself seemed somewhat uneasy about the ambiguity of their relationship. 'We really are going to have to talk about our respective feelings for one another,' she wrote to him one day. 'I've always had the impression, if not the certainty, that they were based on a misunderstanding.'[27] This did not prevent them from becoming long-standing friends.

From October 1954, now that they were preparing to take the *agrégation*, 'the Der's' and 'Coco' were given rooms of their own in the École. But they were neighbours, and they carried on sharing the same car and subscribing jointly to *Le Monde*. Above all, they continued their political discussions. Over the summer, Bianco had the opportunity to go on a long trip to China, with a delegation of people from the Franco-Chinese association (Félix Guattari was also one of their number). On his return, the future author of *Origins of the Chinese Revolution* could not stop talking about it.

Derrida later acknowledged that it was Bianco to whom he owed everything he had managed 'to understand, and to think, in an anxious, critical, ever-changing fashion, about modern China'. [28]

Generally speaking, Lucien was at that time more committed and radical than Jackie, who told him one day: 'If destiny were to give me a chance to play the role of Lenin, I'd quite possibly turn it down.'[29] That year, world events loomed very large for them. On 7 May 1954, with the fall of Dien Bien Phu, the French colonial empire began to collapse. A few weeks later, Pierre Mendès France became Prime Minister, arousing many hopes. But on the night of 1 November 1954, Algeria was rocked by a series of attacks: a hitherto unknown organization, the FLN (Front de Libération Nationale), called for 'freedom to be won back'. On 5 November 1954, the Minister of the Interior, a certain François Mitterrand, stated in the National Assembly that 'Algeria is France' and that 'the Algerian rebellion can lead to only one conclusion: war'. The conflict would last eight years, traumatizing a whole generation and affecting Derrida with particular and lasting intensity.

Another event, this time of much more local importance, marked the start of the new academic year at the École: Jean Hyppolite took over the establishment. He was a great figure in contemporary French philosophy, one of those who would be of real significance for Derrida and one of the first to perceive the latter's philosophical talent. Hyppolite had entered the École the same year as Jean-Paul Sartre and Raymond Aron, and helped to introduce Hegel into France. In the 1930s he attended Alexandre Kojève's famous lectures on *The Phenomenology of Spirit* before translating this fundamental text, with a detailed commentary. For a long time, Hyppolite was a *khâgne* teacher at the Lycée Henri IV, where his pupils included Gilles Deleuze and Michel Foucault. When he took over the École, it was his ambition to restore philosophy to its place of honour on the humanities side. But his temperament prevented him from implementing his plans as much as he would have liked.

Derrida's main discussions in the academic year 1954–5 were definitely those he had with Althusser. Jackie, as nervous about the *agrégation* as he had feared the entrance exam to the École, wanted simply to work and to follow the advice he was given. For the first essay that his *caïman* asked him to write, he took methodical notes on Freud. Then, in a long and highly personal piece of writing, he tried for the first time to bring psychoanalysis and philosophy into dialogue:

When it ceases to be the remorse of philosophy, the unconscious is merely its repentance. Philosophy as such, in its own moment, moves between transparencies: intelligible ideas, 'a priori' concepts, the immediate data of consciousness, pure meanings. But the unconscious is not just a confusion or an opacity. It is mainly a mixture.[30]

The mark Althusser wrote on the first page of the essay was dismissive: 7/20. Admittedly, this was purely a guideline. The main verdict was contained in the comments, which assumed the form of a four-page, warmly worded letter:

> Derrida, we'll have a look at the *details* of this essay together. It would never 'get through' the *agrégation*. I'm not questioning the quality of your knowledge or your conceptual intelligence, or the philosophical value of your thinking. But these will be 'recognized' by the examiners only if you perform a radical 'overhaul [*conversion*]' in the *exposition* and the *expression*. Your current difficulties are the price you're paying for a year devoted to reading and thinking about Husserl, who, as I have to tell you again, isn't a 'familiar thinker' for the jury.

More fundamentally, Althusser thought it was essential that Derrida accept 'the artifice essential to the essay': 'In your piece, it's easy to see that your enemies have been condemned in advance, in fact it's *too* easy: the dice are loaded against them right from the start. To reach this verdict you need to deploy the forms of an ideal court of law: the court of philosophical rhetoric.' Still, Althusser's concluding remarks were encouraging: 'That's enough negative comments. I owe you as much. I'll just add that I think you can take them on board today, so as to avoid deserving them . . . tomorrow.'

For the following essay, 'explanation using simple ideas', the comments were significantly more positive. Althusser criticized the introduction, but thought that the 'discussion of Descartes–Leibniz–Kant' was '*excellent*. (Indeed, the fluency and confidence of your analyses increase as you go on!)' But he still encouraged him to avoid going on at length: 'Don't be over-dutiful towards the classical philosophers.'

At this time, Derrida was drawn between the demands of the looming exam, and his growing interest in Heidegger, already very clear from his dissertation on Husserl. Even though Jean Beaufret sometimes came to lecture at the École, he made no reference at all to Heidegger, despite the fact that he was the latter's main French interpreter. Thus it was with Gérard Granel – who had already passed the *agrégation* but regularly came back to the École – that Derrida started studying Heidegger in the original German. Although 'quite protective' towards Derrida, Granel was a member of a small group of 'precious, esoteric Heideggerean aristocrats' who fascinated and irritated Jackie at the same time. Derrida would remember this when Granel died: 'I was easily intimidated by pretty much anyone, but by him in particular, often to the point of paralysis. In front of him, I always felt like a vulgarian of French culture and of philosophy in general.'[31]

In spring 1955, as the written part of the *agrégation* approached, Derrida suffered the same acute anxiety as he had when trying for the École. The exams were still 'terrifying ordeals, times of anguish and exhaustion' for him, of a kind he would never have to go through subsequently. 'The threat of the guillotine – at least that's what it seemed like – turned those years into years of hell as far as I was concerned. This past was really painful, I never liked the École, in short, I always felt ill at ease there.'[32]

At the beginning of May, Derrida was in such a physical and mental state that he went to see a doctor he did not know, in the rue Cujas, and was prescribed a mixture of amphetamines and sleeping tablets, with dire results. Jackie started shaking all over and was forced to leave the third written exam halfway through, handing in an unfinished paper together with a vague plan. This did not prevent him from passing the written part – but he then topped the list of those who failed the orals. Maurice de Gandillac sent Derrida a letter the day after the results came out, saying how sorry he was at the outcome, especially since he and his colleague Henri Birault had given him a real 'vote of confidence' by giving the 'admittedly shapeless' and sketchy paper he had handed in at the third written exam a high enough mark to enable him to proceed to the orals. Unfortunately, this second part of the *agrégation* did not go any better than the first:

> My colleagues must have told you why they came down hard on one of your arguments, which seemed to get Descartes completely wrong, and for your lecture that, bizarrely enough, focused on a philosopher who happened to have said next to nothing about death. There is no question at all of your talent and, as is the case every year – such is the rule when it comes to the *agrégation* –- we had to allow candidates to pass who were of a significantly lower intellectual 'quality' than some who fell victim to the written or oral exams, since the former students played by the rulebook and were successful by dint of their conscientiousness and their patience. Don't forget that the *'leçon'* ('lecture') part of the *agrégation* isn't an exercise in pure virtuosity, but first and foremost an educational tool which pupils can follow – though this doesn't mean that, once you've rapidly dealt with the things you'd tell your class, you can't address the examiners directly.[33]

Gandillac concluded his letter as encouragingly as possible, pointing out that even Sartre had failed at his first attempt. Another member of the examiners' jury, Ferdinand Alquié, had been more direct, recommending Derrida to 'get more of a proper education', in other words to attend the Sorbonne more assiduously, and to have a more diversified approach on the philosophical level: 'Your three essays are really one essay, you suffer from "monoideism",' he informed Derrida.[34]

The summer vacations in El Biar were overshadowed by this failure, but even more by the worsening of the situation in Algeria. In January 1955, just before his government fell, Pierre Mendès France appointed Jacques Soustelle as Governor of Algeria. Soustelle, an esteemed ethnologist, was deemed to be an open-minded, quite liberal man. Shortly after taking office, he promised that Muslims would be integrated, and planned several important reforms. But it was probably already too late. On 20 August 1955, the FLN organized violent demonstrations in the Constantine area. Armed with axes and cudgels, the insurgents killed 123 victims, including Europeans and Algerians of moderate beliefs. The crackdown was terrible, and caused twelve thousand deaths. The Algerian conflict now intensified into a real war: many Muslims who had so far been reluctant to embrace the idea of independence switched to the side of the separatists, while Soustelle joined the 'ultras'.

In October 1955, Albert Camus started to publish in *L'Express* a series of articles on 'Divided Algeria', in an attempt to define 'a position that would be equitable for all'. Two big divides were opening up, said Camus: one between the European and Muslim Algerians in Algeria itself, and another between metropolitan France and the French of Algeria. 'It is as if the fair trial of the policy of colonization that is at last being held among us had been extended to all the French who live there. If you read a certain sector of the press, it really seems that Algeria is populated by a million settlers with whips and cigars, driving around in Cadillacs.' As for the Jewish population, he pointed out how much they had for years been trapped 'between French anti-Semitism and Arab mistrust'.[35] On 22 January 1956, in Algiers, Camus launched an 'appeal for a civilian truce in Algeria', at a time when he was an object of death threats. His attitude was misunderstood: 'Personally, I have lost interest in any actions except those which can, here and now, spare pointless bloodshed. [. . .] This is a position which satisfies nobody at present, and I already know the reception it will get on both sides.'[36]

Derrida was quite close to Camus's position. But in Algiers, any discussion on the subject was difficult, especially in his family. And in Paris, he was able to talk about it with few people apart from Lucien Bianco, who shared his anti-colonial convictions, while being, as Derrida was, alarmed at the FLN's terrorist actions.[37]

In the academic year 1955–6, the last Derrida was to spend at the École, Maurice de Gandillac invited him on several occasions to the receptions that he and his wife held every Sunday. It was in this salon that Jackie got to know several major figures from the intellectual and philosophical world, such as Jean Wahl and Lucien Goldmann, as well as promising young men like Kostas Axelos, Gilles Deleuze, and Michel Tournier. This was the first time he had gained admittance to a Parisian milieu that had hitherto seemed inaccessible. The previous summer, there had been a *décade** at the chateau of Cerisy-la-Salle devoted to Heidegger, who also attended. This crucial encounter was still being talked about. At a reception at the home of Mme Heurgon, the proprietor of Cerisy, a recording of some of the high points of the *décade* was played. This was a moment that Derrida would never forget:

> I was a student at the École Normale and I heard Heidegger's voice for the first time in a salon of the 16th arrondisse-ment. I can remember one sequence in particular: we were all in the salon, we were all listening to that voice. [. . .] I especially remember the bit just after Heidegger's talk: the questions raised by [Gabriel] Marcel and [Lucien] Goldmann. One of them put the following objection, in so many words, to Heidegger: 'But don't you think that this method of reading or this way of reading or questioning is dangerous?' A methodo-logical, epistemological question. And I can still hear – after the ensuing silence – Heidegger's reply: '*Ja!* It is dangerous.'[38]

But for Jackie, the main event of the year was the somewhat chaotic development of his relationship with Marguerite, the sister of his fellow student Michel Aucouturier. After a long stay in a sanatorium, the young woman eventually returned to Paris in 1954: results of tests on her health were still quite poor, and a serious oper-ation was envisaged, but she refused. 'Once I felt that I was really in danger, I decided to get better,' she remembers. Since returning to Paris, Marguerite had been subjected to a more or less homeopathic treatment, based on a protein-rich diet: every day, she had to eat a whole camembert, two hundred grams of meat, and four eggs, and drink a significant quantity of red wine. This idiosyncratic treat-ment produced a noticeable improvement in her state, enabling her to resume her studies in Russian. Jackie was invited several times to have lunch or play bridge at the home of the Aucouturier family, and grew ever closer to Marguerite. At one of their first meetings, he gave her Camus's *Nuptials*. He revered this *oeuvre de jeunesse*, with its prophetic title. But the book mainly enabled him to give

---

* The conferences at Cerisy traditionally last for ten days – a *décade*. – Tr.

the young woman a glimpse of the Algerian world in which he had grown up.

Marguerite was born in 1932, in a very different environment, and her childhood was particularly eventful. Her father, Gustave Aucouturier, was a former student of Normale Sup: he studied Russian before taking the *agrégation* in history. He met his wife in Prague, where he was working for the Havas Agency, and Marguerite and her two brothers were born there. The Aucouturier family then lived in Belgrade until the German troops invaded in 1941. Not knowing what had become of their father, the three children and their mother fled to Cairo, living in difficult conditions until the end of the war. Then the family settled in Moscow, where Gustave Aucouturier became the Agence France-Presse correspondent: it was here that Marguerite and Michel started to learn Russian. Finally, in 1948, the Aucouturiers returned to Paris so that the children could take the baccalaureate and go on to higher education. As one can see, the young woman was no more classically French than was Jackie: even though she came from a Catholic family, Marguerite would sometimes say that after this childhood spent in diaspora, and having a Czech mother, she sometimes felt more Jewish than Derrida.

In a letter written in the summer of 1956 to Michel Monory, Jackie referred in veiled terms and under the seal of secrecy to the 'terrible period' he had just gone through. The reason was that Marguerite was already involved with another *normalien*, Laurent Versini, a serious young man who was well liked by her parents and had accepted an invitation to the family property in Charente. Initially, this ambiguous situation did not seem to bother Jackie unduly: like many young men of his generation, he often said he did not like marriage or being faithful – until, eaten up with jealousy, he asked Marguerite to choose between him and Versini. Marguerite was probably waiting for just this opportunity to take her decision and go and see her fiancé's mother. When Marguerite explained the situation, Mme Versini asked her in particular to tell her son nothing until the *agrégation* exams were over, so as not to distress him.[39]

For Jackie too, the main thing now was to concentrate on working towards his exam, if he was to stand any chance of finally getting through it. During the weeks preceding the written exams, it was traditional for those preparing to take the *agrégation* in philosophy to go and get 'Althussered' – in other words, let their *caïman* Althusser give them some words of encouragement. Unfortunately for Derrida, Althusser had to leave the École following one of the attacks of depression to which he was already prone. So it was Jackie who endeavoured to reassure *him*, without wishing to 'disturb his peace of mind':

I'm sure that these weeks of rest will have done you good. I was sad to see you so tired, exposed to every agrégativo-administrative wind. In a few weeks, I bet, you'll have got your strength back, and you'll be here again to give us your support over the difficult times before or after the oral exam, with your advice and your presence.

Describing his own situation, Derrida at first feigned detachment:

The period leading up to the *agrégation* is the same every year. Personally, I'm in pretty good shape. A few exercises augur well. An essay on Descartes that de Gandillac thought quite highly of (14.5, 'not being generous, today' – *sic*). Analysis of Kant passage for Hyppolite ('Masterly and excellent', it would have got 'at least 17' – *resic*). I'm not saying this like a good little pupil proud of his good marks – you know, at my age . . . – but because it reassures me, perhaps wrongly, and gives me a bit of a psychological boost before the *agrégation*.

But he could not long conceal how intolerable all this had become to him:

I can no longer, alas, take pride in any praise from de Gandillac or Hyppolite, but I lap it up like a potion, suffering from the *agrégation* like a disease. My God, when will I be able to put this concentration-camp crap behind me? Philosophy – and the rest, as there *is* the rest and it's more and more important – suffers, suffers so much from this captivity in the land of *agrégation*; so much so that I might have gone down with a kind of chronic illness like yours as a result. Do you think we'll be completely cured one day?[40]

With Michel Monory, as usual, he was more direct and no longer even attempted to conceal his malaise. From a bed in the infirmary, where for a week he had been suffering from severe angina, though he was mainly being devoured by anxiety, he wrote the following words to Monory. They now seem prophetic: 'I'm no good for anything except taking the world apart and putting it together again (and I manage the latter less and less frequently).' Just before the written exams, Jackie went off with Robert Abirached to recharge his batteries at the 'Vieux Pressoir', 'a little chateau near Honfleur which discreet philanthropists make available to "exhausted intellectuals"'. He had hoped to pay a visit to Michel, who had just started the chore of military service in Dinan, but he realized this would not be sensible. 'If you could see the state I was in, I'm sure you wouldn't be annoyed with me. This stay in Normandy has done me some good, but I'm washed out and I hardly dare imagine that I'll get through these exams okay.'[41]

The stress of the exam definitely did not suit him. Yet again he was on the edge of a nervous breakdown. This time the written and oral parts of the *agrégation* went off without any disaster, but his results were so-so, if not mediocre, and far less good than what the preparatory exercises had allowed him to expect. Congratulating Jackie on his success, Lucien Bianco encouraged him not to set any store by the 'ridiculously low place' he had achieved. He knew how hard his friend had worked over the last two years, and said that he was mainly happy that Jackie 'at last had the right to try to get a life'.[42]

Derrida waited until 30 August before writing to Althusser, who was still unwell, and had followed the progress of the exams only from a distance – he was not even able to attend the *leçon d'agrégation* of his favourite pupil.* This involuntary desertion did not prevent Derrida from writing to his old *caïman* with considerable affection:

> I have sadly watched as this year drew to a close [. . .] because I'm going to be separated from my best friends, whose pres-ence has been so important for me: you are, as you know, one of them. [. . .] I don't want to express my thanks to you – even though I should – for all that you have given me in your advice and your teaching. I am very aware of what I owe to them, but all the usual formulas of respectful distance with which one addresses a master might damage the affectionate friendship you have always shown me. It is this friendship that I ask you to keep for me, and for which I thank you from the bottom of my heart.[43]

Althusser's reply, too, could not have been more affectionate:

> You'll never know how relieved I was, a fortnight ago, to hear of your success. In spite of everything, and even the favourable opinions I had been picking up before I left, I couldn't help being secretly worried on your behalf, fearing the unpredictable

---

* Hélène Cixous, however, who had just arrived in Paris, *did* attend. 'In June 1956, I just happened to slip into a "theatre", furtively: this was the Richelieu lecture hall in the Sorbonne. I sat on an old wooden bench near the door – so I could make a quick getaway. Far away, ahead of me, his back. He sat there and spoke for a long time. I didn't know him. I can see his back. He's facing an *agrégation* jury, he's going to be sentenced. The subject he is speaking on: "The thought of death". At the end, I leave. The scene stays with me, down to the slightest detail, forever. I didn't see him' ('Le bouc lié', *Rue Descartes* no. 48, 2005: 'Salut à Jacques Derrida', p. 17).

nature of this absurd exam, and the relentlessness of the jury. I can see from where you came in the results that you were spared nothing. Chase this unpleasant reminiscence, and the faces of your judges, from your life and memory as fast as you can!

Allow me to say quite simply that your friendship has been for me one of the most fine and valuable things about these last two years at the École.[44]

And so, in spite of these encouragements (which would not go unheeded), it was on a somewhat bitter note that Derrida left the École Normale Supérieure. Passing the *agrégation*, at the second attempt and with far from flying colours, had forced him to travesty his thinking and his style of writing, to bend to the demands of a discipline that was never his and would never suit him. As he wrote to Michel Monory, this really rather mediocre success 'does not in the least seem like a reconciliation'; it was if he had been allowed to pass 'somewhat reluctantly'.[45] He would remember it all as a real time of suffering, and continued to bear something of a grudge towards the French university system, in which, throughout his life, he would feel 'an outcast'.

Among the various messages his exam success brought him, Derrida must have given particular importance to the letter from his cousin Micheline Lévy. After congratulating her dear Jackie, she confided to him, with a curious mixture of naïvety and insight: 'Instead of being a teacher, I'd like you to have been a writer. [. . .] I'd really like to have read your books (novels, of course), to try to translate you between the lines.'[46] It was to be several years before Derrida would satisfy her wishes.

5

A Year in America

1956–1957

Every year, there are student exchanges between Harvard and the École Normale Supérieure. Jean Prigent, the deputy director of the École, took a liking to Jackie, mainly because he had taught him to drive in the old car he had bought with Lucien Bianco. He duly supported Derrida's application for a bursary as a special auditor at Harvard, officially in order to consult the microfilms of Husserl's unpublished writings, though in fact these documents would not arrive until later.

Contrary to what one might imagine, Jackie was at first unenthused by the prospect of setting off for America: he was terror-stricken at the idea of leaving Paris and his friends. On the other hand, it was the best way of obtaining an extra postponement of army service and avoiding a job in secondary education, which he dreaded almost as much. What worried Jackie most of all was Marguerite's situation. So that she could travel to the United States with him, a work visa was absolutely necessary. And in any case, the Augustus Clifford Tower Fellowship that Derrida was going to receive, to the value of $2,200 for the year, would be quite inadequate for both of them.

More pressingly, Derrida was downcast at being separated from Marguerite during the short vacation period at his disposal. It was mid-August before he reached El Biar. Bianco wondered what his friend would find in Algeria and whether the two of them would long be able to continue 'doing nothing to stop this absurd war'.[1] In every respect, Jackie's stay in Algeria was not a success. This was a result of the political situation, but also because his parents were anxious about his imminent departure for the United States. As he wrote to Michel Monory:

> I'm spending whole days getting ready for this trip, writing bureaucratic letters, filling forms, etc. etc. And I'm also stressed because I don't know if Marguerite [. . .] will be able to come with me, at the same time as me. Ever since we have been . . .

together, which has been for me the *newest* thing in my whole life, I feel I've been caught up in the world, and I'm struggling with all my strength, shedding my blood even, against everything that is of the world, everything which, in the world, constitutes a trap. The prototype is the *'family'*. But I always talk in gloomy, strained terms of what is the greatest joy. [. . .]

I guess you are still in Dinan. I hope you never come to Algiers. The sight of the young soldiers in Algiers really upsets me. Whether careworn or heroic, whistling at the girls or ill-treating the Arabs in the streets, they always look out of place, absurd. My poor Michel, what would they make you do?[2]

In another letter, to Louis Althusser, Derrida described the Algerian situation with remarkable precision:

I still have ten days to spend in this terribly paralysed country. Nothing happens, nothing, nothing that might indicate any political movement or the development of a situation. Just daily attacks, deaths to which you get used, and which people talk about as if they were just an unwelcome shower of rain. But the lack of political awareness, the blindness, are still the same. I've learned nothing from this stay in Algiers, except how to breathe in an air that I wasn't very familiar with. It was apparently the same in the cities of Indochina: frenzy, intensified dynamism, an accelerated orgy of trade, speculation on a future that deceived nobody, a fake cheerfulness; the beaches, the cafés, the streets are all full of people. Between the tanks and the armoured cars, there are more and more American cars; the city looks like a magnificent construction site that indicates the coming of the most peaceful and prosperous future.[3]

A month later, on 30 September 1956, two time bombs would explode in the heart of Algiers, on the crowded terraces of the Milk-Bar, on the place d'Isly, and of the Cafétéria, on rue Michelet, causing several casualties. These two attacks marked a turning-point in the Algerian War. They led to the Djamila Bouhired affair:* the young woman was defended, aggressively, by Jacques Vergès, and sentenced to death, then reprieved after a trial that fiercely divided public opinion.[4]

---

* Djamila Bouhired was a militant in the Front de Libération Nationale in Algeria, and part of the 'bomb network'. She was captured, tortured, and sentenced to death, but Jacques Vergès campaigned on her behalf, and a large swathe of public opinion, alerted to the mistreatment of dissidents by the French army, supported her eventual release in 1962. – Tr.

At the end of August, an official from Harvard told Derrida that he had found a job as an au pair for Marguerite in Cambridge, Mass. So Marguerite could obtain a work visa and go to America with Jackie. But in order to pay for her crossing, she had to borrow money from a female friend. In the Aucouturier family as in the Derrida family, the announcement of the departure of Marguerite and Jackie caused quite a stir.

Michel, Marguerite's brother, had just returned from a year in the USSR: only now did he discover the situation and he could not conceal a certain malaise:

> I was taken aback to learn that the engagement with Laurent Versini had been broken off. I felt partly responsible. Furthermore, Jackie had written my parents a long letter that had really annoyed them: instead of asking for Marguerite's hand in marriage in the traditional way, he set out in detail his very free conception of relationships within a couple. Although he was an old *normalien*, my father had his quite traditional sides. He was not best pleased to see his daughter heading off with this young man.[5]

In El Biar, in the Derrida family, the situation was even more delicate. Marguerite's daily letters finally roused the interest of Derrida's parents. But Jackie waited until the last moment to tell them that their relationship was serious and that Marguerite would be sailing to the United States with him. The announcement of this quasi-engagement with a young woman who was a 'goy', a complete outsider to their world, caused a considerable stir over the next few weeks. Everyone got involved, starting with René, Jackie's older brother, who did not seek to conceal his hostility for the planned marriage.

A maternal uncle, Georges Safar, sent Jackie a letter that greatly irritated him. Even though his uncle assured him that he desired 'neither to approve nor disapprove' of what his nephew was doing, he did want to have a good talk to him when he came back from the United States, to tell him 'what his conscience, his affection, and his experience forced him to say'.[6] There is no doubt that the religious question lay at the heart of his remarks: in the Safar family, as in the Derrida family, endogamy was less the rule than something that just went without saying; you married within your milieu, and often even within the same part of town, as René and Janine had done. But ever since his teens, Jackie had distanced himself from the Jewish community and could not stand the idea of anyone trying to trap him in it. A few days later, he wrote his uncle a letter that seems unfortunately to have disappeared, though one can guess that in it he reacted point by point to his letter, without letting a single detail go unanswered, in the way that he would later make his own in philosophical polemics. Georges Safar was stunned:

> Having written to you in familiar everyday words, you now reply, after dissecting and carefully analysing them (I suppose you're just doing your job) a long, bitter letter, very 'uptight' and sometimes quite impertinent in tone. [. . .]
>
> As for what I had been putting off telling you, it was simply this: what will you do later, the day children come along? I wanted, not to warn you of the possibility, knowing that you'd already thought about it, but to recommend you to weigh it up properly, as [. . .] the problems that you'll have to cope with in the children's upbringing on this point will in my view be insoluble, unless you have already faced up to this future.
>
> Let me add finally, my dear Jackie, that I don't want to see you dissecting, as you did for my previous letter, each of the terms used in it, or even to receive a subtle analysis of them, as in your reply – even if it is not tinged with insolence.

However, the uncle realized that his letter, 'coming after many others', would have found his nephew 'in the position of the gladiator assailed on all sides and, turning his sword this way and that to ward off blows, continues to slice through the air . . . even when he no longer has any enemies around him'.[7]

Only Jackie's female cousins seemed to be pleased about his engagement. Josette advised him 'not to hesitate for a moment, even if there's a bit of friction in the family'. Micheline also said that she was very happy to learn of 'the existence of a future cousin, a pretty Marguerite from Paris, blonde with lovely blue eyes'. She hoped that the quarrel with René would not last, but whatever happened, Jackie must do as he thought best.[8]

Meanwhile, on 15 September, Jackie and Marguerite had embarked in Le Havre on the aptly named *Liberté*. After a wonderful transatlantic journey, they were 'fascinated and thrilled by New York'. They were both seduced and overwhelmed by 'by the mystery of this city without mystery, without history, all on the outside'.[9] Unfortunately, they did not have enough money to see the sights or visit other cities. So they left straightaway for Cambridge, in the suburbs of Boston.

'I was working as an au pair,' remembers Marguerite.

> Mr Rodwin was a professor at MIT, his wife was French and wanted their three daughters to be brought up in French. I had a room in their home, in Arlington Street, near Massachusetts Avenue. It was a pleasant area, right next to the university,

and the work wasn't tiring. Jackie lived on the campus, in the Graduate Center, in a modern building, but it was expensive and strictly off-limits to girls. Even if we sometimes managed to slip past the guards, it didn't make life any easier for us. In comparison with his years at Normale Sup, Jackie had very little money. His bursary wasn't enough, so he gave lessons to some of the professor's children, three mornings a week. That year, we met hardly anybody apart from Margaret Dinner, known as Margot, a student at Radcliffe, the women's college that was the counterpart of the then exclusively masculine Harvard.[10]

Whenever they could, Marguerite and Jackie met up in the extraordinary Widener Library, on the Harvard campus. It was 'the hugest cemetery for books in the world', 'ten times richer' than France's Bibliothèque Nationale, according to Derrida. And it was especially alluring because he had been allowed to ferret around in the reserve stock.[11] He continued to work on Husserl, while systematically reading Joyce's work; throughout his life, he would consider *Ulysses* and *Finnegans Wake* to be the most grandiose attempt ever to bring together in one oeuvre 'the potential memory of mankind'.[12] At that time, Derrida's written English was already excellent, but he felt uneasy about speaking it. Marguerite could express herself more fluently than he could, and with more confidence: ever since childhood, she had been used to speaking another language than her own.

Jackie also took advantage of his stay in Harvard to learn to use a typewriter. Shortly after his arrival he bought himself an Olivetti 32. 'I type very quickly, very badly, making lots of mistakes,' he later confessed. Used to the international keyboard, he would continue for years to buy his typewriters from the United States.

'We spend all our time going for walks, reading and working (just a bit),' he told Lucien Bianco.[13] In his letters to Michel Monory, he was as ever more precise and more melancholy:

> It's a life devoid of events, dates, or any truly human society, more or less. We live by ourselves. Outwardly, life runs at the speed of the most provincial university town. We go 'into town', i.e. Boston, ten minutes' journey by subway, only once or twice a month. Apart from that, we're working, or trying to. Marguerite is translating a dreadful Soviet novel and I'm typing. I'm reading, trying to work, to settle down to something. But all I do is the complete opposite and wonder how it's possible to work without constraint.[14]

At Christmas, they returned to New York. In spite of the cold, they were enthralled, and walked round for days at a stretch. Jackie already loved the city, 'which has a "soul" by being so monstrously beautiful, all on the outside, so "modern" it makes you feel uneasy, and where you feel lonelier than anywhere else in the world'.[15] In their room in the Hotel Martinique, Derrida tried to write 'for himself', as he had not done for years, in notebooks which he seems, unfortunately, to have lost a few years later.

With Margot Dinner and one of her female friends, a German student, they also went to Cape Cod, very well preserved in those days. On another occasion, they hired a car and drove as far as Cape Hatteras, in North Carolina, a wild place whose beauty made a great impression on them. It was on this trip into the heart of America that they came up against the brutality of racial segregation. At the end of the 1950s, signs saying 'Whites Only' could still be seen everywhere. Much later, Derrida would tell his friend Peggy Kamuf about one episode that could have ended badly. They had stopped to pick up a black hitchhiker. The man was amazed that he'd been picked up by a couple of white people, and showed clear signs of nervousness that Jackie and Marguerite could not understand. The hitchhiker was probably imagining the problems that would inevitably have arisen if they'd been stopped by the police: this type of contact between races was at the time completely prohibited. Luckily, the trip finished without incident.[16]

When Derrida arrived in the United States, the result of the 1956 presidential campaign seemed like a foregone conclusion; it ended in November with Eisenhower's crushing victory over his Democrat rival, Adlai Stevenson. Apart from that, international news was too sparse for Derrida's liking and he was soon missing the political discussions he had enjoyed at Normale Sup. Bianco had bought him a subscription to the weekly selection of *Le Monde*, but it reached him only belatedly. In the letters Derrida received from his former *cothurne*,[*] Bianco commented on the turbulent events of the day: the Budapest uprising, the Khrushchev report and its repercussions, the rise of Nasser and the nationalization of the Suez Canal.

What was of much greater concern to Bianco and Derrida was the worsening of the situation in Algeria. Under the government of Guy Mollet, military service had just been extended to twenty-four months. In less than two years, the numbers of the French Army had risen from 54,000 to 350,000 men, while tens of thousands of young Algerians were now going underground. Robert Lacoste, the new governor general, opted for an even more hard-line approach than had Jacques Soustelle. On 7 January 1957, he entrusted the 'pacification' of Algiers to General Massu, who was in command of

---

[*] Room-mate. – Tr.

the 10th division of parachutists. In spite of the aggressive surveillance to which the city, including the Kasbah, was subject, attacks
continued, especially in the grandstands of the city stadium and the
stadium in El Biar.

Bianco gave Derrida some news about their old fellow student
Pierre Bourdieu, who was doing his military service in Algiers,
working in the Lacoste cabinet. He had written a brochure on
Algeria, 'whose tone and form, and even content, are fortunately
completely different from other publications of the general government; I was pretty relieved,' noted Coco. For them too, the prospect
of service was looming. Jackie had suggested that they try to enlist
together, so as to make the two years less awful. But there was
nothing to guarantee that this plan would work. At the same time,
Jackie was finding out from other ex-students about the possibility
of joining the navy: several of them had assured him it was 'the cush-
iest job'. There was an exam to take, with a long essay on a theme
linked to the sea – easy enough for a *normalien*, but an excellent
knowledge of English was also required, which was a bit trickier.

In February, Derrida received a long letter from Michel Monory,
in which he was glad to find his friend 'whole and entire', in spite of
the long separation. He in turn wrote his friend an immensely long
letter in which he wallowed in nostalgia for the years they had been
so close. In the loose-limbed and repetitive style of this letter, we can
already see the style that Derrida would make his own many years
later, in 'Circumfession' or *The Work of Mourning*, for example:

> I often feel as if I'd been laid really low, by a nasty unknown
> fever, when I yield, helplessly, to 'Memory'. It's something ter-
> rible, so much bigger and stronger than us, and it plays around
> with the little lives we lead every minute. Never do I feel myself
> existing as much as when I remember, and never do I feel
> myself dying so much. And I love you rather as if we had been
> nursed together, nourished by this same memory, and nour-
> ished by this same death. We die together, don't you think – we
> die to everything we have loved together, or die together, now,
> to everything that is merely the next day?
>   I don't want to start saying what I remember, since it would
> seem as if I'd forgotten the rest, and I never forget a thing. But
> all the same, there are certain images that leap into my heart,
> like a refrain that drags others along in its train: one evening
> after [the restaurant] 'Lysimaque', a light and our school uni-
> forms, and a dirty floor in the *thurne de musique*, a walk down
> the boulevard Saint-Michel holding the *Van Gogh* book that I
> hadn't opened yet and that now, after the Mediterranean, has
> crossed the ocean, the metro station Europe and me waiting for

you outside the Lycée Chaptal, down in the dark, before going
to see the *Dialogue des Carmélites*, the dark stairs of the *lycée*,
those in the rue Lagrange, the little words over the doors, all
those disappointments, a walk under the arcades of the rue de
Rivoli, near Concorde, the day I had come back from Algeria,
hesitations at the crossroads, *and so on and so forth,** and the
English poets . . . all of this like so many little signs of a life
urging them on, life in full, fully present, all of this like a net
dropped into the sea. [. . .]

When I remember all this, it hurts, it hurts first because I'm
remembering it, quite simply, and then because I'm thinking
how far apart we are now, and how much we had been dreading
this.[17]

When they were finally free of their military obligations, Jackie
wanted Michel and himself to be able to teach in the same town,
hoping thereby that they could revive the passionate friendship they
had shared at the age of twenty. More immediately, he sympathized
with the travails of his friend:

So you're off to Algeria, and this is the reply that will have been
given – ironically and tragically – to our old plan. And there
was me trembling at the thought of getting you to come to my
family – where we'd have been so ill at ease: what I now suggest,
if you're in Algiers or environs, or passing through, is that you
stop off there and make yourself at home, move into my room
and take all your meals there, get your washing done, etc. Don't
hesitate. You know, they're really nice, however depressed I
sometimes felt there. [. . .] I have to write to Bourdieu, he's a
soldier, but in a detachment at Headquarters in Algiers. He
tells me he wields some power and I'll tell him about you.

That same month, Derrida got back in touch with Althusser, first
apologizing for not sending him any news for so long. He felt unable
to tell him much about his travel impressions, since he had seen only
New England so far. As he did not have much money, he would not
be able to cross the United States from the East Coast to the West
Coast, as Althusser had advised him. But he gave his old *caïman* a
particularly severe description of the way philosophy was taught
in Harvard. 'In general, it's poor, elementary stuff. In comparison
with these vast and pompous façades – behind which they glean with
enthusiasm and youth, but also with inexperience and innocence –,
the Sorbonne is an old worm-eaten house through which the spirit

---

* In English in the original. – Tr.

blows in hurricanes.' The only class he had any time for was one
on modern logic, in which he was learning 'a load of things about
Frege, the young Husserl, etc.'. But basically, what Jackie seemed
most discontented with was himself:

> Although I've decided to work by myself, I still haven't done
> much. I'm already anxious to see how a year of total freedom
> is coming to an end – a freedom that I won't enjoy again for a
> long time [. . .] and I was expecting so much from it. [. . .] This
> year will have left me with a strong aftertaste of impotence.
> Until now I'd been pretending that external [causes] had left me
> paralysed, and I wanted to convince myself that once I'd passed
> the *agrégation*, I'd burst forth like a torrent. But in fact it's
> almost worse than before. Of course, I always contrive to con-
> sider myself as a martyr of the current crisis in foundations, of
> the death-agony of philosophy, of the exhaustion of a culture.
> In the vanguard of all these deaths, all one can do is keep
> silent so as, at least, not to miss their 'phenomenon'. Joking
> apart, nothing gives one such a sense of this crisis [. . .] than
> the total change in philosophical climate from one country
> to the next. When you see what happens to philosophy in an
> American book or translation, the impossibility of translation,*
> the eccentricity of the themes, the shift in areas of interest, the
> importance of teaching and local values . . . .[18]

Derrida said how much he was longing to see Althusser again, in
the apartment that the latter had finally been given in the École. He
would like to talk to him about the recent events in Algeria, about
the Budapest uprising, and their repercussions in Paris. He would
also like to talk about the planned 'short impersonal work' which
he was trying to settle down to, 'when he felt able': a translation,
with introduction, of *The Origin of Geometry*, a text of about thirty
pages, already mentioned in the penultimate chapter of his *diplôme*,
and a piece that he considered to be one of Husserl's best. But he did
not know whether he would have the right to publish his translation,
since he had still received no reply from Louvain.

This project would probably be the launching pad for the thesis
that would usually be the next stage of his career. For a *normalien*,
this was 'scarcely a decision'; rather a way of following 'a more or
less natural' course.[19] In this thesis, Derrida wanted to set out the
problems that most preoccupied him: those of science, phenomenology, and, above all, writing. He had in fact embarked on the work
even before he had left for Harvard:

---

* Or: the mischief of translation, *la traduction impossible.* – Tr.

Straight after the *agrégation*, I remember going to see Jean Hyppolite and telling him: 'I want to translate *The Origin of Geometry* and work on that text' – because there was a brief elliptical remark on writing, on the necessity for communities of scientists and scholars to constitute communicable ideal objects on the basis of intuitions of the mathematical object. Husserl said that writing alone could give those ideal objects their final ideality, that it alone could enable them in some way to enter history: their historicity came from writing. However, Husserl's remark was ambiguous and obscure: so I have been trying to articulate a concept of writing that would allow me simultaneously to account for what was happening in Husserl and, if need be, to raise questions for phenomenology and phenomenological intuitionism, and also tackle the question that continued to interest me: that of literary inscription. What is an inscription? When and in what conditions does an inscription become literary?[20]

Even though he had not yet registered the subject of his thesis, Derrida asked Hyppolite whether he would be willing to supervise it. The director of the ENS immediately agreed. 'Make the most of your stay,' he wrote. 'As for philosophy, I have confidence in you and I know that you won't forget it. I think your projected translation of *The Origin of Geometry* is an excellent idea.'[21]

Maurice de Gandillac also remembered Derrida, and gave his former student some methodological advice that he hoped would prove reassuring. The contents of the thesis would take shape as and when required, he assured Derrida. 'Let its existence precede its essence. I strongly advise you to start writing without any preconceived plan. As you continue, you'll see more and more clearly where you are and where you're going.' Gandillac wanted Derrida to make a start on writing 'before the long parenthesis of military service'. The analysis of the Algerian situation which he set out in the rest of his letter clearly showed a left-wing viewpoint. He deplored the way the French Communist Party was, in spite of the efforts of Althusser and several others, so hesitant. 'The Party apparatus paralyses reflection and the watchword "unity of action" blocks any real opposition to Mollet's policies in Algeria.'[22]

Derrida was given a much more brutal reminder of the war when Michel Monory sent him a letter from his barracks in Brazza on 28 April 1957. Jackie was the only person with whom he could share the atrocious scenes he had just witnessed.

Yesterday we had four dead and eighteen seriously wounded, victims of an ambush near Berrouaghia. After a night under a steady downpour, this morning, at dawn, I saw the livid corpses of my comrades, stiff and bloodied; I saw the wounded. But together with these harsh, painful images, I will always see in my mind's eye the seventeen-year-old Arab boy, hanging from a door by his wrists tied behind him, naked, suffering the most violent blows and the most sophisticated tortures all through his body.[23]

Jackie was so shocked that he took a whole day to answer, unsure of how to reply to his friend:

I'm trying to imagine, and I'm horror-stricken. I suppose that the most obvious thing, in the case of a morning like the one you've described, is that any attempt to justify or condemn either group is not just obscene, just a way of quietening one's conscience, but also abstract, 'empty'. And understanding makes you feel a bit more isolated. God won't be able to give any meaning to that, whatever comes out of it all . . .

I'm wholeheartedly with you, Michel. I'd like to talk to you, to tell you everything I'm thinking and feeling now when faced by an Algeria that makes me feel ill, but I'd be ashamed to do so from such a distance, especially to you as you tell me what you can see happening there. [. . .]

I have to go, Michel. I'm thinking about you a lot. If the only thing we can share in this world is despair, I'll be ready to share it with you, always. That's the only certainty that stands up, without lies or blindness.[24]

Jackie knew that he would soon have to start his military service, on his return from Harvard, and he was apprehensive about the 'two-year big black hole' towards which he and Marguerite were anxiously heading. There was a possibility that he might be sent to the front. But Aimé Derrida had been busy for several months, mentioning his son's situation at every opportunity in an attempt to find him a civilian posting. He knew the people who ran the school in Koléa, a little town near Algiers, where people regularly ordered the wines and spirits from him. As they were looking for a teacher for the children of the soldiers, Aimé plugged the fine qualities of his son the *normalien*, assuring them that he was able to teach any subject. Of course, this would still mean two years of relative tedium, but in comparison with the usual military service it would be a doddle.

Jackie and Marguerite had not left for America with the intention of marrying. Indeed, if they were to avoid being separated, there was no other solution. But the idea of a traditional family wedding struck them as unbearable, especially given what had happened when they left home. So, on 9 June 1957, Jackie and Marguerite married in Cambridge, with their friend Margot as sole witness. That evening, after a last dinner with the Rodwin family, the couple took the train to New York before embarking on the *Liberté*. On 18 June, they were back in Paris.

6

The Soldier of Koléa

1957–1959

The newly married couple spent a few days in Paris, where Jackie was unpleasantly surprised to discover that all the books from his years as a teenager and young man, left in a trunk in Normale Sup, had disappeared in his absence. This theft would sadden him for a long time – especially since he was already in the habit of keeping everything.

The main task, during the two months before Derrida started military service, was to patch up things with the couple's families: having been disconcerted by their departure for America, Marguerite's parents, and Jackie's even more, were hurt by the wedding that had taken place so far away, and to which they had not been invited. As Derrida explained to Michel Monory, a few days after his return to El Biar: 'As usual, and perhaps even more seriously, since I'm with Marguerite and because Algeria has become what it is, I'm feeling ill.' Everybody was prowling round them, depriving them of the intimacy to which they aspired. 'Marguerite's family, where I don't feel entirely at ease either, is in spite of everything much more discreet and silent.'[1]

But things soon settled down. Once their disappointment at not being able to throw a big party had faded, Jackie's parents adopted Marguerite, who fitted into their world with remarkable ease. Aimé Derrida was particularly charmed, though he still asked his son with some anxiety whether his future children would have a religious upbringing. 'They'll be self-determining,' replied Jackie, which only partly satisfied his father.[2]

After El Biar, the couple returned to mainland France, and spent a few weeks at Les Rassats, the property of the Aucouturier family, near Angoulême. Although Jackie was very keen to introduce Marguerite to Michel Monory, they missed each other yet again. Jackie returned to Algeria on 24 August and was drafted at the beginning of September. For a month, he attended classes at Fort-de-l'Eau, just outside Algiers, learning how to stand to attention and handle weapons before taking up the teaching post that had been kept open for him thanks to the good offices of his father. 'You see, I'm really lucky and while I don't pull any strings myself, I let others do so my behalf, which isn't much better.'[3] It was a 'cushy number' that it would be ungrateful to complain about, especially to Michel.

So, at the beginning of October, Jackie left with Marguerite to take up his posting in Koléa, a small town some 38 kilometres to the south-west of Algiers, on hills overlooking the plain of the Mitidja. For just over two months, as a second-class soldier in civilian dress, he taught the children of old Algerian soldiers, including quite a number of orphans. Some pupils would join the resistance straight after the *troisième*. In this École Militaire Préparatoire, Jackie and Marguerite would lead a somewhat monotonous life, albeit one which involved a lot of work for him. He had twelve hours of French in the *cinquième* and *quatrième* years, to which he soon adapted, as well as two hours of English in the *troisième*. Every Thursday, in Algiers, he also gave two hours' French to a small group of trainee secretaries; he found these hours very tedious, but the wages were sufficiently good to pay for the room he and Marguerite rented in a villa in Koléa. When one reckons in the need to mark work, the administrative tasks, the translations of newspaper articles for the general government, and even running the school's football, it is easy to understand why he felt he had never had less time for himself.

In material terms, the school worked very well and allowed Jackie and Marguerite to enjoy the life of village schoolteachers. Other aspects were less pleasant, as Derrida explained to Michel Monory:

> The children are likeable, friendly and vivacious, I never get bored in class and always start in a good mood, but contact with the staff, both military and civilian, is really difficult, and sometimes unbearable. The two hours of mealtime in the mess and the class councils are torture.[4]

Derrida's situation was of course less difficult than that of many others – first and foremost, Michel, whose strenuous period of service ended only in December 1957 –, but life in Koléa was all the same far from easy. Marguerite can still remember the battles that took place nearby:

> At night-time, it was a real war. We could regularly hear gunfire. Horrible things happened. One evening, an FLN leader was executed; they then dragged him into the Kasbah, his neck tied to a jeep, before leaving the body outside a mosque. They were probably trying to intimidate the Algerians, but of course this kind of provocation merely stoked their hatred. To crown

it all, the dogs in the barracks started barking every time Jackie passed by. 'They take me for an Arab,' he used to say, and he was probably right, as his complexion was very dark, as usual when he came back to Algeria.

After a few weeks, Jackie and Marguerite bought a 2CV, which meant they could go to Algiers whenever possible. On Friday evenings, they almost always shared the Sabbath meal with Derrida's parents. On other evenings they would dine with Pierre Bourdieu, to whom they were very close throughout this period. Bourdieu had been appointed to the military cabinet of the general government, where he worked as an editor. At the end of 1957, freed from his military obligations, he became a lecturer at the University of Algiers and embarked on a real piece of fieldwork across the whole country. These years in Algeria constituted a definitive turning-point in Bourdieu's intellectual development: he had initially planned to be a philosopher, but now started to turn towards sociology.[5]

Derrida came to the general government once a week; his job was to translate the main things that were being written in English about North Africa. This enabled him to be remarkably well informed and even to gain access to a large amount of information that was censored in France. During this period, Lucien Bianco was in Strasbourg, far from his wife, nicknamed Taktak, and their baby Sylvie. Coco's mood was anxious and glum: he was doing his service as a teacher in a school for NCOs, which exposed him to the bullying behaviour common to old-style military barracks. In many respects, the situation of the Biancos was like that of the two Derridas: more than the work, it was the context that was irksome. If only they could have been together in Koléa, to 'share what we're feeling [. . .], instead of shunning our companions all the time'.

For several months, evidence of torture in Algeria had stirred widespread controversy in France. On 11 June 1957, Maurice Audin, a twenty-five-year-old mathematician, a lecturer at the science faculty in Algeria and a member of the PCA (the Parti Communiste Algérien, dissolved in 1955), was arrested by parachutists. According to his guards, he escaped on 21 June, but nobody ever saw him again. He was probably tortured in El Biar, in the sinister 'Villa des Roses', where one of the officials was none other than the young lieutenant Jean-Marie Le Pen, deputy at the National Assembly. The mathematician Laurent Schwartz and the historian Pierre Vidal-Naquet had just set up the Audin committee and were trying to find out the truth behind his disappearance. The inquest would last until 1962: it concluded that Audin had been murdered.

Bianco had just been gripped by the book *La Question*,* written by one of Maurice Audin's companions, Henri Alleg, recently published by the Éditions de Minuit and immediately censored.[6] In spite of the risks, Lucien circulated the book as much as possible among his acquaintances. These revelations of torture helped to harden his position on the war. He hoped that after these months of separation, Jackie and he were still occupying the same political position.

> I don't know how this war and all these sinister absurdities strike you now, where you are. It seems to me that the only outcome can be independence, after everything that's happened, and our only hope is that this independence (which won't solve anything) will be proclaimed as soon as possible, and the massacres stopped. Perhaps you completely disagree? Give me a few thoughts on the subject, if it doesn't sicken you too much.[7]

Derrida did give him a few thoughts – much more than a few. For events had suddenly accelerated: on 14 May 1958, he settled down to write a letter sixteen dense pages long, relating hour by hour what they were living through in Koléa. They had just experienced some awful days, 'with rage in our hearts and more alone than ever, in prey to the surrounding stupidity, the most abject and malevolent imaginable, a real nightmare', a stupidity that was 'pitiful when it missed its aim', but terrifying each time it threatened to be effective. They had been really afraid, physically, and had taken refuge in their room, glued to the radio. Jackie wrote to Lucien and his wife now that peace and hope had returned, even if these still seemed very fragile. He attempted to tell them about it all in detail, mainly to 'satisfy this need to exchange ideas and to talk, a need that has been suppressed so much these last few days that it has made us want to throw up'.

It had all started, for them, on 12 May, when the newspapers had just announced the demonstration organized in Algiers for the following day, in memory of three soldiers of the contingent who had been taken prisoner by the *fellaghas* (independence fighters) and shot in Tunisia.

> That evening, in the mess, the stupidity around us was particularly aggressive. Of course, although in general we showed our disapproval only in a negative and silent way, we were found out, and hostility towards us found a silent and hypocritical expression. There was an atmosphere of denunciation,

---

* Translated as *The Question*, also in the sense of torture. – Tr.

anonymous letters, thought police. That morning, I hadn't been forgiven for suddenly leaving a group that was optimistically, cheerfully, and excitedly reading out the various leaflets published by 'ultra' organizations and, the evening before, for having unpacked in the teachers' common room a Russian book sent to Marguerite by Michel [Aucouturier]. You can't imagine [. . .] how the unanimity of these sly, cowardly imbeciles is intolerable when one has to face them alone, even when one is as certain as one can be.

That evening, at table, the talk was of Pierre Pflimlin, who was to be formally invested as head of government in Paris the next day. He was being criticized both for planning to extend military service to twenty-seven months and for wanting to pull out of Algeria 'whatever he says'. There were 'too many ambiguities in his speech', added a captain whom Jackie had found relatively open-minded up until then.

Marguerite waved her hand in a way that spoke volumes and aroused silent but violent reactions on the part of some of those near us. [. . .] I was already on the verge of blowing a fuse. Just when the conversation was about to turn to the incidents in Algiers, I decided to walk out of the mess, partly because I couldn't breathe in such a suffocating atmosphere of stupidity and partly to show that I despised what was happening in Algiers and was only interested in events in Paris. [. . .] Just then, out came a few phrases on the radio, talking about the demonstrations 'devoted to the memory of the three glorious French soldiers who had been vilely . . . etc. . . .'. [. . .] We left [. . .] followed by the furious gaze of everyone else there.

Once he was in the yard outside, Jackie could not help but imagine what the group of soldiers were saying about him: 'he doesn't give a damn about the murdered French soldiers', 'anyway, he's a Communist', 'his wife isn't French', 'he's a Jew', 'he reads *Le Monde* and *L'Express*', 'his wife translates Russian books' . . . And suddenly, at the end of his tether, he started sobbing: 'The idea that this gang of bloody idiots, all cosy in their unassailable, invulnerable clear consciences, their clear consciences as thick as elephants' hides, could condemn me as a "traitor" who approved of murder and terrorism, suddenly got to me.'

Needing more information, Jackie and Marguerite switched on Radio-Alger, which they usually viewed as a decent station, but participants in the putsch had just taken it over. A message from General Salan was announced, but 'after half an hour of waiting and bland music, a new voice, urgent, feverish, and silly, monstrously silly', declared that a Committee of Public Safety led by Massu had been formed and taken over the destiny of Algeria.

There's a lot of confusion about it all, no one is sure about the names of the members, people keep getting added or taken off. Salan's out of it. Of course, we're scared. The tone of the news is terrifying. It hinted at the worst possible things, violent racist attacks, the hunting down of 'defeatists', the invasion of Tunisia, etc. We spent the whole night, sick with worry and fear, calculating the chances of a coup d'état, imagining the different consequences it would have, for better and for worse. We thought of the better consequences only in the abstract, to reassure ourselves, dreaming of regrouping the forces of the Left in France, a purge in Algeria, hasty negotiations, the FLN softening its line when faced with a government that had managed to resist, etc.

Now that he had been brought to power by rioters, Massu sent a telegram to Paris demanding the creation of a 'government of public safety, which alone could preserve Algeria as an integral part of metropolitan France'. The deputies, who did not think much of this intrusion, invested Pierre Pflimlin in office as planned. This meant breaking off with Algiers. On 14 May, at 5 a.m., Massu issued a new appeal: 'The Committee for Public Safety implores General de Gaulle to break his silence in view of the establishment of a government of public safety that alone can save Algeria from being abandoned.'

On reassuming his post at school, following those terrible moments, Jackie regained some of his serenity – witness the rest of his letter to Bianco:

The weather is very fine and, as on every morning in my life, I can't understand the anguish of night time when the sun is shining. People are calm, the Left is regrouping, the socialist deputies of Algeria will hold firm, the power of the 'ultras' will suffer, and they will no longer terrorize the government and the ministers of Algeria as they have done since 6 February. Fascism will not pass. [. . .]

In the afternoons, I teach. During the second hour, I almost passed out. I hadn't been able to swallow a single morsel all day long. I apologize for these grotesque details. But never had my faith and my fear as a democrat seemed so very 'gross', and the fascist danger so close, so concrete, so invasive. And all this at a time when I am so alone, without friends, without any prospect of getting away, a soldier in a land that's 'sealed off' and, as we can now see, has never known democracy, has no tradition of

it, offers no centre of resistance to a dictatorship of colonists
supported by the army. [. . .]

I'm at a complete loss, can't settle to anything, a second-class
soldier lost in an ocean of malevolent stupidity and I'd like to
be in Paris – even if it were occupied by fascists –, as a civilian,
with a few friends, and able to play even a modest role in some
resistance movement . . . What damn awful luck![8]

Meanwhile, events were accelerating. On 15 May, General Salan,
who held both civil and military power, addressed the crowd assembled in the Forum d'Alger, concluding his speech with the words:
'Long live France! Long live French Algeria!', and finally, 'Long
live de Gaulle!' General de Gaulle had been ejected from office in
1947 and was still hoping to give France more stable institutions;
he now emerged from his reserve, and declared that he was 'ready
to assume power in the Republic'. For several days, Algiers was the
scene of impressive demonstrations, 'bringing together crowds of
every origin gathered under the unfurled French flag to demonstrate
to metropolitan France their unanimous desire to remain French'.[9]

Jackie had decided not to send his letter to Lucien Bianco in case
it was opened, as were all those written by suspects and 'those with
files on them', a group to which he was convinced he belonged. A
few days later, he added a postscript to his voluminous letter before
giving it to his brother, who would post it in France. Under the
pressure of events, Jackie's tone was more militant than it had ever
been: 'We are here living in a world of absolute pre-fascism, totally
powerless, with our only hopes residing in some Popular Front or
in the better aspects of de Gaulle to sweep away the rottenness.
Fascism will not pass!' On 28 May, indeed, a big antifascist march,
led by Pierre Mendès France, took place in Paris. 'I'd love to have
been in the Place de la République yesterday evening,' wrote Jackie.

On that day, René Coty, the French President, launched his own
solemn appeal 'to the most illustrious of Frenchmen'. On 1 June,
General de Gaulle was invested in office by the National Assembly,
with 329 votes to 224. He was granted full powers for six months,
with the task of establishing a new Constitution. On 4 June, in
Algiers, he gave a speech that cannot be summed up merely in the
famous and ambiguous words 'I have understood your position' [*je
vous ai compris*] to which it is often reduced.

I know what has been happening here. I can see what you have
been trying to do. I can see that the path you have opened up
in Algeria is the path of renewal and fraternity. I mean renewal
in every sense. But that is the point: you wished this renewal
to start at the beginning, in other words with our institutions,

and that is why I am here. I mean fraternity, because you are providing us with the magnificent sight of men who, right across the board, whatever communities they come from, are united in the same ardour, holding each other by the hand. Well, I take note of all this in the name of France and I declare that from today, France considers that, throughout Algeria, there is but one category of inhabitants: there are just people who are fully French – fully French, with the same rights and the same duties. This means that we must open paths that, hitherto, have remained closed to many. It means that we need to give the means of living to those who did not possess them. It means that we must recognize the dignity of those whose dignity was questioned. It means that we need to ensure that those who doubted whether they had a homeland can be assured that they do.[10]

Derrida was clearly ambivalent about de Gaulle. In the French political context, he felt more to the Left. But for him, as for all the Jews of Algeria, General de Gaulle was the man who, in 1943, put an end to the anti-Semitic measures and re-established the Crémieux Decree. As for the present situation, the 'de Gaulle at his best' whom he mentioned at the end of his letter to Bianco was doubtless the man who, in the spirit of the 4 June speech, would enable the different communities living in Algeria to exist together in a completely transformed country. And indeed, over the next few months, important reforms were launched, starting with that of the electoral system, under the direction of Paul Delouvrier, the general government's delegate. But at the same time, the French army led by General Challe was using a 'steamroller' strategy to try to crush the FLN, which, though momentarily weakened, soon rallied. The war was clearly far from over.

Lucien Bianco and his wife had been very touched by Derrida's long letter and the firmness of his convictions: 'For anyone who knows you, it's significant and revelatory to hear you saying again and again: "fascism will not pass!" (I remember your justifiably harsh irony when some Communist at the École kept bleating this slogan on every occasion).'[11] The Biancos would be in Paris for a few weeks, from 10 July onwards, and suggested putting Marguerite and Jackie up in their apartment. But this time, it was Lucien's turn to be worried: following a bad report, he was threatened with being sent 'to an operational unit in Algeria',[12]) which would oblige him to leave his young wife and their baby in France. Derrida would do all in his power to bring the whole family to Koléa.

Lucien Bianco arrived in Algeria on 1 September 1958 and at first went to his posting, not far from Constantine. Sickened at having to take part in this unjust war and tolerate his captain's support for continued French rule in Algeria, Coco hoped to be appointed to Koléa, but could hardly dare to believe this would happen. He told Jackie he was ready to teach French, or even German, if there was no post available in history and geography. In fact, he would even agree to 'sweep the classrooms if it means being in Koléa'.[13] On 15 September, his appointment was officially declared: abandoning the uniform and constraints of military life, he returned to Koléa on the 25th, teaching the same pupils as his old *cothurne*.

For a year, Lucien Bianco, his wife 'Taktak', and their baby daughter Sylvie would share the same house as the Derridas, eating at the same table in the mess, some distance away from the officers. This did not prevent relations with them from being very tense. Another conscript who had attended classes with Derrida in Fort-de-l'Eau, unable to bear the conversation of the 'ultras' a moment longer, got up with his plate one day and went over to the table of the Derridas and the Biancos. 'This way, at least, I've made things clear,' he shouted.

In Paris, the situation evolved rapidly. The referendum of 28 September asked the French to ratify the Constitution of the Fifth Republic: it went through with a 'yes' vote of nearly 82 per cent. A few weeks later, parliamentary elections took place. Still registered in Paris, Derrida asked Louis Althusser to vote for him by proxy, even though they did not share the same opinions. The two men wrote to each other in a manner implicit or metaphorical enough to get past censorship. Althusser merely explained that he would do 'whatever was necessary': 'I'll vote for who you tell me in the first round. And if he has to withdraw before the second round, I'd follow your instructions. I hope you're still in the teaching body, and that now that it's autumn the atmosphere has become less stormy. Tell me what the weather forecasts are saying.'[14] And a few weeks later, he assured him: 'You have voted as you wished . . . Here is your card.' But the end of the letter shows that their political tendencies were different: 'In spite of this, I wish you a Merry Christmas and assure you of my faithful friendship.'[15]

On 21 December 1958, General de Gaulle became the first President of a Fifth Republic that had been tailor-made for him.

The closeness of the Derrida and Bianco couples made the following months much less difficult. They were preoccupied by the war and spent hours listening to the radio and reading the papers. Every week, Jackie and Lucien went together to buy *France-Observateur*. The bookstore in Koléa ordered just two copies, and they wondered who on earth the other buyer could be: many considered this weekly publication to be anti-French, and they had to remain very discreet. The Biancos and Derridas often read the same books: *Doctor*

Zhivago by Pasternak, which Michel Aucouturier had just translated; *Zazie in the Metro* by Queneau; and novels by Henry Miller
and Faulkner brought back from the United States. Marguerite
was translating *The Life of Klim Samgin*, a rather dull novel by
Gorky. As for Jackie, he sometimes tried to resume work on his
introduction to *The Origin of Geometry*, but, with his nineteen
hours of classes per week in Koléa, the three hours in Algiers for the
managerial secretaries, a few private lessons, and the translation of
English newspapers for the general government, he had hardly any
time left over for himself.[16] As he explained to Michel Monory:

> All this, as you can imagine, reduces considerably any chance
> I have of solitude, in other words of breathing. Outside certain
> 'periods' where a devilish craving springs up in me, when I feel
> that I'm seeing the world upside down and walking on my head,
> I can accept it all [. . .], with little sighs that are soon forgotten,
> and the somewhat anaesthetized and dully resigned serenity of
> those who continue to live because they have forgotten that the
> air has become rarefied.[17]

In spite of the distance, the academic world could not be completely forgotten. In February 1959, Maurice de Gandillac suggested
that his former student participate in the 'Cerisy Talks' that were to
take place during the summer, on the theme 'Genesis and structure'.
Derrida could talk about Husserl, using his dissertation as a basis.
But essential, in de Gandillac's view, was the 'free and easy discussion' of the talks that would take place 'in the middle of the lush
Normandy countryside'. There would be 'phenomenologists, dia-
lecticians (idealist and materialist), logicians and epistemologists,
historians of the economy, art and language, ethnologists, biologists,
etc.'. And the conversations would be led 'in the most accommodat-
ing way possible' by Lucien Goldmann and de Gandillac himself.[18]
Although he was apprehensive about this first public conference,
Derrida could not fail to agree to this flattering suggestion.

It was also in this year – and not in 1957, as he would say when he
belatedly defended it – that he officially registered the subject of his
thesis, with the title 'The ideality of the literary object'. Even though
the work was explicitly influenced by Husserl, it was to lead Derrida
towards a completely personal set of problems – in the direction
that, ever since his teens, had been of most importance to him:

> It was then for me a matter of bending, more or less violently,
> the techniques of transcendental phenomenology to the needs
> of elaborating a new theory of literature, of that very peculiar
> type of ideal object that is the literary object [. . .]. For I have
> to remind you, somewhat bluntly and simply, that my most

constant interest, coming even before my philosophical interest, I would say, if this is possible, is toward literature, toward
that writing that is called literary.

What is literature? And first of all, what is it to write? How is
it that writing can disturb the very question 'what is?' and even
'what does it mean?' To say this in other words – and here is
the *saying otherwise* that was of importance to me – when and
how does an inscription become literature and what takes place
when it does? To what and to whom is this due? What takes
place between philosophy and literature, science and literature,
politics and literature, theology and literature, psychoanalysis
and literature? It was here, in all the abstractness of its title,
that lay the most pressing question.[19]

Jean Hyppolite was probably perplexed by this unusual subject
with its still vague outlines, but accepted the projected thesis, while
assuring Derrida that he could change the title once he had made
progress with the writing. Hyppolite declared that he was happy
to learn that the translation of *The Origin of Geometry* was almost
finished. Confirming that he was prepared to publish the text in the
series he directed, 'Épiméthée', he invited Derrida to write to the
Presses Universitaires de France so that they could take the necessary steps with the Dutch publisher of the *Husserliana*. Hyppolite
announced that he would not be able to read the translation
properly before the vacation, but his first impressions were very
favourable. He advised Derrida to embark without delay on the
commentary, with the hope that his military activities would not
absorb too much of his energy. Soon he could return to France and
start his real career. 'Keep me informed about your relations with
secondary education,' concluded the director of Normale Sup. 'You
can rest assured that I'll be thinking of you and your future plans.'[20]

Even though he still had a few more months in Koléa, Jackie was
indeed wondering what would become of him after the long inter-
mission of his service. There was some question of *terminale* classes
in the *lycée* at La Flèche, a rather remote town in the middle of the
Sarthe, but soon his former fellow student Gérard Genette informed
him that there might be a post with him in Le Mans, with a *terminale*
and an *hypokhâgne*, a prospect which seemed much more attractive.
The headmaster was trying to get rid of M. Fieschi, a philosophy
teacher who was much too eccentric and laid-back for his taste.
Genette had spoken to him about Derrida in more than flattering
terms. Now they would need to make contact with the ministry
so that these plans could take shape. If it all worked out, Derrida
would still need to decide whether it would be better to live in Paris
or settle in Le Mans. The question could be summarized as follows:
'Travel (with two return journeys per week) is physically and espe-

cially mentally draining, but life in Le Mans is not much fun.'[22] After a few months, Genette himself had given up the attempt to live in Paris.

In spite of the friendly tone of the correspondence, the two young men as yet hardly knew each other. When they had both been at the École, Genette had been both a specialist in literature and a Communist militant, thus not very close to Derrida. When Soviet tanks rumbled into Budapest in 1956, Genette left the Party.[*] He had just got married, and his wife, Raymonde, nicknamed 'Babette', said she was eager to meet a man who had been described to her as 'gentle and complicated'. However, in order for Derrida actually to be taken on at Le Mans, a rather traditional headmaster still had to be reassured. As Genette explained, maliciously:

> Of course, as a philosopher, you are by definition suspected of many things, in particular of believing in philosophy – they can hang you for that. Take the opportunity to tell him that you only believe in results, i.e., of course, in exams. [. . .] As for the moral climate, re-read the episode [in Stendhal's *Red and Black*] where Julian Sorel enters the seminary, while bearing in mind the progress made by science and the police over the last century.[23]

Jackie and Marguerite viewed this appointment as quite a positive thing. It was flattering to be given a *hypokhâgne* post at the first attempt. The Genettes seemed to be potentially pleasant companions, and were already busying themselves to help the Derridas move. And above all, Le Mans was only two hundred kilometres from Paris: Marguerite, who was hoping to take up her ethnology studies again, would be able to make one or two return trips a week without too much difficulty.

But a more exciting prospect suddenly seemed to open up. On 16 January, the day after his twenty-ninth birthday, Derrida received

---

* Derrida mentions this episode in his interview with Michael Sprinker concerning Althusser: 'With the repression in Hungary in 1956, some of those Communist intellectuals began to leave the Party. Althusser didn't and, I think, never would have. Gérard Genette, who was a Party member until 1956, told me that he went to see Althusser after the Hungarian uprising to tell him of his worries, his anxieties, his reasons, and probably to ask his advice. Althusser apparently told him: "But if what you say is right, then the Party would be wrong." And this seemed impossible, demonstrating *ex absurdo* that what Genette was saying needed to be corrected. And Genette told me with a laugh: "I drew the conclusion from this extraordinary formulation, and immediately left the Party." (I am translating from Derrida's transcription, unpublished in French, preserved at IMEC.) [See also the translation in E. Ann Kapler and Michael Sprinker, eds, *The Althusserian Legacy* (London: Verso, 1993), p. 199. – Tr.]

one letter from Louis Althusser and another from Jean Hyppolite. Althusser was really happy to forward 'a piece of news full of hopeful signs': after months of tricky negotiations, Hyppolite had put forward Derrida's name for the post of *maître assistant* in general philosophy that was to be created at the Sorbonne. The assembly of professors had finally agreed. Everything now depended on Étienne Souriau, the director of studies in philosophy, and on the minister himself. Even though he claimed to be optimistic, Hyppolite advised Derrida to carry on looking for jobs in secondary education until the new post had been confirmed, so as to be ready for all eventualities.[24] But things made good progress: less than a week later, Souriau officially proposed that Derrida take up a job at the Sorbonne as 'head of the *travaux pratiques* for the *agrégation*': 'Do you want this post? If so, it's settled.' Derrida quickly accepted, just before setting off for Normandy and the chateau of Cerisy-la-Salle. His participation in the *décade* on 'Genesis and structure' came just at the right time; it would enable him to renew his links with a world which, by force of circumstance, he had almost completely lost sight of over the past three years.

The 'Talks', held from 25 July to 3 August 1959, were in the end directed by a trio comprising Maurice de Gandillac, Lucien Goldmann, and Jean Piaget. Several figures active in contemporary intellectual debate took part, including Ernst Bloch and Jean-Toussaint Desanti, as well as some 'young bloods', such as Jean-Pierre Vernant and Jean-Paul Aron. Derrida would remember this *décade*, the first in a long series, very vividly:

> I drove a little 2CV and, over the following days, I took some famous people out to Normandy meals where the white wine flowed. They included Jean Piaget, Desanti, old Breton (the latter two became great friends) as well as the Hungarian psychoanalysts Nicolas Abraham and Maria Török[*] – it was the first time that I had met them here, too: they were striking out on their own path between psychoanalysis and phenomenology. The presence of Ernst Bloch, whose work I did not yet know, was in many respects the 'crossing of a frontier', all the more significant in the Europe of those days when the discussions were full of references to Marx, with Goldmann's presence aiding the process.[26]

The title 'Genesis and structure', echoing Jean Hyppolite's book *Genesis and Structure of Hegel's Phenomenology of Spirit*, was here used as such, without any complement of object. The papers and

---

* She was often known professionally as Maria Torok. – Tr.

conversations were 'interdisciplinary' long before that word became common: they moved from the analysis of bureaucracy to that of biology, from mathematics to the myth of races in Hesiod, and from linguistics to religious ideologies. 'A head-on, encyclopaedic treatment like this could never have taken place in a university.'

For Derrida, the *décade* was a real baptism of fire. Although he was one of the youngest participants and had still not published anything, he intervened in several discussions throughout the 'Conversations'. It was he who, rather sharply, launched the discussion after Jean Piaget's paper:

> I remember the juvenile impudence with which I had the nerve to object, as a young dog smitten with genetic phenomenology, to the psychologism of the great Piaget, whose scholastic system I had studiously learned a few years earlier when working for my certificate in child psychology. This happened on the first evening, and throughout the *décade*, Piaget treated the bold, naïvely insolent young man that I then was with a sort of ironic deference, both irritated and protective. He nicknamed me '*the phenomenologist*'.[27]

On the morning of Friday 31 July, in the chateau's library, Derrida delivered his first lecture, reading out some twenty immaculately composed pages. Even though the theme overlapped that of his *diplôme*, he had written a new text reflecting his most recent research. On this day, one of the concepts that would become fundamental in his work, that of *différance*, made an appearance for the first time. Admittedly, pretty much throughout his paper, he used the ordinary word *différence*, but the philosopher was clearly giving it a particular meaning. And in the middle of the text, *différance* – with an 'a' – is there in black and white, albeit furtively: 'This irreducible difference is due to an interminable *delaying* [*différance*] of the theoretical foundation,' he writes.[28]

Another 'first time', just as important, was the fact that Derrida took the opportunity of these Cerisy 'Conversations', and the forthcoming publication of this paper, to swap his first name Jackie for that of Jacques. And he was annoyed when Maurice de Gandillac happened to call him 'Jackie' in public. From now on, his 'real' first name was kept for the use of family and a few old friends.

After a few days' holiday at Les Rassats, then El Biar, Jackie and Marguerite returned to Koléa at the beginning of September for the last weeks of military service. Time dragged, and they could not wait to move back to Paris and start a new life. Derrida knew that he would be very busy writing his Sorbonne lectures and he wanted to discuss them with Althusser: 'If you like, when I get back, I'll submit my plans, texts, topics, etc. to your authority and experience. I think I'll often be needing you, your advice and recommendations.'[29]

To Michel Monory, Derrida described a situation that was a bit hazy and indecisive, but still potentially involving the job of lecturer at the Sorbonne:

> Nothing official as yet, but it's more or less certain; I just need the secondary sector not to block my move. I was told at the beginning of summer [. . .] and I accepted, both delighted and terrified, with my terror bordering on total panic and remaining much more constant and present than my delight. I'm very lucky, you see, but I'm one of those people who can't enjoy their luck. Instead of rubbing my hands in glee, I'm running round like hunted beast, working feverishly in a breathless chaos . . . It's stupid, I hope that when I have to face the monster I'll recover my wits, I'm trying in the abstract to convince myself that, after pulling such faces in this old house, it would be surprising if I hadn't turned into a bit of an old monkey . . . According to the rumours, I owe this piece of luck to Hyppolite, and a little bit to de Gandillac.

Derrida hoped that, on his return to Paris, he would be able to see Michel frequently. Yet again, it was an opportunity for him to rekindle memories. Whether these were happy or unhappy, he could not help but cherish them. Already, he loved his past, all his past:

> I have the impression that I can hear again, right up close, our winters in the rue Saint-Jacques. For me they increasingly have the voice of a golden age, a curious golden age, dark, difficult, with a silent but echoing splendour; and, knowing that I'm coming back to Paris and can see you again, I have the impression that I've gone round in an unreal circle in the interval. [. . .]
> If you had any chance of finding accommodation for us . . . I remember that winter when it rained, when I was exiled here, when I turned my back on my family. And I wrote to you, on this table, asking you to find accommodation. I have to say that you hadn't been successful, but you were so sincerely sorry to have been useless! Anyway, just see if by any chance . . . it's our latest problem.[30]

The following weeks were very confused. Without realizing it, Derrida had become caught up in manoeuvrings that suddenly left him in the lurch. On 30 September, he received a very curt letter from M. Brunold, the general director of secondary education: 'given the importance' of the *hypokhâgne* post for which Derrida had applied and to which he had been appointed, it was impossible to agree to his being placed at the disposal of Higher Education. Once he was free of his military obligations, Derrida would have to take up his post in the *lycée* at Le Mans.

As soon as they were informed, Althusser and Hyppolite tried to get to the bottom of this 'murky affair'. In spite of their interventions in high places, they rapidly realized that the situation had become irreparable. On 6 October, Althusser said that he was 'deeply saddened' at the way things had turned out, 'for you mainly and also for me, as I hoped you'd be right close to the École'.[31] For his part, Genette, who for months had been trying to keep the headmaster sweet, found the situation alarming: 'Give me some news, even if it's vague or bad, since this continual uncertainty is starting to get me down.' But, in practical terms, the decision had been made. Derrida, feeling somewhat bitter, downcast by the plots and power-plays in which he had been entangled, now wanted to start at Le Mans as soon as possible.

Meanwhile, the Algerian situation had reached a major turning-point. On 16 September 1959, General de Gaulle gave a speech that was broadcast on radio and television, in which he mentioned the solution of 'self-determination' for the first time, offering a choice between three formulas: 'complete *francisation*', 'association', and 'secession'. Of course, 'the shape of future consultation will need, when the time is ripe, to be set out and fixed. But the route has been laid out. The decision has been taken.'[32] In the view of the new electoral body, this amounted to independence: the supporters of French Algeria felt betrayed.

The war still continued in Algeria itself, and Derrida was glad that he had finally finished his military service. Not for a moment did he imagine that his year in Le Mans would be one of the most difficult in his life.

7

Melancholia in Le Mans

1959–1960

Since spring, Genette had been tireless and patient. But some pupils in the *hypokhâgne* class at Le Mans who wanted to pursue their studies in philosophy were a bit less patient than he was and had already left for other schools. These long procrastinations had just one advantage as far as Genette was concerned: 'The Headmaster keeps telling himself that he now needs to turn on the charm if he's going to keep you as long as possible. You'll see what a gracious creature he is!'[1]

Finally liberated, the Derridas arrived in Le Mans in mid-November. They initially lived in a furnished flat. But they were soon able to move into a big modern apartment block on the rue Léon Bollée, just a hundred metres down the road from the Genettes, who continued to do all they could to help them, giving them the addresses of decorators and second-hand dealers. Genette remembers with amusement that 'Jacques could sometimes be pretty obstinate. As he needed to coat a set of beech wood bookshelves in linseed oil,' Genette recommended that he add a dose of paint dryer. 'He ignored this detail, which in his view was unnecessary, and for months found that his books were as greasy as doughnuts.'[2]

In material terms, life in Le Mans was more comfortable than in Paris. Otherwise, Genette made no bones about the fact that it would be difficult to find a less civilized city in France. 'The intelligent bookseller, the local writer, the fashionable café, the little clubs, the visiting lecturers – all of this is as unknown here as at the North Pole.'[3] The old city, which has now been carefully revamped, was in 1959 nothing but a 'big sleepy village, where grass grows in the streets with their haphazard cobbles'.[4] The boys' *lycée* to which Derrida had been appointed was the only one in the city; it was right next to the cathedral, and on some days you had to go through the cattle market to reach it.

To begin with, Derrida seemed reasonably satisfied with his new situation, if we are to believe a letter he sent to his cousin:

For this year at least, we're in this big but peaceful provincial city of Le Mans. It has several advantages, fortunately: it's at the gates of Paris (2 hours by train!); I have some interesting teaching to do (philosophy in *hypokhâgne*) that leaves me a lot of free time, and above all we've very quickly managed to find a really suitable apartment.[5]

Derrida taught two classes, which meant some fifteen hours per week. In the literary *terminale*, there were only about fifteen pupils. In the *hypokhâgne*, where, by special dispensation, both boys and girls were admitted, there were almost thirty, not all that brilliant in the main. The audiences were thus a little 'rustic', very different from those Derrida had been hoping to have in the Sorbonne. This did not stop him preparing his lessons meticulously, even if he did not have time to write them out in full as he later did. Far from teaching a standard course, he wanted to communicate the philosophical preoccupations closest to his heart at the time. But perhaps he had taken the headmaster's demands for seriousness too literally. He probably also sought to make up for his shyness by a display of somewhat frigid authority. His pupils would be mainly left with the memory of a difficult and over-demanding teacher. The three eyewitnesses who have shared their experiences with me all agree.

Albert Daussin, then a pupil in *hypokhâgne*, mainly remembers a 'handsome young man, dark-complexioned, with the profile of a Roman medallion', who would sometimes, when class was over, talk nostalgically about North Africa. Otherwise, he was not specially close to his pupils and often gave the impression that he lived in a world of ideas and thoughts to which they would never gain access. 'I seem to remember that he introduced us to the thought of Hegel in such a complex language that few of us could follow him! Our marks demonstrated our inability to follow Derrida's words – it seemed clear that they were in a different dimension, way beyond our capacities for absorption.'

As for Paul Cottin, he was struck by Derrida's seriousness and concentration, very different from the Voltairean irony of Genette and the bohemian charm of Pascal Fieschi, the philosophy teacher they had had the previous year.

Derrida gave nothing away. He seemed to dislike anecdotes and amusing examples. He did not try to make himself liked, but to give us solid, well-structured lessons. His lessons were demanding, but they were at an intellectual level that was too high for us. He placed a little too much trust in our intellectual abilities. The level of our *hypokhâgne* was quite unlike that of a class at Louis-le-Grand or Henri-IV. I remember him talking to us at length about the *Critique of Pure Reason*. In fact, he

tended to bring everything back to Kant. 'You can tell a great
philosopher from the way you find him at every crossroads,'
he used to say. He would screw up his eyes when he was telling
us about particularly difficult things, as if he wanted to help us
absorb his ideas better.

More positive are the memories of Njoh Mouellé, who would
pursue her studies in philosophy before becoming a government
minister in Cameroon.

Jacques Derrida was quite reserved and didn't mix much with
his students. But he did take part in the dinner that we organized with the whole class. Genette and he were the only teachers
who looked after us on that occasion, accompanied by their
wives. He wasn't very chatty, and didn't crack many jokes. One
day, he burst out to one of our classmates who always had a
smile on his lips: 'Listen, Pellois, your permanent hilarity really
gets on my nerves . . .' His lessons were both substantial and
serious and, as I'd been pretty good at philosophy since *terminale*, I personally followed them with great interest. He made
it possible for me to find my feet in Kantianism. I regularly got
good marks from him. Perhaps this was because I was already
really interested in philosophy.[6]

The more the months went by, the less did Derrida attempt to
conceal his disenchantment. Genette was pleased to have set up
'a nice little team' with him but realized that his former fellow
student considered the post as a second best. Derrida brooded over
his failure to get the Sorbonne job as if he were being persecuted.
Initially, his malaise expressed itself in a period of hypochondria.
Every day, he discovered new and alarming symptoms. He feared
cancer or some other deadly illness, and the various doctors whom
he consulted did not manage to allay his anxieties. During the third
term, his depression became evident – his 'big depression', he later
called it, since he would never experience one so serious.
    When Derrida arrived in Le Mans, he was unwilling to confess
the depth of his disappointment. And all at once, he collapsed under
his despair. He had suffered for years before passing the exam to
Normale Sup, then the *agrégation*. He had put up with twenty-seven
months of military service, waiting for the day when life would
finally open up before him. All this effort, just to end up here, standing in front of pupils who did not understand what he was telling
them, with colleagues who could talk about nothing but holidays
and sport! All this, to wear himself out preparing his lessons and
marking boring schoolwork! For months, he had not managed to

work on anything personal. He no longer felt up to staying in touch with his closest friends. In conditions like this, how would he ever manage to finish off a thesis? True, Jean Hyppolite assured him that in the new academic year he would be appointed to the Sorbonne, where a job as *assistant* in general philosophy awaited him: 'I've already told them you'd accept. I reckon it's a very favourable opportunity for you.'[7] But after the disappointment of the previous autumn, Jackie mistrusted illusory hopes and feared that he might have to stay for years in a dull place like Le Mans.

And now, to crown it all, the headmaster insisted that Derrida, being the last teacher to arrive in the *lycée*, should write and deliver the speech on prize-giving day. Genette remembers the gloom into which this request plunged Derrida:

> I can still see him, lying in his bed, explaining to me that he was quite unable to compose this 'ridiculous secular homily': 'No, come off it, that I *can't* do, I've got nothing to say to those bloody idiots.' But the headmaster insisted. To try to put Derrida on a suitable track, I reminded him that the *lycée* building was an old school of the Oratorians, and Father Mersenne must have passed through it – the philosopher and scientist, the friend of Descartes, Pascal, and Gassendi. I suggested he deliver a speech in praise of Mersenne, and even offered to gather a few documents to assist him in his task.[8]

Derrida had something else to worry about: the famous twenty-four hours of the Le Mans races that were due to take place on 25 and 26 June, creating hubbub throughout the city. After having given his last classes as well as he could, he left with Marguerite for the countryside and did not return until just before 14 July, to deliver the aforementioned prize-giving speech on the stage of the new theatre in Le Mans. At this juncture, his appointment as lecturer at the Sorbonne was confirmed. Marguerite and he got rid of the few pieces of furniture they possessed and set off to look for accommodation in the Paris region. Then they left for Prague to stay with Marguerite's family, in their little 2 CV. Even though this journey to the other side of the 'Iron Curtain' roused his interest, Jackie could not dig himself out of his hole. On his return, he was so low that he decided to consult a psychiatrist. Anti-depressants had just been invented: the first were put on the market in 1958. Jackie was prescribed Anafraline, which quickly produced beneficial effects, but caused several side-effects: hot flushes, tremors, etc.

When Maurice de Gandillac wrote to him at the end of the summer, he said he was sorry to hear of Derrida's 'serious health problems'. He hoped that his new post at the Sorbonne would mean he was soon his old self again.

Your appointment was a foregone conclusion, since it was only the ill-will of the managers in the secondary sector that had prevented our decision last year from being implemented. M. Hyppolite and myself emphasized your right to the job and no other candidate was put forward. However, you mustn't have any illusions about the amount of free time this job is going to leave you with. But it's true that the subjects you have to teach will perhaps be closer to your own research.[9]

8

Towards Independence

1960–1962

The Derridas quickly found an apartment in Fresnes, in Val-de-Marne, very close to Orly airport. It was a four-room flat in a brand-new block on the way to Versailles. Marguerite, who had resumed her studies in ethnology, was about to begin a one-year apprenticeship in the basement of the Musée de l'Homme, then start a thesis with André Leroi-Gourhan on the particular features of the liturgy of the Sephardim of Algiers, especially the funeral rites she had observed during the two years she had spent in Koléa.[1]

As for Jackie, he was still feeling low in spirits and dreaded having to take up his new post. 'I didn't know the year had ended so badly for you, like some of the dark days of the first years in Paris,' Michel Monory wrote.[2] Fortunately, the new academic year did not start until 24 October, which gave him a bit of time to prepare his lectures. As the sole *assistant* in general philosophy, Derrida was working under several professors. The burden of work was considerable and he was soon 'caught up in the absurd whirlpool of teaching and Paris. Ever since October, I've been so busy I've hardly have time to draw breath, without a moment to pause and live life.'[3] Anything more than the essential work, which was already substantial, seemed too much for him. And commuting between Fresnes and Paris was less easy than he had hoped.

All the same, compared with his year in Le Mans, the change for the better was considerable. Once the effects of his depression had started to fade, Derrida appreciated his new job at its true worth. 'Of those four years,' he later said in 1992, 'all I can remember is this: I was happy teaching then, more than I've ever been in higher education since.'[4] In fact, this was the only truly university job he would ever have in France. In one of his last texts, a homage to Paul Ricoeur written for the Cahier de l'Herne devoted to the latter, he looked back on that period at the Sorbonne:

In those days, the *assistants* occupied a strange place, which it's difficult to imagine now. I was the only *assistant* in 'general

philosophy and logic', free to organize my classes and my seminars however I wished, and working only in the most abstract
sense under all the professors whose *assistant* I officially was:
Suzanne Bachelard, Canguilhem, Poirier, Polin, Ricoeur, and
Wahl. I rarely saw them apart from at exams except, perhaps,
towards the end, Suzanne Bachelard and Canguilhem, who was
also a paternal and admired friend to me.[5]

As there was no syllabus in general philosophy, Derrida was at
liberty to choose his subjects. He gave entire lecture courses on
Heidegger's *Kant and the Problem of Metaphysics* and 'What is
metaphysics?', but he also discussed themes such as 'Irony, doubt
and the question', 'The present (Heidegger, Aristotle, Kant, Hegel,
Bergson)', and 'Thinking means saying no', and he gave a commentary on Claudel's formula, 'Evil is in the world like a slave
who brings up water from the well'. His reputation soon grew, and
people crowded into his lectures. In the Cavaillès lecture hall, over a
hundred and fifty students piled in, and those who had not taken the
precaution of turning up half an hour early had to remain standing.
After a few months, Derrida was forced to divide the students into
two groups and to repeat the sessions of *travaux dirigés.*[*]
    In spite of the difficult material conditions, typical of the way the
Sorbonne worked at the time, many students would vividly remember Derrida's lectures from those years. Françoise Dastur recalls a
profound philosopher, albeit one who was still very traditional in
his manners.

> He seemed shy and even somewhat clumsy. He read out
> extremely dense lectures, several of which were quite magnifi-
> cent. I particularly remember 'Method and metaphysics' and
> 'Theology and teleology in Husserl'. It was Derrida, together
> with Ricoeur, who initiated me into the phenomenology of
> Husserl and the thought of Heidegger. However, though he
> sometimes referred to Sartre, he never mentioned Merleau-
> Ponty. He demanded a great deal from his students, but gave
> them a great deal in return, and was happy to spend a few
> minutes answering questions at the end of each lecture.[6]

Jean Ristat, who would soon become a friend of Derrida's,
remembers a teacher who was friendly and attentive most of the
time, but who could also be merciless on occasion.

> I remember him flying into a terrible rage during oral exams,
> since several of the students he was examining hadn't read the

---

* Similar to seminars, with the focus on student discussion. – Tr.

Critique of Pure Reason. But he was always available for those who showed real passion for the subject. Sometimes, he'd take us to the 'Balzar' to continue the discussions over a drink. Listening to students, being approachable, were highly unusual in the university in those days.[7]

Meanwhile, the Algerian situation was developing rapidly. It was increasingly the main topic of conversations at the Sorbonne and elsewhere. In Derrida's family as in that of most *pieds-noirs*, resentment against de Gaulle continued to rise. In the referendum on self-determination held on 8 January 1961, the 'yes' vote massively outnumbered the 'no' vote, with 75 per cent in metropolitan France and 70 per cent in Algeria: for the first time, Muslims had an opportunity to vote. On 7 April, the Evian negotiations began, opening up the way to independence. Some people refused to accept it. On the night of 21–2 April, four generals – Challe, Jouhaud, Zeller, and Salan – tried to rouse the soldiers and *pieds-noirs* to revolt, in an attempt to keep Algeria as part of the French Republic. In just a few hours, they managed to seize control of Algiers. On Sunday, 23 April, in a televised speech that became famous, de Gaulle denounced 'the attempt made by a bunch of retired generals', ordering that every means be put into action to block them. The putsch failed, but the OAS (Organisation Armée Secrète) continued, in an increasingly bloody manner, to fight for Algeria to remain French.

It was at about the same time that Pierre Nora, one of Jackie's old fellow pupils at Louis-le-Grand, brought out a book on *The French of Algeria*, published by Julliard. Shortly after receiving this volume, Derrida replied to Nora in a letter of nineteen typewritten pages, single-spaced – a letter that I will quote from extensively, as it seems to me so illuminating. It sets out his convictions on the Algerian situation in a way he had never expressed them before and would never do again. In this detailed analysis, he also showed ethical and political preoccupations that his publications would not reveal until many years later.

Derrida says that he had read the work with unremitting and enthusiastic interest, during days that were in his view dismaying and, so to speak, unreal. He thanks Nora for having written a book with 'the merit, rare and difficult, on this subject [. . .] of being almost constantly *just* [*juste*] in the double meaning of the word,* in its content and its conclusions'. This did not stop him from deploring its tone, 'which, in general, reveals – more than what is actually said – the fundamental attitude of the person writing'. The work often struck him as 'rather harsh in its aggression', and even imbued

---

* I.e. both correct and fair. – Tr.

with 'a desire to humiliate'. 'When you say that you have "never heard a French Algerian replying with a proper argument", I can only conclude that you haven't met enough of them.'

Derrida assures him that he had long since 'within himself, in silence, put the French Algerians on trial', but he is striving to remain even-handed, now that the wind is turning and there is an increasing chorus of criticism from right and left alike. And, as if to avenge himself for his over-long silence, he wants to give Nora the thoughts he has long been accumulating on this subject so close to his heart. It seems to him that his former fellow pupil has, in his book, concealed several elements of a hopelessly tangled situation:

> Isn't it difficult to lay the blame for all of France's policies in Algeria over the past 130 years on something like the French Algerians (in spite of their massive and unremitting guilt, which should neither be overlooked nor diluted on the pretext of sharing it round)? If, as you say, the French Algerians have indeed been the 'makers' of their own history and misfortune, this is true only if, at the same time, one points out that all governments and the whole army (in other words the whole French people in whose name they act) have always been the *masters*.

Derrida is particularly angry with the Left, 'which has never managed to bring about socialism in France, or decolonization anywhere else'. Another point annoys him: like most French people in France, Nora has minimized the diversity of the French Algerians and their capacity for change, treating them instead as a homogeneous, eternal entity. In particular, he has produced a caricature of those 'liberal' French of whom, without saying it in so many words, Derrida feels part. Yet in his view, this is a group which deserves something other than a dismissive condemnation, since it is torn between belonging to France and its support of the principle of decolonization. Of course, this often forces those 'liberals' into ambiguous positions, even a kind of impotence. Nonetheless:

> [They are the ones] who, whether Communist or not, kept political and trade-union life going before the war, and it was in their midst that people such as Alleg, Audin, and Camus thought and acted. They were the ones who, after '45, made it possible in Algiers to elect a progressive-Communist city council in Algiers (Yes! . . .) and who subsequently did good work by collaborating with Algerian delegates, the avowed militants of the nationalist parties. They were the ones who, up until '57, kept touch with nationalists, at a time when war, repression, and terrorist attacks were starting to make many things impossible.

Derrida also criticized Nora for having suggested that the average income of French Algerians was higher than that of French people in France, whereas the reverse was the case, and only a minority of colonists enjoyed any real economic privileges. He took advantage of a long note to sketch out a critique of Marxism:

> This means, perhaps, that the notion of 'colonial system' cannot be understood *essentially* and *always* on the basis of the *sole* idea of *profit*, short-term or long-term. It is perhaps the whole of Marxist dogma about colonization, economic imperialism (and the phases of capitalism) that needs to be revised, especially as it has ultimately left its mark – sometimes anonymously – on the most banal and unquestioned definition of the colonial phenomenon.

As he always did in the case of those to whom he felt close, Derrida defended the complex and nuanced positions of Germaine Tillion and Albert Camus, even if these positions were used by some people 'to support interests that neither of them defend'. It is not so easy to talk of 'objective complicity', rejecting an argument because it has been used by 'ultras'. Unless one is careful, it is easy to fall into dogmatic and sectarian positions that all start in this same way, whether they are revolutionary or not. 'With Germaine Tillion, you say, "we were ripe for Gaullism before de Gaulle". Maybe. Personally, I often regret that this was not even more true, for Algeria, and even earlier . . . .'

In connection with Camus, who had died the previous year, Derrida set out a more circumstantial analysis than anywhere else:

> Firstly, I found *excellent* the intention behind the few pages that you devote to *The Stranger*. I've always read this book as an Algerian book, and all the critico-philosophical apparatus that Sartre plonked on top of it seems, in my view, to lessen its meaning and its 'historical' originality, hiding them from view, maybe even from Camus himself, since he took himself too quickly to be [. . .] a great thinker. [. . .] Not all that long ago, I often judged Camus the way you do, for the same reasons [. . .]. I don't know now whether this is right, and whether some of his warnings will not appear, tomorrow, as signs of elementary lucidity and moral challenge. Many things, *all of his past* to begin with, make it possible to Camus to be credited with a pure and clear *intention*.[8]

This French-Muslim Algeria, for which Camus had always striven, is what Derrida too wishes for. And even though he knows that this dream has become an anachronism, he continues to think that it was by no means the façade of an 'Algeria-as-our-Papa-wished-it'.*

A few weeks later, Nora thanked him for these 'pages so dense and so profound that it would need a second book' to reply to them. He felt that he had acted as a catalyst for Derrida's personal thoughts, and that he was lucky enough to harvest their ripe fruit. Nora wanted to meet so that they could discuss the matter at greater length. He acknowledged that he had written the book in a rough-and-ready way. 'I thought I would relate my stay, reflect on the things I had seen – but if I had attacked the subject in its full scope, head-on, I would have written a whole thesis, and this would have paralysed me.'[9]

The two men spent a long evening together at the end of June, discussing things freely and without attempting to reach any conclusions. Derrida said he was pleased at this exchange of ideas. Even though the discussion sometimes seemed to go round in circles, their disagreement was, in his view, just 'another way of agreeing with one another or disagreeing with ourselves. And how can anyone think seriously about Algeria – or anything else – without ending up in that position?' He thought he could sense that Nora would like to speak his mind on certain points, for example by replying to an account published by Derrida. But 'there is no question – for reasons too many to mention – of writing an article'. The need to protect his family was probably one of these reasons. However, he had no objection to all or part of his long letter being published anonymously, as coming from 'a friend from Algiers'.[10] This plan seems not to have led to anything concrete.

A few weeks later, from El Biar, Derrida sent a new letter to his former schoolmate:

> I'm having a strange holiday here: between a bit of work [. . .] and the pleasures of the sea, the day is taken up, in the midst of this strange society, brooding over unthinkable problems. And I realize that I love this country more and more, love it madly, which does not contradict the aversion I have long stated for it.[11]

---

* In an excellent article, 'Liberalism and the Algerian War: the case of Jacques Derrida' (*Critical Inquiry* no. 36, winter 2010), Edward Baring provides a detailed analysis of Derrida's attitude towards the Algerian War, comparing this letter to Nora with a piece of history homework that Derrida wrote in *khâgne* in 1952, on the 'Causes, characters and first consequences of French colonization from 1888 to 1914'. If we go along with Baring's view, the attitude and conceptions of the future author of *Monolingualism of the Other* remained, for a long time, those of a colonist. Later in his text, he refers – as if to deplore it – to the fact that Derrida did not sign the 'Manifesto of the 121' in 1960. In my view, this is to ignore the fact that Derrida was at the time completely unknown – nobody would have dreamed of asking him to sign, and if he had done so, he would have placed his family, still living in Algeria, in grave danger.

This was to be his last summer in Algeria; probably he guessed as much without admitting it to himself. For French Algerians, fear had become tangible. An elderly man was murdered in El Biar, just a short distance away from the family home. Charlie, the son of one of Derrida's female cousins, came to live in Fresnes for a year, with Jackie and Marguerite, as his family was gravely concerned that he might be assassinated. Here he developed a liking for work and study, and later said that this stay had saved his life.

It was in this unsettled context, in July 1961, that Derrida finally completed his Introduction to *The Origin of Geometry*, the manuscript of which he had written on paper headed 'Faculty of literature and human sciences, History of colonization'. At the start of the academic year, he brought the typescript to Jean Hyppolite, who said he was eager to see it in print. In October, in one of his most laconic letters, Hyppolite assured Derrida that he had read 'with great interest (this is not just an empty formula)' this meticulous analysis 'which closely follows the meanders of Husserl's thinking'.[12] This opinion, in its brevity, could hardly quieten Derrida's considerable anxiety at submitting this first text.

On 24 November, he sent a long letter to Paul Ricoeur, in a very deferential tone: he was keen to submit his Introduction to him before it was published by the Presses Universitaires de France: 'Your judgement is worth more to me than that of anyone else.' In particular, Derrida wanted Ricoeur to endorse the several allusions he had made to the latter's works; he said he was 'especially troubled by the problem of references to living philosophers', and afraid he might not be finding 'the right tone'. He also regretted not having told Ricoeur, on their first encounter, of 'the huge and faithful admiration' that he had for his work, and he wanted to explain 'the accidental reasons' for which he had not asked him to supervise his thesis.[13] A few weeks later, surprised that he had not received the least reply, Derrida had to re-write his letter and send it off a second time, since Ricoeur had lost it. Fortunately, Derrida had kept a rough draft, as he did for all his official correspondence in those days. Ricoeur apologized for his carelessness, and said this time how touched he was by the way his young *assistant*'s letter was so full of 'confession and modesty':

> I can sense perfectly well how difficult it is to get the tone right from one generation to another. In the United States, I used to think that relationships are easier, in the same circumstances, between academics. Allow me to tell you that I would very much like to see the differences (that our reciprocal position makes inevitable) disappear in communication and friendship. Let us place our trust in the boldness of expression, and in time.[14]

Over the following two weeks, Derrida and Ricoeur would grow closer, having lunch or dinner together several times, with or without their wives. But Derrida was still very shy and socially ill at ease. As for Ricoeur, snowed under as he was by his own obligations, he seems not to have read the Introduction to *The Origin of Geometry* closely before it was published. So, in order to get a more frank and direct opinion of his manuscript, which he was still doubtful about, Derrida turned to Althusser.

After an attentive reading, his old *caïman* assured him, on 9 January 1962, that he had never read a text 'so scrupulous and so *profoundly* intelligent on Husserl. Intelligent *in depth*, going beyond the usual picking out of contradictions, seeking out the most hidden intention to account for and explain the enigmas of expression.' He was convinced that Derrida had gone much further than other interpreters, who 'throw in the towel when things get too tough': 'You carry on to the bitter end, and even if one can decide not to be a Husserlian (which is very difficult when reading you . . .), it is easy to see how one could be such, and what being one actually means.' He said how happy he was to recognize in this introduction the point of departure for Derrida's current thinking: writing, 'transcendental' pathology, language. 'You must go on: the pages you have already produced on writing are full of meaning and big with promise.' In Althusser's view, the whole text was first-rate. 'I started reading it on returning from holiday (rain, snow, fog): it brought me light and much joy.'[15] He took this opportunity to invite Derrida to call by and visit him in his lair at Normale Sup: he would especially like to discuss in more detail Husserl's relations with Hegel and Heidegger.

This invitation did not go unheeded. In the short term, it helped Derrida gain a little confidence. He dreamed only of 'being able to replace this artificial, inhuman and industrial stress of producing "courses" and "publications" with a living, shared work carried out in the freedom of dialogue'. The Sorbonne exhausted him: his lectures seemed to meet with approval, but he complained at having to spend most of his time marking student work that was often boring. 'There are days when, overcome by tiredness, all I can get from the whole business is a sense of being worn out, worn down, sacrificing myself for an abstraction.'[16]

At that moment, the Algerian question forced itself on Derrida's attention more brutally than ever. Since the beginning of 1962, the OAS had extended its action to metropolitan France. There were several bomb attacks in Paris, including one on Sartre's apartment; another attack, aimed at André Malraux, disfigured a four-year-old girl. The forces of the Left finally came together and launched a 'National Committee of Action against the OAS and for a Negotiated Peace'. On 8 February, a demonstration was banned and then savagely repressed by the Prefect of Police, Maurice Papon: nine people were killed when they were forced against the barriers of the Charonne metro station. Five days later, a huge procession paid homage to the victims.

The Evian agreements were signed on 18 March 1962. The ceasefire was supposed to take effect the following day. The conflict had left 400,000 dead, of all categories, the vast majority of them being Algerian. From April onwards, Europeans started to leave en masse for metropolitan France. But Jackie, who still hoped that the different communities might be able to coexist, advised his parents to remain in El Biar. A few weeks later, there was a general stampede. Most people were taken by surprise, especially those Jewish families who, like the Derridas and the Safars, had been settled in Algeria for so long that that they had never dreamed they would have to leave the country. Crowds jostled on the quays, even though ships were now taking on considerably more passengers than the authorized limit. Endless queues of cars formed on the road from Algiers to the Maison Blanche airport. Many people preferred to destroy their luggage and set fire to their cars rather than abandon them.[17]

It was Derrida's sister and her family who arrived first. As Marguerite recalls,

Towards the end of May, we received a telegram from Janine and her husband to say they were coming, without any further details. We spent two whole days in Orly, not knowing which plane they might have managed to get on board. There was complete confusion. Finally, Janine came alone with her three children: Martine, Marc and Michel. Everyone found a provisional refuge at our place in Fresnes. There were eventually seventeen of us in our four-room flat. We had got a few beds together, but the children slept on the floor, on cushions.

Martine was eight at the time. She still remembers some aspects of their stay clearly.

It was pretty complicated to organize. Jackie often took my brother Marc and me to Paris. Sometimes, he'd have to leave us for quite a while inside his 2CV, in the courtyard of the École Normale Supérieure – or maybe it was the one in the Sorbonne? He told us that he was going off to feed 'Sophie the Whale' with tins of sardines. He asked us to be patient, as 'Sophie' was quite prickly and he was the only one she would allow near her . . . It took me several years to understand that Sophie was philosophy.[18]

A few weeks later, it was the turn of René and his family to leave Algeria.

At first, it had been the OAS who tried to stop us from leaving. More recently it had been the FLN. We were requested to be on one side or the other; those who were considered as 'lukewarm' were particularly hated. We abandoned our chemist's shop in Bab El-Oued, and left on 15 June. All we took were bits and pieces, like for a holiday. But it was high time for us to go. On the road to the airport, there was yet another kidnapping that day.[19]

When the referendum finally came, on 1 July, there was a crushing majority in favour of independence. Even without waiting for the official results, a jubilant crowd invaded the streets of Algiers, brandishing green and white flags with the red star and crescent. The *pieds-noirs* who had not yet returned to France got a move on now that they were faced with a choice between 'the suitcase and the coffin'. Two weeks later, just after examining at the Sorbonne, Jackie returned to El Biar to help his parents pack a few things. René was reluctant to set foot in Algeria again; he had witnessed too many horrors during the final weeks he had spent there. Pierrot, Janine's husband, and his brother Jaquie Meskel also left with Derrida and his parents, trying to save as many of their things as possible, but Pierrot and Jaquie were immediately threatened and had to go back to France in a hurry. So, in spite of the risks he too was running, Jackie remained alone with his parents. The following days, they did their best to clear René's house, then Janine's, leaving the villa in the rue d'Aurelle-de-Paladines until last to be cleared. But the containers were already full and they could take little with them. They closed the door behind them, hoping that they would be able to get back a few months later, once the situation had calmed down. The place was immediately filled by neighbours, who actually paid them rent for the first months. Then the house, which Aimé and Georgette had only just finally paid for, became the property of the Algerian state. In France, René and Pierrot would need to become embroiled in a great deal of bureaucracy in order to prove they had a right to stay and find businesses to take over. Gradually, like many other 'repatriated' people, the whole family ended up together in Nice.[20]

Even though he had long since left El Biar, Derrida would never forget the pain of this loss. Over the years, he would refer with increasing frequency to his inconsolable 'nostalgeria', a neologism which he had not invented, despite what one might imagine. It was originally the title of a poem by Marcello Fabri, written in the 1920s:

> Algiers, I dreamed of you as if you were a lover,
> perfumed you were, and filled with sunshine and hot spice;

you are even more beautiful now you are so far, the rain
here, the rain attires, as if it were a magic spell,
the grey of the sky with all the gold of your sun . . .[21]

Over and above the wounds on the family and personal level, the
Algerian War also constituted one of the stimuli for all Derrida's
political thinking. In France, for years, he would avoid speaking in
public about a subject that remained too controversial. But in an
interview he gave in Japan in 1987, he acknowledged that, while he
had approved of the Algerians' struggle for independence, he had
long hoped for 'a solution that would allow the French Algerians to
continue to live in that country', 'an original political solution that
was not the one that actually came about'.[22]

He remained faithful to this conviction, one that was fundamental but not at all widely shared. On 22 June 2004, in the last televised
broadcast in which he ever took part, he declared that he favoured,
for Israel and Palestine, a different problematic than that of two
sovereign states, before adding: 'Even between Algeria and France,
although I approved of the independence movement, I would have
preferred there to be a different type of settlement, one from which,
in fact, the Algerians would have suffered less, and which would
have spurned the rigidly unconditional terms of sovereignty.'[23]

Derrida's late discussions of forgiveness and reconciliation, of
the impossible and hospitality, are in my view, in several respects,
echoes of this Algerian wound. During the 1990s, thanks to the
'admirable' figure of Nelson Mandela, the situation of South Africa
was, as it were, a confirmation that the model he had imagined
for Algeria was not necessarily illusory. When he gave his opinion
about apartheid and what had followed, or the Israel–Palestine conflict, he would never stop thinking about Algeria, of the Algerian
within him, without which all the rest would be incomprehensible.

'My adolescence lasted until I was thirty-two,' Derrida stated in
one of his last interviews.[24] The completion of his first book, the
definitive adoption of a new first name, and the independence of
Algeria were events of the year 1962 that marked the end of an era.[*]
The consequences of this break would make themselves apparent
over the following months.

---

[*] Jean-Luc Nancy also considers this same year, 1962, as a major turning-point. In
his text 'The independence of Algeria, the independence of Derrida', he compares
the appearance of the concept of *différance* with the independence of Algeria, where
the issue was less a 're-founding in an origin than the invention of an "origin" yet to
come' (*Derrida à Alger: Un regard sur le monde*, Arles: Actes Sud; Algiers: Barzakh,
2008, pp. 19–25).

PART II
Derrida

1963–1983

1

From Husserl to Artaud

1963–1964

The Origin of Geometry was published under the name of Husserl alone, with the words 'translation and introduction by Jacques Derrida' appearing only after the title. This first publication was official confirmation that Derrida had finally abandoned the first name 'Jackie'. This was a more serious decision than might appear, for someone who would soon be turning the question of the signature into a fully fledged philosophical theme. As he explained:

I changed my first name when I began to publish, at the moment I entered what is, in sum, the space of literary or philo-sophical legitimation, whose 'good manners' I was practising in my own way. In finding that Jackie was not possible as the first name of an author, by choosing what was in some way, to be sure, a semi-pseudonym but also very French, Christian, simple, I must have erased more things than I could say in a few words [. . .].[1]

In many respects, *The Origin of Geometry* was a curious book, mainly for quantitative reasons: Husserl's text occupied only 43 pages of the French edition, whereas the Introduction comprised 170. But above all, its oddness resided in a fundamental ambiguity. In its first pages, Derrida's aim is presented in modest terms: 'Our sole ambition will be to recognize and situate one stage of Husserl's thought, with its specific presuppositions and its particular unfin-ished state.'[2] Taking him at his word, one might believe that he was simply attempting to get as close to Husserl's intentions as possible. In fact, the more the reader plunges into this labyrinthine analysis, strewn with very lengthy footnotes, the more does Derrida seem 'driven by the somewhat inordinate ambition to introduce us to Husserl's phenomenology as a whole',[3] if not to raise questions about the whole enterprise. And in the last pages there appear, as yet allusively, concepts destined for a great future in Derrida's own work, those of *originary delay* and *différance*.

Apart from Paul Ricoeur and Tran-Duc-Thao, Derrida barely refers to contemporary philosophers. One can sense an urge to go straight to Husserl's text, bypassing the official interpreters. Sartre is never quoted, and when Derrida mentions Merleau-Ponty, he does nothing to hide the fact that he is 'tempted by an interpretation dia-metrically opposed to that of Merleau-Ponty'.* In the very middle of his Introduction, however, Derrida develops an unexpected parallel between Edmund Husserl's endeavour and that of James Joyce. Over several pages, he contrasts 'the univocity investigated by Husserl and the equivocation generalized by Joyce'. The former seeks 'to reduce or impoverish empirical language methodically to the point where its univocal and translatable elements are actually transparent', while the latter puts to work a writing that brings out 'the greatest potential for buried, accumulated, and interwoven intentions within each linguistic atom', a writing that 'circulates through all languages at once, accumulates their energies, actual-izes their most secret consonances'.[4] This strange parallel, quite out of kilter with the rest of his commentary, seemed mainly to bring Derrida the phenomenologist face to face with his own double, haunted by literature and by a writing beyond all intention [*vouloir-dire*].

In spite of the technical nature of this first publication, Derrida was far from abandoning more literary projects. Having attempted several times to collaborate in literary reviews, he envisaged writing a short book with Michel Monory, who, on his return from military service, was teaching French in Orleans. Monory had written his *diplôme de lettres* on '*Gaspard de la nuit* and the birth of the poem in prose'. Derrida suggested that the two of them write a volume on Aloysius Bertrand, the author of *Gaspard*, for the series 'Poètes d'aujourd'hui', published by Seghers.[5] The idea would probably

---

* Strange as it might appear, Derrida had hardly any personal contact with Maurice Merleau-Ponty. He seems to have seen him only once, in 1950 or 1951, when the author of *Phenomenology of Perception* was an oral examiner for the entrance exams in philosophy to Normale Sup. According to Françoise Dastur, Derrida also had a telephone conversation with Merleau-Ponty, around 1956 or 1957, as he was embarking on the translation of *The Origin of Geometry*. During the four years which Derrida spent at the rue d'Ulm, he never went to hear Merleau-Ponty at the nearby Collège de France, where the latter taught from 1952 to his death in May 1961. In 1959–60, while Derrida was in Le Mans, Merleau-Ponty devoted his lectures to what he called 'the unthought' of Husserl, focusing mainly on *The Origin of Geometry* (these *Notes de cours sur 'L'origine de la géométrie' de Husserl* were published by Presses Universitaires de France in 1998). But Derrida's and Merleau-Ponty's investigations developed in total independence from each other. In spite of the violence of his attacks on Sartre, Derrida felt many more affinities with the latter, and had read much more of his work. He came back to Merleau-Ponty in *Memoirs of the Blind* (1990) and above all in *On Touching: Jean-Luc Nancy* (2000), but there was always a highly critical tenor to his remarks.

have borne concrete results if the publisher had shown any enthusiasm at all, instead of informing them that he could not possibly
'envisage [. . .] the publication of a book on Aloysius Bertrand',
since his list was full for years to come.[6] But perhaps this rather
unusual plan was really an attempt to rekindle a great friendship
that was starting to fade?

Though it passed unremarked by the media and the non-specialist
public, the appearance of *The Origin of Geometry* was noticed and
hailed in philosophical circles. The great epistemologist Georges
Canguilhem, whom Derrida sincerely admired and whom he sometimes referred to as his 'philosophical superego', was the first to
congratulate him:

> It has been a long time – many months – since I have read a book
> right to the end, at a single sitting, dropping everything else to
> do so. This is the measure of the quality of your work, since I
> read your Introduction to *The Origin of Geometry* without a
> break, and with unprecedented intellectual satisfaction. [. . .]
> Initially, I smiled when I saw how long the Introduction was
> compared to the text itself. But I'm not smiling now – instead,
> I'm glad the Introduction is so long, since in the final analysis
> it's all necessary. There's not a single word of padding. [. . .] I
> wasn't the first to place my confidence in you – that was Jean
> Hyppolite. My confidence simply took its cue from his, but it is
> now fully justified.[7]

In presenting his compliments to Derrida, Canguilhem hoped that
his work 'would be as productive as this success promises'. This was
not mere lip service: he was the main person responsible for ensuring
that the Introduction to *The Origin of Geometry* was awarded the
prestigious Jean-Cavaillès prize.

A few weeks later, Michel Foucault, whose reputation had been
made with the publication of his *History of Madness* in 1961, also
expressed his enthusiasm to his 'dear friend':

> Before thanking you for your Introduction to *The Origin of
> Geometry*, I wisely waited until I had read it, – and re-read it.
> Now I have done so. And all that remains for me to tell you,
> rather dumbly, is that I'm filled with admiration. A few more
> words: I knew what a perfect connoisseur of Husserl you are;
> as I read you, I had the impression that you were bringing out
> quite different possibilities of philosophizing which phenom-
> enology constantly promised but also perhaps sterilized; and
> that these possibilities were in your grasp, were coming into
> your grasp. Probably the first act of philosophy for us – and for

a long time to come – is *reading*: and your reading clearly presents itself as such an act. This is why it has such regal honesty.[8]

Even in the Sorbonne, this first publication led to some very
welcome reactions. Paul Ricoeur launched a seminar reserved
for researchers that was entirely devoted to Husserl. He wanted
Derrida to present his work on *The Origin of Geometry* at the very
first session. 'This invitation is the expression [. . .] of my admiration for your book that I have only just now been studying.'[9] Over
the next few months, Derrida often took part in the discussions at
the seminar, in an atmosphere both friendly and rigorous. Some
of the microfilms made in Louvain are kept in Paris: in a very late
letter, Ricoeur mentioned the work on these manuscripts that he
had shared with Derrida – the manuscripts had aroused both men's
'admiration for an oeuvre of exemplary intellectual honesty'.[10]

The publication of *The Origin of Geometry* also added lustre
to Derrida's prestige among the best students at the Sorbonne.
According to Françoise Dastur,

> at the beginning of the sixties, in spite of the sudden death of
> Merleau-Ponty, phenomenology still appeared the dominant
> philosophy. When it came to *travaux dirigés*, Derrida advised
> students who so desired to form small groups, each of them
> working on a precise theme in Husserl's phenomenology. In
> this way, I took part in two working groups that met outside
> the university once a week, the first focusing on the *Logical
> Researches*, the second, set up by Germanists such as myself,
> embarking on the translation of *Ideas II*. Derrida himself would
> come to work with each of these groups once a term. For most
> of us, this was an amazing opportunity to immerse ourselves in
> Husserl's thought, under the guidance of one of those who had
> contributed most to asking fundamental questions about it.[11]

In a few months, as if to make up for lost time, Derrida's situation
evolved spectacularly. He made important contacts; he was asked
for articles and conference papers on all sides. He had spent years
finishing the Introduction to *The Origin of Geometry*, and was
about to write several fundamental texts on very different subjects.
It was as if these commissions were revealing him to himself; as he
explained in a letter to Foucault, he was now in search of a style of
writing that would be his own:

> University work, in the form assigned to it at present within our
> society – university society in particular – distracts me painfully
> [. . .] from what would be for me the essential task, vital (and

deadly too – which is why whatever conceals this task protects me and reassures me at the same time): a type of *philosophical* writing in which I can say 'I', tell my story without shame and without the delights of the *Journal métaphysique.*[12]

Jean Wahl had invited Derrida to speak at the prestigious Collège Philosophique on the subject of his choice. Derrida decided to talk about the *History of Madness*, which had made a powerful impression on him, even though, on his first reading, he had not concealed from Foucault 'at bottom, a rather muted protest, unformulatable or as yet unformulated', giving him a desire to write 'something like a paean to reason that would be faithful to [his] book'.[13] A year later, he very cautiously sketched out to Foucault the plan of a text that would later become famous, completely transforming his relationship with his old teacher. He had re-read Foucault's book over the Christmas break, he told him, 'with an ever-renewed joy' and was now trying to 'put together a paper' that would focus on the pages devoted to Descartes: 'I think I'll try to show – basically – that your reading of Descartes is legitimate and illuminating, but at a deep level that in my view cannot be the level of the text you are using and that, I think, I will not read altogether the same way that you do.'[14]

The postscript of the letter is somewhat barbed, too. Derrida thanked Foucault for the radio broadcasts he gave every Monday evening. He had been particularly struck by the one on Antonin Artaud, the previous week: 'I have long shared everything you say and seem to think about Artaud. He's another I'd need to re-read, or to read better and more patiently . . . .'

On Monday, 4 March 1963, at 6.30 pm, at the Collège Philosophique, 44, rue de Rennes, opposite the church of Saint-Germain-des-Prés, Derrida gave his first major paper in Paris. It was called 'Cogito and the history of madness'. Foucault was present in the audience. Derrida began by hailing the *History of Madness*. He had been Foucault's pupil, and found himself in the delicate position of the 'admiring and grateful disciple' just as he was about, if not to 'dispute', at least 'to engage in dialogue with the master'. But Derrida soon showed his true colours:

My point of departure might appear slight and artificial. In this 673-page book, Michel Foucault devotes three pages – and, moreover, in a kind of prologue to his second chapter – to a certain passage from the first of Descartes's *Meditations*. In this passage, madness, folly, dementia, insanity seem, I emphasize *seem*, dismissed, excluded, and ostracized from the circle of philosophical dignity, denied entry to the philosopher's city, denied the right to philosophical consideration, ordered away from the bench as soon as summoned to it by Descartes – this last tribunal of a Cogito that, by its essence, *could not possibly be mad*.[15]

However partial it might appear, the reading of this passage nonetheless involved a great deal in Derrida's view. If we are to believe him, in fact, 'the sense of Foucault's entire project can be pinpointed in these few allusive and somewhat enigmatic pages'. Following the first of Descartes's *Metaphysical Meditations* word for word, and going back to the original Latin, Derrida patiently and methodically questioned the reading that Foucault had proposed. And little by little, many of the book's postulates, including the very definition of madness, were cast into doubt or undermined by his analysis.

Foucault's first reaction was really rather positive. He seemed ready to take on board Derrida's critique, without any hint of the violent polemic that would break out nine years later.

The other day, as you can imagine, I wasn't able to thank you in the way I would have wished: not really, not only for the over-indulgent things you said about me, but for the immense and marvellous attention you gave to my words. I was impressed – so much so that, off the cuff, I was taken aback and pretty clumsy in what I managed to say – by the *rectitude* of your remarks that went, unerringly, to the heart of what I wanted to do, and beyond it. This relationship between the Cogito and madness is something that, without the least doubt, I treated too cavalierly in my thesis: via Bataille and Nietzsche, I came back to it slowly and by way of many detours. You have magisterially showed the right road to take: and you can understand why I owe you a profound debt of gratitude.

It would be wonderful to see you again [. . .] as soon as you like. And please believe in my deepest and most faithful friendship.[16]

A few months later, Foucault was still reassuring Derrida, although in a more nuanced way, when the question arose of publishing the text of the latter's paper in the *Revue de métaphysique et de morale*: 'As for your text being published, in the final analysis I think it's a good thing (I'm here speaking egotistically): only the blind will find your critique severe.'[17] And after 're-reading with passion' the text in its published version, he said that he was again 'convinced that it gets to the heart of things and in such a radical, such an all-embracing way that it simultaneously leaves me in an aporia and opens up to me a whole way of thinking that I hadn't thought of'.[18] These friendly relations were to last for several years. We will later discover how and why they deteriorated.

The publication of *The Origin of Geometry* enabled Derrida to resume contact with several of his old classmates from Louis-le-Grand and Normale Sup. Michel Deguy, already the author of four works, including two collections of poems published by Gallimard, suggested that Derrida send some texts to the prestigious review *Critique*. Founded by Georges Bataille in 1946, the review had been edited since his death in July 1962 by Jean Piel, his brother-in-law, who had set up an editorial committee comprising Roland Barthes, Deguy, and Foucault.

For a young intellectual at the beginning of the sixties, *Critique* was an ideal place for publication. Other former fellow pupils of Derrida's, such as Abirached, Granel, and Genette, had already contributed to it, as had most of the significant authors of that generation. Unlike *Les Temps modernes*, *Esprit*, or *Tel Quel*, *Critique* did not issue forth from any clique or clan. As Bataille had wished, the review was a general one. Month by month, it offered, on the books published in France and abroad, studies that aimed to be more than mere reviews: 'Through [these studies], *Critique* seeks to give an overview, as complete as possible, of the various activities of the human mind in the fields of literary creation, philosophical research, and work in history, science, politics and economics.'[19]

Deguy – who published the first article on Derrida in this review, 'Husserl in a second reading'[20] – could offer 'almost as much space as you wish' in *Critique*.[21] With Derrida, he did not yet know that the 'almost' would be appropriate. The latter initially thought of writing a review of Emmanuel Levinas's *Totality and Infinity*. But as he sensed that he would need the peace and quiet of the summer to write it, he first envisaged an article on an essay by Jean Rousset that had recently been published by José Corti, *Form and Signification: An Essay on Literary Structures from Corneille to Claudel*. Foucault was also pleased about this first collaboration with *Critique*.

For Derrida, at this time, writing was a serious business, requiring total commitment. After accumulating notes, he wrote the text by hand, in a ritual of great solemnity:

> For the texts that mattered to me, the ones I had the slightly religious feeling of 'writing', I even banished the ordinary pen. I dipped into the ink a long pen holder whose point was gently curved with a special drawing quill, producing endless drafts and preliminary versions before putting a stop to them on my first little Olivetti, with its international keyboard, that I'd bought abroad.[22]

He completed the article at the end of April 1963 and sent it to Jean Piel, who reacted almost immediately, with both enthusiasm and perplexity. The text was of such high quality and raised questions of such contemporary importance that he would be very happy to publish it in *Critique*. But he was dismayed by its length – some forty pages; perhaps it would be better to cut it into two. Derrida was not thrilled by this idea, and Piel finally decided to publish 'Force and signification' in one go, in the June–July double issue.

The conditional phrase with which the article opens is towering, majestic, and melancholy at once: 'If it recedes one day, leaving behind its works and signs on the shores of our civilization, the structural invasion might become a question for the historian of ideas.'[23] Structuralism would peak publicly in France only three or four years later, but for the young Derrida it was no longer anything more than a hangover from the past, a survival.

The tone of 'Force and signification' comes from who knows where – perhaps from Maurice Blanchot? With the loftiness of its views, the diversity of its reference points – Leibniz and Artaud, Hegel and Mallarmé –, this text seems to have landed from nowhere, but it manifests a style of thought and writing which Derrida's readers must have felt they would need to take seriously. Even though the article was a positive review of Jean Rousset's book, it undermined its basic presuppositions, dealing a series of deadly blows to what Derrida cruelly called 'the worst exhilaration of the most nuanced structural formalism'. 'In the rereading to which we are invited by Rousset, light is menaced from within by that which also metaphysically menaces every structuralism: the possibility of concealing meaning through the very act of uncovering it.'[24] To paraphrase the celebrated words of Malraux, what we here witness is the wild intrusion of philosophical concepts into literary criticism. This long article, which, four years later, would be the opening essay in *Writing and Difference*, perhaps comprises the founding act of what would soon be known as cultural studies.

In 1963, Derrida seemed tirelessly productive. Having made his name as an excellent Husserl specialist, he was turning into an important figure on the Parisian intellectual scene, someone to reckon with. Shortly after the birth of his first son Pierre, on 10 April, he threw himself into writing a new article for *Critique*, a shorter text on a recent work published by Gallimard: *The Book of Questions* by Edmond Jabès. The writer, whom Derrida did not yet know personally, had been born in Cairo in 1912, in a French-speaking Jewish family; as a Jew, he had been forced to leave Egypt in 1956 during the Suez Crisis. A first collection of poems, *I Build My Dwelling*, published in 1959, was simultaneously hailed by Supervielle, Bachelard, and Camus. *The Book of Questions* was the first instalment of a cycle of books that would run to seven volumes.

The article 'Edmond Jabès and the question of the book' bears no resemblance to a traditional commentary. Quoting Jabès at length, slipping in between his sentences so as to draw them out, the text rests on a form of empathy. This was the first time that Derrida had tackled the theme of Judaism; the closeness of Jabès's preoccupations to his own seemed evident:

> For Jabès, who acknowledges a very late discovery of a certain way of being part of Judaism, the Jew is but the suffering allegory: '*You are all Jews, even the anti-Semites, for you have all been designated for martyrdom*' (*Livre des questions*, p. 180). He must justify himself to his blood brothers and to rabbis who are no longer imaginary. They will all reproach him for this universalism, this essentialism, this skeletal allegorism, this neutralization of the event in the realms of the symbolic and the imaginary.

> > '*Addressing themselves to me, my blood brothers said:*
> > "*You are not Jewish. You do not come to the Synagogue . . .*"'[25]

But Derrida was equally fascinated by the link, constantly suggested by Jabès, between writing and Judaism: the 'difficulty of being a Jew, which coincides with the difficulty of writing; for Judaism and writing are but the same waiting, the same hope, the same depletion'.[26]

The text would not be published until February 1964. But Jabès got wind of it through friends and wrote to Derrida for the first time on 4 October 1963. Straight after reading the manuscript, he communicated his enthusiasm to Derrida: 'It's excellent stuff, and I must tell you as much straightaway. [. . .] The paths you open up are those onto which I ventured without knowing in advance where they would leave me. Reading you, I find them traced out so clearly that I have the feeling I have always known them.'[27] A few months later, he again thanked Derrida for his lucid study: 'I am indebted to you for this great joy. From now on, those who have read you will be able to read me in depth.'[28] This was the start of a close friendship with Jabès and his wife Arlette; the couple lived in the rue de l'Épée-de-Bois, near Normale Sup, and this made it easy for them to meet.

As well as this close relationship with Jabès, Derrida formed another and even more essential friendship with Gabriel Bounoure, a figure who was of some importance in those days, though he is now pretty much forgotten. Born in 1886, and therefore already very old by the time Derrida came into contact with him, Bounoure had published only a single book, *Hopscotch on the Square*, in the series 'Cheminement' edited by Cioran. But his regular columns in the *Nouvelle revue française* and various other reviews turned him into the most influential poetry critic of his time. He helped to gain recognition for Max Jacob, Pierre Jean Jouve, Henri Michaux, Pierre Reverdy, and Jules Supervielle, and then discovered Georges Schehadé and contributed a preface for Jabès's first book, which had been written, claimed Jabès, 'under his gaze'.[29] An alumnus of the École Normale Supérieure, Bounoure joined the Resistance from the start, and taught at the universities of Cairo and Rabat; he also appeared as one of the main figures in the dialogue between Arabic and Western civilization, a question in which Derrida was already deeply interested.

On Jabès's insistence, Derrida sent Bounoure offprints of all his first articles, accompanied by long letters. And Bounoure replied each time, very attentively. From the very first exchanges, even though they had yet to meet, Derrida wrote in the most intimate and confidential tone. He described his uncomfortable situation, and laid bare his fragility and his hesitations:

> Your letter touched me more than discretion will permit me to say. Nothing can encourage me as much as knowing that you understand me, that you understand me with the confident and generous fellow-feeling that you have so kindly shown me. You can rest assured that I value it fully – my admiration for you has long since prepared me for it. These encouragements, your authority, are things which I greatly, urgently need. For countless reasons, but in particular because I live in one society . . . that of philosophers, and in the margins of another – the literature of Parisians – where I feel very ill at ease, very alone, forever threatened, by malevolence and misunderstanding, forever longing to turn my back on it, without knowing exactly on *what*. I like teaching, but it is rather exhausting and, basically, distracts me (insofar as it provides me with a very worthy alibi and opportunities for what is known as 'success') from what I feel is the essential thing for me, distracts from what I would like to write – something that requires another life.[30]

The two men met in Paris in spring 1964. The friendship between the young philosopher and the man who in his eyes was there to 'shed light on this strange path' soon became particularly intense. Derrida was touched and intimidated to see turned on him an attention whose 'generosity, force and rigour' he had 'long since known'.

> Apart from the courage I draw from your closeness, which reassures and confirms me, there is the *affection*, of course, which is born within us since we know we are *together* affected by, exposed and assigned to the *same* wind, to the presence of

the same questioning. This is why it is of great importance to my life that, after reading you, I have met you and that we have talked together.[31]

Derrida's most important article from this period was the one that he devoted to Emmanuel Levinas. It was the first substantial study of this philosopher, born in Lithuania in 1906 and thus fifty-eight when the article came out. He had been a friend of Blanchot since the 1920s, a friend of Husserl and then Heidegger, a prisoner in Germany throughout the Second World War. In 1947, he published his first major work, *Existence and Existents*. Since then, he had regularly taken part in teaching at the Collège Philosophique, while running the teacher training school of the Alliance Israélite Universelle. His thesis, *Totality and Infinity*, was published in 1961, in a somewhat small print run, by Martinus Nijhoff at The Hague. It was thanks to Paul Ricoeur that Derrida discovered the work straightaway, as he reminded him in a late letter:

I remember a day which I imagine you have forgotten (it was in 1961 or 1962, I was at the time your *assistant* in general philosophy at the Sorbonne), when we were walking together in your garden. You had just read *Totality and Infinity*, before a dissertation viva – I think you were one of the examiners. I had still not read it and knew only Levinas's 'classic' – and extraordinary – works on Husserl, Heidegger, etc. The following summer, I in turn read *Totality and Infinity* and started to write one long article, then another – and his thought has never since left me.[32]

Derrida took advantage of the relative tranquillity of summer 1963 to write his article 'Violence and metaphysics: An essay on the thought of Emmanuel Levinas'. But as he typed it out, he soon realized that it was 'long, much too long'.[33] Michel Deguy confirmed this when acknowledging receipt of the text: '*You've written a whole book!!* With the system of notes that you use, it all adds up to a hundred or so pages!'[34] Either Derrida should agree to reduce his study to some thirty pages or so, with Deguy's help if required, or he should seek a publisher to turn it into a fully fledged book. But this second solution would probably be difficult to bring off, given the fact that Levinas was at the time little known.

At the beginning of December, Deguy returned to the attack, and adopted a rather firmer tone: 'What would you say if I proposed [. . .] cutting up and butchering your article? Would you suffer intensely to see it amputated, shrunken like a Bushman's head, at the careful hands of someone else?'[35] Then it was Jean Piel who asked Derrida to try to revise his article, since it seemed to him 'essential that an article on Levinas should appear in *Critique* before too long'.[36] He took this opportunity to tell Derrida that he set great store by his collaboration and that all his plans for 1964 would be welcomed with open arms.

Derrida discussed this 'monster' text with Deguy, mulling over the possibility of cutting it down without ruining it. But the sacrifices he would need to agree to would be huge. On 30 January, he abandoned the idea of publishing his study in *Critique*, hoping that Piel would not be cross: 'Let me take this opportunity to tell you what a privilege it is to be able to collaborate with *Critique* and that I feel it is a real honour that the Editor has been so welcoming.'[37] In the end, it was Jean Wahl who agreed to publish 'Violence and metaphysics: an essay on the thought of Emmanuel Levinas' in two issues of the *Revue de métaphysique et de morale*.

This essay, even more than 'Force and signification', begins in a grandiose, magisterial tone, completely different from a critical review. In the first pages, in fact, the focus is not on Levinas, but on philosophy as such:

> That philosophy died yesterday, since Hegel or Marx, Nietzsche, or Heidegger – and philosophy should still wander toward the meaning of its death – or that it has always lived knowing itself to be dying [. . .]; that philosophy died *one day*, *within* history, or that it has always fed on its own agony, on the violent way it opens history by opposing itself to non-philosophy [. . .]; that beyond the death, or dying nature, of philosophy, perhaps even because of it, thought still has a future, or even, as is said today, is still entirely to come because of what philosophy has held in store; or, more strangely still, that the future itself has a future – all these are unanswerable questions.[38]

Thereupon, Derrida embarks on what he tells us is a 'very partial' reading of the work of Emmanuel Levinas, especially the encounter it stages between 'two historical speeches' (or 'discourses'*), 'Hebraism and Hellenism'. The remarks seem quite modest: 'First of all, in the style of commentary, we will try to remain faithful to the themes and audacities of a thought – and this despite several parentheses and notes which will enclose our perplexity.' And Derrida insists on the difficulty of such a project: because the 'stylistic gestures (especially in *Totality and Infinity*) can less than ever be distinguished from intention', he fears 'the prosaic disembodiment into conceptual frameworks that is the first violence of all commentary'.[39]

---

* The French is *paroles*. – Tr.

Ever since the first weeks of 1964, Derrida had been attending Levinas's Tuesday evening classes at the Sorbonne and regularly going up to talk to him at the end. Derrida hoped to use the few months remaining before the publication of his immensely long article to prepare the author of *Totality and Infinity* for its appearance. For while the study was overall very flattering, it also made several critical points. Levinas had sent Derrida a signed offprint of his new text, *The Trace of the Other*, and Derrida began by sending him his previous articles, addressing him in timid and cautious terms:

> I have long hesitated – even after they had been published – to send you these 'dead leaves' . . . Mainly because they did not deserve it, but also because I was anxious not to oblige you, very indiscreetly, to talk or write to me about them. Having to decide whether or not to send out offprints, and whether it is friendlier to do so or to abstain, always makes me very unhappy.
>
> Then we talked about Jabès, and then I thought that what I occasionally try to say in these pages is sometimes linked, in another way, with what I ventured in the text you will soon read in the *R[evue] de M[étaphysique]* . . . So I have made so bold as to send you these three occasional texts, really 'occasional' [*de circonstances*], if we can suppose that there really are 'occasions' [*circonstances*] in this case . . . Anyway, by all that they have led me to say or announce, I feel, as always (and as I did the other evening when, on parting, we uttered the names of Hegel or É. Weil) as close to your thought and as far from it as it is possible to be; which is contradictory only in terms of what you call 'formal logic'.[40]*

In October 1964, Derrida immediately sent the first part of the published article to Levinas; he enclosed the manuscript version of the rest, asking Levinas to excuse the state it was in: 'When you see it, you'll understand the hatred I can sometimes inspire in the secretaries of reviews, printers, etc.' With a mixture of confidence and apprehension, he awaited Levinas's reaction to those 'reckless pages'.[41] The author of *Totality and Infinity* replied frankly:

---

* It is interesting to note that, though Levinas and Derrida got to know each other at the Sorbonne in January or February 1964, contact between them could have been established shortly afterwards by a quite different means. On 19 June 1964, Jacques Lazarus, of the French Section of the World Jewish Congress, wrote to Aimé Derrida that he had had an opportunity to talk to M. Levinas, 'a specialist in the philosophy of Husserl': 'I told him that your son, Professor Derrida, had written a work upon that philosopher. M. Levinas would be very happy to get in touch with him and I would be most obliged to you if you would be so kind as to give me his address.'

I immediately want – after a first reading – to thank you for sending me your texts, with their dedications, for all the trouble you have taken to read me, comment on me and refute me so vigorously. [. . .] I must tell you of my great admiration for the intellectual power deployed in these pages, so generous even when they are ironic and severe. Heartfelt thanks for everything.[42]

'Violence and metaphysics' also won Derrida his first letter from Maurice Blanchot, a close friend of Levinas since the 1920s. He had already read Derrida's previous articles with considerable interest, but this time he made sure he told him 'how helpful' this work was for him and how he would be 'happy to continue to take part in the movement of [his] reflections'.[43] This was the start of an essential friendship that lasted for nearly forty years.

In 1964, Jacques Derrida and Philippe Sollers became acquainted. Even though he was six years younger than Derrida, Sollers had been an important figure since the publication of his first novel, *A Strange Solitude*. In 1958, the work was hailed by Mauriac and Aragon, shortly before Sollers founded the review *Tel Quel* with Jean-Edern Hallier. In 1961, he won the Prix Médicis for *The Park*, his second novel, and resolutely embarked on a series of modernist experiments. He had recently become greatly interested in philosophy. When *The Origin of Geometry* came out, he was immersed in Husserl's *Logical Investigations*. So, on reading Derrida's Introduction, Sollers was very struck by the parallel between Husserl and Joyce; he devoted a short note to the work in the thirteenth issue of *Tel Quel*, in spring 1963. Derrida was touched, and sent him offprints of 'Force and signification' and 'Cogito and the history of madness'.

The tone of Sollers' first letter, on 10 February 1964, was extremely warm; he told Derrida that the two texts had been of the highest interest to him, even if his 'philosophical incompetence' made it necessary for him to proceed intuitively in the debate with Foucault. 'It is striking to note, in any case, that once again – and this is no coincidence – thought and "literature" (when both authentic) can communicate radically with one another. This sort of mutual questioning is very revelatory, isn't it?'[44]

At the same time, Gérard Genette, who had just been appointed *assistant* at the Sorbonne and had already published in *Tel Quel*, invited the Derridas to a 'a dinner of clever clogs with Sollers and perhaps Barthes' on 2 March 1964, in his apartment in Savigny-sur-Orge, in Seine-et-Oise. Sollers and Derrida met up again in June, this time at Michel Deguy's. The two men immediately hit it off, and Sollers was soon asking Derrida for an article for *Tel Quel*, on the subject of his choice. Derrida promised to think about it as soon as he was freed from the busy exam period.

The months from April to July were indeed fully occupied by Derrida's university tasks. He had to set and mark several exams at the Sorbonne, as well as prepare pupils at Normale Sup for the *agrégation* (I will return to this in the next chapter); there were also several bread-and-butter jobs to be done in those years. As Gérard Genette relates:

> In 1963 and later years, Jacques and I, like Jean Bellemin-Noël and Élisabeth de Fontenay, would earn a bit of pocket money by marking papers on 'general knowledge' (essays and 'précis' work) and acting as oral examiners for the same discipline for the entrance exam to the École de Hautes Études Commerciales. There was a legend going round on campus that Derrida often set as a subject 'the yoghurt pot', which – I don't know why – annoyed him greatly.[45]

It was also in the spring of 1964 that Derrida met a certain Hélène Berger, who would soon be better known under the name Hélène Cixous. She was to be one of his closest female friends for forty years. She was an *assistante* in English at the University of Bordeaux, and writing a thesis on James Joyce. On 11 April 1964, she wrote to Derrida for the first time, having read with both pleasure and interest his Introduction to *The Origin of Geometry* as well as his first articles. She felt inevitably drawn to reading Joyce 'from a Husserlian point of view'. But although she was 'a philosopher at heart', she was not a professional, and wanted to discuss with Derrida several points that were giving her problems.[46]

This first 'Joycean rendezvous' took place on Saturday, 30 May at the café Le Balzar, 'the public bar being the Joycean place *par excellence* – where all knots are untied and all puzzles solved'.[47] On this occasion, Hélène Cixous realized that Derrida had a real passion for Joyce that went far beyond the few lines he had published about him at the time. But they discovered that they had several other points in common, including their origins: Cixous had been born in Oran to an Ashkenazi mother and a Sephardi father, and grew up in Algiers, where she frequented the same places as Derrida in his youth: the Jardin d'Essai, the Lycée Bugeaud, and many others. They felt equally close when they talked about their experiences in the French university system and its hidebound ways. 'When I met Derrida, I was at war with the institution,' she remembers.

> As I talked with him, I told myself that there must be other people of his calibre in the French academic system, people who were determined to shake things up. But I very soon

realized that he was really unique. A very deep sense of complicity grew up between us. Thanks to him, I had the feeling
that I didn't need to live just in the company of the dead, the
authors of the great texts that I was reading.[48]

That year, 1964, was definitely one for striking up or deepening
already-existing friendships. Shortly before the summer, together
with his son Pierre, who had only just turned one year old, Derrida
went to Brittany to see Gabriel Bounoure. He had wanted to write
to him as soon as he got back, but he had yet again been 'seized by
the university monster, which had thrown [him] up, exhausted, on
the shore only at the end of July'. This did not stop Derrida being
charmed by the presence – 'deep, radiant, benevolent' – of Bounoure
and by the attention 'both generous and fully devoted to the present
moment' that he showed him throughout his stay. But Derrida
himself was in such a state of exhaustion that he felt 'more incapable than ever', after these months of uninterrupted oral exams, 'of
uttering the shortest sentence'. His fatigue was 'so profound, and
accompanied by a certain bitter distaste for the profession', that he
sometimes felt he had lost the ability to speak. He sadly acknowledged as much: 'My natural way of speaking has become the most
artificial way – that of teaching or that of writing.'[49] He hoped to
have an opportunity to see Bounoure again as often as possible, on
each of his (too infrequent) trips to Paris.

It was at this time that Jacques and his wife settled on a way
of organizing their summer holidays to which they would always
remain faithful, with a few exceptions.

They would spend August with Marguerite's family at Les
Rassats, an old, somewhat dilapidated farm with a big garden, a
few kilometres outside Angoulême. A small annex was set apart for
them, but Jacques did not have a proper office there and so had to
work in conditions of some discomfort. Apart from Marguerite's
parents, her two brothers and their respective families also occupied
the house. Michel Aucouturier, Jackie's old classmate at Normale
Sup, had been appointed to a university post in Geneva; his thesis
was on Marxist literary criticism in the USSR, and he continued to
translate and write on the works of Gogol, Tolstoy, and, above all,
Pasternak, in whose work he specialized.

As for September, they spent it in Nice or its immediate environs,
now that Derrida's parents, and soon his brother and sister too, had
moved there. But while Jacques was always happy to get back to
the beaches of the Mediterranean and go for long swims, the small
apartment his parents occupied in the rue Delille did not make work
very easy. There is general agreement that Derrida was not really
a holiday type of man. August and September were the most pro-

ductive months in the year for him, when he needed to prepare his lectures and write the articles or papers that people were starting to request on all sides. So, in order to enjoy a bit of peace and quiet, he would get up even earlier than during the rest of the year. He swallowed a cup of coffee, and started writing at 6 a.m., knocking off for breakfast at around 9 a.m., then attempting to carry on working until at least lunch, in spite of the noise and commotion around him.

At the beginning of August 1964, when Derrida was still exhausted by the overwork of the previous months, Sollers repeated how much he would like to publish an article by him in a forthcoming number of *Tel Quel*. Derrida, who had 'a great liking for *Tel Quel*', had for some months been thinking about a text which could be entitled 'Writing (or the letter) from Hegel to Feuerbach'. But he was afraid the text would be too long for a review.[50] Sollers liked the subject, and would be happy to publish the text in two issues, so long as it did not exceed fifty or so pages in length. But he also asked Derrida whether he might not have 'something to say about Artaud' for a special issue he was preparing.

On 30 September, back in Paris, Derrida had to admit that the text on writing had, unfortunately, got bogged down on his arrival in Nice. He had only just got back to it, but thought he would not be able to polish it off for quite a while. As for Artaud, Sollers' letter had rekindled the desire to re-read him, something he had not done since his teens, and maybe to write something about him. 'But here too, I'd need time. My job will soon be making its presence felt.'[51] Two months later, in spite of his various classes and other professional obligations, the article on Artaud had made good progress; it would be called 'La parole soufflée'. Derrida hoped to finish it during the winter break.[52]

2

In the Shadow of Althusser

1963–1966

In the very busy year of 1963, Derrida also returned to the rue d'Ulm. Straight after the publication of *The Origin of Geometry*, Althusser invited him to 'hold forth a bit' on Husserl to his students. Derrida was not the only person asked to speak in this context. While the École did not provide any teaching of its own, it was frequently the site for lectures and seminars. Thus, for several years, Jean Beaufret ran a small group of Heideggereans, a quite exclusive coterie. Michel Serres, Pierre Bourdieu, and several others came from time to time to speak at the École during these years.

But Derrida's situation soon turned out to be different from that of those occasional lecturers. On 20 March, Althusser told him of a conversation he had just had with Jean Hyppolite, who was about to leave his post as director of the École for a chair at the Collège de France. The author of *Genesis and Structure of the 'Phenomenology of Spirit'* gave a warm welcome to the idea of seeing Derrida one day return to the École as a *'caïman'*, i.e. an *agrégé-préparateur*. But this might take some time. Meanwhile, Hyppolite intended to talk to Georges Canguilhem about the matter, so as to facilitate Derrida's move from the Sorbonne to Normale Sup, while not treading on too many people's toes.

At the beginning of September 1963, Althusser learned of the suicide of Jacques Martin, his closest friend. His grief would leave him in a fragile state for many months, and this no doubt played a part in his rapprochement with Derrida. Perhaps the new director, the Hellenist Robert Flacelière, quickly realized that Althusser would need help and support. Either way, in 1963–4, Derrida, still an *assistant* at the Sorbonne, was appointed *maître de conférences* at the ENS, with forty-eight hours of classes to be divided out over the year.

'Who will ever write, without giving in to any sort of socio-academicism, the history of this "house" and its filiations? This would be an almost impossible but indispensable task for beginning to understand the various "logics" of French intellectual life in this century,' Derrida declared in one of his dialogues with Élisabeth Roudinesco.[1] In fact, when Althusser brought him in to teach there, Normale Sup was enjoying a particularly dazzling period. A group of brilliant young philosophers had begun their studies there in 1960: they included Régis Debray, Étienne Balibar, Jacques Rancière, and Pierre Macherey. They had become Communists largely because of the Algerian War and together debated at length about Marxism and possible ways of reinvigorating it. They went to Althusser, who as yet had published nothing but a short book on Montesquieu and a few articles, and asked for his help in their theoretical work, over and above his role as *caïman*.

In 1961–2, Althusser's seminar was devoted to the early Marx: the following year, it focused on 'the origins of structuralist thought'. In 1963–4, Althusser worked on Freud and Lacan. He was interested in the dispersed works of Lacan, and asked his best pupils to read them: this was because he had been struck by a homology between the return to Freud advocated by Lacan and his own research into Marx's texts.

Althusser's scrutiny of Lacan was important in at least two respects. At that time, within the French Communist Party, psychoanalysis was still considered to be a 'bourgeois science'; the article 'Freud and Lacan', which was published in 1964 in one of the Party's reviews, *La Nouvelle Critique*, marked the opening up of radically new terrain. But Althusser's intervention was just as decisive within the context of the French universities, where psychoanalysis remained little known. As Élisabeth Roudinesco notes, 'for the first time, Lacanian texts were read from a philosophical perspective that amply exceeded the framework of clinical practice'.[2]

It was also Althusser who, with the support of Flacelière, advocated the moving of Lacan's seminar to the École Normale Supérieure. Lacan had just been through a period of grave crisis: banished from the Société Française de Psychanalyse together with several of his associates, 'excommunicated' as he would put it, he decided to give a new twist to his teaching. He moved away from the traditional structures within which he had hitherto worked, and chose the theme of the 'four fundamental concepts of psychoanalysis' to discuss in front of this much bigger but less specialized audience. On 15 January 1964, in the Dussane lecture hall, the first session of his new seminar was a solemn occasion. Claude Lévi-Strauss was in the audience, as was the psychiatrist Henri Ey. Apparently Derrida did not attend this inaugural session. He was probably detained by an obligation at the Sorbonne, as, in previous years, he had often gone to hear Lacan at Sainte-Anne, sometimes in the company of Michel Deguy.

'From that day on,' writes Roudinesco, 'over a period of five years, the Salle Dussane would be the privileged meeting place of a new Freudian France, one more cultured, more philosophical, and more influential than the previous one.'[3] Within the École, the consequences were immediate and far-reaching. In the following session, Jacques-Alain Miller, who had only just turned nineteen, intervened in the seminar for the first time: 'Rather good, your fellow,' Lacan immediately wrote to Althusser.[4] Impressed by this attempt to read his work as a whole, Lacan replied at length to Miller during the session on 29 January. The dialogue between the old psychoanalyst and the young man would continue uninterrupted, and marked a major turning-point in Lacanian discourse.

In comparison with the bold new approach of Althusser, Derrida initially seemed, in spite of his youth, a more traditional kind of teacher, 'a replacement *caïman*', in the eyes of Régis Debray. But the Introduction to *The Origin of Geometry* made a great impression on Étienne Balibar and his classmates. That year, Derrida gave them three demanding courses on authors barely mentioned by Althusser: the first was on *Thought and Movement* by Bergson, the second on Husserl's *Cartesian Meditations* – a difficult work, of which he gave a memorable analysis –, and the last was called 'Phenomenology and transcendental psychology'.

   As far as the *agrégation* was concerned, Derrida at this time shared Althusser's view. Whether students were Marxist, Lacanian, or structuralist, they should 'go through the motions' for the purposes of the exam: it was essential to master the specific rhetoric of the essay or the *leçon*, irrespective of any philosophical or political question. Derrida himself had suffered enough from exams to have a precise idea of what was needed to pass them. But even in this area, things were starting to move. In 1964, the team of examiners for the *agrégation* was changed: the president was no longer Étienne Souriau, but Georges Canguilhem. The new team would be much more open to contemporary philosophers, to epistemology, to phenomenology and even to psychoanalysis. In these circumstances, having been taught by Althusser and Derrida for the exam would become a real advantage.[5]

   Derrida's qualities as a teacher were all the better appreciated as, just before the written exams, Althusser again fell ill. In April 1964, he felt at the end of his tether, 'at a sort of intellectual dead end', 'with all the symptoms of a very unpleasant "dry" depression'. He left the École for several weeks, asking Derrida whether he could 'keep the boys' enthusiasm going in the run-up to the exam . . . even if just by having a chat with them'.[6] Althusser regretted that he had been leading a crazy life for the past months and apologized to Derrida for having had time to talk to him only in snatches in the corridor.

The situation soon became more serious. It rapidly became obvious that Althusser was completely unable to help just when the *agrégatifs* would have needed him most. In spite of his heavy workload at the Sorbonne, and the texts he was writing, Derrida took over without demur. 'I don't know where I am . . . I've just had a sleep treatment,' Althusser wrote to him shortly after the written exams. 'How are the lads? And how are you? I've gone and inflicted this heavy chore on you without warning, despite really not wanting to.' Althusser was back in the hospital in Épinay-sur-Seine, where it had been possible for some days past to visit him: 'I hardly dare tell you that I'd be overjoyed to see you, but it's at the back of beyond. [. . .] A heartfelt thank you for all that you are *doing* – and thank you first of all for being what you are, who you are.'[7] As he was often to do, Derrida travelled to Épinay to see him in the clinic.

On 10 June, Althusser complained that he would need to endure hospitalization for some time. 'Serious relapses mean my return to reality is not so easy.' So he would not be able to see his pupils again before the oral exams, as he had hoped. On 3 August, he started to feel better, and wanted to express his thanks to Derrida: the *agréga-tion* results of the philosophy students at the École were exceptional, and he knew how much Derrida's presence had helped. 'I won't go into details, as you wouldn't let me speak, but it's true all the same.'[8]

While Derrida was now aware of the seriousness of Althusser's psychological state, the latter also knew of the fragility to which his former student was prone, and did not fail to mention this when necessary. As Althusser wrote, as he gradually emerged from his crisis:

> I realized that you were more than a witness of my adventure: not only did it force a huge amount of work on you, under which you might have been crushed, but it must have left you with a sort of bad taste, a lingering memory that took you back to times that had been difficult for you. You were a witness, of course, but also perhaps, through what was happening to me, a witness (via a third party) of something that resembled the past. For all that you have done and said to me, and also for all you have kept to yourself, I am profoundly grateful.[9]

This affection, this closeness, would not fade over the years, at least during the periods of Althusser's depression and internment, periods that returned almost every year: 'I bless you for existing and for being my friend,' Althusser wrote to Derrida. 'Keep up your friendship for me. It counts among the few rare reasons I have for believing that life (even when full of drama) is worth living.'[10]

But this period, in which Althusser began psychoanalysis under René Diatkine, was also when he wrote the texts that would soon make his name. 'Philosophical exchanges between us were rare, not to say non-existent,' Derrida later told Michael Sprinker.[11] This was not always the case. On 1 September 1964, Derrida gave Althusser an in-depth analysis of the article that the latter had sent to him – 'Marxism and humanism', which was to become the last chapter of *For Marx*, the following year. Derrida's discussion was both frank and friendly:

> I found the text that you sent me *excellent*. I feel as close as one possibly could to that '*theoretical anti-humanism*' that you set out with as much force as rigour, I fully realize that it is your position, I also understand, I think, the meaning of the notion of 'ideological' humanism at certain times, the necessity of ideology *in general*, even in a Communist society, etc. I was less convinced by everything that links these propositions to Marx himself. There is probably a great deal of ignorance in my mistrust and in the feeling that other – non-Marxist – premises could lie behind the same anti-humanism. What you set out on pp. 116 et seq. shows clearly the way Marx broke away from a *certain* humanism, a *certain* conjunction of empiricism and idealism, etc. But the radicalization often appears to me, in its most powerful and alluring moments, very Althusserian. You'll tell me that the 'repetition' of Marx must not be a 'recitation', and that deepening and radicalizing him is being faithful to him. True. But in that case don't we end up with the same result if we start out with Hegel or Feuerbach? And then, though every-thing you say about over-determination and the 'instrumental' conception of ideology satisfies me completely – about the con-sciousness-unconscious too, although . . . – the very notion of ideology bothers me, for philosophical reasons that are, as you know, far from 'reactionary'. Quite the opposite, in fact. The notion strikes me as still imprisoned by a metaphysics and by a certain 'inverted idealism' that you know better than anyone in the world. I even have the impression, sometimes, that it hampers you yourself. . . . We'll have to talk about all this, with Marx's texts to hand . . . and you'll have to make me read.[12]

At the start of the 1960s, a post as *assistant* was limited to four years. So Derrida would inevitably have had to leave the Sorbonne in autumn 1964. A few months earlier, Maurice de Gandillac had advised him to ask for two years of complete leave under the aegis of the CNRS,* so as to complete his thesis. He did so. According

---

* The CNRS, or Centre National de la Recherche Scientifique, is a prestigious state-run organization for research in the sciences, social sciences, and humanities. – Tr.

to Jean Hyppolite, Derrida's candidacy was straightforward and there would be few obstacles, especially since he himself was part of the commission.[13] But the prospect of these two years of pure research scared Derrida more than they allured him. Even though his memory of the years he had spent at Normale Sup as a student were quite painful, he was very tempted by the post of *caïman* in philosophy:

> Through all the suffering, the alluring and fascinating model of the École has left its mark on me, so when Hyppolite and Althusser suggested that I go back when I could have gone elsewhere [. . .], I quit the CNRS to return to the ENS. Whatever criticism I may make of this École, at that time it was a model, and teaching there was a sort of honour and gratification that I had neither the courage nor the desire to turn down.[14]

On leaving the Sorbonne, Derrida wrote a long letter to Paul Ricoeur to tell him of his 'nostalgia, already' and his 'immense gratitude'. He would keep an excellent memory of those four years at the Sorbonne and thought that he had definitely benefited from them, 'both in terms of the profession, and in terms of philosophy, especially where the profession and philosophy, for those of us who are lucky enough, are one and the same'. Even though Derrida still felt fragile, he was sure that, thanks to this sojourn in the Sorbonne, he had been given a valuable boost:

> All of this was possible only because I worked under your direction and at your side. The generous and friendly confidence that you showed me was a profound and constant encouragement. [. . .] Please consider me henceforth as not just your honorary but your permanent *assistant*.[15]

Maurice de Gandillac was glad that Derrida's appointment to Normale Sup was rapidly confirmed, which freed his post at the CNRS and allowed Althusser to be given 'the invaluable collaboration that Hyppolite's departure made more necessary'.[16] But he lost no time reminding Derrida of the importance of the theses that he would need to write, and hoped that his new tasks would give him enough free time to complete them 'as quickly as possible', since *caïmans* had too much of a tendency to let the years slip by.[17] De Gandillac's surmise would prove to be all too accurate. Absorbed by his various planned articles, Derrida explained to Hyppolite that he had barely done any work on his main thesis over the summer of 1964. But he had started an 'essay' on writing in Hegel and Feuerbach, or rather 'between Hegel and Feuerbach', which should enable him to settle on the concepts and the main set of problems that he would need for his thesis. He hoped that this work might lead to a short book that he would submit for inclusion in the 'Épiméthée' series.[18]

In 1964–5, for his first official year as *caïman*, Derrida gave a set of lectures on 'Heidegger and History' that were original enough for him to think he might get them published by Les Éditions de Minuit. Unfortunately for him, the passions of his students were currently being aroused by very different questions: this was the year of the famous seminar 'Reading *Capital*'. In ten or so sessions that soon led to a book, Althusser and his colleagues – Étienne Balibar, Pierre Macherey, Jacques Rancière, and Roger Establet – developed the concept of a 'symptomatic reading' and set out the idea of an 'epistemological break' separating the young Marx, still in thrall to Hegel, from the mature, fully Marxist Marx. Derrida attended some of the sessions, but he felt isolated and ill at ease, as he explained much later in a long interview on Althusser and Marxism that he gave to Michael Sprinker and that was not published in French:

> This whole problematic struck me as probably necessary within the Marxist field that was also a political field, marked in particular by the influence of the Party – of which I was not a member and which was emerging, if I may say so, only slowly from Stalinism [. . .]. But at the same time, I found this problematic – I wouldn't say untutored or naïve, far from it –, but, let's say, too neglectful of the critical questions that I then thought were necessary, maybe against Husserl and Heidegger but at any rate *through* them. [. . .] I had the impression that their concept of history should have gone through this questioning. [. . .] Their discourse seemed to me to yield [. . .] to a 'new-style' scientism, which I could question, but of course I was paralysed, since I didn't want my critiques to be confused with the coarse, self-interested critiques that were coming from the Right and the Left, especially from the Communist Party.[19]

Derrida felt all the more condemned to silence because the discourse of the Althusserians was accompanied by a sort of 'intellectual terrorism' or at least 'theoretical intimidation'. 'To formulate questions in a style that appeared, shall we say, phenomenological, transcendental or ontological was immediately considered suspicious, backward, idealistic, even reactionary.' And yet history, ideology, production, class struggle, the very idea of a 'last instance' still remained, in Derrida's view, problematic notions that were not properly questioned by Althusser and his followers.

I could see in this flight a failure, whether in thought or politics. Inseparably. [. . .] The fact that 'fundamental' questions or questions about foundations, about its own premises, its very axiomatics, were not being asked [. . .], this was something that I saw as a lack of radicalness and a still too dogmatic contribution to its own discourse, and this could not be without political consequences in the short or long term. [. . .] Their concepts were not sophisticated, differentiated enough, and there's a price to be paid for that.[20]

These debates all took place within a small coterie of people 'over-educated in the art of interpretation'. As in a virtual game of chess, everyone tried to anticipate the opponent's moves, attempted to 'guess the other's strategy to the finest detail':

There were camps, strategic alliances, manoeuvres of encircle-ment and exclusion. [. . .] The diplomacy of the period, when there was any (war by other means) was the diplomacy of evasion: silence, you don't quote [. . .]. Personally, there I was, the little youngster, to some extent, it wasn't altogether my generation. But at the same time, there was no open hostility. In spite of these differences and disputes, I was part of one and the same big 'camp', we had common enemies, a lot of them.

When he came across this late interview with Michael Sprinker, Étienne Balibar realized how much Derrida must have suffered at being marginalized and practically silenced in this way. But he acknowledged that, in the mid-sixties, a sort of fortress had formed round Althusser, creating a quite intolerable situation.

In reality, it didn't bother us that Derrida wasn't a Marxist, we had a great deal of esteem for him, both as a philosopher and as a person. In fact several of us spent an evening with him in Fresnes. We felt there was a certain complicity between Althusser and him, without either of them being in hock to the other. It was a pedagogic, but not an ideological team.[21]

On the pedagogic level, Derrida's role was still crucial, since Althusser, exhausted by running the seminar 'Reading *Capital*' and finishing *For Marx*, had suffered a nervous breakdown at the end of spring 1965. Only in July was he able to show any concern for the results of the *agrégation*, especially for Régis Debray. Though he had entered the École at the top of his year, this brilliant student – already highly active politically – had attended it only intermittently. Derrida quickly informed Althusser of the results: Bouveresse was first, Mosconi fourth, and Debray fifth. 'I'd been reassured after his

leçon, which is why I'd telephoned him to give him some encouragement. [. . .] Lacan's daughter came first too, equal with Rabant's
wife. There it is. I always find this *agrégation* atmosphere difficult to
breathe in, you need to see the comedy of the final results.'[22]

Among the candidates whose success was a matter of some
importance to Derrida was Briec Bounoure, Gabriel's grandson.
Even though he was not a *normalien*, Derrida had helped him at a
distance to work towards the exam throughout the year. 'You must
especially reach the exam with the necessary freedom and flexibility
to spot the exact specific nature of the subject, so as not to rush down
some well-known, reassuring path, and to *organize* your discussion,'
he impressed on him.[23] But Briec disappeared off to Brittany the day
after the written exams, without even waiting to find out the results,
wondering whether he should not rather opt for a life as a deep-sea
fisherman. Canguilhem, who knew that Derrida was friendly with
this young man, told him to get in touch with him as soon as possible: 'Tell the boy that he can do whatever he wants in the oral. Given
the marks he got in the written exam, he's going to pass, come what
may.' A few weeks later, Derrida was pleased to be able to write to
Gabriel Bounoure that his grandson's *leçon* had been judged 'the
most philosophical heard so far'. Derrida had really been hoping he
would pass, and 'it would have been heartbreaking if any words of
discouragement had deprived him of success'.[24]

In October 1965, *For Marx* and the collective *Reading 'Capital'*
launched the 'Théorie' series published by Maspero, which aroused
considerable interest, first in France and then in several other
countries. Over the following months, Althusser was the object
'of a passion, an infatuation, and an imitation evoked by no other
contemporary figure'.[25] To many people, he appeared as 'the secret
pope of world revolution'.[26] In November 1966, Jean Lacroix
reported in *Le Monde* that the two most-cited names in papers
handed in by candidates for the philosophy *agrégation* were those
of Althusser and Foucault; it was not uncommon to find the names
of very young philosophers such as Rancière, Balibar, or Macherey
mentioned.[27]

At Normale Sup, the UEC – Union des Étudiants Communistes
(Union of Communist Students) – was tearing itself apart. The
'Italian' tendency – the most open, like the PCI – had hardly any rep-
resentatives at the École. The struggles took place mainly between
the orthodox wing, favourable to the Party and the USSR, and the
'Maos' or Maoists, led by Robert Linhart. The 'Maos' soon left
the UEC, which they viewed as 'revisionist', founding instead the
UJCml – Union des Jeunesses Communistes Marxistes-Léninistes
(Union of Communist Marxist-Leninist Youth). Althusser, who
made no bones about his interest in Mao Zedong's theoretical texts,

followed a complex strategy: he pushed his students into radical positions, but did not for a moment envisage leaving the Party himself.[28]

Several little reviews were set up in the École in the space of a few months. The first, the *Cahiers marxistes-léninistes*, opened with a formula of Lenin's that was hardly likely to arouse much enthusiasm in Derrida: 'Marxist theory is all-powerful because it is true.' After an issue which, in Linhart's view, devoted too much space to literature, Jacques-Alain Miller, Jean-Claude Milner, and François Régnault broke away and set up the *Cahiers pour l'analyse*. This review was run by the 'circle of epistemology' and followed a line that might be called 'Althussero-Lacanian'.[29] Derrida would publish his first text on Lévi-Strauss in it – a chapter of the future *Grammatology* –, and the *Essay on the Origin of Languages* by Rousseau, on which his seminar that year was focusing, would also be republished in it.

While his prestige remained vastly inferior to that of Althusser, Derrida was starting to make a name for himself at the École, and several students were following his courses avidly. 'There were soon two opposite sides,' remembers Bernard Pautrat.

Althusser reigned over a dogmatic and sometimes contemptuous side. Derrida represented the other side: more open, he was suspected of idealism by many. But there were still a good twenty or so of us following his courses. His highly novel way of reading philosophical texts enthralled me. I became a follower of his quite quickly. In 1964, he advised me to do my master's dissertation on Nietzsche, under the supervision of Paul Ricoeur. Without realizing it, I became something like the first Derridean.[30]

Even among the most highly politicized students, some, such as Dominique Lecourt, whom Derrida would encounter several times over his career, followed his teaching with great interest.

Initially, I was planning on becoming an archaeologist. It was Derrida who determined my path, after a first essay written at his request. 'You're a philosopher,' he wrote at the top of my piece when he had marked it. For five years, I never stopped being his pupil and following his seminar, in spite of the sarcasm of my comrades on the *Cahiers marxistes-léninistes*, who viewed him as a useless and woolly-headed metaphysician. Personally, I never wanted politics to drive me away from Derrida and I think he was quite grateful for that. Althusser and Canguilhem were my two main reference points, but with Derrida I could sense that something very important was going on. I went to see him every time there was some point I couldn't clear up, and each time he was very happy to talk to me. I was attached to him as a teacher and as a person. Under his apparent reserve, there was a fire by which I liked to come and warm myself.[31]

At the end of summer 1966, a few weeks after coming top in the *agrégation* exam, Bernard Pautrat sent Derrida a letter that he would remember. He expressed his gratitude – a gratitude that went far beyond the support Derrida had provided during the year leading up to the exam, and was really thankfulness for his presence, his 'really encouraging attention', and 'the irreplaceable depth' of which he had been such a sturdy example:

I think that, in the École, you yourself have a very tough and poorly rewarded job. We have often showed an irritating 'philosophical passivity'. That's why I'm taking the liberty of telling you that your work was not, in spite of everything, a waste of time. Without guides such as you, and Althusser, I would long since have wandered away from philosophy; as you know, without you, our idea of philosophy would have been paltry and unattractive.[32]

3

Writing Itself

1965–1966

However great the quality of his first publications, Derrida was still in a very fragile state of mind. The encouragement of friends was essential to him – that of Gabriel Bounoure first and foremost. As Derrida wrote to him in the first days of 1965: 'Everything you tell me about the essay on Levinas encourages me, and *gives* me a great deal of strength. I need it, of that I am sure. And perhaps the strength that you claim to perceive is merely the strength of this need, in other words a great infirmity that in some way is crying out for help.' Derrida felt that the place in which he was working was that 'of an evasion, of a dissimulation where everything suddenly hazes over in a sort of black clarity'. Bounoure's support enabled Derrida to venture into those zones where the older man had gone before him:

> You have been there before me, and better than me – there at the centre of this experience (let's call it by the names of those who have risked body and soul to explore it: Nietzsche, Heidegger, Levinas, Blanchot). You have seen me coming. Writing for you, I would henceforth be better able to guide my fumbling words. You see, I am still seeking serenity, and seeking to be understood. What else can one do? But I know that the serenity you bring me now is by no means a comfort, and to be understood as one fumbles one's way along doesn't mean settling down into certainty. The other serenity, probably the bad kind of serenity, is that of the university, the École where my teaching consolidates me in another way, duller and more effective, although this serenity tries to meld with the other sort.[1]

Another, much younger person who shared Derrida's interests was assuming great importance for him, as a friend and a writer: Philippe Sollers. Derrida had been deeply moved by his new book, *Event*; he sent him a long letter, timid and really rather awkward, apologizing for his 'phrase-making':

Over and above the expectations that *Event* touches off in
me, over and above all the ways in which you are preceding
me on a path which I think I recognize from a place beyond
memory, over and above all that my comments could say,
coiling around your book which is already its own commentary, in other words effacing itself as it writes itself [. . .] and
writing as it withdraws [. . .], over and above this commentary that I dare not undertake, that I dare not tear from its
ongoing momentum within me, I admired – is it allowed? – the
writer, the marvellous sureness which he maintains at the very
moment he stands on the front line and the ultimate peril of
writing [. . .].[2]

The tone becomes more personal when Derrida confesses how much
Sollers' book awakens in him the love of a literature before which
he feels fragile and, as it were, intimidated. 'Will you be annoyed if
I tell you that, yet again, you have written a very beautiful book? At
all events, I'm very happy, for – I'd never dare say this in public – I
still love beautiful books and believe in them. I still have, I have
kept from my youth, a certain amount of literary devotion.' The
postscript shows the very high level he has assigned to Sollers' book:
'Have you read *Awaiting Oblivion* by Blanchot? He's just sent it to
me, I don't know why, two years after it came out. I read it just
before *Event*. Despite countless differences, there is something of a
fraternal link between the two.'

Sollers was, as may be imagined, deeply touched by the generosity
of this reading. He was pleased by this 'unreserved communication'[3]
and the ideas that came with it, and drew much closer to Derrida
over the following months. Their correspondence was prolific and
their encounters frequent. On Derrida's part, one senses the desire
for a friendship in which the two would almost merge into one, like
the friendship he had enjoyed with Michel Monory.

Derrida's first essay on Antonin Artaud, 'Le parole soufflée',
was published in March, in issue 20 of *Tel Quel*; in the same special
number appeared a text by Sollers, another by Paule Thévenin, and
eleven published letters from Artaud to Anaïs Nin. Derrida's article
proposed an innovative reading of an as yet little-known author. In
1965, only the first five volumes of the *Oeuvres complètes* had been
published by Gallimard.

In this superb article, Derrida begins pondering the particular
difficulty of holding a discourse about Artaud. Too many commentaries merely enclose him within ready-made categories, denying
yet again 'the enigma of flesh which wanted properly to be named
Antonin Artaud'.[4] Even the fine discussion by Maurice Blanchot
tends to treat him as a case, without the 'untamed' quality of his
experience being really taken into account.

If Artaud absolutely resists – and, we believe, as was never done before – clinical or critical exegeses, he does so by virtue of that part of his adventure (and with this word we are designating a totality anterior to the separation of the life and the work) which is the very protest *itself* against exemplification *itself*. The critic and the doctor are without resource when confronted by an existence that refuses to signify, or by an art without works, a language without a trace [. . .]. Artaud attempted to destroy a history, the history of the dualist metaphysics which more or less subterraneously inspired the essays invoked above: the duality of the body and the soul which supports, secretly of course, the duality of speech and existence, of the text and the body, etc. [. . .] Artaud attempted to forbid that his speech be spirited away [*soufflé*] from his body.[5]

On the publication of this issue of *Tel Quel*, Derrida received a phone call from Paule Thévenin, editor in chief of the *Oeuvres complètes*. Derrida had not yet met her: she told him how much she had liked the article. She repeated her praise in a long letter, spelling out the importance of this text for her:

I must thank you: basically, this is the first, or almost, time that something seems to have been given to me. If I except Blanchot's articles, one or two sentences of Foucault's in the *History of Madness*, I had felt for fifteen years that I was working in a vacuum, and never encountering any response. Of course, I'm not identifying with Antonin Artaud. It's just that I thought his work was one of the most important of our day, that it was worth, more than worth all the time I was devoting to him, and that until now I hadn't met anyone who told me that I wasn't mistaken. It's in this sense that I thank you, as I thank Philippe Sollers. But in his case, I had long since known what he thought on this matter.[6]

Thévenin and Derrida soon met and struck up a friendship. Henceforth, Thévenin kept Derrida abreast of her research and regularly sent him as yet unpublished texts by Artaud. She had gathered together Artaud's papers on the very day he died, in controversial circumstances, and she deciphered them with both passion and patience for the expanding *Oeuvres complètes*.[7]

It was at the home of Paule and Yves Thévenin that Marguerite and Jacques Derrida met a small circle of major artists and writers, at dinners that the couple organized regularly in their apartment on the boulevard de la Bastille. Among the usual guests were Francis Ponge, Pierre Klossowski, Louis-René des Forêts, Michel Leiris,

Pierre Boulez, and Roger Blin. But above all, there was Jean Genet, with whom Derrida was to form a close bond.

Genet occupied a particular status in Paule Thévenin's eyes: she fed him, typed out his texts, did his washing, and looked after his papers. For her, he was rather like 'a second Artaud, a living Artaud'.[8] Thévenin was also in search of new critical discourses to rekindle interest in Genet's work, a work which had been a bit smothered by Sartre's celebrated *Saint Genet: Actor and Martyr*, published in 1952 as volume I of Genet's *Oeuvres complètes*.

At their very first encounter, something very powerful happened between Derrida and Genet. Thévenin was a little apprehensive at leaving the two men alone for a moment while she cooked dinner. But when she came back from the kitchen, she found them absorbed in such intense conversation that she felt almost like an intruder. Usually, Genet hated intellectuals or at least mistrusted them. But with Derrida, friendship was immediate, and never faded thereafter. When they met, Genet was going through a difficult period: Abdallah, who had been his companion for seven years, had committed suicide in 1964. Genet had given up writing and burned several manuscripts; he no longer wanted to hear a word said about literature, at least not his own. This did not hinder a great sense of closeness, which Derrida described to Thévenin:

> Will you please tell Jean Genet, when you can find the words and the opportunity, what I will never dare to tell him, will never be able to tell him: that for me, it's a real *feast* – sober, peaceful, inner, but true – to meet him and talk with him, to listen to him, to witness his way of being. [. . .] Of all the people I've been lucky enough to meet at yours, he's the one I love the most.[9]

Genet was sometimes as intimidated by Derrida as the latter could be by him. The most burning philosophical issues preoccupied Genet, as is shown by this fragment from a long letter he wrote to Derrida:

> When you left Paule's apartment, the last time we met, I still had a great number of things to say to you, especially to ask you. [. . .] I wish [. . .] you could tell me whether it's by thinking, carefully, that one manages, in philosophy, to '*choose*' determinism – or its opposite. By what intellectual operation does one make this choice? Does it come quite naturally, following an act of faith? Like a throw of the dice that is justified after it's taken place? Why am I a Communist? Thanks to a generous temperament rationalized after the event? Or a nationalist, why, and how? Is not the irrational – the aleatory – at the start

of any philosophical commitment? I can see, or think I can see, how one justifies a choice, but I don't know how the choice is made. In my view, one first naturally inclines towards it and then finds reasons for it. [. . .] It's a problem which you and your youngest pupils have solved, I'm sure, but *I* can't. One day you'll have to tell me.[10]

For Derrida, in 1965, as often, the start of the summer was rather glum. He had stayed in Fresnes by himself, while Marguerite and Pierre were in Charente, and he felt that his work was making little progress. 'I have the impression that I can see pearls out of reach, like a fisherman afraid of the water even though he's a connoisseur of pearls,' he wrote to Althusser.[11] But 'this little text on *writing*' that he finished with difficulty at the end of August before sending it to *Critique* would soon be considered one of his major works.

Jacques and Marguerite agreed for once to take a real holiday and spent the whole of September in Venice, at the Lido. They went with Pierre, just turned two, and also with Leïla Sebbar, an Algerian student who was, so to speak, his official baby-sitter. A few years later, she became a respected writer. This was Derrida's first trip to Italy, one of the countries he would love the most, and one of the few to which he would often return for non-professional reasons.

On his return, he found a letter from Michel Deguy saying how much he had enjoyed the article 'Writing before the letter'. A few days later, Jean Piel confirmed that he wished to publish this 'extremely dense, rich and novel study'[12] in *Critique*, even though its length meant that it would need to be published in two parts, in the issues of December 1965 and January 1966. As Derrida frequently acknowledged, this article, a sketch of the first part of the book *Of Grammatology*, was the 'matrix' that would govern the rest of his work.

Following the prevailing rule at *Critique*, the text presented itself to begin with as a review of three works: *The Debate on Writing Systems and Hieroglyphics in the 17th and 18th Centuries* by M.-V. David, *Gesture and Speech* by André Leroi-Gourhan, and the conference proceedings *Writing and the Psychology of Peoples*. But the questions discussed in 'Writing before the letter' went much further. Derrida evoked in premonitory terms 'the end of the book', before introducing the concept of 'grammatology', or the science of writing.

In particular, the article proposes a minute analysis of the presuppositions behind Saussure's linguistics, a major reference-point for all structuralist thinking. While Derrida endorses the central idea of difference as the source of linguistic value, he considers Saussure's thought as still too dominated by *logocentrism*, that 'metaphysics of phonetic writing' which has for too long forced writing into a subsidiary role. But the ambition announced in these pages is not limited to questions of linguistics or anthropology. Derrida extends the methods of Heidegger, leading to the 'undermining of an ontology which, in its innermost course, has determined the meaning of being as presence and the meaning of language as the full continuity of speech', and working 'to make enigmatic what one thinks one understands by the words "proximity", "immediacy", "presence"'.[13]

One major concept, the one by which Derrida's thought will often be designated, also appears in the article: that of *deconstruction*. It is in his 'Letter to a Japanese friend' – a friend who could not find a satisfactory equivalent in his own language – that Derrida gave the clearest explanation for his choice of word:

> When I chose this word, or when it imposed itself upon me, [. . .] I little thought it would be credited with such a central role in the discourse that interested me at the time. Among other things I wished to translate and adapt to my own ends the Heideggerean words *Destruktion* or *Abbau*. Both words signified in this context an operation bearing on the *structure* or traditional *architecture* of the fundamental concepts of ontology or of Western metaphysics. But in French the term 'destruction' too obviously implied an annihilation or a negative reduction much closer perhaps to Nietzschean 'demolition' than to the Heideggerean interpretation or to the type of reading I was proposing. So I ruled that out. I remember having looked to see if the word *déconstruction* (which came to me it seemed quite spontaneously) was good French. I found it in Littré. The grammatical, linguistic, or rhetorical senses [*portées*] were, I found, bound up with a 'mechanical' sense [*portée 'machinique'*]. This association appeared very fortunate [. . .].[14]*

On a more anecdotal level, we may note that the verb 'to deconstruct' had not been entirely forgotten when Derrida started to give it new life. In 1960, it was used in a popular song by Gilbert Bécaud, 'The absent one', to words by Louis Armade, a poet and high-ranking official:

---

* Here is the definition of the word 'deconstruct' (*déconstruire*) in the Littré French dictionary:
'1. To disassemble the parts of a whole. Deconstruct a machine so as to transport it elsewhere.
2. Grammatical term. To carry out a deconstruction. To deconstruct lines of poetry, suppressing metre so as to make them similar to prose. [. . .]
3. To deconstruct oneself. To lose one's structure. "Modern erudition attests that, in a region of the ancient Orient, a language that had reached its perfection had deconstructed and deformed itself by the sole law of change, a law natural to the human mind." (Villemain, *Preface to the Dictionary of the French Academy*).'

How heavy it is to bear the absence of a friend
The friend who every evening came to this table
And who will never return, death is miserable
As it stabs you in the heart and deconstructs you.

On the publication of its first part in *Critique*, 'Writing before the letter' created a real stir in intellectual circles. Michel Foucault expressed his enthusiasm for 'such a liberating text': 'In the order of contemporary thought, it is the most radical text I have ever read.'[15] Emmanuel Levinas assured Derrida that he too had been 'captivated by these incandescent, arborescent pages': 'In spite of all your loyalty to Heidegger, the vigour of your point of departure announces the first new book since his own works.'[16]

As for Gabriel Bounoure, he again expressed his admiration for 'all these capital texts'. And Derrida thanked him in lyrical terms: 'What a help for me it is, this marvellous, generous attention that keeps watch over me and whose presence, for two years now, has been ceaselessly accompanying me on my travels. How immensely lucky I am! I'll never be able fully to express my gratitude.' He regretted just one thing: the geographical distance that stopped them meeting up as often as he would have liked.

I need your advice so much, and your vigilant experience, the light of your culture. I have long known it, but your last letter – from an 'old Arab' as you call yourself – confirms me in this feeling. I'd so much like you to tell me about Ibn Massara, Corbin, Massignon.[17]

According to François Dosse, the author of a monumental *History of Structuralism*, 1966 marked the high tide of this new paradigm. It was the year of *The Order of Things* by Michel Foucault – an unexpected bestseller –, of the violent polemic between Roland Barthes and Raymond Picard on the *Nouvelle Critique*, and of the huge volume of the *Écrits* in which Lacan brought together texts hitherto dispersed. While Derrida did not publish a book that year, and was still unknown to the public at large, several articles and lectures confirmed that he was a highly significant figure, one of the 'great minds of the century', as François Châtelet made so bold as to say in *Le Nouvel Observateur*.

This was also the period in which Derrida gradually built up a new entourage with more writers in it than philosophers and academics. Derrida, very attentive to the books people sent him, wrote long letters, affectionate and detailed, to friends such as Edmond Jabès and Michel Deguy, and also to the authors of *Tel Quel* or those close to the review, such as Jean-Pierre Faye, Marcelin Pleynet, Jean Ricardou, and Claude Ollier.

He would enjoy a long friendship with Roger Laporte, five years older than he was and close to Blanchot and Levinas. The vast project Laporte was gradually putting together, under the title 'Biography', was bound to fascinate Derrida. The essential thing for Laporte was to 'reverse the relation, established since the beginning, between living and writing': 'Whereas ordinary life precedes the way we narrate it, I have wagered that a certain life is neither anterior nor exterior to writing [. . .] one cannot narrate a story that has not yet taken place, a completely original [*inouïe*] life to which only writing would grant access.'[18]

The first volume, *Vigil*, was published by Gallimard in 1963, but Derrida discovered it only in 1965, on the advice of Michel Foucault. He expressed his enthusiasm so keenly that Laporte soon sent him the manuscript of the second instalment, *A Voice of Consummate Silence*. Derrida was just as susceptible to this exploration of the limits of language, often close in tone to the mystics and negative theology: 'I am profoundly convinced, against Wittgenstein, whose words you no doubt know, that "what we cannot speak about we must (*not*) pass over in silence."'[19] Laporte's work struck Derrida as a mirror of his own investigations, fascinating and scary simultaneously. In many ways it represented what he dreamed of moving towards, while at the same time feeling a need to protect himself from it by philosophy:

> I think right now that your enterprise has meaning, that it is, in my view, writing at its most radical. And that's why it allures me, and that's why it is only painfully and impotently that I renounce that type of writing. [. . .] Standing near this limit is *threatening* in at least two respects, and that's why I am keeping away from it as much as *possible* so as not to be destroyed by the threat (feast or death) and as close as *possible* so as not to doze off. Threatening to *life* – to that minimum of serenity indispensable for its maintenance, and for vigilance – and, on the other hand, threatening to *Discourse* (or writing). [. . .] I often have the feeling that through my '*fear*', which one day I will be able to put behind me, I have fled from the route of the *heart* that you have managed to follow. [. . .] So I am trying to do the same as you, with an extra mask – that is to say, between my 'life' and my 'thought' an extra detour, a supplementary 'other' and a very painful (believe me) indirect discourse.[20]

Thanks to Marie-Claire Boons, a Belgian psychoanalyst close to Philippe Sollers, Derrida also met Henry Bauchau, a writer still practically at the start of his career even though he was over fifty. He had settled in Gstaad, in Switzerland, where together with his wife he ran a luxury boarding house for young American girls, the Institut Montessano, but he regularly came to Paris for his training analysis, and attended Lacan's seminar whenever he could. In 1966, his first novel, *Torn Apart,* had a great impact on Derrida:

> It's an *admirable* text, if I may say so without effusion or con-
> ventional politeness: admirable in depth and clarity, in force
> and discretion. To my knowledge it's the first literary *work* in
> which, with such mastery, the resources of psychoanalysis and
> the act of poetry are mingled, interwoven, and even merged
> in such an authentic and originary way. [. . .] Apart from the
> poetic beauty and the accomplishment, it is exemplary for a
> literature that really must go through 'analysis' and do more
> than borrow its fetishes.[21]

If Bauchau's first novel had impressed Derrida so much, this was also because, for the first time, he had immersed himself methodi-cally in Freud, whom he had not read before except in a 'very fragmentary, insufficient, conventional' way.[22] Until the mid-sixties, he explained, he had not taken on board the necessity of psycho-analysis in his philosophical work. Conversations with Marguerite had certainly helped to send him in that direction: she had just begun a training analysis which she was financing by translating several essays by Melanie Klein.[23]

At the invitation of André Green, Derrida proposed a first paper on Freud, in March 1966. Green, anxious to open the Société Psychanalytique de Paris up to structuralism and modernity, had expressed the wish to host in his seminar a debate on Derrida's recent articles, but the latter's contribution went far beyond this framework. Under the title 'Freud and the scene of writing', he analysed in detail two little-known texts, the 'Project for a scientific psychology' of 1895 and 'A note upon the "mystic writing pad"' of 1925. Unlike Lacan, Derrida sought to show that the unconscious was based on a hieroglyphic writing rather than on the spoken word. Turning Freud into an essential ally in the deconstruction of logocentrism, he accorded a major importance to the concepts of supplementarity (*après-coup* – in German, *Nachträglichkeit*) and 'delaying' (*à retardement*; *Verspätung*):

> That the present in general is not primal but, rather, recon-
> stituted, that it is not the absolute, wholly living form which
> constitutes experience, that there is no purity of the living
> present – such is the theme, formidable for metaphysics, which
> Freud, in a conceptual scheme unequal to the thing itself, would
> have us pursue. This pursuit is doubtless the only one which is
> exhausted neither within metaphysics nor within science.[24]

Though Derrida spoke in front of just a score of people that evening, in a little room of the Institut de Psychanalyse, in the rue Saint-Jacques, this innovative re-reading of Freud's texts impressed the audience. But it was really the publication of an expanded version in issue no. 25 of *Tel Quel* that brought him several positive reactions: 'More and more, where would we be without you?' Roland Barthes wrote to him.[25]

Even though he had a considerable capacity for work, Derrida often described himself in his letters as 'a beast hunted down by teaching and family duties, with no time to draw breath between lessons, marking, errands, obligations of every kind'.[26] Shortly before, he thought he was on the verge of a heart attack and doctors reassured him only with difficulty. Geneviève Bollème, whom he had seen recently in her lovely home in Cunault, near Saumur, recommended that he take better care of himself: 'Your social life seems to me the downside of your growing fame. They will both increase, but you must defend yourself from the former in order to protect the latter.'[27] Derrida would find it very hard to follow this advice.

Jean Hyppolite, who had very much admired 'Writing before the letter', wanted to publish an expanded version of the article in the series 'Épiméthée'. But Jean Piel and Jérôme Lindon, the latter of whom ran Les Éditions de Minuit, wanted to launch a collection of essays as an extension of the review *Critique*. And they were very keen for *Of Grammatology* to be the first volume in the series – a prospect that could not have been more flattering for Derrida. Between the huge article published in *Critique* and the seminar he had just given at Normale Sup, 'Nature, culture, writing or the violence of the letter, from Lévi-Strauss to Rousseau', he had all the material necessary. But much of it still existed only in the form of notes – a plethora of index cards and scraps of paper, with jottings on the most varied things, including vaporetto tickets.

At the beginning of summer 1966, Derrida felt worn down, almost out of his mind. He felt a great craving for a vacation, for some peace and quiet, so that he could dedicate these months free of teaching to making progress with his writing projects. But after a few weeks of solitary work in Fresnes, then a 'suffocating' conference in the Dolomites, on death and tragedy, he was on the verge of a breakdown: 'I've been forced to endure a period of "nervous" exhaustion not far removed from "despair". I've had to leave Paris against my intentions, to get some rest here with Marguerite, Pierre, and two nephews, as my brother-in-law is ill and has asked us to look after them.'[28]

Among the things that kept him going was his friendship with Philippe Sollers and his close relationship with *Tel Quel*; this review enabled Derrida, in highly favourable and supportive conditions, to keep together the philosophical, anthropological, and literary questions that he cared most about. He was glad that Sollers shared his work with him, sending him to read, hot off the press, his articles 'Sade in the text' and 'Literature and totality'. Derrida found them 'wonderful', assuring Sollers that the piece on Mallarmé had 'taught him *a lot*'. He was sure: with these two texts, and Pleynet's essay on Lautréamont, which was also 'powerful and right', 'the next *Tel Quel* will cause a stir, stir things up. It will be this autumn's happening. The unity of the whole thing's obvious, blindingly obvious.'[29]

Sollers was equally enthusiastic. That year, 1966, was the year in which for him Derrida was *the* thinker, the one who gave a philosophical framework for the question of 'textuality'. In his view, it was a matter of some urgency to gather together Derrida's articles, which for him were a source of 'a never-ending series of reflections', and to put them together as a volume for the series 'Tel Quel'. He was convinced that only a book would be able to give such an original way of thinking the impact it needed. Sollers often felt that Derrida was saying something that nobody really understood, that 'nobody *can* understand', and that Derrida himself was finding it very difficult to 'explain to others'. This resistance played some part in his own admiration, at a time when he had just embarked on the difficult venture of a new fiction to be called *Numbers*. He wanted to get Derrida to imagine a text 'that would bear on what we "think" on the level of myth, being its crazy trace . . . I won't be telling *you* anything new if I say (without complaining) that it's a real hotchpotch.'[30]

At the end of summer, Derrida was still in a 'depressive state', overwhelmed by an exhaustion that he could not pull himself out of, and that rekindled his hypochondriacal tendencies. Trying to work, and not making much headway, he waited impatiently for a new lease of life. And when he started teaching at Normale Sup again, he also groused about the 'interminable and often tense "conversations" with young people who devour [my] liver'.[31]

On 16 September, Derrida explained to Jean Piel that he had bitten off more than he could chew. The project was taking off, but actually writing it was taking longer than he had hoped, especially since he had needed to spend part of the summer working on a text about Husserl, which was to become *Speech and Phenomena*. So the book he had promised would be at least two months late. The editor of *Critique* gave him a friendly, understanding reply. Above all, he did not want to harass Derrida; 'when it's an essential text that's being composed', the project needed time to ripen. But he should not delay too long, either: the exceptional interest with which the first part had been greeted justified Derrida concentrating all his efforts on finishing this impatiently awaited book.[32]

On 30 September 1966, Derrida told Piel that he had started typing up *Of Grammatology*. In spite of a trip to the United States that had tired him out and slowed him down, he hoped to send him the whole work round about the end of November. 'Anyway, let's say that things are done and that the final stage of tidying up the text can start now.'[33] But a few days later, a new factor came into play: Jean Hyppolite and Maurice de Gandillac were encouraging him to present *Of Grammatology* as a *thèse de troisième cycle*, which could then be transformed into a *thèse complémentaire*. This was a tempting proposal, since it was a task from which he would thus be freed on the day he defended his *thèse principale*. Derrida wanted to pay due attention to this university side of things, which he had 'long neglected'.[34] It would be better to make this concession, even if it imposed a few editorial contortions on him: according to the strict rules of the time, the book actually needed to be printed a few weeks before the thesis viva, but it could not be put on sale in bookshops until the viva had taken place. Piel, understanding as ever, agreed to this new constraint and the extra delay it forced on him.

Presented by Derrida as an additional chore in an already taxing period, the trip to the United States would have a decisive effect on his career. This was the famous Baltimore conference, 'The Languages of Criticism and the Sciences of Man', that two professors at the prestigious Johns Hopkins University, Richard Macksey and Eugenio Donato, had organized as a showcase for the recent developments in French thought. While structuralism had been very much in vogue that year in Paris, it was still totally unknown in the United States, either in bookshops or on campuses. With the help of René Girard, Macksey and Donato had drawn up a list of first-rate guests, including Georges Poulet, Lucien Goldmann, Jean Hyppolite, Roland Barthes, Jean-Pierre Vernant, and Jacques Lacan.

From 18 to 21 October, all the speakers were given accommodation in the same hotel, the Belvedere. It was here that Lacan and Derrida were introduced to one another for the first time: 'So we had to wait to come here, and abroad, in order to meet each other!' said Lacan with 'a friendly sigh'.[35] Subsequent events are related in detail by Élisabeth Roudinesco:

The following evening, at a dinner hosted by the organizers, Derrida raised the questions which concerned him about the Cartesian subject, substance, and the signifier. Standing as he sampled a plate of coleslaw, Lacan replied that *his* subject was the same as the one his interlocutor had opposed to the theory of the subject. In itself, the remark was not false. But Lacan then added, 'You can't bear my already having said what you want to say.' Once again the thematic of 'stolen ideas,' the fantasy of owning concepts, the narcissism of priority. It proved too much. Derrida refused to go along, and retorted sharply, '*That* is not my problem.' Lacan was being made to pay for his remark. Later in the evening, he approached the philosopher and laid his hand gently on his shoulder. 'Ah! Derrida, we must speak together, we must speak.' They would not speak . . ..[36]

Lacan had become something of a star in France, and was eager to impose his presence at the Baltimore conference. He probably wanted this trip, his first to America, to become as mythical as Freud's in 1909. Giving a paper on the second day, he first insisted that he speak before the other psychoanalyst present, Guy Rosolato, and the latter's wife took umbrage. But in particular, he started to give his paper in English, a language that he was far from speaking fluently, before shifting into an almost incomprehensible mixture of English and French. The title itself was enough to leave anyone nonplussed: 'Of structure as an inmixing of an otherness prerequisite to any subject whatever'. The translator soon threw in the towel. The public was flummoxed. The organizers were taken aback by what was perceived as a 'huge bad joke'.[37]

Derrida spoke on the afternoon of the third day, just before the conclusions. This did not stop his paper – 'Structure, sign and play in the human sciences' – appearing as the most important given at the conference. Georges Poulet, whose work was the polar opposite of Derrida's, nonetheless sang the praises of this 'admirable paper' to all those who had not been lucky enough to be there, especially J. Hillis Miller, who was to become one of Derrida's staunchest supporters in the United States.[38] David Carroll, a student who had only just started at Johns Hopkins, was also dazzled by this young and unknown philosopher: 'We were just discovering what structuralism was, and he came and started to call into question what we were starting to learn. I immediately realized that it was an event.'[39]

It is true that, way beyond the texts of Lévi-Strauss under analysis, Derrida's paper did not draw back from setting out a number of significant markers. Some formulations would become canonical in the United States, once 'French theory' made its impact there. Derrida, yet again positing the need to break away from the 'ethic of presence' and the 'nostalgia for origins', focused on the way signs could be substituted for one another, freed from any tyranny from the centre. He sought to replace the old hermeneutics that dreamed of 'deciphering a truth' with a mode of interpretation that 'affirms play and tries to pass beyond man and humanism'.[40] It was a matter, however, not of moving on from philosophy, but of reading philosophers in a really new way. In a few powerful paragraphs, the whole programme of deconstruction was set out.

In the debate that followed Derrida's paper, Jean Hyppolite confessed that he was both admiring and lost: 'I can't see exactly where you're going,' he told him. 'I too was wondering whether I know where I'm going,' replied Derrida. 'So in response I'll say that I'm trying to get to the point where I myself don't know where I'm going.' As for the sociologist Lucien Goldmann, a humanist Marxist, he saw Derrida's remarks as the most radical version of the questioning of the subject. This inspired a strange comparison, in rather poor taste:

> I feel that Derrida, whose conclusions I do not share, is playing the role of a catalyst in French cultural life, and I pay homage to him for this reason. He reminds me of when I first arrived in France in 1934. At that time there was a strong royalist movement among the students; and all of a sudden there appeared a group that was also defending royalism, but by demanding a Merovingian king![41]

Derrida had not finished with Lacan. A few weeks after his return from Baltimore, he received the great tome of the *Écrits*, with a signed dedication: 'To Jacques Derrida, this homage, which he can take however he pleases.' Derrida, usually so prolix, reacted a few weeks later with a short letter, the only one he would ever send Lacan:

> I have received your *Écrits*, and would like to thank you very much. The dedication which came with them could not, as you knew, fail to surprise me. An impregnable text, I thought at first. On second thoughts, adding, as your overture invites us to, my own ideas, I changed my mind: this dedication is true and I should receive it as such. 'True' is a word about which I know that you have your own ideas.
>
> As for the book, rest assured that I am very much looking forward to having the time to read it. I will do so with all the attention of which I am capable.[42]

But before he could fulfil his promise, a personal incident was to complicate a relationship that had already got off to a bad start. Derrida related it in detail to Élisabeth Roudinesco, for her *Lacan & Co.* The anecdote is significant; let me quote it at length:

> A year after Baltimore another dinner took place in Paris, at the home of Jean Piel. Lacan clasped Derrida's hand warmly in his oily palms and asked him what he was working on. Plato,

the pharmakon, letter, origins, *logos* and *mythos*: He was preparing a text for *Tel quel.* [. . .] Once again, [Lacan] announced how curious it was that he too had already spoken of the same themes. His students could vouch for it. Derrida spoke to the psychoanalyst and told him the following anecdote. One evening, as his son Pierre was beginning to fall asleep in his mother's presence, he asked his father why he was looking at him. 'Because you're handsome.'

The child reacted immediately by saying that the compliment made him want to die. Somewhat troubled, Derrida tried to figure out what the story meant.

'I don't like myself,' the child said.

'And since when?'

'Since I've known how to talk.'

Marguerite took him in her arms, 'Don't worry, we love you.'

Then Pierre broke out laughing, 'No, all that isn't true; I'm a cheater for life.'

Lacan did not react. Some time later, Derrida was dumbfounded to read the anecdote in the text of a lecture by his interlocutor delivered at the French Institute in Naples in December 1967. Lacan recounted it as follows: 'I'm a cheater for life, said a four-year-old kid while curling up in the arms of his genitrix in front of his father, who had just answered, 'You're handsome' to his question, 'Why are you looking at me?' And the father didn't recognize (even when the child in the interim pretended he had lost all taste for himself the day he learned to speak) the impasse he himself was foisting on the Other, by playing dead. It's up to the father, who told it to me, to hear it from where I speak or not.[43]

Deeply hurt by the almost vindictive exploitation of this private conversation, Derrida would not pursue any personal relationship with Lacan. But he made sure he read his *Écrits* very closely.

4

A Lucky Year

1967

The letter which Derrida sent to Gabriel Bounoure on 12 January 1967 showed the extent to which, even after his recent successes, the old writer's judgement remained essential to him. The tone was lyrical, sometimes enigmatic, and in any case very much out of line with the tone Derrida used with all his other correspondents:

> I will never be able to express my gratitude. [. . .] There is nothing so precious, in the growing desert, as a complicity like yours. And I am often afraid of not being worthy of it. Then, to reassure myself, I allow myself to be inspired by my confidence and by my admiration: I conclude that what I am writing is of any interest only because of the interest you say you find in it. And I need to believe this, especially because I am walking on ground that's forever giving way. [. . .]
>
> Here, there's a mixture of agitation, turbulence, and profound silence. We are living through a strange period: one of the greatest disquiet and an equal sterility. Clamours on every side, faced with the current collapse, crazed cries and crackups, but also a profound, dead silence, for those who can hear it. In all this, I am trying, despite my despair, to maintain a kind of calm that will not be – too much – one of blindness and deafness; to grant to this period itself, so as not to lose my head completely, a craftsman's labours (teaching, turning out short pieces of writing). Marguerite and Pierre – both of them touched by your affectionate and loyal thoughts – both help me in this in a reliable and really life-affirming way.[1]

Since his return from the United States, Derrida assured Bounoure, he had been working very hard, 'though mainly going over the same points, organizing them properly'. As for Bounoure himself, he had now settled for good at Lesconil, in the southern part of Finistère. Derrida regretted that they could meet up only rarely, and hoped that their shared plan of travelling to Morocco – a land with which Bounoure was very familiar – would work out soon. As he would say a littler later, his relationship with Bounoure continued to sustain him in a permanent and fundamental way. Without this 'terrible proximity' that brought them together, it seemed to him that nothing held together any more, 'not even this game with nothing and nonsense, not even this desperate rigour that still needs to regulate the game and the relationship with death'. So Derrida dreamed of 'very long, durable, interminable meetings, interspersed with shared readings and ideas, punctuated by those great elliptical exchanges that mark a great complicity'.[2]

One of the surprises of the beginning of 1967 was a renewal of the relationship with Gérard Granel. A sort of reversal of the power relations between them was soon evident. Granel, who had so intimidated Derrida during their time at Louis-le-Grand, the 'prince of philosophy' before whom he felt himself to be invisible, had heard many good things about his recent articles and was eager to discover them. Derrida quickly sent him a series of offprints, including in particular 'Writing before the letter' – the double article from *Critique* – and 'Freud and the scene of writing'. Granel fully expressed his enthusiasm:

> Reading your two great texts, the same day (and half the night) that followed their arrival, was something like a constant revelation and *jubilation*. Since such was the case, why not say it as simply as that? [. . .] I have the feeling that a completely essential voice [*parole*] – sorry! a 'writing' [*écriture*] – has seen the light through you.[3]

Even though he knew that Derrida would soon revise these articles, developing them for other people to read, Granel said he was really happy to have discovered them 'in this rough form in which a thought is born and breaks through. There are breaks and leaps in them, and sometimes a prophetic chiaroscuro, that are more revelatory than any tamer text will ever be.' The two men soon started to write to one another frequently. Granel had been teaching at the University of Toulouse for several years and was now completing his thesis on Husserl. He needed to come to Paris at the beginning of May and his keenest wish was to have a long 'pow-wow' with Derrida, so struck was he by the conjunction between their two ways of thinking.[4]

Jean Piel, who valued Derrida more and more, regularly asked for his advice on articles that were submitted to him for *Critique*. When consulted on one of the earliest texts by Alain Badiou, an article on Althusser, Derrida's reply was both frank and open-minded:

I've just read Badiou's text. Like you yourself and Barthes,
I find it at least irritating in its tone, the author's pomposity,
the 'marks' he hands out to everyone as if it were prize-giving
or the Last Judgment. I still think that it's important. [. . .] I
don't think there's any doubt of this, and am all the more prepared to grant it this importance because I am far from feeling
'philosophically' ready to follow him in his arguments or his
conclusions.[5]

Piel quite naturally suggested that Derrida enter the review's
editorial board, together with Deguy, Barthes, and Foucault.
Decisions would continue to be reached on an informal basis: meetings were often held at Piel's home, in Neuilly, and included lunch or
dinner. But while *Critique* did not want to follow any public 'line',
the review was, in those days, remarkably lively, with a good grasp
of current issues. The series of books that started coming out under
its name in 1967 increased its influence and prestige.

Even though typing the text took longer and was more difficult
than expected, Derrida and Piel still hoped to see *Of Grammatology*
come out before the summer, at the same time as *Writing and
Difference*, which Sollers was preparing for publication by Seuil, in
the series 'Tel Quel'. For *Of Grammatology*, the dates were complicated: the work had to be printed before the beginning of May, so
as to be submitted officially to the three members of the doctoral
jury, but in no case was it to come out in bookshops before the viva,
scheduled for June.

Derrida soon had to inform Sollers that *Of Grammatology* would
after all not come out before September. He wondered whether it
might also be necessary to delay *Writing and Difference* so that the
two works would not be separated. He was anxious about them
seeming too fragmented if published apart – the various references
from one volume to the other might fall flat. For him, it would
even be better to publish on the same date the 'little Husserl book'
whose proofs he was expecting: 'I am increasingly inclined to think
that it would be to everyone's advantage if the whole lot came out
in September.'[6] This was not Sollers' opinion: he preferred not
to change what had been agreed on and to publish *Writing and
Difference* in spring.

This book, one of Derrida's most famous, was a big tome of 436
pages, which brought together, in a slightly revised form, most of
the texts he had published in reviews since 1963, respecting the chronology of their first publication and readers to 'join the dots' when
it came to what linked one text to another. The volume opened
with the article on Jean Rousset, 'Force and signification'. It was
followed by 'Cogito and the history of madness', 'Edmond Jabès
and the question of the book', 'Violence and metaphysics, an essay

on the thought of Emmanuel Levinas', '"Genesis and structure" and phenomenology', [7] 'La parole soufflée', 'Freud and the scene of writing', 'The theatre of cruelty and the closure of representation' (Derrida's second text on Artaud), 'From restricted economy to general economy, a Hegelianism without reserve' (an article on Georges Bataille, published in *L'Arc*), and 'Structure, sign and play in the discourse of the human sciences' (the Baltimore paper). The work ended with 'Ellipsis', an unpublished piece on Jabès, dedicated to Gabriel Bounoure.

For Derrida, *Writing and Difference* was his first really personal book, the first in which his name appeared as author. As he would throughout his life, he sent several signed copies to his friends, past and present. Opinions among his old classmates from Louis-le-Grand or the rue d'Ulm were divided. Jean-Claude Pariente was very positive: 'I am glad to rediscover, in a more mature and as if sublimated form, of course, the philosophical élan of the Jackie of my youth, and the conceptual liveliness that means that your writings never leave one indifferent.'[8] But though Jean Bellemin-Noël started off by saying that he was 'profoundly happy' to see Derrida 'among the "great" of our world, and increasingly above a good number of them',[9] he soon admitted that most of the texts in the volume went 'over his head' and, in short, left him rather cold: 'I immersed myself in your book sooner than I had imagined. I haven't read it all and, even out of friendship, I won't read it all.'[10] Several of those he had once been close to did not reply, including Michel Monory.

Luckily, other readers – some of the most important – expressed great enthusiasm. Michel Foucault, who knew almost all the texts collected in *Writing and Difference*, had just read them through one after another and was struck by the 'admirably discontinuous work that they comprise':

> In their juxtaposition, in their interstices, an amazing book comes into view, one which has been written non-stop in a single line, from the very first. The reader realizes that he has read without realizing it not just the texts themselves, but this text within the texts which now appears. I don't need to tell you how eager I am to read the ones announced.[11]

A few weeks later, Emmanuel Levinas wrote to thank Derrida, though he also expressed his reservations. He had taken this opportunity to reread the pages devoted to his work, 'in which so much sympathy is joined with so many incompatibilities'.[12] Derrida wrote to him on 6 June 1967, just after the outbreak of what would soon be called the Six-Day War. 'Glued to the radio' since the start of the conflict, he admitted that he had for some time been 'obsessed by

what was happening over in Israel'. This certainly helped to bring
him closer to Levinas.

After commenting on the texts which Levinas had just sent him
– probably the enlarged edition of the work *Discovering Existence
with Husserl and Heidegger* –, Derrida set out, in this long letter
as perhaps on no other occasion, his conception of philosophical
dialogue: a difficult, demanding dialogue, which can take place only
through texts. It is not a matter of trying to bring things together
when this is impossible, and even less a matter of 'discussing', but
of posing the conditions of a face-to-face that is as respectful as it is
intransigent:

> You know, through the texts which you write and those which
> I write, and through the attention they bring to bear on one
> another, if I may say so, what difference and what proximity
> comprises their 'dialogue'. And this too is 'fraternal'. And more
> is said in this exchange than we can hope to get into a letter.
> More in this exchange and in our day-to-day work: as far as
> I'm concerned, in everything I do your thinking is in a certain
> way present. It is doubtless diverted from its course, in some
> way, but it is necessary. Sometimes contested, as you know,
> but in some way necessary at the very time thinking breaks in.
> Without being able to explain it here, I'd say that for two or
> three years, through a certain movement that 'Violence and
> metaphysics' does not yet show, I have felt, in another way,
> both closer to you and further away.[13]

Derrida was much less thrilled by the more academic issues that
needed to be addressed. The very traditionalist Henri Gouhier was
to be chairing the jury and writing the report on the viva for the
thèse de troisième cycle. The reader will perhaps remember that in
1951 he had gratified Derrida with a mark of 5/20 in a *licence* exam,
assuring him that he could come back and take it again the day he
agreed to 'accept the rules and not *invent* where he needs to be better
informed': with *Of Grammatology*, his wish was granted! Derrida
hoped for more attention and goodwill from the second member of
the jury, Paul Ricoeur, but the latter would do no more than give the
text a quick read-through. He apologized to Derrida . . . thirty-three
years later: 'I disappointed you when I greeted the thesis that you
submitted to me with silence, as I later learned.'[14]

As for Maurice de Gandillac, he acknowledged a few weeks
before the viva that he had not 'really read' the work, but he said he
sensed how he wanted the discussion to go. In any case, they would
not have a great deal of time to study the work, since the session
could not last for more than two hours. So it would be impossible to
discuss the whole thing seriously:

The essential thing is that you gain the qualification you are seeking; your renown will not increase thereby (the survey in *Les Temps modernes* indicates that you already belong among the Paris locomotives, though you do not belong to any of the terrorist groups), but we will be glad to be able to tell you officially of the esteem we have felt for you for such a long time.[15]

In actual fact, the viva was not to proceed as serenely as de Gandillac suggested. As Derrida told Michel Deguy, 'beneath the academic laurels and the professions of admiration, beneath the "open-armed" welcome' that Henri Gouhier mentioned, the session was 'an act of war – bitter, raging – in which all the current tensions weighed down on the debate, with the exception of my text, which none of them had managed to read'.[16] In a letter to Gabriel Bounoure, Derrida insisted on what had struck him as 'a profound lack of understanding', and even as 'a blinding resistance', especially on the part of Ricoeur, which surprised and hurt him. 'And the misunderstandings built up, even among those who were quick to applaud. I don't feel at home either in the university system [. . .] or outside the university system. But is it a matter of being at home?'[17]

This was all the more dismaying because it was just the *thèse annexe* that was being examined, and so Derrida was far from having put his university obligations behind him. Developing the subject of his *thèse d'État*, he agreed with Jean Hyppolite that he would put forward a new interpretation of Hegel's theory of the sign – more specifically, 'of speech and writing in Hegel's semiology', though he did not really know when he would find the energy to write it.[18]

Meanwhile, after these months of uninterrupted work, Derrida was in Nice, where he told everyone he was doing nothing: 'I'm in the sea and the sunshine from morning to evening, so I can rediscover something of the climate of the other shore. And I'm letting things settle.' He had 'the violent longing to shed my skin, my old skin', and dreamed of writing something completely different, or of 'taking up very old, very archaic plans, buried under the urgent tasks of Paris and university life'.[19] Unfortunately, he would soon need to be thinking of his classes for the following year, on Hegel and on the logic of Port-Royal. 'I could do with at least one year of absolute peace and quiet . . . Even talking about it will make me drop dead.'[20]

His correspondence with Philippe Sollers was still regular and friendly. 'I always think of you,' the writer assured him, 'as one of the sole "authorities" to whom I feel any desire to show what is happening – and being written – through me.'[21] Derrida had wanted to write to him sooner, but time had gone by very quickly, between 'feeling a bit suffocated by family life, pretty numbed overall' and the 'renewed "Nuptials" with the Mediterranean'. 'In my present state of idleness, which I had not experienced for long months, a new piece of work is perhaps coming into being in silence and new measures being taken.'[22]

That year, the friendship between Sollers and Derrida would encounter its first snag, directly linked to a newcomer: Julia Kristeva. She had arrived from Bulgaria in December 1965 to do a doctorate in comparative literature, and had met Goldmann, Genette, and Barthes, and Sollers shortly after. The beauty, intelligence, and charisma of the young woman, her prestige as a 'foreigner',[23] created an immediate sensation. The new reference points she brought with her – Mikhail Bakhtin, the Russian formalists – and the concepts she rapidly coined, such as intertextuality and paragrammatism, ensured that she had made a name for herself on the Paris intellectual scene within a few months. She published her work first in the Marxist review *La Pensée*, then, starting in spring 1967, in *Critique* and *Tel Quel*.

To begin with, Kristeva's relations with Derrida were excellent. She was captivated by Derrida's highly original way of reading Husserl. In particular, she thought that he was the only philosopher capable of linking a phenomenology already filtered through psychoanalysis with literary experience.[24] But a first incident soon raised its ugly head: Sollers told Derrida he was very annoyed with him for having shown to François Wahl Kristeva's article 'Meaning and fashion' (a discussion of Barthes's *System of Fashion*) before its publication in *Critique*. When Derrida admitted that he was surprised and hurt by this rebuke, Sollers immediately apologized; nothing, he said, was more intolerable to him than the idea of a misunderstanding between them. But he wanted to add a few details:

> Kristeva: the question, here, is more serious than you seem to imagine. On the subject of the appearance, as sudden as it was decisive, of these new ideas, there have been many flurries, many discussions, many little things. I'm thinking of F. Wahl telling me that the article on Bakhtin published in *Critique* was 'crazy'; I'm thinking of some argument over how Miller and Badiou had uttered a radical condemnation of the text that *Tel Quel* has published; I'm thinking of some psychoanalyst who has launched out on a violent attack on some of her work; I'm thinking of the way that, as in a test tube, all the symptoms of what used to be called a cabal, of the finest vintage, have made their appearance.[25]

The truth, undisclosed in this letter as in their meetings over the next few months, was that Derrida was not told one essential fact: Kristeva and Sollers had fallen in love and then got married, in total privacy, on 2 August 1967. At that time, they both insisted on keeping this secret, if not clandestine.[26]

Meanwhile, Marguerite and Jacques returned to Fresnes at the start of August to await the birth of their second child. Jean – Louis Emmanuel – Derrida was born on 4 September 1967, a little earlier than expected, which did not stop him from seeming healthy and tranquil. The choice of these three first names was no coincidence: Jean was Genet's first name, Louis that of Althusser, Emmanuel that of Levinas. Over the days following the birth, Derrida had to take over domestic responsibilities, something to which he was not used. With two children, the Fresnes apartment was becoming really cramped. Jacques and Marguerite started to think about buying a new house. Even though the state of their finances was soon to improve, thanks to the seminar that Derrida started giving a small group of American students, they soon realized that they would need to move a bit further away from Paris.

1967 was definitely a year of births, for two new books by Derrida were published in the autumn.

Speech and Phenomena was published by Presses Universitaires de France, in Jean Hyppolite's series. This short work presented itself as a mere 'introduction to the problem of the sign in Husserl's phenomenology'. But in actual fact, the book developed the questions discussed in *Writing and Difference* and *Of Grammatology*, focusing, in another way, on the privilege granted to presence and voice throughout the history of the West. As Derrida explains in the introduction:

> We have thus a prescription for the most general form of our question: do not phenomenological necessity, the rigor and subtlety of Husserl's analysis, the exigencies to which is responds and which we must first recognize, nonetheless conceal a metaphysical presupposition? [. . .]
>
> What is at issue, then, in the privileged example of the concept of sign, is to see the phenomenological critique of metaphysics betray itself as a moment within the history of metaphysical assurance. Better still, our intention is to begin to confirm that the recourse to phenomenological critique is metaphysics itself, restored to its original purity in its historical achievement.[27]

The problem, in Derrida's view, is in short the deepest ambition driving Husserl's investigations: the desire to liberate an 'original' lived experience and reach 'the thing itself', in its 'pure presence'. In *Speech and Phenomena* he endeavours to bring out the philosophical implications 'of the interdependency that one must accept between what is called thinking and a certain interplay of signs, marks or traces'.[28]

In the eyes of several philosophers, *Speech and Phenomena* is one of Derrida's major works. Georges Canguilhem and Élisabeth de Fontenay expressed their admiration to him on their first reading. The great Belgian phenomenologist Jacques Taminiaux has also professed a passion for this work, placing it on the same level as Levinas's *Totality and Infinity*. And Jean-Luc Nancy considers it even today as one of the peaks of Derrida's oeuvre:

> *Speech and Phenomena* remains in my view the most magisterial and in many respects the most exciting of his books, since it contains the heart of his whole operation: moving away from self-presence; and *différance* with an 'a' in its difficult relation between infinite and finite. For me this is really the heart, the driving force, the energy of his thinking.[29]

Of Derrida's three 1967 works, however, it was *Of Grammatology* that was to remain the most famous. In particular, it was through this work that he thought he would start to make a name for himself in the United States. On Derrida's own admission, the book is, however, composed of 'two heterogeneous passages put together somewhat artificially'.[30] The first part, 'Writing before the letter', was an enlarged version of the article published in *Critique*: it was here that the fundamental concepts were put in place. The second, 'Nature, culture, writing', began with an analysis as patient as it was implacable of a chapter in *Tristes Tropiques*, with 'The writing lesson' showing the stratagems used by the author to link the appearance of violence among the Nambikwara with that of writing.

Subjecting Lévi-Strauss's ethnological discourse to critique just after questioning Saussure's linguistics was a deliberate move on Derrida's part. They were the two pillars of structuralist discourse, a discourse which Derrida judged to be at the time dominant in the field of Western thought, but which was in his view trapped 'by an entire layer, sometimes the most fecund, of its stratification, in the metaphysics – logocentrism – which at the same time one claims rather precipitately to have "gone beyond".'[31]

Lévi-Strauss made no attempt to conceal his irritation. Shortly after the first publication of this chapter in the fourth issue of the *Cahiers pour l'analyse*, he sent a caustic letter to the review's editors:

> Do I need to tell you how grateful I was for the interest shown me in your recent publication? And yet I can't shake off an awkward feeling: aren't you playing a philosophical farce by scrutinizing my texts with a care that would be more justified if

they had been written by Spinoza, Descartes or Kant? Frankly, I don't think that what I write is worth so much fuss, especially *Tristes Tropiques*, in which I didn't claim to be setting out any truths, merely the daydreams of an ethnographer in the field – I'd be the last to say there is any coherence in them.

So I can't avoid the impression that, by dissecting these clouds, M. Derrida is handling the excluded middle with all the delicacy of a bear. [. . .] In short, I'm surprised that minds as agile as yours, supposing they have deigned to read the pages of my books, didn't ask themselves why I make such a casual use of philosophy, instead of rebuking me for so doing.[32]

But Lévi-Strauss occupied only one chapter of the book. The crucial section of the second part of *Of Grammatology* was devoted to Jean-Jacques Rousseau, especially the *Essay on the Origin of Languages*, a short and at the time almost forgotten work that Derrida boldly linked to certain passages of the *Confessions*. Contrasting works of a very different level and style, attentive to their least details, Derrida proposed a new type of reading, which might be likened to the free-floating attention of psychoanalytical listening. Following the traces of the word 'supplement', often associated with the adjective 'dangerous', Derrida showed how Rousseau linked it sometimes to writing and sometimes to masturbation, for both of which he showed a fascinated mistrust.

Reading of the kind Derrida practises 'must always aim at a certain relationship, unperceived by the writer, between what he commands and what he does not command of the schemata of the language that he uses'.[33] It is a 'signifying structure that reading must *produce*', even when the work pretends to efface itself behind the signified contents that it transmits. At the polar opposite of the academic tradition, the discourse of philosophy or of the human sciences is approached as a text in the full sense of the word.

The publication of *Of Grammatology* more than confirmed the interest aroused by the double article in *Critique*. On 31 October, in *La Quinzaine littéraire*, François Châtelet reviewed it, devoting an enthusiastic full page to it under the title 'Death of the book?' On 18 November, Jean Lacroix, in charge of the philosophical coverage in *Le Monde* since 1944, devoted an entire article to Derrida, half a page long. The first lines were a real accolade:

Philosophy is in crisis. This crisis is also a renewal. In France, a whole constellation of (relatively) young thinkers are transforming it: Foucault, Althusser, Deleuze, etc. We now need to add to these names that of Jacques Derrida. Known to a small group of enthusiastic *normaliens*, he has just revealed his talent to a wider public by publishing three books in six months, including *Of Grammatology*. Through the attention he brings to bear on the problem of language, he seems close to the 'structuralists'. He does them justice and acknowledges that thinking, across the world, has been given a formidable impetus by a sense of disquiet over language, which can only be a disquiet of language and within language. He distances himself from this tendency, however, insofar as – like the iconoclast he is –, far from deriving inspiration from a scientific model, he is still in thrall to the philosophical demon. [. . .] Derrida's aim is not the destruction, but the 'deconstruction' of metaphysics. The foundational concepts of philosophy enclose the *logos*, and reason, within a sort of 'closure'. This 'closure' needs to be smashed, we need to attempt a break-out.[34]

The concept of '*différance*' was also introduced in this reliable, positive analysis, as were those of '*gramme*' and 'trace'. Jean Lacroix underlined the crucial link between Derrida's philosophy and those of Nietzsche and Heidegger, while avoiding several of the misunderstandings that would later come about. 'Derrida', he emphasized, 'does not want to privilege writing at the expense of speech.'

Three days previously, in *La Tribune de Genève*, Alain Penel had enthusiastically hailed an author who 'questions Western thought'. This time, the emphasis was on *Writing and Difference*. The praise was unreserved and sometimes uncritical:

After him, Marx, Nietzsche, Heidegger, Freud, Saussure, Jakobson, Lévi-Strauss, etc, appear dull. This is because Derrida shows himself to be more radical than they are, insofar as his thinking puts all others to the test, aiming successfully to be a reflection on contemporary reflection. By showing thereby that metaphysics continues to poison Western thought, Jacques Derrida makes his mark as the boldest contemporary thinker. His works cannot fail to constitute a new, superior field for the reflections of all those – critics, philosophers, teachers, students – who are interested by developments in our culture.[35]

The book had been eagerly waited and brought its author a huge postbag. Sollers, who had already read the complete manuscript in the summer, had immediately called it 'a quite brilliant text'.[36] Kristeva was very touched to have received a signed copy of the book, as a 'sign of complicity': she thanked Derrida for all that she already owed to his work and for all that she would continue to draw from it.[37] She would soon be sending him a series of questions, which he would answer at length in writing, under the title 'Semiology and grammatology'.[38] As for Barthes, he was in Baltimore when he thanked Derrida warmly: *Of Grammatology* was, in this place, 'like a book by Galileo in the land of the Inquisition, or more simply a civilized book in Barbary!' A judgment which, in retrospect, seems quite piquant.

For it was also from the United States that another warm letter arrived, announcing an equally fruitful relationship: that in which Paul de Man told Derrida how much he had been 'thrilled and interested' by *Of Grammatology*. He expected this work to help in the 'clarification and progression of [his] own thinking', something which Derrida's Baltimore paper, and their first conversations, had already suggested.[39] As they talked over the breakfast table at the conference the previous year, the two men had realized that they were both interested in their different ways in the *Essay on the Origin of Languages*. This was the origin of a friendship which became deep and enduring: after this first encounter, Derrida would say, nothing ever separated them, 'not even a hint of disagreement'.[40] Shortly thereafter, de Man published a fine review of the book in the *Annales Jean-Jacques Rousseau*, which was followed by a major, more critical article,[41] but in particular he very quickly started encouraging his students at Cornell to look into this new thinker.

Samuel Weber, who was then writing his thesis under de Man's supervision, remembers hearing him talk about Derrida at the beginning of 1966, even before the Baltimore conference:

Just after he read 'Writing before the letter' in *Critique*, he spoke to me about it with enthusiasm. I immediately read the article and it blew me away. It rapidly seemed to me that Derrida was doing what Paul de Man was trying to do. So de Man would have had every reason to feel at least ambivalent about him, but I never felt this was the case. He felt neither jealousy nor resentment for him, just a frank gratitude.[42]

It was at de Man's request that, at the end of autumn 1967, Derrida gave a seminar in Paris on 'the philosophical foundations of literary criticism' for a dozen American students from Cornell and Johns Hopkins. His course fascinated them mainly because Derrida was particularly open to dialogue and individual contact. Like several others, David Carroll remembered this time with special intensity, since it was also here that he met his future wife:

This Paris seminar turned all my ideas on literature – most of them, admittedly, received ideas – upside down. To put it in crude and hasty terms, Jacques presented those attending the seminar who were expecting something else, or who, like me, didn't know what they were expecting, with something completely new: a double, and doubly critical, mode of questioning and type of analysis. He gave a class every week, a class that was simultaneously philosophical and literary, showing complex and contradictory relationships, both internal and external, between literature and philosophy. I was overwhelmed, we were all overwhelmed, by Derrida's style, by his way of reading, of asking questions, of analysing texts. Everything was up for questioning, everything was up for discussion, and in a different way. And in order to do this, it was especially necessary to find another voice, another style, another writing. Nothing was the same as before.[43]

Gérard Granel did not simply congratulate the former boarder at Louis-le-Grand for 'all these births, books and a child pell-mell!'[44] While Derrida, now the only reader who counted in his view, immersed himself in his still unpublished thesis on *The Meaning of Time and Perception in E. Husserl*, Granel was writing for *Critique* a detailed review of the three recent volumes, 'Jacques Derrida and the erasure of origin'.

In these twenty pages, he hailed the arrival of a profoundly new kind of writing. He was probably the first to use the adjective 'derridien' in French. The opening lines cannot fail to have touched his former classmate: 'Already a whole work – but one that is not at all a "work"; already a whole style of writing, in one year unfurled over our heads like a banner. A beautiful sight in the sky and bright in its new colours.'[45] But while singing the praises of Derrida and his 'strategy', which manages to remain 'respectful and kind', Granel does not draw back from showing rather more malice towards Levinas – he does not see how Levinas could 'wriggle out of the net that Derrida has tightened round him' – and especially towards Foucault:

> An implacable patience, a fearsome gentleness, are also evident in the 'few remarks' that Foucault brings down on himself for the treatment he metes out to Descartes in the *History of Madness*. This is perhaps where we can see most clearly how a 'particular point', initially lost in the middle of the work, enables us to penetrate gradually, and then all at once, into this work even when it is already open, its implications laid bare. Indeed, all we need to do thereafter is to transport (not even to transpose) the now evident inadequacies of the *History of Madness* into *The Order of Things* for the essentially undefined notion of archaeology underlying the whole enterprise to fall apart.[46]

Foucault, who had hitherto encouraged Derrida 'with his warm friendship', wanted Derrida to oppose, if not the publication of the

Algiers, early twentieth century.
(Derrida: personal collection)

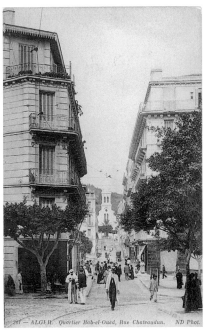

Jackie Derrida, aged two.
(Derrida: personal collection)

Sitting on the car with his father, his mother, and his brother René.

(Derrida: personal collection)

Family group: Jackie is in the middle, on his mother's knees.

(Derrida: personal collection)

At the corner of the Boul'Mich and the rue Soufflot, the favourite cafés of Derrida and his friends in the early 1950s.
(Private collection)

The École Normale Supérieure in the rue d'Ulm (© Jean-Philippe Charbonnier/Rapho) at the period when Louis Althusser (above) was teaching there.
(© Fonds Louis Althusser/Archives IMEC)

Jacques Derrida, c. 1960, in Prague, in Marguerite's family.
(Derrida: personal collection)

Paul Celan.
(© Photo Gisèle Celan-Lestrange/
Fonds Paul Celan/Archives IMEC)

Michel Foucault.
(© Bettmann/CORBIS)

Philippe Sollers
in the early 1960s.
(© AFP)

Emmanuel Levinas
in 1988.
(© Ulf Andersen/Gamma)

Paul Ricoeur in 1970.
(© Yves Leroux/Gamma)

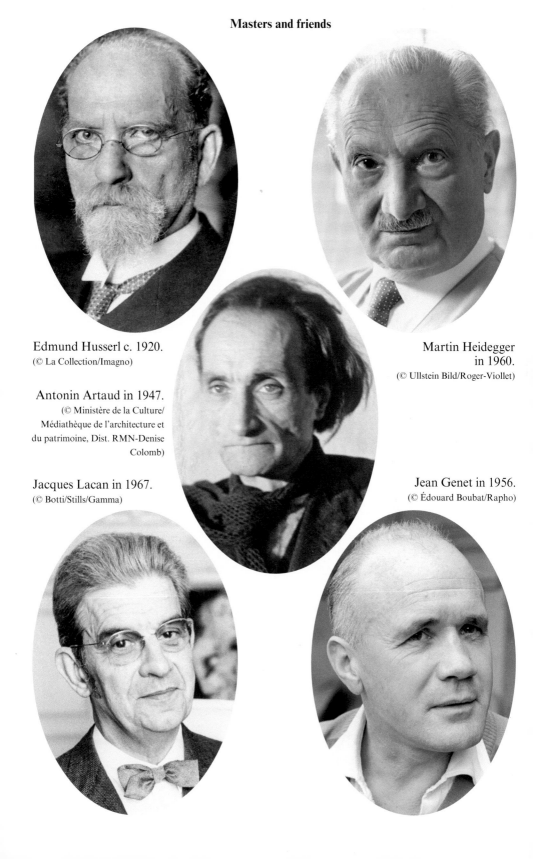

Masters and friends

Edmund Husserl c. 1920.
(© La Collection/Imagno)

Martin Heidegger
in 1960.
(© Ullstein Bild/Roger-Viollet)

Antonin Artaud in 1947.
(© Ministère de la Culture/
Médiathèque de l'architecture et
du patrimoine, Dist. RMN-Denise
Colomb)

Jacques Lacan in 1967.
(© Botti/Stills/Gamma)

Jean Genet in 1956.
(© Édouard Boubat/Rapho)

1950–1, second year of *khâgne*. Jackie is in the third row, third from right. On his right, his friend Michel Monory. The teacher is Roger Pons.

(Derrida: personal collection)

1951–2, third year in *khâgne*. Jackie is in the front row, fourth from left.

(Derrida: personal collection)

At the Lycée Louis-le-Grand, first year of *khâgne* (1949–50), wearing the grey boarders' overcoat.
(Derrida: personal collection)

The three boys from Algiers in *khâgne*. From left to right: Derrida, Jean Claude Pariente, and Jean Domerc.
(Derrida: personal collection)

In an Algiers street, shortly before his departure for Paris.
(Derrida: personal collection)

At the wheel of his father's car.
(Derrida: personal collection)

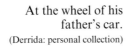

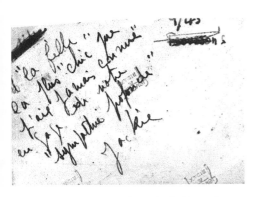

Jackie at fifteen. The photo is dedicated to one of his girlfriends.
(Derrida: personal collection)

In El Biar with his friends in the football club (Jackie is in the second row, smiling).
(Derrida: personal collection)

With his mother, summer 1950.
(Derrida: personal collection)

At the primary school in El Biar, 1939. Jackie is in the second row (second from right).
(Derrida: personal collection)

At the Lycée Ben Aknoun in 1946 (third row, third from left). In the
second row, the blurred face is that of Jackie's friend Fernand Acharrok.
(Derrida: personal collection)

On the ship *Le Liberté* taking Jacques to the United States for the first
time with Marguerite, in 1956.

With his sons, Pierre, born in 1963 (right), and Jean, born in 1967 (below).
(Derrida: personal collection)

On *Le France* in September 1971 with his niece Martine Meskel.
(Derrida: personal collection)

Cerisy-la-Salle: the Nietzsche conference in 1972. From left to right: Gilles Deleuze, Jean-François Lyotard, Maurice de Gandillac, Pierre Klossowski, Jacques Derrida, and Bernard Pautrat.

(© Archives de Pontigny-Cerisy)

Cerisy-la-Salle, 1975, with Francis Ponge.

(© Archives de Pontigny-Cerisy)

Tableau vivant of the painting *The Massacre of the Innocents*, c. 1975, in the house
of the Adamis in Arona. In the foreground, Jean, Marguerite, and Jacques Derrida.
On the right, Camilla Adami; in the background, Valerio Adami.

(Derrida: personal collection)

The sisters Sylviane (on the left) and
Sophie Agacinski, Paris, July 1966.
(© Rue des Archives/AGIP)

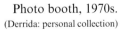

Photo booth, 1970s.
(Derrida: personal collection)

Letter from Jacques Derrida to Gérard Granel, sent from Nice, 29 December 1989. Most of Derrida's correspondents found his handwriting extremely difficult to decipher.

(Derrida: personal collection)

whole article, at least this extremely brutal paragraph. But Derrida, now a member of the editorial board of *Critique*, reminded Foucault of his own self-imposed rule: 'not to intervene, either for or against, on any article concerning [him]'.[47] The consequences soon made themselves felt: these few lines, though modified at the request of Jean Piel, led to a serious cooling of the relationship between Derrida and Foucault. In Derrida's view, Granel's article was even the precipitating factor that led to Foucault's violent riposte in 1972.

Granel wanted nothing to do with this unpleasant quarrel. In the long letter he sent to Derrida a few weeks after the publication of the article, he said yet again that he was struck by the 'unexpected closeness' of their work, the 'community of destiny suddenly revealed, as if, having for ten years been a prisoner in a *maximum isolation cell*, [he] had suddenly heard an Other knocking on the wall or on the pipes'. He felt that only the two of them could make progress in philosophy, since 'Heidegger is going to die, and in any case [their] writing, though it is based on his work, begins after him'. Jean Beaufret did not do the work one might have expected of him, and all the rest was lost in the anonymity of 'disciplehood'. Apart from what interested Derrida and him, there was nothing but Marxism, neo-Thomism, and the Sorbonne – in short, 'various forms of an irremediable erring'.[48]

The first interview Derrida gave appeared in December 1967 in *Les Lettres françaises*, the cultural weekly edited by Louis Aragon. In this minutely rewritten article, the author explained to Henri Ronse, in a deliberately labyrinthine fashion, the relation between the three works he had just published:

> *Derrida*: One can take *Of Grammatology* as a long essay articulated in two parts (whose juncture is not empirical, but theoretical, systematic) *into the middle* of which one could staple *Writing and Difference*. *Grammatology* often calls upon it. In this case the interpretation of Rousseau would also be the twelfth 'table' of the collection. Inversely, one could insert *Of Grammatology into the middle* of *Writing and Difference*, since six of the texts in that work preceded – *de facto* and *de jure* – the publication in *Critique* (two years ago) of the articles that announced *Of Grammatology*; the last five texts, beginning with 'Freud and the Scene of Writing,' are engaged with the grammatological opening. But things cannot be reconstituted so easily, as you may well imagine. In any case, that two 'volumes' are to be inscribed *one in the middle of* the other is due, you will agree, to a strange geometry, of which these texts are doubtless the contemporaries.

Ronse: And *Speech and Phenomena*?
Derrida: I forgot. It is perhaps the essay which I like most.
   Doubtless I could have bound it as a long note to one or
   the other of the other two works. [. . .] But in a classical
   philosophical architecture, *Speech* . . . would come first
   [. . .].[49]

Even more than Husserl, Heidegger had become for Derrida the
essential philosopher, the one with whom he would continue to
argue. In his interview in *Les Lettres françaises*, he explained that he
felt towards him an 'extreme ambivalence', a 'vexed admiration':[50]

What I have attempted to do would not have been possible
without the opening of Heidegger's question. [. . .] But despite
this debt to Heidegger's thought, or rather because of it, I
attempt to locate in Heidegger's text – which, no more than
any other, is not homogeneous, continuous, everywhere equal
to the greatest force and to all the consequences of its questions
– the signs of a belonging to metaphysics, or to what he calls
ontotheology.[51]

From a concrete point of view, it was at this period that there
began a to-and-fro relation between Heidegger and Derrida that
would continue for several years. Pierre Aubenque – an alumnus
of Normale Sup, a great Aristotle specialist, mentioned flatter-
ingly by Derrida in *Of Grammatology* – was at the time teaching in
Hamburg. He needed to invite Heidegger to dinner, and the latter
told him he was keen to find out about the most up-to-date French
philosophy; he seemed to take a particular interest in structuralism.
'I won't fail to sing your praises . . .', Aubenque informed Derrida.[52]
   In a note in his recent work *Do We Need to Deconstruct
Metaphysics?*, Pierre Aubenque mentions this conversation. On the
evening they met, in the last days of 1967, Heidegger showed considerable curiosity about Derrida's work. Though he was usually so
ready to vaunt the philosophical merits of the German language, he
had even agreed to pay close attention to the subtleties of a concept
that was deeply embedded in French:

He seemed especially interested in the theme of '*différance*', and
we spent a long time trying to translate this term into German.
We couldn't. The two meanings of the French word '*différer*'
are expressed in German by two terms: *verschieden sein* (to
be different) and *verschieben* (to defer, to postpone). In spite
of a vague homophony, these words have two different roots.
Derrida's play on words is possible only in Latin (where the
verb *differre* has two meanings) and in the Romance languages.

English, which uses two related words – 'to differ' in the first sense and 'to defer' in the second – constitutes an intermediate case. Heidegger was forced to admit: 'On this point, French goes further than German.' And he asked me to transmit to Derrida his great eagerness to meet him, though unfortunately this did not happen.[53]

It is important to note that, while Derrida also wanted to make the acquaintance of Heidegger, he wanted to do so in a suitable context. The French disciples of the master of Freiburg irritated him too much for him to imagine going to the Thor seminar the following year – near the home of René Char, in l'Isle-sur-la-Sorgue – even though Granel and Deguy would be taking part. Heidegger conceived these private seminars as lectures and the participants as pupils in a 'Kindergarten', whom he cross-questioned brusquely. Given the difficulties of translation and 'the strangeness of the relationships short-circuited by Fédier and an immediate entourage that was really ridiculous', Deguy was convinced that Derrida would never have stood it.[54]

5

A Period of Withdrawal

1968

Henry Bauchau and his wife Laure ran a luxury boarding school in Gstaad, with rooms spread out among three chalets. At the invitation of the Bauchaus, the Derridas spent two Christmases in succession here. Their long evenings together gave rise to a real friendship, both intellectual and intimate. A few weeks later, Henry Bauchau wrote what a vivid memory he had of the times they had spent together:

> For us, this encounter, in the snow, as if in some odd timeless zone, was a kind of event. Admittedly, the new ideas played a part, but contact and the personalities involved were much more important. I was very struck by the mixture of rigour and gentleness in your own personality, your extreme openness to everything. [. . .] Something happened in the course of these few days, something I do not seek to define, but something that was of great significance for Laure and myself.[1]

In a later letter, Bauchau emphasized how important this meeting had been for him:

> It was less your thinking than yourself. From this mixture of gentleness and firmness, rigour and everydayness, a way of listening to this time without rejecting any of it, especially paternity. To move beyond the world of the Father without denying the links of paternity – this gave me a great deal to think about when I saw the four of you.[2]

Bauchau, already a novelist, was, however, disconcerted by a conversation in which Derrida told him that he was writing for a 'very definite, restricted' audience, one that would then be in a position to transmit his thought. In his reply, the author of *Writing and Difference* came back to this decision, explaining that his type of work involved applying one's strength in the right way: mediations were crucial if he was to have any chance of being understood: 'I'm convinced that addressing "the man in the street" directly means not being understood by him, or anyone at all, or in any case producing only paltry effects.'[3]

For now, at all events, Derrida was far from addressing the man in the street. While he was active in the early months of 1968, he spoke only in very specialized contexts. On 16 January, he spoke at Jean Hyppolite's seminar at the Collège de France: his paper was called 'The pit and the pyramid: An introduction to Hegel's semiology'. This text, later reprinted in *Margins of Philosophy,* was the sole trace of the thesis subject that he had registered a few months earlier.

Hyppolite was still Derrida's faithful ally in academia, as this eloquent letter proves: it was written in support of Derrida's inclusion in 'the list of those qualified to teach in higher education':

When I first met M. Derrida, at the École Normale, where he was my student, I had the impression, which is not that frequent, of having come across a real, authentic philosopher. I felt, in spite of the difficulties and sometimes the obscurities of his research (on Husserl), that I could have confidence in him. This confidence has not been belied, but I did not know how successful his first works were going to be, even though he had done nothing to curry favour, and made no concessions – for which I congratulate him. [. . .] The main thesis, which I am supervising, could have been written on the basis of his work on Husserl, but J. Derrida asked me if he could discuss the subject in Hegel. When one supervises such a philosopher, one can only let him make the running. [. . .] J. Derrida's work exists; his inclusion in the list of those qualified to teach in higher education will acknowledge its existence and his qualities as a philosopher and a teacher. I am more than favourable to it: I have no reservations in recommending him.[4]

1968 marked the start of Derrida's journeyings: he was already starting to be a frequent traveller. On 25 January, he took the train for Zurich together with Gérard Genette and Jean-Pierre Vernant, for a conference organized by Paul de Man as a sort of continuation of the Baltimore conference. Genette was to remember vividly the night he had to spend with Derrida, during this brief stay in Switzerland:

De Man had put everyone up in a delightful hotel in the old city, but for lack of space he had crammed Jacques and me together in the same twin-bed room. [. . .] It was at lights-out time that my temporary *cothurne* realized that he had left his pyjamas behind – but not, fortunately his portable typewriter. The typewriter made up for the lack of pyjamas, so he asked me whether the noise of him working would bother me. Of course, my reply was conciliatory, so he spent a good part of his night, and mine, [. . .] typing, I suppose for some other future conference, a paper whose tenor I might have been able to infer, if my ear had been more absolute and better trained, from the acoustically differentiated sonority of his typewriter keys.[5]

It is not going too far to deduce that the pages Derrida was so hastily typing were those of the paper on '*La différance*' that he gave the next day, on Saturday, 27 January, at 4.30 p.m., in the amphithéâtre Michelet in the Sorbonne. For the first time, he had been invited to present his work to the Société Française de Philosophie, a somewhat intimidating assembly from which, unfortunately, two of his allies were missing: Emmanuel Levinas and Maurice de Gandillac – they were both examiners at a thesis viva.
The opening of this text was to remain celebrated:

I will speak, therefore, of a letter.
Of the first letter, if the alphabet, and most of the speculations which have ventured into it, are to be believed.
I will speak, therefore, of the letter *a*, this initial letter which it apparently has been necessary to insinuate, here and there, into the writing of the word difference; and to do so in the course of a writing on writing, and also of a writing within writing whose different trajectories thereby find themselves, at certain very determined points, interacting with a kind of gross spelling mistake [. . .].
Therefore, preliminarily, let me recall that this discreet graphic intervention, which neither primarily nor simply aims to shock the reader or the grammarian, came to be formulated in the course of a written investigation of a question about writing. Now it happens, I would say in effect, that this graphic difference (*a* instead of *e*), this marked difference between two apparently vocal notations, between two vowels, remains purely graphic: it is read, or it is written, but it cannot be heard.[6]

In the discussion that followed this paper, which was both a recapitulation and a new foundation, the first reaction – that of Jean Wahl – was rather positive. But it was followed by an irritated reaction on the part of Brice Parain, who compared this *différance*, which is 'the source of everything' and which 'cannot be grasped', to negative theology. Derrida totally denied this. Then Jeanne Hirsch, a traditional humanist, criticized 'a certain contemporary philosophical style', wondering whether it was not the symptom of a 'lack of humility in one's way of saying what needs to be said'. She was annoyed by Derrida's mode of expression: it would be better if 'the way of saying things went unnoticed'. What bothered her even more, in a concept such as *différance*, was a way of using the language that had entered French philosophy only under the influence of German. Derrida replied that this expression, which had not passed unnoticed, was exactly the subject that he had been focusing on. Then he added, ironically: 'Perhaps I am indeed under the influence of this German philosophy which you mentioned. [. . .] But in the field of philosophy, is German influence a bad thing?'[7]

A few days later, Georges Canguilhem wrote to Derrida to say that he had gone home filled with delight, and enthusiasm, from the conference, even though it was far removed from his own preoccupations, but he confirmed that his colleagues had really not liked it. This was probably the moment when the breach between Derrida and French philosophical institutions started to open. Considered up until then as talented and promising, Derrida had now become a real pain, with his three books published in one year, his articles in non-specialist reviews, and the aura that was starting to surround his name, in France and abroad.

On 31 January, he set off for London, at the instigation of his former student Jean-Marue Benoist. He spoke at a conference on Rousseau, on 3 and 4 February, and gave a paper that later became 'The linguistic circle of Geneva'. During this first visit to Britain, he also went to Oxford, where he again gave his paper on 'La différance'. But his British audience were even less impressed than the members of the Société Française de Philosophie. The words 'deconstruction' and '*différance*' were deemed to be ugly, and the paper as a whole created a 'chilly consternation', rapidly followed by an explosion of wrath on the part of Alfred Jules Ayer, the great figure of logical positivism, who lost his cool. Derrida would never forget this first incident: he would remember it when he met with similar misadventures in Oxford and Cambridge later on.[8]

Even though Derrida found the rhythm of all these journeys and requests for papers was 'becoming absurd' and felt that it would 'have to stop',[9] his lectures and classes abroad were only just starting. His name was circulating more and more, and articles on his work were starting to be published in several countries, including in the prestigious *Times Literary Supplement*. The first concrete proposal came from Germany. Samuel Weber had discovered Derrida thanks to Paul de Man two years previously. He was currently teaching at the Free University in Berlin, and Peter Szondi, the head of department, had asked him to organize a seminar on structuralist literary criticism and very much hoped that Derrida would agree to give a paper. 'As a great admirer of your works, I am sure that you will find in Germany a large and important audience.' He was convinced that Derrida's ideas could have 'a highly favourable influence on the development of the human sciences in Germany'.[10]

Shortly thereafter, Derrida's first visit to Berlin gave rise to a revealing misunderstanding. Sam Weber came to meet him in the small airport of Berlin-Tegel, situated just outside the city. One of Weber's friends had already met Derrida: she described him as 'looking a bit like a young rogue in a black jacket'. But reading Derrida's first texts must have played at least as big a part in Sam Weber's image of Derrida:

I was imagining a sort of revolutionary. In the concourse, I spotted a handsome man who looked a bit like Vittorio Gassmann, with a velvet shirt open at the chest and a series of thriller magazines under his arm. I told myself: 'Well, that's what the philosopher of the future looks like.' I went up and greeted him; he thanked me for coming to fetch him and we headed off towards my Beetle convertible. His first question somewhat surprised me: 'Is there a swimming pool at the hotel?' I was impressed. 'We're really in the post-philosophical era,' I thought. But I told him, a bit embarrassed, that he probably wouldn't have time to go swimming before the conference. 'What conference?' my passenger asked. 'I've come about a film. I'm a producer.' Finally realizing my mistake, I turned back and spotted outside the airport a gentleman in a grey suit, looking lost and sheepish, trying vainly to hail a taxi. Derrida – the real one – looked up, saw me, saw my passenger – who was laughing heartily at the situation – and understood what had happened. A little later, he asked me how I had managed to confuse him with the other man. 'Er . . . You know . . . The violence of metaphysics . . .,' I told him. He was hurt, and retorted: 'Violence perhaps, but not brutality!' . . . The story doesn't end here: when I took him back to the airport, on the Sunday, we saw the false Derrida at the bar, surrounded by several pretty girls he must have been recruiting for his film. He indicated us with his eyes, and leaned towards them, tittering, as he told them what had happened . . . . The fact of the matter is that, in those days, Derrida was still not very sure of himself. He dressed rather drably, like a traditional professor, and was ill at ease in social situations. Only gradually did he free himself up, inventing a public persona for himself and a form of erotic identity that he made his own.[11]

This story left its mark on Derrida, and he often mentioned it on his later trips to Germany. But this first stay in a Berlin that was already in a state of great unrest was mainly important for the start of his relationships with Peter Szondi, the founder of the Institute of Literary Theory and Comparative Literature and one of the most respected contemporary professors, even among student protesters. The son of the great psychiatrist Leopold Szondi, Peter Szondi was born in Budapest in 1929, into a Jewish family. In 1944, the whole family was deported to Bergen-Belsen, before benefiting from a bargain made with the Nazis and sent to Switzerland in the 'Kastner train'.[12] Peter Szondi remained traumatized by survivor's guilt for the rest of his life, as did his great friend Paul Celan. It was thanks to Szondi that Derrida make the acquaintance of this major poet – whose path he had sometimes crossed in the rue d'Ulm since 1964:

> It so happens that Celan was a colleague of mine at the École Normale Supérieure for many years without me knowing him, without us really meeting. He was the German lector. He was a very discreet, very self-effacing, inconspicuous man. In fact, one day, in the office of the Director of the École, there was a discussion of various administrative matters and the Director himself said something that suggested he didn't know who Celan was. My Germanist colleague spoke up: 'But, Monsieur le Director, do you know that we have here as lector the greatest poet in the German language?' This shows the Director's ignorance, but also the fact that Celan's presence was, like his whole being, like all he did, extremely discreet, elliptical, self-effacing. This explains why for a few years, when I was his colleague, we did not get to know each other.[13]

When Szondi in turn came to Paris, he finally introduced Celan to Derrida and the two men exchanged a few words. A few meetings ensued, always brief and practically silent: 'The silence was his as well as mine. We would exchange signed copies of our books, a few words, and then disappear.' Celan was no more voluble at a lunch with Derrida at the home of Jabès and his wife: 'He had, I think, a rather grim experience when it came to his relationships with many French people.' It needs to be remembered that, at the time, there were hardly any translations of Celan. And even though Derrida knew enough German to work closely on philosophical texts, Celan's language remained for him at this time enigmatic, more or less inaccessible. He would take many years to read him properly.

It was in somewhat strange circumstances that Derrida got to know another writer who had fascinated him since his teens, Maurice Blanchot.

It all started with a volume of homage to Jean Beaufret, *The Endurance of Thinking*, which his old pupil François Fédier had started to organize in 1967, asking for contributions from Kostas Axelos, Michel Deguy, René Char, Maurice Blanchot, Roger Laporte, and several others. Derrida did not immediately say yes: 'I initially hesitated because, basically, I did not feel particularly close to Beaufret, with whom I had a good personal relationship; but I did not feel Beaufretian, or Heideggerean in the Beaufret way.'[14] Fédier turned on the charm for Derrida, and was so insistent that the latter agreed to give a paper he had already written, the result of a seminar: 'Ouisa and Grammè: Note on a note of *Being and Time*'.

A few weeks later, over a lunch at Fresnes, Roger Laporte related a few anti-Semitic remarks made by Beaufret, one of them concerning Levinas. Derrida was thunderstruck, probably more than Laporte might have imagined. The next day, he wrote to Fédier to tell him about this grave and awkward problem:

> I have just been informed – and this is for me *absolutely* surprising and shocking – of some remarks made on several occasions by Jean Beaufret, remarks that are in a word *massively, clearly,* and *vulgarly* anti-Semitic. *It is absolutely impossible for me*, in spite of my stupefaction, to cast any doubt on the authenticity of what I have heard. [. . .] I am drawing this conclusion, at the least, and you must of course be the first to know: I am obliged to withdraw my text from this collection of homages; my decision is irreversible but I will keep it secret and, if you agree, we can find some external pretext to explain it. [. . .] The text which I had given you was the sign that not only am I not part of any 'plot' against Beaufret, but that I was even willing to contribute to breaking a certain circle or cycle that I felt was intolerable [. . .] as far as the whole problem [. . .] of Beaufret was concerned.[15]

In spite of Derrida's discretion, Fédier soon found out that the 'informer' was Laporte. He warned Beaufret, who immediately protested against 'the circuit [. . .] of whispered defamation', asking for a face-to-face explanation. The confrontation took place a few days later in Derrida's office. Pale with emotion, Beaufret vigorously denied the remarks attributed to him, while Laporte felt that he was now the one on trial. He came out of the meeting in such a state that his wife Jacqueline took the initiative and alerted Blanchot, who was so 'tormented' by the matter that he emerged from the hermit-like existence in which he had lived for many years. At the beginning of February 1968, Derrida and Blanchot met for the first time so that they could mull over the right attitude to adopt.[16]

Blanchot did not immediately realize that the person attacked by Beaufret was none other than Levinas. On 10 March, without withdrawing his text from the Beaufret tribute, he asked Fédier to add the following dedication: 'For Emmanuel Levinas, to whom, for forty years, I have been bound by a friendship that is closer to me than I am myself: in a relation of invisibility with Judaism.'

On 2 April 1968, Blanchot and Derrida co-signed a letter that they intended to send to all those contributing to the volume. They explained that after 'a difficult debate' they had decided to include their contributions in the volume after all: Beaufret had denied that he had uttered the most serious of the remarks in question, and rejected the interpretation given to the others, so they had not felt they had a right to pronounce, by withdrawing, 'an accusation so serious that it would have simultaneously meant a sentence of guilty'.[17] But these letters, sent by Blanchot to the publisher for forwarding, would never reach their addressees.

After this period, a bit too full of turmoil for his taste, Derrida felt the desire to settle down to some quiet work. That year's *agrégation* programme allowed him to rediscover such 'inexhaustible' authors as Plato and Hegel. As he wrote to Gabriel Bounoure, 'in spite of the huge library of books that academics have written on them, you always have the feeling that you haven't yet *begun* to read them. This is basically what interests me the most.'[18]

The article 'Plato's pharmacy', published in two issues of *Tel Quel* (winter and spring 1968), to some extent marked a new, freer, more explicitly literary tone. The first lines were to become famous:

A text is not a text unless it hides from the first comer, from the first glance, the law of its composition and the rules of its game. A text remains, moreover, forever imperceptible. Its law and its rules are not, however, harbored in the inaccessibility of a secret, it is simply that they can never be booked, in the *present*, into anything that could rigorously be called a perception.

And hence, perpetually and essentially, they run the risk of being definitively lost. Who will ever know of such disappearances?[19]

The last paragraphs are just as striking:

The night passes. In the morning, knocks are heard at the door. They seem to be coming from outside, this time . . .

Two knocks . . . four . . .

– But maybe it's just a residue, a dream, a bit of dream left over, an echo of the night . . . that other theater, those knocks from without . . . [20]

This did not stop the main part of this long article – springing as it did from a seminar at Normale Sup – from proposing a minute, quasi-philological reading of the *Phaedrus*. Derrida had, as we have said, learned Ancient Greek only belatedly, but he now seemed to move in it quite easily. While using a standard French translation, the one by Léon Robin published by Budé, he constantly went back to the original text and retranslated passages, especially each time the word *pharmakon* occurred. This term, whose traces Derrida followed closely in his reading of Plato, had in fact been translated sometimes as 'remedy', sometimes as 'recipe', 'poison', 'drug', or 'philtre'. Since these variations seemed to him quite pernicious, he endeavoured to bring out the extent to which 'the malleable unity of this concept, or rather its rules and the strange logic that links it with its signifier, has been dispersed, masked, obliterated, and rendered almost unreadable not only by the imprudence or empiricism of the translators, but first and foremost by the redoubtable, irreducible difficulty of translation'.[21] The question was all the more far-reaching in that this concrete term, now a 'philosopheme', seemed in his view to play as central a role in Plato's work as did 'supplement' in Rousseau. Hemlock itself, the potion that Socrates was sentenced to drink, 'is never called anything but a *pharmakon*'.[22] The question of the inscription of the philosophical text in its language, and thus the matter of translation, would become constant preoccupations of Derrida – especially because the foreign versions of his own texts would keep forcing him to confront them.

At the end of an evening spent together, Philippe Sollers gave Derrida the manuscripts of his two new books, *Logics* and *Numbers*. Derrida already knew most of the essays gathered in *Logics*, but he was deeply impressed by *Numbers*. He was soon immersed in 'this arithmetical and theatrical machine', 'this implacable numeration and these seeds innumerable in number'.[23] He very quickly expressed the desire to write something, while being fully aware of the resistance of this strange fiction, imbued with reflexivity:

> I dream of a genius idea – but I have no genius – or a way of writing that would allow me to 'get stuck in', so that within the dimensions of an article I could both write a text, master your machine and yet present it as something to be read enrolled around its consumed self. I've never taken on such a difficult task, one both necessary and risky. And if I finish it, it will all have been said, by you first and foremost, in *Numbers* already and in that remarkable, in every respect, interview in *La Quinzaine*.[24]

While his friendship with Sollers again seemed unclouded, relations with Jean-Pierre Faye had become very prickly. Faye was five years older than Derrida, a writer but also an *agrégé de philosophie*:

on the entire editorial board of *Tel Quel*, he was the only one who was not an autodidact. Without ever being close to one another, the two men had long had a more than merely polite relationship. In 1964, Derrida sent an appreciative letter to Faye about his novel *Analogues*. And Faye had on several occasions said how much he admired Derrida's work. When he received his copy of *Writing and Difference*, Faye assured him that 'Freud and the scene of writing' was the 'most exciting' piece of philosophical writing that he had read for years.[25] And after immersing himself in *Of Grammatology*, he again told Derrida that, in his view, Derrida's path was 'the one that counted, and more than any other'.[26]

But the crisis that had been brewing for months between Sollers and Faye broke out in autumn 1967, when Jacqueline Risset and Pierre Rottenberg joined the editorial board of *Tel Quel*. Unhappy at the way the review had been developing, and Kristeva's growing importance, Faye resigned on 15 November. Over the next few weeks, he tried to bring Derrida over to his side and warned him about the way his methods were being 'misused' in *Tel Quel*, especially in a recent text by Rottenberg. Faye said he was particularly shocked by 'the brusque way in which the opposition between speech/writing had been *equated* with that in class struggle between bourgeoisie/proletariat'.[27]

Faye immediately set up his own review, *Change*, also published by Le Seuil. Sollers viewed this as a stab in the back. Faye wrote several times to Derrida, inviting him to lunch in the hope of making an ally of him. But Derrida kept his distance, and stayed friendly but firm. From then on there was a degree of mistrust between the two men. Faye shortly afterwards remarked that he had asked himself 'a few questions' while rereading *Of Grammatology*, and invited Derrida to discuss them with him,[28] but there was no reply.

The ideological landscape in this period was as complex as it was changing, and the confrontation between *Tel Quel* and *Change* can be understood only as part of a much wider configuration. After the Argenteuil Conference in 1966, the French Communist Party embarked on a new policy towards intellectuals. The monthly *La Nouvelle Critique*, which enjoyed a relative autonomy within the Party, opened up to avant-garde movements, and in particular to *Tel Quel*, whose work suddenly started to be considered as 'of a high literary and scientific level'. Three flamboyant young women incarnated modernity in the review: Catherine Clément, Élisabeth Roudinesco, and Christine Buci-Glucksmann. Derrida would have dealings with them several times in the course of his career.

At the end of 1967, the editors of *La Nouvelle Critique* prefaced an interview with Sollers and other contributors to the review, stating how greatly 'this work merits our sympathy and can teach us quite a bit'.[29] It was in this spirit that, on 16 and 17 April 1968, the first Colloque de Cluny took place, on the theme 'Linguistics and Literature'. Derrida did not attend, but his work was frequently mentioned. Over and above the themes under discussion, the explicit purpose of the gathering was to 'break the many walls that separate different fields' to 'find grounds for a fruitful exchange'.[30] In the view of one of those who took part, both sides could feel a certain satisfaction: the Communist Party could finally emerge from its dogmatism and sclerosis, while the avant-garde could feel anchored by its responsibility and political activism. The concrete results of this theoretical rapprochement were soon evident: on 24 April, *Les Lettres françaises* devoted its first page to Jacques Henric interviewing Sollers under the title 'Writing and revolution'.

Neither the Communist Party, nor *Tel Quel*, saw May 1968 coming. Neither did Althusser or Derrida, even though they came into daily contact with the most politically active students. Vincent Descombes puts the matter very well, when he described May '68 as 'a month in which the French educated classes had the surprise of their lives. The revolution which had been spoken of for so long was triggered off without warning. Yet perhaps this revolution was not a revolution after all . . . [. . .] The first victim of the upheaval was the man professing to knowledge, the teacher [. . .].'[31]

The events broke out at the Sorbonne on 3 May, with a demonstration against the closing of the university at Nanterre and a number of students being brought before the disciplinary commission. Within days, the whole Latin Quarter was in uproar. From 9 May onwards, the movement started to reach students in the provinces and developed extremely rapidly. Two days later, the main trade unions called for a general strike. On 13 May, a crowd nearly a million strong marched through the streets of Paris, from the Gare de l'Est to the Place Denfert-Rochereau. This demonstration, the biggest since the Liberation, temporarily united students and workers, chanting 'Ten years, that's enough!' and 'Happy Birthday, General!' Marching with the *Tel Quel* writers, Derrida bumped into Maurice de Gandillac who, to his dismay, asked him how he was getting on with his thesis.

Those weeks of tumult, in which it was difficult to travel between Paris and Fresnes, brought Derrida into closer contact with Jean Genet, and he had dinner with him privately on several occasions. Derrida was later to remember vividly their nocturnal strolls through Paris, sometimes walking together until daybreak. 'Genet, in those streets without cars, in this completely immobilized, paralysed country, which had run out of petrol, kept saying: "Ah, how beautiful! Ah, how beautiful! Ah, how elegant!"'[32]

Maurice Blanchot, whom Derrida continued to see on a regular basis, was also filled with enthusiasm. The author of *Thomas the*

Obscure and *The Space of Literature*, whose health had been precarious for years, even seemed to find a kind of renewed vigour in the movement: he was at all the demonstrations, all the general assemblies, and took part in composing pamphlets and motions, and suggesting one of the finest slogans of May '68: 'Be realistic, demand the impossible.' For the radical Blanchot, there was nothing to be lost and so nothing to be saved. He was impelled by an exultation of pure revolt, intensified by a fascination for anonymous writing, a sudden act of vengeance against 'the misery of the isolated mind'.[33]

In an interview with François Ewald, Derrida later recognized that he personally had not been 'what they call a *soixante-huitard*':

Though I then participated in demonstrations and organized the first general meeting of the time at the École Normale, I was on my guard, even worried in the face of a certain cult of spontaneity, a fusionist, anti-trades-union euphoria, in the face of the finally 'freed' speech, of restored 'transparence', and so forth. I never believe in those things . . . [. . .] I was not against it, but I have always had trouble vibrating in unison. I didn't feel I was participating in a great shake-up. But I now believe that in this jubilation, which was not very much to my taste, something else happened.[34]

Admitting that his distance probably contained 'a sort of crypto-Communist legacy', Derrida spoke in more detail about his attitude to the student movement in his interview with Maurizio Ferraris:

I did not say no to '68', I took part in the demonstrations, I organized the first general assembly at the École Normale. Still, rightly or wrongly, my heart was not 'on the barricades'. What really bothered me was not so much the apparent spontaneity, which I do not believe in, but the spontaneist political eloquence, the call for transparency, for communication without relay or delay, the liberation from every sort of apparatus, party or union. [. . .] Spontaneism, like workerism, pauperism, struck me as something to be wary of. I wouldn't say my conscience is clear on this matter and that it's as simple as that. These days [. . .], I would be more cautious about formulating this critique of spontaneism.[35]

Derrida was not alone in his failure to grasp the full extent of the events. Althusser, who had pushed many of his students into politically radical positions, including Maoism, was completely at a loss; he spent the spring and part of the summer shut away in a clinic. Robert Linhart, the founder of the Union des Jeunesses

Communistes Marxistes-Léninistes (Union of Communist Marxist-Leninist Youth), went into a sleeping cure, as he too had fallen prey to psychological problems. As for Sollers, May 1968 was the moment when he decided to align himself with the positions of the Communist Party, which was overall very hostile to the student movement: according to the collective texts published in the summer number of *Tel Quel*, May 1968 corresponded merely to the fleeting emergence of a non-Marxist, even 'counter-revolutionary' leftism.

Even though it would have immense repercussions, the movement had started to lose impetus by 30 May. Nearly a million demonstrators marched down the Champs-Elysées in support of General de Gaulle. A few weeks later, the general elections gave him a crushing majority. On 10 July 1968, Prime Minister Georges Pompidou was dismissed and replaced by Maurice Couve de Murville.

During this time, the Derrida family were finally able to move into the brand-new detached house they had bought in Ris-Orangis, a good twenty or so kilometres south-east of Paris. They would not be moving again. For Derrida, keeping his distance from the capital was not due merely to economic necessity. To the Paris apartment, which for him was synonymous with promiscuity, he preferred a house with a garden, in countryside which was not really countryside.

He spent the beginning of summer in Nice, without Marguerite or the children. After the upheaval of the previous months, these days seemed to be doing him good, as he told Henry Bauchau:

> In this silence and idleness, it's a welcome return, even a welcome regression: there's the Mediterranean of my childhood, in which my body can really immerse itself. And then – another return to the mother. I'm living alone with my parents, something I haven't done for twelve years . . . I know you can understand this strange experience . . .[36]

Derrida was contemplating writing a whole book about Plato. But meanwhile, he was mainly busy with *Numbers*. His enthusiasm for Sollers' novel was as intense as before and he regretted, after all these months, that he had still not finished the text he wanted to devote to it: 'This book is extraordinary and I don't feel able to measure up to it, especially in an "article". "Dissemination", however, is making progress, it's already too long and, and as I'd foreseen, it will need two issues of *Critique*.'[37]

After reading this article, almost as long as the fiction that had inspired it, Sollers again thanked Derrida, however derisory this might seem after such a gift: 'I'll insist for a simple reason: you'll enable me, if I'm strong enough, to advance further into the darkness. What you give me is really a crazy and unhoped-for support.'[38] The facts of the matter were more ambiguous. For this moment of extreme closeness also marked a subtle form of rivalry between the fiction and the commentary on it. Mixing almost inextricably his text together with Sollers', the philosopher had managed to give the writer the feeling of a 'carnivorous osmosis'.[39] Thrust would soon lead to parry.

At the beginning of May, Derrida joined Marguerite and the children at Les Rassats. Eager to see Sollers and Kristeva again, in calmer circumstances after 'all the jolts and all the silences' that had kept them apart since the spring, he took advantage of this brief stay in Charente to go and spend a day in their company in the Île de Ré. But shortly after this meeting, a new event came along to threaten their relationship. On 20 August, troops of the Warsaw Pact invaded Czechoslovakia to crush the 'Prague Spring'. While Aragon and *Les Lettres françaises* clearly came out against the Soviet intervention, the *telqueliens* took a harder line and claimed they supported it. As Sollers wrote to his friend Jacques Henric: 'You mustn't count on me to disarm, not even for a second, the Red Army (not to mention the Bulgarian tanks for which I even feel a guilty passion). The whiffs of a sordidly self-interested humanism wafting up are the last straw as far as I am concerned.'[40] At a dinner, Paule Thévenin launched 'into a violent diatribe, denouncing the Czech counter-revolutionaries and singing the praises of the Soviet Union', which led to a severe chill in relations.[41] It is easy to guess why: Marguerite Derrida, whose mother's family lived in Prague, viewed things with, let us say, a different eye.

Summer 1968 was also marked by the start of a venture in which Derrida would play a role both discreet and essential: the creation of Vincennes. Within the highly conservative government formed by Maurice Couve de Murville, Edgar Faure, the new Minister of Education, was an exception. A liberal and a modernizer, he enjoyed the confidence of General de Gaulle, who, while still reeling from the May '68 movement, had realized that the French university system needed to change as a matter of urgency.

On Monday, 5 August 1968, Raymond Las Vergnas, the new Dean of the Sorbonne, set out to Edgar Faure his dream of a university completely different from those that then existed in France, a university open to workers, in particular those without a baccalaureate, where the education given would be flexible and interdisciplinary, where professors competent within their fields could be recruited even without the qualifications traditionally required. This project did not emerge from nowhere. It was mainly the fruit of conversations that Las Vergnas had had with Hélène Cixous. A few months earlier, in an astonishing show of institutional strength, he had

sent this young woman to fill a post as professor at Nanterre even
before she had had the viva for her thesis. Given a grandstand view,
she had observed the events of May with the greatest attention,
surprised by their extent and the desire for total upheaval that they
demonstrated.

Just after his meeting, Las Vergnas announced to Cixous that the
Minister was entrusting her with a 'prefabricated new university, an
offshoot of the Sorbonne in the forest of Vincennes'.[42] He asked the
Joyce specialist, whose address book was already impressively full,
to help him set up an experimental university. Derrida was the first
person Cixous contacted. On 7 August, she sent him a telegram (the
house in Ris-Orangis still had no telephone): 'Need advice plans
pilot University.'[43]

As Cixous later explained:

I asked Jacques Derrida to be my adviser (in secret: he wasn't
appointed, but was acknowledged by Las Vergnas). Through
him, I could also be sure of recruiting a commission of experts,
a scholarly circle that would guarantee the quality of those
recruited, including Georges Canguilhem, or Roland Barthes.
For scholarly legitimacy was of course the *condition* of the
venture.[44]

Derrida showed no desire to go and teach in Vincennes himself.
At the time, he still felt quite at ease at Normale Sup. But this project
for an experimental university interested him and he was heavily
involved in the preliminary discussions held in Cixous's apartment in the rue Lhomond, with François Châtelet, Jean-Claude
Passeron, Jean-Pierre Richard, Lucette Finas, Gérard Genette,
Tzvetan Todorov, and a few others. Derrida's role was naturally
crucial in laying the basis for the department of philosophy, but he
was just as enthusiastic about the introduction of psychoanalysis,
which at the time was not taught in any university. Since at that
period Lacan and his colleagues did not wish to have anything to do
with it, Derrida suggested entrusting responsibility for the department to Serge Leclaire, a doctor and psychoanalyst of Lacanian
allegiances, and had his choice ratified by Canguilhem.[45]

For some months, Derrida had also been pulling strings to help
Bernard Pautrat escape from the *lycée* where he had been dying of
boredom. Though barely twenty-four, he was suddenly plucked out
and sent to the rue d'Ulm to assist Althusser and Derrida with the
philosophy students. With the arrival of Pautrat, Derrida could call
on the services of an accomplice, almost a disciple. The Marxist grip
on the École was very tight, and Althusser had probably wanted to
maintain some balance within the school. Pautrat was, to be sure,
close to the '*mao-spontex*', those leftists characteristic of the scene

straight after May '68 who favoured the revolutionary spontaneity of the masses rather than parties and structured organizations. But he was mainly a reliable, brilliant philosopher who had come top in the *agrégation* and was perfectly 'Derrido-compatible'.[46]

Pautrat was delighted about his imminent arrival at Normale Sup. But he had worrying news of Althusser, whose state of health was improving only slowly: he would be away for at least the whole of October. This came at a particularly inconvenient time, since Derrida himself was preparing to leave Paris until the end of November: the Americans had been so dazzled by his performance in 1966 that they had invited him to teach at Johns Hopkins for two months – a proposal he could hardly turn down, if only because of the financial perks. So Pautrat would have to look after the philosophers at the start of the academic year by himself. As he put it: 'I'll do my best, of course, to cope, but I can't deny I'm more than a little anxious about it.'[47]

At the end of September, Jacques and Marguerite flew to the United States with their two sons: Pierre was just over five, and they had just celebrated Jean's first birthday. It was in the house in Cloverhill Road, in Baltimore, that he would take his first steps.

Derrida was prone to worry, and had been nervous about this stay. In fact everything went as well as it could have done. He soon struck up a friendship with Richard Macksey, director of the Humanities Centre at Johns Hopkins and co-organizer of the 1966 conference. Derrida appreciated his 'magical hospitality' and his incredible personal library, 'the most miraculous and dependable'[48] that he would ever encounter. He made a pilgrimage – which would become a repeated ritual – to the tomb and the room of Edgar Allan Poe.

The first seminar Derrida gave at Baltimore took up and amplified the one he had given at Normale Sup on 'Plato's pharmacy'. But he also proposed readings of Baudelaire, Artaud, Nietzsche, and, especially, Mallarmé, sketching out what later became 'The double session'. As Derrida in those days taught in French, only a score of listeners came along. But many of them were bowled over, including J. Hillis Miller, then close to Georges Poulet and the Geneva School, who became one of the great figures of deconstruction in America. As Miller remembers:

When I turned up at the first session, I was afraid my French might not be good enough for me to follow. But I was straightaway fascinated by the power of Derrida's discourse. It was extraordinary, I'd never heard anything like it. Very quickly, we became friends, and got into the habit of having lunch together once a week. To begin with, each of us spoke his own language, then he started to talk to me in English.[49]

While the start of Derrida's stay in America was quite 'calm, slow and unhurried', a real whirlwind of lectures – the first in a long series – started in mid-October. Over the next few weeks, he went to New York, Yale, Providence, Washington, Buffalo, and Chicago. As he wrote to Sollers:

> I keep asking myself, from the depths of my old, neurotic vulnerability, how I survive – pretty well, basically – this series of exhibitions of a travelling salesman that I felt I would be quite unable to carry out. I manage without too many disasters, for the salesman and, dare I hope, for the merchandise (I note this since you are part of the latter . . .). [. . .] I am still living in *Numbers*, and everything I do here – in particular, but not only, the classes – constantly brings me back to it, makes the numbers work, over and above the dissemination that I left behind me on my departure.[50]*

In New York, at the conference on 'Philosophy and Anthropology', he gave an influential paper that would long be remembered: 'The ends of man'. As he would make it a habit of his, Derrida immediately underlined the circumstances in which he was speaking: 'Every philosophical conference necessarily has a political significance,' he insisted, especially if it is supposed to be international; its very possibility is inseparable from the 'form of democracy':

> Such, in its most general and schematic principle, is the question which put itself to me during the preparations for this encounter, from the invitation and the deliberations that followed, up to acceptance, and then to the writing of this text, which I date quite precisely from the month of April 1968: it will be recalled that these were the weeks of the opening of the Vietnam piece talks and of the assassination of Martin Luther King. A bit later, when I was typing this text, the universities of Paris were invaded by the forces of order – and for the first time at the demand of a rector – and then reoccupied by the students in the upheaval you are familiar with. [. . .] I have simply found it necessary to mark, date, and make known to you the historical circumstances in which I prepared this communication. These circumstances appear to

---

* From New York, Derrida sent Sollers a proposal for a lecture tour in American universities, which in his view had two advantages: to confirm the presence of *Tel Quel* and his own in the United States – henceforth, '*Tel Quel* is considered the most original and reliable French cultural product of the day' –, and going home having pocketed $1,500 to $2,000 net profit (i.e. some 5,000 to 7,000 euros today). Sollers did not follow this proposal up, largely for political reasons.

me to belong, by all rights, to the field and the problematic of our colloquium.[51]

The rest of his address – with its text emblematically dated to 12 May 1968 – endeavours to answer the question 'What does France think about man these days?' In it, Derrida mentions Hegel and Kojève, Sartre and Nietzsche, but the focus was on Heidegger and his 'Letter on humanism'.

While this paper and his other contributions were well received, Derrida was soon complaining about these unremitting, exhausting journeys. He spent only two or three days a week in Baltimore, and the rest of the time travelling, 'like a sleepwalker, not even or barely noticing the places, the lecture halls, the people, his own discourse, etc.' He claimed he wanted to put a quick end to 'this machinery and the pleasure one can sometimes take in it'.[52] But this frenzied rhythm did not stop him appreciating the American style of education and its comfortable, peaceful character – poles removed from the permanent tension prevailing at Normale Sup. At Johns Hopkins, Derrida's presence aroused great enthusiasm: the originality of his reference points, the force of his concepts, and also his personal availability ensured his reputation for a long time to come. When Gérard Genette occupied the same post, over the following two autumns, he emphasized how much Derrida had left 'a dazzling memory, for countless good reasons, plus this one: the only nice Frenchman since Lafayette. *All* the others are arrogant.'[53]

In Paris, meanwhile, intense and often fraught negotiations on Vincennes continued. In spite of this distance, Derrida was concerned about the fate of some of his friends, such as Lucette Finas and Michel Deguy. As Genette told him:

> Everyone feels, three times a day, shunned, then welcomed, then again shunned, depending on the wheeling and dealing, the pressure of external forces, and the skilful but very complex manoeuvrings of Las Vergnas, who is in the final analysis the only one who decides for the time being. [. . .] All this is very difficult, it's no longer the merry throng that started the ball rolling, a few 'principles of reality' have resurfaced.[54]

Maurice Blanchot himself, who might have been thought to have kept a great distance from this petty academic bargaining, felt obliged to become involved. He was glad that Derrida had escaped these 'very troublesome debates' by virtue of his distance. Even though he regretted having to take part, he tried to prevent rivalries between different circles and cliques of intellectuals 'mobilizing the students in the guise of more disinterested demands'.[55]

Pautrat, meanwhile, informed Derrida of the negotiations concerning the department of philosophy. He was in regular contact
with alumni of the École Normale who might be interested in
teaching at Vincennes. But discussions on this matter were no easier:

> The first reactions of Balibar and a few others were very
> negative, for political and personal reasons, but the latest
> news suggests that there might be a sudden U-turn: Badiou,
> Miller, Balibar, Macherey and others might apply – for posts
> that are, after all, limited in number. Serres would be pre
> pared to come, and Foucault's great regret is that he can't call
> on Deleuze, who's just been urgently hospitalized for a very
> serious pulmonary tuberculosis.[56]

At the École Normale Supérieure, just one memorable incident
occurred during Derrida's absence. At the request of a few new
students, who had been taught by him in *khâgne* at Henri-IV, Jean
Beaufret had been invited to give a lecture for the first time in years.
Despite a certain reluctance, Derrida did nothing to stop this. But
on the day Beaufret spoke, a group of leftists – led by Philippe
Castellin, who had come top in the entrance exam to the École in
1968 – prevented him from speaking. When he learned about this
boycott, Derrida asked Pautrat to phone Beaufret and offer his
apologies, saying that he was unable to do so in person: the events
of the beginning of the year had left their mark.

Towards the end of November, Pierre informed his parents: '[W]e
have to return now, I'm losing my French.'[57] For Derrida, too, it
was high time to go home to Paris. But the journey involved several
difficulties. The plane that had taken off from Baltimore was caught
in bad weather, which meant the Derridas missed their connection
at Boston. Derrida found this delay and the whole chaotic journey
a real trial. On the flight the following day, he spent the whole
time tense and hunched up, clenching his fists tightly. And when
Marguerite coaxed him to relax, he replied, furiously: 'Don't you
realize that I'm keeping the plane in the air by the sole force of my
will?' He was traumatized for a long time, and for several years he
refused to get back into a plane.[58]

Return to life in Paris was difficult, especially because of a significant event that had occurred during Derrida's stay in the United
States: Jean Hyppolite, his thesis supervisor and long-standing
protector, had died of a massive heart attack on the night of 27–8
October. As Derrida explained twelve years later, at his thesis viva,
this loss was not just a moment of great sadness for him; it was also
a way of drawing a line and moving on: 'By a strange coincidence, it
[Hyppolite's death] marked at that date – the autumn of 1968, and

it was indeed the autumn – the end of certain type of membership in the university.'[59]

Hyppolite's death did indeed appear as a symptom and a symbol. As Vincennes mobilized energies, the old Sorbonne was on the retreat, especially in philosophy. After the retirement of Henri Gouhier, Jean Guitton, and Jean Grenier, nobody could see how their chairs would be filled, what would happen to the lectures, and who would draw up the syllabus and the schedule. According to Maurice de Gandillac, 'the old professors reacted to the events [of '68] in such different ways that their collaboration is very difficult. Almost none of them is immune from protests.'[60]

A few weeks later, Gandillac, who hoped to obtain 'a sort of sabbatical year', sent Derrida a moving letter that gives a good idea of the atmosphere. He asked him to forgive the 'anxieties' which the other members of the examining jury and he himself had 'clumsily' expressed at the viva the year before, especially since there had been analogous difficulties with Deleuze. Gandillac realized that the events of May had 'sounded the death knell [*glas*] for a certain type of ceremonious relationship'. 'It is you, now, who are a master – a difficult master. As for us, panting after the movement and eager to carry on learning, it is sometimes hard to adapt. Forgive us, as our hearts are in the right place.'[61]

But if the old masters were all at sea, Derrida himself and many of the professors of his generation were almost as disoriented. Teaching in the United States – or in Tunisia, in the case of Foucault and Barthes – gave them a provisional refuge from an almost intolerable French academic situation – one that was at all events incompatible with the serious work Derrida hoped to accomplish. Jean-Claude Pariente, who was teaching in Clermont-Ferrand but had come to Normale Sup to give a seminar on Rousseau, could understand the weariness of his old comrade as he returned to 'this world that's pretty broken down'. 'Here, we're exhausted by all the commissions, meetings, discussions . . . Yes, we set and marked the exams and started teaching again at the end of November, but it needed a constant presence and a permanent state of alert.'[62]

As in the previous year, the Derrida family went to Gstaad, to the Bauchau home, for the Christmas vacation. Once again, it was an opportunity for long conversations. With real clairvoyance, Henry Bauchau encouraged the author of 'Plato's pharmacy' to launch out on a more literary form of writing, as a letter from a short while later confirms:

> I wonder whether you have started to write outside philosophy and yet with 'all your bags and baggage', as you put it so well. I reckon that's where you'll end up, there's a part of you that

only a poem could express. [. . .] But perhaps you still want to see things too clearly, where the place of the poem is obscure . . .[63]

It was also poetry that Derrida discussed in one of his last letters to Gabriel Bounoure. Beginning with a quotation from Mallarmé – 'I stand amid the hubbub of a shore tormented by the waves' –, he added that the 'waves' had indeed been very powerful since his return to France. But he especially wanted to share with Bounoure a nice story about his son Pierre. Hardly five and a half years old, and barely able to read, Pierre was fascinated by Mallarmé and trying to learn by heart the opening line of 'Hérodiade': 'Abolished, and her fearful wing in tears.' In the United States, Pierre had already flattered himself on being able to give his occasional female student childminders some help in interpreting Mallarmé:

> So for a while, sometimes interrupting his games, he's been bringing a little chair and a little table into my study, asking me to 'pass over your Mallarmé' and sitting there seriously, opening the book always at the same page and wearing himself out over the difficulties of the same text, probably chosen for its brevity: 'A dream in a dream'! That being said, apart from these little Mallarmean simperings, Pierre is a continuous upwelling of poetry, sometimes quite incredible – and this for us represents the miracle of the everyday.[64]

As for Derrida himself, in thrall to too many 'petty tasks and petty anxieties', he dreamed 'of distance, retirement, of a long, uninterrupted period'. He felt that his social and professional life was destroying his strength, and this vexed him all the more since he could see no way out. On the invitation of Briec Bounoure, he was to go to Brest on 23 May, to give a paper called 'The library on fire' ('La bibliothèque en feu') or, if preferable, 'The library at stake' ('La bibliothèque en jeu'). He was mainly looking forward to seeing Gabriel Bounoure again. But things turned out differently. The old writer died on 23 April 1969, one month before this trip, which thereupon lost its main raison d'être. Derrida had lost an important conversation partner – one of the few in whom he could completely confide.

6

Uncomfortable Positions

1969–1971

At the start of the academic year, in autumn 1968, while Derrida was in Baltimore, a series of lectures began, organized by *Tel Quel*'s 'Theoretical Study Group' in the heart of Paris's Saint-German-des-Prés area. These evening gatherings, part of the still turbulent wake of the May events, attracted huge audiences. It was Philippe Sollers who opened the cycle on 16 October. The two following sessions were led by Jean-Joseph Goux, a young scholar whom Derrida had much admired since the publication in *Tel Quel* of his 'Marx and the inscription of labour' and 'Numismatics'.

Fascinated by *Of Grammatology*, Goux boldly extended Derridean thought to several new fields. 'It's the most interesting thing I've read about Marx,' Derrida told him after the publication of his first article. And though he had not been able to attend the double lecture 'God, father, phallus, language', he was greatly interested by this text when he did read it.[1] Goux embodied to perfection the spirit of the collective volume *Théorie d'ensemble* (*Collective Theory*) which 'Tel Quel' published at this time: they wished to transcend traditional disciplines, if not to unify them, at least to build real bridges between the most radical Marxism, a Freudianism revised by Lacan, and the theory of writing.[2] It is probably no exaggeration to see a sort of 'Gouxo-Derridean' inflection in a concept such as *phallogentricism*, which Derrida came to prefer increasingly to logocentrism from the early 1970s onwards.

In January 1969, a few weeks after Derrida's return to France, three evening gatherings of the Theoretical Study Group were devoted to 'the engendering of the formula' by Julia Kristeva. This involved a reading of Sollers' *Numbers*, as detailed as Derrida's 'Dissemination', which appeared at almost the same time in two issues of *Critique*. But Kristeva's point of view, distinguishing between 'genotext' and 'phenotext' to establish 'semanalysis', was very different from Derrida's. 'As regards *Numbers*,' Sollers now acknowledges, 'it could be said that there was a theoretical competition between Derrida and Kristeva.'[3] This is also the impression of Goux, who was at the time friendly with all three protagonists:

> There was doubtless an anxiety on the part of Sollers that Derrida would have too great an impact on *Tel Quel* and his own work. Beyond the homage, Sollers must have read Derrida's immense article on *Numbers* as an attempt at appropriation. Sollers was flattered and at the same time scared by this text, which was much more than a commentary. And Derrida's growing prestige must have seemed dangerous, just when it was mainly important to foster the rise of Julia Kristeva as the main theorist of the review.[4]

But for now, any conflict was muted, if not virtual, and everything seemed to be passing off for the best. On 26 February and 5 March 1969, Derrida presented to a packed hall a lecture that bore no title, but was later published in *Tel Quel* as 'The double session'. Over the years, Derrida had gained considerably in confidence: what he proposed on these two evenings was more a performance than the delivery of a traditional lecture. As Catherine Clément wrote to him shortly afterwards:

> What you are doing is rather like an incantation, and differs from it by an appeal to writing; like a mime, and differs from it by the non-representable; like opera – a marriage of voice-gesture-body-setting – and differs from it by the absence of distance; like a clown [. . .], and differs from it by the lack of difference among the signifiers: none of them is privileged, as being more fertile in un/reading than any other.[5]

It was Mallarmé, long since one of Derrida's fetish authors, who was the centre of 'The double session'. And it was, *inter alia*, the foundations of thematic criticism that he endeavoured to deconstruct, in the shape of its most ambitious realization: Jean-Pierre Richard's *The Imaginary Universe of Mallarmé*.

> It is obvious – and this will later receive further confirmation – that the fact that we have chosen to focus on the 'blank' and the 'fold' is not an accident. This is both because of the specific effects of these two elements in Mallarmé's text and precisely because they have systematically been recognized as *themes* by modern criticism. Now, if we can begin to see that the 'blank' and the 'fold' cannot in fact be mastered as themes or as meanings, if it is within the folds and the blankness of a certain hymen that the very textuality of the text is re-marked, then we

will precisely have determined the limits of thematic criticism itself.[6]

According to Derrida, the blank designates the diversity of blanks that appear in the text '*plus* the writing site [. . .] where such a totality is produced'. There is, however, no question of turning the blank of the page of writing into 'the fundamental signified or signifier in the series. [. . .] This "last" blank (one could equally well say this "first" blank) comes neither before nor after the series.'[7] Nothing either can or should arrest the interplay of slippages and drifts at the heart of writing. Instead of the hermeneutic concept of 'polysemia', Derrida wanted to deploy that of 'dissemination'. This new mode of writing, which he was here starting to put into practice, would find its most radical application five years later in *Glas*.

On a completely different level, spring 1969 was marked by the departure of General de Gaulle. After the crisis of the previous year, he had attempted to regain some personal legitimacy. So regional reform acted as the pretext for holding a referendum. On 27 April, the 'no' votes won. As he had said he would, de Gaulle resigned on the following day. A few weeks later, Georges Pompidou, his former Prime Minister, was elected President.

Even though Derrida was always a man of the Left, he did not share the gut hostility to de Gaulle of many of his contemporaries. In a late interview with Franz-Olivier Giesbert, he even mentioned General de Gaulle as the only politician he had really admired, apart from Nelson Mandela: 'Even when I was anti-Gaullist, in the sixties, I was fascinated by a person like that who could marry everything – vision and calculation, idealism and empiricism. Skilful and cunning like all good politicians, he stood head and shoulders above them with his grand ideas, his verbal felicities, and the theatrical performances of his press conferences.'[8] On this subject, Derrida was the complete opposite of Maurice Blanchot, who loathed de Gaulle with a permanent and virulent loathing. A few days after the General's departure, Blanchot even wrote to Derrida: 'I have to admit that, for a moment, I felt myself breathing more easily and, waking in the middle of the night, wondering: "But what's happening? Some weight has been lifted? Ah yes: de Gaulle."'[9]

In the rue d'Ulm, another departure perturbed spirits even more than the General's: the departure of Jacques Lacan. Since 1964, every Wednesday just before noon, the pavements of the rue d'Ulm had been invaded by flash cars and pretty women. Lacan himself turned up in his Mercedes 300 SL, before entering the Salle Dussane, where a dense throng piled in to attend his seminar. People smoked very heavily, especially since the master himself set the example; the resulting smoke was so dense that it passed up through the ceiling and drifted through the floor above, rousing frequent complaints. In the eyes of the Director of the École, Lacan was simply a trendy lecturer and a thorough nuisance to boot. He had been seeking a pretext to get rid of him for some time. As Dominique Lecourt remembers:

> One morning in 1969, Robert Flacelière called me into his office, which was unusual, and told me: 'M. Lecourt, you're a philosopher – I've noticed you've been attending Lacan's lectures on truth and I'd like to know what you think about them . . . In your view, is it serious stuff? Personally, all that business about the phallus, I find it obscene . . . The reason I'm asking you is that M. Derrida and M. Althusser tell me it's serious stuff.' The scene was like something out of *Ubu Roi*. I tried to argue a case, unaware that he'd already decided to send Lacan packing. Flacelière found that this trendy, provocative approach had nothing in common with the École's real mission. But when he wanted to act out his resentment and kick Lacan out, there was uproar.[10]

On 26 June 1969, Lacan made public the letter of exclusion that 'Flatulencière' had sent him: yet again, he felt he was being exiled as a public enemy. Immediately after the end of the session, several faithful listeners, including the artist Jean-Jacques Lebel, Philippe Sollers, Julia Kristeva, and Antoinette Fouque, a major figure in French feminism, improvised an occupation of the Director's office. The situation rapidly turned nasty: Philippe Castellin – who had already led the revolt against Jean Beaufret the previous year – started smoking Flacelière's cigars, and then slapped him on the face.[11] Sollers merely appropriated a pile of headed notepaper, which he jubilantly used over the following months. But the whole affair went beyond the merely anecdotal. 'The question of Lacan played a part in distancing me from Derrida,' Sollers acknowledges. 'Like Althusser, he was still in certain respects an institution man. Both of them gave Lacan only lukewarm support, while at the time he was in a dreadfully isolated position, abandoned by his daughter Judith as well as by his son-in-law. It was in this period that I started to draw closer to him.'[12]

In the rue d'Ulm, the 'maos' had long been in the majority, at least as far as the philosophers were concerned. Dominique Dhombres, who entered the École in 1967, remembers that 'it took just a year for me to shift from Paul Ricoeur to Mao Zedong, then to working in a factory, as was the custom'. Luckily for Derrida, several pupils of more Heideggerean sensibilities arrived at Normale Sup at the end of the 1960s: Emmanuel Martineau, Jean-Luc Marion, Rémi Brague, Alain Renaut, and Jean-François Courtine, among others.

Bernard-Henri Lévy entered in 1968. In his book *Comedy*, he gave a colourful account of his first meeting with Derrida:

> Then came the beginning of the academic year. The master received, in private, the new students in that office in the rue d'Ulm of which we had all dreamed. There he was. In flesh and bones. Younger than I had imagined. Pleasanter, too. Almost friendly. Good heavens! The philosopher, the giant, the pitiless deconstructor, the mysterious writer of whom I could never have guessed that he had a doctrine on such trivial questions as a 'thesis outline', a 'topic for a Masters', a 'syllabus for a *licence* or for the *agrégation*' – could it be him, that immense personality, that travelling companion of *Tel Quel*, that artist, just like, quite simply, taking the time to welcome his new pupils and talking to them in a language that was the same as that of all normal professors? Yes. It was indeed him. I could weep at the thought. I was so moved that I was speechless. 'Who are you? What do you do? Are you a Germanist? A Hellenist? A Kantian or Nietzschean? A dialectician *à la* Hegel or *à la* Plato? An idea, in a word? A concept?'[13]

Lévy was so intimidated to find himself at last face to face with the master, all of whose books he had read, that he could manage no more than to introduce himself as a friend of Benesti: a cousin of Derrida's, a prosperous chemist in Neuilly, from whom Lévy obtained his supply of amphetamines. The allusion to this cousin – who considered 'Jackie' as the family failure, even though he was apparently a 'dab hand' in his field – caused a considerable chill and brought this first meeting to an end. Having 'mixed up Plato's pharmacy with Benesti's' was an 'unforgivable gaffe', a mistake which, in Lévy's view, compromised his relationships with Derrida for good.

However, they got on better over the next few months. Like many students at the École, the future 'BHL' felt a priori more drawn to Althusser. But Derrida was more present and much more accessible. During one conversation, he helped the future author of *Barbarism with a Human Face* to avoid a dreadful mistake.

> Derrida did me an enormous favour in 1970! I'd reworked the papers on Artaud and Nietzsche that I'd given at his seminar and I really wanted to turn them into a book. In *Le Monde*, I'd seen an advert for a publisher who was looking for manuscripts to publish . . . La Pensée universelle! I sent them my text, my heart beating. They replied that they were interested. But they needed 10,000 francs to defray costs. When I told him this, Derrida burst out laughing: 'You're mad – it's a con!'[14]

Despite the increasing popularity of his seminar, Derrida sometimes dreamed of leaving the 'gilded fortress' of the École and going
back into the university system. Though he had abandoned the idea
of writing a traditional thesis since the death of Jean Hyppolite,
the new opportunities opened up in the wake of May 1968 seemed
to involve less burdensome modes of entry. He confided in Pierre
Aubenque, now a professor at the Sorbonne, whose reply was
encouraging. He said he had recently had a long conversation with
Maurice de Gandillac on the subject of two or three philosophers
who could take advantage of the new regulations, whereby they
could put forward published work as a thesis: 'We talked mainly
about you and Althusser, and Gandillac didn't think there'd be any
major obstacles, especially for you.'[15] But he would need to investigate further, since there were few precedents. Over the autumn
of 1969, Derrida and Aubenque both talked the matter over with
Canguilhem, who would be fully in favour, on a personal level, but
was worried about the reluctance on principle of several colleagues,
at least initially. The project was shelved for a long time.[16]

Things were easier in foreign universities, where Derrida was being
welcomed with growing enthusiasm. He returned to Berlin at the beginning of July 1969, then regularly over the next year, giving a seminar
in the Department of Comparative Literature to some forty or so students. During these trips, he made the acquaintance of a young man
from Luxembourg, Rodolphe Gasché, whose son became one of his
most reliable supporters, and wrote an account of *Of Grammatology*
at Hans-Georg Gadamer's request before embarking on a translation
of *Writing and Difference* for the great publishing house Suhrkamp.
Derrida also met Werner Hamacher, who, like Gasché, later spent a
long period at Normale Sup, auditing the seminar, and who became a
staunch Derridean, in the United States and Germany.

At the Free University, Berlin, where the pressure of Marxism
was as great as in Paris, it was with Samuel Weber that Derrida
had the closest professional and personal relationships. He also
continued to be close to Peter Szondi, even though the latter,
increasingly isolated within his own department, viewed the evolution of the seminar with mistrust. Szondi wrote to a friend, with a
hint of bitterness: 'People are increasingly indulging in an esoteric
style of reading, *à la* Derrida (it is painful for me to say this, since I
like Derrida a great deal); they fantasize about texts, as Liszt wrote
fantasias on themes by Bach.'[17*]

In Britain, too, there was increasing interest in deconstruction.
On 25 September 1969, a long, serious review of *Of Grammatology*

---

* Peter Szondi committed suicide in Berlin on 18 October 1971, just over a year
after Paul Celan and, like him, by drowning.

appeared in the *Times Literary Supplement*, by Philippe Sollers; it aroused considerable curiosity.[18] At the invitation of Alan Montefiore, whom he had met at Cerisy back in 1959, Derrida went to Balliol College in February and May 1970. 'I brought him over partly out of a spirit of contrariness,' recalls Montefiore.

> His work and that of other French philosophers was looked down on in Great Britain. I was swimming against this current, publishing regular reviews of what was coming out in France in *Philosophy*. But for my students, and even often for me, Derrida's works were still very difficult to get a handle on. I'd asked him to let those taking part in these encounters speak before he did, so they could ask him about what they didn't understand. In discussions of this kind, he was remarkably clear.[19]

In France, this period was marked by several polemics, these days largely difficult to get excited by. Now that the Communist Party has lost most of its prestige and influence, it is not easy to realize how important it was straight after 1968, at a time when many young intellectuals decided to join the Party so as to ward off pressure from the extreme Left. Antoine Casanova, who was at the time the editor in chief of *La Nouvelle Critique* and, since 1970, a member of the Central Committee, acknowledges that, these days, it is almost impossible to understand the 'advances, limits, blindspots, and difficulties in escaping from previous frameworks of thought, action, and argument' that then preoccupied the Communists.[20] Far from being monolithic, the Party was home to several intellectual tendencies, which sometimes clashed over somewhat strange issues.

On 12 September 1969, *L'Humanité* published a long article by Jean-Pierre Faye with the title 'Comrade Mallarmé'. Even though Sollers and *Tel Quel* were his main targets, Faye was implicitly attacking Derrida. He vigorously protested against the idea that the whole history of the West was founded on the '"debasing" of writing, its repression at the hands of speech'. In his view, certain people had even managed 'to identify, quite seriously, speech to the bourgeoisie and writing to the proletariat'. Faye went even further than this caricature.* With his cryptic references to Heidegger and

---

* In 1967, in his interview with *Les Lettres françaises*, Derrida reacted angrily to this reading. Never, he assured readers, had it been for him a question of rehabilitating writing against speech or protesting against the voice. The main thing, in his view, was to analyse the history of a hierarchy and not in the least to oppose 'a graphocentrism to a logocentrism, [n]or, in general, any center to any other center' (*Positions*, p. 10). It is far from clear that Derrida's more enthusiastic commentators have always shown the same caution.

the notion of *mythos*, he tried to cast a shadow of political suspicion over Derrida, suggesting a link between his work and the 'retrograde revolution' that brought Hitler to power.

Derrida abstained from any reaction. But the following week, a double response appeared in *L'Humanité*. One came from Claude Prévost, a member of the editorial board of *La Nouvelle Critique*. The other was written by Sollers:

> Alluding to the theory of writing that we consider to be scientifically founded by the pathbreaking book by Jacques Derrida, *Of Grammatology* (1967), M. Faye, who in any case comments on no more than a fragmentary aspect of the work, which he misinterprets, states peremptorily that it constitutes a continuation of Nazi ideology. This suggestion is extremely grave. Not only does Derrida criticize Heidegger at several points, but to insinuate that this work might have the least point in common with Nazism is an act of *defamation*. Targeting simultaneously Derrida through *Tel Quel* and *Tel Quel* through Derrida, M. Faye claims (always by insinuation) that we have '*identified speech with the bourgeoisie and writing with the proletariat*'; that we support the view that '*history has not stopped going backwards in the West*', etc. But statements such as these can absolutely not be found anywhere either in Derrida or in *Tel Quel*.[21]

Rather curiously, Faye wrote to Derrida that the remarks attributed to him about the latter

> constitute a gross lie. Those who have put this lie into circulation bear the responsibility for it. As for myself, let me say clearly, and publicly, that your name has never been mixed up with any of that, in this tone. Let me also express the esteem and admiration that I have had for your work, as you well know, for several years.

He also said he would like to have with Derrida 'that friendly conversation' that they had been planning to have for several months. However, Faye asked Derrida, 'provisionally' and 'to avoid any further wilful misinterpretation', not to make this letter public.[22] On 10 October, he published in *L'Humanité* a statement to 'clear matters up': in it, he insisted that he had nothing but esteem and admiration for Derrida and his philosophy.

This did not stop the polemic from dragging on in *Tel Quel* and *Change*; indeed, the atmosphere deteriorated even more. In *La Gazette de Lausanne*, Faye, who had been working for several months on the philosophical roots of Nazism, attacked Derrida explicitly, claiming that in his work there was 'a sort of blindspot marked by the influence of the philosophy of Heidegger and by what is, in that philosophy, already a blindspot, an ideological *stain* [*tache*] whose origin lies in the most regressive elements of German ideology between the wars'.[23] From now on, the relationship between Derrida and Faye would be one of permanent hostility – and this would have far from negligible consequences a decade or so later.

One result of these dark quarrels was that Derrida became close to Jean-Louis Houdebine. He was a member of the Communist Party, ran the review *Promesse*, and was a friend of Sollers and Kristeva. He published articles frequently in *La Nouvelle Critique*, and was eager to open it up more to modern trends. This was not always an easy task: while a new gathering at Cluny was being organized, Houdebine wrote to Derrida to say how much his philosophy was 'sidelined, repressed' within the Party. 'This is due to very deep resistances that are difficult to overcome,' as Sollers had warned him.[24]

The second Cluny conference, held from 2 to 4 April 1970, took as its theme 'Literature and Ideologies'. Derrida, who had not taken part in the first conference, missed this one as well, but his work often came up, leading to a violent clash on this occasion between *Tel Quel* and *Action poétique*, the review edited by Henri Deluy that was also linked to the Communist Party but was much more eclectic. Tensions ran so high that one of those present actually fainted. The young linguist Mitsou Ronat, a close friend of Faye, was given the task of attacking Kristeva, with no holds barred. Élisabeth Roudinesco laid into Derrida, comparing his work with Jung's. When he heard about this, Derrida was flabbergasted.

Roudinesco still remembers these quarrels vividly:

That evening, the *telqueliens* complained to the organizers about the violence of the attacks. Mitsou Ronat and I were given an official rap on the knuckles and we had to negotiate for much of that night to ensure it wouldn't be made public. Christine Buci-Glucksmann and Catherine Clément were chosen to respond to us the following day. We seemed to be in a minority, but in actual fact *Tel Quel* had lost its battle for intellectual and literary control of the Party. They'd been trying to impose a 'line', a single, rigid theory, something we absolutely wanted to avoid. It was largely because of this setback that Sollers became more radical and moved towards Maoism the following year.[25]

These quarrels may have attacked Derrida's work but they did not really involve him, and were far removed from the questions that he was really interested in. In 1969 and 1970, he started to form new alliances.

He began exchanging views with Jean-Luc Nancy, a young assistant lecturer at the University of Strasbourg. It was Nancy who took the initiative, sending Derrida an article in which he discussed his work, before it was published in the *Bulletin de la faculté de lettres de Strasbourg*. Derrida sent him in return a long letter which showed how well he knew the young philosopher's work:

> I already knew, having read your work several times in *Esprit*, that we were bound to meet or that, at least, our paths would cross. Your letter and your article surpass my expectations: warmest thanks.
>
> I won't be able to answer all the questions – decisive and incisive – that you formulate, both discreetly and forcefully. I also wonder about them, as you can probably guess, and the perplexity that you express openly in your letter, as you know [. . .] is one that I cannot fail to share. [. . .] Yes, too, on the matter of 'ideology', of 'science'. We read our 'contemporaries' in a similar way. We need to work. But it's a minefield, more than ever.[26]

At the end of his letter, Derrida mentioned the text in which he thought he had gone 'furthest' in discussing the matters raised by Nancy: 'The ends of man', a paper that he was preparing for a conference in Brussels, once he had given it in New York. He offered to send him this text: he did not envisage publishing it in France, at least not for the time being: 'I'm not really interested in publication just now, I'm even rather scared at the prospect. And I think this state of affairs is going to last.'

Nancy was very touched by this letter; the intimacy of its tone meant he felt less isolated. But he did not know whether he would be up to a meeting with Derrida – he was worried he might not be able to 'unpack correctly my no doubt rather inchoate intuitions'. Nancy came from a very different background from Derrida. Born in Bordeaux in 1940, into a Catholic family, he had been shaped by the JEC, the Jeunesse Étudiante Chrétienne (Christian Student Youth). After several attempts to get into Normale Sup, he had done a Masters under the supervision of Paul Ricoeur. He had originally gone to Strasbourg to study theology, but he soon moved away from the subject. Here, Lucien Braun, then an assistant lecturer in the Department of Literature, introduced him to Philippe Lacoue-Labarthe.

> We immediately got on really well, even though we were very different. Philippe was an atheist, more political than me, more literary, too. He'd published a few things in *Le Nouveau Commerce* and was still close to Gérard Genette, a teacher he'd

had in *hypokhâgne* in Le Mans, before being Gérard Granel's student in Bordeaux. Coming across *Of Grammatology* from different angles, we'd both been excited by it. Derrida represented living philosophy for us: there was somebody doing philosophy right in front of our eyes, producing concepts that we would have to work with. Derrida had provided the missing link in the chain from Hegel to Heidegger; he enabled me to read Husserl. Braun was afraid I might leave for Nanterre, where Ricoeur wanted me to be his assistant. He intuitively realized that if he brought Philippe and me together, he'd be able to keep both of us . . . May 1968 was a time of great upheaval in Strasbourg. There were many debates and a great desire for radical positions. We were very distrustful of the Communist Party, vaguely attracted to Maoism, but even more fascinated by Situationism – Philippe especially.[27]

At the beginning of 1970, Nancy and Lacoue-Labarthe invited Derrida to take part in a seminar on rhetoric, within the context of the newly established 'Groupe de recherches sur les théories du signe et du texte' ('Research Group on Theories of the Sign and the Text'). Gérard Genette and Jean-François Lyotard also attended. The paper which Derrida proposed, with the title 'The white mythology', was a fragment taken from his seminar at Normale Sup:

It'll be about the status of metaphor in the text of philosophy, aimed at bringing out the 'metaphysical' traits of the concept of metaphor that may guide and thereby neutralize this problematic. [. . .] The pretext, if not the guiding thread, of this analysis will be a passage from *The Garden of Epicurus* by Anatole France (yes!). The real guiding thread goes from Nietzsche to Heidegger.[28]

Derrida went to Strasbourg for the first time on 8 and 9 March 1970. This meeting, in many ways a milestone, was recounted in detail by Lacoue-Labarthe in an eloquent homage improvised shortly after Derrida's death:

He was one of our first three guests in the little 'research group' that Jean-Luc and I had managed to set up, after '68. What struck me – three things, unforgettable: the infinite sadness of his gaze, as he came out of the station with Genette and before he saw Jean-Luc and myself, who had gone to pick him up; it was the gaze of Kafka in the photos, of Celan too (and indeed, his first words were to tell us of the death of Celan, which he had just heard about). His incredible mastery, then, in his paper 'White mythology', which left me stunned, floored, stammering, shamefaced, when I needed to respond shortly afterwards (but then, immediately, his benevolence, dazzling, his kindness, much more than just an attentive understanding: his smile . . .). Finally, that evening – and against all expectations –, his gaiety, his vivacity, or rather the joy that could, all of a sudden, be so characteristic. [29]

A few months before this homage, the last time Derrida went to Strasbourg, Lacoue-Labarthe and Nancy had together related other memories of that stay:

We remember a walk along the Ill: Philippe went ahead with Genette, Jean-Luc followed with Derrida (Lyotard hadn't arrived yet). Genette and Philippe knew each other and were chatting away; but Jean-Luc was discovering Derrida's capacity for silence and was rather nervous about finding himself reduced to pointing out in turn the Rohan palace, the cathedral, the old customs house, none of which really called for any response . . . On the other hand, a bit later, he became more talkative, and told us a recent story about one of his sons, still very young, who'd headed off on his bike, on a main road, without permission. The fear Derrida had felt was still tangible. We were a bit surprised: we'd just learned that you don't always have to talk philosophy with a philosopher, and that the place for work is in texts. [30]

The bonds between Nancy and Lacoue-Labarthe rapidly grew stronger, and led to several joint projects.

It was at about the same time that Derrida got to know Sarah Kofman, whom he soon introduced to the two adoptive Strasbourgeois. Born in Paris in 1934, the daughter of a rabbi who had been arrested and deported in 1942, she had lived the entire latter stages of the war as a child in hiding, in particularly dramatic circumstances that she revealed only in her last book, *Rue Ordener, rue Labat*. She became acquainted with Derrida in 1968. Kofman was writing her thesis on 'Nietzsche and metaphor', with Jean Hyppolite as a supervisor. When he died, she asked Derrida to step in; as he was not officially qualified to do so, it was Gilles Deleuze who eventually took over. This did not stop Kofman being one of the most faithful members of the audience at Derrida's seminar in the rue d'Ulm, and she became a close colleague.

In June 1970, Derrida was mainly preoccupied by the health of his father, which rapidly deteriorated. Aimé had been suffering from nephrenic colic for a while, and lost weight to an alarming degree. The doctors diagnosed a stomach ulcer, then a depressive condition.

The summer was overshadowed by this worsening illness, as the doctors could not come up with any precise diagnosis. Jacques was irritable and exhausted and unable to work on the text on Condillac he had brought with him to Nice. 'My father's illness has given me, and is still giving me, so much anxiety that I've lost all my strength and courage,' he wrote to Nancy.[31]

Hospitalized for pleurisy, Aimé Derrida died on 18 October 1970, 'after two months of anxiety, uncertainty, and even enigma'.[32] In fact, he had probably been suffering from pancreatic cancer – the same illness from which Jacques himself would die, at exactly the same age.[33] Over the last two weeks, Derrida travelled increasingly between Paris and Nice; he continued with his visits, to support his mother, and these trips were all the more exhausting as he still refused to take the plane. Shaken by this death, which he had not been expecting, he felt haggard, lost, 'barely able to keep up a professional façade'.[34]

Things at the École Normale Supérieure had been very restless over the post-'68 years, but it went through a real crisis at the start of 1971. In February, a strike continued for several weeks. The Action Committee known as 'Damocles', which had been fomenting the movement, decided to organize a big party to celebrate the centenary of the Commune. Over five thousand people were welcomed to the École on the evening of 20 March 1971. But the organizers of the party could not keep control and the night ended in violence. The war memorial was vandalized, several rooms were pillaged, as was the library, and a fire was started. On the morning of Sunday, 21 March, the École looked like a battlefield. President Georges Pompidou, an alumnus, was deeply shocked. He took the unprecedented step of asking Olivier Guichard, the Education Minister, to close the École for two weeks. When he learned that Robert Flacelière had been away on the evening in question, the President was furious, and demanded his resignation. Pierre Aubenque, who was quite a close colleague of Derrida's, was initially suggested as a replacement director for the École. But Pompidou preferred to call on the top student of his own year, the Hellenist Jean Bousquet, to restore order.[35]

A few weeks after these events, Derrida left for Algeria, with Marguerite, Pierre, and Jean, for a fortnight. He was due to give a series of lectures at the University of Algiers, but he was mainly looking forward to revisiting the places he had known in his youth, for the first time since summer 1962. Unfortunately, the visit was far from being a success, as he told Roger Laporte:

> This trip was difficult in every way. A depressing return to the 'archaic' places of my childhood; a country that you are

really glad to see has attained independence, and, basically, is functioning okay, but also bogged down in dreadful problems (unemployment, over-population, etc.) that are visible at first glance; a university full to bursting (18,000 students) but without any political liberty (the student union has been dissolved, there's very strict ideological control, the right of assembly and putting up political posters forbidden, etc.). Then the discomfort with the children, rain almost all the time. So we came back home earlier than expected.[36]

This did not stop Derrida from falling prey to violent attacks of '*nostalgeria*' over the following years. In letters to his friend Pierre Foucher, who had long been teaching in Algeria, he said how much 'this whole buried past still worked on [him] silently but powerfully'.[37] 'I sometimes have fits of nostalgia so strong I could fall over backwards in a faint. I'm hardly exaggerating. As soon as I get the opportunity (time, money), I'll go and spend a few days there.'[38]

Like several of his contemporaries, Gérard Granel had been in a state of deep intellectual crisis ever since May 1968. Before then he had seemed to take little interest in politics; now he put it foremost among his preoccupations. He sent Derrida the texts he had recently published and asked him questions on several points, beginning with 'the enigma of his silence on Marx'.[39] Admittedly, he was not the first to do so, but he was the only one to whom Derrida bothered to reply at such length, and so frankly. 'If I'd seen where the "main thing" is, in Marx and in everything that's at issue in his name, if I'd managed to read this whole field in a way that was not *regressive* in comparison with what "I" am attempting elsewhere [. . .], I'd have had my say on Marx,' he wrote to Granel.[40]

Of course, he explained, some people thought that you need to express an opinion on everything. For instance, he had just been asked to take part in an interview on atheism, for a volume in which Jean Rostand, Claude Lévi-Strauss, Edgar Morin, and François Jacob would also hold forth on the subject, but he 'of course' told the purported interviewer of his 'definite silence' on the matter. Likewise he turned down a radio programme on Blanchot, even though the latter was one of the authors who counted most for him.*

---

* The letter of refusal which Derrida sent to the Belgian radio and television authorities was completely characteristic of his attitude to the media at that time. He mistrusted the lot of them, even those that were the most attentive to and respectful of his work. 'You may know how greatly I am convinced of the significance of the thought of Maurice Blanchot – whose true importance has not yet been appreciated – and how much it counts for me. This is the main reason for which it seems to me difficult to "talk" about it in a radio interview, to "decide what I think"

The text of the author of *Capital* was 'stratified, diversified, has no "truth"', but it was currently being subjected to an interpretative strategy that Derrida deemed, 'in the main, metaphysical and regressive'. However, he did not wish to attack this strategy head-on, since in the circumstances it would be a reactionary move. 'I'll never fall into anti-Communism, so I'm shutting my mouth. And I know this annoys everyone, and that certain people don't much care, as you do, to "respect" my silence.'

Acknowledging that his attitude 'may wrongly give the impression of apoliticism, or rather "apraxia"', Derrida finished this long letter by announcing, as it were, what would twenty-two years later become *Specters of Marx*:

> I will never emerge from this silence until I have done the work. And this work, I can sense, knowing as I do my style and my rhythms, will never give rise to a 'conversion', but to oblique incisions, sideways shifts, following this or that unnoticed vein in the Marxist text or the 'revolution' of which it is the discourse. [. . .] Meanwhile, what else should one do than work within the limits of the rigour of which one is capable [. . .] and to act 'on the left' every time one can, in the field one perceives or looks over, when the situation is clear enough for this, without having too many illusions about the microscopic effects of any such 'action'.

'To act "on the left" every time one can': this would continue to be Derrida's line of conduct, even though he was accused by some people of taking a stance only belatedly. When the situation seemed 'clear enough' to him, he would reply without wavering to requests made of him. On 12 November 1970, he signed the petition against the censorship to which *Eden Eden Eden* by Pierre Guyotat had fallen;* co-signatories included Jérôme Lindon, Jean-Paul Sartre, Simone de Beauvoir, Pierre Boulez, Michel Foucault, and a great number of writers, those of the New Novel and *Tel Quel* among others. Two weeks later, he replied, along with four hundred French intellectuals, to the appeal launched by *La Nouvelle Critique* demanding that Angela Davis be set free. On 19 January 1971, in *L'Humanité*, he signalled for the first time his support for the Palestinian cause: after the repeated acts of bloody aggression by the Jordanian army, he signed an appeal 'against any attempt to

---

and bring together my ideas about him in a few minutes on the basis of a few questions. I sincerely regret this: please understand my scruples' (letter from Derrida to a representative of the RTB, 13 December 1969).

* This attracted controversy for its linguistic experiments and alleged obscenity. – Tr.

liquidate the Palestinian resistance', calling on 'public opinion and all democratic forces to bring about a political solution that cannot be envisaged apart from the right of peoples to self-determination'.[41]

A few months later, the George Jackson affair saw him getting much more personally involved. Jackson was a Black militant, incarcerated in a Californian prison; after the death of a white warden during a riot, he was unjustly accused of murder together with two other Black prisoners. But the book in which Jackson relates his story, *Soledad Brothers*, had a profound impact on American public opinion and turned this young twenty-eight-year-old American Black into a symbol of the struggle of the Black Panthers. The work was published in French by Gallimard with a preface by Jean Genet, who had spent three months with Black revolutionaries, and engaged on a veritable tour round American universities with them. In July 1971, when Jackson was due to be sentenced, Genet launched an appeal for a committee of support for the imprisoned Black political militants,* then asked the signatories to add their own contributions to a book about Jackson.

Derrida wrote his reply on the crossing to the United States, in the form of a letter to Genet. But on 21 August 1971, two days before his trial was due to begin, Jackson was shot down by the police, officially for attempted escape. The book lost its raison d'être and the very subtle piece written by Derrida was never published. While restating his support for the cause of Black prisoners, he told Genet of his reluctance about the form chosen. He was mainly concerned that such a work might reduce 'this huge issue to a more or less literary, or even publishing, event – to an intelligentsia busy whipping up signatures and providing itself with a certain French, even Parisian, image'.

> That's why I'm still hesitating to take part in the collective action you mentioned to me; and that's why I fear the way that

---

* The appeal was accompanied by a manifesto by Genet called 'For George Jackson', reprinted in his posthumous work *The Declared Enemy: Texts and Interviews*, ed. by Albert Dichy, tr. by Jeff Fort (Stanford, Calif.: Stanford University Press, 2004) – first published in French in 1991. In the penultimate paragraph of this manifesto, Genet wrote: 'I have come to that part of my speech where, to help save the blacks, I am calling for crime, for the assassination of whites' (p. 69). In its radical violence, such a phrase flies in the face of *all* Derrida's political positions, throughout his life. It may well be felt that the signatories – who included Maurice Blanchot, Marguerite Duras, Pierre Guyotat, and Philippe Sollers – read and approved merely the appeal on behalf of Black prisoners, and not the contents of Genet's accompanying manifesto. At all events, thanks to Hadrien Laroche, the author of the book *Le Dernier Genet* (Paris: Seuil, coll. 'Fiction & Cie', 1997), for drawing my attention to this problem. It calls for a long analysis which I cannot embark on here.

people might one day place such importance on the 'literary talent' (which must also be acknowledged, of course, you're quite right, and it's not you that I'm suspecting here – it should also be used, I agree) of the 'poet' Jackson. And other similar traps. Will we ever know who's laying a trap for whom in this scenario? [. . .] With the best will in the world, with the most sincere moral indignation against what remains, of course, intolerable and unacceptable, what people say they are trying to free might then be imprisoned anew. A crime domesticated.[42]

Whether or not they were published, these concrete acts of solidarity were far from being sufficient to meet people's expectations. Among those closest to Derrida, some were even more impatient than Gérard Granel to get some reaction out of him to the theoretical questions that seemed to them the most urgent, starting with Marxism-Leninism. This was the case with Jean-Louis Houdebine and Guy Scarpetta, the editors of *Promesse*. Originally, this was a poetry review based in Poitiers, but Houdebine and Scarpetta gradually transformed it into a satellite of *Tel Quel*. When, in May 1971, they asked Derrida for an in-depth interview, the author of 'The double session' immediately realized what was at stake. 'What an ideological situation over the past few months! And what violence in the confrontations!' Houdebine had recently written to him.[43] Derrida agreed to face up to this violence.

The interview took place in his office at Normale Sup on the afternoon of 11 June 1971.[44] Even though the discussion was probing, the tone remained perfectly courteous. Derrida, who said that he had accepted such an interview for the first time, was admired greatly by both Houdebine and Scarpetta and for his part he had no intention of evading their questions. Though he had not reacted publicly to the attacks of Jean-Pierre Faye and Élisabeth Roudinesco, he did so now, clearly, firmly, and sometimes ironically. While restating his support for Sollers and *Tel Quel*, he refused to be enrolled under the banner of dialectical materialism, insisting that there would be 'no theoretical or political benefit to be derived from precipitating contacts or articulations, as long as their conditions have not been rigorously elucidated'. Between the work of deconstruction that he himself was carrying out, and the Marxist panoply of concepts, 'the conjunction cannot be *immediately given*'.[45] What had appeared as 'necessary and urgent' to him in the historical situation which they shared was 'a general determination of the conditions of emergence and the limits of philosophy, of metaphysics'. Replying implicitly to Faye, Derrida maintained that Heidegger's text was of great importance to him, comprising 'a new and irreversible advance, all of whose critical resources we are far from having exploited'. This had not prevented him from marking, 'in *all* the essays' he had published, 'a *departure* from the Heideggerean problematic'.[46]

The next day, Houdebine thanked Derrida warmly for his patience in replying to all their questions. But a few days later, when he informed Sollers about the interview, he described 'a position more defensive than offensive', a great number of 'precautions', and much 'prudence'.[47] Things were far from over. On 1 July, Houdebine sent Derrida the transcript of the interview, together with a letter of markedly Leninist inspiration, part of which would be published as an appendix to the interview. Derrida, for his part, did not merely review his remarks with minute attention; he added a very long note, extremely vigorous in tone, on Lacan – another subject.

> In the texts that I have published so far, the absence of references to Lacan, in effect, is almost total. This is justified not only by the aggressions in the form of, or with the aim of, reappropriation that Lacan, since the appearance of *De la grammatologie* in *Critique* (1968) (and even earlier, I am told), has proliferated, whether directly or indirectly, in private or in public, in his seminars, and from 1965 on, as I was to notice myself reading them, in almost *each* of his writings. [. . .] This constriction of discourse – which I regret – was not insignificant, and, here too, called for silent listening.[48]

When Derrida had written his first articles, he stated, he had known only two or three of Lacan's texts, even though he was already 'assured of the importance of this problematic in the field of psychoanalysis'. Ever since, on reading the *Écrits* closely, he had discovered several of the main themes that he was himself endeavouring to question: 'a telos of "full speech" in its essential tie [. . .] to Truth', and 'a light-hearted reference to the authority of phonology, and more precisely to Saussurean linguistics', together with an absence of any specific probing of the 'question of writing'. He announced that he had been greatly interested by the 'Seminar on *The Purloined Letter*' and would soon be coming back to it.[49] This he did in November 1971, in a lecture at Johns Hopkins University, probably the same as that also given at Yale.

On 30 July, Houdebine said he had received the revised and enlarged interview. The whole piece comprised, in his view, 'an important text, a series of highly productive markers in the ideological field of the new academic year'; he had no doubt that it would 'have quite an impact'.[50] Derrida insisted that the text not be shown to anyone before publication, scheduled for November. This did not stop Houdebine from describing the contents of the interview – including the note on Lacan – when he met up with Sollers and Kristeva on the Île de Ré.

The 'new academic year' did indeed start in a highly radical-
ized atmosphere. At *Tel Quel*, the pressure of the Maoists was
increasing. In June 1971, Sollers got Seuil to publish *Daily Life
in Revolutionary China*, the extremely enthusiastic piece of reportage brought back by a friend of Althusser's, Maria Antonietta
Macciocchi. This book made Derrida feel uneasy, and he asked
his old friend Lucien Bianco what he thought of it. The author
of *Origins of the Chinese Revolution* made no attempts to conceal
his exasperation at this clumsy piece of propaganda for a
Cultural Revolution whose bloody brutality was often ignored by
Europeans. As Derrida put it in a late text, his friendship with
Bianco had very soon put him on his guard against 'the obscurantist terror that was waxing so eloquent in certain quarters',
especially 'at a time when the most alarming, the most threat-
ening, and sometimes too, the most comic dogmatic slumbers
dominated the stage of a certain Parisian "culture"'.[51] For now,
he avoided the subject as best he could. In spite of the hardening of political positions, dialogue with Sollers remained very
friendly, as with Kristeva, who had just officially come onto the
review's editorial board. *Dissemination* was in production and
it seemed self-evident that Derrida would take part in the conference 'Artaud/Bataille' that *Tel Quel* was organizing for the
following summer in Cerisy.

All the same, as in 1968, it was a relief to set out for the United
States. The Derridas travelled by ship, in the middle of August,
since Derrida had still not overcome his phobia of flying. Jacques
and Marguerite were accompanied by their two sons, and also by
their niece, Martine Meskel – Janine's daughter – who had just
taken her French baccalaureate in Nice. 'During my childhood,' she
remembered,

> Jackie was in some ways my 'American uncle' [my exotic ben-
> efactor]. His travels to distant parts made me dream. In July
> 1971, as I was impatiently awaiting the results of my French
> baccalaureate, he told me: 'I'd love to take you to the United
> States, but you realize it depends on the marks you get in the
> *bac.*' In actual fact, he already had the results in his pocket and
> they were good . . . A few weeks later, we embarked together on
> the steamer *France*. I remember that Jacques pointed out the
> distance between the luxury of the ship and the poverty of
> the American Blacks whom he supported in their struggles.
> On the crossing, I felt immersed in an intellectual atmosphere
> that was quite new for me. Marguerite made me read a few
> works by Freud, and Jacques a few dialogues by Plato. The fol-
> lowing year, I immediately got good marks in philosophy, and
> that helped me decide what I wanted to study.[52]

The first weeks were basically given over to tourism. With their first car, a white Citroën Ami 6 which they had brought on board the *France*, Marguerite and Jacques wanted to show as many things as possible to Martine and their children – Pierre was eight, and Jean would celebrate his fourth birthday during their stay in America. 'We stayed in New York for a few days,' relates Martine Meskel. 'Jacques was happy and proud to show me round this city, which he already knew very well. He insisted on us driving through Harlem; at times, he filmed it all as he drove. He said we shouldn't stop off there, as it was dangerous, but he still thought it was important to take us there.'

They stopped over in Boston, and then all travelled on together to Montreal, where the fifteenth congress of French-speaking philosophical societies took place, from 29 August to 2 September. Paul Ricoeur gave the inaugural lecture. Derrida spoke just afterwards, giving the paper 'Signature, event, context', a reading of Austin that would give rise, a few years later, to a polemic with John R. Searle that would create many ripples. But for now, it was with Ricoeur that Derrida had a long and lively discussion that subsequently continued through their respective writings.[53]

Martine left shortly after, to enter *terminale*. Over the following months, during a very mild autumn, Jacques, Marguerite, and their two sons rediscovered Baltimore and their friends from Johns Hopkins. They were put up in a huge apartment where Scott Fitzgerald had lived. Jacques's mother and one of his aunts came to join them for a few weeks. Even though Derrida had a heavy teaching load, the first weeks were very pleasant:

> Professors and students very welcoming, university administration incredibly 'well-oiled', easy-going. The comfort and 'user-friendliness' of everything constitute – in the library, for instance – a spectacle, an object in themselves. Of course, the bathload of *dough* in which everything happens makes everything easier. And then this is, apparently, one of the most peaceful of the American universities: politically, socially. Some students complain about this. They're the ones, too, who know Paris, have spent a year there, and are following politico-literary events in Paris on a daily basis, as if they lived between Gallimard, Maspéro and Le Seuil.[54]

Among these students, there were some who already knew Derrida's work well as they had attended the Parisian seminar he gave to a select few, in an annex of Cornell and Johns Hopkins on the Place de l'Odéon. This was the case for Alan Bass, who became one of his best American translators:

In Paris, the course Derrida had given us in 1970 was on Lautréamont; I'd been fascinated by his approach and started to read him methodically, stuffing my texts with quotations from his work. In Baltimore, his seminar was mainly a reading of Lacan and especially the 'Seminar on *The Purloined Letter*'. In order to understand Lacan properly, I decided to read Freud as systematically as possible. This was my introduction to psychoanalysis, which was later to become my profession. Derrida really liked the piece of work I did at the end of that series of classes. He invited me to his apartment, with Marguerite and the children, and had a long talk with me. I remember it as if it were yesterday: Jacques Derrida in person was sitting next to me and correcting my grammatical mistakes! A few days later, Hillis Miller, who was teaching at Johns Hopkins and was one of Derrida's most fervent defenders, suggested that for my thesis I should do an annotated translation of *Writing and Difference*. I felt that I was being offered an extraordinary opportunity. Jacques and Hillis spoke to me about my future and the role they were planning for me. The following year, in the New York Public Library, I began to translate *Writing and Difference*, checking all the references one by one. When there was a quotation from Leibniz's *Monadology*, I read the whole work.[55]

At that time, Derrida's reputation in the American university world was limited to small circles. This was firstly because he taught in French, and so to a restricted number of students, but mainly because none of his works was as yet available in English. The first translation, by David B. Allison, was of *Speech and Phenomena* (followed by 'Form and meaning' and 'Differance') in 1973.[56] Then, while Alan Bass concentrated on *Writing and Difference*, Gayatri Spivak, a former student of Paul de Man, started to translate *Of Grammatology*. But neither work would be published for several years. So, in the short term, it was through individual lectures and meetings that the principles of deconstruction gradually spread across the United States. From mid-October, while continuing to teach at Johns Hopkins, Derrida began to make weekly trips to other universities. Paul de Man had just left Baltimore for Yale, and this move would soon have important consequences. For now, he asked Derrida to give a paper on the theme 'Literature and psychoanalysis' for the Department of Comparative Literature. So, unlike what had happened when Derrida first visited Yale, he would have a 'passionately interested audience' who would have read his work, de Man assured him.[57] Indeed, 'The factor of truth',* a draft of the text

---

* This is best known as 'Le facteur de la vérité', with the word *facteur* also meaning postman. It is included under this title in *The Post Card* – Tr.

of the same name, delighted the audience. At Johns Hopkins, on 6 November, Derrida gave another important paper, 'Qual Quelle', on the occasion of the hundredth anniversary of Valéry's birth; he had immersed himself in the latter's oeuvre for the first time since his teens, and would often refer to it subsequently.

Throughout his stay in America, Pautrat and Althusser gave Derrida news from the rue d'Ulm. The new director had arrived: Jean Bousquet, a former classmate of Pompidou, a 'handsome old chap, rather demagogic', but 'definitely more subtle and polite than his predecessor'.[58] Derrida was not to worry himself *'the slightest little bit* for the École and its philosophers':[59] everything was going fine.

But his two colleagues and friends were especially keen to keep him informed about the turbulence in Paris: this was no less than it had been in autumn 1968, during his previous stay in Baltimore. Sollers had congratulated Bernard Pautrat on his book *Versions of the Sun: Nietzsche's Figures and System*, recently published by Seuil. But he had in particular told him in detail all about the big event of the day. It concerned *Daily Life in Revolutionary China*. In September 1971, the banning of Macciocchi's book from the *Fête de L'Humanité** had hastened Sollers' break with the Communist Party. So Derrida would need, before his return, to get used to the new situation, as 'the adjective "revisionist" is now being handled with such aplomb – naturally, easily, innocently'.[60] In the headquarters of the Éditions du Seuil, in the rue Jacob, the *Tel Quel* office was plastered over with *'dazibaos'*,[†] many of them the work of Marcelin Pleynet. The most piquant, perhaps, was this one: 'Two conceptions of the world, two lines, two paths: Aragon or Mao Zedong? Comrades, you must choose!'[61]

Meanwhile, Althusser was involved in a complex set of manoeuvres. Even though there was no question of his leaving the Party, he had recently met Houdebine, who had just devoted an entire issue of *Promesse* to him. What he had heard about the forthcoming interview with Derrida had greatly intrigued him: 'I think that he'll forward it to me before publication, if you like. As you know, I'd like to *understand* what you write, and not just make do with a few *aperçus* and fragments.' Perhaps this interview would help him get more of an insight into what his former pupil was thinking. 'The striking thing is that until now, none of the people whom you annoy has been able to put forward a critique that's up to the

---

* This was an annual fair and showcasing of books and pamphlets endorsed by the Communist Party. – Tr.

† *Dàzìbào*, literally 'big character announcement': a handwritten poster usually for propaganda.

sheer *level* of what you're writing.'[62]   The issue of *Promesse* with its major Derrida interview came out on 20 November, shortly before the new *Tel Quel*, 'so as to enjoy a period of exclusive sales'.[63] As Houdebine had foreseen, it did not go unnoticed, and the sales were better than usual. But something else happened: without giving any warning to Derrida – who was appalled when he discovered –, Houdebine immediately sent the issue to Lacan, explaining that the long note about him had been added belatedly: 'This is why, in the issue as published, there is no reaction from us to the critical remarks made by Derrida, with which we are far from always agreeing. But we haven't concealed this disagreement from Derrida [. . .], without however dreaming of censoring him.' In his letter, Houdebine assured Lacan that any reply he might care to give would be published in the review.[64]

Derrida returned from the United States on 7 December. Over the next two weeks, he was overwhelmed by a sort of avalanche, 'mainly because of the current hubbub in our little Parisian circus'.[65] He felt torn between his intellectual integrity and his desire not to break off with a close friend and a milieu that was still important to him. With the publication of *Dissemination* in the offing, in the 'Tel Quel' series, Sollers composed an enthusiast preface: 'Dissemination is both, in the wake of an inscription without reserves, risk, dispersion *and* the strictest constraint. The most difficult thought, the most abrupt *and* the most playful.' Derrida, meanwhile, had left several signs of complicity within the future book: not only was a quarter of the volume devoted to *Numbers*, but he made a few flattering remarks about Julia Kristeva, Marcelin Pleynet, and Jean-Joseph Goux; and he occasionally quoted Marx, Lenin, Althusser, and even the *Writings* of Mao Zedong. But not even all of this would be enough.

7

Severed Ties

1972–1973

It was New Year, 1972. This was the time of year to exchange good wishes, a habit to which Derrida would remain faithful, and he sent Henry Bauchau, whom he was sorry he had not seen for a long time, a long and rather melancholy letter:

> The life I've been leading, that many of us have been leading, worse luck, is becoming more and more depressing and absurd, mainly because of our sterile, inattentive, abstract busyness, which means that every day is swept up into social life, the worst days and the best too. I'm increasingly frustrated by everything that stops me seeing friends, talking with them, sharing time with them. And there are more and more things that stop me, they keep piling up, bringing me slowly and surely to a kind of intolerable and fatal suffocation. [. . .] The 'Paris' scene is asphyxiating – and empty, too.[1]

A few days later, he sent Sollers an affectionate letter, in which there was nonetheless a certain embarrassment, about the manuscript of his novel, *Lois* (*Laws*): 'I'm sorry for being so late. I wanted to re-read it. And I'll have to read it again, of course, more than once. [. . .] Difficult, ultimately impossible to write about *Lois*. The text is a minefield. At every moment, you risk [. . .] landing on a bad square on the board (prison, pit, labyrinth, etc.). But what a game!' This is very far from the enthusiasm he had immediately expressed after his first reading of *Numbers*.

Over the next few days, things speeded up. On 18 January, Derrida informed Houdebine that he had responded to an interview request from Antoine Casanova, the editor in chief of *La Nouvelle Critique* – and he had done so in spite of the now total breaking off of relations between *Tel Quel* and the Communist Party. But this meeting, he insisted, by no means indicated that he was going over to their side. 'I had told you how I thought things would develop, and I was quite right. I restated well-known "positions" and very firmly, very clearly expressed my disagreement with the way *Daily Life in Revolutionary China* had been banned at the *Fête de L'Humanité*. And this took up most of the interview. Nothing significant apart from that.'[3]

That same evening, Jacques and Marguerite were invited to have dinner at the home of Paule and Yves Thévenin, together with Sollers, Kristeva, and Pleynet. But time went by and the three *telqueliens* did not appear. Derrida and Paule Thévenin soon learned that this was a 'rap on the knuckles' – in reprisal for the meeting with Casanova.[4] Thévenin and Derrida were aghast at this attitude and immediately drew the consequences. The very next day, they separately informed the organizers of the Cerisy conference that relations had been 'broken off' with Sollers and the *Tel Quel* group, and so they would not be taking part in the scheduled *décade* on Artaud and Bataille. In his letter, Derrida said, 'I regret this, but my decision is final, and I thought it best to inform you straightaway so that, if you think it appropriate, you can make it public.'[5]

When he realized the situation, Sollers tried to salvage what he could, by purporting to distinguish between Derrida's attitude and Paule Thévenin's:

Jacques,
I guess everything can happen without *too* much of a fuss, no?
    You know that I've thought about it and think I need to show my fundamental commitment re the Macciocchi affair.
    Could you please say:
    (1) to Paule: that I don't think there's any point in suggesting that we're going to attack her (because of her work) – we will, of course, *never* do so.
    (2) to Yves: that whatever happens, Julia and I will continue to be his grateful friends.
Thank you for this favour.
Best to Marguerite.
For you, everything that you know *from other sources* (it's written).

Sollers added a PS: 'Is it absolutely necessary for Paule to start telling everyone that she *and* Derrida have broken off relationships with *Tel Quel*?'[6] In actual fact, there was nothing left to salvage, even though *Dissemination* was to be published a few weeks later in the 'Tel Quel' series. Derrida hoped to stay on friendly terms with a few of the group's outsiders, especially Jacqueline Risset – she lived in Italy, far from all these dramatic twists and turns –, but he no longer had any time for Sollers, Kristeva, or Pleynet, who would have no compunction about attacking him.

The brutality that was soon to be the rule was not just individual; it was characteristic of the period. On 25 February 1972, just over

a month after these events, the Maoist activist Pierre Overney
was murdered by a guard at the gates of the Renault factory in
Billancourt, as he was handing out leaflets calling for a commemoration of the massacre at the Charonne metro station, ten years
previously. On Saturday, 4 March, the day of his funeral, nearly two
hundred thousand people marched through Paris, from the place de
Clichy to the cemetery of Père-Lachaise. Jean-Paul Sartre was near
the coffin. Michel Foucault and many other leading figures were
in the crowd. And it is said that, on that day, Althusser declared:
'It's leftism that they are burying.'[7] In retrospect, Overney's death
marked a crucial moment: the time when the French extreme Left
avoided resorting to a more than verbal violence.

Derrida was deeply affected by the break with Sollers, with whom
he had been close friends since 1964, but he always refused to say
any more about it, inviting his readers 'on the one hand to "read the
texts", including his own, and especially those of the collection and
the review in the years '65–'72, [. . .] and on the other hand not to
trust "at all" the public ["grossly falsifying"] interpretations-recon-
structions of this final sequence by certain members of the *Tel Quel*
group'.[8] This long silence on Derrida's part means that his exchange
of letters with the young Belgian philosopher Éric Clémens, a friend
of Goux and Pautrat and a member of the editorial board of the
review *TXT*, is of all the more interest.

There was a rumour going round that Derrida was 'practically
a member of the French Communist Party,' wrote Clémens in a
letter of 4 March 1972. To counteract this malicious rumour, he
wanted Derrida to publish in *TXT* a sort of update, a 'Supplement
to *Positions*', as it were, in which he would reply 'not to *Tel Quel*,
but to the question of [his] political relation to, and/or [his] interest in, China and the Cultural Revolution', so as to emerge finally
from his 'ambiguous' stance. Like many other young intellectuals of that period, Clémens was becoming increasingly radical.
But he was trying not to give up on philosophy, or at least on
Derrida's, on which he had for several years been giving a seminar
at the University of Louvain. 'We fantasized that the deconstruction of metaphysics would open a door to the Cultural Revolution,'
Clémens remembers today. 'We would have liked Derrida to take
the crucial step, as we had done.'[9]

Although Derrida was very irritated by this initiative, he did
reply, explaining his position vis-à-vis the events of the last
few months in a way he would never subsequently do. He said,
however, that he had read Clémens's letter without pleasure,
and felt it was 'a pressure', or at all events 'a pressing request for
accounts and guarantees' to which he did not have the slightest
intention of yielding:

I try never to define my position, in a theoretical or political debate, by giving way to any potential or actual haste or intimidation. It's difficult, it's never purely and simply possible, but trying to do so is a (theoretical and political) rule that I have hitherto observed. My break with *Tel Quel* also has – though not only – this meaning.[10]

So it was only 'in the name of friendship' and without any view to publication in *TXT* that Derrida agreed to reply to Clémens. But he argued his case point by point, in detail. On the question of the Communist Party, to begin with: 'The fact that there are people claiming today – to whom, and with what credibility, I have to wonder – that I'm an ally, even a member, of the Communist Party, hostile to China (!!!!), is something that, not to put too fine a point on it, just makes me laugh.' As far as China was concerned, he said he was not in principle opposed: he even made more concessions to Clémens that in all his public texts:

On the historico-theoretical level, and in the field we share, I don't think I was the last (litotes) to refer to it. [. . .] On the most contemporary political level, nothing against it, either. The fact remains that between this *clear* fact (the need for a positive reference to the Cultural Revolution) and all the consequences to be drawn from it [. . .], there lies the space of a rigorous, difficult analysis: I have not carried out this analysis, but I can't see any evidence that it has been carried out anywhere else, probably for reasons that are already susceptible to analysis. In any event, I really must maintain the coolest vigilance towards everything that people might try to propose to us on this subject.

As for the 'split, in all its aspects – not at bottom theoretical, perhaps', mentioned by Clémens at the end of his letter, Derrida feared that his correspondent was simplifying things just a little bit too much. Admittedly, the final incident was ridiculous, but it would not have taken place 'without a charged, long-standing, complex background', impossible to analyse in a mere letter. 'It was intimated to me that it was judged unacceptable for me to *meet* (later on it was added, [. . .] *that I meet without consulting Tel Quel*) Casanova from *La Nouvelle Critique*.' This brief encounter had, however, been without any practical consequence, any commitment on his part: 'If my gesture – agreeing to this meeting without asking for the "authorization" of *Tel Quel* – has any political significance, it is this one, which I completely take upon myself: these days, it is not *forbidden* to meet a member of the CP, or a sympathizer of the Communist Party, and even less to discuss matters with him.'[11]

The relations between Derrida and the Communist Party are worth dwelling on. Michael Sprinker's interview on Althusser is again a source of valuable insights here. Though Derrida was never either a member of the Party, or a fellow-traveller, this is because Stalinism, even in its milder forms, had been unacceptable to him ever since he had seen it at work at Normale Sup at the beginning of the 1950s. And the Marxist dogmatism to which he had been subjected ever since his return to the École as *caïman* had of course not made things any easier. As he told Michael Sprinker, he viewed the French Communist Party and the Soviet Union as incompatible with the democratic Left which he espoused.

> Personally, I saw the Party as being closed up in a suicidal politics already then. It was losing. It had two alternatives: either it hardened its Stalinism and would lose through losing its electorate (and thereby becoming isolated in Europe) or else it would transform into reformism, a moderate socialism of the social democratic type and would lose also, since the Socialist Party already occupied that space. That was the dilemma, the fatal aporia. [. . .] In a certain sense, [Althusserianism] represented a tough current in the French Communist Party. And from this standpoint, it was even more suicidal than the Party. Although in another sense it was less so because it sought to regenerate a true theoretical thinking to which I sincerely believe it is correct to pay homage.[12]

None of this stopped Derrida, just after his break with *Tel Quel*, from drawing close to several members of the Party, starting with Jean Ristat, whom he had known and liked for many years: having been a student of Derrida's at the Sorbonne, Ristat had published a first book, *The Bed of Nicolas Boileau and Jules Verne*, which Derrida thought was 'admirable'. One of his subsequent works, *Le Fil(s) perdu* (*The Lost Son/Thread*), was a sort of versification of 'Plato's pharmacy'. But at this time, Ristat was mainly known as an associate of Aragon. He started writing for *Les Lettres françaises* in the mid-sixties, taking up cudgels on behalf of the avant-garde, especially *Tel Quel*, until Sollers and his accomplices suddenly broke off relations with the Party.[13]

It was Ristat who conceived and coordinated the special issue of the review *Les Lettres françaises* dedicated to Derrida on 29 March 1972. The list of contributors to these twelve large-format pages was prestigious. After original artwork by André Masson on the cover, there were the names of, among others, Roland Barthes, Catherine Backès-Clément, Hubert Damisch, Jean-Joseph Goux, Roger Laporte, Claude Ollier, Paule Thévenin, and Jean Genet. The latter, who had published nothing for several years, took the trouble to write a brief letter of homage during one of his brief stays in Paris. Treating Derrida as a pure writer, Genet quoted the first lines of 'Plato's Pharmacy' before stating:

> For us, this opening is as celebrated as the first page of [Proust's] *Young Girls in Flower*, just as new, and yet torn from our own selves by Jacques Derrida, who makes it his own and now makes it ours. It will be ours more and more, and less and less his. [. . .] The first sentence is alone. It is *totally* alone. But let us read lightly, with a nimbleness that is, if possible, as subtle as Derrida's, simply, guided by the playfulness of the words, as the full sense of the sentence trembles sweetly and bears it on towards the next. The usual, coarse dynamism that leads a sentence to the next seems in Derrida to have been replaced by a very subtle magnetism, found not in the words, but beneath them, almost under the page.[14]

So for Genet, it was important to 'read [*lire*] gently. Laugh [*rire*] gently as the words make their unexpected entrance. Accept above all what is offered to us with good grace: poetry. Then the meaning will be handed to us, in reward, and very simply, as in a garden.' Coming from a writer for whom Derrida had the greatest admiration, this eloquent homage cannot have failed to touch him.

It was also in the form of a short letter to Jean Ristat that Roland Barthes intervened, while saying he was sorry not to be able to 'collaborate fully' in the issue. The lack of time was probably not the only reason for this. Barthes was very close to Sollers and in a very delicate situation at this time when everyone was being forced to take sides. Nevertheless, in the few lines he wrote, admiration and gratitude are expressed with clarity and force:

> I belong to another generation than Derrida and probably his readers; so Derrida's work has had its impact on me, in the middle of life, of work; the semiological enterprise was already fully formed in me and partly achieved, but it risked staying imprisoned, enthralled by the phantasm of its scientificity: Derrida was one of those who helped me to understand what was at issue (philosophically, ideologically) in my own work: he knocked the structure off balance, he opened up the sign: for us, he is the one who *unpicked the end of the chain*. His literary interventions (on Artaud, on Mallarmé, on Bataille) have been decisive, and by that I mean: irreversible. We are indebted to him for new words, active words (and in this respect his writing is violent, poetic) and a sort of incessant deterioration of our intellectual comfort (the state in which we feel too comfortable about what we think). Finally, there is in his work something

that is kept silent, and fascinating: his solitude comes from
what he is going to say.[15]

Derrida was particularly touched by this text. A few days later, he
thanked his 'dear friend' for his 'sovereign and generous opening'
and took the opportunity to tell Barthes, as he had never before
done, how greatly his work had counted for him.

> Even before I started writing, [your work] was always there,
> helping me like an irreplaceable critical resource, but also like
> one of those glances of solidarity, whose rigour never limits
> one, but instead lets one, makes one write. And this bond,
> which also proceeds from the solitude, yes, of which you speak,
> is for me, in my work, so familiar, secret, discreet that it never
> becomes the object of a discourse.[16]

Maurice Blanchot, he added, was the only other person with whom
he could have a similar relationship 'of closeness, of gratitude, and
complicity', and to whom he could express this 'in such a naked,
trusting way'. Coming from Derrida, this was quite a compliment.
On both sides, in spite of the break with *Tel Quel*, esteem and friendship continued to prevail, even though the two men rarely met. And
Derrida would write a superb text, 'The deaths of Roland Barthes',
shortly after the tragic death of the author of *Camera Lucida*.[17]

In the view of Sollers and the *telqueliens*, any move towards Ristat,
in other words towards Aragon too, appeared as an act of war.
On 30 April was published the second issue of the *Bulletin du
mouvement de juin 1971*, a little 'home-made' publication edited by
Marcelin Pleynet. In this booklet, which began and ended with a
poem by Mao Zedong, Derrida was attacked twice over. The title
of the first text was to remain celebrated: 'Ô mage à Derrida' ('Oh
Derrida's magus' – but also, ironically, 'Hommage à Derrida'). The
article itself, in all its clumsy phrasing, is an anthology piece:

> A special issue of *Les Lettres françaises* against the leftists and
> the 'rogue' Overney? No, a special issue for the philosopher
> Jacques Derrida. So could Aragon's rag be a political sponge?
> Philosophy, as any fool knows, has nothing to do with politics,
> unless, of course, esotericism is now part of the ideological
> arsenal of the pcfr [*sic**]. And how can one have any doubts,

---

* The lower case letters indicate all the esteem felt by the author of the article for
the PCF (French Communist Party). As for the letter 'r' at the end, it is the initial
of 'revisionist', one of the great insults of the day. In the following sentence, 'change
course' is of course an allusion to *Change*, the review run by Faye and scorned by

when we see Jean Ristat, spiritual son of Aragon-Cardin, changing course. [. . .] This issue is not short of a paradox or two, so let us savour this one: Derrida's book *Dissemination*, which is a pretext for this gathering of intellectuals electing by plebiscite the policies of the pcfr, takes its title from an essay of a hundred pages (a third of the book) which Derrida devotes to Philippe Sollers' novel, *Numbers*. Need we say that we find practically no trace of Sollers' work, or even of Derrida's work on Sollers, in this issue of *Les Lettres françaises*?[18]

The second article, signed 'Ideological struggle at the front', bore the title 'Derrida or the anti-yellow peril'. The attack was simultaneously brutal and sheepish. After all, the author of *Writing and Difference* had long been one of the pillars of *Tel Quel*:

29 March – *Lettres françaises* – Homage to Derrida.
[. . .] Revisionism delights in the texts of the idealist philosopher Derrida published over two years ago. Eclectic ecstasies. Ragbag of revisionist intellectuals (the socialite backès-clément and the Marxist Jean Genet). Obviously, as soon as anyone refers to Revolutionary China, it all becomes much clearer. Derrida, a specific moment in the history of the avant-garde, a philosopher who is formed of nothing but the shameful abandonment of all philosophical struggle in the shape of revisionism. But intelligent idealism, 1,000 times better than dumb materialism. Derrida today is absorbed, *overtaken* by the avant-garde in a scientific theory of ideologies. Revisionism, with its back to the wall, lauding to the skies mere crumbs. Wheeling and dealing: revisionism lives only by exploiting the past achievements of the same avant-garde which denounces it.[19]

Barthes's participation in this issue of *Les Lettres françaises* was, of course, ignored.

At Pierre Overney's funeral, Bernard Pautrat bumped into Michel Foucault: 'So,' the latter asked him, 'what are you up to? Still philosophical scribbles?' [20] Through Pautrat, the attack was clearly aimed at Derrida, whom Foucault had just critiqued twice over. This polemic, exactly contemporary with the split with *Tel Quel*, but on a quite different level, would become one of the best-known in modern philosophy.

---

the *telqueliens*. As for June 71, chosen as the name of the movement, it is the date on which Macchiocchi's *Daily Life in Revolutionary China* was published. Many other allusions could be spelled out.

It had all started in Japan, a few months earlier, when the editor of the review *Paideia*, Mikitaka Nakano, had submitted to Foucault the outlines of a special issue to be devoted to him. One of the authors was planning to write a text on 'Foucault's discourse and Derrida's writing', taking this opportunity to translate 'Cogito and the history of madness'. But Foucault's annoyance at Derrida's article had increased in proportion with the latter's fame; he suggested that his Japanese correspondent add an unpublished piece by himself, the 'Reply to Derrida' that he had been mulling over for some time.

In this text, which was for him something of a warm-up, Foucault acknowledged that Derrida's analysis was 'undoubtedly remarkable for its philosophical depth and the meticulousness of his reading'. Insisting that he had no intention of replying point by point, but rather of adding 'a few remarks', Foucault began by shifting the debate onto the ground of principles. This was a cunning move: he was out to make deconstruction seem akin to the most traditional and indeed the most normative French philosophy. Philosophy *à la* Derrida, claimed Foucault, set itself up as the 'law' of all discourse. One failed to live up to it – strange faults that are 'like a blend of Christian sin and Freudian slip'. 'The smallest "snag" will suffice for the whole apparatus to be laid bare.' In Foucault's eyes, this conception of philosophy leads it to situate itself 'on the far side and the near side of any event'. 'Not only can nothing happen to it, but everything that can happen is already anticipated or enveloped by it.'[21]

At the time he wrote the *History of Madness*, Foucault thought that he himself had not freed himself sufficiently from the postulates of philosophical teaching, since he had been 'unable to resist placing at the head of one chapter, and therefore in quite a privileged place, the analysis of a text by Descartes. This was no doubt the most expendable part of my book, and I willingly admit that I should have omitted it, had I been more consistent in my casual indifference towards philosophy.' But Foucault did not turn away from direct confrontation: after these preliminaries, he turned to the celebrated pages in Descartes and attempted to dismantle Derrida's analysis.

Things might have gone no further, remaining at a distance, in a limited-circulation publication. One can imagine Japanese readers feeling a bit lost when faced by this minute comparison of the Latin and French versions of a short passage in the *Metaphysical Meditations*. But Foucault was out to draw blood: he took the opportunity of the republication of the *History of Madness* by Gallimard to add two appendices. In the second, under the poetic title 'My body, this paper, this fire', he resumed and expanded his argument against Derrida. Compared with the article in *Paideia*, the tone has become noticeably harsher. Foucault conducts his argument on two fronts: he is out to destroy Derrida's position *and* to best him on his own ground. Foucault embarks on a methodical confrontation of Descartes's text and Derrida's commentary on it. The irony is unremitting, and the desire to wound obvious. Foucault mimics the philologists and Latinists, without avoiding the 'scribble' mentioned to Bernard Pautrat. He is attempting to gain the advantage on every front at once, showing that he understands better than Derrida the letter of Descartes's text, even though this is not his main objective. In short, having left his original enthusiasm far behind, he gives a thorough going-over to an essay that he deems to be a failure, as he might have done at Normale Sup at the start of the 1950s.

The last two pages are scathing, and through the attack on 'Cogito and the history of madness' are aimed at Derrida's whole methodology:

> It might well be asked how an author as meticulous as Derrida, and one so attentive to texts, managed not only to allow so many omissions, but also to operate so many displacements, interventions and substitutions. But perhaps we should do that while remembering that Derrida is recalling an old tradition in his reading. He is well aware of this, of course, and this faithfulness seems, quite rightly, to comfort him. He is reluctant, in any case, to think that classical commentators missed, through inattentiveness, the importance and singularity of the passage on madness and dreaming.[22]

On one fact at least, Foucault claims he agrees with the author he is trying to crush. It was not out of inattention or casualness that the classical interpreters had smoothed over the difficulties of this passage in the *Metaphysical Meditations*, it was 'systematic':

> It is part of a system, a system of which Derrida is today the most decisive representative, in its waning light: a reduction of discursive practices to texual traces; the elision of events that are produced there, leaving only marks for a reading [. . .].
>
> I would not say that it is a metaphysics, metaphysics *itself*, or its closure, that is hiding behind this 'textualisation' of discursive practices. I would go much further: I would say that it is a historically well-determined little pedagogy, which manifests itself here in a very visible manner. A pedagogy which teaches the student that there is nothing outside the text, but that in it, in its interstices, in its blanks and silences, the reserve of the origin reigns; that it is never necessary to look beyond it, but that here, not in the words, of course, but in words as crossings-out, in their *lattice*, what is said is 'the meaning of

being'. A pedagogy that inversely gives to the voice of the masters that unlimited sovereignty that allows it indefinitely to re-say the text.[23]

'Little pedagogy': the expression became notorious. For Derrida's detractors, of whatever stamp, it was as if Christmas had come early. (John R. Searle himself unerringly referred to it, in a later polemic, even though this highly technical discussion on Derrida was far removed from his own preoccupations.) Deconstruction aroused fear, it seemed to shake the foundations of metaphysics and Western thinking, and here it was being identified with the most scholastic, the most worn-out of traditions, as if Derrida, the champion of dissemination, were nothing more than a trifler.

Foucault sent the new edition of the *History of Madness* to his old friend and former pupil. In the dedication, he asked him to 'forgive [me] for this too slow and partial response'.[24] Two years later, Foucault would again have a go at Derrida in an Italian interview, describing the latter's relation to the history of philosophy as 'pitiful'.[25] The time for argument was over: Foucault wanted to crush an enemy, even though he claimed he loathed this kind of attack, in one of his last interviews.[*] The two men would not speak to each other for a long time, and even avoided anywhere they might meet. And this quarrel was one of the things that would soon lead Derrida to distance himself from *Critique*.

Derrida's close relationship with Jean-Luc Nancy and Philippe Lacoue-Labarthe assumed added importance after these two spectacular breaks. On one of the first evenings they spent together in Ris-Orangis, they talked it over at length. Derrida wanted to give these two young philosophers, whom he increasingly admired, as much help as he possibly could. Though he did not have the least power in the university world, he assured them of his support on the publishing side, especially when it came to *Critique* and the Éditions de Minuit.

---

* 'I like discussions, and when I am asked questions, I try to answer them. It's true that I don't like to get involved in polemics. If I open a book and see that the author is accusing an adversary of "infantile leftism" I shut it again right away. That's not my way of doing things; I don't belong to the world of people who do things that way. I insist on this difference as something essential: a whole morality is at stake, the one that concerns the search for truth and the relation to the other. [. . .] The polemicist [. . .] proceeds encased in privileges that he possesses in advance and will never agree to question. On principle, he possesses rights authorizing him to wage war and making that struggle a just undertaking; the person he confronts is not a partner in search for the truth but an adversary, an enemy who is wrong, who is harmful, and whose very existence constitutes a threat' (Foucault, *The Foucault Reader*, ed. by Paul Rabinow, Harmondsworth: Penguin, 1991, pp. 381–3).

He also invited them on several occasions to Normale Sup, together or separately, to speak on the subject of their choice. Nancy and Lacoue-Labarthe suggested a seminar on Lacan, an idea which Derrida welcomed. 'After the interview in *Promesse*, this might have looked like something of a conspiracy,' Nancy admits.

> But in actual fact, we wanted to read Lacan properly, for our own benefit first and foremost, and then for our Strasbourg students. Our work consisted for the main in focusing line by line on 'The instance of the letter', one of the major texts in the *Écrits*. Initially we couldn't understand much of it. Gradually, we worked out what came from Hegel, from Bataille, and from Heidegger.[26]

At this period, Derrida dreamed of forcing the École to evolve. For instance, he thought of recruiting a few *normaliens* outside of the usual system of competitive exams, and based simply on their real abilities. He also wished to foster interdisciplinary research and open up a real forum for research, but at every point he came up against the conservatism of the institution. The new Director, Jean Bousquet, invited him, rather maliciously, to go back to teaching the Latin of Descartes. Derrida was offended, and asked Jean Bollack and Heinz Wismann to set up a seminar to study Greek philosophical texts from a new point of view. Having started his study of classical Greek belatedly, Derrida never stopped trying to deepen his approach to the language and thought of Greece, and was particularly scrupulous in the way he quoted the texts.

In March 1972, Deleuze and Guattari's *Anti-Oedipus* was published by Éditions de Minuit, in the 'Critique' series, and was hugely successful. On the stylistic level, its difference from Derrida's earlier works was evident, with its famous opening: 'It is at work everywhere, functioning smoothly at times, at others in fits and starts. It breathes, it heats, it eats. It shits and fucks.' From the theoretical point of view, as Vincent Descombes noted, while Deleuze seemed to have 'succeeded in the Freudo-Marxist synthesis where everyone else had tried in vain, it was because he adopted an irreverent style which meant, in the end, that his synthesis was neither Freudian nor Marxist'.[27]

Derrida reacted with irritation and hostility. At a dinner with Gérard Granel, he went so far as to attack the bestseller so violently that Granel abandoned the discussion.[28] In Derrida's words, *Anti-Oedipus* was a 'very bad book (confused, full of contorted disclaimers, etc.) but an important symptomatic event, to judge from the demand to which it is clearly meant to supply and the way it has been welcomed by a very broad and dubious sector of opinion'.[29]

These cantankerous remarks were fairly obviously not just theoretical; they were also aimed at Foucault, a long-standing friend and ally of Deleuze. Derrida was convinced that 'a sort of unbroken, homogenous front, involving "*Change – Tel Quel* – Deleuze – Foucault"' was being drawn up, and this front appeared worrying to him, in several respects. 'As they'd like to give credence to the idea that all they have to confront is the French Communist Party (with which, as you know, I have no truck whatsoever, and which deep down mistrusts "us", no doubt correctly) you can imagine the effect of isolation this has, of being "hunted down".'[30]

As the irony of the calendar would have it, the Nietzsche conference, held in Cerisy from 10 to 20 July 1972, came straight after another celebrated *décade*, in which Derrida had also been scheduled to speak: the one which *Tel Quel* dedicated to 'Artaud/Bataille', enrolled under the banner of the Cultural Revolution. The participants might almost have met. The sessions on 'Nietzsche, Today?', led by the strange couple Maurice de Gandillac and Bernard Pautrat, gave rise to several stormy scenes. A number of groups were present: the ancients and the moderns, but also the Deleuzians and the Derrideans. At the opening session, Pautrat candidly set out the issues facing the assembled listeners: 'We all know more or less what to expect from a conference such as "Nietzsche, Today?" [. . .] Everybody has already had his or her say on Nietzsche, and there's no possible compromise between all these desires.'

Relations between the participants remained generally muted, but there were still several theoretical confrontations. One member of the audience asked Deleuze 'how he expects to manage without deconstruction'; the latter replied, courteously but firmly, that this 'method', even though he 'admire[d] it', had nothing to do with his own.

> I really don't set myself up as a commentator on texts. A text, for me, is simply a small cog in an extra-textual practice. It's not about commenting on the text by a method of deconstruction, or a method of textual practice, or other methods, it's about seeing what use it is in the extra-textual practice that extends the text.[31]

This was not far removed from the criticism that Michel Foucault had expressed a few months earlier, in more clearly radical terms. Derrida also remembered seeing Jean-François Lyotard writing in the room. '"You're working up to the last minute," I said to him. And he replied, with a smile, "*I'm sharpening my weapons*", and the friend-foe was clearly identifiable.'[32] This period just after 1968 was no longer a time for commenting on the texts of the tradition (even in a new way), but one for changing the world.

Derrida, who was among the first speakers, presented one of those never-ending lectures that would soon become legendary in Cerisy. His text filled over fifty pages in the conference proceedings published the following year in the 10/18 series; it would then become a separate little book, *Spurs*. While the title announced was 'The question of style', Derrida immediately revealed that 'woman will be [his] subject':

> There is no such thing as a woman, as a truth in itself of woman in itself. That much, at least, Nietzsche has said. Not to mention the manifold typology of women in his work, its horde of mothers, daughters, sisters, old maids, wives, governesses, prostitutes, virgins, grandmothers, granddaughters, big and little girls. For just this reason, then, there is no such thing either as the truth of Nietzsche, or of Nietzsche's text.[33]

He proceeded to trace these feminine figures, affirming that '[t]he question of the woman suspends the decidable opposition of true and non-true [. . .].The hermeneutic project which postulates a true sense of the text is disqualified under this regime. Reading is freed from horizon of the meaning or truth of being [. . .].'[34]

Sarah Kofman, herself a Derrida specialist, opened the debate in resounding terms: 'I wished first of all to thank Derrida for his most eloquent paper. He spoke in the most magisterial way and he's left us with nothing more to say . . .' But Heinz Wismann, though acknowledging that the style of the paper would doubtless affect that of later work, put to Derrida a probing philological question: is the truth, in Nietzsche's view, '*Frau*' or '*Weib*'? 'It's *Weib*,' Derrida immediately replied. But Wismann felt that, in his paper, Derrida had constantly mixed up these two German words: though both of them mean 'woman', they have almost opposite meanings: *Frau* is a noble, respectful word, while '*Weib*, which has a rather deprecatory connotation, designates woman insofar as she arouses desire, the female, even the prostitute. [. . .] So we'd need to follow in Nietzsche's text the interplay of *Frau* and *Weib* if we are to understand fully the metamorphosis of truth.'[35]

The question that opened up the most far-reaching perspectives came from Fauzia Assaad: 'Might one night find, at the limit of your text, a possibility of doing philosophy in a feminine way?' Delightedly, Derrida picked up the ball and ran with it: 'Is that a personal question? I too would like to write like (a) woman. I try . . .' The statement did not go unnoticed. This Cerisy conference, and the book in which its proceedings were published, played an important role in the reception of Derrida by feminists, especially in the United States. Between Derrida and women (who had been so often ignored by the Western philosophical tradition), an alliance was soon to be formed. A personal factor probably played a part in this process.

The borders between public and private life are one of the most delicate questions which a biographer encounters. And the long love affair between Derrida and Sylviane Agacinski that started in 1972 is one of the major difficulties the present biographer has had to face. Agacinski was not willing to present her own account, and the immense correspondence that she exchanged with Derrida will apparently be inaccessible for a long time.*

While we should respect everyone's privacy and Derrida's oft-repeated liking for secrecy, we should also bear in mind his remarks on an even more celebrated affair, that between Hannah Arendt and Martin Heidegger. Derrida referred to it at a seminar on 11 January 1995, in words which were doubtless carefully weighed:

> I think that one day, when it comes to Arendt and Heidegger [. . .], we will need to talk openly, fittingly, philosophically, with due seriousness and at appropriate length, of the great shared passion that bound them together over what might be called 'a whole life', across or beyond continents, wars, the Holocaust. This singular passion whose archive, so to speak, with its count-less historical threads, inextricably political, philosophical, public and private, manifest or secret, academic and family, is slowly being revealed [. . .] this lifelong passion deserves better than what generally enshrouds it – an embarrassed or discreet silence on the one side, or, on the other, vulgar rumour or whispering in the corridors of academia.[36]

---

* The reader may recall that Derrida, who kept the least little scrap of paper, in his last public conversation with Jean-Luc Nancy and Philippe Lacoue-Labarthe related how, one day, he had destroyed a correspondence 'with grim determination': 'I destroyed a correspondence that I should not have destroyed and I will regret it all my life long' (*Rue Descartes* no. 52, 2006, p. 96). Like other people, no doubt, I first thought that these destroyed letters were those from Sylviane Agacinski. But this auto-da-fé is also referred to in *The Post Card* as having occurred several years before Jacques and Sylviane met: 'The most beautiful letters in the world, more beautiful than all literatures – I began by tearing them up on the banks of the Seine, but it would have taken twenty-four hours [. . .]. I packed it all back in the car and in a suburb that I did not know, where I chose to wind up, I burned everything, slowly, at the side of a road. I told myself that I would never start again' (*The Post Card*, p. 33). I do not know where the letters sent by Agacinski to Derrida are now; but it is known that he did not destroy them. And, according to acquaintances, nearly a thousand letters from Derrida have been preserved by Agacinski. In the pages of the present work, the reader will have had a chance to appreciate how talented a letter-writer Derrida was; so one may indulge in dreaming of these letters and hoping that they will be published one day, even if far in the future.

Likewise, though Derrida declared that he was rather shocked by the publication, in 2001, of the correspondence between Paul Celan and his wife Gisèle, this was not because he was hostile in principle, but because he deemed that such an edition might be misleading without other love letters being published also, notably those to Ingeborg Bachmann and Ilana Shmueli.[37]

Sylviane Agacinski, the grand-daughter of a Polish miner who had come to France in 1922, was born in 1945, and grew up in Lyon. As a pupil at the Lycée Juliette-Récamier, she studied drama, as did Sophie, her elder sister, who went into the theatre professionally and married the actor and humorist Jean-Marc Thibault. Sylviane studied in the Faculty of *lettres* at Lyon, where she attended the lectures of Gilles Deleuze, among others. She moved to Paris in 1967, worked freelance for *Paris-Match* for a year, and actively participated in the events of May 1968. 'Breathtakingly beautiful' in the opinion of many of those who knew her at the time, she would like to have become an actor. But she eventually resumed her studies, and was taught by Heinz Wismann, among others. She came top in the written exam for the CAPES in philosophy, passed the *agrégation*, and taught in Saint-Omer and Soissons, and then in the Lycée Carnot in Paris, in the *classes préparatoires* for the École des Hautes Études Commerciales.

Sylviane attended Derrida's seminar at the École Normale Supérieure from 1970, with her then boyfriend, the writer Jean-Noël Vuarnet, and started an affair with Jacques in March 1972, during a conference organized in Lille by Heinz Wismann. She broke off with Vuarnet before the *décade* at Cerisy and the atmosphere was very tense. Derrida started his paper with a few sentences filled with double meanings:

> From Basel in seventy two (The Birth of Tragedy) Nietzsche writes to Malvida von Meysenbug.
> From this, Nietzsche's letter, I shall snip out the bits and pieces of an erratic exergue: ' . . . *At last my little bundle* (or the little envelope (*pli*): *mein Bündelchen für Sie. Will it ever be revealed, what was thus* named *between them?*) *is ready for you, and at last you hear from me again, after it must have seemed I had sunk into a dead silence (Grabesschweigen) . . . we could have celebrated a reunion like that of the Council of Basel (Basler Konzil), which I recall with warm memories . . . .*'[38]

This was the first of the coded messages that Jacques and Sylviane were to exchange so often, from one book to another, up to at least *The Post Card*.

As at many of the Cerisy conferences, at least in those days, there was more than work in the air. Jean-Luc Nancy, who was thrilled to discover the place, remembers that this *décade* was swept along 'by a Dionysian mood' characteristic of the years in the wake of 1968: 'There were talks and discussions in every corner and every sense, it was a little intellectual orgy, but a sensual orgy too.'[39] Many people embarked on affairs, more or less discreetly. Derrida already had the reputation of being a seducer, and this was not his first fling. But it was probably the first one that turned passionate. To escape the somewhat stifling atmosphere of the château, Jacques slipped away on several evenings with Sylviane, to Deauville or Cabourg. His stay at Cerisy was, in any case, very brief; he left halfway through the conference, as he had said he would.

Over the next few weeks, Jean-Noël Vuarnet, who had been badly shaken, alluded in veiled terms to the intellectual and emotional tensions that had left their mark on Cerisy. From then on, Sylviane and he 'fell out for good'.[40] In his own letters, Derrida kept quiet about his relationship with the young woman even to his closest friends, but he could not hide his turmoil. To Philippe Lacoue-Labarthe, who told him about the last days of the *décade*, in particular an anti-Derridean outburst from Jean-François Lyotard, he wrote:

> I feel the same: what I remember of this conference, which has left me with more than one painful, very painful memory, is fortunately – with a sense of trust that I don't often have, increasingly rarely in fact – being able to meet with a few friends, you first and foremost. And this sustains me. As I was sustained by everything shown in the magnificent text you gave me to read: rigour, sobriety, the absence of all complacency, the openness to what really does need to be hunted down, these days, in the places where if I might say so, saving your presence, not many of us are on the prowl. [. . .] In the current situation – where as you can imagine I often feel very ill at ease and very alone – this relationship that I have just evoked and that I have with very few people (almost nobody apart from yourself, Nancy, and Pautrat) is absolutely vital to me.[41*]

With Lacoue-Labarthe and Nancy, a veritable alliance was being established. During the conference, on a stroll through the grounds of the château, Derrida mentioned to them Michel Delorme and the new publishing house run by the cooperative structure Galilée that he was launching. He suggested that they extend their study

---

* This letter is written in red ink, like most of those Derrida sent between August 1972 and the end of the following year. This habit annoyed some of his correspondents, beginning with Paule Thévenin, who dated the difficulties in her friendship with him from that time.

on Lacan and publish it as a short book rather than a long article, promising to recommend this project to Delorme. He himself was finishing off a text on Condillac that was going to be used as the preface to the latter's *Essay on Human Knowledge* and would eventually become *The Archaeology of the Frivolous*. But he was feeling tired and doing things 'slowly and unenthusiastically'. 'The Condillac is, if I may say so, a routine piece of work,' he explained to Roger Laporte.[42]

Work was interrupted by the correction of the proofs of two books that were coming out with Éditions de Minuit in the autumn: *Margins of Philosophy* and *Positions*. On his own admission, Derrida was a poor proof-corrector and this tedious task cast even more of a shadow over the weeks he spent in Nice in the little apartment on the rue Parmentier. In the letter he sent to Michel Deguy, he made no attempt to disguise his bad mood, but he did conceal from his old friend the factor that must have greatly contributed to it: the impossibility of seeing Sylviane:

> Never have holidays been so burdened down, wiped out, poisoned by 'families'. The discomfort and promiscuity, the overcrowding are such that writing a postcard requires considerable ingenuity. You can imagine the rest. Another fortnight's irritation and nervous exhaustion. A terrible mess – for us, at any rate, and for what we might be doing with our time; the children are radiant.[43]

Just like 1967, the year 1972 meant for Derrida the publication of three new works: after *Dissemination* – published in spring by Éditions du Seuil in conditions rendered difficult by the quarrel with *Tel Quel* –, *Margins of Philosophy* and *Positions* came out with Éditions de Minuit in the autumn. In *La Quinzaine littéraire*, Derrida tried to explain to Lucette Finas, to whom he was very close at the time, the links between the two main volumes, insisting that there was no break between them:

> Apparently, of course, *Dissemination* is mainly concerned with so-called 'literary' texts: but it is also an attempt to question the 'taking-place' – or not – of the literary. Apparently, of course, *Margins of Philosophy* deals with or encounters, hails within view of, philosophy. These are often discourses of provocation, and in any case have been received as such – lectures given to solemn university audiences, sometimes swathed in Frenchness (Collège de France, Société Française de Philosophie, Société de Philosophie de Langue Française) or not. [. . .] So these two books are not bound together by any peaceable, academic linking of literature with philosophy, revised and corrected

by the faculty of letters and human sciences. Instead, they
question the border and the passage, the oppositional complicity that that has been constituted between these suburbs
[*arrondissements*] of our culture.[44]

The general press, whether or not it was kindly disposed, found it
really difficult to review these works. So *Le Monde* simply contented
itself (it was midsummer) with a brief notice that could hardly have
been more laconic: in it, *Dissemination* was described as a 'difficult
and essential work for those who wish to follow the development
of Derrida's thought, one of the most important of our day'. And
the following month, the newspaper mentioned among the autumn
publications 'two works by this renowned philosopher: *Margins
of Philosophy*, ten unpublished texts that reaffirm the need, in the
face of ideology, of a rigorous and generative "deconstruction";
Positions, three interviews on work in progress'. This did not give
much help to potential readers.

However, even *Elle* was talking about Derrida, albeit in rather
farcical terms. A few months earlier, Jacqueline Demornez had
referred to 'those unwritten laws which will colour the year '72'.
Among the passwords, now that *The Order of Things* is no longer
the height of fashion, one should always – she assured her readers –
drop the name of Derrida and say that 'his last book, *Dissemination*,
is the best thing ever written on drugs. If anyone asks you to go into
a little more detail, defend your point of view by quoting the author:
"In any case, a text always remains imperceptible."'[45]

On 2 December, in *Le Journal de Genève*, John E. Jackson described
Derrida as 'a difficult author, but the only contemporary philosopher admired by Heidegger', the one 'whom he considers, it is
said, as the only contemporary philosopher worthy of the name'.[46]
While the formula was rather bold, the curiosity of the author of
Being and Time for that of *Writing and Difference* seemed as intense
as ever. In Strasbourg, Lucien Braun, who knew Heidegger well,
had tried on several occasions to organize a meeting, insisting on
the informal character it would need to have. On 16 May 1973,
Heidegger replied to his request, saying that he was looking forward
to 'making the acquaintance of Monsieur Derrida, who [had]
already sent [him] several of his works', but he had taken on too
many engagements for the next few weeks and wanted to postpone
this visit to the autumn.[47]

At all events, Heidegger continued to find out about Derrida. At
what was to be his last seminar, in September 1973, he welcomed to
his house the Belgian phenomenologist Jacques Taminiaux. After
three quarters of an hour spent talking about this and that, he
abruptly asked: 'Monsieur Taminiaux, I've been told that Jacques

Derrida's works are very important. Have you read them? I'd be very grateful if you could explain in what way they are important.' Taminiaux felt all the more awkward since only ten minutes or so remained before the ritual interruption of the conversation by the philosopher's wife, and since, too, he was obliged to express himself in German:

> I couldn't tell him about 'deconstruction' without falling into a trap, since his own use of the word *Destruktion*, prior to and different from Derrida's, stood in the way. As for *différance* with an 'a', just you try, without pedantry, when you think in a Romance language, translating it into German and, to crown it all, in front of the thinker of ontological difference. Since, the day before, Heidegger had discussed his relationship with Husserl via the *Logical Investigations*, I charged ahead into an impossible summary of *Speech and Phenomena*. [. . .] I rushed into an ultra-schematic identikit portrait of the issues at stake in Husserl's distinction between expression and index. From Heidegger's reaction, I very quickly realized that my effort had failed: 'Ach so! Sehr interessant!' he said, hastily adding: 'But in what I've written, I think there are things very similar to what you've just said.' As Madame Heidegger was coming in to bring the conversation to a close, I was barely able to stammer: 'Yes, yes, no doubt, he owes a lot to you, but it's still completely different.' [48]

In October 1973, Philippe Lacoue-Labarthe informed Derrida that Heidegger was too tired and had asked for the planned meeting to be postponed again; he did not want to give up hope, however: 'Since Heidegger seems keen on it, this meeting really will happen.'[49] But it was not to be: the health of the master of Freiburg gradually declined until his death on 26 May 1976. The planned meeting never came off. It is not clear that Derrida really wanted it to happen: the chance of a meeting worthy of the name was very slender.

Another major figure was central to Derrida's relations with the two philosophers from Strasbourg: Jacques Lacan. Reading the manuscript of *The Title of the Letter*, which extended the analysis they had set out in their discussions at Normale Sup, Derrida made no attempt to disguise his admiration for this 'very prudent, skilful, and impregnable rigour. It would be a wily customer who could catch you out.' [50] Curiously, 'impregnable' (in French, '*imprenable*') seems to have been a word that Derrida associated with Lacan: it was the same word he had used in 1966, when thanking Lacan for his vast work. But the adjective had slipped from being applied to the fortress of the *Écrits* to this subtle and rigorous study.

The book by Jean-Luc Nancy and Philippe Lacoue-Labarthe was published at the beginning of 1973. The two authors sent it to Lacan with a deferential dedication. He did not reply in person, but he referred to their work at length in his seminar, at the session on 20 February:

> Today, and in a way that will perhaps strike some people as paradoxical, I'm going to recommend you to read a book of which the least that can be said is that it concerns me. This book is called *The Title of the Letter* and it has been published by Galilée, in the series 'À la lettre'. I won't give you the names of the authors, who seem to me on this occasion to be playing the role of second fiddles.
>
> This is not to diminish their work, since I will say that, as far as I am concerned, it was with the greatest satisfaction that I read it. I wish to subject your audience to the ordeal of this book, written with the worst of intentions, as you will find out in the last thirty or so pages. I cannot encourage it to be broadcast enough. [. . .]
>
> So let's say that it's a model of good reading, so much so that I can say I regret never having obtained, from those close to me, anything equivalent.[51]

As soon as they left the session, many members of the audience rushed out to buy a copy. Rumour spread rapidly and Galilée had to reprint the work quickly. 'This success was very ambiguous for us,' Nancy remembers. 'Our being treated as Derrida's minions was hurtful for us and annoying for Derrida. While we had explored some of his intuitions in greater depth, we alone were responsible for this text. But for a long time, forever perhaps, this book meant that our two names were associated with his.'[52]

Ever since the polemic with Michel Foucault, relations between Derrida and *Critique* had not been simple. He continued to give his opinion on the articles that Jean Piel submitted to him; now and again, he would pass on a text from an author he thought highly of, such as Luce Irigaray, Lucette Finas, or Jean-Michel Rey. But Derrida found that Piel did not always share his enthusiasm as much as he had hoped: this was the case with *The Childhood of Art* by Sarah Kofman, which Piel refused to publish at Minuit, before trying to publish a severe critique of it in the review.

On 4 August 1973, Derrida sent Piel a long typewritten letter: 'after, as they say, mature reflection', he had decided to leave the editorial board of *Critique*. He mentioned personal reasons, and emphasized the interest that he had shown, for ten years, in the review and later the series associated with it: 'This collaboration has been quite long-lasting and friendly: I am particularly keen not to give my departure the appearance of a betrayal.' Even though Derrida insisted on the risk of excessive dispersal of his efforts and his increasing fatigue, it was evident that the malaise had other reasons behind it:

> I particularly need, in order to pursue or gather together what I am trying to do myself, to take up more distance and freedom, in particular to withdraw, as far as possible, from a Parisian scene from which I feel more estranged than ever. [. . .] It is probably an illusion, but I would like to provoke (in myself), at least superficially, a certain renewal . . .[53]

At Piel's request, Derrida agreed to join the review's committee of honour, a wider circle that did not involve anything concrete: 'In that way it will be impossible to interpret my withdrawal as a breaking off, and I am grateful to you for allowing me to mark this so clearly.' Piel had asked Derrida to tell him, 'in all frankness and friendship', what concrete reasons lay behind his distance, but Derrida assured him that there were none. Anything he might add would not be any more concrete; 'anecdotal, perhaps', but it was from the anecdotal scene more than anything that he increasingly wished to withdraw.[54]

On the Parisian scene, however, he was far from being invisible. At the start of summer 1973, *Le Monde* devoted a double spread to 'Jacques Derrida, the deconstructor', with a caricature by the cartoonist Tim, who presented him as an Egyptian scribe with an impressive head of hair. Lucette Finas, who had organized this presentation, insisted that 'Derrida has, overall, been given a much warmer welcome abroad than he has in France.' Most of his works had been translated into a dozen languages, she claimed, exaggerating a little, before explaining briefly, and as informatively as possible, concepts such as trace, *différance*, supplement, pharmakon, hymen, and so on.

In the same issue, Christian Delacampagne, an ex-*normalien* who was now a regular collaborator on *Le Monde*, attempted to define deconstruction. Since 'metaphysics as a whole, in other words our culture as a whole', should be considered as a *text*, deconstruction was, first and foremost, an act of reading. To deconstruct 'is not to demolish, to beat naïvely against a fortress with one's fists. Since the middle of the nineteenth century, the death of philosophy has been on the agenda, but the sentence is difficult to carry out: the death of philosophy must be philosophical.'

Strangely enough, Philippe Sollers also contributed to his homage, in a way far removed from the attacks that had appeared in the *Bulletin du mouvement de juin 1971*. Derrida's contribution to literature was, in his view, 'of absolutely decisive importance: with "grammatology", a new relationship between literary practice and philosophy has been founded'. Derrida had formulated a question which philosophy had always failed to ask itself, one that aimed at transforming the very status of literature. While Sollers made no direct mention of the previous years' quarrel, he nonetheless expressed a few reservations, in a somewhat paternalistic tone:

> The crisis, the sheer excess produced by Derrida, may be productive, but only if he in his turn is not encircled by academic utilization. For we need to distinguish between the considerable work accomplished by Derrida and the 'Derrideanism' that has developed at breakneck pace. [. . .] I think that he himself will need to overcome the way his discourse may become reassuring.[55]

The review *L'Arc*, meanwhile, wished to devote a complete issue to Derrida. Catherine Clément submitted a list of contributors in which there were more writers than philosophers in the traditional sense: Hélène Cixous, François Laruelle, Claude Ollier, Roger Laporte, Edmond Jabès, and so on. This did not stop Derrida from abruptly rejecting the transcription of the interview that he had given Clément: he said he had neither the time nor the strength to reduce those sixty pages to the required form and dimensions, especially since he was far from satisfied by what he had improvised. 'The few interviews in which I have taken part have always left me, more or less depending on the case, discontented (with myself, of course).'[56]

Risking sabotaging the whole project, Derrida refused with equal vigour to have any photo of him to appear in the review, even less on the cover, as had been the practice in all previous issues of *L'Arc*. He later explained this intransigence to Didier Cahen, in the radio programme 'Le bon plaisir':

> During the fifteen or twenty years in which I tried – it was not always easy to do with publishers, newspapers, etc. – to forbid photographs, it was not at all in order to mark a sort of blank, absence, or disappearance of the image; it was because the code that dominates at once the production of these images, the framing they are made to undergo, the social implications (showing the writer's head framed in front of his bookshelves, the whole scenario) seemed to me to be, first of all, terribly boring, but also contrary to what I am trying to write and to work on. So it seemed to me consistent not to give in to all this without some defence. This vigilance is probably not the whole story. It is likely that I have a rather complicated relation to my

own image, complicated enough that the force of desire is at the same time checked, contradicted, thwarted.[57]

Nonetheless, the issue was finally published, with an Escher print on the cover: a procession of little alligators who escape from a sheet of paper before returning to it. In the introductory text, 'The wild one', Clément analysed what, in her view, constituted 'Derrida's deviance':

He is not in his place, not like the others, he is wild. A philosopher? Yes, by profession, since he teaches philosophy; more a writer, perhaps. An academic? Yes, no doubt, since he is a *maître-assistant* at the ENS; but exiled into a sphere of activity that he is subjecting to a powerful critique. [. . .] The material of philosophy has no privilege for him, no more than any other: 'literature', 'theatre'; and the uncertain field of texts whose status is indeterminate (narrative? biography? song? poem?) are places in which the words of the language can be worked over. Now, the method of deconstruction is always coming close to *fiction*. [. . .] This issue of *L'Arc*, in an ideal perspective, demands to be read as a collective fiction of which Derrida would be the title, the pre-text.[58]

Standing out from this collection of essays was the contribution by Emmanuel Levinas, entitled 'Quite otherwise'. The author of *Time and the Other* began by hailing the importance of 'these texts, exceptionally precise and yet so strange' published by Derrida, and wondered whether his work cuts across 'the development of Western thought with a line of demarcation, like Kantianism, which separated dogmatic philosophy from criticism'. He could hardly have been more flattering. Except that, characterizing the work of deconstruction, Levinas then went on to propose a terrible, ambiguous image:

To begin with, everything is in place, after a few pages or a few lines, as the result of a redoubtable questioning, nothing is left in which thought can dwell. Over and above the philosophical implications of the propositions, this is a purely literary effect, the new frisson, the poetry of Derrida. Whenever I read him, I again see the exodus of 1940. As it retreats, the military unit arrives in a locality which still suspects nothing, where the cafés are open, where the ladies are shopping in the 'novelties for ladies' section, where the hairdressers are hairdressing hair, the bakers are bakering, the viscounts meeting up with other viscounts and telling one another stories about viscounts, and where everything is deconstructed and desolate an hour later, the houses, closed or left with their doors open, emptying of their residents swept away by a river of cars and pedestrians through streets restored to their 'profound yesterdays' as roads, traced in an immemorial past by the great migrations.[59]

The text comes to a more serene ending, with Levinas acknowledging that he neither can or will 'prolong the trajectory of a thought in another direction than that in which its word [*verbe*] is disseminated', and that he is even less inclined to indulge in 'the ridiculous ambition of "improving" a true philosopher'. 'To come across him on his path is already a good thing, and it is probably the very mode of the encounter in philosophy. While emphasizing the fundamental importance of the questions asked by Derrida, we wanted to express the pleasure of a contact at the heart of a chiasmus.'[60]

Derrida, who had become increasingly interested in Levinas's work since the first long study he had written on it, nearly ten years earlier, wished to remember only the things in this article that brought them close to one another. He immediately wrote to thank him:

Dear friend,
From the bottom of my heart (of the chiasm), thank you. Allow me to tell you quite simply that your generosity has touched me – that you know [. . .] that we dwell *together* in, I will not say the same, but a strangely refined X, an enigmatic affinity. When all the landmarks disappear (cultural, historical, philosophical, institutional), when everything is 'deconstructed and desolate' by war, this austere complicity is – for me – vital, the last sign of life.[61]*

A few weeks after this special issue of *L'Arc*, Fayard published the first book entirely devoted to Derrida. *Écarts* had been organized by Jean Ristat and brought together four essays: 'The throw of the dice/D.'s move/and (is) Judas' by Lucette Finas, 'An "unheimlich" philosopher' by Sarah Kofman, 'A double strategy' by Roger Laporte and 'Marginal note on a text in progress' by Jean-Michel

---

* Derrida alluded to his article several times in their later correspondence. On 6 March 1976, he wrote to Levinas: 'I don't express properly, or enough, how touched I am by the way you send me your texts, and everything they give me to read, to think. Forgive me. The strange relationship that you have so lucidly and generously defined, "contact at the heart of a chiasmus", is still for me a living experience. Especially since, on this chiasmus – and such is the logic of the chiasmus – I feel unstable enough to pass over, often, to your side. [. . .] Across the distance, the silences, the dispersion, all the difficulties that make encounters so rare, please believe in my proximity, very attentive and very friendly, very cordial – for I am sure that at the heart of the chiasmus the heart must always prefer itself.'

Rey. Jean-Noël Vuarnet had initially been approached, but said no – for reasons that, we may surmise, were more personal than theoretical.

The work was often difficult and sometimes unhelpfully mimetic, but it did help to reinforce Derrida's stature. The author of *Margins of Philosophy* was admittedly rather on the sidelines, but he could not be ignored. The critiques to which his work had just been subjected were a direct consequence.

8

Glas

1973–1975

Glas, in all its formal complexity, did not come from out of nowhere. Jean Genet's text on Rembrandt published in *Tel Quel* in 1967, 'What has remained of a Rembrandt torn into very regular little squares and flushed down the toilet', was already divided into two unequal columns, as would be 'Tympan', the first text in *Margins of Philosophy*. But above all, just before embarking on *Glas*, Derrida had begun another planned book in two columns, *The Calculus of Languages*, on Condillac. The unfinished manuscript preserved at IMEC comprises seventy-eight typewritten pages: clearly, the sheets of paper were introduced into the typewriter twice over, with two different justifications (i.e. right or left). From time to time, each of the texts is interrupted by a few blank lines, which enables Derrida to master the correspondences between the two columns, despite the rudimentary DIY methods at his disposal. After a while, the second column abandons the art of writing according to Condillac to make room for a commentary on 'Beyond the pleasure principle', an essay of Freud's to which Derrida would return at length in *The Post Card*. Otherwise, *The Calculus of Languages* is fairly well behaved – far from the typographical and stylistic effervescence of *Glas*.

The manuscript of this in every way exceptional text has, unfortunately, been mislaid: there is no trace of it in Irvine, or in IMEC, nor apparently at Galilée. But Derrida described the genesis of *Glas* on several occasions. In particular, his correspondence with Roger Laporte, one of his main interlocutors at this time, is full of invaluable details. Laporte, who had been appointed professor at Montpellier in 1971, had initially felt very isolated there, but he soon struck up a friendship with Bruno Roy, who ran Fata Morgana. This small publishing house, which aimed to be 'at the crossroads of artisanal excellence and literary exigence', had already published short texts by Foucault, Deleuze, and Levinas, as well as *The Madness of the Day* by Blanchot. It was this publisher to whom Derrida at first wanted to send the highly idiosyncratic work of which he was thinking. In April 1973, in a letter to Laporte, he mentioned for the first time a planned book in two columns, on Genet's work. In his mind, this was just a volume of seventy to a hundred pages, 'with a rather complex typographical composition' – in other words, a project that seemed to suit Fata Morgana down to the ground. In spite of the usual overwork involved in preparing his students for the *agrégation*, Derrida was ready to announce, on 30 June, that he was working regularly on this text and that the Condillac had been 'left to one side for a while'.[1]

It was over the summer, first in Les Rassats and then in Nice, that Derrida wrote most of the work, in a sort of fever, with no tools other than his little mechanical typewriter. He very quickly discovered that *Glas* was taking on a form and a size that would inevitably cause problems for manufacturers and publishers. But the more progress he made, the more he also had 'the impression (superstitious, anxious, neurotic – it's almost the real subject of this text) that it was the last thing he [was] writing, and also the first book (composed, planned as such)'.[2]

In the radio programme 'Le bon plaisir', broadcast on France-Culture, he said that he had first completed the text on Hegel that had emerged from the 1971–2 seminar on 'Hegel's family', 'while bearing in memory, so to speak, or in planned form', the text devoted to Genet.

> The two main bands lived together in my memory as I was writing them, and it was then, belatedly, that I calculated where to insert the Judas holes, on the bodies of the two columns. But, concretely, it was done in a very artisanal fashion, which must have required several rewritings, goings over, cutting and pasting on the manuscript, on the page, of an ultimately artisanal kind. But the artisanal was to some extent mimicking the ideal machine that I would like to have built so as to write the thing all in one go.[3*]

Over the weeks, the text 'grew in a somewhat monstrous way', and Derrida realized that finishing it off and getting it published would involve several difficulties. He was discontented with the extract from *Glas* that appeared in September 1973 in the issue

---

* In a later interview, he went into more detail: 'It was well before computers that I risked the most refractory texts in relation to the norms of linear writings. It would be easier now for me to do this work of dislocation or typographical invention – of graftings, insertions, cuttings, and pastings – but I'm not very interested in that any more from that point of view and in that form. [. . .] *Glas* – whose unusual page format also appeared as a short treatise on the organ, sketching a history of organology up to the present – was written on a little mechanical Olivetti' ('The word processor', in *Paper Machine*, pp. 25–6).

of *L'Arc* devoted to him; it 'went against everything [he] wanted', mainly because it simply reproduced a fragment from the section on Genet, without giving the least idea of how the whole thing should look.[4]

With the start of the academic year and the various engagements accepted by Derrida, his rate of writing slowed down. But he still hoped to finish the work over the Christmas vacation. Given the dimensions that *Glas* had assumed, the plan to publish it with Fata Morgana no longer made sense: Bruno Roy's publishing house specialized in short books and could not take on such a technically complex and financially risky project. So the work would be published by Galilée, a house that Derrida increasingly approved of and whose name in any case harmonized wonderfully well with the verbal chains around which the text was organized – from the gladiolus (*glaïeul*) to the gob of spit (*glaviot*), from galleys (*galères*) to glory (*gloire*).

Studying the project with Michel Delorme and the layout artist Dominique de Fleurian, Derrida started to realize how difficult and expensive it would be, in concrete terms, to produce the book. Page layout would take months of work, making countless meetings and constant adjustments inevitable. Created a good ten years or so before word processing came on the scene, together with computer-assisted publication, *Glas* was, for the author as well as the publisher, an extraordinary technical feat. One needs to remember that in those days, first proofs came in the form of scrolls on thermal paper that needed to be cut and pasted by hand on a luminous table. The least little change meant you had to start all over again. The work was printed, states the colophon, on 27 September 1974, and was published in the 'Digraphe' series edited by Jean Ristat. The first run was of 5,300 copies; it would take years for the entire run to be sold.

It was the book's material aspect that most impressed at first sight. *Glas* was a volume of twenty-five centimetres by twenty-five, a highly unusual format, especially for an essay. The cover was austere and grey; there was not the least blurb. When you open the book, you are even more surprised:

First: two columns. Truncated, at top and bottom, and carved in their sides too: cuts, tattoos, incrustations. A first reading can suggest that two texts, rising one against the other or one without the other, do not communicate. And in a certain deliberate way, this remains true, as far as the pretext is concerned, the object, the language, the style, the rhythm, the law. A *dialectic* on the one side, a *galactic* on the other, heterogeneous and yet indiscernible in their effects, sometimes leading to a real hallucination.[5]

Glas was a radicalization of the work begun in *Margins of Philosophy* and *Dissemination*, but it was also, in its own way, a continuation of Mallarmé's dream of 'The Book'.* Compared to traditional norms, it was the height of provocation. Without beginning or end, divided up in many different ways, playing havoc with typographic conventions, the book also lacked any scholarly apparatus: there were no footnotes, and there was no bibliography whatsoever. In particular, *Glas* juxtaposed 'the interpretation of a major canonical corpus of philosophy, that of Hegel, with the rewriting of a more or less outlawed poet-writer, Genet':

> This contamination of a great philosophical discourse by a literary text that is reputedly scandalous or obscene, and of several norms or kinds of writing by each other, could appear as violent, already in the 'page layout'. But it rejoined or reawoke an old tradition: that of a page ordered in a different way in its blocks of texts, of interpretation, of inner margins. And thus, too, the tradition of another space, another practice of reading, of writing, of exegesis. This was, for me, a way of assuming the practical consequences of certain propositions in *Of Grammatology* concerning the book and the linearity of writing.[6]

Marked as it was by the *Zeitgeist*, *Glas* can also be read as a reply to Deleuze and Guattari's *Anti-Oedipus*, which had so irritated Derrida. For, whatever the provocations and textual games of his work, Derrida refused to abandon the rigour of argument. The left-hand, most continuous column came out of the seminar of 1971–2: Derrida followed one thread, that of 'Hegel's family', from its most biographical version to its most conceptual aspects; the text offers a detailed analysis of a few chapters in the *Principles of the Philosophy of Right*. The right-hand, much more broken column drifts across Genet's entire oeuvre, bringing out the omnipresence of flowers in it and, through them, the very name of the author.[†] The path, however, is left free and open: unlike Sartre in his *Saint Genet: Actor*

---

* The little-known article on Mallarmé published by Derrida in early 1974, in the collective volume *Tableau de la littérature française*, in certain ways resembles a 'reader's guide' to *Glas*. Following a French syllable such as *or* [French for 'gold', among other things – Tr.] in undecidable games that sweep it far beyond signifier and signified, Derrida focuses on 'those infinitely vaster, more powerful and interwoven chains, [. . .] unsupported, as it were, always suspended.' 'So what we are left with is the way the "word", the packets of its decomposition or its reinscription, never identifiable in their singular presence, finally refer only to their own interplay, and actually never emerge from it to lead towards anything else' ('Mallarmé', in *Tableau de la littérature française*, vol. 3, Paris: Gallimard, 1974, p. 375).

† Genet = *jennet* (horse), but *genêt* = the flower 'broom'. – Tr.

and Martyr – which Derrida criticizes several times – Derrida never claims to be giving 'the "keys" to the-man-and-the-complete-work, their ultimate psychoanalytico-existential signification'.[7]

Glas poses real difficulties for reading: literally, the reader does not know where to start. It is impossible to follow the two columns in parallel, page by page, since the argument soon starts to dissolve. But it would be even more absurd to read one column as a whole and then the other: this would be to deny the profound unity of the volume and fail to recognize the ceaseless echoes that bounce from side to side. So it is up to readers to invent their own rhythm, to read the pages in sequences of five, ten, or twenty, then to retrace their steps, constantly glancing across at the other column. Readers must construct the relation, implicit in the text, between the family according to Hegel and the absence of family according to Genet, between the reproductive sexuality theorized in the *Principles of the Philosophy of Right* and the homosexual expenditure of the *Thief's Journal* or the *Miracle of the Rose*.

Glas is a permanent challenge to traditional reading – whether philosophical or literary – and is addressed to an *unlocatable* reader, as much at ease in Hegel's as in Genet's texts. This can be stated in more Derridean terms: this is a reader *to come*, as if invented by the book.

While most booksellers were puzzled, not really knowing what to do with this book of unusual format and uncertain genre, the critical reception was positive. On 1 November 1974, in *La Quinzaine littéraire*, Pierre Pachet devoted a double-page spread to this 'disturbing endeavour'. A few weeks later, at the beginning of the *Figaro littéraire*, Claude Jannoud benevolently referred to 'The Gospel according to Derrida', though he did wonder whether it was still philosophy. But for Jean-Marie Benoist, in *L'Art vivant*, it was exactly in this challenge that the force of the project lay: '[P]hilosophical writing, religious writing, poetic writing, body, sex, and death, everything explodes at the tolling of this knell [*glas*], a unique enterprise in today's current French textual production.' *Le Monde* was openly enthusiastic: on 3 January 1975, Christian Delacampagne hailed the 'qualitative leap' represented by this volume:

> Finally, Jacques Derrida has given us his first book. Yes, you read me right: his *first* book. His previous works – from *Speech and Phenomena* to *Dissemination*, via *Of Grammatology* – were merely collections of articles. *Glas*, however, is the first book conceived and composed by Derrida as a *book*. Not that it is a smooth, unified text, continuous and linear: in reality, it is the complete opposite.[8]

But the reactions of friends and colleagues to this work were at least as important to Derrida. Althusser, even though his personal style was the polar opposite of Derrida's, sent him a lyrical letter. He had placed *Glas* on the coffee table of his living room, and sang its praises to anyone who dropped by:

Personally, I read you mostly in fragments – sometimes more in one fell swoop, but in the evenings. Slowly. Always on the coffee table where there's no question of working but of listening to whoever's talking opposite me, – I read and it's like listening to you. [. . .] You've written 'something' extraordinary. You know this better than we, your readers, do. You've got in ahead! because *you've written*, but we'll catch up, only to discover that you've moved on . . . That's why I'm making haste and speaking the language of my belatedness: I was bowled over, Jacques, by this text, this book, its two columns, their double monologue and its complicity, the toil and the gleam, the neutral and its pain, the dreary and its splendour – and the *internal* repetitiveness, along each 'track', of that contrasting choir. Please forgive me for these ridiculous words, but it 'says' *completely new* things, that go past Hegel and Genet; it's a philosophical text without precedent *which is* a poem of a kind I've never come across before. I'm still reading.[9]

Even more surprising, Pierre Bourdieu was also very warm in his praise:

Dear pal,
I want to thank you, very sincerely, for your *Glas*, which I've read with great pleasure. I was interested by your graphic experiments, *inter alia*. I'm also trying, following another logic, to break the forms of traditional rhetoric and your endeavour has given me a great deal of encouragement. On the content, as far as I can sense, – it's not so easy to touch bottom . . . . – I think that we could agree on many points. I sometimes tell myself that, if I did philosophy, I'd like to do what you're doing.[10]

In the United States, *Glas* roused the enthusiasm, in particular, of Geoffrey Hartman, Paul de Man's colleague at Yale. In this strange book, he saw the consummation of one of the dreams of the German Romantics, especially Friedrich Schlegel: 'Symphilosophy', a symbiosis of art and philosophy.[11]

With Paule Thévenin, things were much more difficult. On 20 October 1974, Derrida shyly and awkwardly sent her the volume. A few months earlier, he had given her the part concerning Genet to read; she had been severe, judging the text to be 'unfinished', 'too hastily written', and above all 'less cunning than Genet'.[12] Shortly after the book's publication, Derrida heard from several quarters the rumour that she was leading a 'real campaign of denigration' against *Glas*. He sadly rebuked her for this; she replied very aggressively:

> So you want to pick a quarrel with me. I've known that for a long time. And believe you me, it goes back much further than *Glas*. Or rather, and it's perhaps this which has made me react to the reading of this book, *Glas* tolls the bell for many friendships, as I've read in it. And the web you have woven leaves little room for manoeuvre to anyone who wants to try to defend themselves. [. . .]
>
> Basically, you've taken your break with Philippe Sollers very badly. And, to resolve the matter, you had to make a clean slate of everything that might remind you of the privileged relationship that linked the two of you together. There were stooges involved. Never mind them. They never mattered. In order to get rid of the very memory of that period, you had to unburden yourself of everything that had mattered to some extent: Antonin Artaud, me. Through Genet, in *Glas*, that's what I read. You won't get me to believe that with the sword [*glaive*] of the gladiolus, you didn't want to decapitate the *gli** of Sollers' glottis.[13]

Thévenin claimed that she had abstained from talking about the book, except as regards its material aspect, which she felt was too unrefined. She did, however, admit that she had broken her silence on the matter on two occasions, notably at a dinner with the 'people from *Digraphe*'. In reality, if she found this book difficult to take, it was probably because she had the impression that Derrida wanted to steal Genet from her, just as others had tried to take over Artaud, when she would have liked both writers to belong to her alone. Between Thévenin and Derrida, relations would be chilly for over two years, during which time they avoided seeing one another. And their relationship would never be as free and easy as in its first years.

One reaction counted for much more in Derrida's eyes: that of Genet himself. He knew better than anyone that Sartre's analysis, in *Saint Genet: Actor and Martyr*, had left Genet with writer's block for over ten years. As Derrida explained in a late interview, there had been on Sartre's part 'a project of explanatory mastery that

---

* The word *gli*, not found in 'standard' French, occurs in Michaux's poem 'Glu et gli' ('Glue and gli'), a gleeful piece of verbal jazz which riffs, as does *Glas*, on 'gl-'. – Tr.

again imprisoned Genet in his truth, in a truth supposedly inscribed in his originary project' – an explanation all the more aggressive in that it failed to recognize the writing as writing.[14] With the long drift proposed in *Glas*, Derrida absolutely did not want to arrest Genet in his career, 'to draw him back, [. . .] to bridle him'. He had emphasized this in the middle of his text: 'For the first time I am afraid, while writing, as they say, "on" someone, of being read by him. [. . .] He almost never writes anymore, he has interred [*enterré*] literature like no one, [. . .] and these (hi)stories of *glas, seing,* flower, horse ought to make him shit.'[15] After the publication of *Glas*, Derrida would be very touched when Genet said a few friendly words to him on the subject, almost furtively, but he took great care never to mention it to him again.

One of the nicest surprises that came about as a result of this typographically so inventive book was curiously oral in nature. On 3 November 1975, Jean Ristat and Antoine Bourseiller, the theatre director and friend of Jean Genet, organized a public reading of *Glas* at the Théâtre Récamier. The pages of the book were projected onto a screen, while Maria Casarès and Roland Bertin read extracts. The experience touched Derrida deeply, as he wrote to Bourseiller:

> You have succeeded in doing something that I thought was impossible. And I could not admire more the fact that you were even prepared to take the risk. During the performance, you gave me the – strange – joy of reconciliation (with what I had written there and what came to me from elsewhere, altogether acceptable). It was really good. And not just for me, as I now know. Everyone experienced the scene as a sort of theatrical and revolutionary mass, powerful, sober, uncompromising – and they owe this to you, and know they do.[16]

That same day, Bourseiller described to Derrida how much joy the evening had given him, as well, before making a suggestion:

> In fact, reading *Glas* [. . .], what had struck me, was the tragic sense that emerged from it, and was there throughout Monday evening's performance, tangible. [. . .] There were moments that were 'crude' theatre, in the industrial sense of the term, both during the rehearsals and in public. [. . .] There was no longer any question of a philosophical text, no longer any question of modernity, but of theatre. You can't mistake the meaning of silence in a theatre.
> So, dear Jacques Derrida, let me cut to the chase: you need to try to write a dialogue, quickly, without bothering about

whether it's theatrical or not, simply, instead of the two columns, and a page layout, writing it in the form of a Platonic exchange(!), situating it in time, in place, but above all, let me insist, without worrying whether the content is dramatic or not. The subject you choose will inevitably be the fire that we will then just have to set on the stage. I sincerely believe, after this experience of reading you, that you're also an author of a certain, as yet indefinable, form of theatre, something eloquent and at the same time moving. [. . .] Try it – what have you got to lose? In comparison with your own research, nothing but the constraint of a form.[17]

Bourseiller's intuition was quite correct. Though he had not yet done so, Derrida would launch out, over the following months, into modes of writing that, without being conceived directly for the theatre, adopted the form of a dialogue. This was the case with 'Pas', published in the review *Gramma* in 1976 before being reprinted in *Parages*. And he was very happy to create audio versions of two of his works: *Cinders* first – with Carole Bouquet –, then 'Circumfession', which he read alone, superbly, in its entirety.[18]

Glas was the occasion for an important meeting, with the painter Valerio Adami. The poet Jacques Dupin, who ran the publishing arm of the Galerie Maeght, suggested that Derrida join forces with a painter to produce a silk-screen mixing drawing, painting, and writing. He also suggested the name of Adami and presented his work to Derrida. A lunch date was fixed for October 1974, but before the scheduled meeting, Jacques and Marguerite came across Adami and his wife Camilla in another context:

By a curious chance, a few hours after leafing through his catalogues, I was fortunate to meet him at the home of friends we had in common, in the rue du Dragon, where we'd both been invited for dinner. And it was here that I saw Valerio's face for the first time. The lines of his face, his style of drawing, and his drawing [*graphie*] as such – the way he writes, traces letters –, all of this seemed immediately, in my view, to constitute a world, an inseparable configuration. [. . .] It all came together that first evening, in the unity of action of twenty-four hours, as Joyce would say.[19]

This was the first time that Derrida ventured to write about a pictorial work. But the meeting was not based merely on an aesthetic attraction. Adami was a man of great literary and philosophical culture, drawn to works and authors about whom Derrida, too, was passionate:

In Adami, what seduced me immediately and allowed me to draw near to his painting, to get into it, so to speak, was of course that while he is an absolute draughtsman, and painter, in spite of it all he welcomes into the space of the works which he signs various arts, especially literature – you find in it phrases, texts, characters from literature, the family of writers, Joyce or Benjamin for example.[20]

For the silk-screen they were going to produce together, it was Adami who took the initiative, suggesting that they base it on *Glas*, which had just been published, and whose plastic qualities had struck him greatly. As Derrida related:

He chose a passage, isolated a phrase and asked me to write it then sign it in pencil on a piece of paper – then he set to work. He soon presented me with a drawing that swiftly became a massive picture on which he had written the said phrase, through an immense fish caught on a hook. His work was a response, so to speak, to what was written in *Glas*. He counter-signed the passage in question, taking up a teenage poem, with the following line of verse: 'Glue of the pool milk of my death drowned', which I discuss at length in the work.[21]

Derrida and Adami went on to sign together five hundred large-format silk-screens. Then, for Maeght's review *Derrière le miroir*, the philosopher wrote a text entitled '+ R (Into the Bargain)' This was not really a piece of art criticism: Derrida developed his ideas on the letter and the signature, the line and frame, before focusing on the question of technical reproducibility in Walter Benjamin and the issue of the art market. Derrida, as ever very sensitive to matters of context, pondered in particular the effects generated by his own intervention: 'What happens when a surplus-value is placed *en abyme*?'[22]

What might have been no more than an ephemeral collaboration was soon transformed into a profound and enduring friendship with Adami and with his wife Camilla. From 1975 onwards, the Derrida family stayed on several occasions in the Adamis' large house in Arona, on Lake Maggiore. This was a huge palace, partly destroyed during the war, rich in stories and legends, a little intimidating for the children. The first and second floors were completely occupied, while on the third an independent apartment had been arranged for friends who came from pretty much all over the world, from Mexico, Venezuela, India, and Israel. As Adami relates,

[T]here was room for everyone in this rather tumbledown, decadent place, which regained its youth in the summer. We'd go for a walk in the vast grounds where there were magnificent trees. In the villages nearby, there were five cinemas. Every evening, we'd go and see a different film. It was thanks to this villa that I was able to preserve such faithful and deep friendships.[23]

For Derrida, these weeks at the Adamis' were closer to real holidays than the times he spent in Nice or at Les Rassats. Of course, he got up very early and worked all morning. But the rest of the time he was able to relax. He enjoyed conversations with Adami as much as the affectionate teasing of his wife: 'I often used to provoke him,' remembers Camilla Adami,

which disconcerted him a little, since he was more used to talking to men. In spite of his love of women and his closeness to feminism, he still had a bit of a misogynistic side, like many men of his generation. But when he felt he could trust you, he could be very witty. We used to joke a lot, perhaps because he'd left his usual circles behind. And he loved dancing . . . He would also agree to experiences that were quite unusual for him: every year, Valerio would direct a tableau vivant inspired by a classical picture, such as *The Miraculous Draught of Fishes* or *The Massacre of the Innocents*. Jacques cheerfully joined in, with Marguerite and the children.[24]

9

In Support of Philosophy

1973–1976

As far as publishers were concerned, Jacques Derrida always insisted on his independence. From the very first contract he ever signed, he struck out the 'preferential clause' that tied him to submitting his following works to the same publisher. His main links were, for many years, with reviews rather than publishing houses: he was less close to Éditions de Minuit than to Jean Piel and *Critique*, less close to Éditions du Seuil than to Philippe Sollers and *Tel Quel*. On both these sides, relations had become difficult if not impossible. As for the Presses Universitaires de France, who had published his first works on Husserl, they were a much too traditional publishing house for the projects he was now developing. And since his quarrel with Foucault, it was clear that Gallimard would have nothing further to do with him.

For Michel Delorme and Éditions Galilée, Derrida showed immediate enthusiasm. The small scale of the publisher, its cooperative character, and the attention it paid to the material aspect of books were all factors that appealed to him. After the success of *The Title of the Letter*, Derrida wanted to go further and produce a real series. At the end of summer 1973, he discussed this at length with Delorme, who seemed 'ready for anything', as Derrida wrote to Philippe Lacoue-Labarthe. He wanted the latter, as well as Jean-Luc Nancy and Sarah Kofman, to help manage the project. At the end of October or beginning of November, Derrida suggested that they meet up in Paris 'to look over all eventualities, systematically and in minute detail, with all the papers to hand'.[1]

The Speculative Remark by Jean-Luc Nancy, which Derrida greatly admired, was to figure among the first titles, as well as *The Jewish Figures of Marx* by Élisabeth de Fontenay and *Camera Obscura* by Sarah Kofman. Derrida was convinced that the philosophical series they were envisaging answered a real need. It could rapidly assume 'a very necessary and very active place'.[2] One of Galilée's advantages was the speed with which it could react: things were soon licked into shape, and the first books came out at the end of 1973, even though the series 'La philosophie en effet' only really started up the following autumn.

Derrida was very pleased at these first developments, especially since it was also Galilée which began publication, in January 1974, of a new review whose title had been his suggestion: *Digraphe*. The publishing editor was Jean Ristat; on the editorial board he was initially aided by Jean-Joseph Goux, Luce Irigaray, and Danièle Sallenave. So *Digraphe* appeared as a friendly review – and aimed to be a new *Tel Quel*. Derrida published work in it on several occasions, including the long text 'Parergon', which came out in issues 2 and 3, but he took care not to get too involved in its day-to-day running.

At the start of the 1970s, the idea of community was far more than a word or a concept for Jean-Luc Nancy and Philippe Lacoue-Labarthe. Both of them were fascinated by the first wave of German Romanticism – that of the Jena group, in which poetry and philosophy were indissociably linked; they were shortly to publish a major book on it, *The Literary Absolute*.[3] Even though Nancy and 'Lacoue' had very different temperaments, they taught together, often wrote in collaboration, and worked on many projects together, especially at the TNS, the Théâtre National de Strasbourg. But above all, as Jean-Luc Nancy wrote, 'their personal and family lives' formed 'a quite new kind of symbiosis' that led to them living in the same house on the rue Charles-Grad. Inspired by the idea of utopia, this quasi-phalanstery was considered by many Strasbourgeois as a decidedly subversive place: the spirit of '68 continued to mix everything together, for a good decade: 'forms of life and ideas, political schemas and social, sexual, and cultural representations'.[4]

Personally, Derrida could not have felt further from such an ideal and such a lifestyle, as he said at his last meeting in Strasbourg with Nancy and Lacoue-Labarthe:

> This writing or this thinking involving two, three, or four hands has always been a fascinating, admirable, enigmatic vision for me, but still just as impossible and unthinkable today. Nothing seems as unimaginable to me, and I feel this as my own limit – as unimaginable as, in the private life that was indissociable from the public experiences I have mentioned, the way they lived as a family community.[5]

This did not stop Derrida from suggesting that 'La philosophie en effet' be run by a quartet: the idea of a collective work immediately appealed to him. Sarah Kofman suggested the word *Mimesis*, which struck him as an open, unifying concept, linking 'the theoretical and practical themes of repetition, production and reproduction, reflection, image, idol, icon, simulacrum, mimicry, double, mask, identification, etc.'[6] Derrida suggested to the four people in charge of the series two other authors: Bernard Pautrat and Sylviane Agacinski. All six of them got together at the end of June 1974 to decide on the volume's contents. As Nancy recalls: 'This was when Philippe and I realized that the relationship between Jacques and Sylviane was not just philosophical.'[7] *Mimesis*, which Derrida placed great faith in, was the young woman's first publication, and he was obviously keen to highlight it. But he proceeded with some subtlety, and did not impose his will on his fellow authors:

> Have you thought about the order of texts in the volume? Personally, I'm not happy with any choice that presupposes an interpretation or hierarchy, I'm strongly tempted by putting the authors in alphabetical order – it's arbitrary enough to neutralize the question of semantic or systematic order. That way, it would start with the least 'public' name, and I can see all sorts of advantages in this. Tell me frankly what you think.[8]

Derrida hoped that the volume could come out very quickly and devoted the beginning of summer to writing his own text, 'Economimesis', a provocative reading of a few fragments from Kant's *Critique of Judgement*. He wrote to Lacoue-Labarthe:

> I'm looking forward to reading your texts, and this common publication – like everything we do together – gives me great pleasure. [. . .] With *Mimesis*, we should trigger a real uproar around the beast, stir/scare the theoreticalizing populace, make it chase after the cattle as if we were unleashing merry hell at a cattle market or opening wide – to the exit, I mean – the doors of a country show. I can just see this scene.[9]

This agitprop tone and these banal metaphors are extremely rare in Derrida's correspondence, and confirm that, in his view, *Mimesis* was a real war machine and a sort of continuation of *Glas*. But for all sorts of reasons, the volume was held up.

Derrida devoted the rest of summer 1974 to the text that Nancy and Lacoue-Labarthe had requested for the special number of *Poétique* that they were preparing with the title 'Literature and philosophy mixed'. He chose to rework his 1971 lecture on Lacan's 'Seminar on *The Purloined Letter*'. But the article started to grow much longer than anticipated, which – together with the actual contents of the text – caused him some anxiety. When he sent it to the two authors of *The Title of the Letter*, he asked them to tell him 'quite frankly and brutally' if anything struck them as 'false, grossly mistaken or totally inadequate in this reading, or indeed too displeasing in the quarrel'. In a clear echo of the misadventures that had occurred three years earlier with the interview in *Promesse*, he insisted that, apart from themselves and Genette, the manuscript should be read by no one, in particular at Éditions du Seuil: 'Since, I'm sorry to say, I know everyone in that circle, I have very reasonable reasons for formulating this demand.'[10]

Lacoue-Labarthe immediately reassured Derrida, on every point: length was no problem, since the issue had been conceived to be organized around his text, and of course they would not give the manuscript to anyone to read, especially not François Wahl, Lacan's interlocutor at Seuil. As for the contents, he found 'The factor of truth' consistently impressive: 'The absence of any hitting "below the belt" – and even the esteem and the sort of liking for Lacan's work that shines through – divest this quarrel of any unpleasantness' – especially since this quarrel had been expected for several years.[11]

Despite Lacoue-Labarthe's words, this article, one of Derrida's best-known, is also one of his harshest. To begin with, it is not just any text from the *Écrits* that he lays into, but the one Lacan had chosen to put at the head of the volume, thereby conferring a strategic role on it. But in particular, Derrida suggested that Lacan's position was actually quite traditional: comparing the 'Seminar on *The Purloined Letter*' to Marie Bonaparte's analysis of Edgar Allan Poe, he recognized in it 'the classical landscape of applied psychoanalysis'. Poe's novella was investigated as if it were merely 'an "example"', and literary writing, far from being analysed as such, was placed in 'an *illustrative* position'.[12] Even though Lacan constantly evoked the signifier, the text's formal structure was ignored, just when, and perhaps insofar as, its 'truth', its 'exemplary message', were supposedly being deciphered. As Derrida emphasized, Poe's story was much craftier than the commentary on it. And one of the essential questions thus became: 'What happens in the psychoanalytic deciphering of a text when the latter, the deciphered itself, already explicates itself? When it says more about itself than does the deciphering (a debt acknowledged by Freud more than once)? And especially when the deciphered text inscribes in itself *additionally* the scene of the deciphering?'[13]

What needed to be deconstructed, in this minutely detailed reading of Lacan, was also the primacy which Lacan gave to the phallus. With the concept *phallogocentrism*, Derrida had been endeavouring for some time to show that the logos and the phallus were two manifestations 'of one and the same system', inseparable from the Western metaphysical tradition: 'erection of the paternal logos (discourse, the dynastic proper name, king [*roi*], law [*loi*], voice [*voix*], self [or 'ego': *moi*], veil [*voile*] of the I-the-truth-I-speak, etc.) and of the phallus as "privileged signifier" (Lacan)'.[14] This was a major issue, since feminism was at this time making major theoretical advances. Luce Irigaray – whose books *Speculum of the Other Woman* and *This Sex Which is Not One* caused quite a stir in 1974 – did not conceal what she owed to Derrida in her attempt to think feminine sexuality in terms other than those prescribed by the economy of phallic power and the Freudian tradition. The book *The Newly Born Woman*, published by Catherine Clément and Hélène Cixous in 1975, developed similar themes. Between Derrida and what would soon be known as 'feminine studies' a real alliance was established. His relationship with Sylviane Agacinski surely played a part.

This period, immensely busy on the French scene, was also the time when Derrida's American career really started to take off. Until now, Derrida had stayed in Baltimore for only two long periods in 1968 and 1971. The rest of the time, he organized a seminar in Paris with a group of students from Johns Hopkins and Cornell. A third stay of over two months in Baltimore had been scheduled for 1974, but Derrida had declined it the year before, explaining that insurmountable obstacles prevented him from going:

> These are mainly difficulties to do with school: the children's, first and foremost. Pierre has just started at the *lycée* and Jean at 'big school', and in each case we have been warned about the consequences of an absence of three months from school. And it would be too psychologically painful for me to be separated from them for such a long time. There is my school too: they have made no bones about the fact that my many absences (trips to give lectures or classes, especially when they last a while) were not to the taste of the management and students of the École – especially since one of my colleagues, Althusser, is often ill and has, as the result of a serious relapse, just had to leave the École to be hospitalized; no one can as yet be sure how long he will be away.[15]

Derrida assured his correspondent that this decision was a very tough one, since he had excellent memories of his previous times at Johns Hopkins and had made many friends there. As he would probably not be able to go for the next few years, he recommended that they invite Lucette Finas in his stead, a suggestion that met with a lukewarm response. The real situation seemed a little more complicated than he had stated. In a letter to Paul de Man, Derrida said that he wished to have a talk about all this with him, since his relations with Johns Hopkins had been 'making [him] feel awkward for some time'.[16] He probably did not have a real counterpart on the campus. Paul de Man immediately grabbed this opportunity and,

together with J. Hillis Miller, started working at having Derrida
'transferred' to Yale, for much shorter stays. By the end of April
1974, de Man assured him the arrangements were essentially all in
place: 'Enthusiasm for your presence, however intermittent, in Yale
will not fail to triumph over the administrative obstacles.'[17]

If this project could be envisaged, it was mainly because, the previous year, Derrida had started flying again, overcoming the phobia
from which he had been suffering since autumn 1968. This was an
essential condition for him to appear at seminars in Berlin every
fortnight, at Samuel Weber's invitation. He had managed to cope
with the first plane flights only by stuffing his face with pills, but
he gradually grew calmer. So it was now possible to envisage relatively short stays in the United States. During this transitional year,
Derrida went there for two weeks in October 1974, dividing his time
between Johns Hopkins and Yale.

In January 1975, de Man was able to confirm officially Derrida's
appointment for three years to a post as visiting professor at Yale.
The conditions were excellent: Derrida's arrival was scheduled for
September, before the new academic year at Normale Sup, for a
stay of about three weeks. He was to give a seminar to a group of
graduate students, on the subject of his choice, in twenty or so sessions: the six or seven first ones were in Yale, the others in Paris
with the American students who were doing an additional course.
He was paid an annual sum of $12,000 (the equivalent, these days,
of about 33,000 euros) – a significant amount, even though Derrida
would have to pay for his accommodation and most of his travel.[18]
This engagement ended his previous contract with Johns Hopkins,
but the students of that university, like those from Cornell, could
continue to attend the Paris seminar.

Yale, situated in New Haven, Connecticut, some 120 kilometres
north-east of New York, was one of the richest and most prestigious
universities in the United States. In the field of literary studies, it
was also the cradle of the New Criticism, the dominant current from
the 1920s to the beginning of the 1960s. But the deciding factor in
Derrida's eyes was the role played there by de Man. Ever since their
first encounter in 1966, based on their common interest in Rousseau,
the bond between the two men had continued to deepen. Although
he was in charge of a literature department, de Man gave philosophy an essential place: for him, Hegel, Husserl and Heidegger
were essential reference points. The great mutual esteem between
the two men soon turned into a 'rare experience of friendship'. As
Derrida wrote, shortly after returning home from his first stay:

Those three weeks in Yale, with you, now seem even more
like a paradise lost, already somewhat unreal, violently tugged
away by everything that harasses me and tears me to pieces

here. What I most appreciated, as I've already told you, very clumsily, was your attentive and affectionate closeness. And as well as the time and energy that you lavished on me [. . .], I was very touched by this discreet attention for the 'difficulty' on the basis of which, within which I exist and try to work. I feel that you can understand it, that you can see it behind whatever may strut around in pedagogical self-assurance or the games of writing. This 'difficulty' (I absolutely refuse to use any other word) is, today, worse than ever.[19]

Derrida said he was already looking forward to his next stay and 'the lessons to be drawn from this first experience'. De Man was equally enthusiastic. He, too, felt that he had found the accomplice he needed if the Department of Literary Studies were to grow to its fullest extent:

I can't tell you how much good your stay did all of us, your friends here, all those who listened to you with passion, and myself in particular. The results of your teaching are starting to appear. I've seen several students who wish to continue working with you and will go to France next year, and a group of young teachers has come together spontaneously and is meeting every week to read and discuss your early works. It is literally the first time for very many years that a group of people from varied backgrounds has gathered together in Yale to pursue an intellectual goal. In fact, everyone's been bored since you left and things seem really grey and monotonous in your absence.[20]

In France, the main struggle in the years 1974–6 was to set up the Greph, the Groupe de Recherches sur l'Enseignement Philosophique. For Derrida, this was not just a militant activity distinct from his personal work. As he later explained in an interview, it appeared to him at this time that any activity of philosophical deconstruction that bore only on concepts and contents would to a great extent miss its target: 'It would remain a sort of purely theoretical enterprise if it did not take on the institution of philosophy.' After focusing on the question of the margins and frames of the philosophical text, Derrida thought that it was crucial to examine the 'institutional edges' – the practice of teaching, the master–pupil relationship, the form of exchanges between philosophers and the way that philosophy was brought within the field of politics. And so, together with a small group of friends, he embarked on a 'practice of institutional deconstruction'.[21]

Current affairs played a part in this decision. Nearly six years had gone by since May 1968, and there was a widespread feeling that the university system had been reclaimed by conservative forces.

The starting point for what was soon being called the Greph was a protest against the particularly reactionary report published by the jury of examiners of the philosophy CAPES in 1974: referring to pedagogical requirements, the jury stigmatized the effects of new philosophical tendencies evident in the answers handed in by candidates, and advocated a return to the most academic norms. A few weeks later, some thirty or so teachers and students adopted the 'Pilot Study for the Constitution of a Research Group into the Teaching of Philosophy'. While some of the questions raised were historical or theoretical in nature, others touched on concrete and sometimes urgent problems concerning exam syllabuses, the form that exams – including competitive exams – should take, the way juries of examiners were set up and norms for evaluation established, the recruitment of teachers and their professional hierarchy, the place reserved for research, and so on.[22]

The political context accelerated things: Georges Pompidou died in office on 2 April 1974, and on 19 May, Valéry Giscard d'Estaing was elected President, narrowly beating François Mitterrand, the Union of the Left candidate. In March 1975, the new Minister for Education, René Haby, proposed an overall rethink of secondary education – including philosophy.

Even before the details of the reform were widely known, Derrida reacted in a two-page article in *Le Monde de l'éducation* under the title 'Philosophy repressed'. In a style that could hardly have been more direct, he claimed that the teaching of philosophy would be affected 'more profoundly than any other discipline' by the planned measures:

> Since the new Terminales are organized according to a totally 'optional' system, there would no longer be any required teaching of philosophy in the only class in which, up to this point, it has been offered. Philosophy would be given three hours a week in the 'première': about as much, on average, as in the sections of the Terminales that receive the least today. Even before examining the grounds for or aims of such an operation, let's move on to what is irrefutable: the number of hours reserved for philosophy, *for all students*, is massively reduced. Philosophy was already the only discipline confined to a single class at the end of the final year of secondary studies; it would still be contained in a single class, but with fewer hours. Thus an offensive that had proceeded, in recent years, more prudently and deceitfully is openly accelerated: the accentuated dissociation of the scientific and the philosophical, the actively selective orientation of the 'best' students toward sections giving less room to philosophy, the reduction of teaching hours, coefficients, teaching positions, and so forth. This time,

the plan appears clearly to be adopted. No systematic introduction to philosophy could possibly be attempted in three hours a week. How can one doubt that? Since students will have had no other access to philosophy as such during *their entire studies*, the candidates for the 'philosophy' option will be more and more rare.[23]

Derrida rejected any corporatist-style defence. His combat was explicitly political. The 'destruction of the philosophy class' that in his view was imminent would have the main effect of 'stopping 'most lycée students from exercising philosophical and political critique. Historical critique as well, since history is once again the target associated with philosophy':

> In the lycées, at the age when one begins to vote, is the philosophy class not, with the exception of history, the only place in which, for example, texts on theoretical modernity, those on Marxism and psychoanalysis in particular, have some chance of being read and interpreted? And there is nothing fortuitous in the fact that the pressure from those in power has become continually more pronounced against this class and certain of its instructors and students since 1968 and the 'protests' that developed in the lycées.[24]

In Derrida's view, maintaining, in a purely defensive way, the teaching of philosophy in *terminale* in its existing form would mean giving weapons to the forces of repression. While fighting the Haby Reform, he wanted also to promote an idea that was close to his heart, that of extending philosophy lessons to other classes in secondary schools and thus to younger pupils:

> Let us quickly forestall the self-interested objection of those who would simply shrug. There is no question of transporting into the sixième a teaching that is already impracticable in Terminale. But rather of accepting here, as is done in all other disciplines, the principle of calculated *progressive stages* in initiation into, apprenticeship in and acquisition of knowledge. As everyone knows, in certain conditions – and it is these which must be given their freedom – the 'philosophical capacity' of a 'child' can be very powerful. The progression would concern as much the questions and texts of the tradition as those of modernity. [. . .] In particular, critical articulations would need to be made between this philosophical teaching and the teaching of other subjects, which is itself being transformed. Or rather, they would need to be *reorganized*: after all, who can doubt that a very definite philosophy is *already* being taught

through French literature, languages, history, and even the sciences? And has anyone ever paid attention to the real difficulty of teaching these other subjects? Or religious instruction? Or moral education?[25]

The Greph was officially set up on 15 January 1975, and would play a major role in the fight against the Haby Reform, which greatly increased its visibility. Effectively supported by Roland Brunet, a teacher at the Lycée Voltaire, Derrida was also aided by a small group of twenty to thirty persons, including Élisabeth de Fontenay, Sarah Kofman, Marie-Louise Mallet, Michèle Le Doeuff, Bernard Pautrat, and Jean-Jacques Rosat. There was also his niece Martine Meskel, who was then working towards her *licence* in philosophy, and, above all, Sylviane Agacinski, who played a very active part. It was probably she who helped to make Jacques aware of the problems raised by the teaching of philosophy in *terminale*, a reality of which he had only distant and somewhat unhappy memories.

Even though the movement developed throughout France, the provisional seat of the Greph was established at the École Normale Supérieure, where most of the meetings also took place. For Derrida, who did not have the least secretarial help, the administrative and practical aspects soon became very burdensome. As Marie-Louise Mollet remembers:

He did more than play his part, and never drew back from the most humdrum tasks. One of the things that struck me most at the time was the fact that he behaved in the same way to all the participants, whatever their qualifications, functions, and social status. There was a very friendly atmosphere in our meetings, with a ferment of ideas and a desire for innovation that seemed to make him happy.[26]

The battles in which the Greph was involved were given added point by the institutional problems that Althusser faced. In June 1975, he took his doctorate on the basis of work already published at the University of Amiens. But a few days later, the Universities' Consultative Committee refused to add the author of *For Marx* to the list of those able to teach as university lecturers. Althusser's eminence gave a considerable echo to the appeal drawn up by Derrida and widely spread by the Greph:

All those interested in philosophical activity, political theory, political struggles (etc.) will not need us to remind them of Althusser's work [. . .]. It is well known that, in France and the whole world, this work has profoundly affected, renewed, fertilized the field of Marxist thought. And not only

Marxist thought. It manifestly represents, in France and the whole world, one of the most powerful and most lively of philosophical trends. [. . .]

It is true that, given the novelty of the questions it raises, by the style of intervention or exposition it inaugurates in the universities, by its open link with political practice, this work disturbs the guardians of a certain power and a definite tradition in the philosophical institution. With all the inelegance of fearful resentment, these guardians have just erected a barrier against him whose political character they can no longer conceal.[27]

Of course, discriminatory measures such as these did not merely strike at Althusser, but his case did have the merit of illustrating, in a spectacular fashion, the political dimension of the problem: supported by 'the most reactionary forces in teaching', government policy was proceeding on 'a brutal bringing to heel of schools and universities'. Replies to the Greph's appeal arrived *en masse*. The Giscardian authorities and members of the Universities' Consultative Committee would bear a deep grudge against Derrida and his colleagues.

As the institutional landscape froze, Normale Sup remained in many respects a space of independence and freedom. Derrida, eager as ever to open up the École, invited as often as he could the thinkers he rated highly, including Jean-Luc Nancy, Philippe Lacoue-Labarthe, Heinz Wismann, Jean Bollack, and a few others. His own seminar was increasingly prestigious. As Lacan's had been, it was mainly frequented by an audience from outside, even though the theme chosen was always linked to the *agrégation* syllabus. Denis Kambouchner, who started attending when he was still a *khâgne* pupil at Louis-le-Grand, before becoming a friend of Derrida's, gives an excellent description of the ritual of this seminar, where one in two of the sessions was devoted to Derrida's meticulously composed analyses and the other to a freer discussion:

Essentially, these sessions constituted lessons in reading, not in the traditional shape of the *explication de texte* or analysis of doctrines, but in a hyper-interrogative way that adopted many registers, brought out to a remarkable degree the least singularities of the texts studied, made bold comparisons between the most cardinal and the most apparently contingent elements, laid bare key themes and complex structures at the heart of neglected passages, crisscrossed the history of philosophy or culture to make us aware of certain parallel structures, and in short reconstituted, in successive approaches, the 'gestures' of an author by setting him on a 'stage' that was at once huge and yet always intimate, whose configuration we would not have suspected hitherto. Although Derrida actually always sought in his writings and his teaching the greatest demonstrative clarity, this teaching was demanding, and what was at issue in it could often evade many people. [. . .] [Derrida,] who one day gave as a rule 'not to smooth out the folds', very quickly set you in the midst of them, probably with the idea that practising philosophy meant taking an interest, right from the start, in certain complications, and accepting them.[28]

Work with students at the École was highly individualized. In spite of an already overburdened timetable, Derrida would devote a great deal of time to seeing the students in his office on the first floor, and paid an unusual degree of attention to the worries of each of them. As Kambouchner recalls: 'Everything that came from him, gestures, verbal replies, was energetic and at the same time very concentrated. Never any approximation, never any slackening; frequent pauses. He was there in front of you, already at that period, like a block of power and memory.'[29]

Whatever their different philosophical positions, Althusser, Pautrat, and Derrida continued to form a pedagogical trio that most of the students greatly appreciated. Each piece of work submitted by students was corrected twice over, leading to a detailed analysis. And almost every Tuesday, the three *caïmans* met to listen to the 'practice lectures' given by the *agrégatifs*. Souleymane Bachir Diagne, a student at the end of the 1970s, remembers these sessions clearly:

Practising the 'lecture' was an important moment: everyone had to present a class on the subject which the *caïmans* had chosen for us, then they would 'take over'. Derrida had the fabulous ability, in his comments, to gauge what the student's intention had been, then what had become of it in his lecture, and why. He had a remarkable way of seeing the arguments of other people from the inside. Over and above the *agrégation*, he really helped me to make progress in my own way of thinking. While I was at the École, I submitted two pieces of writing to him: an essay on Nietzsche's *Genealogy of Morals*, then a text on philosophy in Africa and discussions on the very idea of 'African philosophy'. Derrida had talked to me about this work, and eventually advised me to 'think of it all together'. This had intrigued me: for me, an essay on Nietzsche and a text on African philosophy had comprised two different exercises on unrelated subjects. But that's just it: what Derrida taught me with this remark, which I have thought about, was that they weren't just 'exercises': writing on this, and then on that. To think together meant bringing to light what I wanted to do: this meant going via Nietzsche *and* the discussion of African philosophy. I still live my philosophical life with that advice in mind.[30]

On the editorial level, things had soon turned sour. Relations with Galilée had completely failed to live up to their promises. In March 1975, Michel Delorme turned down *Mimesis*, mainly with the excuse that there was a 'publishing crisis' of which *Glas* had just been one of the victims.[31] Derrida had hoped to change publishing practices; he was profoundly disappointed.

For several months, Jos Joliet, a former student of Derrida's who worked for Flammarion, acted as an intermediary. In April, the teams of 'La philosophie en effet' and of the review *Digraphe* joined the publishing house in the rue Racine. Even though the series was still run by the team as a whole, Henri Flammarion insisted that Derrida look after 'the technical side', a rather heavy responsibility for which he had neither any real competence nor any particular liking.

After these tumultuous months, Derrida spent the beginning of summer 1975 writing *Signéponge*, a lecture that would take up a whole day at the Francis Ponge colloquium in Cerisy, at the start of August,. This text was essentially about the role of the signature, as if it were making Ponge's whole oeuvre derive from 'the chance of his name'; it paid almost mimetic homage to a poet he had liked since his teens. The first lines were an address rather than an *incipit*:

FRANCIS PONGE – from here I call him, for greeting and praise, for renown, I should say, or renaming.

Much would depend on the tone I want understood. A tone is decisive, and who shall decide if it is, or is not, part of discourse?

But then he is already called Francis Ponge. He will not have waited for me to be called himself.

As for renown or renaming, that is his thing.[32]

As often, alas, the rest of the summer did not bring Derrida the respite he had hoped for. After some exasperating and expensive problems with his car that put him in a bad mood, the family sojourn in Menton was not very successful, as the apartment rented by his mother turned out to be 'uncomfortable and noisy, barely tolerable'.[33] However, he needed to prepare his classes for the autumn, while writing 'Pas', a long dialogue on Blanchot, in which a 'manifestly masculine' voice was confronted with another voice, 'rather feminine'.

Derrida returned to Paris even more tired than when he had left, with 'a need for silence, for rest, for gentle strolls' that he did not manage to satisfy. On his return from Yale, at the beginning of October, he found so much work waiting for him that he could not hide his dejection. 'I'm exhausted, everything is beyond me (in particular the Greph, the École, Flammarion, Joliet and Sarah . . .),' he wrote to Lacoue-Labarthe as he polished off *Mimesis*.[34]

This work, published in November 1975 by Aubier-Flammarion, had the appearance of a manifesto for the series 'La philosophie en effet' as well as being a theoretical counterpoint for the work of the Greph. When *La Quinzaine littéraire* brought the six authors together for a debate discussion, Derrida declared right from the start that *Mimesis* was not a book of philosophy, but a work that, in its writing and in its themes, 'is trying to shift the philosophical, to reinscribe it in fields which it has always apparently dominated'.

> Against this 'belief' in philosophical hegemony, we are plugging the code and the norms of philosophical discourse into others that are not recognized as philosophical, such as Hoffmann, Brecht, and a few other places. In short, it is not a book whose norms follow what is expected these days from a philosophical discourse, by those norms which still control, powerfully, scholastically, so many books that claim to be anti-philosophical.[35]

A more radical approach was deployed in *Le Monde*. Christian Delacampagne emphasized that the authors had sought to express themselves as one: 'Here is the result: an interview, probably the first of its kind, signed "collectively".' One of the contributors insisted that *Mimesis* 'does not "bring together" contributions on a "theme"'. The book attempted, instead, to 'undermine the idea of "contributions" signed by several "authors"'. And indeed, in the very strange text that acts as a preface, 'a fictive *I*, neither singular nor plural, nor collective, refers to six so-called "proper" names'.[36] Subtle and sophisticated, such an attitude is the polar opposite of the massive return of the subject and authorial ego that was characteristic of the *nouvelle philosophie*, whose moment of triumph was approaching.

However active and efficient the way he managed his many activities, Derrida continued to feel dissatisfied by the life he was leading. In a letter to Paul de Man, he described perfectly the ambivalence he felt:

> The 'Parisian scene' (as I call it, for short, to simplify matters), and everything that keeps me tied up in it, tire me and discourage me – to the point of despair. They stop me working and I dream of some kind of break, conversion, retirement. But I'm not going to start complaining all over again. In fact, in spite

of the desperate gaze I keep fixed on this scene, which I know too well, in some ways, I still have the strength – where do I get it from, I don't know? – of doing things, performing in it (seminars, the Greph, publishing . . .). But every evening I tell myself it can't last.[37]

In 1976, in the United States, Derrida's fame continued to spread rapidly. In the words of Richard Rand, a former student of de Man who became one of Derrida's American translators:

The development of what was rather simplistically called 'the Yale School' was mainly Paul de Man's doing. He had a great influence on his students, coupled with an extraordinary political sense for everything that concerned relations between the universities. He was ambitious in the noblest sense of the term. In spite of his vast culture and the quality of his personal work, he started to study under Derrida, as it were, as he immediately perceived his greatness and guessed that he would be able to shift the lines of force in the American academic world. It was de Man who played the decisive role in getting Derrida known in the United States. Like Derrida, Paul de Man had a combative, if not warlike, temperament. He regularly wrote in the *New York Review of Books*, often very scathingly. 'We must draw blood,' he would sometimes say. This taste for polemics also helped to bring him closer to Derrida.[38]

Whereas in France the reception of Derrida's work occurred on the margins of university institutions, in the United States it was within the top-flight universities, and via a set of more traditional mediations, that it acquired its legitimacy and started to spread among a broader public. As the sociologist Michèle Lamont explained in a celebrated article, Derrida's success in the United States was not a given: it needed first to go through a 're-framing' that transported it from the field of philosophy to that of literary studies, then to its dissemination across an increasingly far-flung university network.[39] The context, after all, was completely different from the one that Derrida had known in France: the references that were most widely shared by his first French readers – Saussurean linguistics, Lacanian psychoanalysis, Althusserian Marxism – were not part of the cultural baggage of his American audience. And above all, the latter were not as a whole greatly acquainted with philosophy; it was mainly through Derrida that they discovered Hegel, Nietzsche, Husserl and Heidegger.

At Yale, there were more students at Derrida's seminar every year, even though he spoke in French and discussed authors who were not much translated, such as Francis Ponge and Maurice

Blanchot. It has to be said that Derrida acquired an increasing mastery of the specific features of the American system of education. After the seminar, which began at 7 p.m. and continued quite late, several members of the audience met up in cafés such as George and Harry's or the Old Heidelberg to continue the discussion over a glass of something.[40] The rest of the week, Derrida made himself extremely available. One Yale professor underlined this point immediately after Derrida's death: '[H]e was a particularly charismatic teacher who really changed the lives of a lot of his students.'[41] Many of those to whom he generously gave so much of his time during those years would soon be appointed to professorships pretty much throughout the United States, often with his support, and would foster the spread of his influence over the following decades.

A young woman, Gayatri Chakravorty Spivak, played a decisive role in the reception of Derrida in the United States. On arrival from Calcutta in 1961, she worked on a thesis supervised by Paul de Man before discovering, with real excitement, *Of Grammatology*. Spivak devoted several years to this extremely tricky translation. When she came to Paris in summer 1973, she met Derrida several times, and asked for advice on the various difficulties she encountered. In 1974–5, at Brown University, Providence, she gave a seminar on Derrida on which was based the long introduction that she added to her translation before it came out with the Johns Hopkins University Press in 1976. This text, about a hundred pages long, and decidedly more accessible than the work it prefaced, went on to be a manual for generations of American students. Even though Spivak's translation met with some criticism and had to be revised several times, *Of Grammatology* achieved astronomical sales of nearly 100,000 copies.[42]

In his absorbing study *French Theory*, François Cusset gives a good description of the 'crucial shift' brought about by Spivak by presenting Hegel, Nietzsche, Freud, Husserl, and Heidegger as so many 'proto-grammatologists':

> The Americans will henceforth see Derrida less as the heterodox continuation of the philosophical tradition, or even the one who dissolves its text, than as its sublime end-point, a sort of empyrean of critical thought for which these German precursors would have merely prepared the way. [. . .]
>
> Beginning in 1976, what was as yet only a theoretical programme will find itself read, studied, and soon set to work in certain graduate literature courses, especially at Yale and Cornell. One began gradually to *apply* deconstruction, to draw from it the modalities of a new 'close reading' of the literary classics, and to find in the latter, as though through a magnifying glass, the mechanisms by which the referent is dissipated, the content ceaselessly differed/deferred by writing itself.[43]

In Derrida's view, quite apart from any consideration of career, the essential element of his annual stays in Yale continued to be his personal and intellectual bond with Paul de Man. No sooner was he back in Paris, overwhelmed by the mass of problems waiting in his in-tray, than he said that he was full of nostalgia:

I dream of the trips between New Haven, Moon Bridge, and Bethany, of all those days (happy days, yes!) that they punctuated, like something distant and mythical that I have not managed to retain. And – a little more each year – I receive those moments in Yale as the signs of your friendship, of a very rare, very precious friendship, which despite or through that discretion echoes in me clearly, profoundly, all the more distinctly because something is becoming more rarefied in me, the space of friendship is shrinking strangely, dangerously, as the other (I don't know what to call it, the other of a certain worldly society) grows broader, increasing the number of its networks, its machines and its traps. [. . .]

Those who are amazed (you, sometimes) by my activity, my zeal for doing or writing things, don't always see (but *you* see it) from what fundamental disabused, weary disbelief (I dare not any longer even call it scepticism or nihilism) it rises.[44]

Publishing problems were doubtless weighing on Derrida more than any others. For the first time, he had a series that he and his friends could publish in. But their capacity for decision-making remained subordinate to the publishing house's real managers, and this frequently irritated him. To get the projects close to his heart published by Aubier-Flammarion, Derrida was often required to add long prefaces to them. This was the case for William Warburton's *Essay on Hieroglyphics* and in particular for *The Wolf Man's Magic Word* by Nicolas Abraham and Maria Torok. 'Fors', the long essay that Derrida wrote over the summer of 1976, was in many ways a fraught text.

If Derrida had continued to draw closer to psychoanalysis, ever since his first discussion in 'Freud and the scene of writing', this was largely due to his friendship with Abraham and Torok. Derrida met Abraham for the first time in 1959, at the conference on 'Genesis and Structure' in Cerisy-la-Salle. Abraham, born in Hungary in 1919, had initially been a philosopher. In 1958 he became a psychoanalyst, and tried to combine Husserlian phenomenology with the thought of Freud, in a field where 'neither phenomenologists nor psychoanalysts' ventured.[45] With his partner Maria Torok, he was also the main person to introduce the work of Sandor Ferenczi into France.[46]

The friendship between the two couples had consequences that were not merely theoretical. Towards the end of the 1960s, it was Abraham and Torok who convinced Marguerite Derrida to undertake a training analysis; they also recommended to her Joyce McDougall, an analyst greatly influenced by Donald Winnicott and Melanie Klein.[47] The admission of Marguerite to the Société Psychanalytique de Paris was far from straightforward. In 1974, she was initially 'referred', to the great surprise of René Diatkine, one of those who had been supervising her. At a meeting, one of the training analysts apparently remarked to him: 'You really need to realize that if you accept Mme Derrida, you'll be opening the door to Jacques Derrida.' Marguerite was accepted the following year, and opened a practice in the rue des Feuillantines, but she tried to keep as far away as possible from the institutional struggles that were tearing the psychoanalytical milieu apart.[48]

For Derrida, writing 'Fors', the long preface to *The Wolf Man's Magic Word*, was a 'perilous exercise for all sorts of reasons', overshadowed as it was by the death of Nicolas Abraham one year previously.[49] But the book fascinated him and he wanted to try to make the work of those two marginal figures in psychoanalysis better known. Abraham and Torok had focused on the memoirs of the Wolf Man, one of Freud's most famous patients, and put forward in *The Wolf Man's Magic Word* a new reading of this case which had attracted numerous commentaries, including those of Lacan and of Deleuze and Guattari. Rereading with a fresh eye the remarks and dream narratives of the Wolf Man (whose real name was Sergei Pankejeff), they brought out the interplay between the four languages that played a crucial role in his personal story: Russian, German, English, and French. Abraham and Torok also introduced a series of new concepts, such as 'the rind of the ego' and the 'crypt', a sort of 'false unconscious filled with phantoms – to wit, fossilized words, live corpses, and foreign bodies'.[50]

Published in October 1976, *The Wolf Man's Magic Word* was a great success, especially among the Lacanians – which greatly irritated Lacan himself. On 11 January 1977, he attacked the work at length in his seminar, settling several accounts at the same time. The first concerned philosophy – in general but mainly in particular:

I've got a thing here which, I have to say, has filled me with terror. It's a series that's come out with the title 'La philosophie en effet'. Philosophy in effect, in effects of signifiers, that's exactly what I'm doing my best to pull out of, I mean I don't think I'm doing philosophy, you always do more philosophy than you think, there's nothing more slippery than this area; you do it, too, when it suits you, and it's certainly not what you can feel proudest of.[51]

A little further on, Lacan tackles slightly more specifically what had 'rather frightened him', treating *The Wolf Man's Magic Word*, 'by a certain Nicolas Abraham and a certain Maria Torok', as if it were a rather untimely echo of his own discourse on the Wolf Man. But he soon returned to what in his eyes was the main thing: Derrida's preface. It was the first time Lacan had talked about Derrida since the publication of 'The factor of truth' in *Poétique*. And he did so with no holds barred.

> There's one thing that, I have to say, surprises me even more than the spread, the spread – which I know perfectly well is happening –, the spread of what is called my teaching, my ideas [. . .], one thing that surprises me even more: not the fact that *The Wolf Man's Magic Word*, not only does it float along, but it's breeding, it's the fact that someone I didn't know – to tell the truth, I think he's in analysis – that I didn't know was in analysis – but this is a mere hypothesis – it's a certain Jacques Derrida who's written a preface to this *Magic Word*. He writes an absolutely fervent, enthusiastic preface in which I think I can perceive a throbbing that is linked – I don't know which of the two analysts he is dealing with – what is certain is that he couples them; and I don't think, I have to say, even though I set things going in this path, I don't think this book, or this preface, are in very good taste. Under the rubric of delirium, that's the way I'll tell you about it, I can't say it's in the hope you'll go and see; I'd even prefer you to give up such an idea, but anyway at the end of the day I know that you'll rush to Aubier-Flammarion, even if only to see what I call an extreme.[52]

And Lacan went on to conclude that he was 'scared' by what he felt 'more or less responsible for, namely having opened the sluice gates of something that [he] could just as well have shut.' The remark on Derrida's apparently being in analysis unleashed the hilarity of the audience; he was soon informed about it. Others did not hesitate to relay the rumour afterwards, as Derrida mentioned in *The Post Card*.* Ten years later, he returned to the incident at the conference 'Lacan with the Philosophers'.[53]

---

* 'In Montreal, during a very well attended lecture, Serge Doubrovsky had wanted to get a certain effect from some news that he believed he could bring to the knowledge of his audience: I was supposed to be in analysis! A swollen head, don't you think? [. . .] Remark, I'm not so surprised. Once that upon the appearance of the *Verbier* [*Magic Word*] and of *Fors* Lacan let himself go at it right in his seminar (while running the risk of then retracting the faux-pas under ellipsis in *Ornicar* [. . .]), the rumour in a way became legitimate' (*The Post Card*, pp. 202–3).

In his comments on 11 January, Lacan made a sideswipe at
another great friend of Jacques and Marguerite Derrida, René
Major, even if he did not name him, merely mentioning 'the spread
of [his] teaching to that something that is at the other extreme of
analytic groups, which is that thing that goes around under the
name Institut de Psychanalyse'.[54] Major had been the director of
this institute since 1974.

Major, born in 1932 in Montreal, arrived in Paris in 1960 and
met Jacques and Marguerite Derrida thanks to Nicolas Abraham.
In 1966, he was an enthused member of the audience when Derrida
gave his paper 'Freud and the scene of writing', and started to read
Derrida's works methodically. Derrida very soon told him: 'They'll
make you pay very dearly for the interest you're showing in my
work, I can promise you that.'[55] Within the French psychoanalytic
movement, Major soon occupied an original position. In 1973,
together with his friend Dominique Geahchan, he set up a working
group that, the following year, took the name 'Confrontations', and
met with considerable success. Major was also in charge of a series
published by the Aubier-Montaigne imprint, and it was Derrida
who suggested the title: 'Psychoanalysis Taken at Its Word' ('La
psychanalyse prise au mot').[56]

Throughout the late 1970s, 'Confrontations' strove to tear down
the walls between the groups and societies that were confronting
one another on the French psychoanalytical scene. As Élisabeth
Roudinesco explains, the seminar organized by Major at the Institut
de Psychanalyse, in the rue Saint-Jacques, was 'an open space in
which representatives of different varieties of Freudianism came to
speak of their dramas, conflicts, and works without having to initiate a split'.[57] But the debate was not just an internal one: Major also
invited personalities from the intellectual scene such as Clément,
Kristeva, Baudrillard, Nancy, and Lacoue-Labarthe.

It was in this context that, on 21 November 1977, 'Confrontations'
welcomed the author of *Glas* and 'The factor of truth'. This memorable session – which would constitute the last part of the book *The
Post Card* – was prepared with great care, almost like a theatrical script. The audience was flabbergasted by Derrida's power of
improvisation, even though in fact it was all written out, including
Major's remarks. Extending the dialogue from a distance which
had set them at loggerheads for over ten years, Derrida seemed to
address Lacan directly, trying, as it were, to outdo him verbally. Far
from sticking to the position of a philosopher outside this milieu
and its quarrels, he made no attempt to conceal how redoubtably
well informed he was. He would later define himself as 'a friend of
psychoanalysis', but he here waxed ironical over the idea of the 'slice
of analysis' and the division 'into four slices' of the world of French
psychoanalysis:

In France there is not an analytic institution cut into four slices that it would suffice to adjoin in order to complete a whole and to recompose the harmonious unity of a community. If it were a cake, it would not be a *quatre-quarts* [four fourths, i.e. pound cake].

Each group [. . .] allegedly forms the only authentic analytic institution, the only one legitimately wielding the Freudian heritage, the only one that develops this heritage authentically in its practice, its didactics, its modes of formation and of reproduction. [. . .]

Consequence: to go do a *tranche* (which is not at all of the whole [*qui n'est pas du tout*]) in another group (which is not of the whole [*qui n'est pas du tout*]) is to *tranche*-fer onto the non-analyst, who then can counter-*tranche*-fer onto the analyst.[58]

10

Another Life

1976–1977

Ever since the early 1960s, Marguerite had freed Jacques from most of the constraints of everyday life. To enable him to work in the most favourable conditions, she took on every aspect of domestic life, including money matters and the children's education. This did not stop Derrida being an affectionate and attentive father. As Pierre says:

> I don't remember him telling us many stories or really playing with us when we were little, but he was tender and loving and could give time to us. Later, he didn't help out much with schoolwork. It's true that Jean and I were always very good pupils, which sometimes made him proud. Both my mother and he were rather easy-going and rarely said no to us. The evenings when there were guests, I tried to stick around as long as possible. I clearly remember evenings with Paule Thévenin, Sarah Kofman, Jean Genet, Jean Rista, Camilla and Valerio Adami, Chantal and René Major . . . .[1]

Jean, his younger son, remembers a father who was almost always working:

> From when we were very young, we were used to seeing him shut himself away, and we weren't tempted to go in without good reason. The handle on his study door was placed in the upright position when he didn't want to be disturbed. This was a code that my brother and I knew and respected. But throughout our childhood, he travelled much less than later on, and he was at home almost every evening. When the TV news was on, he asked us to be quiet, then he'd enjoy watching a film or a serial. Even though he thought what was on TV not much good, he must have got something out of it. I think that it was a form of therapy for him. He was generally very open towards us and didn't intervene much. For instance, he took care not

to have much direct influence on what we were reading. What *was* difficult to deal with was his permanent anxiety: when we were little, he was afraid we'd go and play outside or wander a bit too far away; later on, motorbikes and drugs were real nightmares for him. When he was angry, this was always due to anxiety, especially if we came home later than we'd said we would.[2]

Derrida's friends all emphasize how much he wanted to keep his sons near him, and how easily he worried about the least little thing. As Camilla Adami remembers:

In many respects, he behaved like a Jewish mother. He could telephone two or three times during a meal if there was any-thing to worry about. But his anxiety was also an emotional matter. If the children didn't come to give him a goodnight kiss in the evening, he immediately got really upset. A 'goodbye' spoken without warmth was enough to make him depressed.[3]

This family life, which Derrida was so keen to preserve, had since 1972 been given a severe jolt by his relation with Sylviane Agacinski. Haunted by this secret, he observed the greatest discretion possible and never appeared with her outside meetings on Greph or pub-lishing business. Only a few close friends, such as Lucette Finas, sometimes invited them as a couple. But among those close to Derrida, many guessed at this other side to his life.[4] Pierre himself understand, as early as age eleven or twelve, that there was another woman in his father's life:

At home, a telephone line was reserved for his use: one day, I picked up the receiver and it was Sylviane at the other end: she was embarrassed and brought the conversation to a swift end. A little later, there was a scene that might have come out of a novel. My mother, Jean, and I had gone into Paris on some outing. We happened to come across Jacques and Sylviane, in a situation that was quite unambiguous. But there wasn't any big scene: my mother behaved as if there was nothing wrong and we said hello to Sylviane as if she were just a colleague . . . I even think that we went to have a drink together in a café.[5]

In private life, whether with Marguerite or Sylviane, the situation was not an easy one and created moments of crisis and bouts of mel-ancholy. In several letters to Roger Laporte, who himself was prone to feeling low, Derrida referred in veiled terms to 'this whole web' in which he was paralysed and suffocating. He sometimes expressed the desire to 'start out on another, a new journey'.[6] A few months later, he insisted: 'Life is, for me, too, increasingly burdensome, difficult, barely possible. Don't even feel up to talking about it.'[7] But that whereof he could not speak, he tried to write. For the first time since a stay in New York, in 1956, he started to keep a diary, one of the forms that was most important for him:

> If there's one dream that's never left me, whatever I've written, it's the dream of writing something that has the form of a diary. Deep down, my desire to write is the desire for an exhaustive chronicle. What's going through my head? How can I write fast enough to preserve everything that's going through my head? I've sometimes started keeping notebooks, diaries again, but each time I abandoned them [. . .]. But it's the biggest regret of my life, since the thing I'd like to have written is just that: a 'total' diary.[8]

At the beginning of the Christmas vacation of 1976, Derrida started keeping two notebooks. The one, small in format, contained precise notes about circumcision: this was 'the book of Élie', which he had started to think about shortly after his father's death, at the end of 1970. The other, a bit bigger, was a Canson album whose cover would be reproduced, in 1991, in the book he wrote with Geoffrey Bennington.[9] Prior to any concrete plan, it was first and foremost a matter of writing for the pleasure of wielding the pen, 'to take up a pen, after the typewriter', on drawing paper that was 'thick, a bit rough'. But during this time of inner crisis, the notes rapidly took a very personal turn, gradually sketching out the fragments of a fascinating self-analysis.

For example, Derrida tried to draw up a list of all the blows he had received during his youth, soon realizing that they were 'always linked to racism, one way or another': 'No trauma, for me, perhaps, which is not linked on some level with the experience of racism and/ or anti-Semitism.' Several passages dwelt on circumcision, which definitely struck him as 'a *good* thread to trace one's way, in a new direction, through autobiography'.

On 23 and 24 December, he wrote a great deal. Gradually, a real project, of considerable scope, started to emerge:

> If I don't invent a new language, a new 'style', a new *phrase*, this book will have failed. This doesn't mean that I have to start there. Quite the opposite. Starting in the old language and drawing oneself (and the reader) towards an idiom that would eventually be untranslatable into the language of the beginnings.[10]

The question he had to face was that of an 'après-*Glas*', something that went further than *Glas*, and which he could attain only 'laboriously, gradually, while ceasing to publish [. . .] for a long time'.[11] What Derrida wanted, in short, was to find a very different tone from those he had deployed until then, to reach a sort of 'language without code'. This was 'the old dream, the only one that interested [him]', the dream he had already mentioned in conversations with Gabriel Bounoure and Henry Bauchau:

> To write from this place, with this tone, one that will finally make me appear from the other side, even if unrecognizable. For I have been misunderstood – radically, and not in the usual simplistic sense. A writing that nothing in what people know, have known, have read by me would have enabled them, or me, to anticipate. To keep of this book only what will have been – by me today – unrecognizable, unforeseeable.

He hoped, now, to be in a position to write this work planned since 1970, shortly after the death of his father, and never tackled since. Circumcision would play an important role in it, but that did not mean that the book would turn into an essay. Derrida wanted to relate many other things in it, including his depression in Le Mans. He would go back over his dead brothers and 'all the family silences'. What he wanted to change the most profoundly was his way of approaching writing. For this book to be really other, he would need to emerge from philosophical discourse, 'tell a lot of stories', 'launch out unrestrainedly into anecdotes':

> Independently of the content, whether it be more or less interesting, this *relation to the anecdote* is itself what needs to be transformed. It is, *in me*, choked, screwed up, repressed. All the 'good reasons' for this repression must be subjected to suspicion. What is being hidden, forbidden? Fear of the doctor: what will he discover? And I mean the traditional doctor, not even the psychoanalyst.[12]

The notebooks also contain a few dream narratives, together with a rudimentary analysis:

> Dream. Taking part in a national political meeting. I start to speak. Accuse everyone. (As usual: I never form alliances and shoot in every direction: completely alone. Fear is an alliance, and that sense of security that maintains the alliance. I'm really afraid of this, which means there is nothing heroic about my solitude – instead, something fearful and cowardly: 'they can't catch me here' – and I start to seek the cause in 'flight from

alliance'* and disgust with 'community'. This very word makes me sick.)†

These – largely unpublished – notebooks cannot be read without a sense of unease. Even more than the most personal letters, these pages are located on a fragile frontier between the private and the public. As Derrida writes: 'Anyone reading these notes without knowing me, without having read and understood *everything* of what I've written elsewhere, would remain blind and deaf to them, while he would *finally* feel that he was understanding easily.'[14] While their contents were often very intimate, these notebooks nonetheless form part of the collection of manuscripts that Derrida decided to deposit at the University of California, Irvine. And in 'Circumfession', one of his finest texts, he referred to them frequently and quoted long excerpts from them, in a somewhat reworked form. As for the 'Envois' in *The Post Card*, which he started on a few months after these notes, they are an almost direct extension of them. Once one has taken cognizance of these notebooks, it is impossible not to take them into account.

Over and above any literary or philosophical question, it is clear that Derrida was at this time going through a very deep crisis. The 'atmosphere of disaster' in which he felt he was moving made him, on some days, unable to write. The way he was being torn apart by his love affair, and the reproaches with which he was confronted on both sides, rekindled his melancholy tendencies and made his anxieties about death more tangible than ever. As he noted on 31 December: 'The split in the ego, at least in my case, is not a piece of transcendental patter.'

I am (like) one who, returning from a very long journey (outside everything, the earth, the world, men and their languages), tries

---

* Or from the covenant. – Tr.
† This almost antagonistic relationship with the question of community is one of the things that so distinguishes Derrida's thinking from that of Jean-Luc Nancy. In 1983, the latter published, in the review *Aléa*, a long article with the title 'La communauté désoeuvrée' ('The idle community'), which later became a book. Maurice Blanchot developed these ideas in *La communauté inavouable* (*The Shameful Community*) published by Éditions de Minuit in 1984. Both Nancy and Blanchot attempted to rethink the idea of community at a time when the Communist utopia was collapsing. As we have just seen, several years before this debate became a major issue for his colleagues, Derrida rejected the idea and the 'very word' of community. It probably remained in his view associated with forms of belonging to which one is subjected rather than which one chooses, whether ethnic or religious. It should not be forgotten that many Jews talk about 'the Community' without further specification: a reality from which Derrida had wished to escape in 1942 (the school called 'the Alliance' in the rue Émile-Maupas), as well as when he got married. As we shall see in the third part of this book, much of Derrida's later work concerns a projected 'new International', freed from any communitarian model.

to keep *after the event* a logbook, with the forgotten, fragmentary, rudimentary instruments of a prehistoric language and literature. Tries to understand what has happened, and to explain it with pebbles, pieces of wood, the gestures of someone deaf and dumb before there was anyone to teach the deaf and dumb, the fumblings of a blind man before Braille . . . And they're going to have to piece things together with that. If they knew, they'd be afraid and they wouldn't even try.[15]

On 3 January 1977, after a 'terrible day' of which he refused to say any more than that 'it is in itself more than a world', the notes started to become less frequent. They ceased completely at the end of February, when some drama occurred about which he remained silent, because 'you should never say anything about a secret', but which we can assume had to do with his love life.

For the first five months of 1977, the letters I have managed to find are really much more infrequent than usual. And on 21 February, Derrida wrote to Paul de Man that, if he had been late sending him the programme for the seminar he was scheduled to give in Yale the following autumn, this was because he had 'for rather longer than usual been thinking of stopping'.[16] Evidently, Derrida was ensuring a minimal service, writing little and travelling even less.[17]

His time in Oxford at the beginning of June was the basis for those 'Envois' that would fill half of *The Post Card*. This strange and superb correspondence would attain a very complex and almost undecidable status – to which I return later – when it was published, but everything suggests that the original version, which was as yet not linked to any planned book, was written for Sylviane Agacinski. The first fragment is dated 3 June 1977:

Yes, you were right, henceforth, today, now, at every moment, on this point of the *carte*, we are but a minuscule residue 'left unclaimed': a residue of what we have said to one another, of what, do not forget, we have made of one another, of what we have written one another. Yes, this 'correspondence', you're right, immediately got beyond us, which is why it all should have been burned, all of it, including the cinders of the unconscious – and 'they' will never know anything about it.[18]

The second 'Envoi', dated the same day, is even more lyrical. The form of the letter takes over from the private notebooks while allowing for a form of address, a sort of soliloquy:

and when I call you my love, my love, is it you I am calling or my love? You, my love, is it you I thereby name, is it to you that I address myself? I don't know if the question is well put, it frightens me. But I am sure that the answer, if it gets to me one day, will have come to me from you. You alone, my love, you alone will have known it.[19]

It was on 2 June that Derrida came across the famous postcard representing Socrates and Plato that would be at the heart of the volume. Extracted from a thirteenth-century fortune-telling book, this paradoxical image seemed to address him directly, as if to rekindle his long-standing meditation on the relation between speech and writing:

> Have you seen this card, the image on the back [*dos*] of this card? I stumbled across it yesterday, in the Bodleian (the famous Oxford library), I'll tell you about it. I stopped dead, with a feeling of hallucination (is he crazy or what? he has the names mixed up!) and of revelation at the same time, an apocalyptic revelation: Socrates writing, writing in front of Plato, I always knew it, it had remained like the negative of a photograph to be developed for twenty-five centuries – in me, of course. Sufficient to write it in broad daylight. The revelation is there, unless I can't yet decipher anything in this picture, which is most probable in effect. Socrates, the one who writes – seated, bent over, a scribe or docile copyist, Plato's secretary, no? He is in front of Plato, no, Plato is *behind* him, smaller (why smaller?), but standing up. With his outstretched finger he looks like he is indicating something, designating, showing the way or giving an order – or dictating, authoritarian, masterly, imperious. Almost wicked, don't you think, and voluntarily. I bought a whole supply of them.[20]

His reflections on this image continued through several letters, then the correspondence broke off provisionally on his return home from Britain on 11 June.

While Derrida felt somewhat better, he was still not completely himself. Once freed from his obligations in the rue d'Ulm, he wrote for the review *Macula* a very long text in dialogue form about Van Gogh's shoes, as discussed by Martin Heidegger and Meyer Shapiro. This piece of work exhausted him, he wrote to Sarah Kofman: 'I couldn't find my way to the end of it and don't know what they'll think about it. I feel tired and a bit discouraged by what I'll need to do this summer, especially the Yale classes.' Sarah was depressed too, as often. Derrida advised her to take some rest – advice he was also giving himself, even though he found it very difficult to follow: 'We need a pause, a slow rumination, a time for "repair". The ideal would even be to stop teaching for a while.' He wondered whether he might not find some way of suspending his seminar for a year. For now, he left with his family for Conca dei Marini on Italy's Amalfi Coast, where the Adamis had rented a house: 'I'm going to swim as much as possible. I'm in poor shape physically. I've put on weight (as always when I'm tired) and I feel as heavy as a bag of lead.'[21]

Derrida was thrilled to discover this region, and greatly impressed by the ancient and still very well-preserved site of Paestum. This was also the first time he had visited Pompeii, a place which he liked to revisit in later years. Nonetheless, August did not live up to all his expectations. Perhaps this was because he had not fulfilled his desire of 'jumping over towards Sicily', something he had dreamed of doing with Sylviane.[22] This was probably also because he had not really managed to relax. He explained all this in a long letter to Philippe Lacoue-Labarthe, asking him to share its contents with Jean-Luc Nancy.

> I've been trying to work and to work on myself in a slightly different way, but it's difficult, at the moment, to say how much I've succeeded. In short, I came home yesterday [. . .] exhausted and overwhelmed-worried-discouraged by what lies ahead. I'm leaving on the 10th for Yale (the schedule is overladen there, too). Anyway. [. . .] Joliet has asked me to write a text for 'Champs', so I'll revamp 'Le facteur de la vérité', preceded by an essay on *Beyond the P[leasure] P[rinciple]* and a preface, the whole to be called *Freud's Legacy*. I'd thought I might finish it this summer, but I'm late. I still hope to submit the manuscript at the end of October for publication in the winter or spring.[23]

In every respect, the piece was far from the shape that *The Post Card* would finally assume, in 1980. At this stage, the 'Envois' were not part of the project at all.

On 10 September 1977, Derrida left for Yale, but the absence of Paul de Man, who was on sabbatical in France, meant that his stay there was less agreeable than in previous years. 'Your influence in the United States is growing, with all the aberrations and hardenings of position that this implies,' de Man had told him.[24]

Having left them to one side for eight months, Derrida resumed his notebooks on 12 October, just before his return from the United States. These personal notes are interwoven with the writing of the 'Envois', a manifestation of that new 'writing without interruption that has been sought since the beginning', and in which autobiography takes its full place, in a lyrical and often painful way.

> I have lost you [*Je t'ai perdu(e)*]: I no longer possess you, no longer possessing you, provoked your loss, I have forced you into the loss of yourself.

And if I say – as is true – that at this moment I am losing life, this oddly comes down to the same thing, as if 'my' life were that other which I was forcing to its loss.[25]

[. . .] and today when the event which marks the interruption in February (re)occurs, is confirmed after the event [*après coup*] as if it had not taken place but needed time to coincide with itself anew, no one will never know the secret from which I write and the fact that I say it changes nothing.[26]

During Derrida's stay in Yale, his house in Ris-Orangis had had some work done on it, transforming the attic into an office which he reached by a ladder and in which he could not stand upright. While he now had a place of his own, he felt this move to be a sort of exile in which he was cut off from his nearest and dearest:

I will call this attic (and the person who gave it to me, made me climb up into it, live, work, separate myself, circumvent myself, and circumdecide myself) my SUBLIME.
   Subliminal, under the heaven, the workshop and departure lounge for my sublimation, my separation accepted, my renunciation loved, the serenity of disaster. Already feel like dying here. Then, the trapdoor is closed. I am respectfully enclosed, not having known or been able to touch me, love me for what I am, I would have been.[27]

This uncomfortable attic in which Derrida would work for many years would disconcert his American visitors when they came to visit him in Ris-Orangis. In winter, the little electric radiator did not make much difference to the cold and Derrida had to write with his neck wrapped in a scarf, swathed in pullovers, and sometimes an overcoat. Harold Bloom, one of the major figures in the Yale School, 'expressed his dismay and surprise that this was where the great works signed "Jacques Derrida" got the green light, upstairs in an unheated attic'.[28]

But, for now, discomfort was not Derrida's most pressing problem. In many ways, his new situation was like the promise of a *vita nova*. What he was seeking was the form of a writing that would enable him to 'find himself again, after having been (by whom?) for so long *lost*'. Autobiography made its entry into his work more directly than before. During the autumn of 1977, Derrida would embark on several texts that used the form of the 'log-book' and took over from the private journals in which he now stopped writing.
   It was probably not entirely a coincidence if the longest part of Sylviane Agacinski's first book, *Aparté: Conceptions and Deaths*

of Søren Kierkegaard, published in March 1977 in the series 'La philosophie en effet', took the very free form of a 'journal "of reading"', a form which, the author writes, 'seems to sanction groping, wandering, and rehashing; it lifts the prohibition that ordinarily falls on digression; in principle it is tolerant of a certain disconnectedness'. 'At any rate, should it be necessary to provide a thread or gist here, then we might say that from one end to the other end in every sense of the word, it will be a question only of *breaks* or *ruptures*.'[29] It is as if the dialogue between Sylviane and Jacques were being continued, in an admittedly encrypted way, through the books they published that year.

The first words of 'Living on' – a long essay meant for the collective book *Deconstruction and Criticism* – echo with particular force if we remember the period Derrida had just lived through: 'But who's talking about living?' And the immensely long note at the foot of the page that runs along at the bottom of the main text opens with this note: '10 November 1977. Dedicate "Living On" to the memory of my friend Jacques Ehrmann.'[30] Ehrmann had been responsible for Derrida's first visit to Yale and was the author of, among others, a text entitled 'The death of literature' . . . The constraint which the five representatives of the so-called 'Yale School' had imposed on themselves was that they would all discuss Shelley's poem 'The Triumph of Life' in their own individual way, but, in a symptomatic reversal of expectations, Derrida referred much more to *Death Sentence* and *The Madness of the Day* by Blanchot.

The tonality of 'Cartouches' was equally sombre. This text, which was originally to be called 'Log-book', accompanied 127 drawings by Gérard Titus-Carmel depicting little mahogany boxes in the shape of tiny coffins, 'pocket size coffins' as Derrida called them. The first entry was dated 30 November 1977; the last 11 and 12 January 1978. Well before the meditation on 'date' that Derrida composed a few years later in 'Shibboleth: For Paul Celan', the themes of the 'only time' and 'the crypt' are powerfully set out here:

7 January 1978
When the date itself becomes the place of a crypt, when it stands in for it.

Will they ever know why I inscribe this at a given date? Throw of a *die*.

Le date [cf. *la date* "the date"] has also been used [in French] : *le date* [the thing given, the *datum*]. *There is* the date of today, they'll never know anything about what was given to be lived in it – and taken away.

The date itself will stand in for a crypt, the only one that remains, save the heart.[31]

11

From the Nouveaux Philosophes *to the Estates General*

1977–1979

Ever since the beginning of the TV programme *Apostrophes* on 10 January 1975, the French media landscape had experienced a major change of direction. The programme, chaired by Bernard Pivot on Antenne 2, every Friday at 9.30 p.m., assumed a major place in literary and intellectual life. The mere presence of an author on the panel often increased his or her sales considerably, and a brilliant performance could transform a difficult work into a best-seller.

The broadcast rapidly transformed editorial practices, encouraging the emergence of a new generation of authors who had grown up with television and could use the medium with ease. They wanted to bypass the traditional modes of legitimation and address the general public *directly*. The convergence of their interests with those of *Apostrophes* was ideological as well as being a consequence of the media involved: what counted for Bernard Pivot was less the books than the debate they could arouse. This favoured the great questions of the day, starting with that of totalitarianism. Solzhenitsyn – whose *Gulag Archipelago* had been translated into French in 1974 and caused a huge stir – was one of the first guests. As for the *nouveaux philosophes*, they would always find a major platform for their ideas on *Apostrophes*.[1]

On 27 May 1977, Pivot even offered them a real launch pad, with a special broadcast entitled 'Are the *nouveaux philosophes* on the left or the right?' On the panel were Bernard-Henri Lévy, André Glucksmann, and Maurice Clavel, on the one side, François Aubral and Xavier Delcourt, the authors of *Against the Nouvelle Philosophie*, on the other. The *nouveaux philosophes* were judged to have performed more brilliantly than their detractors. The sales of the first book by Bernard-Henri Lévy (soon nicknamed 'BHL' for short), *Barbarism with a Human Face*, soared the very next day, and soon hit 80,000.

Widely supported by the mainstream media, including *Le Monde* and *Le Nouvel Observateur*, the 'new philosophy' split the intellectual world. The controversy was all the fiercer as several of these young authors had been educated at Normale Sup, as contemporaries of those whom they were now attacking. Like his friend Maurice Clavel, Michel Foucault had supported André Glucksmann in 1975, when Le Seuil brought out *The Cook and the Man-Eater*. Philippe Sollers, who had broken away from Maoism shortly after his return from China, formed a real alliance with Bernard-Henri Lévy, and methodically took up the cudgels on behalf of his books. Roland Barthes voiced his support for *Barbarism with a Human Face*, allowing *Les Nouvelles littéraires* to publish the letter he had written to its author. By contrast, Gilles Deleuze spat out his venom in a short pamphlet, *On the Nouveaux Philosophes and a More General Problem*. He started right off by saying that 'their thought is crap':

> I can think of two possible reasons why it is such crap. To begin with, they proceed with gross concepts, as gross as a hollow tooth: law, power, master, world, rebellion, faith, etc. This means they can mix things up grotesquely, creating schematic dualisms: law versus rebel, power versus angel. At the same time, the feebler the thought content, the more self-important the thinker, and the more the subject of utterance gives himself airs despite the emptiness of the actual utterances. [. . .] With these two procedures, they destroy work. [. . .] This massive return to an author or an empty subject inflated by vanity, and to stereotypical schematic concepts, represents an obnoxious reactive force.[2]

In the rest of his text, Deleuze compared the methods of the *nouveaux philosophes* which the plans set out in the Haby Reform: they both involved 'a serious dumbing-down of the "programme" of philosophy'. But what counted for him, much more than for Lévy or Glucksmann, was the profound modification that this 'marketing enterprise' had inflicted on intellectual life: 'Indeed, it is the submission of all thought to the media; by the same token, it gives these media the minimum intellectual endorsement and complacency to stifle the creative attempts that would enable them to move forward on their own initiative.'

Derrida had deliberately kept out of the controversy. But at the end of the summer, Jean Piel asked him to contribute to the special issue of *Critique* that he was putting together on the theme 'What use is philosophy today?' He made it perfectly clear that the idea had come to him when he saw 'the indecent, sickening, and ridiculous display of the so-called work by those who pass themselves off under the name "the *nouveaux philosophes*"'. Piel drew up a questionnaire, 'quite neutral in appearance', and sent it to a considerable number of philosophers whom he esteemed 'and also to many who are still very young'.[3] Jean-Luc Nancy and Philippe Lacoue-Labarthe, who had been asked to contribute, were hesitant. Derrida would have preferred that neither he nor they contributed to the issue, since they had no idea in whose company they would find themselves, and what would come out of it:

> I don't want to judge Piel (there would be too much to say, and if I left *Critique*, it was only after I had spent considerable time weighing up the effects of his practice, but never mind that), but one thing is sure: for a long time he's done nothing positive in 'our' direction, and he is motivated mainly by the desire to defend against the *nouveaux philosophes* something which I personally am not sure I support [. . .].
>
> The analysis of the scene that has produced the big neophilosophical bubble is not something to be improvised, especially not in a letter, but we can agree on one point, I think: the forces that are currently dominant in it, or are taking advantage of it, are of such a nature that they grow every time anything advances onto their ground, or speaks as loudly as they do, even (and especially) when it is to attack them. Some apparent, clearly demarcated silences, some indifferent perseverances, on another ground, can sometimes be more effective, more intimidating.[4]

A few days later, Derrida said the same to Piel, but his tone was different. Of course, he felt very concerned by the question that had been asked, especially the question of the *nouveaux philosophes*. And naturally, he had wondered what might be 'the answers that would be the most efficient, relevant, political, etc., and the most *affirmative* too', apart from the 'distaste' that 'the grim phenomenon' aroused in him. But he was just about to leave for the United States for five weeks, and his schedule there was packed. Now, if he did want to write anything, Derrida said, he would want it to be a close analysis, so that he could really measure up to a phenomenon that he considered to be profound and important, 'in spite of or because of the symptomatic paltriness of the work produced and the agents who are pushing themselves in it':

> In a force field that is obviously so favourable to it and at present conditions all forms of public exchange, the neophilosophical circus can easily grow and extend its territory, in short draw advantage from anything that *takes up a position towards it*. [. . .] You know that neo-philosophy – and this is no coincidence – can avail itself of powerful loudspeakers in all the press apparatuses, from *Marie-Claire* to the *Nouvel*

Obs, from *Playboy* to *Le Monde*, from France-Culture to TF1, Antenne 2, France 3 – not to mention other, more surprising and closer media? [. . .] All these phenomena, despite their lack of 'philosophical' interest, nonetheless interest me greatly, very indirectly. And they at least deserve a long, complex analysis that discusses pretty much everything and goes quite some way back in time.[5]

Even though, at bottom his position was not very different from Deleuze's, Derrida disagreed with the strategy of the latter's short pamphlet. But he remarked to Daniel Giovannangeli – who wrote the first thesis on Derrida's work at the University of Liège – that the discourse of the *nouveaux philosophes* made him feel like writing something about Marx, though he added that he would not do so, since this would mean giving them a surplus value which they did not deserve.[6] A few months earlier, he had stated in an interview in *Digraphe*:

You know to what extent I have remained unmoved in the face of various episodes of 'Marxist' or pseudo-Marxist dogmatic eruptions, even when they were attempting to be terroristic or intimidating, and sometimes very close to places I was passing through; well, I find even more ludicrous and reactive the hastiness of those who today think they have finally landed on the continent of post-Marxism. They are sometimes one and the same, but who would be surprised by that? You are aware of the new Parisian consensus and all the interests that are knotted together by it.[7]*

---

* The relations between Bernard-Henri Lévy and Derrida were much more fraught and ambiguous than they might seem. In an article in *Le Magazine littéraire* in May 1974 (well before *Barbarism with a Human Face* had made him famous), Lévy stated that Derrida was 'not a guru', and attacked Derrida's disciples rather than the master himself: 'There are Derrideans, and yet there is no such thing as Derrideanism. Jacques Derrida has disciples, and he is not a *maître à penser*. This is perhaps the main ambiguity of his texts, the key to their hermeticism and their legendary difficulty. Derrideans? They constitute, as it were, our new *femmes savantes*. A strange race of philosophers who gravitate around the rue d'Ulm and the reviews of the avant-garde. They speak the language of the master and mimic his least little tics. They write "difference" with an *a* and read Greek in the original. They go to seminars in the same way that others go to mass or to market: to seek the last rites or the latest trendy concept. Today it's "hymen", yesterday it was "pharmakon", the day before yesterday "the arch-trace". You don't quite understand? They tell you in reply that there's nothing to understand: these aren't "concepts", but "textual work".' However, according to Lévy, the real issues involved in Derridean deconstruction were political: 'They touch on the most sensitive point of our theoretical situation: the destiny and status of Marxism. Everyone is talking of *going beyond* Marxism: Derrida is perhaps the first to *outflank it*.' Some twenty years before Derrida's *Specters of Marx*, this is quite an insightful remark. And Lévy concluded:

Meanwhile, the publishing activities of Derrida and the three co-directors of 'La philosophie en effet' were being pursued at Aubier-Flammarion in often difficult conditions. Sales of the Greph's collective work, *Who's Afraid of Philosophy?*, published in paperback, rapidly topped 10,000 copies, but the four people in charge of the series found it extremely difficult to find an audience for some of the works that they thought of most importance. On 4 April 1978, Derrida complained bitterly about this in a long letter that he sent to Mme Aubier-Gabail, the woman who ran the Aubier publishing house in the impasse Conti, where the volumes of 'La philosophie en effet' were now published. He had just learned that she was refusing to publish one of Walter Benjamin's main works, *The Origins of German Baroque Drama*, which mean that nobody else could translate it either. In the view of the directors, however, it had always been clear that certain foreign works, deemed to be important and useful to their strategy and their research, would be given a place in the series. 'This is the case with Benjamin's work. My surprise – which is really quite unbounded – is all the more in this case, as it is a "classic" work, quoted everywhere in the world, fundamental in many respects, scandalously poorly known in France.'[8]

The publisher replied in some embarrassment, on this point as on the other difficulties raised by Derrida. A month later, as most of the problems were still unresolved, he called into question the transfer of 'La philosophie en effet' to Aubier, and asked for the series to be returned to the parent publisher, where logistical support should be more easily assured. Henri Flammarion had already agreed in principle and the transfer to the rue Racine was effected quickly. But this change of address was far from solving all the problems. Derrida, who remained the main link with the publisher, found the work this involved him in very irksome, as he moved from department to department. On 8 August 1978, he complained about this to Sarah Kofman, whose book *Aberrations: The Becoming-Woman of Auguste Comte* was due to be published shortly afterwards, as was Derrida's own work *The Truth in Painting*, due to come out directly in paperback, in the 'Champs' series, though the many illustrations were creating practical difficulties. 'I came out of it all exhausted, but all the same reassured. Let's hope that we won't be disappointed again. If we are [. . .], I'm throwing in the towel next year.'[9]

'There are definitely some good things about such a byzantine approach, which produces unsuspected effects. Derrida's solitary and obstinate labour is already part and parcel of the great tradition of philosophies of the hammer. These harsh, rough-edged, demanding philosophies are first and foremost vast demystifications. These redoubtable, glacial thoughts attack conformisms wherever they may be. In the fairground of ideologies, the Derridean hammer is perhaps one of our criteria of rigour.'

Over the next few months, things did not get any easier – quite the opposite. For Philippe Lacoue-Labarthe's book *The Subject of Philosophy: Typographies 1*, the typesetter made a mess of all the Greek quotations, which meant that publication had to be deferred. Nancy and Lacoue-Labarthe, who by force of circumstances could help Derrida only from afar when it came to publishing matters, wondered whether it was worth bothering about a series if they had to work in such conditions.[10] Derrida, swamped by work and tasks that were often unrewarding, said that he, too, was 'tired, disappointed, discouraged'. And also, unfortunately, completely powerless. The problems that had arisen at Flammarion were, he said, the same he had encountered at Seuil, Minuit, and the Presses Universitaires de France. He wanted to talk about it in detail with Lacoue-Labarthe and Nancy. With Kofman, it would unfortunately be impossible. 'She is for me, with me, more "difficult" (how can I say it?) than ever. And this doesn't help sort out our common problems, of course. [. . .] I'm very tired at having to expend so much energy, in such a repetitive and ineffectual way.'[11]

One thing was certain: Derrida refused to envisage their series being transferred to another publisher. 'Anywhere else, let's not forget: it would be [François] Wahl or [Jean] Piel: much worse in either case.' The basic problem was one of economics: 'La philosophie en effet' published demanding books that sold few copies – they were miles away from those which the public was now snapping up:

> With *The Testament of God* [Bernard-Henri Lévy's new work] we wouldn't have met with any delays, and not only because there isn't any Greek in that book, I suppose, but because *all* the conditions of its production and 'launch' are, as you know, different. So long as we're not writing for all the Poirot-Delpechs* in the world and what they represent, we'll be fighting on in difficult, almost impossible conditions. [. . .]
>
> Now, do we need to keep the series? This is clearly the question you're asking and, I have to say, I've been asking myself the same question for a long time. Here, our analyses and our plans do not inevitably or completely coincide. In any case, everyone will need to make a choice and assume his or her responsibilities. Personally, I've never had the least 'motivation' for organizing (even collectively) a series. The interest which, very late in the day, drove me to this one was not, as you know, a personal interest (you can see what I mean by that: ease, comfort, power [. . .]). So, no personal interest, but on the contrary – and at the cost of certain personal interests – let

---

* Bertrand Poirot-Delpech was a conservative journalist, novelist, and Academician. – Tr.

us call them theoretico-political aims that interested me, yes, and that interested you too, I think. [. . .] It would just need you no longer to be convinced for that to be a sufficient reason for abandoning it; in addition, I'd also be following the most 'natural' tendency of my tastes and my rhythm.[12]

In spite of this 'natural tendency', Derrida felt obliged to take up the cudgels again on behalf of philosophy. Although the Haby Reform had been passed in June 1975, it had been delayed, though not abandoned. It was meant to be implemented at the start of the new academic year 1981; so it was high time to react. In March 1979, twenty-one well-known figures (including François Châtelet, Gilles Deleuze, Jean-Toussaint Desanti, Élisabeth de Fontenay, Vladimir Jankélévitch, and Paul Ricoeur) launched an 'Appeal' for a meeting of the Estates General of philosophy. Roland Brunet initiated the process, but things would never have become as far-reaching as they did without the constant involvement of Derrida. The Appeal rapidly attracted over 2,500 signatures.

The Estates General opened on the morning of 16 June in the *grand amphithéâtre* of the Sorbonne. About one thousand, two hundred people took part, from all over France. The only downside was that few students turned up; admittedly, the dates chosen were not very practical for them. Vladimir Jankélévitch, who had shown his solidarity ever since the start of the Greph and its struggles, opened the proceedings. Stating clearly that 'the teaching of philosophy is threatened in its very existence', he hailed 'the far-sightedness and courage' of Roland Brunet and Jacques Derrida. Of course, for the time being, the danger was covert rather than explicit: 'Nobody apparently wants anything bad to happen to philosophy, everyone wants it to do well: they want to "modernize" it, dust it down, open its windows to "the modern world".' But behind 'these suave promises', the aim was gradually to diminish the place of philosophy and to reduce the number of those who taught it.[13]

Derrida then spoke, presenting 'in a personal capacity' what the philosophy of these Estates General should be. Naturally, he spoke against the Haby Reform and in favour of the preservation of a minimum of four hours of philosophy for all pupils in *terminale*, but in particular he developed the idea that he felt to be of the most importance, that of 'the *extension* of philosophy teaching to the whole second cycle in *lycées*'. Unfortunately, he could not stop himself reopening an old quarrel, that which over the past two or three years had set philosophers in the universities against the young trendies. Derrida refrained from naming his adversaries, but everyone found them all the easier to recognize because Bernard-Henri Lévy had made another noted appearance on *Apostrophes* two weeks before the Estates General:

Today, neither among those philosophers who are in the slightest bit awake, nor among those who have even just a little bit lost their innocence and have trained themselves to a degree of discernment in these areas (publishing, the press, television), would anybody dare to speak up for the vitality or rigour of philosophy by referring to a big part, the major part, one might say, of what has been for some time exhibited on the most prominent shelves, what noisily claims to be philosophy in every sort of studio. Since a relatively recent and very definite date, the loudest speakers have been given the loudest loudspeakers without (in the best cases) wondering why, all of a sudden, newspaper columns and airwaves were being handed over to them so that they could talk *like this* and say *just that*.[14]

A reply soon materialized. The Saturday afternoon and Sunday morning were devoted to work in groups, but the Sunday afternoon was taken up by a new plenary session meant to bring it all together and reach some conclusions. It was during this session, chaired by Jean-Luc Nancy, that a major incident was to occur.

Bernard-Henri Lévy arrived with a small group of friends, including Dominique Grisoni, who in 1976 had brought out the collective book *Politiques de la philosophie* to which Derrida has contributed, together with Châtelet, Foucault, Lyotard, and Serres. By Lévy's own admission, they were not interested in the Haby Reform. They had come to the Estates General spoiling for a fight. 'Most of those people had continually taken sides against me for two years,' he relates. 'I considered them to be my enemies. I said to myself that there were two different ways of defending philosophy. This was the theme of many of my interventions of that time. So I was at war with the university system. And the university system paid me back by being at total war with me.'[15] Dominique Grisoni was the first to move: he interrupted Derrida from the back of the hall. It was suggested that he speak using a microphone, like the other participants, but the audience, most of whom wanted to carry on with the proceedings as planned, immediately started to boo him. Since Grisoni could not make himself heard, BHL tried to 'avenge his comrade'. 'I came down and moved towards the podium. They tried to stop me speaking. I wanted to get onto the podium to take the microphone, and pushed my opponents out of the way. Derrida came down in person to give them a hand, and we came to blows, like in the time of his teenage brawls, and mine.'[16]

After this moment of confusion, Jean-Luc Nancy announced that 'Bernard-Henri Lévy can speak as soon as the assembly is ready to hear him,', but he had to insist that the people on the podium agree to leave it. The following exchanges, which were recorded in the volume published shortly afterwards, are worth quoting:

B.-H. Lévy: I am amazed to see that when somebody (I've been
given leave to speak, so I will) starts to explain something
here, to put on trial the institution of philosophy, to put on
trial those men who for years have benefited from this system
and who react only when they feel threatened, that person
is told to shut up. [. . .] I'm amazed that, when I myself am
given leave to speak, a certain number of men come over to
grab the mike from me and trigger an incident. As far as I'm
concerned, that's what I wanted to say: I've been amazed
ever since yesterday to hear people putting the media on
trial: do you think it was the philosophy professors who were
the first to denounce the Gulag? It was television and the
media. Do you think that it's in his capacity as a philosophy
professor that, a year ago, when Brezhnev came to Paris,
Glucksmann opened his 'opinion column' to three dissidents
from the East and caused a scandal? That was the media. It
wasn't the Estates General of philosophy. I'm amazed that
today, as 76,000 Vietnamese are castaway by the Malaysian
government, nobody even mentions the fact. I'm amazed
that, the day before Corsican militants are scheduled to
appear in the State security court, including a philosophy
teacher, Mondoloni . . .

Derrida: We've discussed him already. Stop talking rubbish.

B.-H. Lévy: Perfect. My apologies. In that case let me say I'm
amazed that people have been talking about anti-media vigilance. They used to talk about anti-fascist vigilance. If that's
why you're holding Estates General of philosophy, I'm not
just amazed, I'm extremely disappointed.

S. Agacinski:. I'd just like to say a word to B.-H. Lévy: he was
here yesterday, but he didn't feel like speaking out since
he'd come alone. Today, he's turned up with friends who've
started yelling from their seats to sabotage the assembly and
take over this whole enterprise.[17]

There are divergent accounts of what happened next, and the
book that records the interventions and debates of those two days
allows us to build up only a partial idea of this confrontation,
several 'inaudible' passages of which could not be transcribed. Lévy
now claims that he was 'expelled from the hall' and then 'thrown
into the rue de la Sorbonne'. At a panel discussion organized by
the review *Esprit* a few months after these events, Derrida gave a
very different version, mentioning 'a brief and minor scuffle', before
adding:

I would not linger over this incident, which, by the way, is very
illuminating, if I had not just learned that, if we are to believe

an interview between P. Sollers and B.-H. Lévy, the latter claims to have been 'beaten up' at the Estates General. 'Beaten up!' One can hope that such an eloquent defender of human rights knows the meaning of and weights this expression [. . .].[18]

Given the great number of participants and the stir which the Estates General caused in the media, Derrida was forced to agree to having photographs taken of him, albeit reluctantly. In this respect, too, the weekend in question was a turning point. But Derrida's relations with the press remained difficult. For example, shortly before the event, he refused to allow *Le Matin* to publish an interview he had given Catherine Clément, since he was dissatisfied with the transcription. She told him in no uncertain terms how disappointed she was: this interview was to have been the main piece in a special number on the Estates General and it seemed to her insulting that, 'in such an incredibly casual way', Derrida had decided to withdraw it, 'unilaterally and without any possible discussion'.

It's clear you know nothing about a journalist's profession. [. . .] Academics despise and sometimes hate journalists: you are one of their number. [. . .] No doubt you are a great philosopher. But this gives you no right at all to despise those who *also* work in language. [. . .] I also think that it's incredible you can't get out of this deadlock, since it's clear that your relations with the press are full of problems on every side, and it's easy to guess why, if you always behave the same way.[19]

Clément had hit the nail on the head, in many respects. Derrida's mistrust of the press and the media, like Bourdieu's, would last for a long time, leaving the field open to the *nouveaux philosophes*, who occupied the territory without any qualms.[20]

But the impact of the Estates General was not just confined to these events, however spectacular. On the institutional level, the extent of the mobilization had a considerable effect. On television, on the evening of 16 June, the Minister for Education claimed not to understand what – in the presidential decree affecting the implementation of the Haby Reform, which had not even been finally decided on – could be so alarming for philosophy; there must have been misinformation or misunderstanding.[21] The efforts of Jacques Derrida and Roland Brunet had not been altogether in vain: while the most innovative ideas of the Greph would remain a dead letter, the Haby Reform was never implemented and the teaching of philosophy in *terminale* was safe for a long time to come.

12

Postcards and Proofs

1979–1981

At the symposium on the work of Peter Szondi held in Paris on 23 June 1979, Derrida met someone whose importance would soon become apparent. He related it immediately, in one of the 'Envois' of *The Post Card*:

> On the way out, diverse presentations. 'With you, one can no longer present oneself,' a young American (I think) woman says to me. She gives me to understand that she has read (before me, therefore, she was just coming from the US), '*Moi, la psychanalyse*', in which I let play, in English, the so-difficult-to-translate vocabulary of presentation, of presentations, of '*introductions*', etc. As I was insisting on getting her name (insisting is too strong), she said 'Metaphysics', and refused to add a single word. I found this little game rather clever and I felt, through the insignificant frivolity of the exchange, that she had gone rather far (I was told afterward that she was a 'Germanist').[1]

Avital Ronell tells the story rather differently:

> I'd come to this conference with my friend Gisèle Celan-Lestrange, Celan's widow. At that time, my status was unclear: I was still something of a student, even though I'd already begun teaching. I wasn't prepared for this meeting, on that day. I didn't think there would be so few of us in the hall. During the break, Derrida came over to me and asked me who I was. I don't know why I replied: 'But . . . don't you recognize me?' He gazed at me in embarrassment. 'Er . . . no, I don't think so.' I insisted. 'Really? But that's not very nice. I'm metaphysics.' I was staging myself like an effect of his text. He was dumb-struck, a bit lost: 'So, you're metaphysics . . .?' I'd been hoist by my own petard, and more or less obliged to carry on with the game. I added something like: 'Yes, and I don't much like the way you've been treating me up until now . . .'[2]

Avital Ronell had been born in Prague in 1952. Her parents, Israeli diplomats, had lived in New York since 1956. She started her studies there before going to the Free University in Berlin, working with Jacob Taubes, a rabbi and professor of hermeneutics. In 1979, the year she met Derrida, she obtained her doctorate at Princeton. Ronell would very rapidly become a close friend of Derrida, and one of the most original and striking figures in the Derridean movement. 'I was working on Goethe and Eckermann at that time,' she explains.

I was fascinated by the figure of Eckermann, the one who could take down the remarks of his master, reassure and amuse him. I admired Eckermann's extreme, perfect passivity. Shortly before that, Gadamer had told me I should find a master, since a real thinker couldn't avoid leaning on a master. So I must have fantasized about becoming Derrida's Eckermann. I very quickly thought I could sense and understand his immense solitude, and I wanted to throw a rope to him. In those days, his fame was spreading rapidly. More or less consciously, Derrida was building up a sort of team for himself, disseminated across the world. In that team, I could play the role of 'Minister for Germanic Affairs'. I applied for this post and I obtained it. For several years, we had many sustained conversations on Goethe, Kleist, Hölderlin, and Kafka.

Ever since its publication in 1976, *Of Grammatology* had continued to enjoy considerable success. Two years later, Alan Bass's remarkable translation of *Writing and Difference* was published by the University of Chicago Press.[3] By this stage, deconstruction was now in fashion, and Derrida was much sought after. At the end of summer 1979, he went on a major conference tour of North America with the older of his two sons, Pierre, who was then sixteen. As the latter remembers,

What impressed me the most was the energy he could draw on. We changed city almost every day. Every time, there was the plane journey, a lunch, a long conference session, then generally a cocktail and a dinner that went on until late. The pace of a real rock star. After a few days, I'd been brought to my knees, which greatly surprised my father. He was in better shape than ever. I felt that the trip was galvanizing him.[4]

This did not stop Pierre from remembering his trip with pleasure, especially his meetings with Paul de Man, in Chicago and Yale.

Derrida said that he, too, had enjoyed this experience: 'It was very strange, rich and ultimately very mysterious.'[5] But Pierre stayed for only part of the tour, before returning to Ris-Orangis to start his *terminale*. From 24 September, Derrida gave a three-week seminar in Yale on 'The Concept of Comparative Literature and the Theoretical Problems of Translation'. Then he went to Montreal for a conference on 'Nietzsche's Otobiography' and two days of free discussion with some of those most enthusiastic about his work, such as Claude Lévesque, Christie V. McDoland, Eugenio Donato, and Rodolphe Gasché.[6]

Jacques and Marguerite Derrida were generous hosts. Many colleagues, translators, and even students were invited to their home in Ris-Orangis. During the 1979 Christmas holidays, Avital Ronell was a guest on several occasions. Pierre, still not seventeen, was a brilliant young man, passionate about music and literature. He and Avital were soon involved in a love affair. Jacques was surprised and uneasy. However liberal he was, he was worried about the age difference: Avital was eleven years older than Pierre. Perhaps Derrida also felt that she was too closely tied to his own world. As for Pierre, he hankered after independence. 'My father and I had never been very close,' he remembers.

> As I grew up, I tried to establish a real relationship with him, but we always kept a certain distance from one another, even physically. From a very young age, I felt the need to protect myself, keeping secret almost everything that was important for me. My affair with Avital played a revelatory role. The fact that I wanted to leave home just after the baccalaureate was something he couldn't understand. When I hesitated to embark on *hypokhâgne*, envisaging a sort of sabbatical year, he was even more dismayed. He asked friends we had in common – for a long time, I'd mainly hung out with people older than myself – to try to get me to change my mind. As far as my studies were concerned, in fact, they succeeded.[7]

Avital confirms that things were not always easy, at least not initially. 'Jacques worried about my relationship with Pierre, just as he worried about everything that concerned his children. His worries certainly did make life complicated for us. At the same time, my relation with Pierre was a way of becoming part of the family. And Marguerite was as kind to me as one could possibly be.' In June 1980, just after the *bac* – which he passed with flying colours – Pierre moved into Tzvetan Todorov's old apartment with Avital. 'For me, those years in Paris correspond to a really lovely dream,' remembers the woman whom Derrideans would long continue to call 'Metaphysics'.

In another context, with other protagonists, things could have turned into a soap opera. With Derrida I zigzagged between the two poles of private, family life and intellectual life. Our relation was very fraught and sometimes very complicated. Often, I was there to make him laugh, like a jester. So I had the right to tell the king the truth. Curiously, in spite of this family closeness, we continued to address each other with the formal *vous*. To my mind, this was the *vous* discussed by Levinas, which marks an even more authentic intimacy.[8]

Derrida finished *The Post Card* at the beginning of summer 1979, before leaving for the United States. It was so that he could finish the 'Envois' that he bought an electric typewriter. In this long series of love letters, Derrida was going back to his first desire, which led him 'toward something that literature makes room for better than philosophy', this 'idiomatic writing whose purity, I realize, is inaccessible, but about which I continue to dream'.[9] The letters on which he based *The Post Card* have disappeared or are inaccessible, so all suppositions are permitted and even encouraged: 'You might consider them, if you really wish to, as the remainders of a recently destroyed correspondence,' Derrida announces in the prologue.[10] Even if the text regularly states how it has been constructed, it enjoys throwing the reader off the scent. It is a question of taking the letters away in advance 'from every centre of, as they say, genetic criticism. Not a sketch will remain to uncover the traces.'[11]

Everything is stated in the 'Envois', but in a way strewn with carefully laid booby traps, which renders forever undecidable the frontier between the private and the public, between self-disclosure and fiction. This does not stop Derrida leaving in the text 'all kinds of references, names of persons and of places, identifiable dates, identifiable events, they will rush in with eyes closed, finally believing to be there and to find us there and to find us there when by means of a switch point I will send them elsewhere to see if we are there'.[12] Of the immense original correspondence, only fragments remain, since one of the rules Derrida imposed on himself was to retain only what could be '*combined*' with the three other texts in the volume – 'To speculate – on "Freud"', 'Le facteur de la vérité', and 'Du tout' – as if the 'Envois' comprised merely an exorbitantly long preface. And there is nothing to prove, of course, that some of the letters were not written after the event, specially for publication.

Jean-Luc Nancy was the first to react to the almost complete manuscript of *The Post Card* when Derrida sent it to him. He received it at the same time as Sarah Kofman and Philippe Lacoue-Labarthe, as one would expect, since the work was to be published in their series. In spite of its length, he read it very quickly, especially the 'Envois', so greatly was he 'enthralled, captivated, and some-times moved'. 'Independently of any decision on publication, this text touches me, I feel like saying, parodying the way you use words, it touches, it does nothing but that, touching (and reaching its destination, too), it's a text of tact and skin.' Nancy admitted to feeling 'almost a kind of regret that "Envois" isn't a separate book', even though he knew that, by itself, this text would have a different status, leaving philosophy for literature.[13] He would not be the only one to nurse this fantasy.

The Post Card is in fact a cunningly composed work, just as powerfully divided into two as *Glas*, even if the cut is not as clearly demarcated visually. A same set of problems circulates through the whole volume, 'between the posts and the analytic movement, the pleasure principle and the history of telecommunications, the postcard and the purloined letter, in a word the transference from Socrates to Freud, and beyond'.[14] But between the 'Envois', which occupy the first half of the volume, and the three following texts, the style of writing and the mode of exposition are almost entirely different. 'To Speculate' comes out of a seminar given at the École Normale Supérieure with the title 'Life death'; this is a detailed, fascinating analysis of Freud's *Beyond the Pleasure Principle*, but we also meet Socrates and Plato. As for 'Le facteur de la vérité', the methodical re-reading of the 'Seminar on *The Purloined Letter* by Lacan', we have already discussed it, but this fundamental text also resonates with the rest of the work. *The Post Card* ends with 'Du tout', the fake-improvised encounter with René Major published for the first time in the review *Confrontation*. The reader who can really read these four texts, then link them together, is a rare if not utopian one.

The translation of the 'Envois' was to be of an even more fear-some difficulty than Derrida's other texts, apart from *Glas*. When he read the text for the first time, Alan Bass, who was far from being a novice, had the impression that it would be as complicated as trying to translate Joyce into French. Derrida acknowledged that the 'Envois' were very encrypted and agreed to provide Bass with explanations, comments, and suggestions whenever required. 'Most of this work was done by letter,' Alan Bass recalls.

> He would send me my pages back with many annotations. But we had at least one long session together in a railway station buffet, while he was between trains. There were many details that would have escaped my notice if he hadn't drawn my attention to them. For example, in the sentence '*Est-ce taire un nom?*' ['Is this to keep silence about a name?'], you also have to read 'Esther', which is one of the forenames of his mother, but also a biblical name that plays a very active part in the book. In

spite of all my efforts, many of these effects disappeared in the translation.[15]

Hans-Joachim Metzger, the German translator of *The Post Card*, would find the work equally demanding. 'On reading your questions,' Derrida wrote to him, 'I see yet again that you have read the text better than I have. That's why a translator is absolutely unbearable, and the better he is, the scarier he is: the super-ego in person.'[16]

At the end of winter 1980, when he sent *The Post Card* to his friends, Derrida seemed to be making more or less systematic use of the formula 'yours' (*à toi*), which created a few additional misunderstandings. Every reader – especially when female – could feel that the book was meant for him or her in person. Élisabeth de Fontenay described exactly the unease the work aroused:

> I feel, when faced with *The Post Card*, as if I were an old English spinster, a sort of Brontë sister, living through a love affair, which has nothing to do with a love affair by proxy, as you can well imagine. It would instead resemble divine sainthood. And the naïvety of my first impression of this book now overwhelms me, for a long time. And I will hold to this first-degree reading of a book that is perverse enough to make room for me in this way.[17]

But for some readers, especially Derrida's closest friends, the allusions to reality at the centre of the 'Envois' seemed barely tolerable. Pierre remembers how he recoiled from the work. 'When *The Post Card* was published, I sensed how much private life, how many disguised confidences, even how much exhibitionism there was in the book. I had no desire to be confronted with it, at any case in this form, and this no doubt played its part in the fact that I read relatively few of my father's books.'[18]

The articles that came out were mostly positive. They all focused on the first part of the volume, somewhat reductively. In his *Journal de lectures*, the writer Max Genève waxed enthusiastic about the 'the finest epistolary novel since Crébillon *fils*'.[19] In *Les Nouvelles littéraires*, Jane Herve also hailed 'the Derrida factor' (or 'Postman Jacques' – *le facteur Derrida*), albeit in a rather heavily ironic style, while Philippe Boyer, an old associate of the review *Change*, devoted a full-page spread to *The Post Card* in *Libération*, under the title 'A philosopher's love letter':

> In literature as in agriculture, the main principle is that everyone should stay at home to look after the cows properly. Novels should be written by novelists, cookery books by gastronomes,

philosophy by philosophers . . . But what happens when, all of
a sudden, Jacques Derrida decides to tackle literature *mano a
mano* and give birth to a love story where we were expecting a
theoretical treatise?[20]

Even though the press was positive, there were far fewer reviews
than for Derrida's previous works. It must be said that, since the
beginning of 1980, there had increasingly been signs of change in
France. On 5 January, Lacan signed the letter dissolving the École
Freudienne de Paris before retiring into silence; he passed away on
9 September 1981. Roland Barthes suffered an accident from which
he never recovered, and died on 26 March 1980. On 15 April, it was
Sartre's turn; fifty thousand people followed his funeral procession,
probably sensing how much was being buried with him. In fact,
the ideological climate was changing rapidly. Marxism had been
fragile since the mid-1970s, and now gave way to an equally arrogant 'liberalism'. The publishing world, too, was being transformed.
Difficult works were less fashionable than ever, and several of the
intellectually more demanding series ceased publication.

One revelatory symptom of the new Zeitgeist was the creation,
at Gallimard, of the review *Le Débat*. Pierre Nora, who had played
a key role in the rise of structuralism, clearly wanted to turn over a
new leaf. In the opening declaration, 'What can intellectuals do?', he
gave the impression he was attacking the authors of his own series,
the 'Bibliothèque des sciences humaines' and the 'Bibliothèque des
histoires', starting with Michel Foucault. In issue 3 of the review,
under the title 'Human rights are not a policy', Marcel Gauchet,
the editor in chief chosen by Nora, laid into Lacan and Derrida
with considerable vehemence. The coarsest aspects of the *nouveaux
philosophes* seemed to have found their epigones. Now nothing
stopped those who wanted to denounce the 'master thinkers':

> Beyond the field of political notions, we will need to show
> clearly how the innumerable versions of anti-humanism that
> have been developed are part of, or connive with, the mental
> universe of totalitarianism. Two examples: Lacan's denuncia-
> tion of the subjective lure [*leurre*] swept away by the chain of
> signifiers, and Derrida's vision of writing as the process of
> difference in which the identity of the proper is dissolved.[21]

In academia, one interesting possibility seemed to be within reach. At
Nanterre, Paul Ricoeur had found 1968 and its sequels very difficult
to cope with – he had even had a dustbin emptied on his head.[22] At the
end of the 1970s, after several heart scares, he decided to stop teaching
at Nanterre as well as the phenomenology seminar he ran in the rue

Parmentier. Even though his relation with Derrida had gone through some tricky patches, and the 'Derridamania' that was starting to spread in the United States had occasionally irritated him, Ricoeur could imagine only one person as his successor – his former *assistant* at the Sorbonne. In his view, the author of *Speech and Phenomena* was the only one able to extend, even if in a critical fashion, his research on Husserl and phenomenology.[23] And so, before handing in his resignation, Ricoeur informed Derrida, in complete confidence.

Derrida replied in a long letter on 1 July 1979, just a few days after the Estates General of philosophy. After 'days and days of hesitation and reflection – and of anguish', he decided it would be better to turn down the possibility that Ricoeur had 'so generously opened up'. This was not just because of the uncertainties and obscurities of the process on which he would need to embark to submit a thesis *sur travaux*,* nor because of his tense relations 'with a certain university authority', it was mainly because he was unsure he wished to take on such a heavy responsibility:

I am a little scared, yes, scared, that these new burdens, this new life, might make it even more difficult to pursue a certain type of work, or even action or struggle, which I feel I must continue. It is, more on my level, a small responsibility, but a responsibility all the same. The École Normale is not the ideal place for this, but, ultimately, I have the impression right now that, for a little longer, my freedom to work will be less limited. *I may be making a serious mistake* and it is highly possible that I will regret my decision. But at the moment I cannot see clearly enough to reach any other decision. I do not have the strength to do so.[24]

Derrida signed off his letter by saying how much he had been 'moved, profoundly encouraged', and, as it were, 'justified' by the trust Ricoeur had just shown him. The latter in turn said that he was very touched by the frankness of Derrida's explanations: 'To say that I can understand your reasons would not go far enough. I have the deepest respect for the intellectual integrity that I can discern in your position.'[25] He took this opportunity to assure his former antagonist of his deep affection.

But, in November, the problem of Nanterre raised its head again, now more urgently. One Saturday morning, after an hour's journey under a heavy downpour, Ricoeur found only one student waiting for him in the room where he was to give his *agrégation* class. He was furious, and went straight up to the office to ask to take early retirement.[26] Several of Ricoeur's friends then went to see Derrida and managed to overcome his reluctance, assuring him that his

---

* A doctorate awarded on the basis of work already published. – Tr.

election would be a mere formality. An opportunity like this would probably not come by again for a long time.

The first stage in applying for the post was to submit a state thesis *sur travaux* as quickly as possible. Jean-Toussaint Dessanti, whose work Derrida admired even though it was far removed from his own, assumed the role of thesis supervisor, and Maurice de Gandillac was to chair a jury which also included Pierre Aubenque, Henri Joly, Gilbert Lascault, and Emmanuel Levinas. The title chosen to subsume the ten publications submitted was 'The inscription of philosophy: research into the interpretation of writing'. To make his work more likely to 'pass', Derrida decided to leave out his most risky works: *Glas*, *Spurs*, and *The Post Card*.

The viva took place on Monday, 2 June 1980 at 2 a.m., at 46, rue Saint-Jacques. The room was packed and the weather was scorching. Derrida, wearing a blue suit, shed his jacket before speaking.[27] Summarizing his intellectual career in the very fine text 'Punctuations: The time of a thesis', he did not seek to disguise his extremely ambivalent relations with the university system, acknowledging that he had long neglected his thesis, before deciding not to submit one. On his change of attitude, of course, he could give only a veiled and allusive explanation:

> Only a few months ago, taking account of a very wide number of different factors that I cannot analyze here, I came to the conclusion, putting an abrupt end to a process of deliberation that was threatening to become interminable, that everything that had justified my earlier resolution (concerning the thesis, of course) was no longer likely to be valid for the years to come. In particular, for the very reasons of institutional politics that had until now held me back, I concluded that it was perhaps better, and I must emphasize the 'perhaps,' to prepare myself for some new type of mobility. [. . .] Perhaps because I was beginning to know only too well not indeed where I was going but where I was, not where I had arrived but where I stopped.[28]

In his opening statement, Pierre Aubenque, rather irritated by the celebrity of the candidate and the crowd that had thronged into the room, announced that he would play 'without demur his role as judge, in accordance with all the academic criteria in force'.[29] In contrast, with great generosity, Levinas hailed the event which this viva constituted, assuring the listeners that it was 'an exceptional ceremony' and so could not 'obey the consecrated rites':

> The significance of your oeuvre, the extent of your influence, your international audience, the number and quality of the pupils and disciples gathered around you in Paris, have long

placed you among the master figures of our generation. But the fact that a philosopher such as you should sit – even for just a few hours – in the place you are and obliged to reply to questions comprises a circumstance that we really need to make the most of – that, at least, is what I personally am going to do [. . .]. This viva is something of a symposium. We must not waste this opportunity.[30]

In spite of a somewhat bewildering intervention from Jean-Toussaint Desanti, the viva went well. So the first stage towards becoming Ricoeur's successor had been completed. People would wait quite a while for the next move . . .

On 23 July 1980, one week after Derrida's fiftieth birthday, a symposium of a different nature, more open and friendly, began at Cerisy-la-Salle. Édith Heurgon, who ran the centre, and the programme adviser, Jean Ricardou, had for several years wished to organize a conference about the author of *Glas*, but Derrida had been extremely reluctant. At the end of 1977, when the conference proceedings of *Ponge: Inventor and Classic* came out, Heurgon reiterated her proposal. This time, Derrida accepted in principle, on condition that there would be a dialogue on his work and not a celebration of his name and his oeuvre. Not wishing to be involved with the programme or the choice of guests, he suggested that Jean-Luc Nancy and Philippe Lacoue-Labarthe run the *décade* together. It was to be called 'The Ends of Man', the title of one of the most influential texts in *Margins of Philosophy*.

The programme drawn up by Nancy and Lacoue-Labarthe was full and challenging. Among the speakers were Sarah Kofman, Sylviane Agacinski, Luce Irigaray, Barbara Johnson, Louis Marin, Rodolphe Gasché, and Werner Hamacher. But the conference also included a series of small-group seminars on such questions as psychoanalysis, literature, translation, politics, art, philosophy, and education. However great their desire to avoid any impression of being star-struck, people competed to have Derrida attend their session.

The conference began with a sharp exchange between Derrida, on the one side, and Luc Ferry and Alain Renaut, already a duet, on the other. After their presentation on 'The question of ethics after Heidegger', Derrida accused them of 'ideological confusionism', and rebuked them for having right from the start distanced themselves '*irreversibly*' from Heidegger. Even though he claimed that he had never had 'an attitude of dogmatic, unreserved acquiescence' towards Heidegger, Derrida could not accept the simplifications in which they had just indulged in order to put the author of *Being and Time* in his place. The debate rapidly became more heated and the pair quickly left Cerisy. Five years later, in *French Philosophy of the Sixties*, they would attack Derrida directly.

Jean-François Lyotard's paper, 'Discussions, or phrasing "after Auschwitz"', was another high point, albeit much more pacific. Eight years after the tensions of the Nietzsche conference, Derrida was very touched by the 'generous gesture' Lyotard was making by attending this *décade* on his work. In his turn, he would speak at the conference 'The Faculty of Judging', on Lyotard, in the summer of 1982. The two men continued to draw closer and to exchange views.

The many participants at 'The Ends of Man' were extremely diverse, both in nationality and intellectual tendency, and the conference was the forum for some real dialogues, even discussions on fundamental questions and sometimes probing investigations. Like Philippe Lacoue-Labarthe, Jean-Luc Nancy would remember this *décade* vividly:

> For us, it was an exciting – intoxicating? – responsibility, having to run a *décade* at Cerisy. But it was an encounter of exceptional richness and intensity, definitely because, at that precise moment, Derrida, on the one hand, and the theme, on the other, represented what I would call a 'big gun' in everybody's interests, expectations, and questionings. It seemed to us that we could grasp the form or the forms of a possible mode of thought for a world coming into being, beyond '68, but still confident in its momentum and impelled by the spur of political necessity.[31]

The enthusiastic atmosphere lasted until the last day, 2 August. When the time to sum up and bid farewell arrived, one of the Japanese participants, Yasuo Kobayashi, stood up and made a statement that everyone would remember:

> Since people have mentioned feelings, let me express here my own personal feelings. [. . .] I came here – but not without anxiety, not without fear. And then [. . .], I have come to the point where I can tell you, without knowing to whom I am speaking: I love you. In my feelings, this is friendship in Blanchot's sense. For this reason, I thank you – and yet again, let me tell you: I love you.

One of the indirect consequences of the conference was the renewal of relations with the publishing house Galilée, which had worsened five years earlier shortly after the publication of *Glas*. The initial intention had been to bring out *The Ends of Man* in the 'Champs' series, but Flammarion refused to allow more than one volume for the proceedings, which would have meant only a tiny number of the papers could be published, and none of the debates.

As he recounted in a letter to Nancy and Lacoue-Labarthe during August, 'by a strange twist of fate', Derrida met Michel Delorme at the Fondation Maeght in Saint-Paul-de-Vence and mentioned these difficulties to him.

> He was immediately eager and enthusiastic (in his own style, which you know – he had heard about the conference). He suggests publishing it all in one big volume as early as next January or February if the manuscript is submitted in October. He wants to do things in grand style – nice cover, big circulation, etc.!!! All this happened in ten minutes' conversation on the stairs: I told him that I'd talk to you about it without delay, as the final decision is yours.
>
> What do you think? Personally, while regretting the loss of the Flammarion 'paperback', I feel that Galilée is the best solution because it will be quick and Delorme is obviously very keen.[32]

Nancy and Lacoue-Labarthe naturally expressed their agreement with Derrida's analysis, and looked forward to this almost exhaustive publication (there were gaps in the recording of some of the discussions). But the technical organization of the manuscript was very time-consuming: the work would need to be shared. 'You can at least count on Sylviane and me,' Derrida announced.[33] The project was completed with remarkable speed, without the delays experienced at Aubier and Flammarion. In spring 1981, a huge volume of 704 dense pages, with an original cover by Valerio Adami, was published by Galilée. In spite of the many contributions, noted Nancy and Lacoue-Labarthe in their introduction, the proceedings of this conference could give only a very partial idea 'of what really took place, over ten summer days, at Cerisy: confrontation (sometimes a real clash), questioning (sometimes real interrogation), collaboration and friendship (sometimes a real party atmosphere)'.[34]

Autumn was marked by a tragedy. On Sunday, 16 November 1980, at 7 a.m., Louis Althusser, who had left the clinic for a few days' leave, hammered on the door of Pierre Étienne, the doctor at the École Normale Supérieure: 'Pierre, come and see, I think I've killed Hélène!', he yelled, wild-eyed. The doctor slipped on a dressing gown and went with the man who had been his friend for over thirty years. Hélène Althusser, *née* Rytmann and known in the Resistance by the name Légotien, was lying at the foot of her bed, strangled. As Dominique Dhombres relates,

> Louis Althusser was extremely agitated. 'Do something or I'll set the bloody place on fire,' he told the doctor. He kept

repeating the same sentence: 'I've killed Hélène, what comes next?' Dr Étienne called the Sainte-Anne hospital to have him interned. The ambulance arrived some ten minutes before the police, alerted by Jean Bousquet, the director of the ENS. Louis Althusser fell into such a state of prostration that Guy Joly, the examining magistrate who went that evening to Sainte-Anne, decided not to tell him that he had been charged with murder. The philosopher seemed unable to understand the meaning of this judicial act.[35]

However dreadful it may have been, this turn of events did not come entirely as a surprise to Althusser's friends. 'Since I'd known him, I'd never seen him in such a state,' remembers Dominique Lecourt.

They'd been trying out a new medicine that obviously didn't suit him. Sometimes it was impossible even to visit him, he was so off his head. However, Diatkine had allowed him out of the clinic, saying that this was the 'resolution crisis'. He had always been under the spell of Hélène and Louis, both of whom he was treating. But Althusser continued to be in a bad way. Some of us were afraid he might commit suicide. Hélène often phoned me to bring me up to date. Derrida and I regularly discussed Althusser's state, with anxiety as much as with sadness.[36]

As soon as they had placed the most famous Marxist philosopher in the world in an isolation ward, the doctors started to seek out his family. 'In reality, Althusser didn't have any,' explains Étienne Balibar, 'as his nephew was at that time very young. So they turned to the École, which had long since replaced his family, so to speak. They immediately informed Derrida, whose behaviour throughout the whole period was admirable.'[37] On that grim Sunday morning, he was among the first to arrive, at the same time as Régis Debray, with whom he had re-established communications the year before during the preparations for the Estates General of philosophy. Together they went to the Sainte-Anne hospital and waited for hours, without being allowed to see Althusser.[38]

The next day, the headlines were full of this major event. *Le Quotidien de Paris* would lead a veritable campaign against Althusser and the École Normale Supérieure. However, on the first day, information was quite confused and discussion confined to a 'Mystery at Normale Sup':

The question arises of whether or not he [Althusser] is directly responsible for the death of his wife. But yesterday, a veil was immediately drawn over the night's events. The director of the

École, M. Bousquet, was unavailable for comment. The concierge had been instructed to remain discreet. As for the École's doctor, he replied to our questions straightaway: 'People are over-dramatizing the situation, Louis Althusser's wife passed away overnight, and he has fallen prey to a deep depression.' But perhaps the doctor was merely seeking to ward off the spectre of public rumour from the famous establishment.[39]

On the Tuesday morning, on its front page, *France-Soir* soberly confirmed that it was indeed a case of murder: 'Psychiatrists are examining Althusser. The magistrate has not been able to inform him of the charge as the philosopher is not in a fit to state to understand.' The tone was much more brutal in *Le Quotidien de Paris*, which devoted an entire page to the affair, with a venomous editorial by Dominique Jamet: 'So many precautions, Messieurs, so many reticences, so many pious lies, so many pens dipped repeatedly into the inkwell until they no longer come out again, so many friendships, to the point of complicity, so many silences or half-silences, some stemming from self-censorship, others, in all probability, from political or social censorship.'[40]

The most exorbitantly right-wing hatred broke out: to believe the editorial writer, the police would have been called immediately if the murderer had been anyone else, but Althusser was an 'eminent member of the Communist Party' as well as belonging to the 'French intellectual establishment':

He is on the side of the mighty, although he has turned his kind gaze to the poor. [. . .] Are there then state privileges? Should a philosopher never get his hands dirty? And who are these people who arrogate such a right, one that lies outside common law? [. . .] How dare the paragons of virtue who protest against inequalities and class justice attempt to organize this inequality for their own benefit?

On Wednesday, 19 November, Jamet returned to the attack: 'Althusser, the scandal', proclaimed *Le Quotidien* on page one, before describing 'the amazing corporative plot woven by all those many people who claim they want to suppress classes, no doubt so that they can preserve castes'. And the newspaper pondered, quite seriously: 'Should we be afraid of philosophy?' Jean Dutourd also held forth in *France-Soir*, while the extreme right-wing weekly *Minute*, describing the philosopher as an *'anormal supérieur'** wrote in a sadly predictable fashion: 'How typical is the Althusser affair

---

* 'Superior abnormal', with a 'pun' on École Normale Supérieure. – Tr.

– Communism in a nutshell: it starts in the mists of philosophy
and ends in a sordid Grand Guignol episode.' Like the Minister
of Justice, Alain Peyrefitte, an alumnus of the ENS, they wanted
Althusser to be put on trial.

During these initial days, 'crushed by emotion, [. . .] Jacques
Derrida, loyalest of the loyal, refused to make any comment'.
More than ever, he mistrusted the press. 'Too upsetting' were the
only words he uttered to the journalist from *Le Monde*.[41] This did
not stop him from taking action, quickly and effectively. On 18
November, he wrote a letter on headed ENS notepaper, co-signed
by several colleagues. Louis Althusser was at present not fit to
choose a lawyer, they explained. 'We thus feel that it is our duty to
ensure, however provisionally, that he is defended, and this is why
we, who constitute his family of friends, are asking you to be Louis
Althusser's lawyer.' [42]

The expression 'family of friends' was a perfectly accurate
description. Over the weeks following the tragedy, Derrida, Debray,
Balibar, and Lecourt spared no effort. As soon as they were given
permission, they went to see Althusser in the closed wing of Sainte-
Anne, while doing their best to find a solution to the various
problems that arose. Derrida took as much as possible onto himself,
but he was hit hard. Jos Joliet was alarmed to see him 'so anguished,
so wounded', and offered to help in whatever way he could.[43]*

Judicially speaking, the matter was delicate. The examining magistrate had concluded that there was no ground for prosecution,
since psychiatric disorders had deprived Althusser of discernment
and any control over his actions at the time of the event; this condemned Althusser to indefinite psychiatric internment, but it meant
he would avoid interrogation and trial.[44] Although this decision,
reached on 23 January 1981, corresponded precisely to the situation,
it rekindled the polemics on the support and the special favours the
philosopher might have been able to draw on. The following day,
the *procureur de la République* – France's equivalent of the Attorney

---

* Even before the Althusser affair, it appears that Derrida was suffering from a
renewed bout of anxiety. The tenth anniversary of his father's death surely played
a part in this. In a letter to Philippe Lacoue-Labarthe, he mentioned the photos he
had been willingly allowing people to take of him, contrary to his habits, over the
last few weeks, 'as if [he] were going to die'. His first visit to Morocco had gone very
badly, in spite of the excellent welcome he had received: 'I really thought I was going
to die on the day I arrived in Morocco. [. . .] I managed to come back to something
or other, life, or a kind of apparent normality, to give four papers, to walk along the
Ocean, even to dance, alone, in front of musicians from a sect invited by my friend
Khatibi, in my honour, etc. And now I'm trying to set off again, but it's touch and
go' (letter from Derrida to Philippe Lacoue-Labarthe, n.d., probably October 1980).
As far as Marguerite remembers, Derrida phoned Khatibi in the middle of the night,
before leaving his hotel and going to stay with him.

General – decided to remove any ambiguity by reminding everyone that there was nothing exceptional about this procedure.[45]

Medically speaking, things were no simpler, as Dominique Lecourt relates:

> Shortly after the drama, Dr Diatkine asked Derrida, Debray, Balibar and me into his office. Crushed by his responsibility, panic-stricken at the idea he would be asked to give an explanation, he held forth in an incredible fashion, thanking us for not placing the blame on him. He continued to deny the facts. 'What we know,' he said, 'is that Hélène is dead, but I am equally certain that Louis couldn't have killed her, since it's technically impossible.' In Sainte-Anne, Althusser had been placed under the supervision of a young psychiatrist with whom a strange relationship was developing. Just as Diatkine had long been, he was falling under Althusser's spell, and starting to believe that Althusser knew more about his own case than the psychiatrist himself did.[46]

Since internment was bound to be indefinite, Sainte-Anne was not the best solution. With Diatkine's support, Althusser asked to be transferred to the Eau vive clinic at Soisy-sur-Seine, where he had already been treated on numerous occasions. But the request was turned down by the Prefect of Police, without any official explanation. Derrida, Balibar, and Lecourt intervened yet again:

> We greatly regret, in the patient's interest, this negative decision. It is clear, on the admission of the very doctors who are currently treating him, that the emergency service in which he now is does not suit long-term treatment. [. . .] In our view, such an authorization would not constitute a particular favour, but a decision dictated by logic and humanity.[47]

In June 1981, Althusser was discreetly transferred to Soisy-sur-Seine. Over the following months and years, Derrida continued to pay him regular visits. As Étienne Balibar explains:

> Jacques Derrida was the senior member of our group. He took things in hand, acting with both intelligence and generosity. In Soisy, he went to see Louis almost every Sunday; he acted like a relative, taking him back to their house in Ris-Orangis whenever Louis was allowed out. When Jacques was abroad, it was Marguerite who took over . . . This loyalty was all the more remarkable in that Althusser had a very ambivalent relation with Derrida: it was a strange mixture of admiration, affection,

and jealousy. When he was in a manic phase, Louis could be very mordant, even if he often disguised his aggression as irony. 'I've seen the greatest living philosopher,' he would tell us. It was all a matter of his tone of voice.[48]

Other worries plagued Derrida at this time. On 8 August 1980, shortly after the end of the Cerisy conference, Jacques Brunschwig, a professor at Nanterre and the cousin of Pierre Vidal-Naquet, sent him an embarrassed letter. The recent thesis defence had admittedly removed one obstacle, but new difficulties had arisen. To begin with, Paul Ricoeur's post had been suppressed. When a new post was created, one of his colleagues, annoyed that the job seemed to have been reserved for Derrida, decided that he would apply. Brunschwig explained, uncomfortably, that the atmosphere at Nanterre had deteriorated over the past few months: 'Unfortunately I am far from being able to announce to you the unanimous election, without any hitches or off-stage plotting, that you might have expected.' He suggested that Derrida ask for further advice before announcing that he was applying.

From that moment on, things went from bad to worse. Derrida's hesitations irritated several of the professors at Nanterre, who had the impression that he was playing hard to get. According to his old classmate Alain Pons – by now Professor of Political Philosophy at Nanterre, but not part of the group responsible for overseeing the succession to Ricoeur –, Derrida's failure was largely the result of petty meanness: it was feared that Derrida might be a nuisance, and people were jealous of his celebrity. But one should not underestimate the pressure brought to bear by the Minister for Universities, the extremely reactionary Alice Saunier-Séité: having had the buildings at Vincennes razed to the ground,* she barred the path of the man who had founded the Greph and set up the Estates General of philosophy. Now, in order to obtain the post of professor at Nanterre, Derrida still had to jump through one institutional hoop: he had to be auditioned by the CSCU, the Conseil Supérieur des Corps Universitaires. This was to remain one of his worst memories.

Dominique Lecourt, who was turned down the same day, remembers the scene vividly.

---

* After the destruction of Vincennes and its move to Saint-Denis, the Minister had stated: 'What do they have to complain about? Their new buildings will be located between the rue de la Liberté, the avenue Lénine and the avenue Stalingrad, and they'll be surrounded by the local Communists' (remarks quoted by Claude-Marie Vadrot, 'Quand Vincennes déménage à Saint-Denis', *Politis* no. 30, April 2008, p. 32).

At the beginning of March 1981, [Derrida and I] were both subjected to the same ordeal. It so happened that I had to go into the interview just after him. I saw him coming out looking as white as a sheet: 'I'm never setting foot in this institution again. You can do what you like, but as far as I'm concerned, it's all over.' Later on, he told me that certain members of the jury had amused themselves by reading extracts from his books out aloud, in as sarcastic a manner as possible. Several colleagues hated him for his brilliance, his strangeness and his total absence of concessions. With the Greph and the Estates General, he had brought the wrath of the Inspection Générale down on his head. This audition was a sort of vengeance for them.[49]

When it came to the vote, Derrida had only one supporter. And it was Georges Labica, a specialist in Hegel and Marx, who obtained Ricoeur's old position, thereby also inheriting the Laboratory for Phenomenology, 'even though he had never attended the least session at the seminar in the rue Parmentier'.[50] For Derrida, the failure was compounded by humiliation: after many hesitations, he had decided to defend a thesis *sur travaux* only because he had been assured that the job was being kept for him.[51]

In this period of electioneering, in which the race between Giscard and Mitterrand was turning out to be particularly close, the affair was reported a great deal in the French press and even abroad. And Derrida received several letters from friends and colleagues who were indignant at this 'stupid decision' that would merely increase 'the divorce between living thought and the university'.[52] But it would take more than this to calm him down. For several weeks, health worries, which he hoped were not serious, had left him feeling tired and listless. Above all, Marguerite and he had just found out that their son Jean was suffering from diabetes, a piece of news that distressed and alarmed them.

On 8 May 1981, Derrida told Paul de Man of the many various difficulties he had just gone through:

The Nanterre affair ended in the worst possible way, probably the most predictable, too, and I don't know what my brief university future in this country is going to consist of. For the time being, I'm staying at the École in the hope that the political change (I hope it happens but am not convinced) that's perhaps been in the air for some days will allow me at least some respite there.

The winter was tough, at least since February, since I've been 'paying for' a great number of things [. . .] with a fatigue (physical and mental) of a kind I haven't experienced for a long time.

[. . .] After the 'work' of the autumn (teaching, several articles, conference papers, trips until February), I endured – it was triggered or signalled by those attacks of 'renal colic' (apparently no kidney stones) – a travail of body and soul, I mean of conscious and unconscious in the shape of nervous exhaustion and boundless discouragement.[53]

This anguish in the face of 'what resembled the worst of things', especially since the symptoms seemed similar to the malady that had killed his father, did not stop him dealing as best he could with work in progress. But it probably played a part in the aggression shown by Derrida in a debate with Hans-Georg Gadamer. He acknowledged as much twenty years later, in a posthumous homage to the great German philosopher of hermeneutics:

Some people criticized me for never having really entered into the open dialogue that Gadamer had initiated in April 1981 at the Goethe Institute in Paris and from which I seemed to have withdrawn. I am inclined to think that they were not wrong.

The reply he gave to my own replies, during our encounter in 1981, ended with these words, and, filled with admiration for his benevolence, his smiling generosity and his perspicacity, I would like to say that I completely agree with him: 'Any reading which seeks to understand is merely a step on a path that never comes to an end. Anyone who sets out on this path knows that he will never get "to the end" of his text; he is grasped by it. When a poetic text has touched him to the point that he ends up by "entering" it and recognizing himself in it, this presupposes neither agreement nor confirmation on his part. One abandons oneself so as to find oneself. I don't think I am so far away from Derrida when I emphasize that we never know in advance what we will be when we find ourselves.[54]*

To his pleasant surprise, the political change which Derrida said he hoped for, albeit without great conviction, actually happened. On 10 May 1981, François Mitterrand was elected President, and at the parliamentary elections on 14 and 21 June 1981, a 'pink wave' gave the Socialist Party and its allies a very large majority. Pierre Mauroy was appointed Prime Minister, Jack Lang Minister for Culture, Alain Savary Minister for Education, and four communists were brought into the government. While he was happy at this new state of affairs, Derrida was unaware of just how important it would soon be for him. He did not want to hear anything more about

---

* And each other – *on se trouvera*. – Tr.

France, especially not the French university system: 'Are things going to change now? As regards everything to do with teaching and culture, I am inclined to be as cautious and reserved as possible.'[55]

In the United States, Paul de Man was still a peerless ally. In spite of increasingly explicit resistance, he managed, with the support of J. Hillis Miller, who was in charge of all matters concerning graduate students, to renew Derrida's contract as visiting professor. As was the case in Oxford and Cambridge, the Department of Philosophy at Yale did not conceal its hostility to Derrida and the whole wave of French theory. One of the professors, Ruth Marcus – a pure positivist and specialist in formal logic – even turned it into a personal campaign, trying year after year to stop a man she considered as an impostor from coming to Yale. The violent polemic that set Derrida against John R. Searle in several issues of the review *Glyph* contributed to increased tensions with the proponents of analytical philosophy.* But deconstruction also had several opponents among literary scholars, now that its success had made it a threat to traditionalists. Only departments of comparative literature gave it an enthusiastic welcome.

It was mainly from a personal point of view that the relation with Paul de Man had become essential for Derrida, taking over from his friendships with Michel Monory, Gabriel Bounoure, and Philippe Sollers. The trust that de Man had placed in him for several years was of the highest importance to him, and Derrida assured him that he drew '*indispensable* strength from it': 'This has long been true and is so today *more than ever*.'[56] Over the following months, several events would bring the two men even closer together. In spite of the extreme discretion he maintained, especially about the years

---

* The row began with the translation of the conference paper 'Signature event context', mainly devoted to John L. Austin, in the first number of the review *Glyph: A Journal of Textual Studies*, created by Sam Weber in 1977. In its second issue, the review published a reply by John R. Searle, 'Reiterating the differences: A reply to Derrida', reproaching Derrida in a somewhat self-satisfied way for not having understood Austin and speech-act theory. Derrida reacted with as much violence as irony in a long article called 'Limited Inc a b c . . .'. Since Searle had acknowledged his debt to several of his colleagues, Derrida treated him throughout his text as a collective entity: 'In order to avoid the ponderousness of the scientific expression "three + n" authors, I decide here and from this moment on to give the presumed and collective author of the reply the French name "Société à responsabilité limitée" – literally, 'Society with Limited Responsibility' (or Limited Liability) – which is normally abbreviated to *Sarl*.' This way of conducting the polemic did not correspond to the codes governing university confrontations in America and aroused lasting resentment. For example, Searle would refuse to allow his text to be reprinted next to Derrida's in the volume *Limited Inc* which gathered all the evidence, first in the United States (*Limited Inc*, Evanston, Ill.: Northwestern University Press, 1988 – the above excerpt is on p. 36), then in France (Paris: Galilée, 1990).

before his arrival in the United States, de Man referred one day in
conversation to a novel by Henri Thomas whose main character was
based on him: this text, called *Hölderlin in America* when first published in a review, was given the title *The Liar* when it came out with
Gallimard. 'It's less flattering, but much more truthful,' de Man
added, in premonitory fashion, in a 1977 letter.[57] Ever since then,
Derrida had been looking for the book in a more or less desultory
way. It was during the Easter holidays of 1981 that he finally found
it, in a second-hand bookstore in Nice. As soon as he had read it,
he wrote to de Man: 'I can't tell you any more, but all the same, I
can't remain silent about the fact that reading *The Liar* [. . .] has
made a great impression on me, even overwhelmed me, has in any
case roused deep echoes in me, "unheimlich", in other words with
and without surprise. But I'm already saying too much.'[58] It is true
that the subject of the novel is far from anodyne. Chalier, the main
character, is accused of bigamy: before marrying a young American
woman, he has sworn on oath that he has never been married or
divorced, but an inquiry later reveals that he has been married in
Europe, with two children. 'What did anyone know about those
years before America?' the narrator wonders. The question would
rebound tragically on de Man a few years later. And Derrida reread
Henri Thomas's novel closely, probably dreaming of the confidential details to which this reading might have given access if de Man
and he had not shared the same liking for secrets.[59]

After the trials and tribulations of the start of the year, the summer
of 1981 was rather 'restorative' for Derrida. 'I'm not working, so to
speak, or I'm letting myself work [. . .] without knowing, less than
ever, where I'm going, where it's going – but fortunately "it's going"
better than at the worst times of this winter.'[60] Pierre was in New
York, with Avital's family, and the news about Jean's health was a
little more reassuring. But Derrida was all the more anxious about
the new academic year since, for the first time in several years, he
could not spend the start of the autumn in Yale.

The mathematician Georges Poitou had just succeeded Jean
Bousquet as head of Normale Sup and many of the teaching staff
there were worried at the possibility of 'a new policy, perhaps a
new structure'. In Althusser's absence, Derrida's presence during
the first days of term had become indispensable. But this situation
made him feel oppressed and sad: 'At times I have an overwhelming
nostalgia (I am measuring my words) for my autumns in Yale. What
a life . . .',[61] he confided to de Man. At Yale too, even though they
knew he would be coming in the spring, Derrida was greatly missed.
Geoffrey Hartman admitted: 'I'm afraid we've all become addicted
to your presence, and September seems very empty without you.'[62]

Derrida continued to kick his heels at Normale Sup. Even though he remained accessible to his pupils and attentive to their personal careers, things had become very difficult since Althusser's departure. An essential bond had been broken and the École had become in Derrida's eyes inseparable from this tragedy. At the same time, his relations with Bernard Pautrat were growing more distant. As the latter relates:

> Whatever he may have said, Derrida encouraged his associates to behave like disciples, and he fostered a kind of mimicry. Actually, that's how I myself behaved for a few years, without altogether realizing, so great was my admiration for him. But after a while, I could see how much he obeyed the old principle 'he who is not for me is against me': as soon as there was a difference of opinion, or he suspected one, he drew the consequences. Being with him meant you gave him complete support. Now quite apart from the fact that I'm not a model of obedience, in my view there cannot really be a Derrida school, because deconstruction is primarily a style – his and his alone. All he leaves his disciples with are leftovers. This is one thing that, in a sense, makes him resemble Heidegger, the philosopher who probably obsessed him the most. Of course, people such as Nancy and Lacoue-Labarthe have tried to avoid this failing, and perhaps they've succeeded since they were already professionally formed when they started to work with him. This was not true of me. So I had no other solution than to escape from that attraction to find my own orbit. And then I have to confess that Derrida, the man I had loved and admired so much, had given place to another, always busy, forever checking his diary, then his watch, always between two meetings and two telephone calls. This is understandable and acceptable, although it didn't strike me as being very 'philosophical'. But just then, I have to admit, I found it a bit difficult to put up with his never-ending complaints: 'If only you knew . . . I don't have a minute to myself . . . etc.,' while he'd obviously done everything to build up this life of turmoil and celebrity.[63]

However weary he may have been, Derrida did not finally give up his work at Normale Sup during the last months of 1981. In one last attempt, probably hoping to take advantage of the arrival of a new director and the recent political upheavals, he drew up quite a radical plan to transform teaching at the École. Apart from philosophy, he pondered the future of the whole Literary School, detailing in a thirteen-page typewritten document a few 'propositions for a preliminary project'. His initial judgement was severe: 'The interests of the state and the nation decree that we do not allow [. . .] the potential of a still thriving and productive institution for research and teaching to be weakened or destroyed.' So it was important to define 'the conditions of survival and then the development of the Literary School'. Up until now, Derrida stated, the latter had never been given the means to live up to the research vocation laid down in the official texts. Without weakening the traditional recruitment by competitive examination and the system of *khâgnes*, it would be a good idea in his view to open up as soon as possible 'another space' by recruiting independent researchers 'at another level and following different criteria'. Research centres should also be created, preferably looking towards new disciples or original themes, and leading to a specific diploma. After adding some initial details on the way these centres would operate, Derrida concluded that such a development was in his view the only future for the Literary School: 'This very ambitious project will have no chance unless people are determined to invent the following: new forms of work, new courses and atypical "careers", research themes that hitherto have not been investigated in the university system, in other institutions, or even anywhere in France.'[64]

The project garnered several reactions – mainly positive, at least as far as the basic idea was concerned – and led to several meetings. But in the meanwhile, a real rebellion was being fomented against Derrida: at the beginning of December 1981, Emmanuel Martineau, an alumnus of the ENS and a Heidegger specialist, turned against his old teacher, launching a ten-point appeal to his 'comrades'. He asserted that Derrida was using the *agrégation* seminar as a pretext 'for "cunning" verbal acrobatics deprived of any seriousness and any philosophical sense, and, what is more, perfectly inadequate for preparing a candidate for the *agrégation* exam, which is notoriously difficult'. He also judged that Derrida's personal production, which was 'pure literature and had nothing to do with philosophy in general, nor with the history of philosophy in particular', constituted a 'case history both depressing and over-abundant' for all those who respected 'our doctrinal tradition'. In consequence, he called on the students to 'resist'.[65] The first effect of this appeal was the drawing up of a petition in support of Derrida.

However grotesque, this polemic hurt Derrida and reinforced even more his desire to leave Normale Sup as soon as he could, especially since the project of reform that he had attempted to launch soon got bogged down. It had become difficult for him to give his seminar in a place where, he thought, students could not in any case quote him or follow his working methods if they wanted to pass the *agrégation*.'They didn't even need to be warned, they just knew,' and so they protected themselves from any form of contagion.

> And so I alienated myself, I forgot *myself*. I tried to forget myself whenever I corrected an essay. When I was giving a class

it was a different matter. I've always been able to do what I wanted in seminars. But when I corrected essays and presentations for the *agrégation*, I was carrying out what were, for me, exercises in absolute depersonalization.[66]

Then, as the year ended, a bolt from the blue struck that was to have profound repercussions on Derrida's situation.

13

Night in Prague

1981–1982

Ever since the crushing of the Prague Spring, in August 1968, the situation in Czechoslovakia had been especially grim. President Gustáv Husák had imposed a 'normalization' process that made the country one of those most closely aligned with the USSR. In December 1976, a petition with the title 'Charter 77' started to circulate, demanding that the government respect its own commitments to freedom. Among the authors and first signatories of the Charter were the dramatist and future president Václav Havel, the diplomat Jiri Hajek, the writer Pavel Kohout, and the philosopher Jan Patočka, a former pupil of Husserl and Heidegger. However minimal the demands expressed in the Charter, the authorities rapidly came down hard on its instigators. After a long, brutal interrogation, Patočka had to be hospitalized and died of a brain haemorrhage on 13 March 1977.

In Oxford, in 1980, a group of teachers set up the Jan Hus Educational Foundation, which took its name from the Czech religious reformer who had been burned as a heretic in Constance in 1415. Its aim was to aid Czech universities by organizing secret classes and seminars, bringing in banned books, or giving financial support to the publication of *samizdat* literature. One of the founders of the association, Alan Montefiore, was then dividing his time between Britain and France. His wife, Catherine Audard, also a philosophy professor, soon launched the French branch of the association. Its statutes were laid down on 4 August 1981. The great historian and former member of the Resistance Jean-Pierre Vernant was elected president, while Derrida took on the post of vice-president; he was particularly sensitive to the question of Czechoslovakia as he had travelled there several times and was kept regularly informed of the situation by the maternal branch of Marguerite's family.

The organizers of the Jan Hus Foundation did not merely send money. They took it in turns to visit Czechoslovakia, even though they knew that the risks involved in travelling there were far from insignificant and necessitated several precautions. The first missions were marked by several incidents: their luggage was meticulously searched, books were confiscated, and they were accompanied to the border in the middle of the night.[1] On Saturday, 26 December 1981, the date scheduled for Derrida's departure for Prague, the situation was extremely tense throughout the entire Soviet bloc: less than two weeks previously, General Jaruzelski had decreed a state of siege in Poland. Without being hostile to the reason for this visit, Marguerite would have preferred it to be postponed to a more favourable time. But Derrida, whose timetable was already difficult to manage, would not hear of the date being changed.

Marguerite's intuitions were immediately confirmed: at Orly airport, even before he embarked, Derrida had the sense that he was being followed. As soon as he arrived in Prague, there was no room for doubt: he was subjected to constant surveillance, as he related on his return to the audience of his seminar, in words that put a light-hearted spin on events:

> In the morning, at my hotel, I could already sense police activity. I turn round and I see the hotel proprietor look at the clock and grab the phone to announce where I am heading. I notice someone following me and tell myself, 'am I really being tailed?' – for me, this was the start of the experience of being tailed – or 'isn't it my anxiety that's forcing me to imagine I'm being tailed?'
>
> I get into the metro compartment, he was still there, he gets in next to me [. . .] and at that point I say to myself: I need to shake him off. So I summoned up my knowledge of novels and psychology, I tried to remember all the techniques of the genre. The metro stops. The doors stay open for a few seconds, and I have to jump out at the last minute . . . but get stuck in the metro.[2]

Before reaching the rendezvous point assigned to him, Derrida, anxious to protect the anonymity of his contacts, again tried to throw off his pursuer, darting through shops and passages. But at every stage, the man set to tail him was still there, impassively waiting.

Professor Ladislav Hejdánek was a signatory of Charter 77 and had resumed the tradition of the seminars 'in camera' that had previously been held at the home of Patočka. It was at Hejdánek's that a few students and colleagues had gathered to listen to Derrida. The subject he discussed had nothing directly political about it: as at the seminar he was giving that year at the École Normale, Derrida spoke on Descartes and his relation to language. His remarks were quite technical and of interest to only part of the audience; one of the students even asked how this kind of philosophy could be useful to them in their situation. At the end of the session, the conversation became more informal. Derrida alluded in veiled terms to the way he had been tailed, before voicing his surprise that his hosts expressed themselves so directly, despite the more than likely presence of microphones.

Derrida was checked as he left the building, just after the seminar, but this did not lead to anything further. 'Kein Problem!' the policeman assured him as he handed back his passport. Feeling increasingly uneasy, Derrida went to pick up a few things from the hotel and then went to stay with one of Marguerite's aunts, Jirina Hlavaty; he decided that he would not give the second session scheduled for the seminar. On Tuesday, 29 December, worried at the lack of news, Professor Hejdánek tried in vain to reach him at the Central Hotel. Then he contacted the French Embassy, where he was assured that nothing unusual had been reported to them: Derrida was to take the plane as planned, in the early afternoon on the next day.[3]

It was at the airport, at baggage control, that the trap closed on Derrida. Just as he stepped forward, the customs official gave way to a 'huge guy' who emerged from behind a curtain. Derrida was led into a little room where his bag was minutely examined: a sniffer dog was brought in for the task. To begin with, Derrida could not understand what was happening to him, thinking that the customs official was looking for manuscripts. As he later told the journalist of Antenne 2: 'I'd imagined every kind of possible scenario: being questioned, deported [. . .], but never had I dreamed of a machination of this kind, with drugs. And yet, from literature and journalism, I was acquainted with this scenario.'[4] The customs officer asked him to tear open the grey cloth lining of his bag. Derrida himself pulled out four extremely suspicious-looking little brown packets . . . Other customs officers arrived in the room, and were soon joined by police, who informed him that he was under arrest and took him to the nearest station.

Accused of 'producing, trafficking and transferring drugs', Derrida defended himself vehemently: why would a professor of mature years come to Czechoslovakia to set up as a debutant trafficker? 'I was told, firstly, that it was unlikely that the drug could get into my case without my complicity, and secondly that it was well known to all police services that drugs were often transported by people who would not usually be suspected – diplomats, intellectuals, singers, etc.'[5] Had Paul McCartney not been arrested in Japan two years earlier?

Even though the interrogation was in many respects just a piece of make-believe, it dragged on for six or seven hours. And it was in vain that Derrida repeatedly asked that his family be informed and the French Embassy alerted.

The prosecutor, the police chief, the translator, and the lawyer assigned to me knew very well why this trap had been set, they knew that the others knew, were watching each other, and conducted the whole comedy with an unshakable complicity. [. . .] I knew the scenario and I did, I think, everything that *had* to be done. But how to describe all the archaic movements that are unleashed below that surface [. . .]?[6]

Shortly after midnight, Derrida was taken to the prison of Ruzyne, next to the airport. The cold, the snow, the huge and sinister building: all of this, including the insults and brutality to which he was subjected, gave him a strange sense of having already lived through it all. To begin with, he was alone in his cell; he kept banging with his fists on the door, repeating the word 'embassy' and 'lawyer' until one of the wardens threatened to hit him. Around 5 a.m., a Hungarian gypsy was brought into the cell, but he did not speak a word of English. Touched by the philosopher's distress, his companion in captivity helped him to clean the place as well as they could. Then, to while away the time, the two men started to play noughts and crosses, with Derrida marking out the grid on a paper handkerchief.

On the morning of 31 December, the future author of *Force of Law* was subjected to the painful formalities of incarceration. 'I have never been more photographed in my life, from the airport to the prison, clothed or naked before putting on the prisoner's "uniform".'[7] He was taken into another cell, where there were already five young men, five 'kids' he would later call them, with whom he could make conversation in English. They explained the fate that probably awaited him: he would eventually be put on trial, then sentenced to jail, most likely for two years. Derrida started to imagine what would happen to him during this long period of isolation and without a single book. For several hours, 'in a terrified jubilation', he fantasized that imprisonment could open up onto a paradoxical deliverance, allowing him to write without constraint and without anyone asking him to, on and on.

In Paris, news of Derrida's arrest arrived only belatedly. In the late afternoon of 30 December, Marguerite had first waited for him in vain at Orly airport. It had been announced that his flight had been delayed, then cancelled, but there was nothing very alarming about this in the middle of winter. It was only that evening that Marguerite received a call from her aunt, who had been alerted by a lawyer: 'She was furious: "Jacques has been arrested. You can see what a vile country we live in! I'm ashamed, I'm really ashamed . . .". Since I supposed that her phone was bugged, I tried in vain to calm her, in case she in turn ended up being harassed.' Pierre was in the United States with Avital Ronell. Marguerite had her parents staying with

her in Ris-Orangis for a few days; Jean, then fourteen years old, was
with her too.

Panic-stricken, Marguerite first phoned Catherine Audard, who
gave her the number of her contact, Denis Delbourg, an old student
of Derrida's, in charge, *inter alia*, of East–West relations in the office
of Claude Cheysson, Minister of Foreign Affairs. 'I phoned him
straightaway,' Marguerite remembers.

> He told me he'd sort it out as soon as he could, the following
> morning, but this wasn't enough to calm me down. I wanted
> him to act straightaway, and he eventually promised. Around
> 6 a.m., I decided to phone Régis Debray, who was then a close
> adviser of the President. A few hours later, he assured me that
> François Mitterrand was taking the affair very seriously, saying
> that he was prepared to recall the French Ambassador and
> threaten the Czechs with economic sanctions.

News of the arrest was very quickly made public. Jacques Thibau,
general director of Cultural Affairs at the Quai d'Orsay, phoned
Catherine Clément, who edited the culture pages of *Le Matin*, and
asked her to give as much publicity as possible to Derrida's arrest:
with the agreement of Claude Perdriel, she decided to put the news
on the front page of next day's issue. As soon as the first newsflashes
came out, the telephone never stopped ringing in the house in
Ris-Orangis and Marguerite went into action:

> I stayed in my dressing gown all day, as I didn't have time to
> get dressed or even really grasp what was happening. Roland
> Dumas, whom we had met several times at Paule Thévenin's,
> called me to offer his help. He was prepared to set off for
> Prague with me straightaway, but he was the only one who
> asked me whether it was possible that Jacques had really been
> smuggling drugs.[8]

Meanwhile, the Ambassador of Czechoslovakia in Paris, Jan
Pudlak, was summoned to the Quai d'Orsay. At 4 p.m., he was
received by Harris Puisais, the official in charge of countries in the
East and an intermediary well known to the Russians, as well as
Denis Delbourg, who conducted the interview because of his closeness to Derrida and intellectual circles. The Ambassador could not
understand why this affair was causing such a fuss, right up to the
highest levels of state. Denis Delbourg was a young diplomat at the
time but he has a very precise memory of this conversation:

> After I had told him of our surprise and our condemnation
> of this arbitrary arrest on the pretext of possessing drugs,

the Ambassador replied with aplomb that the circulation of illicit substances in French universities, with the complicity of teachers, was widely known, and his country was justified in suppressing this traffic! I interrupted him: 'Do you know who Professor Derrida is? Professor Derrida is an austere man, who enjoys the highest of reputations in all academic circles in France and abroad, and you won't find anyone who will believe such an accusation for a single second.' I remember using the word 'austere' while wondering *in petto* whether the concept of austerity would be validated by the philosopher himself, but I was using the language that I deemed the most appropriate when faced with a representative of the Communist moral order ... And while I was speaking, I saw the Ambassador, who was taking notes, write this word, 'austere', in a little notebook. I continued: 'I am myself a pupil of Professor Derrida's, and I can mention a number of his former students, classmates, or friends, who have passed through the École Normale Supérieure in the rue d'Ulm and now occupy high positions, starting with Régis Debray, adviser to the President . . .' At the end of the interview, though the Ambassador was still keeping up the same language, the expression on his face had changed, and I imagine that he was starting to wonder seriously what he had got himself involved in. There's no doubt that in Prague, on the other hand, the authorities knew what they were doing, and were testing our reactions.[9]

In reality, the Czech services had not been fully aware of Derrida's celebrity. The storm of protest that broke out in a few hours, in the media, the ministries, and even at the Élysée, made them realize their blunder. In the evening, Gustáv Husák was informed that France was demanding the immediate liberation of the philosopher. Neither Prague nor Moscow wanted an open crisis with France; the Czech president had no other solution than to comply.

On the night of 31 December–1 January, the police who had arrested Derrida the day before came to release him, this time deferentially. As Kafka had been frequently mentioned during the previous day's questioning – Derrida, who was writing the paper 'Before the law' for the Lyotard conference, had been to Kafka's tomb during his stay in Prague – the lawyer told him, 'in an aside: "You must have the impression of living in a Kafka story." And then later: "Don't take things too tragically; consider it a literary experience." I responded that I did take it tragically, but first of all for him – or for them, I don't remember exactly.'[10]

Exhausted, Derrida arrived at the French embassy just as the decorations for the New Year's Day reception were being taken down. He was taken to a room where he rested as well as he could, rereading the Prague sections of Chateaubriand's *Memoirs from Beyond the Grave*. The following afternoon, he took the train for Paris, accompanied by an employee of the embassy to the German border. At Stuttgart, he was met by a team from Antenne 2 and the journalist Sylvie Marion interviewed him at length.

On his arrival at the Gare de l'Est, on 2 January at 7:30 a.m., Derrida was assailed by journalists and photographers. Diplomats, colleagues, students, and friends had all come to see him. But Derrida hardly had time to say hello. He left with Marguerite and Jean for the studio of Antenne 2 to view, with the journalist, the interview that had been filmed in the train: it was a delicate matter and he was anxious not to compromise anyone by a clumsy phrase.[11]

For a contemporary TV viewer, the sequence broadcast on the 12:45 p.m. news is very strange, especially since the philosopher was given an unusual amount of time, seven minutes, to relate what had happened to him. Derrida expressed himself slowly, especially to start with, and without looking at the camera. After describing the context of his visit to Prague, he agreed to relate the facts, but tried hard to avoid sensationalism and self-pity:

> So I was thrown, I think that's the right word, into a dungeon. [. . .] I hesitate to describe the brutality of the thing, which in one sense was commonplace and in another was reserved for me alone, I think. Then, it was the kind of day any common law prisoner spends. For the same reason, I won't describe it, but for me it was extremely intimidating to experience something – starting with the door of the cell closing on you, the prisoner's uniform – that I knew only through pictures or books. And so it was in the middle of the following night that, this time with a great deal of courtesy and academic deference for Monsieur le Professeur, they came to free me. In between, I had no idea of what was going on outside. [. . .]
> I couldn't know whether the French authorities, my family, etc., had been informed, or even knew where I was. And it was intimated to me it could take at least a few days, at least until the end of the holiday period, before the embassy was told and could make contact with me, and that the trial could take, after a preliminary inquiry of two months, for an indefinite period, and that the sentence laid down for this type of accusation was two years, involving both myself and other Czech intellectuals, in a trial which could be imagined as following all sorts of scenarios.
> Personally, what I wish to remember from this sequence and what I wish other people to remember is that this was a

machination aimed primarily at intimidating and discouraging all those who, whether intellectuals or not, intend to travel to Czechoslovakia, in particular to demonstrate their solidarity with those there, Chartists or not Chartists, who are struggling for human rights to be respected. Yes, they are the ones I would like to salute, since they are struggling in really heroic – in other words obscure and anonymous – conditions.[12]

Another extract from the interview was broadcast on the 8 o'clock news that evening. Although he was still under an official charge, and wanted the investigation to be brought to a proper conclusion, Derrida forcefully demonstrated his desire that the mission of the Jan Hus Foundation should continue, so as to show solidarity with Czech dissidents. He himself stated that he was prepared to go back there.

That same day, Jean Genet came to spend the evening in Ris-Orangis with Paule Thévenin. He pressed Derrida with questions, as if this arrest had made the two men even closer: 'So, prison, did you discover how it smells? . . . And did you suspect it was your friends who had put you in this situation?' On this last point, Genet had guessed correctly: Derrida had been consumed by near paranoid feelings during his imprisonment. And even though he tried to put a brave face on events now that he was back, for example by relating his story in an almost humorous way to the audience at his seminar, the whole business had come as a terrible shock. According to several of his friends, images of Prague would come back to him for months: he would regularly have the feeling that people were following him, eavesdropping, or hunting him down.[13]

On 8 January, Derrida wrote to President Gustáv Husák to demand that he be given an official apology and cleared of any accusation. Transmitted by the diplomatic services, this letter would lead, eighteen months later, to nothing more than a vague attestation from the Czech Foreign Ministry certifying that 'no criminal proceedings had been set in motion' against him. Derrida eventually got back his personal belongings, but, despite several requests, his tampered-with bag was never returned.[14]

In spite of the various demonstrations of sympathy that flowed in as a result of his arrest, one had particular importance: the letter that Philippe Sollers sent him, ten years almost to the day since they had broken off relations:

My dear Jacques
Ouf!
    It's at times of high intensity such as these that you realize who you love. The radio, at dawn.

Strangely, what I saw in front of my eyes was your *handwriting*, straightaway.

Never mind, here we are in a real novel, with the Pope, drugs, police, Embassies – and the rest.

Hello Poe! *Of course!*

Happy New Year – very best wishes as well as to Marguerite (I have been thinking a lot of all of you).[15]

Derrida's reply, on a postcard showing the old Jewish cemetery in Prague, showed how sore the wound still was:

Thank you, thank you for your letter. What you say goes straight to my heart.

So that's what it will have needed (prison and the rest!).

Never mind, your gesture is just like what I'd liked in our friendship, over nearly ten years, already ten years ago . . .

You must know it, but I have to, or prefer to, say it: it's through rigorous loyalty to that past friendship that, when confronted with the worst things (aggression, insults, demeaning denigration, etc.), I have kept silent, a silence to which, of course, I now return. After your letter, this silence will perhaps have a different taste for me, and it's this in particular for which I want to thank you. Yours.[16]

Derrida would go no further and would ostentatiously turn away from Sollers when the latter came up to him at some reception or other. This break was, for him, final.

The same was not true of Michel Foucault, who had spoken on radio as soon as he heard of Derrida's arrest to demand his liberation. The two men resumed contact, initially at a distance. But some time later, when Foucault invited Jacques and Marguerite Derrida to an evening at his home, at the request of an American professor who was dropping by at the Collège de France, Derrida was greatly touched by the quality of his welcome. Foucault's premature death, on 25 June 1984, did not give them time to become really close again. But it was with real generosity that Derrida returned to Foucault's work in 1991, on the occasion of the thirtieth anniversary of *Madness and Civilization*, when he began by referring to their former friendship, then 'this shadow that made [them] invisible to one another, that made [them] not associate with one another for nearly ten years', claiming that this 'stormy discussion' was itself part of a history that he loved 'like life itself' and like all his past.[17]

In Czechoslovakia, the Derrida affair had a significant and highly positive impact for the image of France. The activities of the Jan

Hus Foundation resumed almost immediately. As Étienne Balibar, who played a very active part in it, remembers,

We knew that we risked being hassled, searched, even robbed of the books we were bringing. But we were convinced that, after this fiasco, the biggest risks were behind us. Even after the fall of the Berlin Wall, the Czechs and Slovaks didn't want the Jan Hus association to cease its activities. Even today we still continue to help doctoral students.[18]

Jacques and Marguerite learned what had really happened only years later, from the lips of Ladislav Hejdánek, the professor of philosophy at whose home the clandestine seminar had been held. In 1981, a provincial official had just been appointed to the head of this local police service. He wanted to draw attention to himself by some act of distinction and so had set up the whole thing by himself. Of Derrida he knew nothing, except that he was a member of the annoying Jan Hus Foundation which was giving support to dissidents. The plot had not been directed against Derrida at all; it could have been aimed at any other foreign visitor. Knowing nothing of Derrida's celebrity, the official had not for a moment imagined the international repercussions that his arrest would entail. His excessive zeal backfired: he was demoted and sent back into the provinces. And much later, after the 'Velvet Revolution', he was himself arrested for drug trafficking.

For Derrida, the Prague affair remained a traumatic memory, a sort of echo of that grim day in October 1942 when he had been expelled from the Lycée Ben Aknoun. It was if his entire life had been 'framed by two sets of bars, two heavy, metal interdictions': 'Whether they expelled me from school or threw me into prison, I always thought the other must have good reasons to accuse me.'[19] This arrest brought him centre stage, without his having asked for it. But it was without the least doubt one of the things that led him to *lay himself open* more and more, especially in the political arena. 'All things considered,' he wrote, 'my arrest in Prague in 1981 constituted the voyage that, in my whole life, was most worthy of the name.'[20]

14

A New Hand of Cards

1982–1983

In the spring of 1981, Jacques Derrida had greeted the coming to power of the Left with a more muted enthusiasm than most French intellectuals. Admittedly, his mood was then particularly dark. In November 1981, in the major interview he gave *Libération* under the title 'In praise of philosophy', he wondered what place the new socialist government intended to give philosophy. François Mitterrand had been well disposed towards the struggles of the Greph and the Estates General of philosophy and had stated before the elections that, if he won, the teaching of philosophy would be 'maintained and developed'. Derrida thought it was a matter of some urgency to remind him of these commitments.[1]

Ever since the Prague affair and the direct intervention of the Élysée in his liberation, the situation had evolved in a highly positive direction. Derrida had been informed on several sides that philosophy would not be forgotten. But he was not the only one to be actively supporting it. On 19 January 1982, a few days after speaking at the conference 'Creation and Research' organized by Jack Lang, Jean-Pierre Faye contacted Jean-Pierre Chevènement, the Minister for Research and Industry, while François Châtelet attempted to set up an experimental department of philosophy at Paris VIII, the former University of Vincennes that had been broken up by Alice Saunier-Séité. Eager to bring all these initiatives together, Chevènement organized a working lunch on 13 March 1982. This meeting can be considered to mark the founding act of the Collège International de Philosophie.

As Dominique Lecourt explains,

Philippe Barret, an ex-*normalien* and technical adviser in the minister's office, played a major role in this project. One might even say that he was the kingpin. Barret was perfectly well aware of Derrida's role in the Greph and the Estates General of philosophy. He knew that nothing could be done without him. He wanted to involve him in the initiatives of Faye and

Châtelet, and he wanted to add me to the team so that the philosophy of science wouldn't get left out. What he'd forgotten was the old hostility between Derrida and Faye. The latter was not best pleased that it was Derrida rather than he who had been entrusted with the coordination of the project, though this seemed natural to Châtelet and myself.[2]

The mission for the creation of the Collège International de Philosophie was set up on 18 May 1982. In the shape laid down by the minister, the project followed on directly from the work of the Greph and the Estates General of philosophy:

Philosophical research in France currently occupies a still modest place, limited to certain often quite separate domains in universities and the CNRS. [. . .]
 At a time when the government is preparing to extend the study of philosophy in secondary education, it is important that research applied to this discipline be assured of the conditions and instruments best adapted to its flourishing. [. . .]
 From this point of view, it seems to be opportune to study the conditions of creation of a Collège International de Philosophie, a centre of research and training for inter-scientific research, able to foster innovative ideas, open to new research and pedagogic experiments, and capable of setting up organic relationships with analogous institutions abroad.[3]

On 25 May, a mail shot went out through France and several other countries, while the press reported on the project. Services were offered from all sides, in every shape and form, from pretty much the whole world. Some days, several dozen of them arrived, many of them addressed personally to Derrida. As he told Paul de Man, he was living in 'a state of crazy hyperactivity almost completely foreign to [his] interests and tastes, against a background of anxiety at the vanity, the risks, the obstacles' of everything to do with the Collège International de Philosophie – especially as the project was developing 'amid pitfalls and eagerness, hatreds and battles' that he left it to de Man to imagine. As for his personal situation, Derrida, as often, took a rather sombre view of it all:

Strangely, and really rather suspiciously, the new regime is showing me a great deal of 'symbolic' deference, sending me countless signals, but without ever committing itself to anything (for example for a rather more decent post that shows no sign of coming). They are giving me the most promising signs, but they are no more than signs and – since I'm rather familiar with these situations – I can't exclude the possibility that it will all come to a very sticky end.[4]

This did not stop Derrida accompanying Jack Lang to Mexico at the end of July for the world conference of ministers of culture. In a memorable speech, Lang denounced American cultural imperialism. Derrida thanked him a few days later for what had been, for him, 'a very enriching experience, an opportunity and an honour'. He was very happy about the 'friendly complicity of these few days', and hoped that the Collège International de Philosophie would be able to count on his advice and support.[5]

Pierre was really rather precocious and passed the exam for Normale Sup at his first attempt, at the age of nineteen. For Derrida, this brought back many memories: 'Exactly thirty years ago, to the day, I entered the same establishment, at the age of twenty-two, after two failed attempts and what suffering . . . a strange experience, a strange situation, isn't it?' he wrote to Paul de Man.[6] After hesitating between literature and philosophy, Pierre finally chose philosophy, since the classes seemed to him more open and interesting, even if literature remained his predominant passion. But becoming a philosopher when you have the name Derrida was far from self-evident. 'When I told one of my teachers that I'd made this decision, he told me I was committing suicide,' Pierre remembers.[7]

Unfortunately another piece of bad news cast its shadow over the end of the summer. Although Paul de Man had not been well for several months, he could not make his mind up to seek medical advice. In July 1982, worried by his state, Geoffrey Hartman and his wife arranged for him to see a doctor, who immediately sent him to New Haven for a proper examination. An inoperable tumour was diagnosed, right next to the liver. Derrida was among the first to be informed by de Man, initially by telephone, then in a letter that was almost serene in tone:

> Since I've been back home, I've been much better and I'm starting to eat, to sleep, to walk a bit, and to enjoy the discreet pleasures of convalescence. All this, as I was telling you [on the phone], seems prodigiously interesting to me and I'm enjoying myself a lot. I knew it all along but it is being borne out: death gains a great deal, as they say, when one gets to know it close up – that 'peu profound ruisseau calomnié la mort' [shallow stream calumniated as death].* Anyhow, I prefer that to the brutality of the word 'tumeur'.[8]

---

* A quotation from Mallarmé's sonnet in homage to Verlaine. – Tr.

Over the following months, Derrida and de Man would write to and phone each other very frequently. Illness and the threat of death made their relation more intense than ever.

In 1982 – some time after a proposal from Marguerite Duras that came to nothing – Derrida agreed for the first time to appear in a film. *Ghost Dance*, a feature by the English director Ken McMullen, made him play himself, next to Pascale Ogier, in a strange but memorable way. The first scene is very short but repeated *ad nauseam*: it takes place in the café Le Sélect, in front of a Titus-Carmel poster. Between the takes, the pretty young actress explains to the philosopher what 'eye-line' means in cinematic terms – the way you look each other in the eye. This experience left its mark on him.

Another, much longer sequence, took place in Derrida's office. As Ogier asks him whether he believes in ghosts, he launches into a veritable discourse on spectrality, a theme that would soon become central to his work:

Do you start off by asking a ghost whether he believes in ghosts? Here, the ghost is me ... The minute I'm asked to play my own role in a more or less improvised film scenario, I have the impression that I'm letting a ghost speak in my place. Paradoxically, instead of playing my own role, I'm unconsciously letting a ghost ventriloquize myself, in other words speak in my place. [. . .] The cinema is an art of *phantomachia*, [. . .] it's an art in which ghosts are allowed to return. [. . .] All this needs at present to be discussed, in my view, in an exchange between the art of the cinema, in its most unprecedented aspects, never seen before, and something psychoanalytic. I think that cinema + psychoanalysis = science of the ghost. [. . .] I think that the future belongs to ghosts, that technology increases greatly the power of ghosts.[9]

Derrida evokes the ghosts of Marx, Freud, and Kafka ... and of the woman he is talking to. How could he have imagined that the actress would die in 1984, at the age of twenty-four, thereby giving this exchange a disturbing resonance that he would later mention several times?

At the end of my improvisation, I was to say to her: 'And what about you, do you believe in ghosts?' And, repeating it over and over, at least thirty times, at the request of the film-maker, she says this little sentence: 'Yes, now I do, yes.' And so, already during shooting, she repeated this sentence at least thirty times. Already this was a little strange, a little spectral, out of sync, outside itself; this was happening several times in one. But imagine the experience I had when, two or three years later, after Pascale Ogier had died, I watched the film again in the United States, at the request of students who wanted to discuss it with me. Suddenly I saw Pascale's face, which I knew was a dead woman's face, come onto the screen. She answered my question: 'Do you believe in ghosts?' Practically looking me in the eye, she said to me again, on the big screen: 'Yes, now I do, yes.' Which now? Years later in Texas, I had the unnerving sense of the return of the specter, the specter of her specter coming back to say to me – to me here, now: 'Now . . . now . . . now, that is to say, in this dark room on another continent, in another world, here, now, yes, believe me, I believe in ghosts.'[10]

Another death, much closer to him, soon came to haunt him. On 3 April 1983, while Derrida was in Yale, his nephew Marc, the elder son of Janine and Pierrot Meskel and brother of Martine, died in a car accident. This brutal death would remain, for him and for the whole family, 'a terrible heartbreak'.[11] Derrida always kept Marc's picture near his desk, next to those of his father and his little brother Norbert.

Since summer 1982, the meetings on the CIPH, the future Collège International de Philosophie, became more frequent. In a letter to Derrida, Jean-Pierre Faye had said how much he was looking forward to their two projects converging: 'The years of work in common that will doubtless be planned will thus come about under the sign of our solidarity.'[12] Unfortunately, the reality was quite different, and there were never-ending quarrels.

As Dominique Lecourt relates:

We hadn't initially realized how much Derrida and Faye hated each other and how much damage from the past they were carting around. At the beginning, François Châtelet tried to mediate, but he quickly fell ill. Jack Lang and François Mitterrand himself had seemed to support Faye, allowing him to hope that he might be able to preside over the destinies of the Collège. He was convinced that Derrida had stolen his place. There was no let-up in the tension between them and there were more and more clashes, on every kind of pretext. There were endless problems over keys, who got what office, etc.[13]

Disagreement was just as great on more fundamental matters. Faye dreamed of bringing scientists together with artists in a grand and prestigious establishment; he was fascinated by René Thom, Ilya Prigogine, and questions such as 'self-organization'. For Derrida, the priority was to provide a place for transversal research on new themes still coming into being, as well as to avoid the Collège International de Philosophie rapidly turning into an institution just like the others. As he explained in *Libération*:

> We have foreseen original arrangements that ought to ensure a deontology that is as rigorous as possible. There will be, for example, no [professorial] chairs, no permanent positions, only contracts of relatively brief duration. Thus, minimal structure, collegiality, mobility, opening, diversity, priority given to research that is, precisely, insufficiently 'legitimated' or under-developed in French and foreign institutions.[14]

For Derrida, the main thing was to contrive a rigorous selection of research projects in a place that should not thereby become 'a "centre for advanced studies", aristocratic and closed, nor even a centre of higher education'. He was eager that the Collège should be exposed to 'the most irruptive provocations of the "sciences", of "technology", of the "arts".' But he also wanted – and this was an idea that had always been close to his heart – to be able to recruit speakers and programme organizers without paying too much attention to academic qualifications.

On Monday, 10 October 1983, Laurent Fabius – who had succeeded Jean-Pierre Chevènement –, Jack Lang, and Roger-Gérard Schwartzenberg officially established the Collège in its provisional premises, 1, rue Descartes, within buildings that had previously belonged to the École Polytechnique. A two-headed structure was set up: on the one hand, there was a 'Collège provisoire', of which Derrida was unanimously elected director; on the other, an 'Haut conseil de réflexion', an advisory body directed by Faye. But instead of muting the tensions, this dual organization simply intensified them. It had initially been laid down that every decision would be signed by the two directors – including the programme for all the seminars –, but the risk of paralysis immediately reared its head. After the threat of a collective resignation of the Collège provisoire, a more flexible version of the internal regulations was adopted. Faye was pleased that agreement had been reached and again expressed his hope that the two bodies 'would fertilize one another'.[15]

Relations with the outside world were just as difficult, since even before its opening, the Collège International de Philosophie had aroused many desires and fantasies. Many people hoped to get their dream job there. So Sarah Kofman complained to Derrida that she had not been included in any of the 'guiding bodies'. He assured her that he had soon realized that it would be 'wrong, unacceptable, and tactically clumsy' for there to be, apart from a few more distant allies such as Jean-François Lyotard, 'more than one friend of the, so to speak, gang of four or the Daltons'.* And since some figures from outside Paris needed to be included, he suggested the names of Philippe Lacoue-Labarthe or Jean-Luc Nancy, and Marie-Louise Mallet from Lyon. This circumstantial explanation did not stop Kofman from feeling excluded.[16]

Derrida would also have liked to have given a leading position to Avital Ronell, whose academic career had yet to take off, in spite of the prestigious qualifications she had obtained at Princeton and Berlin. She says:

> So long as the electors just read my CV everything was fine, but the minute they met me, things got worse. My temperament must have played a part. And the fact that I was a woman didn't help, of course. When the CIPh was set up, Derrida wanted me to play an important role in it. Since I spoke English, German, and French fluently, and was well acquainted with those three worlds, there was talk of me looking after international exchanges, a dimension that was really important to Derrida. But in the end it didn't work out and I got a job at Berkeley, which he wasn't very pleased about, since in his view it was an 'enemy' fief, mainly because Searle was there. For me – I was happy to define myself as a 'loyal warrior' on behalf of deconstruction, this was an extra reason for going there: there were battles to be fought on the West Coast of the United States, where Derrida was not much in evidence at the time. But he sometimes mistrusted me. He'd told me, in the first days of our relationship, that one day I would make war on him, whereas I'd decided that this would never be the case, at least not on my initiative.[17]

The creation of the Collège international de philosophie obliged Derrida to intervene in the media more than he had done hitherto. During the summer of 1983, a two-page interview was published in *Libération*, topped by a big, rather romantic shot of the philosopher that seemed to contradict the headline: 'The Collège will have no president.' On 9 September, it was the turn of *Le Nouvel observateur* to allow 'Derrida the unsubdued' to speak. The way he was presented shows very clearly how he was perceived at the time:

> If philosophy, which was threatened even in the *lycées* during Giscard's term, is today honored in the form that is most welcoming to the future of intelligence, it is thanks to Jacques

---

* The Dalton Gang were outlaws in the American West in the late nineteenth century. Here the phrase is equivalent to 'the usual suspects'. – Tr.

Derrida, the principal instigator of the Collège International de Philosophie that has just been created under the aegis of three ministerial offices. And yet, this fifty-three-year-old thinker-writer is, in France, at once famous and unknown, respected and ignored. Not well-liked by the universities that act as guardians of stagnant knowledge, he is also exceptionally discreet on the public stage. Jacques Derrida does not play the game. An explorer of the margins, he causes the limits of philosophy, psychoanalysis, literature to vacillate in his multiform work. This thinker who travels willingly through the works of others – Husserl, Kant, Freud, Nietzsche, Genet, Jabès, Levinas, Leiris – has often been reproached for the difficulty of his style. While making every effort to keep things simple, he explained to Catherine David what are, in his opinion, the misunderstandings and traps that today threaten thinking.[18]

It was in this interview that Derrida agreed for the first time to provide some autobiographical information, and talk about Algeria, anti-Semitism, his formative years, and the Prague affair. His attitude towards the media was starting to change. Whatever his reluctance, he now knew that he could not do without them. In April 1981, the monthly *Lire* launched a wide-scale survey aimed at identifying the most influential French intellectuals. Claude Lévi-Strauss came top, followed by Raymond Aron, Michel Foucault, Jacques Lacan, and Simone de Beauvoir. Bernard-Henri Lévy came ninth. Derrida's name appeared nowhere in this list of thirty-six celebrities; even though, at this time, his work was not aimed at the general public, this absence must have hurt him.

Ever since the rebellion against him in autumn 1981, the situation at Normale Sup had been far from settled. The new regime at the École had brought in more vexatious measures against the philosophy *caïmans*, imposing fresh and hitherto unknown administrative constraints. More than ever, Derrida wanted out. But this would mean him finding a new job, which the Collège International de Philosophie just could not provide him with. In August 1983, in a letter to Rodolphe Gasché, he mentioned the possibility of moving to the École des Hautes Études en Sciences Sociales. A post directing studies on 'philosophical institutions' could be created for him. The election would take place in November. 'And although they're telling me I have every chance of getting it, experience has made me extremely cautious and mistrustful as regards anything that depends on the *académie* and my dear colleagues. I will remain so until the last moment.'[19]

Even though Lucien Bianco, director of research at the Hautes Études for several years, assured him that he need have *no* worry',[20] Derrida was still apprehensive. In November, as the election approached, he insisted that his old friend 'Coco' support him as actively as possible:

> I'm sorry to bother you again with this problem. I wouldn't dare do so if it wasn't such a serious matter for me and the time left to me in these accursed institutions. [Jacques] Revel himself, [the historian] – I've seen him – seemed (not to dramatize things) worried enough to want you to be there on 9 December. When he told me as much, I realized that a few votes might swing it either way. I feel very awkward and very guilty about asking you, even if you're the only person I can talk to right now (what a world!). If you could come and try to convince your friends, I'd be somewhat reassured.[21]

On the evening of the vote, Derrida was in Venice for a conference. But he asked Bianco to call Marguerite straightaway, whatever the result: 'All this makes me really sad, for countless reasons, but what can one do?' The author of *Origins of the Chinese Revolution* was well aware of the temperament of his former *cothurne* and his solidarity was unstinting:

> I'll be there. [. . .] I'd already decided to phone Marguerite, I didn't want to leave anyone else with the task of telling you the result, *which cannot fail to be good*. Don't worry: I know that you will worry, all the same, but you have no reason to do so. In two weeks, it's goodbye to the ENS! After, you'll have every opportunity to moan about that other 'accursed institution', the EHESS, but at least it's a cushy number.[22]

None of this completely reassured Derrida. A few days later he also pleaded his own case to Gérard Genette, even though he had not seen the latter much for several years. The wound from Nanterre still stung, and Derrida wished at all costs to avoid a new failure:

> You probably know that I'm a candidate for a post at the EHESS, and the vote takes place on 9 December. If you have no objection to this candidacy (now my only chance of not spending the rest of my professional life as a *maître assistant* in this École, which has become 'unbearable' to me), can I ask you to attend the session? I wouldn't have dared to ask you for your support if things were not *very serious* for me and if alarming rumours had not reached me: I do not know where they come from and I am not sure how serious they are. And I can't properly talk about them – and even then only hesitantly – except to two or three friends . . . Forgive me for this gesture. Affectionately.[23]

Fortunately, the election went off as Bianco had foreseen. In many ways, this new post in the École des Hautes Études would be a real liberation for Derrida. However, a few days later, bad news from the United States reached him. Paul de Man's illness had considerably worsened. The two men were closer than ever: almost every day they had long phone conversations together. Derrida was shocked by the state of his friend:

> Just now on the phone, I could feel such weariness in your voice, I myself was so disappointed to learn that any improvement had still not appeared and I felt so powerless that I was lost for words. But you know, don't you, that my heart is with you and that my thoughts accompany you at every moment of this ordeal. With you I wait and look for the signs, and I would so much like to help you be patient until your strength returns.[24]

On 21 December, de Man succumbed to his cancer. Cancelling a scheduled trip to Poland, Derrida went to the United States shortly afterwards. Little could he have imagined what consequences this death would soon have for him and for deconstruction.

PART III
Jacques Derrida
1984–2004

1

The Territories of Deconstruction

1984–1986

In a public discussion with Hélène Cixous in March 2003, Derrida mentioned a question that someone had already asked him at a conference in summer 1984. 'Why did you say it was in 1984?' asked Cixous. The short dialogue that ensued was less trivial than may appear:

> *J.D.*: Because it's a date, and I very clearly remember that it was in 1984, and because 1984 was a very strange date or year for me, and it was the year I did that little thing on Joyce [*Ulysses Gramophone*], and gave it again, a few months later, in Urbino. That's where it happened, the . . .
>
> *H.C.*: And you can remember the date? What a guy!
>
> *J.D.*: No, 1984, I'm not going to bore you with that, I have reasons to remember that year, because it was one of the strangest years in my life . . . that's all.
>
> *H.C.*: He's got a capacity for remembering things that stupefies me.
>
> *J.D.*: Not at all! I'm profoundly amnesiac and there are just some things that stay with me.[1]*

If 1984 really was more than just busy in terms of work and travel, Derrida remembered it first and foremost for a private reason, one that could not be stated in the context of that public debate with Cixous. The year had started with a real shock: Sylviane Agacinski

---

* I can vouch for the importance of that year from an altogether more personal point of view. On 21 August 1984, Derrida sent Marie-Françoise Plissart and I the text of his essay on the photo album *Right of Inspection*, and wrote: 'Will you ever forgive me for this long delay? If I could describe my "life", since last summer, you might agree that I can plead mitigating circumstances.' The phrase had, at the time, seemed merely part of the rhetoric of a perpetually overworked and particularly punctilious man. It was only when I came to write this book that I fully understood it.

had informed him that she was pregnant. The question of having a child had come up between them ever since 1972. Their 'absolute happiness' had started to turn sour in 1978: by mutual agreement, but not without considerable heart-searching on each side, Sylviane resorted to an abortion then. But this time round, she was thirty-eight. Jacques said that he felt paralysed, unable to face a child even though he had dreamed of it as an event both desirable and imposs-ible.* His bond with Marguerite was, in his view, indestructible, and paternity was a matter of too much significance for him to agree to it in a half-hearted way. He let Sylviane decide for herself, but assured her that he would accept whatever decision she came to. He himself could not support two family homes. As for Sylviane, she found herself facing the most serious decision of her whole life. The issue was not just her insurmountable difference of opinion with Jacques, but, more than anything else, the birth of a child. She had to make this vital choice: there was no easy way out.[2]

The relationship between Sylviane and Jacques had already gone through more than one rough patch, but on every occasion their passion had survived. This time, the disagreement was fun-damental, and their affair never recovered. They did not break up all at once, however. Derrida and Agacinski had a great many friends in common and were working together on several projects. She entered the Collège International de Philosophie in 1986 as programme director and member of the steering committee, and then joined the École des Hautes Études en Sciences Sociales as a *professeur agrégée.* And, until 1996, she continued to publish in the series 'La philosophie en effet'. When Sylviane and Jacques hap-pened to find themselves meeting in the same professional context, their relationship appeared quite untroubled, at least in the first years.[3]

Daniel Agacinski was born on 18 June 1984; Jacques chose his first name. Sylviane brought up the child by herself and then, from 1990 onwards, with Lionel Jospin, whom she married in 1994.

---

* The theme of the child runs obsessively through the 'Envois' in *The Post Card,* written between 1977 and 1979. But the child is also designated as something impossible. 'To the devil with the child, the only thing we ever will have discussed, the child, the child, the child. The impossible message between us. [. . .] Whatever you do I will approve, and I will do so from the day that it was clear that between us never will any contract, any debt, any official custody, and memory even hold us back – any child even' (*The Post Card,* pp. 25–6). 'Between us, I have always believed (you don't, I know) that the absence of filiation would have been the chance. The bet on an infinite, that is, null genealogy, the condition for loving each other (*s'aimer*) finally. It happens otherwise, the child remaining, alive or dead, the most beautiful and living of fantasies, as extravagant as absolute knowledge. As long as you don't know what a fantasy is, nor of course, by the same token, what knowledge is' (ibid., p. 39).

Apparently, Derrida saw Daniel at least once, shortly after his birth. But he did all he could to keep the birth of his third son secret, especially from his mother, his brother, and his sister. While he said nothing to Pierre and Jean, this did not stop them from becoming rapidly aware of the situation. 'I learned about Daniel's birth from the gang, quite early on,' remembers Pierre.

> Ever since childhood, I'd seen a lot of my father's associates, and some of them had become friends of mine. In spite of all the precautions he tried to take, quite a few people were in the know. And in any case, Philippe Lacoue-Labarthe, Jean-Luc Nancy, René Major, and a few others continued to see Sylviane long after the split. In our family, by contrast, there was total silence, and still is. The subject just couldn't be mentioned.[4]

It was, however, on Marguerite's advice that Jacques decided to recognize officially this child whom he barely knew on 6 March 1986. But the confusion waxed all the greater, since Derrida later told Élisabeth Roudinesco that it is recognition much more than genetics which defines paternity:

> Identifying a genitor is not the same as designating a father. The genitor is not the father! The father is someone who *recognizes* his child; the mother recognizes her child. And not only in a legal sense. The obscurity of the question lies entirely in this 'experience' that is so hastily called 'recognition'. Beyond or on this side of the law, its modalities can be diverse, complex, convoluted; they can spread, become stabilized or destabilized in the course of a history whose end is never determinable. It is this 'experience' that will give rise to a very complex inter-weaving of symbolic possibilities – and that will found a bond (always more or less stable or fragile, never assured) between the 'moment of the genitor' and the 'symbolic moment'.[5]

As for Sylviane Agacinski, questions about sexual difference, especially maternity, became a main topic in her thinking, and this decisive experience flowed into that reflection. She wrote on the question of relations between masculine and feminine, filia-tion, and conflict within the couple in *Drama of the Sexes: Ibsen, Strindberg, Bergman*[6] and on the interplay of biological and bio-graphical in *Body in Pieces*.[7] In a tellingly symptomatic way, one of the chapters in *Parity of the Sexes* is called 'Freedom and fecun-dity'; Agacinski here distances herself from Simone de Beauvoir's feminism, stating that '[n]othing proves that a woman can only be free through the denial of one of her most beautiful and gratifying possibilities':

We often suppose that woman, as mother, is used and made
an instrument of by man. But we forget that the concern with
descendants does not belong exclusively to men. From this
point of view, the 'instrumentality' is necessarily reciprocal,
and the question of knowing which one uses the other, which
one makes a means or an instrument of the other, is not easily
decidable. This is confirmed today, now that procreative and
contraceptive techniques have given women control over their
own reproduction. Nietzsche writes in *The Gay Science* that
for a woman 'man is only a means: the end is always the child.'
This provocative affirmation is in the process of coming true,
women ultimately choosing with which man and at what
moment they will have children.[8]

The beginning of 1984 was an emotional time for Derrida for
other reasons. Although he was unable to attend Paul de Man's
funeral, he did cancel a long-standing plan to go to Poland so that
he could take part in the homage to de Man organized at Yale
University on 18 January. He spoke only briefly, however, having
'the strength for only a few very simple words': 'At a later time, I
will try to find better words, and more serene ones, for the friendship
that ties me to Paul de Man (it was and remains unique), what I, like
so many others, owe to his generosity, to his lucidity, to the ever so
gentle force of his thought.'[9]
    Over the following weeks, Derrida did indeed write three long
papers – 'Mnemosyne', 'The art of memoirs/memories', and 'Acts:
The meaning of a word given' – which he gave in French at Yale,
in the spring, before repeating them in English at the University of
California, Irvine, near Los Angeles, on what was probably his first
visit there. With these homages, a new period in his life seems to have
opened up, dominated by memory, first and foremost, with which he
claims that his relationship was as passionate as it was painful:

> I have never known how to tell a story.
>   And since I love nothing better than remembering and
> Memory itself – Mnemosyne – I have always felt this inability
> as a sad infirmity. Why am I denied narration? Why have I not
> received this gift [. . .] from Mnemosyne?[10]

Dominated, too, by mourning, from which memory was in his
view inseparable, these three papers, developing Derrida's meditation begun in 'The deaths of Roland Barthes', inaugurated the long
series of homages to the dead collected in *The Work of Mourning*.
This kind of speech is immediately in thrall to a certain impossibility, since it is mainly addressed to someone who is now past all
address:

[D]eath reveals the power of the name to the very extent that the name continues to name or to call what we call the bearer of the name, and who can no longer answer to or answer in and for his name. And since the possibility of this situation is revealed at death, we can infer that it does not wait for death, or that in *it* death does not wait for death. In calling or naming someone while he is alive, we know that his name can survive him and *already survives him*; the name begins during his life to get along without him, speaking and bearing his death each time it is pronounced in naming or calling, each time it is inscribed in a list, in a civil registry, or a signature.[11]

The word '*Mémoires*', which Derrida chose as title for the volume eventually published in the United States, should be taken in every sense, including the most literal ('memories'). This homage to Paul de Man was an opportunity for him to look back over his own career and, as it were, draw up an initial appraisal. For just over twenty years, his work had been built up of mainly circumstantial pieces, with articles, conference papers, and seminars. His books, with the exception of *Glas*, were collections in which the overall argument was revealed only in a pointillist fashion. But by now, in the United States – where more and more of his work was being translated – Derrida was being taught, and overviews of his work were being published. In 1983, Jonathan Culler's *On Deconstruction* came out: its avowed aim was 'to describe and evaluate the practice of deconstruction in literary studies', but also to analyse it 'as a philosophical strategy'.[12] Just as Gayatri Spivak had attempted to do, Culler wished to grasp Derrida's thought as a whole and make it usable. This transformation of a challenging body of work – extremely disseminated as it was, and almost inseparable from the texts on which it commented – into a kind of universal method would create several misunderstandings which Derrida laboured tirelessly to combat.

The three papers on Paul de Man were not a matter of commemoration alone. They were also polemical. For two years, articles against de Man, Derrida, and the Yale School had been growing ever more frequent in the press. The confrontations, initially confined to academia, spread to a more general readership. The titles of these articles summed up the general reaction: 'The crisis in English studies', 'The word turned upside down', 'Destroying literary studies'. As Derrida wrote:

Certain professors invested with a great deal of prestige, and thus also with a great deal of academic power, launch a campaign against what seems to them to threaten the very foundation of this power – its discourse, its axiomatics, its procedures, its theoretical and territorial limits, etc. In the course of this campaign, they grasp at straws[*]; they forget the elementary rules of reading and of philological integrity in whose name they claim to do battle. They think they can identify deconstruction as the common enemy.[13]

The war extended beyond American soil. Ruth Barcan Marcus, an open enemy of the Yale School, went so far as to write to Laurent Fabius, the French Minister of Industry and Research, to protest against what she thought was Derrida's 'appointment' as director of the Collège International de Philosophie. She claimed:

To found a 'Collège International de Philosophie' with Derrida as director is a sort of joke or, more seriously, raises the question of whether the Minister of State has fallen victim to a piece of intellectual fraud. Most of those who are informed about philosophy and its interdisciplinary connections [*sic*] would agree with Foucault when he describes Derrida as someone who practises 'terrorist obscurantism'.[14]

The Minister merely sent a copy of the letter to Derrida, advising him 'never to walk down a staircase in front of this lady'.

With or without Mrs Marcus, it was proving tricky to establish the Collège International de Philosophie. At the beginning of 1984, the CIPh, as it is often known, really did kick off. Seventy working groups or seminars were set up. But as Derrida explained in the very long letter he wrote to all the organizers, 'these initial successes have been possible thanks to an exceptionally heavy workload that many of us have found crushing'. There were permanent tensions at play. Hoping to overcome them, Derrida proposed a significant change in the internal regulations: in his view, the director of the Collège properly speaking should also head the Haut Conseil de Réflexion, its governing body. This suggestion met with a scathing reply from Jean-Pierre Faye. And yet Derrida was not after any increase in his personal power. As he explained at the end of his letter:

On 10 October 1984, one year after my election, I will give up my responsibilities as director. I have already decided to do this in any case, wherever we have got with the process envisaged. [. . .] I have been forced to take these decisions for deontological reasons, sufficient in themselves, and for personal reasons:

---

* More literally, everything is grist to their mill. – Tr.

overwork, excessive dispersal of activities, fatigue, desire to keep some strength in reserve for another type of work, after what is, after all, three years of service to the Collège.[15]

Throughout this year, in spite of the success of many of its activities, the Collège International de Philosophie continued to be a source of worries for Derrida. He found the administrative tasks especially burdensome as the difficulties with Faye were still unresolved, in spite of several attempts at a rapprochement. But, on a deeper level, it was the very spirit of the CIPh that did not live up to his wishes. As René Major puts it:

> To begin with, Derrida was the life and soul of the Collège, but he didn't stay so for long. With Lyotard and a few other prestigious organizers, he used to come to a great number of the sessions. But quickly – even more quickly than for other institutions – the CIPh was overtaken by – or fell back into – shortcomings that we couldn't tolerate in other contexts. We'd dreamed of a freer, more open, more international system than the one that soon imposed itself.[16]

When the Collège celebrated its twentieth birthday, Derrida did not hesitate to ask, forthrightly, whether it had done any more than just 'survive'. Had the CIPh that had been kept going and grown the one they had dreamed of? 'We must always try to know what price we pay for our continual existence, and what are the limits of the acceptable concessions or compromises or surrenders.'[17] Over and above theoretical arguments, we should not forget that Derrida's own temperament played a part in this rapid move away from the Collège, which was repeated in the case of several other projects.

> I loved the Collège a great deal, since I was one of those who had dreamed of it and founded it. But, very soon, I couldn't stay in the Collège any longer. First, being director is too big a job. And even in general, I'm not enough of a community person to put up with cliques. So I quickly withdrew, while retaining my liking, my solidarity, my friendship for the Collège and for many of its members. But, as a space, it didn't suit me at all.[18]

This underlying reluctance did not, however, stop Derrida demonstrating his solidarity with the Collège International de Philosophie every time it experienced difficulties or its very existence was threatened.

In Derrida's case, as in many others, the United States acted as a hub for internationalization. Translations of his works, initially limited to the major European languages, started to spread pretty much across the world. And he was now travelling more than ever. In 1984 alone, as well as Yale, where he went on two occasions, he presented papers, gave seminars and took part in conferences in New York, Berkeley, Irvine, Cornell, Miami, Ohio, Tokyo, Frankfurt, Toronto, Bologna, Urbino, Rome, Seattle, and Lisbon.[19] Speaking on the most varied subjects, he transformed whatever situation he was in and made it the starting point of his address. The *here and now* became the driving force behind his words. The start of his paper 'Psyche: Invention of the other', which he delivered at Cornell and Harvard, spoke volumes about this habit:

> What else am I going to be able to invent?
> Here perhaps we have an inventive incipit for a lecture. Imagine, if you will, a speaker daring to address his host in these terms. He thus seems to appear before them without knowing what he is going to say; he declares rather insolently that he is setting out to improvise. Obliged as he is to invent on the spot, he wonders again: 'Just what am I going to have to invent?' But simultaneously he seems to be implying, not without presumptuousness, that the improvised speech will remain unpredictable, that is to say, as usual, 'still' new, original, unique – in a word, inventive. And in fact, by having at least invented something with his very first sentence, such an orator would be breaking the rules, would be breaking with convention, etiquette, the rhetoric of modesty, in short, with all the conditions of social interaction.[20]

However prolific his output, and however enthusiastically it was greeted more or less everywhere, Derrida did not feel that he was working 'in the noble sense' of the term.[21] In particular, he did not feel well, physically speaking. As he wrote to Sarah Kofman in September 1984:

> I've had (yet again!) a very difficult summer and I didn't want to moan by letter (rather serious health problems for me: the doctor initially thought the worst. Some possibilities have been eliminated thanks to an ultrasound of my pancreas and liver. That leaves the stomach. I stalled at the prospect of an endoscopy, they'll do it in Paris. I'd lost 6 kilos – and had 8 and 6 pressure . . .). I'm better, and I'll carry on with the examinations next week.[22]

The death of Paul de Man and his break-up with Sylviane probably played a part in the 'gloomy anxieties' that had been nagging at him for months. The medics finally diagnosed a big gallstone that meant that his gall bladder had to be removed at the end of December. This was his first operation, and the first time he had been hospitalized – a real ordeal for 'someone who, in addition, is terrified by the medical world'.[23] The doctors advised Derrida to moderate his activities somewhat, especially his travel. But he paid little attention to this advice.

Among his many other problems, he was worried by publishing issues. Since Flammarion did not intend to translate de Man's *Allegories of Reading*, he was unwilling to give them the book that he had written on his friend. At the beginning of 1985, feeling that he no longer really had a publisher, he discussed with Michel Deguy, a member of the readers' committee at Gallimard since 1962, the possibility of offering the two volumes to that august company.[24] He knew, however – through Jean Ristat and others – that his stock there was not high.

Deguy was more than positive in his reaction. But for the project to be accepted, he would need to find allies. He thought that *Mémoires: For Paul de Man* 'should also be of interest, of special interest in fact, to what is known as a "historian"'. This was an allusion to their old friend Pierre Nora. But the latter showed no enthusiasm. As for Deguy, though he felt 'pretty isolated', he said he was ready to go 'as far as possible'.[25] Over and above the book on de Man, he wanted to get Derrida onto the Gallimard list. But the latter had no illusions about his chances. Deguy notified the official refusal to him two months later. In his book *The Committee*, published in 1988, he returned somewhat scathingly to this episode:

I phoned Pierre [Nora] – at length – since he refused an ad hoc interview. I knew that for a second reading we would need his support and, practically, his agreement. [. . .] Most of his enemies in the academic and intellectual world, especially among the hard-line Heideggereans, acted as if all of Derrida's ideas were 'ridiculous'. Sniggering over a short quotation was their form of argument. I knew, of course, that Pierre Nora and his advisers did not count themselves among the number of zealous supporters of 'Derrideanism'. That was why I wanted to assure myself of his *objective* support. [. . .] This was perhaps to forget too quickly, and among other obstacles, that it is very difficult for contemporaries and friends, who had spent part of their youthful years together at Louis-le-Grand, then the Sorbonne, to recognize the value of one of their number, when they had all been equals, and to contribute to his *historical* destiny. Pierre Nora refused to take any interest in the project, and advised me in conclusion that it was up to me to 'sort it out by [myself]'.[26]

The affair assumed its full significance a few months later, when Gallimard published, in its series 'Le monde actuel', the book by Luc Ferry and Alain Renaut *French Philosophy of the Sixties: An Essay on Anti-Humanism*. Dedicated to Tzvetan Todorov, this pamphlet – which was something of a bestseller – was largely masterminded by Marcel Gauchet and François Furet, who ran the review *Le Débat*.[27] Ferry and Renaut were already known to Derrida: they had both spoken at the Cerisy conference on 'The Ends of Man'; after their presentation, the discussion had been extremely tense.

Attempting to establish 'the unity of inspiration, over and above the polemics and divergences', of an anti-humanist trend in philosophy, *French Philosophy of the Sixties* aimed to proceed 'to an uncompromising dismantling of French Marxism, of French Heideggereanism and of Freudianism *à la française*', before calling for 'the renewal of an authentic critical philosophy'.[28] Foucault, Derrida, Lyotard, Bourdieu, Althusser, and Lacan were the main targets of this attempt at liquidation, whose ideological presuppositions are clear enough. The fourth chapter is devoted entirely to Derrida, whose work is described as a 'hyperbolic repetition' of Heidegger's. For Ferry and Renaut, it can all be summed up in a few extremely simplistic formulae: 'If [. . .] *Foucault = Heidegger + Nietzsche*, and if we can say that [. . .] *Lacan = Heidegger + Freud*, French Heideggereanism can be defined by the formula *Derrida = Heidegger + Derrida's style.*'[29] Farewell to the analyses of Rousseau, Hegel, Husserl, Levinas, and so many others: if we are to believe these two, there is, between Derrida and his model, 'no difference other than one of *rhetoric*':

> French Heideggereanism is therefore dedicated exclusively to *symbolizing* ontological difference. It is indeed *French*, even very French, but only by virtue of its taste, talent, and aptitude for producing *literary* variations on a simple, even poor, philosophical theme, and that a borrowed one. Very closely linked to certain French peculiarities in the approach to philosophical discourse (the essay, the *khâgne*, the aggregation), this taste and this aptitude have been put to the service of one of the most stunning exercises in *repetition* that intellectual history has ever known.[30]

In spite of this coarse-grained analysis, the work would be influential enough for Derrida to return to it, fifteen years after its publication, in *For What Tomorrow. . .*, his dialogues with Élisabeth Roudinesco.[31] Admittedly, it was just when *French Philosophy in the Sixties* first came out that Roudinesco and he had been reconciled, after years of mistrust. This is how she tells the story:

Ever since I'd attacked him, at the second Cerisy conference, by unwisely comparing his ideas with those of Carl Gustav Jung, Derrida had cold-shouldered me. At the meetings of 'Confrontation', every time I spoke, he did not conceal his irritation. But the first volume of *Jacques Lacan and Co.** had been published in 1982 and I was working on the second, in which I felt that he would have an essential place: so we would need to put this old quarrel behind us. At our first meeting in Ris-Orangis, in March 1985, he asked me how I'd be presenting him in my book. I told him he was one of the great readers of Freud, and listed all texts in which he was present. And there were also his relationships with Lacan, Leclaire, Abraham, and Torok, not forgetting René Major ... Our conversations became increasingly free and easy. For instance, he told me in detail about Lacan's indiscretion regarding Derrida's son Pierre.[32]

Derrida asked to reread all the passages concerning him, but made only minor modifications. For her part, Roudinesco's account brings out just how unique Derrida's position was:

The further I advance, the more I realize the importance you have had for the French history of psychoanalysis in the second half of the century. I think that, in the relationship you have to the 'Freud question', your place (and not your theories) is comparable to that of Breton before the war: a contradictory and perpetual questioning. And finally you are the only person to have questioned the work of Lacan in a way other than by mimicry, repetition, adoration, or mere rejection.[33]

Derrida's loyalty to Louis Althusser, another target of *French Philosophy of the Sixties*, was unfailing. In July 1983, Althusser quietly left the Soisy clinic to move back to his apartment in the rue Lucien-Leuwen, in the 10th arrondissement. However, the situation was still very delicate: 'When the sectioning order was lifted,' explains Étienne Balibar, 'there was a kind of scandal, made worse by *Le Figaro*.

As his address had been published, we were very worried. In the entrance hall to the block of flats, they'd given him a false name: Berger. Psychologically, Althusser was still extremely fragile and he kept having to spend further periods in the clinic. I remember one of his manic phases, when Derrida intervened

---

* I.e. the French original. – Tr.

decisively. Althusser had told us that he wanted to make his big come-back, hiring La Mutualité* to organize a meeting on 'Communism today'. We were terrified at this idea, since it would rekindle all the old hostilities. But Louis wouldn't listen to reason. Derrida and I knew from experience that there was no other solution than to have him hospitalized before the depressive phase began. But, in order to avoid the risks and burdens of a long-term internment, we needed to persuade Althusser to ask for himself to be hospitalized. In spite of all my efforts, I hadn't managed to persuade him. Derrida succeeded, after just one meeting, which speaks volumes about the relationship they had. I honestly think that nobody else could have managed.[34]

In spite of ever heavier responsibilities, and ever more frequent trips abroad, Derrida continued to visit Althusser regularly. Sometimes they would go for walks together in the Père-Lachaise cemetery, very close to where he lived. The exchanges of ideas between them were freer and deeper than before. Althusser had started to read or reread Nietzsche, Husserl, and Heidegger. When he was in reasonable shape, he enjoyed discussing them with Derrida, as the latter related in his interview with Michael Sprinker:

Althusser was always fascinated with Husserl and Heidegger without his having ever given any public sign for this fascination. [. . .] For Althusser, if I may be allowed to say it in such a brutal way, Heidegger is the *great unavoidable thinker of this century*. [. . .] how many times did he say to me during the last years in the hospital: 'Listen, you've got to talk to me about Heidegger. You've got to teach me Heidegger.' [. . .] Heidegger was a great (oral) reference point for him and [. . .] he was never one of those who tried to denigrate or disqualify Heidegger's thought, even for the political reasons of which you are aware. But you are very well aware that a certain configuration, even a reciprocal fascination-repulsion between Marxism and Heideggereanism is one of the most significant phenomena of this century. And we have not finished meditating on it, assuming that we have seriously begun to do so.[35]

In March 1985, just as Michel Deguy was trying in vain to get Derrida onto the Gallimard list, the latter renewed contact with Michel Delorme, who ran the Galilée publishing house – he had

---

* A conference centre in the fifth arrondissement of Paris. – Tr.

published the proceedings of the conference on 'The Ends of Man' in 1981 and, perfectly naturally, two years later, the text of the paper Derrida had given on that occasion, 'On a newly arisen apocalyptic tone in philosophy'. But something quite different was now at stake. As Derrida wrote to Jean-Luc Nancy, Delorme was proposing to take over the whole series 'La philosophie en effet', in better conditions than could be offered by Flammarion. He said that he was prepared to publish, without further discussion, four books per year, except for collective works or very big volumes, which would need to be negotiated case by case. Derrida wished to discuss this as soon as possible with Kofman, Nancy, and Lacoue-Labarthe. Personally, he could see 'only advantages to this move, which would also be a homecoming'.[36]

The three co-directors agreed with Derrida's analysis. And the move soon came about: on 15 July 1985, Charles-Henri Flammarion acknowledged, without bitterness, their wish to bring to an end the series which they had been running at Flammarion.

> I understand and endorse this decision, and I would like to thank you for the work of reflection and publication that you have undertaken and entrusted to us. Admittedly, this work has encountered a few difficulties, to which the solution has not always been adequate. [. . .] The fact remains that these ten years will have made it possible to publish some important works that have left their mark, or are destined to do so, on the field of philosophy. It is also true that the intellectual situation, as well as the current state of publishing, has altered, and perhaps calls for new ideas.[37]

For Derrida himself, over and above the series, the move to Galilée was more than just a detail. A real relationship of trust and complicity soon sprang up between himself and Michel Delorme. Galilée was the polar opposite of the big publishing houses – the very model of a 'counter-institution' of the kind Derrida liked, a space of freedom where he could publish what he wanted, as he wanted, at an increasingly sustained speed. Admittedly, Delorme was not really a reader, let alone a partner in philosophical discussions, but this was probably not what Derrida was looking for. In the remarkable catalogue of human sciences that Galilée was about to produce, his work was indubitably the centre: some forty or so books by him would be published between 1986 and 2004. But Derrida was in good company. As well as Kofman, Nancy, Lacoue-Labarthe, and all the writers given a home in their series, Galilée published several fine authors such as Étienne Balibar, Jean Baudrillard, André Gorz, Jean-François Lyotard, Paul Virilio, and many others.

One of Derrida's first books to be published by Galilée, *Parages*, brought together four texts written and published between 1975 and 1979: ' '*Pa*ce not(*s*)', 'Living on', 'Title to be specified', and 'The law of genre'. All four dealt with the fictional works of Maurice Blanchot, especially *Death Sentence* and *The Madness of the Day*. As Derrida explains in his introduction to the volume:

> Other works of Blanchot have been accompanying me for a long time, those that are situated, also improperly, in the domains of literary criticism or of philosophy. [...] But the fictions remained inaccessible to me, as though plunged in a fog out of which only some fascinating glimmers, and sometimes, but at irregular intervals, the light of an invisible lighthouse on the coast reached [*parvenaient*] me. I will not say that from now on these fictions have left this reserve, indeed on the contrary. But in their very dissimulation, in the distance of the inaccessible *as such*, because they open onto it in giving it names [*elles donnent sur lui en lui donnant des noms*], they presented themselves to me again.

Even though the two men had not met since 1968, and exchanged letters only rarely, they were united by a 'friendship of thought' which remained, for both of them, 'one of life's graces'.[39] Blanchot said this in a letter to Derrida, written shortly after a phone call, in August 1985: 'To hear your voice, to have heard your voice was such a moving event that I was barely able to respond. It doesn't matter, perhaps. Since forever, everything has been implicit between us. This goes to the deepest level and is said by not being said.'[40] He repeated this six months later, after receiving *Parages*: 'For this gift made to me, not without peril for yourself, by this book and your books and by everything which at the same time goes beyond them, I cannot express my gratitude enough – that of having been, for a while, your contemporary.'[41]

At the same time, the little book *Shibboleth: For Paul Celan* came out. This was the text of a paper given in 1984 in Seattle. This highly personal reading of a poet who was of increasing importance to Derrida mainly focused on the word that gives the book its title: *shibboleth*, a Hebrew word with many meanings that has come to signify a password – the word that enables one to cross, or prevents one from crossing, a frontier kept under close surveillance:

> The Ephraimites had been defeated by the army of Jephthah; in order to keep the soldiers from escaping across the river [. . .], each person was required to say *shibboleth*. Now the Ephraimites were known for their inability to pronounce correctly the *shi* of *shibboleth*, which became for them, in

consequence, an 'unpronounceable name'; they said *shibboleth* and, at that invisible border between *shi* and *si*, betrayed themselves to the sentinel at the risk of death. They betrayed their difference in rendering themselves indifferent to the diacritical difference between *shi* and *si*; they marked themselves as unable to remark a mark thus coded.[42]

The word *shibboleth* is, beyond any question of its meaning, untranslatable: for Derrida it is a perfect metaphor for poetry. But he also finds in it many other themes dear to his heart: exclusion and covenant, secret and circumcision. As often, his approach was not exactly to the taste of specialists in the writer, those 'experts' about whom he had waxed ironic a few months earlier when discussing Joyce.[43] The great philologist Jean Bollack, who was very close to Derrida at the beginning of the 1970s, acknowledges that their relations deteriorated at the time of *Shibboleth*:

We both spoke at the Celan conference in Seattle. Between us, we maintained a very cordial tone, but our approaches were incompatible. Since 1959, I'd been a friend of Paul Celan, as well as of Peter Szondi. After Celan's death, I had the sense of a debt. Around 1980, I started to work on his texts with all the strength at my disposal. I spent years learning 'Celanian'. And in my view, the reading that Derrida was proposing was too hazardous. I wrote to tell him that you couldn't play that game with texts like Celan's, that you needed to pay more attention to the structures which his poetic language had imposed on itself. I would like to have gone over with him the very phrases that he quoted, to try to understand them in their context. Unfortunately, Derrida had organized his life in such a way that this kind of exchange wasn't possible any more.[44]

Parages and *Shibboleth*, like *Ulysses Gramophone*, which came out a few months later, are demanding works, with a rhythm all their own. They fall neither within philosophy nor within literary criticism. Even though Derrida was just then preparing his first radio broadcast 'Le bon plaisir', with Didier Cahen, most journalists said nothing. Readers were few and far between. In *L'Autre Journal*, Catherine David aptly summarized what was now the prevailing opinion:

The rumour is pitiless: Derrida has gone too far. You can't read him any more. Even philosophers can't follow him. Some of them admit as much with an ambiguous smile. Others wonder what he is getting up to – this thinker who once set the tone for French intellectual fashion by placing linguistics at the heart of philosophy and who now persists in losing himself in the thickets of a disconcerting hermeticism. [. . .] His books have always been difficult, but at least in the old days you knew what he was talking about: philosophy. Since, let's say, *The Post Card*, we don't know any more. He claims that philosophy is also transmitted in the form of love letters, postage stamps, telephone kiosks. He mixes everything up! Let's say no more about him . . .[45]

For her part, David was convinced that, while it is difficult to interpret Derrida, he can perfectly easily be read:

For this, you need to agree to read him the same way you dream, without any instruction manual, with jumps, drops, lapses, open questions. Patiently . . . [. . .] It's not, as it would be for an ordinary reading, about 'understanding'. [. . .] It's about something else, a meticulous path of thought, a contemplation of the detail, the letter, the time of silence. [. . .] In this period with its love of straight lines and short cuts, when common sense has re-established its dominion over the kingdom of thought, slowness and curves as magnified by Derrida have become the modern form of philosophical courage.

While nobody much bothered about Derrida in France, his fame in the United States continued to grow. Deconstruction had moved from departments of French to those of comparative literature, then of English, which enabled its influence to spread dramatically. But resistances developed at the same speed. On 9 February 1986, *The New York Times* magazine declared war on the Yale School and Derrida, 'the man who invented deconstruction'. 'The tyranny of the Yale critics' was the headline on the cover. The tone of the article was equally strident, claiming that, ever since the 1970s, a so-called 'hermeneutical mafia' had extended its sway over literary studies in Yale, and won many of the most prominent critics over to Derrida's ideas.[46]

But at that time, the Yale School was no more than a memory. Ever since the death of Paul de Man, the university in New Haven had lost its main source of attraction. Only the presence of J. Hillis Miller still drew Derrida there. But in summer 1985, Miller told the latter privately that he was not intending to stay at Yale.

After Paul de Man's death, I felt that a page had been turned. The attack on what we represented was getting fiercer the whole time. We could no longer ensure that any of our colleagues got tenure. It was even getting more and more difficult to invite

Derrida. I sensed that the next few years would be much less pleasant and interesting than those we had just lived through. Murray Krieger, a remarkable character, suggested that I move to Irvine, a new university to the south of Los Angeles. He was a professor of English and comparative literature, but in particular he ran the institute of Critical Theory. I was tempted to accept his offer, but I still hadn't made my mind up. In August 1985, I spoke to Jacques in the garden of his home in Ris-Orangis. I can still hear him telling me: 'If you go to Irvine, I'll gladly go too. It will recharge my batteries.' He tended to leave institutions in case he became associated with them for too long and got trapped. But he probably also had, more or less consciously, a desire to 'win the West' . . . When I mentioned the possibility of getting Derrida to come to Irvine, Murray Krieger reacted enthusiastically, understanding the aura this would give to the humanities as a whole. And as he was a close friend of William Lillyman, the university vice-chancellor, the administrative obstacles were dealt with in the twinkling of an eye. When I asked about how much Derrida would be paid, Lillyman immediately asked me what he had been earning at Yale, and then added: 'We can go 50% better and give him tenure for a part-time post as a distinguished professor.' So the transfer happened in 1986.[47]

On moving to Irvine, Derrida took the decision that he would henceforth teach in English, which would enable him to reach much bigger audiences. When it was a rather more formal lecture, he read out a previously translated text. But for seminars, this would have been much too onerous. So Derrida simply annotated the French version and translated his own words directly, initially rather slowly, but soon very fluently. It didn't stop this change of language being a problem for him, theoretically even more than practically. As Samuel Weber remembers:

One day, one of his listeners tried to reassure him: 'Your English is excellent, we can understand everything.' And Derrida replied: 'That's just the problem: I'm merely making myself understood.' He had played with the resources of the French language like a virtuoso; for a long time, he suffered from being able merely to 'communicate' once he started to express himself in English. But his mastery became increasingly more refined. In his last years, he was able to devote a lecture to the shades of meaning between *maybe* and *perhaps*.[48]

Even though they were much less at ease in English than he was, Derrida also encouraged Kofman, Nancy, and Lacoue-Labarthe to set foot in the United States. The situation struck him as being much more open than in France, now that 'French Theory' was all the rage. He wanted their careers to benefit and was always ready to write enthusiastic and effective letters of recommendation. In 1985, Nancy went to teach for two years at the University of San Diego, not far from Irvine, which made it easier for them to meet. To support the publication of Lacoue-Labarthe's *Typography* by Harvard University Press, Derrida wrote a forty-page preface, stating his admiration for 'the force and the exigent character' of his thought:

> What I share with Lacoue-Labarthe, we also both share, though differently, with Jean-Luc Nancy. But I hasten imme- diately to reiterate that despite so many common paths and so much work done in common, between the two of them and among the three of us, the *experience* of each remains, in its singular proximity, absolutely different; and this, despite its inevitable impurity, is the secret of the idiom. The secret: that is to say, first of all, the *separation*, the without-relation, the interruption. The most urgent thing – I will try to work on this – would be to break here with the family resemblance, to avoid genealogical temptations, projections, assimilations, or identifications.[49]

Just after reading this superb text, Lacoue-Labarthe sent Derrida a letter that showed how touched he was. The powerful impact of the pages his friend had just devoted to him left him almost speechless.

> The only word that comes to mind is that I am overwhelmed. Apart from 'mere' narcissism, even though I won't deny that: this is the first time that I can see someone reading me, and that someone is you, not just what you represent, but the fact that my debt towards you in philosophical matters cannot be measured and, as you know, I obstinately consider you to be the master of a school at which I consider myself still to be learning, even though I was never really in the position of being your pupil. But apart from that narcissism, because of what you *give* to these texts about which, in spite of the appearance of the tone, I have always felt so unsure. You show them a trust that I would never have thought possible and I have just started to understand what they were trying to say and what I wasn't able to say.[50]

This period was also marked by meetings with several young philosophers who would go on to have brilliant careers.

Bernard Stiegler contacted Derrida in really quite unusual

circumstances. As he later related in his short book *Passer à l'acte*, it was during a long sojourn in prison near Toulouse that he embarked on studies in linguistics and then philosophy with the support of Gérard Granel. 'Those five years' incarceration were the best thing that happened to me,' he says.

Since time was the only thing I had, I was able to read a few great philosophical oeuvres in a methodical way: Plato, Aristotle, Heidegger, but Derrida too. *Of Grammatology* struck me as a super-human text. After a while, I was so enthusiastic about Derrida that Granel encouraged me to write to him. I took a while to make my mind up, as ever since I'd been in prison, I'd chosen to adopt what I felt was a salutary attitude: expect nothing from outside. So I was very afraid that he wouldn't reply and that this would bug me. In fact, he replied straightaway and in very generous terms. We met for the first time in Paris in October 1982, during one of my periods of parole. In spite of all his efforts to put me at my ease, I was paralysed by my feelings, stupefied to find myself face to face with the author of a text that had had such an impact on me.[51]

During his last months in detention, Stiegler sent Derrida the text on Plato that he was writing and which formed the basis of his *maîtrise* dissertation. Derrida was immediately impressed by the quality of the work. In his letters, Stiegler added personal remarks that were bound to touch Derrida, so soon after his own brief incarceration in Prague. In particular, he said that he was even more apprehensive about his final release than he desired it: 'At present, I've just got to the heart of my work, where I feel almost at ease, and this liberation will, I fear, wreck all my efforts to put myself at the disposal of texts as much as possible – and in this respect, prison is a very virtuous place.'[52]

After Stiegler's release at the beginning of 1983, Derrida continued to follow his philosophical work. But, to the amazement of the man who admired him as an inaccessible master, the author of *Of Grammatology* took an equal interest in his professional future, helping him as much as possible to fit into society. In 1984, Stiegler was appointed for six years as director of the research programme at the Collège International de Philosophie. In 1986, he registered to write a thesis under Derrida's supervision at the same time as his then partner, Catherine Malabou, an alumna of the École Normale Supérieure at Fontenay-Saint-Cloud and an *agrégée* in philosophy.

Since being appointed to a post at the École des Hautes Études, Derrida had been in a position to supervise theses, a task which he took with remarkable seriousness. But for his students, in the French institutional context, the situation brought several risks. As Catherine Malabou explains:

> Approaching Derrida, and *a fortiori* writing your thesis with him, meant you were more or less finished in the university system. In France, everyone who worked with him suffered for it. Even now, the label 'Derridean' still sticks to me, even though my work no longer has much to do with his. Every time I went in front of a panel of examiners, I was given the privilege of having them ask a few – generally malevolent – questions about him. Of course, Derrida had sometimes been provocative, especially towards the Inspection Générale or the *agrégation* examiners, but I think that what mainly bothered people was the independence from institutions that he always embodied. And it was precisely this independence that I loved in him. Never have I met anyone less fazed by possible reprisals or questions of social respectability. He couldn't stand institutional obedience getting in the way of thinking, or the norm winning out over the demands of thinking. On a deeper level, there's something in deconstruction itself which tends to arouse hostility: it's a kind of approach that generates disquiet.[53]

For Derrida, deconstruction was still mainly a way of thinking about philosophy. It was not a doctrine, but a means of analysing the genealogy of the history of philosophy, 'its concepts, its presuppositions, its axiomatics and doing so not only theoretically but also by questioning its institutions, its social and political practices, in short the political culture of the West'.[54] This somewhat restrictive definition did not prevent Derrida from exploring new domains and embarking on hazardous experiences.

Ever since many people had deserted the political field, he had been tackling it increasingly directly. In 1984, the paper 'No apocalypse, not now' discussed the threat of nuclear war and closely scrutinized the language being used by the Reagan administration. Written to accompany a travelling exhibition against apartheid, 'Racism's last word' analyses the particularities of the South African regime and the international complicity from which it profited. This was a case about which Derrida felt particularly strongly. In 1986, he provided a long, powerful piece to the book *For Nelson Mandela* in which fifteen writers – including Nadime Gordimer, Susan Sontag, Hélène Cixous, Kateb Yacine, and Maurice Blanchot – hailed one of the most long-standing political prisoners in the entire world.

In this text, 'The laws of reflection: Nelson Mandela, in

admiration', Derrida goes far beyond a mere homage. He puts forward a veritable analysis of what is most specific about the person, the attitude, and the writings of the former leader of the ANC. 'Why does he also *force* one to admire him?' he wonders. It is mainly because 'Mandela's political experience or passion can never be separated from a theoretical reflection: on history, culture, and above all, law.'[55] What Derrida finds in Nelson Mandela is a figure he had dreamed of ever since the Algerian War: a man able to turn the English democratic model against the proponents of apartheid; a sort of deconstructor in action. 'In all the senses of this term, Mandela remains, then, a *man of law*. He has always appealed to right even if, in appearance, he had to oppose himself to this or that determinate legality, and even if certain judges made of him, at certain moments, an outlaw.'[56] The distinction Mandela establishes between obedience to the law and obedience to an even more imperious conscience is in many respects close to the opposition between law and justice which Derrida was to develop a few years later in *Force of Law*.

At this time, Derrida was also starting to tackle theological and religious questions that would assume an increasing place in his work. In June 1986, he opened the conference 'Absence and Negativity' organized by the Hebrew University and the Institute for Advanced Studies in Jerusalem, with a paper called 'How to avoid speaking: denials'. In a discussion of negative theology and the work of Dionysius the Areopagite (known as pseudo-Dionysius), Derrida conducts a dialogue with his former student Jean-Luc Marion, the author of *The Idol and Distance* and *God without Being*. Comparisons – of a somewhat critical nature – were drawn between Derrida's work and negative theology, a movement which he admitted had always fascinated him:

> I objected in vain to the assimilation of the thinking of the trace or of differance [*sic*] to some negative theology, and my response amounted to a promise: one day I will stop deferring, one day I will try to explain myself directly on this subject, and at last speak of 'negative theology' *itself*, assuming that some such thing exists. [. . .]
>
> Having already promised, *as if in spite of myself*, I did not know *how* I could keep this promise. [. . .] Above all, I did not know when and where I would do it. Next year in Jerusalem, I told myself, in order perhaps to defer indefinitely the fulfilment of this promise. But also to let myself know – and I did indeed receive the message – that on the day when I would in fact go to Jerusalem, it would no longer be possible to delay. It will then be necessary to do it.[57]

This paper, with all its insights, was in many ways a preparation for 'Circumfession'. In a note, Derrida also acknowledged that this was the most 'autobiographical' discourse he had ever risked:

> If one day I had to tell my story, nothing in this narrative would begin to speak of the thing itself if I did not come up against this fact: I have never yet been able – lacking the ability, the competence, or the self-authorization – to speak of what my birth, as one says, should have brought closest to me: the Jew, the Arab.[58]

Several of Derrida's interventions in the mid-eighties concerned the aesthetic field. He proposed a 'reading', in the form of a dialogue, to accompany *Right of Inspection*, an erotic, silent photographic narrative by Marie-Françoise Plissart that would later be rediscovered in the light of Queer Theory.[59] He composed a new study on Antonin Artaud, 'Maddening the subjectile', focusing on the portraits assembled and presented by Paule Thévenin.[60] He ventured for the first time to write about Shakespeare, when his friend Daniel Mesguich directed *Romeo and Juliet* in 1986 at the Théâtre Gérard-Philippe in Saint-Denis.[61] Even though he admitted to an 'intimidated' respect for Shakespeare's work, he would like one day, he said, to become a 'Shakespeare expert'.[62] He would partly realize this ambition with *Specters of Marx*, where the presence of *Hamlet* is almost as powerful as that of Marx.

At the end of 1984, Derrida also played a part in the audacious exhibition that Jean-François Lyotard and Thierry Chaput were planning at the Pompidou Centre, with the title 'Les Immatériaux'. One of the exhibition spaces was to be devoted to the 'Épreuves d'écriture' ('Proofs/tests of writing'): some twenty authors were invited to contribute, including Daniel Buren, Michel Butor, François Châtelet, Maurice Roche, and Jacques Roubaud. Lyotard's idea was to 'gauge the effects of "new machines" on the formation of thought': he offered them an interactive platform for writing. Each of them was to choose a certain number of words from a list and compose short texts, before reacting to the others' pieces. But though this seemed like a stimulating concept, the technology was still in its infancy. With some difficulty, an imposing computer equipped with a modem and accompanied by a simple beginner's manual was installed in Ris-Orangis. When this machine made its entry into his house, Derrida felt that a monster had just been let in. This was his first contact with information theory and, for all his goodwill, he found it extremely difficult to use.[63]

The most unusual project of this period would associate Derrida with two of the most innovative architects of the day: the Franco-

Swiss Bernard Tschumi and the American Peter Eisenman. During the 1970s, like other architects of his generation, Tschumi dedicated himself to new concepts from outside his discipline, especially in the arts, sciences, and philosophy. For ten years, he mainly focused on paper architecture, exhibiting and publishing more than he built. When he won the international competition launched in 1982 for the Parc de la Villette, a huge area of fifty-five hectares on the site of the old Paris abattoirs, Tschumi decided to make a big impression. On this site, which was to bring together the Grande Halle, the Cité de la Musique, the Cité des Sciences, the Géode, and the Zénith, he intended to fashion 'the first park of the twenty-first century', punctuating the space with a network of small red buildings which he called the 'Folies'. As chief architect of this huge project, Tschumi decided to invite other artists to collaborate. He initially wished to get Jean-François Lyotard to work with Paul Chemetov, but the author of *The Postmodern Condition* was rather wary. 'With Derrida, it was just the opposite,' recalls Tschumi.

He showed an immediate interest when I called him and came to meet me at the little agency I then had near the Gare du Nord. I told him about Peter Eisenman, a remarkable architect from New York, born in 1932 but still not very well known, and I introduced them to one another a few months later in the United States. I am still struck by the generosity Derrida displayed. However busy he might be, he always found the necessary time.[64]

Even if he was mistrustful of facile transpositions between architecture and deconstruction, Derrida found the project alluring and exciting. He wrote a fine text on Tschumi's ideas, then agreed to collaborate with Eisenman. Tschumi gave them rather a narrow plot of land, thirty metres by thirty; but they were at liberty to build a 'Folie' here as they wished. Derrida's first contribution was purely philosophical – a text on the 'Chora' – or *Khôra* – in Plato's *Timaeus*, a term that in his view was untranslatable: it refers to the place, the space or spacing, or the site.[65] But as soon as the discussion became more concrete, a curious chiasm came into play. Derrida kept coming back with extremely pragmatic questions – he was worried about the absence of benches, plants, and shelter in case of bad weather –, while Eisenman, irritated by his partner's 'architectural conservatism', kept upping the conceptual stakes. Derrida eventually realized this, and at one of their meetings said: 'Peter, I have a suggestion to make. In this association, let's behave as if you were the dreamer and I the architect, the technician. That way, you'll be the theorist and I'll look after the practical consequences.'[66]

After two years of sometimes difficult discussions, the plan had to be abandoned, mainly for budgetary reasons. And all that eventually remained was a book, *Chora L Works*, which traced the stages of their collaboration. But Derrida was far from finished with architecture. Though it rather twisted some of his ideas, a deconstructivist trend soon emerged in architecture, proposing a strange synthesis of Derridean deconstruction and Russian constructivism. In 1988, Philip Johnson and Mark Wigley set up an exhibition at MoMA in New York, bringing together a series of top architects – Zaha Hahid, Frank Gehry, Daniel Libeskind, Rem Koolhaas, Peter Eisenman, Bernard Tschumi, and the Austrian agency Coop-Himmelb(l)au – under the rubric 'Deconstructive Architecture'. Although Derrida was not involved, the reaction of the French press was negative. Jean-Pierre Le Dantec wrote that Derrida had been 'vampirized by a coterie', and Jean-Louis Cohen reflected that, rather than being a matter of theory, 'this coupling of Russian avant-gardes and the French philosopher seems more to fall under teratology, or the science of monsters'.[67]

2

From the Heidegger Affair to the de Man Affair

1987–1988

Ever since his arrival at the École des Hautes Études, Derrida had been able to develop a theme of his own choosing, without needing to bother too much about the *agrégation* syllabus. The question that had been preoccupying him since 1984 had been that of 'Nationalities and philosophical nationalisms'. Since the autumn of 1986, he had given this theme a more specific twist, giving it the title 'Kant, the Jew, the German'. The issues at stake may have been philosophical, but they were far from academic:

> As you have will already have seen, what interests me in this seminar is the modernity, the past and the future of a certain couple, the Jewish-German couple that in my view is altogether unique, unique in its kind, and without which it is impossible to understand anything of the history of Germany, the history of Nazism, the history of Zionism [. . .] quite a lot of things, in other words, in the history of our time.[1]

Session after session, Derrida patiently examined texts by Fichte and Nietzsche, Adorno and Hannah Arendt, as well as Richard Wagner, Michelet, and Tocqueville – not forgetting Heidegger, the philosopher to whom he returned almost every year, with passion and tenacity. Claiming that 'you can think only in the language of the other', Derrida was explicitly arguing with Heidegger, who, in the famous posthumously published interview in *Der Spiegel*, maintained that 'you think only in your language, in your own language', and Derrida wanted 'to demonstrate the privilege, the excellence, the irreplaceability of Greek and German as languages of thought'.

In the immediate wake of these reflections, in March 1987 Derrida gave the closing paper, 'Of spirit', at the end of the conference organized by the Collège International de Philosophie under the title 'Heidegger, Open Questions'. Derrida scrutinized the trajectory of the word 'spirit' (*Geist*) both in Heidegger's most overtly philosophical texts and in the famous 'Rectoral Address' which he gave in 1933. As Derrida explained in an interview:

> At the moment when his discourse situates itself in a spectacular fashion in the camp of Nazism [. . .], Heidegger takes up again the word 'spirit', whose avoidance he had prescribed; he removes the quotation marks with which he had surrounded it. He limits the deconstructive movement that he had begun earlier. He maintains a voluntarist and metaphysical discourse upon which he will later cast suspicion.[2]

A few weeks after this conference, the trial of Klaus Barbie, reported widely in the media, put the Nazi question back at the top of the current agenda. On 4 July 1987, after a two-month hearing, Barbie was given a life sentence for crimes against humanity by the Cour d'Assises du Rhône. In October the same year, the publication of the book by Victor Farías, *Heidegger and Nazism*, was something of an event. The question, admittedly, was not new: in France, Jean-Pierre Faye, for one, had dealt with the matter at length, and Derrida had faced his attacks as early as 1969.[3] But the debate on Heidegger, like that on Céline, kept resurfacing every fifteen or twenty years.

Although it had been written in Spanish, Farías's book was initially published in France. This was not due merely to the contingencies of publishing. According to Christian Jambet, the author of the preface to this French edition:

> Heidegger has, since the war, become a French philosopher. It is in France that his thought has aroused the most echoes, it is here that it is viewed as the philosophy that is most adequate to the events of modernity. [. . .] For many scholars, his work seems *obvious* in a way that no other philosophy in France has managed, apart from Marxism. Ontology reaches its consummation in a methodical deconstruction of metaphysics as such.[4]

Christian Jambet's remarks almost eclipsed Farías's biographical investigation and were immediately taken up and amplified in the many articles published over the following days. 'Heidegger, Nazi activist and thinker', wrote Georges-Arthur Goldschmidt in *Le Matin* on 15 October 1987: 'Victor Farías's book will stop people philosophizing in circles and force the "Heideggereans of Paris" to face up to the questions that they have always known would at one fell swoop empty of all content the things they had tried to put into their writings.' 'Heil Heidegger!' was the headline in *Libération* the next day; here, too, it was the French Heideggereans who were under attack, with Robert Maggiori accusing them of never having tried to understand 'Heidegger's absolute silence on the monstrosities of Nazism'.

It was at this precise moment that two new works by Derrida were published by Galilée: the short book *Of Spirit: Heidegger and the Question*, as well as the huge collection of pieces, *Psyche*. In what was probably an inevitable misunderstanding, *Of Spirit* was read as a response to Farías, though it was not at all meant to be one. However, Derrida had no intention of evading the issue. In a long interview with Didier Eribon, he referred straightaway to Farías's work, and his remarks were scathing:

> Concerning the majority of the 'facts', I have yet to find anything in this investigation that was not already known, and for a long time, by those who take a serious interest in Heidegger. As for the research into a certain archive, it is a good thing that its results are being made available in France. The most solid of these results have already been available in Germany ever since the work of Bernd Martin and Hugo Ott, which Farías draws on extensively. Beyond certain aspects of the documentation and some factual questions, which call for caution, discussion will focus especially – and it is important that the discussion remain open – on the interpretation, let us say, that relates these 'facts' to Heidegger's 'text', to his 'thinking'. The reading proposed, if there is one, remains insufficient or questionable, at times so shoddy that one wonders if the investigator began to read Heidegger more than an hour ago. It is said that he was Heidegger's student. These things happen. When he calmly declares that Heidegger, I quote, 'translates' 'a certain fund of notions proper to National Socialism' into 'forms and a style that, of course, are his alone', he points toward a chasm, more than one chasm, a chasm beneath each word. But he doesn't for an instant approach them and doesn't even seem to suspect they are there.[5]

In Derrida's view, there was nothing sensational in Farías's book, except for those unaware not just of the more rigorous of previous historians, but also of the reflections on the subject of thinkers such as Maurice Blanchot, Emmanuel Levinas, Philippe Lacoue-Labarthe, and Jean-Luc Nancy. Derrida stated that he himself had registered reservations in *all* his references to Heidegger, from his first texts onwards. And he was now more than ever convinced that, while condemning 'unequivocally both Heidegger's Nazism and his silence after the war', these needed to be analysed in a way that went 'beyond conventional and comfortable schemas'.

Why does this hideous archive seem so unbearable and fascinating? Precisely because no one has ever been able to reduce the whole work of Heidegger's thought to that of some Nazi ideologue. This 'record' would be of little interest otherwise. For more than a half-century, no rigorous philosopher has been able to avoid a 'full and frank discussion' with Heidegger. How can one deny that? Why deny that so many 'revolutionary', audacious, and troubling works of the twentieth century have ventured into or even committed themselves to regions that, according to a philosophy which is confident of its liberal and leftist-democratic humanism, are haunted by the diabolical? Instead of erasing or trying to forget it, must one not try to account for this experience, which is to say, for our age? And without believing that all of this is already clear for us?[6]

Derrida soon found himself at the centre of the polemic – it was just as if, through Heidegger, he was the one under attack. He had been publishing for twenty-five years, and he had been famous in French intellectual circles for twenty years. But for the French public, this was just the second time – the first had been the Prague affair – that he had come to notice.

Victor Farías addressed the philosopher directly in a text called '13 facts for Jacques Derrida', published in *El País* and then reprinted in *Le Nouvel Observateur* and several European newspapers: 'What does Jacques Derrida say? The facts are there, but they have no significance in themselves without a corresponding philosophical interpretation. Even richer than that: Derrida has "found nothing in this investigation that had not been known for a long time".' Whereupon Farías summarized a series of 'extremely important' elements that had been 'completely unknown' before his book, before he concluded his letter by saying: 'If Derrida knew all that, why didn't he tell us? He would have spared me twelve years' work.'[7] Even though several aspects of Farías's work on Heidegger would be questioned and qualified over the following years, his attack bore fruit.[*]

Passions were still running high when, on 27 November 1987, Robert Maggiori published in *Libération* a double-page spread with the title: 'Derrida tient Heidegger en respect' ('Derrida keeps Heidegger at a distance'[†]).The article itself was ambivalent: Maggiori patiently followed the analysis put forward in *Of Spirit*;

---

[*] A few years later, Farías went off the rails when he tried to prove that Salvador Allende 'was actually just a supporter of the "Final Solution"', an anti-Semite, a homophobe, and a sworn enemy of "inferior races": in short, a Nazi disguised as a socialist' (Élisabeth Roudinesco, *Retour sur la question juive*, Paris: Albin Michel, 2009, p. 294). In 2005, the President Allende Foundation brought proceedings against Farías for defamation of the dead.

[†] But with the subtext 'Derrida respects Heidegger'. – Tr.

he underlined its interest and its importance before regretting the fact that Derrida never moved on from a 'conceptual statement' to a 'moral insurrection'. But the conclusion was, all of a sudden, more brutal:

> Let's say things in crude and simple terms: Derrida's analysis is indeed subtle and acute [. . .], but, when it comes to analysing Heidegger's 'utterance', which was aimed not just at settling a point of doctrine or illuminating a concept, but at giving a philosophical determination of Nazism, why make such a fuss? Why hold such unclear ethical or political *positions*? Why does Heidegger's work keep one at a distance, as the sword does its victim?[8]

Derrida was deeply hurt, by the subheadings that divided up the article and seemed to summarize it – 'without ever criticizing a thing', 'not much moral insurrection' – and especially by the word 'fuss [*chichis*]'. Today, Maggiori agrees:

> He was taken aback by that over-familiar word. If I'd written 'precautions' or 'sophistication', he'd probably have found it easier to accept. He sent me a brutal letter just after the article came out, and didn't speak to me for four or five years. His sensitivity was particularly great because *Libération* mattered to him and I was one of the few journalists to write probing articles on works of philosophy. But the press is always inclined to simplify matters, even if only in the headlines and subheadings, for which I am far from being the main person responsible. These were things he never accepted.[9]

A week later, it was the turn of *Le Monde* to react. Roger-Pol Droit devoted a long article to Derrida's two books, for once more clement than the one in *Libération*. He emphasized the books themselves, rather than the polemic launched by Farías and Jambet:

> Famous and unknown, [Derrida] makes disconcerting moves, sidling along the walls between philosophy and literature, dismounting the proper, the name, the word – and the book too, with the result that many people can't, as you say, follow. And yet! What inventiveness there is, clear, incisive, even joyful, in the styles of the volume [*Psyche*] that is being published at the same time as *Of Spirit*! [. . .] What if Derrida were to be discovered in France?[10]

The boil had not yet been completely lanced, however. When the review *Le Débat* devoted a bulky issue to 'Heidegger, philosophy

and Nazism', Mireille Calle-Gruber, in charge of university rela-
tions at the French Institute in Heidelberg, invited Derrida and
Lacoue-Labarthe to a meeting on the subject with Hans-Georg
Gadamer.

The debate was held on the evening of 5 February 1988 in front
of over a thousand people. In many ways, it was exceptional. After
a series of confrontations in France, the Heidegger question was
finally returning to Germany, and in a place fraught with memories:
it was in this very same lecture hall that, on 30 June 1933, Heidegger
had given a speech with the title 'The university in the new Reich'.
The audience had come not just to see Derrida, but also Gadamer,
already a very old man and a local star; it was also the first time
that Derrida and he had spoken to one another since their failed
dialogue in 1981. When the speakers entered the hall, the audience
applauded in German style, banging on the tables.[11]

The encounter was held in French and lasted over four hours;
it was as serene as the subject-matter permitted. Gadamer was
initially able to provide an eye-witness account, as a contemporary, of Heidegger's 'folly'. But this evening also gave him an
exceptional opportunity to emerge from his long discretion on the
period. Derrida started by saying how important Farías's work
was: whatever reservations one might have about it, he said, 'this
book has forced professional philosophers to explain themselves in
a more urgent and immediate way'. Lacoue-Labarthe and Derrida
focused more on the question of Heidegger's silence after the war,
in relation to his Nazi commitments and to Auschwitz. It was this
obstinate silence, maintained even in the presence of Paul Celan,
that remained, in the eyes of Maurice Blanchot and many others,
'a wound to thought'. But could it have been otherwise? Would it
not have been too easy to seek to absolve oneself with a few conventional words of apology? Derrida embarked on a hypothesis that he
himself admitted was risky:

> I think that, perhaps, Heidegger said to himself: I'll not be
> able to utter any condemnation of Nazism unless I can utter it
> not only in a way worthy of what I have already said, but also
> worthy of what happened there. And this was something of
> which he was not capable. [. . .] And I consider that the terrify-
> ing, perhaps unforgivable silence of Heidegger, the absence of
> phrases of the kind we wish to hear, [. . .] this absence leaves us
> with a heritage, leaves us with the *injunction* to think what he
> did not think.[12]

Questions from the audience tried to get the speakers to commit
themselves more clearly. Derrida emphasized that, in 1968, he had
already learned from Jean Beaufret that Heidegger had had a Nazi

party membership card: 'Then, there was the article by Hugo Ott, etc. [. . .] Should we have done anything other than what we did do? Perhaps.' Philippe Lacoue-Labarthe noted that these questions had been debated at length during the Cerisy conference on 'The Ends of Man', but none of this seemed to have counted for anything on the media stage to which the polemic had recently shifted. Derrida restated this position, in a more anxious manner than usual:

> I felt it was more important [. . .], more urgent to try to read Heidegger's texts in the way I can, to teach Heidegger, seeking in his text material on the basis of which I could try to understand what kind of a relationship there might be between the facts of his Nazi commitment and his text. And I thought that this was what I could do best, and that this required patience, a great deal of patience. [. . .] I don't feel that I have forgotten the sense of a responsibility that you would call ethical or political in that area.

Several German and French journalists attended the meeting, which continued the following day with a press conference at the Sole d'Oro, a famous restaurant in Heidelberg whose walls were covered with photos of Gadamer. Then Derrida and Gadamer had a conversation alone together, trying to move on from Heidegger and open the space for a real dialogue.[13]

While Philippe Lacoue-Labarthe's position may have seemed close to Derrida's at this memorable debate, it had already started to diverge. Shortly before, indeed, Lacoue-Labarthe had brought out a text called *The Fiction of the Political*: this was a violent attack on Heidegger, whose philosophy was analysed in terms of 'arch-fascism' and 'national-aestheticism'. According to Philippe Beck, who was then writing his thesis under Derrida's supervision, Lacoue-Labarthe's growing anti-Heideggereanism was one of the factors that led Derrida to move away from him increasingly, while drawing closer to Jean-Luc Nancy.

> Philippe Lacoue-Labarthe always regretted, in my view, that he was never able to play a part in the Situationist International, which was very active in Strasbourg. There was something strategic about his alliance with Derrida, apart from the (real) admiration that he shared with Nancy – and you would expect this. He probably hoped to radicalize deconstruction, in the political sense of the term. But not at any price: Lacoue did not make any pious references to Debord. And we mustn't forget his reading of Benjamin, one he shared with Derrida. As for Nancy, he thinks *with* rather than *against*, preferring, I think, the critique of reason to critical reason.[14]

The Heidegger affair also rekindled older quarrels, starting with the one which had long been brewing with Pierre Bourdieu. While he had greeted *Glas* with an enthusiastic letter, five years later Bourdieu laid into Derrida in no uncertain terms, in the last pages of one of his main works, *Distinction*. Admittedly, this postscript – 'Towards a "vulgar" critique of "pure" critiques' – was officially devoted to Kant's *Critique of Judgment* and the denial of 'the social categories of aesthetic judgement' that could be read in it.[15] But behind Kant, it is undeniable that Bourdieu was attacking Derrida and his reading of Kant in the text 'Parergon' (reprinted in 1978 in *The Truth in Painting*). In his view, although it did bring out some of the hidden presuppositions of Kant's philosophy of the judgment of taste, Derrida's reading is still 'subject to the censorships of the pure reading'. Despite 'transgressing the most binding rules of orthodox commentary', any questioning of the philosophical postulates was, in his view, more apparent than real. 'The supremely skilful game' in which Derrida indulges is merely an apparent transgression; it in fact perpetuates 'the existence and the powers of philosophical reading'.[16]

All things considered, Bourdieu's attack was not unrelated to the one launched by Michel Foucault seven years earlier in the final pages of another postscript, namely the republication of his *History of Madness*. For the author of *Distinction*, it was also a matter of dislodging philosophy from its domineering position. If we are to believe Bourdieu, deconstruction is merely a very sophisticated lure. As he puts it, 'the philosophical way of talking about philosophy de-realizes everything that can be said about philosophy'. However subtle they may be, or precisely because of their subtlety, 'the most audacious intellectual breaks of pure reading' are merely 'an ultimate path of salvation' for a discipline that in his view is threatened with pure and simple destruction.[17]

Derrida did not immediately reply to this critique. But, focusing on the Kantian problematic of the *Conflict of Faculties*, he devoted several sessions in his 1983–4 seminar to the postscript of *Distinction* before returning to it in 'Privilege', the text which opens *Who's Afraid of Philosophy?* Derrida endeavours to demonstrate that Bourdieu is doing exactly the same as he had criticized Derrida for doing: he wanted to give sociology an 'absolute, that is, *philosophical*, hegemony over the multiplicity of the other regions of knowledge, of which sociology would no longer simply be a part'.[18] In a spectacular *coup de force*, Bourdieu thus overturns the ancient hierarchy of the branches of knowledge by turning sociology into the new queen of the disciplines, able to lord it over all the others and reveal what they have left unsaid. Far from being the promised revolution, it was merely an attempted putsch.

This conflict between two disciplines was also a metaphor for the rivalry between two men of the same generation, trained in the same institutions. Originally, Bourdieu had aimed to be a philosopher, like Derrida, but he very quickly changed tack, moving from Husserl to Kabylia, then to sociology, without ever quite bidding farewell to philosophy. As Didier Eribon, who managed to stay friends with both men, illuminatingly puts it:

> Bourdieu was haunted by the figure of Derrida, and many of his remarks on philosophy and his apparent choices in this domain can be explained only by this relationship, more subterranean but more fundamental than those he tried to evince so as better to mask the truth – a relationship with a man whom, deep down, he doubtless considered to be his only equal and his only rival, and who was in any case his interlocutor both privileged and denied (one day he told me: 'There's always someone in your own generation whom you consider right from the start as your rival' . . . before naming his own rival, who, of course, was Derrida . . . You need merely read the postscript to *Distinction* on Kant's aesthetics to realize this!)[19]

As so often, it was Heidegger who acted as a catalyst, rekindling old quarrels that concerned him only indirectly. On 10 March 1988, *Libération* had a double-page spread headlined by the words: 'Heidegger by Pierre Bourdieu: the great crash in philosophy'. This was actually an interview with Bourdieu about his book *The Political Ontology of Martin Heidegger*, a slightly revised version of a text from 1975. Right from the start, Bourdieu's allusions seemed to target Derrida: 'Farías's book has had the merit of forcing Heideggereans to emerge from the lofty reserve into which they had withdrawn.' Philosophy was used to 'abusing its symbolic powers' and treating history and the human sciences with disdain, but here it was forced to face up to positive knowledge. And Bourdieu went so far as to claim that 'if that philosophy, and those philosophers, were dragged under by the great crash of Heideggerean thought, it would not be a loss in [his] eyes'.

Then the attack became head-on, as Bourdieu turned to Derrida's interview in *Le Nouvel Observateur* a few months earlier:

> I found it rather funny that Derrida, who was well acquainted with my 1975 text – he'd read it and I gave an account of it in his seminar without arousing the least objection –, should, in his attempted rebuttal of the sociological analysis, call for a form of analysis able to go beyond the contrast between understanding from within and explaining from without, a programme that I had been proposing for some time, and one which I had, in my view, realized. It has to be said that the debate on Heidegger had placed him in a very difficult situation.[20]

The counter-offensive was scathing. The young English philosopher Geoffrey Bennington, who was at the time staying with Derrida, remembers seeing him being beside himself with anger that morning when he came down for breakfast. 'Derrida, completely furious, showed me Bourdieu's interview in *Libération*. Since I felt he was reacting over-impulsively, I suggested that he wait a bit before sending off his reply. "It's too late for that, the fax has already gone," he retorted.'[21]

Derrida's riposte appeared the following week. For him, it was an opportunity to sort out his relationships with his old classmate. The whole business was far from seeming 'funny'. Let me quote at length this text, which has never been reprinted:

> Of all the debatable (and edgy, so very edgy!) remarks made by Bourdieu, I'll simply quote the one that includes the most flagrant counter-truth. I say *counter-truth* as a way, no doubt, of practising what Bourdieu would probably call a *euphemization*. Yes, of course I knew Bourdieu's text. And yes, indeed, he had presented it in my seminar (actually a seminar of the Greph, in which he was at the time very interested [. . .]). But when Bourdieu dares to claim that he had '*given an account of it at* (my) *seminar without arousing the least objection*', this is *monumentally false*, as some thirty or so participants can bear witness. I was not alone in formulating certain objections – of which there were many.[22]

Derrida took this opportunity to widen the combat and return, in his own 'edgy' way, to older wounds:

> I have *always* found Bourdieu's analyses (and those he inspires) inadequate, both in their philosophical axiomatic [. . .] and in their implementation, in particular when they concern philosophical texts, or more especially texts such as Heidegger's. It is not essential to be a 'Heideggerean' (who is?) or to rest content with 'Heideggerean conclusions' to realize that the set of concepts underpinning Bourdieu's work are pre-Heideggerean. It has never been put to the test of the 'questions' raised by Heidegger. [. . .] And I have far from forgotten or neglected Bourdieu's text – in fact, it was also of him that I was thinking when (for example) I said that we need to get beyond the contrast between reading from an internal and reading from an external standpoint. For I think that the two readings are, in Bourdieu, juxtaposed, and pretty much equally inadequate. In fact, his 'internal' reading, if we could still distinguish it as such, seems even more short-sighted than the other. And not only in the case of Heidegger – this concerns French matters, closer to us.

If I have not written this so directly before now, no more than I have replied to so many of the errors in *Distinction* that would have fully deserved it, this was not so as to avoid having to face troublesome texts, but by a reflex (no doubt old fashioned and out of date, or even too 'distinguished') of loyalty or reticence in wounded friendship. It is true, I often prefer silence [. . .]. Now I am freed from my reserve, thanks to this latest aggression.

As for the end of the letter, it is quite clearly a case of denegation:

One word more: the debate on Heidegger has never placed me in '*a very difficult situation*', as Bourdieu claims in a gesture whose rhetoric strikes me as coming from a kind of electoral sociology; and my serenity has never been affected by it. For, after all, I am to some extent involved – and not only by my last book – in provoking and complicating the said debate. For a long time already, and even recently. Those who sometimes look at my work will know this well.

This page of *Libération* is completed by a short, sober summing up by Bourdieu. Embarrassed by the proportions that the conflict was assuming, he said that he regretted that 'certain unhappily chosen words' in his interview had hurt Derrida. And while he deplored the 'prophetic anathemas' which the author of *Of Spirit* had just used, he preferred, in the name of their 'old friendship', not to inflame things any further. In fact, the two men would soon overcome their differences, and join forces in several combats throughout the 1990s. The basic quarrel between them, however, reappeared in *Sketch for a Self-Analysis*, a posthumously published text by Bourdieu, in which there are several digs at Derrida. In the very first pages, Bourdieu points out that, in his youth, he had been a student at Normale Sup, specializing in philosophy, and thus 'at the summit of the scholastic hierarchy, at a time when philosophy could appear as triumphant'. It was then 'the queen of disciplines', he insists, before acknowledging: 'I have often had occasion to define myself, with some irony, as the leader of a liberation movement of the social sciences against the imperialism of philosophy.'[23]

Coming at exactly the same time as the Heidegger affair, the de Man affair was a real blow for Derrida, since it encouraged facile comparisons. But while the debate on Heidegger was essentially French, the polemic on de Man mainly concerned the United States.

However, it all started in Belgium, with the research carried out by a young Flemish scholar, Ortwin de Graef, who tells the story in these words:

I started my thesis at the University of Louvain in 1986. I planned to write a study on the theoretical and critical work of Paul de Man, but I knew that he came from Antwerp and I'd heard about his uncle, the famous Henri de Man, an important socialist in the period between the world wars who later collaborated with the Germans. Even though it was of somewhat secondary importance when compared with my subject, I was curious to read Paul de Man's first publications, before he left for the United States. In the Archives of Flemish cultural life, there was a dossier on him. I first came across some articles that had appeared in 1942 in the newspaper *Het Vlaamsche Land*. In November 1986, I wrote to *Yale French Studies* to find out whether a publication on this subject might be of interest to them, but they never replied. In spring 1987, I came across the bulky dossier of *Le Soir volé*: 170 articles published between 24 December 1940 and 28 November 1942 in the biggest French-language Belgian daily, at the time kept under tight control by the occupying forces. I familiarized myself with these texts, many of which were quite innocuous but some of which were much more significant, though I didn't quite know what to do with them. In July, an international literary conference took place in Louvain, at which I presented a paper on the theoretical work of Paul de Man. Among the other speakers were Sam Weber and Gayatri Spivak, and I told them about my recent discoveries. As soon as he returned, Sam Weber informed Derrida, who immediately showed the greatest interest in the question. Hastily, just before I left to do my military service, I sent him a series of photocopies, highlighting those that stood out most for ideological reasons.[24]

By the end of August 1987, Derrida was convinced that the articles in question should all be made public, as quickly and widely as possible.

The necessary conditions had to be created so that everyone could read them and interpret them in total freedom. No limit should be set on the discussion. Everyone should be in a position to take his or her responsibilities. For one could imagine in advance the effect that these 'revelations' were going to produce, at least in the American university. One did not have to have second sight to foresee even the whole spectre of reactions to come.[25]

Derrida suggested taking advantage of the conference on academic institutions and politics ('Our Academic Contract: The Conflict of the Faculties in America') scheduled for a few weeks later at the University of Alabama, in Tuscaloosa, to discuss the matter with the speakers, who would include several former students and colleagues of Paul de Man. Derrida was really shaken by this discovery. At the conference, he mournfully handed out copies of a certain number of the articles published in *Le Soir*, including one called 'The Jews in contemporary literature'. On 10 October, the participants held a 'discussion that lasted more than three hours and touched on both the substance of things and the decisions to be made'.[26] Many were shocked and did not know how to react. But Derrida was categorical: the material should be published in full, and they, who had been close to de Man, were the ones who should publish it.[27] Richard Rand, the organizer of the conference, shared his view, and insisted that they act as quickly as possible:

> As a former journalist, I sensed straightaway that the affair was going to blow up. I thought the main documents should be published quickly in the *Oxford Literary Review*, as proof of our good faith. But this strategy was undermined by other people who were not present at the Alabama meeting. They thought that we should act more cautiously, and not rush into things. Unfortunately, Derrida allowed himself to be convinced. For me, this remains a missed opportunity, and I think it was very prejudicial.[28]

Rumours soon started to circulate and the 'affair' broke out in the worst possible way. On 1 December 1987, the *New York Times* announced on its front page: 'Yale scholar's articles found in pro-Nazi paper'. The unsigned article was full of mistakes and half-truths about Paul de Man and the political situation in Belgium during the Occupation. The affair assumed considerable proportions throughout the United States, then in countries where the de Man's name had hitherto been known only to a handful of specialists. The German press was particularly virulent, while in Sweden de Man was labelled 'the Waldheim of postmodernism'.* But the controversial texts remained inaccessible: they were published only in the autumn of 1988.[29]

One of the keys to the de Man affair and the absurd proportions it would assume lay in the watertight separation between two worlds: on the one hand, Belgium, where as a young man de Man had

---

* The Waldheim affair broke out in 1986. After a period as Secretary General of the United Nations from 1972 to 1981, Kurt Waldheim (1918–2007) was then standing in the elections for President of the Republic of Austria. The revelation of his service in the Wehrmacht during the Second World War meant that he was ostracized by several heads of state throughout his period of office, from 1986 to 1992.

published his first articles but where next to nothing was known about the fame later won by the master of the Yale School and even less about the content of his work; and, on the other, the United States, where his career took place but where there was general ignorance about the complexities of the Belgian situation under the German Occupation.

The most surprising thing is that de Man's early articles had gone unnoticed for so long. They had been published under his real name, over a period of two years, in the biggest Belgian daily, and so they were easily accessible. According to Jean-Marie Apostolidès, professor at Stanford, the scandal could very easily have erupted a few years earlier: 'I must be the first person in the United States to have become aware of these articles,' he says.

I was then finishing my book *The Metamorphoses of Tintin* and, as Hergé had published in *Le Soir* under the Occupation, I'd had those papers brought over to the Widener Library at Harvard. One afternoon, towards the end of 1982, Jeffrey Mehlman came up to me in the reading room, just as I was reading one of the bindings of *Le Soir* from the wartime. He had long been close to Derrida, before taking an interest in the early articles of Maurice Blanchot. I told him: 'Since you're interested in intellectuals' troubled pasts, look at what I've just found out about Paul de Man.' And I showed him a few significant passages from the articles that I'd been reading over the previous days, without attaching any particular importance to them. Unlike me, he sensed straightaway that these texts were a time bomb. However, he himself came from Yale, he had known and worked with Paul de Man, and wished to come to Harvard. He encouraged me to reveal the affair myself. If I refused, it was because these articles struck me as conformist and insignificant and because Paul de Man, in my view a secondary figure in literary criticism, did not deserve to be the focus of such polemics. But I promised to keep the newspapers for another week or two before sending them back to Belgium. If he wanted to go through them with a fine-tooth comb, he had the references, he simply needed to ask for them on his next visit to the library. As far as I know, he didn't do so, even though he immediately realized the full implications of the affair, given what I had just shown him. I also mentioned these articles to Barbara Johnson, another of Derrida's colleagues, but she paid little attention: history didn't interest her.[30]

It has to be acknowledged that the de Man trail was very easy to follow for anyone knowing something of the history of Belgium between the wars and under the Occupation. It would have been enough to investigate his links with his uncle Henri de Man (1885–1953), the author of the famous work *Beyond Marxism* who was president of the Belgian Workers' Party from 1938 before supporting the Nazis under the Occupation. Henri de Man was a character of great importance, whose influence during the 1930s went far beyond the borders of Belgium. His former political brother-in-arms, Paul-Henri Spaak, has spoken of him in these terms: 'His errors, which were great, and made him an outcast and an exile, cannot prevent me from saying that he is the most authentic socialist thinker of the twentieth century, and one of the few men who, on certain occasions, gave me the sense that he was a genius.'[31] As for the historian Zeev Sternhell, he grants him an essential place in his book *Neither Right Nor Left: Fascist Ideology in France*, explaining that the 'planism' of Henri de Man 'was, for the socialism of the time, the most thoroughgoing example of anticonformist thinking of the interwar period. Where political theory was concerned, it was an original experiment of great importance.'[32] But Paul de Man's past might still have surfaced another way. The famous critic Georges Poulet, the author of *Studies in Human Time*, a professor at Johns Hopkins and Zurich, was the younger brother of Robert Poulet, a much more radical Belgian collaborator than Paul de Man: arrested and sentenced to death in 1945, Robert Poulet later saw his sentence commuted to exile. Thus it seems unthinkable that Georges Poulet would not have known, at least in outline, about 'Paul de Man's war'. So if the affair did not break out in Paul de Man's lifetime, this was also because nobody wished it to, for as long as he ran the best comparative literature department in the United States.

All those who knew Paul de Man insist on his discretion regarding his life before he arrived in the United States. He had found his vocation in America; everything before that no longer counted. When Geoffrey Hartman asked him one day why he had written so little before 1953, saying that he must after all have published some things before that date, de Man had laconically replied: 'Nothing but journalism.'[33]

At the end of 1987, the scandal unleashed by the *New York Times* assumed considerable proportions. And, as in the Heidegger affair, the polemic soon extended to deconstruction as a whole. Though de Man had been dead for four years, Derrida and his colleagues were alive and kicking. For all the detractors of the Yale School and Derrida's work, this was an unexpected opportunity. According to *Newsweek*, Jeffrey Mehlman, professor of French at the University of Boston, went so far as to declare that there were 'even grounds for viewing the whole of deconstruction as a vast amnesty project for the politics of collaboration during World War II'.[34] This confused view, as absurd as it was mean-spirited, was repeated over the next few weeks: *The New Republic* devoted an article to the theme 'Fascists and deconstructionists', while the *LA Times* spoke of 'The (de) Man who put the con in deconstruction'.

Derrida reacted in the heat of the moment, when the press campaign was far from over. In January 1988, hardly a month after the article in the *New York Times*, he composed a meticulous account of the affair. While its title was poetic – 'Like the sound of the sea deep within a shell: Paul de Man's war' – the text itself came out fighting, much more directly than had any of Derrida's previous work. As the situation dictated, this long article first came out in the United States, translated by his friend Peggy Kamuf, who was already one of his most faithful translators.[35]

'Like the sound . . .' comes across as more of a narrative than an analysis. Derrida, who had said shortly after de Man's death that he had never been able to tell a story, this time found himself obliged to do so. Referring to his discovery of the material in *Le Soir*, he made no attempt to conceal the dismay he had at first felt:

> From the first reading, I thought I recognized, alas, what I will call roughly an *ideological configuration*, discursive schemas, a logic and a stock of highly marked arguments. By my situation and by training, I had learned from childhood to detect them easily. A strange coincidence: it so happens, on top of it all, that these themes are the subject of seminars I have been giving for four years as well as of my last book, on Heidegger and Nazism. My feelings were first of all that of a wound, a stupor, and a sadness that I want neither to dissimulate nor exhibit.[36]

Derrida, happy to go into historical detail, placed the wartime articles published de Man in *Le Soir* in their context. Most of them were innocuous. He then turned to the most problematic in the series, 'The Jews in contemporary literature':

> Nothing in what I am about to say, analysing the article as closely as possible, will heal over the wound I right away felt when, my breath taken away, I perceived in it what the newspapers have most frequently singled out as recognized antisemitism, an antisemitism more serious than ever in such a situation, an antisemitism that would have come close to urging exclusions, even the most sinister deportations.[37]

This did not stop Derrida embarking on a closer reading of the article in question, with an at times excessive ingenuity and generosity. When the young de Man wrote: 'Vulgar antisemitism readily takes pleasure in considering post-war cultural phenomena (after the war of '14–18) as degenerate and decadent because they are *enjuivés*', the author of *Writing and Difference* attributed to the phrase a subtle game of ulterior motives:

> It is indeed a matter of criticizing vulgar antisemitism. That is the primary, declared, and underscored intention. But to scoff at vulgar antisemitism, is that also to scoff at or mock the vulgarity of antisemitism? This latter syntactic modulation leaves the door open to two interpretations. To condemn vulgar antisemitism may leave one to understand that there is a distinguished antisemitism in whose name the vulgar variety is put down. De Man never says such a thing, even though one may condemn his silence. But the phrase can also mean something else, and this reading can always contaminate the other in a clandestine fashion: to condemn 'vulgar antisemitism', *especially if one makes no mention of the other kind,* is to condemn antisemitism *itself inasmuch* as it is vulgar, always and essentially vulgar. De Man does not say that either. If that is what he thought, a possibility I will never exclude, he could not say so clearly in this context.[38]

In writing this long defence of de Man, Derrida knew what risks he was running. He did so out of loyalty to his dead friend and out of concern for justice, giving full scope to his 1984 lectures on the promise which 'has meaning and gravity only with the death of the other': 'I could not know that one day, the experience of such a wound would have to include responding for Paul de Man [. . .], speaking once again, of-him-for-him, at a moment when his memory or his legacy risk being accused and he is no longer there to speak in his own name.'[39]

But 'Like the sound . . .' was also an act of 'legitimate defence', for de Man's early articles had given Derrida's enemies the opportunity to launch a radical attack on *him*. Hardly able to believe their luck, his long-standing opponents – positivist philosophers, conservative humanists, and leftist Marxists – suddenly combined their forces to get rid of a man and a theory that had caused them unease for quite some time. Derrida began by waxing ironical, before counter-attacking:

> One may also wonder, with the same smiling indulgence: but, after all, what does deconstruction (in the singular) have to do with what was written in 1940–42 by a very young man in a Belgian newspaper? Is it not ridiculous and dishonest to extend to a 'theory', that has itself been simplified and homogenized, as well as to all those who are interested in it and develop it, the trial one would like to conduct of a man for texts written in Belgian newspapers forty-five years ago and that moreover, once again, one has not really read? [. . .]

Why do people pretend not to see that deconstruction is anything but a nihilism or a skepticism? Why can one still read this
claim despite so many texts that, *explicitly, thematically, and
for more than twenty years* have been demonstrating the opposite? Why the charge of irrationalism as soon as anyone asks a
question about reason, its forms, its history, its mutations? Or
the charge of antihumanism, with the first question put to the
essence of man and the construction of its concept?

In short, what are people afraid of? Whom do they want to
make afraid?[40]

As so often, it is in the footnotes that Derrida is most direct
and aggressive. He attacks with particular virulence an article by
Jon Wiener called 'Deconstructing de Man' and published in *The
Nation*.

From its title to its final sentence, this spiteful and error-ridden
article gathers within its pages more or less all the reading mistakes I have evoked up until now. It is frightening to think that
its author teaches history at a university. Attempting to transfer onto deconstruction and its 'politics' (such as he imagines
them) a stream of calumny or slanderous insinuation, he has
the nerve to speak of de Man as an 'academic Waldheim' [. . .].
There is thus nothing surprising in the fact that Jon Wiener's
article has provided a model. The author of this article is,
however, famous for his mistakes in *The Nation*: on more than
one occasion, this journal has had to publish strongly-worded
and overwhelming rectifications after the contributions of this
collaborator, who has thus proved to be something of a liability
[*malencontreux*].[41]

The de Man affair caused a considerable stir across American
campuses, leading to several violent quarrels, even within Derridean
circles. On 26 April 1988, David Carroll, who had been among the
first of Derrida's followers, addressed a long open letter to Derrida.
It was not the content of Derrida's remarks that he disagreed with,
but the strategy adopted. He could not understand why Derrida
had taken his defence of de Man so far, or why he had been ready
to take the attacks onto himself and even to 'assume the worst of
what he had written and in a sense assume responsibility for it',
when such writings were diametrically opposed to all his political
convictions and choices.[42] Derrida was too sore to accept these criti-
cisms, however moderate. He furiously annotated David Carroll's
text, and felt that his former student was incapable of reading him.
Relations between the two men would be profoundly undermined
by this spat for several months.

Things were hardly any easier with Avital Ronell:

We had intense disagreements at the time of the de Man affair. He wanted to gather his supporters and form a united front at all costs. This didn't strike me as being a good strategy. Defending Paul de Man's early texts completely and almost blindly shouldn't have been considered as a duty by those inspired by Derrida. But, at the time, he tolerated even less than usual any nuances of internal disagreement. Unfortunately, there was nobody strong enough to persuade him to adopt another strategy, one that would be less aggressive more adequate to the American context. The way he responded, in 'Like the sound . . .', aggravated the situation even more. It was seen as an exercise in textual manipulation, as if the sophistication of deconstructive readings had finally led to this: finding excuses for anti-Semitic articles, getting the text to say anything at all so long as it meant whitewashing it of accusations of Nazism! The whole affair was a disaster. In certain ways, we never got over it.[43]

In the months following the publication of 'Like the sound . . .', the editorial board of the review *Critical Inquiry* received many letters, most of them very violent in tone. 'It's no exaggeration to say that your article has provoked more discussions and led to more extreme reactions than any text that we can remember publishing,' wrote one of the editors of the review to Derrida.[44] Six of these commentaries were selected for publication in *Critical Inquiry*, but since they sometimes brutally attacked Derrida, they were sent to him in good time for him to react. In the last days of 1988, he wrote a long collective response. Immediately translated by Peggy Kamuf under the title 'Biodegradables: Seven diary fragments', this sixty-page article remained unpublished in French, being so closely tied as it was to the American context. Derrida, stung to the quick, reacted harshly against those who had expressed criticism or doubts of any kind. He had been expelled from school in 1942, just as de Man was publishing his articles in *Le Soir*: he now recognized that he found it very difficult to tolerate all the lessons in vigilance that people claimed they could give him on this subject.[45]

Only on 10 March 1990 could a more serene and probing discussion take place in Paris, as one of the Saturday sessions at the Collège International de Philosophie. Michel Deguy, Élisabeth de Fontenay, Alexander García Düttmann, and Marie-Louise Mallet each reacted to *Mémoires: For Paul de Man*, before Derrida responded attentively, without immediately rejecting the objections that some of them had raised. As he acknowledged, these questions

remained 'difficult and challenging' for him. In a dialogue with
Élisabeth de Fontenay, he pondered the silence observed by de
Man, even with Derrida himself:

> I don't know why he didn't tell *me* anything, and why he hardly
> mentioned it to anyone else, to so few people. [. . .] I don't
> have any answer, I don't know, I have only hypotheses. I met
> de Man in 1966, we were very close from 1975 when I went
> to Yale every year for three or four weeks. Paul de Man then
> became, and remains for me, a very dear friend, but we didn't
> know each other very well, we didn't know about our 'lives' – it
> happens!

This was an opportunity for Derrida to discuss his concept of
friendship, and the essential place that he reserved for secrecy. He
did not think that the condition of friendship was familiarity 'or
what people complacently call nearness or acquaintance with the
other'.

> Our 'exchanges', to use that ridiculous word, were always very
> discrete. The signs of friendship were clearly given, but we
> didn't say much to reach other. Neither of us did. When I say:
> perhaps I'd always known or perhaps he thinks that I'd always
> known, I can't rule out the possibility that he said to himself,
> basically: these things are well enough known (since, as we
> now know, he'd talked to others about them), perhaps they're
> going round in rumours, perhaps Jacques Derrida knows about
> them, he doesn't mention them, they're things that go back
> thirty years, let's not talk about them. It's possible. You know
> how things happen 'in society'; someone has a secret, but above
> all he's in solitary confinement [*au secret*], he's the only one
> who doesn't know that everybody knows. [. . .]
>   Why did I never ask any questions? I knew that Paul de
> Man had a complicated history: he'd left Belgium just after
> the war, he'd found settling in America very disruptive, at
> least academically. One day he told me: 'If you want to know
> my life story' – this is the kind of thing we said to each other
> – 'read the novel by Henri Thomas, *The Liar*.' [. . .] I bought
> it, I read it, I was overwhelmed. It was not in the least about
> Belgium, it took place later, in the United States. I wrote to de
> Man to tell him what an impact the book had had on me. No
> reply from him. He himself told me one day, alluding to *Glas*
> and *The Post Card*: 'There are some books by you that I don't
> want to discuss with you. I won't even mention them to you.'
> Friendship can cope with certain silences, with the unsaid and
> the secret that are not necessarily fatal to it.[46]

It was at this meeting of the Collège International de Philosophie that, for the first time as far as I am aware, Derrida tackled the theme of the unforgivable, which would assume such a decisive place in his thought:

> I never know who has the right to ask for a confession, if there is ever a confession, and above all, who has the right to forgive, to say 'I forgive'. The phrase 'I forgive' also seems to me as impossible, or at least impossible to assume with any self-assurance, as impossible as the request for a confession – and perhaps as the confession itself. And yet I've written 'unforgivable'. I'm not sure I was right to do so and in any case I'm not happy about it.

This decidedly difficult period was marked by still more polemics. Jürgen Habermas's book *The Philosophical Discourse of Modernity* was translated into French and published by Gallimard in 1988, having first been published in Germany in 1985. Two of these twelve lectures were devoted to the author of *Writing and Difference*. But since, in Habermas's view, Derrida 'does not belong to those philosophers who like to argue', he announces right from the start that he is going base his discussion on the work of Derrida's disciples, 'who have worked 'within the Anglo-Saxon climate of argument'.[47] It is actually Jonathan Culler's *On Deconstruction* on which he most relies.

Since Habermas had always been a fierce enemy of Heidegger, the filiation which he establishes between Heidegger and Derrida is not in the least a compliment. If we are to believe Habermas, their two philosophical methods coincide almost perfectly: 'The familiar melody of the self-overcoming of metaphysics also sets the tone for Derrida's enterprise; destruction is renamed deconstruction.'[48] So, in the view of Habermas – who is here close to Ferry and Renaut's *French Philosophy of the Sixties* – there is nothing new in Derrida, apart from the tone, which itself leads to a fateful levelling of the difference between literature and philosophy:

> If, following Derrida's recommendation, philosophical thinking were to be relieved of the duty of solving problems and shifted over to the function of literary criticism, it would be robbed not merely of its seriousness, but of its productivity. Conversely, the literary-critical power of judgment loses its potency when, as is happening among Derrida's disciples in literature departments, it gets displaced from appropriating aesthetic experiential contents into the critique of metaphysics. The false assimilation of one enterprise to the other robs both of their substance.[49]

Habermas's reputation and his widespread influence in Germany obliged Derrida to respond, especially since some articles attacking him in no uncertain terms had just appeared in the German press because of the de Man affair. In the *Frankfurter Rundschau*, Manfred Frank said that he was worried that young Germans might fall 'into French hands', extending the suspicion of fascism or 'neo-darwinian' pre-fascism to the whole 'French International' of Derrida, Deleuze, and Lyotard.[50] In the view of Alexander García Düttmann – who had studied at Frankfurt before viewing himself as an associate of Derrida –, Habermas explicitly warned his students against Derrida; at the time, he described his thought as nihilistic, obscurantist, and politically dubious.

In a long note added to the eventual French publication of *Mémoires: For Paul de Man*, Derrida began by waxing indignant at Habermas's method, emphasizing that, in one of the two chapters on him, he is criticized over thirty pages. After pointing out a series of errors of interpretation, Derrida launched a more frontal attack on the very principles of Habermas's philosophy:

> It is *always* in the name of ethics – a supposedly democratic ethics of discussion – it is always in the name of transparent communication and 'consensus' that the most brutal disregard of the elementary rules of discussion is produced (by these elementary rules, I mean differentiated reading or listening to the other, proof, argumentation, analysis, and quotation). It is *always* the moralistic discourse of consensus – at least the discourse that pretends to appeal sincerely to consensus – that produces in fact the indecent transgression of the classical norms of reason and democracy.[51]

All of these themes went to the heart of another important text of 1988: 'Toward an ethics of discussion'. This was the afterword to the book *Limited Inc*, a collection of the pieces in the particularly violent controversy between Derrida and John R. Searle ten years earlier. Returning to Searle's text, 'Reiterating the differences: a reply to Derrida', and his own scathing response, 'Limited Inc a b c . . .', Derrida endeavours to analyse 'the symptoms that this polemical "scene" can still make legible', over and above the precise theoretical contents that were then at stake.[52]

Derrida increasingly realized the level of violence at work in academic and intellectual discussions, including in his own methods. He explained this in a late interview with Évelyne Grossman:

> When I try to think, work or write and when I think that something 'true' needs to be put forward in the public space, on the public stage, well, no force in the world can stop me. It's not a

matter of courage, but when I think that something needs to be said or thought, even in a 'true' but as yet unacceptable way, no power in the world can discourage me from saying it. [. . .] I have sometimes written texts that I knew would cause offence. They were, for example, critical of Lévi-Strauss or Lacan – I knew the milieu well enough, after all, to know that this would cause a stir – well, it was impossible for me to keep it to myself. This is a law, it's like an instinct [or drive (*pulsion*)] and a law: *I cannot not say it.* Between you and me, sometimes when I was writing this sort of text, a bit provocative and polemical in some circles, writing something and then, as I was just drifting off to sleep, half-asleep, there was someone inside me, more lucid or vigilant than the other, who kept saying: 'But you're completely crazy, you shouldn't be doing this, you shouldn't be writing this. You know perfectly well what's going to happen . . .' And then, when I open my eyes and settle down to work, I do it. I disobey that council of prudence. That's what I call the instinct of truth [*pulsion de vérité*]: it *must* be said [*avoué*].[53]

The two years of ceaseless combat which Derrida had just experienced did, however, mark a kind of break. The following period would be characterized by new alliances and by the emergence of an apparently more mellow Derrida. As if in response to these accusations, ethical and political questions would soon move to the centre of the stage.

3

Living Memory

1988–1990

With all his multifarious obligations, his travels, and his increasing correspondence, Derrida was more and more overwhelmed by work. As Avital Ronell notes, he did not have a position as a professor in the French university system, so he had no assistant or secretary to help him, with the result that he had to 'locate, photocopy, collate, and carry everything by himself'. She recalled him 'schlepping his encumbering carton of books to subject himself to a committee's interrogation [. . .]. He was, on some days, his own proletariat, at least according to the standards of American visitors and inscriptions.'[1]

In spite of his stamina, Derrida was sometimes unable to cope. During the autumn of 1987, he became friends with Elisabeth Weber, a young woman who was working on the German translation of *Ulysses Gramophone* and came to see him on various occasions after his seminar to discuss the difficulties she was encountering.

> A few months later, as I was finishing my doctorate, he asked me if I might be interested in giving him a hand, especially with his correspondence. From the beginning of 1988, I went to Ris-Orangis every Sunday to work with him. In the morning, Derrida would dictate answers to the letters that had been piling up during the week. The afternoons were generally kept for the papers, manuscripts and books that he had received, as well as for organizing his library.[2]

But Elisabeth's role soon became more extensive. As she explains:

> After a while, he also entrusted me with the finishing touches and corrections to several books: *Limited Inc*, which brought together the pieces of the polemic with Searle, and the big volume of interviews *Points*. The initiative for this project came from me, if I remember correctly. We discussed in detail which interviews to use from the selection I'd made. I also looked

after the preparation for publication of the manuscript *The Problem of Genesis in the Philosophy of Husserl*, his Master's, which had aroused the intense interest of Françoise Dastur, Jean-Luc Marion, and Didier Franck and that came out with the Presses Universitaires de France in 1990. My task consisted mainly in checking quotations in German, tracking them down in the complete works of Husserl – which did not yet exist in the 1950s –, correcting the translation of them when necessary, and adding the references to translations recently published in French. I worked for him until September 1991, when I got a job at the University of California, Santa Barbara. But we continued to meet up on a friendly basis every time I stayed in France.

Another important collaboration brought Derrida together with a young professor at the University of Sussex, Geoffrey Bennington. Passionate about Derrida's work since the end of the 1970s, Bennington had first acted as his interpreter on his visits to Oxford, and then overseen the quality of translations of his work into English. But Derrida soon asked him to join in a more important project.

In January 1988, I'd published in the *Oxford Literary Review* a long and rather scathing article in which I reviewed several recent books about him. He told me he'd really liked this piece. A bit later, he suggested that I write the book that the Éditions du Seuil wanted to publish about him in their series 'Les Contemporains'. I was flattered – I could hardly believe my luck. For political reasons, Derrida really wanted it not to be anyone French or already identified as a Derridean who wrote this book. So I suggested, at a lunch at Denis Roche's, the director of the series, that Derrida himself collaborate in the volume: perhaps it was the memory of *Roland Barthes by Roland Barthes* that made me think of this. Very quickly it occurred to me that I'd write an analysis of his work without quoting any of it. I worked on it in 1988, while on sabbatical, spending quite a lot of time creating a sort of 'Derrida software' on my computer. I wanted to establish a real database which I would use for writing my text. The further I advanced, the more convinced I became of the solidity and coherence of his work. His way of writing, and his relationship to philosophy, places the commentator in a really difficult position. Derrida puts forward not just a reading of many of the major works in the history of philosophy, but also a rereading of his own texts. On repeated occasions, I found in his books, allusively formulated, ideas that I thought I'd discovered all by myself. I submitted my 'Derridabase' to him at the beginning of 1989. After what seemed to me a very long time, he phoned me and told me how much he had enjoyed it. But he was still very enigmatic about what he was writing. I only knew that he had imposed a material constraint on himself: fifty-nine paragraphs – he was in his fifty-ninth year – that would be as long as MacWrite, the computer program he used, would allow. I still knew nothing of the actual subject.[3]

Between Bennington and Derrida there was a kind of duel between two modes of writing. 'Circumfession' is first and foremost a response to the attempt by 'Geoff' to establish a database.[4] Worried about seeing himself boxed in like this, Derrida tries to write a text that escapes the systematic cartography drawn up by Bennington. Next to a corpus of which the critic 'has not retained intact a single fragment',[5] he reintroduces the body, including his own penis. Just as Bennington's methodical exposition is turning him into an almost acceptable philosopher, Derrida spends his time deconstructing from within the work that is dedicated to him.

For his text, Derrida uses the notes on circumcision begun in his notebooks of 1976–7 (shortly after *Glas*) and 1980–1 (just after *The Post Card*). He had dreamed at the time of writing *The Book of Elijah*, 'a novel in 4 columns, at 4 discursive levels',[6] even if the appearance of the book would not necessarily reflect this so immediately as in *Glas*. Something of this project would subsist in 'Circumfession', where four main motifs are interwoven: a meditation at the bedside of the dying mother, the autobiographical anamnesis, extracts from the notebooks on circumcision, and quotations from the *Confessions* of Saint Augustine. The writing was done in waves throughout the whole of 1989 and the first months of 1990. For Derrida it was a kind of intimate response to his mother's illness, but also a way of coming back to himself after the painful polemics of the past two years.

Georgette Safar had been born in 1901 and so was already very old – bedridden and suffering from Alzheimer's. During her interminable agony, Jacques came to Nice as often as he could, sometimes correcting the proofs of his books at her bedside. The rest of the time, he phoned her almost every day. From the end of 1988, when she suffered an attack that almost killed her, she was 'in a strange lethargy, between life and death, really "hospitalized at home", no longer able to recognize [him], hardly able to speak, see, or hear'.[7] 'Circumfession' is a vast funeral wake, one of Derrida's most audacious texts and probably the most moving. By writing these fifty-nine sentences that it is impossible to quote without truncating them, he wanted to

Part of Jacques Derrida's last
library at Ris-Orangis.

(© Andrew Bush)

Jacques and Marguerite at Cerisy.
(Derrida: personal collection)

On the beach at Villefranche-sur-Mer, with his brother René and his sister Janine.
(Derrida: personal collection)

With Hélène Cixous, 2003.
(© Sophie Bassouls/Sygma/Corbis)

With Élisabeth Roudinesco, 2001.
(© John Foley-Opale)

In his office in Ris-Orangis. (© Carlos Freire)

In the converted loft in Ris-Orangis. 'My sublime,' Derrida sometimes called it.
(© Carlos Freire)

1991, the photographer Carlos Freire followed Jacques Derrida in his day-to-day life: above, at his seminar at the École des Hautes Études en sciences sociales.

(© Carlos Freire)

At the café. (© Carlos Freire)

Visiting Louis Althusser at the clinic of Soisy-sur-Seine.
(© Fonds Jacques Derrida/IMEC)

Serving the tea. Hôtel Saint-Georges, Algiers, 1984.
(Derrida: personal collection)

In Beijing, in September 2001.
(Derrida: personal collection)

At Laguna Beach, California.
(Derrida: personal collection)

With Geoffrey Bennington,
at the time of writing
'Circumfession'.
(Derrida: personal collection)

In Dublin, next to the
statue of James Joyce.
(Derrida: personal collection)

In Heidelberg, in 1988,
with Philippe Lacoue-
Labarthe and Hans-Georg
Gadamer.
(Derrida: personal collection)

With François Châtelet and
Pierre Bourdieu.
(Derrida: personal collection)

Travelling in Cotonou
towards the end of
the 1970s.
(Derrida: personal collection)

Conference on 'The Ends
of Man', Cerisy, 1980.
From left to right, on
either side of Derrida:
Jean-Michel Rey, Sarah
Kofman, and Daniel
Limon.
(© Archives de Pontigny-Cerisy)

With Jorge Luis Borges,
in 1985.
(Derrida: personal collection)

LE MATIN
DE PARIS
Le Matin des Livres

Nº 1510   VENDREDI 1er JANVIER 1982   3,00 F

UN PHILOSOPHE FRANÇAIS ARRETÉ A PRAGUE

Jacques Derrida, professeur à l'Ecole normale supérieure, est accusé par les autorités tchécoslovaques, d'avoir détenu des «médicaments non autorisés».
Délit de droit commun, disent les Tchèques. Provocation politique, pense-t-on à Paris

Le philosophe français Jacques Derrida a été arrêté dans la nuit de mardi à mercredi à l'aéroport de Prague, d'où il n'apprêtait à rentrer en France après avoir rendu visite à des collègues philosophes de l'association Jean-Hus. Les douaniers ont trouvé dans ses bagages des « médicaments non autorisés », et le philosophe a été inculpé de « détention de drogue ». Selon le droit tchèque, il risque deux ans de prison ou une sanction financière. Pour les autorités, en effet, il s'agit d'une simple affaire de droit commun.

A Paris, on estime qu'il s'agit d'une provocation politique qui pourrait bien servir d'avertissement aux intellectuels français solidaires de la Pologne. Le Quai-d'Orsay a convoqué hier l'ambassadeur de Tchécoslovaquie en France, et des démarches diplomatiques ont été entreprises auprès du gouvernement de Prague. P. 7

L'arrestation de Jacques Derrida : un avertissement aux intellectuels français solidaires de la Pologne

Mitterrand : «Nous refusons le système qui opprime la Pologne» P. 3

POLITIQUE	TCHAD
Une interview de Maurice Joyeux	*Progression d'Hissène Habré*
L'un des « historiques » du mouvement anarchiste français, Maurice Joyeux, membre du Conseil économique et social et ancien militant de Force ouvrière juge, pour le Matin, la politique de la gauche au pouvoir. Une politique qu'il regarde avec sympathie mais aussi un peu de scepticisme. P. 2	Les forces d'Hissène Habré sembleraient progresser au Tchad. Si l'on en croit Radio-Tripoli, la ville d'Ati, située à 450 km à l'est de N'Djamena, serait encerclée et de « violents combats » se dérouleraient à Mongo. P. 8

«Le Matin» présente à ses lecteurs ses meilleurs vœux pour 1982

Pologne : Nouvel An «normalisé»

Le Nouvel An polonais s'inaugure sous l'état de siège, même si, pour un soir, il avait été levé. Les condamnations de responsables de Solidarité s'accumulent mais les autorités militaires accentuent aussi leur campagne pour convaincre l'opinion internationale que la normalisation est en bonne voie. Des nouvelles rassurantes sont arrivées en Occident sur plusieurs personnalités de l'opposition dont Tadeusz Mazowiecki, Jacek Kuron et Adam Michnik, dont les informations sur les autres détenus sont toujours très ambiguës.

Le séjour de vingt-quatre heures à Bonn du vice-premier ministre polonais Rakowski s'est principalement soldé par l'annonce que Varsovie avait recommencé à payer les intérêts de sa dette en Occident. Pour l'état de siège, il a déclaré qu'il ne pourrait pas durer « éternellement ».

Une nouvelle législation du travail est instaurée par décret. Le travail est désormais obligatoire pour tous les hommes de dix-huit à quarante-cinq ans. Cette mesure, qui n'aura guère d'effets pratiques étant donné la paralysie de l'économie polonaise, pourrait être utilisée comme un moyen de faire la chasse aux éléments « peu sûrs », à commencer par les quelque quarante mille permanents de Solidarité maintenant au chômage. P. 6

POLOGNE: LE JEU DE L'EGLISE

EST-OUEST LES ARMES DE LA GUERRE ECONOMIQUE

LE NOUVEL **observateur** CETTE SEMAINE

le magazine vidéo de l'année
de l'attentat de la rue Copernic à l'assassinat du président Sadate les grands événements du monde

1981 L'ANNÉE CHOC
RCA VIDÉO

'The Prague Affair': the front page of *Le Matin* on 2 January 1982. At that time, the press had no decent photos of Derrida.
(private collection)

Gare de l'Est: on his return from Prague, Derrida, with his wife Marguerite on his left, replies to journalists' questions.
(© Joël Robine/AFP)

With Paul de Man, in the United States, towards the end of the 1970s.
(Derrida: personal collection)

In June 1979, at the Estates General of Philosophy held in the main '*amphi*' (*amphithéâtre* or lecture hall) of the Sorbonne (© Marc FontaneL/Gamma), there was a brief altercation between Jacques Derrida and Bernard-Henri Lévy.

(© Marc Fontanel/Gamma)

At Cerisy in 1992 for the conference on 'Crossing Frontiers'. From left to right: Marie-Louise Mallet, Jacques Derrida, Michael Levinas, and Michal Govrin. (© Archives de Pontigny-Cerisy)

With Avital Ronell, in 2003 or 2004. (Derrida: personal collection)

Cerisy-la-Salle, summer 2002. 15 July was the birthday of both Daniel Mesguich (first left) and Jacques Derrida. Also visible, from left to right: René Major, Édith Heurgon, and Maurice de Gandillac.

(© Archives de Pontigny-Cerisy)

In Cerisy again, conference on 'The Democracy to Come', with Jean-Luc Nancy, in 2002. (Derrida: personal collection)

May 2002. (© Serge Picard/Agence Vu)

confide to the bottom of this book what were my mother's
more or less intelligible sentences, still alive at the moment I
am writing this, but already incapable of memory, in any case
of the memory of my name, a name become for her at the
very least unpronounceable, and I am here at the moment my
mother no longer recognizes me, and at which, still capable of
speaking or articulating, a little, she no longer calls me and for
her and therefore for the rest of her life I no longer have a name
[. . .]
      the other day in Nice when I asked her if she was in pain
('yes') then where, it was February 5, 1989, she had, in a rhetoric that could never have been hers, the audacity of this stroke
about which she will, alas, never know anything, no doubt
knew nothing, and which piercing the night replies to my question: 'I have a pain in my mother,' as though she were speaking
for me, both in my direction and in my place [. . .].[8]

Georgette Safar died at the beginning of December 1991. And as
Jacques wrote to his old friend Michel Monory, whom he still saw
from time to time, 'this long, long death, lasting for three years,
does not make mourning any easier and is in truth no preparation
for it'.[9]

Exactly contemporary with 'Circumfession' is the text *Memoirs of
the Blind*, which is also very autobiographical and dominated by
pain. It was originally just a matter of Derrida designing an exhibition for the Louvre, selecting a series of drawings, and then writing
a commentary on them. The suggestion simultaneously interested
and alarmed him; he still had no idea of the 'overall approach' he
would adopt. Then in June 1989, he fell victim to an episode of facial
paralysis that immobilized his left eye in particular. It is easy to
imagine his panic. At the beginning of July, he was forced to cancel
a meeting in the Cabinet des Dessins with the three curators who
were supposed to help him choose the images.

I have been suffering for thirteen days from a facial paralysis
caused by a virus, from what is called *a frigore* (disfiguration,
the facial nerve inflamed, the left side of the face stiffened, the
left eye transfixed and horrible to behold in a mirror – a real
sight for sore eyes – the eyelid no longer closing normally: a
loss of the 'wink' or 'blink', therefore, this moment of blindness
that ensures sight its breath). On July 5th this trivial ailment
has just begun to heal. It is finally getting better after two weeks
of terror [. . .]. And so on July 11th I am healed (a feeling of
conversion or resurrection, the eyelid blinking once again, my
face still haunted by a ghost of disfiguration). We have our first

meeting at the Louvre. That same evening, while driving home, the theme of the exhibition hits me.[10]

On 16 July, Derrida had a dream involving blind people attacking him. He was increasingly convinced: 'The drawing is blind, if not the draftsman or draftswoman. As such, and in the moment proper to it, the operation of drawing would have something to do with blindness.' This conviction became the subject of the exhibition and the accompanying catalogue.

The same year, 1989, was marked by another shock, which affected Derrida much more than one might have expected. After the philosophy *agrégation*, his son Pierre wrote his thesis very quickly, supervised by Louis Marin. And thanks to Didier Franck, who had just started a series of philosophical works published by Éditions de Minuit, it was immediately published under the title *Guillaume d'Ockham, le Singulier* (William of Ockham, the Singular). But the young man decided to have it published under the name of Pierre Alféri, his maternal grandmother's surname. In Derrida's library, the book has this winning dedication: 'For you, Papa, to whom I owe much more than a name. For you, Maman, to whom I owe much more than a name.'
On Pierre's part, as he explains, this was not in the least an impulsive decision.

> Ever since my teens, I'd felt that the name Derrida wasn't really mine, that it was already taken, so to speak. If I'd published under my own name, I'd have felt I was being a hermit crab. Of course, I wasn't so naïve as to think that I just needed to sign Pierre Alféri for people not to know who I was. But all the same it gave me a little bit of room for manoeuvre. I didn't ask Jacques about it and at first he wasn't very happy with my decision. In any case, even if it might seem a hostile act, I was ready to defend it, since I felt I had no other choice. I kept this signature for all my other works. 'Pierre Alféri' isn't a mere pseudonym; it's become a name for everyday use, following the *de rigueur* formula.[11]

For Jacques Derrida, the question of the signature had long been an essential theme. He couldn't understand why his eldest son would want to change his name. In his view, it was almost a form of denial. And when Emmanuel Levinas told him that he found this decision 'very noble', he was disconcerted.[12] In his interviews with Maurizio Ferraris, Derrida said:'[T]here is always an inadequacy in the very idea of paternity: [. . .] one can sign neither a child nor a work. Being a father means having the extremely joyful and painful experience of the fact that one is not the father. [. . .] [p]aternity is neither a state nor a property.'[13] And he insisted even more on the question 'of the name one receives or the name one gives oneself' in the short book *Passions*, transforming it into a fully fledged philosophical theme:

> Suppose that X, something or someone (a trace, a work, an institution, a child) bears your name, in other words your title. A naïve translation or a common fantasy: you have given your name to X, so everything that belongs to X [*revient à X*], directly or by a circuitous route, in a straight or an oblique line, belongs to *you*, like a surplus for your narcissism. [. . .] Conversely, suppose that X does not want your name or your title; suppose that, for one reason or another, X frees himself from it and chooses another name, effecting a sort of repeated weaning from the originary weaning; then your narcissism, doubly wounded, will *ipso facto* find itself all the more enriched: what bears, has borne, will bear your name appears sufficiently, powerful, creative, and autonomous to live alone and dispense radically with you and your name. He returns to your name, to the secret of your name, so as to be able to disappear *in your name*.[14]

His eldest son's career worried Derrida for other reasons. He had always admired him, was thrilled by his precocious successes, and was delighted to see him taking up philosophy. But, rather as Jacques had done in Le Mans, Pierre had a breakdown in the middle of his probationary year. And he very soon decided to leave philosophy so as to move into literature, which did not reassure his father, who was as traditional as many others when it came to his children. Derrida explained the problem to Michel Monory: 'Pierre, who couldn't take it any more, has, if I understand correctly, made an attempt to escape from teaching. He has a CNL [Centre National du Livre] bursary for the year, is writing, busying himself with several things and doesn't seem to be much worried about a profession.'[15]

'When I gave up philosophy,' acknowledges Pierre,

> he was extremely worried about my professional future. For one thing, he considered that being a university professor was a nice job. Deeper down, he must have regretted the fact that I was moving away from philosophy and practically no longer reading it. Even his own books, I have to admit that I've read them in a very fragmentary and rather intermittent way. I felt overwhelmed by the increasingly rapid rhythm of his publications: no sooner had I started one that I was receiving one or two more. My personal philosophical development had been very un-Derridean: the texts I was most interested in didn't at all come from him. After studies in ethnology, my brother

Jean worked in philosophy more than me, but he, too, went into areas that were almost entirely safe from Derridean commentaries. He didn't become a professor and found his own field, pursuing personal research, especially into Plotinus and neo-Platonism.[16]

Over the following years, Pierre Alféri and Olivier Cadiot set up the *Revue de littérature générale* and published ten or so works with Éditions P.O.L.; these included *Le Cinéma des familles,* a novel filled with autobiographical details – Derrida would recommend it to several of his friends. But Derrida would continue to be worried by his oldest son's professional situation. 'I've had all sorts of small jobs,' says Pierre.

I've been a bookseller, I've worked in publishing, I've written lyrics for songs. When I translated several parts of the Bible for Éditions Bayard, this wasn't just for the pleasure of writing, it was also my main source of income . . . If the paternal model has played any role in my development, it was that I took over his desire to be a writer. In my own way, I've perhaps taken his desire forward. One evening, he came to the Fondation Cartier, to a performance I'd organized with Rodolphe Burger. There were images projected, readings, music. At the end he came up to congratulate me and said: 'Basically, we're doing more or less the same thing.' He was aware that he was practising philosophy more and more as an artist. He often felt closer to writers, painters, or architects than to academics.[17]

Nonetheless, Derrida still had to deal with professors of philosophy – not always a happy experience. A Commission of Reflection on the subject matter to be taught had been set up at the end of 1988 by Lionel Jospin, then Minister of Education. It was chaired by Pierre Bourdieu and François Gros, and given the task of revising the material being taught while making it more coherent. It was in the framework of this commission that the Commission for Philosophy and Epistemology was established, co-chaired by Jacques Bouveresse and Jacques Derrida and comprising Jacques Brunschwig, Jean Dhombres, Catherine Malabou, and Jean-Jacques Rosat. This small group met for six months, from January to June 1989. In Derrida's view, it was a question of extending the work started in 1974 with the Greph and continued at the beginning of the 1980s with the Collège International de Philosophie. But if he was to gain acceptance for the ideas he felt most strongly about, one of the challenges was to reach some understanding with Bouveresse, who for years had regularly been attacking him; he had said some very harsh things about the CIPh. In spite of this, the two men agreed to work together, both convinced that reform was essential. In an undated note, Derrida described the commission's work very directly:

> The question and the task were as follows: between Jacques Bouveresse and myself, as was a secret to nobody, between the two of us and the other members of the commission – Dhombres, Brunschwig, Malabou and Rosat –, any philosophical similarity didn't exactly leap to the eyes, nor did any resemblance in philosophical styles, practices, methods, or subjects, not to mention the diversity of our professional situations. This diversity was even the rule governing our assembly. Between some of us, people have even, on other occasions, spoken of conflict. So the question and the task were: what do we wish for, in common today? On what can we agree so as to continue the discussion and propose that the discussion be continued? And thus philosophical work? On what could the greatest diversity of philosophers and citizens in this country – whom we will endeavour to represent as best as we can – agree in order to identify problems, form hypotheses, start a discussion, to subscribe, in short, to the principles of a discussion?[18]

This is confirmed by Catherine Malabou:

> To begin with, Bouveresse and Derrida were both on their guard. But things finally went off okay between them. They shared the same view of the problem and could easily agree on a set of proposals. One evening, they even managed to discuss what lay behind their differences: since the Vienna School and the work of Wittgenstein were in certain respects close to deconstruction, why had Derrida never taken any interest in them? They kept up a good relationship until the end of what was a difficult project.[19]

Among the proposals put forward by the commission they were chairing was the idea of including a series of clearly defined questions in the syllabus of philosophy classes. This way of making people's expectations more specific should remedy the mediocre results of too many of the candidates in the baccalaureate and the fear which the discipline aroused in a great many of them.

> If the great majority of answers in the 'bac' do not at present satisfy minimal philosophical demands, this is mainly because the pupils, having to foresee any kind of question, have not been able to prepare anything; as they generally lack basic

knowledge about the questions put to them and the most
elementary familiarity with the given problems, they do not
understand what is being asked of them, and in any case do not
have the theoretical tools to answer.[20]

However moderate these proposals were, they aroused fierce
debate. A petition opposing the report was signed by one thousand
two hundred people. On 18 October 1990, a particularly stormy
session was held in the amphithéâtre Poincaré, rue Descartes. The
teachers present fought against the contents of the report, but
also against Derrida himself, with often highly aggressive attacks.
Catherine Malabou remembers some difficult moments.

> The Société Française de Philosophie and the Association
> Française des Professeurs de Philosophie were the biggest
> detractors of the project, which finally led to its being shelved.
> Jacques knew that he had many enemies in the Inspection
> Génerale, but he couldn't understand why philosophy teach-
> ers were refusing to envisage philosophy being extended to the
> classes of the *seconde* and *première*. Like a trades union official
> abandoned by his base, he was fighting on behalf of people who
> gave him absolutely no support. After this report, he felt sick
> and absolutely refused to ever get involved in this kind of thing
> again.[21]

Jacques Bouveresse emerged from the venture feeling just as crest-
fallen. 'On the content, I continue to think that our proposals were
perfectly reasonable. Shortly before his death, Derrida said, in a
television broadcast, that one had to resign oneself to admitting
that the corporation of philosophy teachers was, in fact, profoundly
reactionary. I can easily imagine what it must have cost him to say
this.'[22]

Just as stressful was another crisis that had erupted a few months
earlier, during preparations for the conference on 'Lacan with the
Philosophers' scheduled to take place at Unesco in May 1990,
on the initiative of the Collège International de Philosophie. The
polemic, launched by Alain Badiou, concerned the place occupied
by Derrida in the wake of Lacan. In his letter to René Major on 12
December 1989, Badiou asked him to change the title announced for
his paper: 'Since Lacan: Is there a Derridean psychoanalysis?' The
presence of Derrida's name in the title of a paper, when he was 'the
only living philosopher to be mentioned anywhere in the entire conference', struck him as being likely to 'saturate the significance' of
all their work.[23] Major and Derrida were appalled by this demand,
which seemed to them a form of censorship.

Things soon took a turn for the worse. Several participants threatened to withdraw from the steering committee if the offending title were kept. Philippe Lacoue-Labarthe, chair of the CIPh that year, was very keen on having Badiou there, as he felt quite close to him politically. A compromise was eventually found, with Major agreeing to replace the second part of his title, 'Is there a Derridean psychoanalysis?', with a mere dash. He would comment on this unusual erasure, turning the incident into the starting point for his paper.

The conference took place from 24 to 27 May 1990 in the great auditorium of Unesco; it was an enormous success. Derrida gave the closing paper. Under the title 'For the love of Lacan', he set out the history of his turbulent relationship with the author of the *Écrits*, sometimes ironically, sometimes admiringly. 'And if I were to say at this point: "You see, I believe that we loved each other quite a lot, Lacan and I . . .," I am almost certain that many of you could not bear it. And for that reason, I am not yet sure as to whether or not I will say it.'[24] Nearly ten years had gone by since Lacan's death and the ideological context that now prevailed had made Derrida feel closer to him.

Whether concerning philosophy, psychoanalysis, or theory in general, what the restoration now in progress attempts to cover up, deny or censure, is the fact that nothing of that which could transform the space of thought in recent decades would have been possible without some explanation with Lacan, without Lacanian provocation (however it is received or discussed) [. . .].[25]

In his paper, Derrida alludes without naming it to the recent *roman à clef* published by Julia Kristeva, *The Samurai*, in which Lacan was turned into Lauzun and Derrida was called Saïda. They were both described as adulterated goods, only good for export, but Derrida was treated more sarcastically. The attack was full-on; the fact this was a *roman à clef* made it even more wounding:

Saïda took advantage of May to pluck up his courage and seize the occasion. His meditations, inspired by *Finnegans Wake* and Heidegger, irritated philosophers and reduced the literature merchants to silence – both bodies were confronted with their own transcendental stupidity. Everyone was tight-lipped, no one was won over. The ceremony used to last nearly there hours, and sometimes there were even two sessions – six hours in all. The survivors could be counted up afterward. They were to be the first fans of the 'condestruction' theory: the word was invented to show that one should never construct without destroying, too. It wasn't a very elegant expression, it sounded downright woggish [. . .]. What exactly did it mean, 'condestruction'? The formerly timid Saïda broke down every word into its minutest elements, and from these seeds produced shoots so flexible he could weave them into his own dreams, his own literature, rather ponderous but as profound as it was inaccessible. This was how he started to acquire his reputation as a guru, which was to overwhelm the United States and the American feminists, who all became 'condestructivists' out of affection for Saïda and endogenous dissatisfaction.[26]

A second crisis erupted a few weeks after the conference. Badiou was furious that Major and Derrida had alluded several times in their papers to the controversy that had set them at loggerheads with him. Feeling that too many privileges had been granted to Derrida for the proceedings not to be unbalanced, he wished to withdraw his text. After a new mediation on the part of Lacoue-Labarthe, a meeting that brought together all those involved took place on 10 August 1990. Yet again, a compromise was found: Badiou agreed to let his text be published, on condition that all the letters and documents relating to the controversy be published as an appendix to the work.

This would all be a matter of mere anecdote if it had not led to a more than passing tiff between Lacoue-Labarthe and Derrida. According to Philippe Beck, who knew all the protagonists well,

> Badiou was isolated just then. He needed to form alliances and drew very close to Lacoue at that time, since both of them were concerned to criticize Heidegger. Lacoue, who was actually very critical of Badiou on certain important points, was torn between Derrida's patient and attentive deconstruction and Badiou's polemical and philosophical manoeuvres. So he decided to show his solidarity with the latter rather than with René Major, which Derrida never forgave him for. But in Lacoue there was, at least at the time, a primacy of political critique at the heart of poetics. The fact that Badiou and Derrida drew close later on obviously puts the whole business in a strange light.[27]

But these events were of course merely a trigger. Many other factors had been leading up to this crisis between two men linked for nearly twenty years by a close friendship. From *Heidegger, Art, and Politics* onwards, Lacoue-Labarthe was overcome by a kind of rage against Heidegger. He could no longer find words harsh enough to describe him. Without saying so explicitly, he held a grudge against Derrida for not condemning him sufficiently. The de Man affair was probably an extra irritant. The question of Jewishness was a real source of tension between the two thinkers. Lacoue-Labarthe was not Jewish, but over the years he had become increasingly philo-Semitic. He felt as if he were experiencing the trauma of the Shoah in his own flesh, almost as much as Sarah Kofman was.[28] But Derrida refused to give Auschwitz any absolute singularity. At a debate at the Collège International de Philosophie, on 11 March 1990, he repeated and clarified his position on the subject, returning to the debate held at Cerisy ten years previously, after Jean-François Lyotard's paper:

> When [. . .] I expressed my disquiet at the way all thinking about the Shoah, genocide, extermination was being centred on Auschwitz alone, this wasn't to relativize Auschwitz. To begin with, the Shoah isn't just Auschwitz. It wasn't to relativize Auschwitz and the extermination of the Jews, it was with the infinite respect, the memory, the bottomless pain that this extermination can arouse in us, to draw from it at least the lesson that other exterminations have taken place, are taking place, may take place; and here too the question of the 'us' remains open; and if we closed it, if we closed the net at that point, that would be very serious for reasons that I don't need to go into. That's all. It wasn't at all in order to relativize or push Auschwitz into the background [. . .]. Not at all, quite the opposite. I think that respect for Jewish martyrdom under Nazism obliges us not to centre all possible martyrdoms on that one.[29]

But above and beyond any philosophical or political question, various personal elements played a decisive role in the confrontation between the two men. Derrida found the self-destructive aspects of Lacoue-Labarthe difficult to take. Although he was finding it increasingly difficult to breathe, he never stopped smoking, morning, noon, and night, sometimes giving the impression of someone living through his last days. His problems with alcohol had become even more worrying. Jean-Luc Nancy sadly remembers: 'Philippe had started drinking, without us realizing. He drank on the quiet, mainly white wine and whisky. His alcoholism became more and more serious and evident, and had a powerful impact on his character. Nothing and nobody could help him.'[30]

Their mutual friends watched helplessly as Derrida and Lacoue-Labarthe drifted apart. Samuel Weber says: 'Gradually, relations between them became more distant, and the clashes more frequent. And yet there a lot of things that made them similar. Philippe was more of a poet and artist than Jean-Luc, who was more philosophical and serious. But Philippe was also more tragic, more depressive.

Perhaps he rekindled Jacques's own anxieties too much.'[31] In Philippe Beck's words, 'Derrida was a tormented Mediterranean. Lacoue-Labarthe stood for many of the things that fascinated him: austerity, political intransigence, closeness to poetry. Lacoue's real dream was probably literary in nature: he thought that Derrida had "found prose", as Badiou put it, and dreamed of inventing poetry like Hölderlin and Celan. This dream obviously had a political significance.'[32]

As Derrida moved away from Lacoue-Labarthe, he became closer to Nancy. The latter had long suffered from cardiac problems but had never bothered to have them treated. It took a major crisis in the summer of 1989 for him finally to become aware of the seriousness of his state. Though Derrida drove himself quite hard, he implored his friend to take things easier: 'Take a rest, don't work too hard when you're travelling, do this for me, write away peacefully, the way we need to, in the calm of the rue Charles-Grad . . ..'[33] He frequently told Nancy how important his thought, his texts, and his friendship were to him: 'Look after your heart, as I do. You need to take walks, not smoke (smoke less), learn to take, in other words to give yourself time, a lot of time . . . .'[34]

On 19 July 1990, Nancy told Derrida that he was soon going to need a heart transplant: if they did nothing, he had only six to seven months left to live. 'Both to harvest my strength and to be ready to undergo a transplant, as soon as a heart was ready, I no longer had any right to leave Strasbourg,' Jean-Luc Nancy relates.

> Jacques made a return trip out specially to see me, which filled me with pleasure but also with fear. Having to wait for a transplant undeniably helped to bring us closer together. He telephoned me the whole time. This was a very impressive gesture, and it struck all my friends. I'd told Jacques, jokingly: 'I'm the best Derridean. I've taken your concept of the transplant* literally.'[35]

Alexander García Düttman confirms how worried Derrida was about his friend throughout this anxious time of waiting:

> Shortly before Nancy underwent his heart transplant, Derrida told me: we need to talk about Jean-Luc Nancy, we need to bring out the value of his work. He suggested to Peggy Kamuf that a special issue of *Paragraph* be devoted to him, and wrote the first paragraph of 'On touching', a long article that would

---

* Or 'graft' – *greffe*. – Tr.

later become a whole book. As if, more than anyone else, he had chosen Jean-Luc as his heir. Because he wasn't just a mimic. Because his work was close and singular at the same time, creating an opening towards Christianity.[36]

In spring 1991, Jacques was in California for several weeks when Jean-Luc announced that he was going to have the operation that same evening. Distressed at being so far from the man who had become his closest friend, Derrida impulsively replied: 'Don't worry, I'll wake up with you.'[37] The operation was a success. Over the next years, in spite of his serious health problems, Nancy would enjoy an unusually active life for someone with a heart transplant.

In the autumn of 1990, Derrida had to mourn another significant death. On 22 October 1990, Louis Althusser died in the hospital de la Verrière, in the department of Les Yvelines. The two men had been linked for almost forty years, and their relationship had been, as we have seen, extremely complex. At the burial, in the little cemetery of Giroflay, it was Derrida who spoke in front of the last faithful friends. While he did not hide what had separated them and sometimes put then on opposite sides, he reiterated how dear this relationship had been to him:

And what remains most present in my eyes, most alive today, closest and most precious, is, of course, his face, Louis's so very handsome face, that high forehead, his smile, everything that, in him, during the moments of peace – and there were moments of peace, as many of you here know – radiated kindness, the need for love and the giving of love in return [. . .].[38]

Five years earlier, Althusser had been deeply hurt by a column in *Le Monde* in which Claude Sarraute had compared him to the Japanese cannibal Issei Sagawa who had killed and eaten a young Dutch woman: charges against him had been dropped on grounds of insanity. Shortly afterwards, Althusser started to write his auto-biography, *The Future Lasts a Long Time*. Right at the start of his narrative, he refers to the 'ambiguous' effects of the fact that he had been declared 'unfit to plead' – which had condemned him to being 'placed beneath a tombstone of silence'.[39] The title chosen would turn out to be prophetic: in 1992, this posthumous publication would have immense repercussions. Over the following years, the publication of several unpublished works by Althusser would bring about a complete revaluation of his life and his work. *The Future Lasts a Long Time* is a quasi-clinical document at the same time as being an attempt at self-analysis; it also constitutes, in little details here and there, an extraordinary posthumous homage to the gigantic figure of Derrida, the 'most radical' of all – the only great thinker of our age and, in Althusser's view, for a long while to come, perhaps, the last.

4

Portrait of the Philosopher at Sixty

In 1992, Jacques Derrida gave Osvaldo Muñoz an interview which concluded with a traditional 'Proust questionnaire'. If this text, meant for the daily *El País*, was in the end not published, this is perhaps because Derrida deemed it a bit too revealing:

What are the depths of misery for you?: To lose my memory.
Where would you like to live?: In a place to which I can always return, in other words from which I can leave.
For what fault do you have the most indulgence?: Keeping a secret which one should not keep.
Favourite hero in a novel: Bartleby.
Your favourite heroines in real life?: I'm keeping that a secret.
Your favourite quality in a man?: To be able to confess that he is afraid.
Your favourite quality in a woman?: Thought.
Your favourite virtue?: Faithfulness.
Your favourite occupation: Listening.
Who would you like to have been?: Another who would remember me a bit.
My main character trait?: A certain lack of seriousness.
My dream of happiness?: To continue dreaming.
What would be my greatest misfortune?: Dying after the people I love.
What I would like to be: A poet.
What I hate more than anything?: Complacency and vulgarity.
The reform I most admire: Everything to do with the difference between the sexes.
The natural gift I would like to have: Musical genius.
How I would like to die: Taken completely by surprise.
My motto: Prefer to say yes.[1]

The convictions and the aporias, the anxieties, the hopes and the flaws, the desire to occupy every place, poetry, memory and secrecy – in a sense, they're all there.

'Jacques was permanently overworked,' explains his son Pierre.

> Too many conference papers and trips, too many commitments
> and obligations, too many texts and books to write. He com-
> plained about being overburdened almost every day, like a kind
> of basso continuo. At the same time, if he was always on the
> breach, he coped with things, he kept going forward. He had to
> *answer*, most often as a matter of urgency.[2]

Quite unlike Melville's Bartleby and his celebrated 'I would prefer
not to', Derrida was the man who preferred to say 'yes'. He had
made this into a way of life, a mode of being. The more the years
passed, the more projects piled up, the more letters he had in his
in-tray, and the more trips there were to organize. He 'overflowed',
writes Michel Deguy, one of the few people who followed his career
from beginning to end. 'The "too-much" was his moderation. But
too much what? Too long, for example. When a "participation"
by Jacques Derrida was announced, his friends' smiles insinuated:
"How long is he going to speak for?" You never know. If he's said
he'll be brief, you'd better make sure he has two or three hours . . . .'[3]

Excessive and wholehearted: this was also how Derrida was in
his relationships, in his sudden enthusiasms as well as his resent-
ments. His kindness, his availability, his friendly ear sometimes had
a reverse side – sudden, intense outbursts of anger. A disagreement
or a momentary clumsiness was enough for you to be disgraced, to
be consigned to the enemy camp. 'He could be hurt very easily,' says
his son Jean. 'There were wounds which the slightest incident could
be enough to reopen. When someone had brushed him up the wrong
way, or attacked him in a text, he never forgot.'[4] In those cases,
he could be harsh and implacable, and even unfair. Claire Nancy
witnessed this: 'Fragile and tormented, Derrida sometimes saw the
world as a football pitch. One day, he drew me a kind of map of the
world: there were countries where he was recognized, those where
his enemies were dominant, and finally those where he was still
unknown.'[5]

This occupation of a terrain on which he was both attacking
and defending made him cautious, mistrustful, and even somewhat
paranoid. However great his successes, he saw nothing but threats.
And even when he occupied the position of master, he still saw
himself as the victim he had on more than one occasion been, especially in institutions. 'There was something childish in his attitude,'
acknowledges Bernard Stiegler. 'An infinite demand for love.' But
there was nothing one-sided about this permanent desire to feel
loved. Derrida was also terribly sentimental and generous to a fault.
He was attentive towards the people he mixed with, interested in
their lives and the lives of their friends. However busy he was, he

would keep in touch with them by writing or telephone, and showed real empathy. He was sincerely affected by their tribulations and was able to share their joys. The day when Alan Bass showed him a photo of his daughter just a few months old, Derrida marvelled at her and said: 'Make the most of it, the time goes so quickly.' He himself had suffered from seeing his children leave home too swiftly for his liking.

Many of those close to him, such as Samuel Weber and Martine Meskel, his niece, also remember his bursts of laughter. Derrida, unlike what he says in some of his texts, loved telling funny stories, but they made him laugh so much – especially Jewish jokes – that he was often unable to get as far as the punch line. 'Laughter to him was like another version of aporia. It was an important dimension to his personality, together with melancholy,' says Samuel Weber.

> I can remember one joke he liked to tell, as it struck me as revealing his own anxieties: A man goes to the doctor and has several tests done. When he comes back a few days later, the doctor tells him: 'No need for you to worry, everything's fine, everything's really fine . . . We're just going to carry out a few more little tests . . .' 'Oh, that's good,' says the patient. 'When exactly?' 'Well, let's say tomorrow morning, as soon as the surgery opens.' That made him laugh a lot. It's the burlesque version of his anxiety about death.[6]

But as his fame and his authority grew, this liking for laughter was expressed less and less often. In public, Derrida appeared more serious, in response to people's expectations of him. In private, his mood was often sombre. Élisabeth Roudinesco is still struck by his incredible tendency to feel guilty, as if he felt responsible for everything that happened: 'A fortnight before his death, referring to the questionnaire that Bernard Pivot used to put out on *Apostrophes*,[*] he told me: "When I arrive in front of Saint Peter, this is what I'll tell him: 'I'm really sorry' and 'the landscapes are lovely'. Remember that."'[7] Derrida was more and haunted by the passing of time, and the thought of death became an increasing obsession. 'Life will have been so short,' he kept saying, using the future anterior that suited him so well. He had a kind of urgent drive to be forever producing something, to get involved in more and more projects, to leave traces. To the people who, like Claire Nancy, rebuked him sometimes for publishing too much, he replied: 'I can't help it. It's my way of fighting against death.'

---

[*] *Apostrophes* was a French TV programme hosted by Bernard Pivot. It was devoted to books and ran from 1975 to 1990. – Tr.

Even though the idea of death never left him, Derrida in many ways lived life to the full. Jean-Luc Nancy insists on how 'the presence of Jacques was powerful, alluring, captivating, impressive – not just as the presence of a great stature, but as a tender and anxious sensibility, as an attentiveness on the alert, as a mixture of availability and reserve. He who contributed so much to deconstructing "presence" was overwhelmingly present.'[8]

In a fine essay written in homage, 'Jupiter among us', Denis Kambouchner also insists on the first obvious physical impact that might surprise those who know Derrida only through his books:

Derrida was a remarkable body: features, voice, skin, gaze, hair, shoulders and body language. [. . .] This body affected you in an intense and characteristic way. [. . .] Listening to Derrida, speaking to him, was not like meeting the Word or some replica of it, but, in the species of a pure capacity for decipherment and indication, an intelligence of a Jupiterian kind (we don't have a Greek word for that). Not an ostentatious Jupiter, thundering and majestic, but an inner Jupiter, with a superior knowledge and precision in his will, and at the same time the life of desire, simple affection, the defiance of fatigue, the imagination always awake, torment never far away, and affirmation reflected so much it became a malady.[9]

When he was a student, Derrida said that he was fragile and ate at the table of those following a special diet. Ever since then, his health had been excellent, though this did not stop him being a hypochondriac and panicking over the slightest potential symptom. He had the heart rate of a sports cyclist or marathon runner, less than fifty beats per minute, which gave him an extraordinary physical capacity and force of recovery. He kept an eye on his food and was not especially fond of wine, which did not stop him being amazed by the knowledge his friend René Major showed in this field. Ever since his time in Koléa, he had given up cigarettes, smoking little cigarillos instead. Under pressure from his son Jean, he finally gave up these as well, and switched to a pipe, which he often forgot to light but with which he liked being photographed. In fact, if he lived a very sober life, constant anxiety about his health was the main reason. He had so many plans, so many books to write, that he wanted to live to a grand old age.

Jean-Luc Nancy was always impressed by Derrida's stamina on his transatlantic trips. After a quick snack, ignoring the time difference, he was able to give a long paper, take part in a debate, and give an interview before putting on a good show at the reception that almost invariably followed. On a trip to Mexico for the Collège International de Philosophie, Derrida confessed to Nancy: 'When

I got there, I was dead beat. I tried to grab forty winks in the car that came to pick me up from the airport. But as soon as I started to speak, any trace of tiredness evaporated.' Then, he added: 'I'm crazy.' In public, Derrida was galvanized by the interest of his listeners. His powers of physical resistance were much greater than in his youth. He said so himself: 'I was more physically fragile then [at the age of twenty], and I would've collapsed from doing a fraction of what I do now. The reception of the work is what gives me this energy.'[10]

One should not underestimate the aspect of oral performance, the almost theatrical quality of Derrida's later texts and, of course, his seminars and interventions. As Michel Lisse notes, a lot of Derrida's texts were written to be performed: 'Sometimes the rhythm slows down, sometimes it speeds up; quotations in German interrupt the French phraseology, several languages mingle. Certain passages, although serious, cause laughter by highlighting aporias or repeating terms.'[11] The writer Max Genève, a long-standing friend, habitually read Derrida's work but had not heard him speak in public; after a conference paper, he said he was 'seduced not merely by the restless audacity of the text itself, but also by its performance, its perfect diction, the energetic gestures, especially the one used to announce quotation marks, which evoked the torero just about to stick in his banderillas or the cowboy wielding a pistol in each hand'.[12] Speaking for hours on end, sometimes for a whole day, taking part in a debate or answering questions in a demanding interview: these were all so many physical performances that, as with great sportsmen, liberated Derrida's dose of endorphins and made him euphoric. Even more than writing, he liked to '*talk* philosophy'.[13] He drew nourishment from his own words and their effect on the audience. For a few hours, all his anxieties could be forgotten. Never, perhaps, did he feel so fully alive as then.

In public, whatever he did, Derrida was now centre stage and attracted attention. He had been so timid and unsure of himself when he came to Paris, he had observed with envy the confidence of someone like Gérard Granel; over the course of the years, he had become increasingly solar. Many of his friends and colleagues referred to his narcissism. If some of them described him as a bit of 'a monster', this was because it went far beyond traditional narcissism: Derrida practised it to excess, thereby questioning the boundaries of narcissism and turning it into a philosophical gesture. The fairest assessment is probably Maurice Olender's: he describes it as 'a radiant narcissism'.[14]

Derrida had an irresistible desire to seduce. And if he almost never spoke of his relationship to women, this was because his obsession with secrecy was greater in this area than in any other.

But many people knew that 'the feminine' was, for him, always in the plural. If Derrida vaunted faithfulness in his reply to the Proust questionnaire, this was because every relationship was for him a unique, irreplaceable event; so he felt capable of faithfulness to many people. Among all the women he knew, Sylviane Agacinski occupied a special place. Never again would he expose himself to that degree; never again did he want to suffer or make someone else suffer as much. But he remained a great seducer, and if he valued his own success and fame, this was also because they made things easier. His immense respect for women, and especially his great willingness to listen to them, rather like an analyst, were redoubtable weapons. As Marguerite Derrida puts it: 'I've always thought that it was mainly through his capacity for listening that Jacques could seduce women.' This quality, rare in a man, even rarer in a personality as strong as his, impressed many of the women he frequented. His friend Marie-Claire Boons is happy to say as much: 'I found in him an absolute ability to listen that I've never come across in anyone else. An abstention from all moral judgement. In every situation, he wanted to go where life was.'[15]

'Love of women was there even before puberty,' he confided one day to Hélène Cixous. 'It was already a mixture of identification and compassion. I felt I was on their side.'[16] As the years went by, he increasingly preferred the company of women to that of men, and indeed he thought that women were his best readers. All the same, in spite of his theoretical alliance with feminists, Derrida loved women who affirmed their femininity and assumed it without hysteria. A woman who did not attract him physically had a hard time trying to interest him, however great her intellectual abilities. 'When we first got to know each other,' says Alan Bass, 'he would often describe himself as "a horrible Mediterranean macho man".'

In spite of ups and downs, the union between Jacques and Marguerite remained essential and indestructible. Nothing could undermine it over the forty-eight years of their life together. According to Avital Ronell, 'Marguerite never considered anyone to be a rival. She always had something nice to say about the women who were close or too close to Jacques, which does not mean that she did not suffer because of them.'[17]

From their earliest encounters, Marguerite had been convinced that Jacques would be the greatest philosopher of his generation. And so her admiration, present right from the start, did not have to keep being restated. And if Jacques was amazed that his wife was not more dazzled by the marks of external recognition that he received, this was because she had not waited for him to meet with success before believing in him. Honours, to which Derrida himself was quite drawn, since he viewed them as a recompense for the difficulties and rejections that he had also suffered, held little importance for her. She would sometimes describe her husband as an 'extraterrestrial', which he rather liked.

To help him with his work, Marguerite had since the beginning of the sixties taken over all the daily tasks and looked after the material side of life: the home, the paperwork, the schooling of the children, the tax returns, and countless other things. 'Jacques didn't even know where the bank was,' she said. 'The employees in the local branch had never set eyes on him. When I took in some documents that I'd got him to sign, some of them asked me laughingly: "So he really does exist, your Monsieur Derrida?"'[18]

Their friend Alexander García Düttman relates: 'Jacques always trusted Marguerite completely. She was beyond criticism. In one sense, you could almost say that he didn't deserve her.' If Derrida enjoyed inviting people round for dinner – friends, colleagues, translators, students –, it was Marguerite who looked after everything, managing, in spite of her own activities, to ensure that the meals were not only ready on time, but delicious as well. She received guests in a way as simple as it was warm, as if all of this was self-evident. And if she was sometimes ironical about her husband, it was in a benevolent, collusive way, without the least nastiness. Derrida was aware of Marguerite's delicacy, her extraordinary way of doing things just right, and nothing that came from her could hurt his feelings.[19]

Ultimately, the only thing that sometimes annoyed Marguerite was Jacques's jealous temperament. 'He wasn't happy when he couldn't reach me straightaway. At every instant, he wanted to know where I was, what I was doing, and with whom. But if I made the mistake of asking him a question of the kind, he said: "Ah, always this reciprocity!"'[20]

In spite of his 'unconditional devotion' to Paris, of which he sometimes said he loved each little alley, knowing that it would survive him,[21] Derrida never wanted to live there. He had grown up on the heights of El Biar, and so a big city always had something suffocating about it for him. The Derrida couple remained loyal to their house in Ris-Orangis, which they acquired in 1968, improving and extending it over the years. Here, in this place to which Derrida was glad to return after every trip away, there were bookcases and desks everywhere. In every room, he left traces. Here, letters that had accumulated since his arrival in mainland France, press articles and the countless editions of his own books in the most varied languages. There, works of philosophy, many of them in tatters as he had read them and annotated them so often. In another room, books he had been sent, signed copies. In the stairwell, collections of reviews. And, separately, 'the literature he loved'. After the years spent in his 'sublime', the little attic where he could not stand upright, he moved onto the veranda, belatedly adding a very big library. If Derrida needed so much space, this was because he kept everything: his old computers, the theses, long essays and other paperwork from students that he had collected over forty years, but also the most insignificant documents. In the garden in Ris-Orangis there was also the cemetery for all the cats in his life, and all the Christmas trees he had transplanted there. The trace, for him, was not just a philosophical concept; it was a reality that affected every instant. Every object, however humble, was charged with the moment of life that it had borne. Any everyday or banal gesture constituted a witness and the promise of a future: 'When I leave a piece of paper around at home or when I make a note in the margin of a book – an exclamation mark, for example –, I always wonder who's going to read that? and *what will my children get out of it, if they ever read that?*'[22]

As Derrida stated on more than one occasion: his principal desire was less to create a philosophical work or a work of art than to preserve a memory. The gaze he turned to his past had the effect of saving him and in some way casting a spell over him:

> I have the fortunate nature that dictates that of no moment in my life – including the worst things I have lived through – have I wanted to say: I would prefer not to have lived this; in this sense, I am always reaffirming, always repeating. So when I say, 'I love what I have loved,' it is not only this thing or person, but rather: I love love, if one can say that, I love every experience I have had, and it's true, I want to keep everything. That is my good fortune. And yet I very rarely have the feeling in the present of being happy, of loving simply what I am living, but in the past everything seems to have been loved, and needs to be reaffirmed.[23]

Ever since he was a young man, Derrida had been a very early riser, around 6 a.m. After a first cup of coffee, he started work. And when, three hours later, he joined Marguerite for breakfast, he sometimes said that he'd finished his day's work, in other words his work for the seminar. After a certain age, he had a short nap after lunch, but he was a little embarrassed to admit it, especially in the first years. When he was alone, he could continue to work indefinitely, forgetting meals and the notion of time. In the film *Derrida* he says: 'When I stay at home by myself all day, I don't get dressed. I stay in my pyjamas and dressing gown.'[24]

The most useful tool, since 1986, was inevitably the computer, with its monumental capacity for memory and storage. 'I can't do without it any more now, this little Mac, especially when I'm working at home; I can't even remember or understand how I was able to get on before it.'[25] He acknowledged that he was as 'dependent on it as a drug addict'. But while the computer rapidly became indispensable to him, he initially found it another source of anxiety. The first times he saw the icon of a bomb appearing on his screen, he really panicked. It needed all the patience of Pierre and Jean to help him tame this object little by little. For while the computer offered Derrida immense possibilities, it also came with a huge danger: that of losing work. In the early days, this happened to him a lot.

I now have at home, I can freely admit, three computers and two of then also have a zip drive, an extra hard disk [. . .] and when I write a long text that's hanging around without being printed out, I never leave the house without making copies of the text in question [. . .]. There are at least ten copies that I leave in different places, because there are also risks of fire, of burglary. And here, in my briefcase, I have my essential current work. This is the neurosis that develops with technology.[26]

When he was not in Ris-Orangis, his anxieties were even greater. During the holidays or when he was about to travel, Derrida copied his work on several disks. He kept one copy on himself, placed another in his suitcase, and left a third one with Marguerite or his brother. When he was at Irvine, he entrusted one copy to J. Hillis Miller in disk form and another in hard copy. As Maurizio Ferraris relates in his short book *Jackie Derrida: rittrato a memoria*, one of the things that made him happy when his archives were taken off to Irvine was that they left him not only a complete set of photocopies but also the photocopier.

In everyday life, Derrida was almost obsessively punctual, especially when it came to catching a train or a plane; woe betide anyone who delayed him. He did not like dinners that dragged on; in the restaurant, he could get impatient if the dishes did not arrive quickly enough. He preferred small gatherings of friends around the table to big official dinners, where his nightmare was finding himself stuck between people he did not know, or who bored him. Alexander García Düttmann remembers:

Together with such intellectual complexity, there were some surprisingly simple and easy-going aspects to him. I once spent several weeks at their home in Ris-Orangis. In the evenings, if Marguerite wasn't there, we had spaghetti for dinner before watching television. Jacques would often doze off shortly after dinner. Generally speaking, he had various strategies to disguise his need for sleep. At conferences, he sometimes held his head in his hands, as if he were lost in thought. In actual fact, he was taking a brief nap, which didn't stop him addressing a highly relevant remark to the speaker at the end of the paper.[27]

Television played an important role in his life, especially when he was travelling. He was happy to admit this: 'I'm more frightened of a hotel room without a television than a house without running water.'[28] This dependency came with a certain sense of guilt:

I spend much too much time, I think, watching television, and I reproach myself at the same time, naturally, for not reading enough anymore or for not doing other things. [. . .] Sometimes I watch bad soap operas, French or American, or programs that give me a greater cultural awareness, such as those on the Arte channel. Political debates, spectacular political encounters in general, *L'Heure de vérité*, *7 sur 7*, or old movies. I could spend twenty-four hours a day watching good political archives . . . And so I watch a little of everything.[29]

On Sunday mornings, while having a workout on the exercise bike, he followed with close interest the Muslim and Jewish religious broadcasts, between 8:45 and 9:50 a.m.[30] In the United States, he could watch televangelists for hours on end, with a kind of fascination. But what gripped him even more, as Peggy Kamuf relates, was the direct broadcast of Congress hearings. Around 1987, at the end of Ronald Reagan's second mandate, he spent a great deal of time watching the procession of witnesses speaking about the affair of the 'Contras' sent into Nicaragua, and the American hostages in Iran. All this, of course, had some influence on the seminars he gave on bearing witness, or perjury.[31]

On the culinary level, Derrida was still influenced by family tradition. He continued to like the cuisine of his childhood. Marguerite learned to cook Algerian couscous without meat: couscous with butter, peas, fromage blanc, and hard-boiled eggs. He enjoyed good cooking, even if his tastes remained quite simple. Avital Ronell – a committed vegetarian – relates that one day, at a dinner with Chantal and René Major, she let one dish go by without taking a helping, which caused a certain embarrassment. When she said she had perfectly decent philosophical reasons for not eating meat, Derrida turned to ask her what they were. So Avital told him what it meant to her to incorporate the body of the other. Shortly afterwards, Derrida, who was extraordinarily receptive to this kind of thing, started to speak of *carnophallogocentrism* rather than *phallogocentrism*.

Later on, with me and in front of me, he said he was a vegetarian. But one day, someone told me he had eaten a steak tartare, as carnivorous a kind of food as you can get. For me, it was as if he had betrayed me. When I spoke to him about it, he initially said I was behaving like a cop. Then he said, neatly: 'I'm a vegetarian who sometimes eats meat.'[32]

After dinners in Ris-Orangis, Derrida would gladly offer to drive home any guests without transport. He enjoyed driving, and always went into Paris by car. He'd learned when still very young, on the job, with his father's car. But since he had never studied the highway code, he had his own ideas about it, which could sometimes lead to spectacular results. He considered, for example, that most 'no entry' signs did not actually apply to him, and that big roads should automatically have priority over smaller ones. At the wheel, he rapidly lost his cool. In traffic jams, he could almost get hysterical. And, to crown it all, whenever he stopped for even a short time he would start taking notes. In a letter to Éric Clémens, he indicated in a PS: 'Excuse the handwriting, I'm writing in the car (what a life!), but I've stopped, not even at a red light. I've just thought of the title for a book: *Written at a Red Light* . . .'[33] But while he was not a reassuring figure at the wheel, he never had an accident.

Marguerite says that they always had Citroëns, less out of any particular liking than because there was a garage not far from the house. 'At one time, he took over his father's DS, but he wrecked it when he forgot to put any oil in. One day, filling up the tank, he used diesel instead of petrol.' Subsequently, he went for modest vehicles, even if he knew how to appreciate a nice car. René Major says: 'I'd just bought a Lotus "Esprit". He started to examine it with great interest, before going into ecstasies over its name: "How extraordinary. I'm just writing a book called *Of Spirit* [*De l'esprit*] . . . Could I give it a spin?"'[34]

While his daily life was for the most part imbued with sobriety, he made an exception for his clothes. While a pupil at Louis-le-Grand, Jackie had been forced to endure the grim grey coat; as a young professor, he had dressed rather drably. But he had changed a great deal since his first trip to Berlin, when Sam Weber had failed to recognize him, as Derrida bore so little resemblance to the way he imagined him. Since the start of the 1970s, he had mainly gone for bright colours, shimmering materials, and marked contrasts. He took care over the way he dressed, even if his rather showy tastes did not meet with uniform approval. As René Major remembers: 'We used to comment on each other's clothes. Chantal and I knew that he could be really quite clothes-conscious. We often gave him ties, and shirts. He valued brand names, especially Kenzo.' And Élisabeth Roudinesco emphasises: 'Perhaps there were two areas he didn't go into: clothes, and his relationship with women.'[35]

For a long time, the Derridas did not have much money. They welcomed bread-and-butter jobs to get by, whether these were Marguerite's translations or Jacques's activities as an oral examiner for the École des Hautes Études Commerciales. But by the end of the 1960s, with his first invitations to the United States and the courses he gave to American students in Paris, they started to be better off. Derrida had a good salary at Yale, then at Irvine and New York, added to his salary in France and his royalties, even if he was in no hurry to pick these up. Of course, his conference appearances brought in more and more. But Derrida was not a man to worry about money and it was never a motive force in his life: he no longer needed to bother about it, and this was enough. Often, he did not even ask about the financial conditions for him to make an appearance. And when he spent many weeks writing a long paper for a conference, he often did this for free. In the United States, he sometimes admitted that he was taken aback by the huge sums demanded by certain other figures in 'French Theory', even though they were less famous that he. In the universities where he taught, he was never one to ask for a rise. This was not a matter of disdain or naïvety; rather, it was not in his nature to talk about money, even less to haggle.

'He hated having to tot up amounts and share the bill at the end of a restaurant meal,' says Peggy Kamuf. 'In any case, he was generally the one who picked up the tab.' He liked to settle the bill discreetly, before it was brought to the table. And he did not like it when people insisted on paying for him, especially when they were younger or less well-off than he was. David Carroll remembers: 'He was the most generous man I've ever met, generous with his time, his energy, his help, his advice, and also his money.'[36] And Alan Bass remembers a friend saying to him one evening: 'But Jacques, it can't be your turn to pay *every time*.'

With his children, he was always generous. But he could also be so with people who, at one time or another, found themselves in great difficulties. And when he did someone a favour, he was discreet and delicate about it. For several years, he did what he could to help Jos Joliet, who had formerly worked for Flammarion and for whose novel *The Child with the Sitting Dog* he had written the preface. In his most painful periods, Derrida never abandoned him. The philosopher's elegance in money matters was a form of sovereignty.

Most of the time, he conducted his life in a regular, if not rather ascetic way. But there was a more Mediterranean tendency to enjoy life in him, one which he endeavoured to repress in the day-to-day. It was while on his travels that he sometimes expressed himself more freely, especially when he wanted to impress young women. In those cases, he was quite susceptible to splashing money about, to big hotels and ephemeral luxury. He probably inherited this taste from his mother, for whom poker had been a major passion. And while Derrida himself seems not to have been much of a gambler, it was with a certain pleasure that he entered the door of a casino or went on a jaunt to Las Vegas during one of his stays in California. In the interview for *El País*, after all, he had admitted, rather unexpectedly, to 'a certain lack of seriousness' as his main character trait.

Derrida had a very odd relation to reading. Marguerite says that one day, at Les Rassats, as she was deep in Balzac's *Splendours and Miseries of Courtesans,* Jacques glanced at what she was reading before retorting: 'Ah, *you've* got all your life ahead of you!' Derrida found it very difficult to read just for pleasure.

> For some time now, I have experienced as a real misfortune the fact that I am less and less able to read without that reading getting involved in a writing project, thus a selective, filtering, preoccupied and preoccupying reading. When I read, it is in short spurts and most often in the middle of writing, of grafting the writing onto what I read. But as for reading in large, welcoming waves, I feel myself more and more deprived of it. It is a real deprivation.[37]

In the books on which Derrida worked, you can see 'the traces of the violence of pencil marks, exclamation marks, arrows, underlinings'.[38] Reading was already a form of work, it was the first stage of writing.

> I read with a project in mind. I rarely read in a disinterested manner [. . .], so I read in an active, selective, too selective way, not passive enough. [. . .]
> I read very impatiently, very quickly, and this selective impatience costs me dear: probably a great number of injustices, of negligences. But very often, opening a book in the middle, this impatience has thrown me towards what I was seeking, or what I didn't know I was seeking but then found. [. . .]
> I realize that it's in writing *on* a literary text that I start to read it and that my first reading, comprised of intermittent flashes, is full of gaps. [. . .] Basically, I read for the purposes of teaching.[39]

The technology of writing had always interested him. He enjoyed pointing out that Nietzsche was the first thinker in the West to possess a typewriter, whereas for Heidegger only handwriting was veritable writing.[40] For a long time, when it came to all the texts important to him, Derrida started writing with a pen, starting over again several times. Only when the text was launched, the tone and the overall point of view sketched out, did he turn to his typewriter.

All those who heard him typing, on his little Olivetti with its international keyboard, then on his electric typewriter, were struck by his speed. J. Hillis Miller says:

> One day, at Yale, I called by with Harold Bloom to take him to lunch. But in the corridor, the clatter of his typewriter was so quick that we didn't dare knock on his door. His creativity seemed linked to the rhythm of typewriting, like that of many American writers. He could really think with his fingers, at the same time as he was writing.[41]

But while he could type very quickly, Derrida worked only in short sequences. After fifteen or twenty minutes, he would get up and start walking around; or he would become absorbed in a book: 'The more something interests me or demands my attention, the more quickly I interrupt my work.'[42] His relation with his body was crucial and the positions in which he worked were in his view far from trivial matters.

> I sometimes write lying down, taking notes when I wake up, after a dream. [. . .] When I write sitting down, I'm managing thoughts, ideas, movements of thought that always come to me when I'm standing up, doing something else, walking, driving, running. When I used to go running (I've stopped now), that was then the most organizing things, ideas, would come to me. I've sometimes gone running with a piece of paper in my pocket to make notes. Then, when I sat down in front of my table [. . .], I was managing, making use of furtive, cursive things, sometimes flashes of inspiration, that always came to me when I was running. I very quickly became aware of this: it was when I was on my feet that good things could come to me.[43]

The best account of his creative process is probably to be found in an encounter with Patrick Mauriès, for a long article in *Libération*:

> When I start to write a text, it's always what I'd call the *tone* that gives me the most trouble. I generally find the tones that occur to me insupportable. The difficulty of writing is always a matter of the pose – the question 'where am I going to place myself?' This isn't something that you can decide all by yourself:

you have to be discovered by the addressee for the tone to be placed. That's basically what the work involves: what addressee am I going to set up for a particular tone to be required of me, and for me to base my work on that request? What is requested of me? Who is asking me for what?[44]

Derrida claimed to produce texts that were generally 'more than an article and less than a book', with the feeling that he was always writing at too great length. He worked on several things at once, 'or rather on just one', he corrected himself, 'with several projects in mind that persecute me'. Rather than writing to commission (*sur commande*), Derrida preferred to speak of occasional writing (*d'occasion*). 'I've practically never written a text without the occasion coming to me from outside; then, of course, I appropriate it – the purely spontaneous thing, "the" book that I have to write, the only one, being indefinitely postponed, put off . . . .'

In his interviews with Maurizio Ferraris, Derrida also insisted on this poetics of the occasion that he had made his own. Accepting an invitation to speak or write was 'a sort of "passive" decision':

I have never planned to write a text. Everything that I've done, even the most composite of my books, were 'occasioned' by a question. [. . .] Why write? I've always have the feeling – at once very modest and hyperbolically presumptuous – that I have nothing to say. I don't feel I have anything in me me that's interesting enough to authorize my saying, 'here's the book I planned all by myself, without anyone asking me for it.'[45]

The question of the commission (*commande*) – or rather of the demand (*demande*) – was thus fundamental to his way of working. The *responsibility* that Derrida imposed on himself was that of constantly *responding* – to the title of a conference, or to the place in which it was being held, or to the person inviting him or the circumstances of the moment. In spite of the criticism often made of him, this was anything but a rhetorical gesture. It was a way of thinking philosophy *in situ*, considering every time he spoke as a specific situation, a *here and now* that would never return and was the very thing that needed to be addressed. A conference paper by Derrida, an intervention at a meeting, was first and foremost a speech act, a performative in Austin's sense; this was a theory that he had critically debated, but it was for him 'one of the major bodies of thought or main theoretical events – undoubtedly the most fruitful – of our time'.[46] It was a matter of describing a context so as better to displace or deconstruct it, even if this meant dwelling on it at length, analysing *by what right* people had come together, even if this ran the risk of seeming never to get to *the real issue*.

Like his readings, Derrida associated his travels with the notion of work, of a mission to be accomplished. Sometimes he even felt that he was following his father's traces: 'Would I be doing the same as he, perhaps, after protesting my whole life against his enslavement? Would my lecture tours be the theatrical, respectable, sublimated version of a humiliated father?'[47] As a new Saint Paul, Derrida practised the strange profession of being a *travelling salesman of thought*. No philosopher has ever travelled more than he did. Actually, the word 'displacement' would be more suitable, since there was in him, he claimed, someone 'who never would travel, who insists on not doing it at all, who insists that he never in fact did'.[48]

> In my primitive French, 'voyage' equals work, servitude, slavery [*traite*]. And a certain shame even, the origin of social shame. The consequence of that, and what governs travel, is this: never associate it with leisure, with idleness, nor even with active tourism, with visiting, with curiosity [. . .]. I 'visit' very little when I travel, no tourism, except by pretence and by dying of boredom when I am forced into it.[49]

His bad conscience was probably forcing him to paint things blacker than they actually were. Catherine Clément remembers seeing Derrida in Japan as radiant as 'a kid filled with excitement', in spite of a more than packed programme. He loved the attention paid to him, the break from everyday rhythms, the charms of an ephemeral return to being a bachelor. Unlike sedentary and family holidays that brought back all his anxieties, travelling was the ideal remedy for depression as far as Derrida was concerned. But as so often, the reality was really rather mixed: while he was happy to set off, he was at least just as pleased to come home.

When Jean-Luc Nancy expressed surprise that Derrida had accepted some invitation that forced him to undertake a long, tiring journey, the reply was always the same: 'They're friends of mine, I can't refuse.' Friendship was the first criterion of choice. Derrida enjoyed meeting up with old friends and returning to familiar places, creating a form of habit. In New York as in Irvine, he invented rituals for himself. In Baltimore, already, what he loved was going back to the house and tomb of Edgar Allan Poe. In Prague, he never missed out on the Kafka pilgrimage. Like everything else, places were of value because of the memories they rekindled. The ones that attracted him most were places already laden with memories.

Trips to Italy occupied a particular place. This was, he wrote in *Counterpath*, the only place to which he would like to 'eternally return'. It was one of the few countries where he had 'sometimes visited without any public or academic "pretext", with "just" friends of the heart and the head.'[50] The south partly replaced an Algeria that was now inaccessible. Derrida loved Naples and Pompeii, Capri, Paestum, and Sicily. Maurizio Ferraris says that one day, in Rende, he said he was thrilled to be in Calabria, because in Algeria he'd often heard about the brigands in Calabria: 'After dinner, we went out for a stroll and Jacques told me how much he'd loved stories about the mafia, ever since he'd been a boy. At that very moment. the music from *The Godfather* wafted out from a nearby house . . . .'[51] North Italy was linked to his friends Valerio and Camilla Adami, with whom he enjoyed a few days' holiday with Marguerite, in Arona in the first years, then in Meina, on the edge of Lake Maggiore. He enjoyed taking part in a summer seminar here. For him this was a real dream, an ideal happiness: 'two or three days in the sun in an amphitheatre overlooking the lake, speaking about something like the origin of the work of art in front of Italian students and artists'.[52]

Travelling was not always such a simple matter. For five years, anxiety had stopped Derrida boarding a plane. He had needed to make a real effort to travel again by plane, but gradually he had started to enjoy it, especially since his status meant that he was invited to travel business or first class. Those long hours of travel were for him a privileged time when, without any risk of being disturbed, he could work intensely, as if in suspended animation, outside of time. But his anxiety had not evaporated; it was merely more diffuse: 'I never go away on a trip [. . .] I never put any distance whatsoever between me and my "house" without thinking – with images, films, drama and full orchestral soundtrack – that I am going to die before I return.'[53]

Derrida's anxiety was also for his family, as if his absence placed them in danger. No sooner had he arrived anywhere than he phoned home to reassure himself. 'As soon as I enter a hotel room, even before looking at its walls (sometimes I don't even see them for several days), I worry about the phone, the local number of the MCI or ATT, and I phone.'[54] He had already done so when he was at Yale, and Paul de Man and J. Hillis Miller came to pick him up at Kennedy Airport: as soon as he had picked up his suitcase, he rushed off to phone. He may have made 'the event', the '*arrivance*', into one of his main themes, but he was forever pleading for '*nothing to happen*', as if nothing could happen without it being something bad.[55]

Derrida had few leisure activities. Playing football, one of the great passions of his youth, had not survived his move from Algeria. He had stopped playing after Koléa and watched football matches on television only occasionally. At the beginning of the sixties, he played tennis regularly: the first image that Sollers kept of Derrida was that of a racket in the back seat of a 2 CV. During the 1980s, he went jogging, something he had picked up during his stays in California, but when he found that the pleasure promised was a little slow in coming, he eventually stopped. He had never liked walking and now avoided it more and more. Only swimming continued to be a real source of enjoyment, but only at the seaside.

Since the period when Michel Monory had dragged him off to the theatre, he tended to find plays boring, Shakespeare apart. Of course, he closely followed the plays of his friends, those written by Hélène Cixous or put on by Daniel Mesguisch, the theatre performances in which Jean-Luc Nancy and Philippe Lacoue-Labarthe played a part. But this was more out of friendship than any real interest.

Cinema was much more important. During Derrida's childhood in Algiers and his student years in the Latin Quarter, he saw a great many films. In Ris-Orangis, things were more complicated. So he mainly went to the cinema when he was in the United States. Unlike Deleuze, who wrote two major works on the subject, there was nothing of the 'cinephile' about Derrida. What he sought from cinema first and foremost was a way of freeing himself from taboos and forgetting his work. In an interesting interview with *Les Cahiers du cinéma*, he extolled this dimension of a 'culture that leaves no traces':

> It's an art that is still popular [. . .]. It's even the only great popular art. [. . .] We really need to let it stay that way. [. . .] When I'm in New York or California, I see a countless number of American films, anything that's on and the films that people are talking about – I'm very good at keeping up. It's a time when I'm free and able to rediscover this popular relation with cinema that is essential to me. [. . .] It's a gift of my youth, and I'm extremely grateful to cinema for bringing me this, getting me out of my professorial role. Cinema remains for me a great hidden enjoyment, secret, avid, greedy, and thus infantile.[56]

He had only a moderate liking for Woody Allen, too European for his tastes. What he really liked were, firstly, films about Mafiosi and what in his view constituted pure American cinema. He never tired of the *Godfather* trilogy, or Sergio Leone's *Once Upon a Time in America* and Cimino's *Heaven's Gate*. 'In cinema I like there to be an intelligence that isn't that of knowledge, or intellectual in quality, but of the way it's directed.'[57] *Le Grand Pardon* by Alexandre Arcady, a family saga set in the world of gang leaders in the Jewish *pied-noir* milieu, was also a favourite. He was quite open about these tastes: asked one day about any influence that the films of Godard might have had on his work or his imagination, Derrida replied with a sincerity that he himself described as brutal, that there had not been the 'slightest influence'.[58] This did not stop him enjoying acting in Ken McMullen's *Ghost Dance*, a rather avant-garde film – admittedly, he was playing himself, alongside Pascale Ogier.

Though, in the interview in *El País*, he had claimed that he dreamed of having 'musical genius', he took little interest in music, apart from the Arabo-Andalusian music of his childhood. He liked jazz, like a lot of people of his generation, and sometimes took the opportunity of a stay in New York to attend a concert. But though he had sometimes met Pierre Boulez at Paule Thévenin's, he showed no liking for contemporary music. Thanks to Pierre Burger, a philosopher before he became a musician, and especially to his own son Pierre, Derrida liked the Strasbourg rock group Kat Onoma and went to hear them several times.

Although he had enjoyed going to museums since his youth, Derrida was unsure of his aesthetic tastes whenever areas outside his sphere of work were concerned. Without false modesty, he admitted to his lack of competence. And when he was asked about the visual arts, he insisted: 'I've never taken the initiative in talking about anything at all to do with those fields. Every time I do so, it's because I have been asked.'[59]

Responding was the very essence of Derrida's work, but it was also what drove his relationships with his friends. Until the beginning of the 1980s, he was an extraordinary correspondent, writing long, detailed letters that, together with his books and seminars, form, so to speak, the third component of his oeuvre.

Derrida was literally overwhelmed by friends from every period, relationships that he tried to keep up to the best of his abilities, in a very generous and individualized way. As Bernard Stiegler says, 'he had an unrivalled capacity for attention, an unbelievable availability for everything and everyone. It was like a demand on himself, to live his thinking to the full.'[60] But in the course of his travels, his classes, and his lectures across the world, Derrida had built up a huge social network which he found it increasingly difficult to cope with. From the middle of the 1980s, he became unable to respond to the requests that assailed him on all sides. Letters and messages came to him from throughout the world: acquaintances from the present and the past, colleagues, students, publishers, translators, journalists. He was asked to give lectures, attend conferences, write articles, provide references, sign petitions . . . But he had neither an assistant nor a secretary; he could no longer manage. His correspondence became more functional, and complaint became a leitmotif – which annoyed some of his close friends. Marie-Claire Boons, to whom he was close in the 1960s, continued to write him long letters full of private details, but could not conceal her frustration: 'You seem inaccessible to me. You don't write to me, you don't reply to me. I'm tired of never knowing how you are reacting to my letters, your own difficulties, your efforts, your hopes.'[61] And when Derrida did reply, it was now briefly, which came as rather a disappointment given the expectations he had aroused.

In 1988, in a letter to his old friend Pierre Foucher, he confessed to a 'serious *epistolarophobia*, a real malady of body and soul' which made it increasingly impossible for him to reply to the letters that were building up, especially when he was travelling.[62] For friends, he now preferred to use the phone. And where he had once sent such eloquent letters in reply to the books people had sent him, he no longer felt up to it. In spite of this difficulty, he never failed to write letters of recommendation when asked by friends or colleagues whom he esteemed. There are dozens of these in his correspondence, beautifully composed and effective. Many of his friends owed part of their careers to his generosity.

Derrida was a wholehearted friend. Whether they were famous like de Man, Althusser, and Nancy, or more obscure, Derrida was absolutely loyal to those he loved. But he was very demanding in return, sometimes too much so. As Stiegler puts it, this was 'the flip-side of his generosity as a friend'. Then he could develop a certain paranoia, and his closest friends could one day find themselves suspected of disloyalty or, even worse, treachery. According to Michel Deguy, 'Jacques was extremely sensitive. He could tolerate only those who accepted his genius without demur.' When a public conflict broke out, he required unstinting solidarity. So, during the de Man affair, he distanced himself from several friends and colleagues because their analysis of the situation differed from his own. For quite different reasons, he stopped seeing Maria Torok, shortly after the death of Nicolas Abraham. Indeed, several of his friends lived in muted fear of a sudden quarrel, and worried that they might find themselves consigned to the side of his 'enemies', those who were 'against him'.

The other side of this harshness was a tendency to complaisance. Alexander García Düttmann acknowledges that he was on more than one occasion irritated by the 'cliquishness' around Derrida. 'It annoyed me that Derrida treated with such consideration people who had little more than their loyalty in their favour. But he wanted to be loved at all costs, even more than to be understood.'[63] Derrida sometimes suffered from the mimicry that he inspired, but in many respects he accepted it and encouraged it. 'I think he was sincerely convinced that most of those who flattered him were people of high calibre,' says Avital Ronell. 'He probably found in his disciples a sort of mirror that reassured him. The problem is that, by dint of his telling them repeatedly that they were extraordinary, many of them started to think they were, and became really insupportable.'[64]

Perhaps he did not wish to see their mediocrity. He was probably not unaware of the services they could render him.

For a long time, in Derrida's public remarks, Algeria and Jewishness went unmentioned. The more the years passed, the more he assumed his origins and gave them a place in his thought and writings. But as with many other things, there was a persistent ambivalence in his attitudes. For example, most of the time he felt he had largely 'effaced and overcome' the *pied-noir* accent he had had in his childhood and teens. But when he heard recordings of himself, he could recognize certain aspects in his elocution: 'I think it isn't violent, it isn't very marked, but it is marked. In the closure of the "e"s, in a certain delivery, in a certain rapidity of elocution, with the mouth a bit closed . . . I don't feel very at ease with this accent.'[65] It was at moments of great emotion or anger that the intonations of Algiers resurfaced, and he found this difficult to deal with: 'My voice, its *authoritarian* aspect, on the one hand, and its accent of *origin*, on the other, which, combined, are what I can't stand and find it even harder to put up with since the effort to keep them under control always, to some extent, fails.'[66]

Derrida's relations with his family were very ambivalent. Once he was Jackie again, he was confronted with his past, and his own resistances. If he was sometimes annoyed and almost ashamed, if he was disappointed that they did not try to read his work and that real topics of conversation were so rare, he was extraordinarily attached to them. But when he discovered that his mother 'had kept almost none, just a few at most' of the cards and letters that he had written to her 'over nearly thirty years, twice a week',[67] he was deeply hurt. This did not stop him returning every year, on the anniversary of his father's death, as if to gather the clan together again. And, every summer, Marguerite and he spent several weeks at Villefranche-sur-Mer, just next to Nice, spending whole days on the same little stretch of beach, as he had done in the old days on the beaches of Algiers. His cousin Micheline Lévy says that he stayed in the midst of the family group and hated anyone to move away even just a little. He wanted to keep his family around him, even if he was silent and absorbed in his reading most of the time.[68]

Whether at Les Rassats or on the Côte d'Azur, holidays were highly ritualized affairs and Derrida's main requirement was that he could work intensely. At Villefranche, they initially stayed in the Hôtel Versailles, but Jacques, who found it too noisy, very soon decided he preferred La Flore, which was also on the hills above the village.[69] It was one of the most beautiful spots in the world, he often told his brother and sister. As was his habit, he rose at 6 a.m. and started work after a first cup of coffee. In the afternoon, he would go for long swims. 'He always said "I feel alive again",' remembers his brother René. Derrida, inclined to vanity, was happy to acquire a suntan and to have a more active physical existence, something that he had to repress in everyday life. He enjoyed the sun and the sea, which he missed in Paris, and which played a part in his love of California. Irrespective of his social life, Derrida was also glad to meet up with old friends and return to places that he loved, such as the Musée Matisse and the Fondation Maeght. Every year, he went back to Èze to carry out a symbolic act: sending a postcard to Blanchot, who had lived there for a long time.

Derrida never rid himself of some of the rather archaic aspects of his family inheritance. As his mother had been a compulsive poker player, she had performed many little rituals so as not to incur bad luck. According to Peggy Kamuf, even though he made fun of himself for it, Derrida remained very superstitious. He would fabricate little secret rites, and carry out all sorts of calculations that tormented him but that meant he would not infringe certain rules. His mother had hated green, and for him this colour was always associated with misfortune. He carefully avoided all clothes in that colour and did not like Marguerite wearing it. This superstition could become an obsession and take a serious turn. Robert Harvey claims that one day, in New York, Derrida held up a conference so that he did not have to sit on a chair covered in green. And this phobia was far from being the only one:

> A family superstition that I still respect today: when leaving, once the threshold has been crossed, never retrace one's steps back inside. It gives rise to comic situations I don't dare describe. Especially when, before a long voyage, mother or sister or wife has already thrown water at you on the doorstep to mark the moment when, having left, only then must you turn around and say goodbye. One returns alive only on that condition.[70]

These were not mere traditions. These beliefs were directly linked to his anxiety. One day when Marguerite retraced her steps to get something she had left inside the house, Derrida asked her: 'What are you doing that for? Do you want me to be anxious all day?' But even though he sometimes felt a vague sense of guilt about this heritage, he tried to turn it into an object of thought, and the theme of spectrality assumed an ever great place in his work. After all, Freud himself had taken an intense interest in these questions, especially in his relations with Ferenczi. In his text 'Telepathy', Derrida examined this sometimes derided interest with curiosity and sympathy. [71]

Derrida, the man of 'too much', was at least as much the man of too little. His solitude was immense, profound. Avital Ronell remembers that he could seem terribly absent, especially at certain meals: 'There were terrible barriers around him. He didn't really seek to establish a relationship in which the other could really confront him. When I initiated something intrusive, he would accept this, but he himself would never have started to place things on such a footing himself.'[72] The dazzling, generous lecturer, the man full of solicitude for his friends and family, managed all his life long to create an almost infallible system to protect his privacy. For a long time already, even apart from his periods of depression, there had been something fragile and secret within him, something that could be expressed only in writing – something essential and impossible, inseparable from the way he viewed philosophy: a demanding, risky path, far from the facilities of dialogue. He acknowledged this one day:

> The philosopher is someone whose desire and ambition are absolutely mad; the desire for power of the greatest politicians is absolutely miniscule and juvenile compared to the desire of the philosopher who, in a philosophical work, manifests both a design on mastery and a renunciation of mastery on a scale and to a degree that I find infinitely more powerful than can be found elsewhere [. . .]. There is an adventure of power and unpower, a play of potence and impotence, a *size* of desire that seems to me, with the philosophers, much more impressive than elsewhere. It is out of all proportion with other types of discourse, and sometimes even with all the rules of art.[73]

5

At the Frontiers of the Institution

1991–1992

At the beginning of 1991, Seuil published in its series 'Les Contemporains' the book *Jacques Derrida*, by Derrida and Geoffrey Bennington. This would long remain the best introduction to Derrida's work. Derrida's contribution to the book did not consist merely in 'Circumfession'. He was also the main author of the part called 'The law of the genre', which, for many years, would constitute the most complete chronology, together with several photos. 'Even if I signed the biographical parts,' explains Bennington, 'he actually wrote most of it. Denis Roche insisted on their being factual elements, but neither Derrida nor I wanted anything resembling a traditional biography. The ellipses are his. I worked on the basis of the material that he was prepared to give me.'[1] While there are several remarks about Derrida's private life, his family, childhood, and youth, including the 'serious depressive episode' in Le Mans, the chronology becomes purely factual once he starts publishing: 'I have selected only the public "deeds", i.e. overexposed ones, or, as they say, "objectively verifiable" on the basis of accessible documents. Everyone knows that these are not always the most significant, the most interesting, or the most determining.' Most of these biographical markers, Bennington emphasizes, were communicated to him 'by J.D. in a rather discontinuous or aleatory way [. . .] with an enthusiasm that was, let's say, uneven.'[2]

On publication, the book earned Derrida emotional letters from several friends of his youth. Continuing to call him 'Jackie', 'so as to go against the current of the official "Jacques"', Jean Bellemin-Noël told him he had read his text with 'tears of intellectual emotion'. 'Circumfession' had made him remember a 'certain form of presence' of Jackie in his life, 'preserved, as if outside of time'. 'I was really very moved by all that. Surprised: attacked, but from on high; and obliged, to keep a brave face on things, to look up.'[3] Other companions of Derrida's younger years, such as Robert Abirached and Pierre Foucher, felt the same thing.

The reviews were very positive, and also insisted on the contribution Derrida had made. In *Le Nouvel Observateur*, Didier Eribon hailed 'Circumfession'. 'With this dazzling narration, in which an impossible biography struggles with the *Bildungsroman* for dominance, the philosopher (the writer?) has given us one of his most magnificently successful performances.'[4] Marc Ragon in *Libération* and Claude Jannoud in *Le Figaro* were equally captivated. Roger-Pol Droit, who reviewed the book belatedly for *Le Monde*, was much more perplexed: in his view, 'Circumfession' was a 'very strange text, almost intolerable with its mixture of shamelessness and cunning, but also its crude and risky simplicity. [. . .] A useful volume for all sorts of readers, this book may also arouse a certain unease, in which it is probably difficult to distinguish between artifice and authenticity, irritation and emotion.'[5]

The drama of 'Circumfession', one of Derrida's most original and accessible texts, is directly linked to the context in which it was conceived. Dialoguing with Geoffrey Bennington's rigorous analysis so as better to deconstruct it, Derrida's text remains quite inseparable from it. Confined to the lower third of the page, on a rather gloomy grey background, it looks like a huge footnote, at first glance quite unalluring, whereas it would – more than other pieces – have merited existence as a work in its own right. We are far from the typographical prowesses of *Glas*, far from the big book on circumcision of which Derrida had dreamed for many years. Of course, the book was designed to look just like this. All the same: Derrida's work here reaches one of its limits, and it alienated many of 'Circumfession''s potential readers. Hélène Cixous, who attaches particular importance to this text and has often worked on it with her students, provides them with enlarged photocopies, without the grey background. In *Portrait of Jacques Derrida as a Young Jewish Saint*, she reproduces a few pages of 'Circumfession' in a large format, scattered with coloured letters and words, thereby doing justice to the beauty of Derrida's text. This beauty is also brought out in the audio version recorded by Derrida for Éditions des Femmes in 1993.[6]

At the same time as Seuil's *Jacques Derrida*, a small work of a completely different kind was published by Minuit: *The Other Heading*. This was the text of a lecture given in Turin, the previous year, at a conference on 'European Cultural Identity' chaired by Giovanni Vattimo. In this important political intervention, Derrida mainly developed the idea that what was 'proper' to a culture was that it was not identical to itself: 'Not to not have an identity, but not to be able to identify itself, to be able to say "me" or "we"; to be able to take the form of a subject only in the non-identity to itself or, if you prefer, only in the difference *with itself* [*avec soi*].'[7] At a time when nationalism was rearing its head again, often in bloody fashion, in the former Yugoslavia as in the ex-USSR, Derrida reflected on the frontiers of Europe. The definition it had constantly sought to give itself, for instance in Husserl and Paul Valéry, was surely a negative form, first and foremost, resting on the exclusion of its other? Derrida was far from identifying completely with that Europe.

I am European, I am no doubt a European intellectual, and I like to recall this, I like to recall this to myself, and why would I deny it? In the name of what? But I am not, nor do I feel, European *in every part*, that is, European through and through. By which I mean, by which I wish to say, or *must* say: I do not want to be and must not be European through and through, European *in every part*. Being a part, belonging as 'fully a part,' should be incompatible with belonging 'in every part'. My cultural identity, that in the name of which I speak, is not only European, it is not identical to itself, and I am not 'cultural' through and through, 'cultural' in every part.[8]

The beginning of 1991 marked a new stage in the reception of Derrida's work, at least in France. In March, *Le Magazine littéraire* devoted a long series of articles to him, presenting him in somewhat uncertain terms: 'A singular character, Derrida has become famous. His name circulates across five continents. He allures and dismays in equal measure. Derrida is the name of an enigma. It was time to provide a key.'[9] The issue also contained a major interview with François Ewald as well as various articles and studies, but the main innovation was probably the photographic reportage by Carlos Freire. By publishing personal photos in the book published by Seuil, Derrida had opened up a breach. The Brazilian photographer showed him at home, in his office, in his attic; we can see his collection of pipes, his little Citroën; we meet him in a café on the boulevard Raspail, just before his seminar at the École de Hautes Études, in the lecture hall with students, then in a salon of the Hôtel Lutétia. In spite of all his friendliness towards the photographer, Derrida lent himself to the image rather than abandoning himself to it. 'He had a slightly hunched way of posing, like a boxer,' remembers Carlos Freire.[10]

This change of attitude irritated some of those who, like Bernard Pautrat, had seen Derrida refusing to have his photo published throughout the 1960s and 1970s:

I'd greatly appreciated his 'anti-media' line. He didn't give interviews, he didn't let people take his photo. I was taken aback when I saw the book he'd done with Bennington, then the first issue of *Le Magazine littéraire* that was devoted to his work. There were photos everywhere, including private or purely anecdotal images. I have to confess that I was disappointed.[11]

In many respects, it can be said that Derrida's career as a teacher was to invent an audience that would suit him, listeners who would come to hear him and to whom he could talk the way he wanted, irrespective of any syllabus and any of the constraints imposed by exams. At the Sorbonne, he was already a bit freer than at the *lycée* in Le Mans. At the École des Hautes Études, he was much freer than at Normale Sup. Over the years, he increasingly gave himself permission to enjoy this situation to the full, without needing any alibis.

Derrida gave his seminars on Wednesdays, between 5 p.m. and 7 p.m., the timetable that he had had at the École Normale. He arrived with an old satchel full of books and folders, and he arranged the sheets of paper and the volumes he would need with meticulous care in front of him. In fact, he continued to write his discourse from the first word to the last, before 'vocalizing' it in the lecture hall, as he improvised.

He had the gift of capturing his audience's attention immediately, in a way sometimes reminiscent of Lacan:

This will be, as usual, as will have been, inevitably, as all my seminars should have been, a short treatise on love. And please do not think that in announcing that I am going to speak to you about love, I am yielding to any demagogy. Given the way I will without delay be speaking of it, I fear that it's more likely that those who have come for a serenade will make a quick exit rather than stay on.[12]

One difficulty, of which he was fully aware, was that he needed simultaneously to address the faithful, probably the majority of his listeners, while also giving those who were coming for the first time a way in. For every 'prologue' was also an 'epilogue', and every new seminar continued where the previous one had left off:

As is the case every year, I have to do the impossible: begin again. Continue to begin, repeat what was said and repeat the new departure. Take up the thread of a seminar where it was broken off, and that is always too soon, to carry on, to what still needs to be done, and it is always too much, the *rest* of the rest still to be done. But at the same time as I begin again, I have to begin for those among you who weren't there last year, or the previous years, since it is in fact the same seminar that has been moving slowly and continuously along for at least six years, with the changes of title ('Nationality and philosophical nationalism', 'Kant, the Jew, the German', 'Politics of friendship', 'Loving-eating-the other', etc.) being mere metonyms for the same preoccupation, the same *focus* for questions in which things have not yet been brought to completion.[13]

Yves Charnet, only just twenty when he first came to hear Derrida, has described to perfection the way he was dazzled:

That voice gently started to weave its spell – on each of the fervent women and each of the captivated men listening –, a spell that would remain, for me, as it were, the signature tune of that shaman of thought. Jacques Derrida would never cease to turn, for the two hours that each memorable session lasted, to turn around his thought. And yes, to make thought turn. American men and women, Japanese men and women, German men and women, young people from all over the globalized world composed that impressive and enthralled audience. [. . .] I must insist on the element of personal beauty, of individual splendour, which [. . .] contributed to the lightning-bolt effect of those words whose poetic energy pierced us. That way of centring the pedagogic space on a body – a body involved in the act of teaching to such an extent that pupils had the physical impression of living through a passion of the word.[14]

Over the years, Derrida's discourse had freed itself from all academic rhetoric. Indeed, he would often treat the philosophical tradition in a zigzag way, indulging in several digressions. In 'Answering the secret', in 1991–2, he focused especially on *Bartleby the Scrivener*, by Herman Melville, but he also referred to 'The figure in the carpet' by Henry James, *Raymond Roussel* by Michel Foucault, *Clé* by Annie Leclerc, the *Metamorphoses* of Ovid, the Book of Job, and the Gospel According to Saint Matthew – not to mention Freud, Heidegger, and Patočka. The two following years were devoted to bearing witness, and Derrida took in works by Kierkegaard, Proust, Celan, Blanchot, and Lyotard, with more unexpected excurses into Hugo, Hemingway, Antonioni's *Blow-Up*, Claude Lanzmann's *Shoah*, and the trial of Rodney King in Los Angeles.

The seminar was his laboratory, an opportunity for him to prepare and test out his new ideas. He began to explore paths that he would follow in his books or his major lectures. But the seminar was also a privileged moment, in which his words could be free, fulfilled, sovereign. Françoise Dastur puts it very well: 'Throughout the years when I followed his seminar, between 1987 and 1994, I also watched as something rare took place: a set of ideas coming into being, and doing so, as it were, without any safety net.'[15] And Avital Ronell confirmed the importance of these moments:

> Even if he devoted himself to it entirely, the seminar cor-
> responded to a kind of quietude. All his obligations were in
> abeyance. For two or three hours, he had the floor, and he
> could speak as he wished. He showed an almost childish pride
> in never stopping for a drink of water. And he refused to envis-
> age any kind of break, which irritated me a bit. But he would
> never have tolerated some people attending only the first part,
> or arriving only at the start of the second.[16]

Though Derrida felt comfortable at the École des Hautes Études, he still dreamed of a place at the most prestigious of French academic institutions: the Collège de France. Bergson, Valéry, Merleau-Ponty, Lévi-Strauss, Foucault, Barthes, and many others had taught there. It was the place for 'consecrated heretics', as Bourdieu called it once – he himself had been professor there since 1982. In spite of his up-and-down relations with him, the author of *Distinction* would have liked to ensure that Derrida was elected to the Collège de France. But when he initially floated the idea in the spring of 1990, at in informal meeting, he encountered stiff opposi-tion. In search of allies, Bourdieu turned to Yves Bonnefoy, who held the chair of poetics.

Bonnefoy and Derrida had known each other since at least 1968; they had both been friends of Paul de Man, whom they felt was scandalously little known in France. After pondering the matter, Bonnefoy decided that the chances of success were high:

> You have a few enemies in the place, but not so many, and it
> would all depend on our scientists. Bourdieu himself aroused
> some suspicions, as he knows, but less than he might believe.
> So for my part I have high hopes, and I've told our friend that I
> was ready to introduce you if he felt it was desirable. This could
> reassure some of our colleagues.[17]

Derrida was very touched by this support. He feared that his can-didacy might involve Yves Bonnefoy in many difficulties, but he was happy that the plan did not seem too desperate a venture. During the autumn of 1990, preliminary negotiations were cautiously pursued. Bonnefoy had made overtures to André Miquel, who was apparently the best placed to weigh up the votes for and against Derrida. If the result was favourable, Derrida could embark on drawing up an official application. Bonnefoy confirmed that he was ready to commit himself 'completely (and happily)' to defending his candidacy, though this would involve a somewhat convoluted strategy:

> Rather than presenting you in terms of pure quality, I feel it will be useful for me to set out my position in terms of the big choices that are worrying certain of my colleagues: showing that you are the antagonist they need to develop their own thinking, in a situation of dialogue that one needs to realize is the innermost vocation of the Collège.[18]

In January 1991, Bourdieu and Bonnefoy felt that the situation had become more favourable. Derrida needed to prepare his 'statement of qualifications and published work' over the summer so that his candidacy could go forward in November.[19] Unfortunately, the 'grand project' failed. Sensing the difficulties, Bourdieu suggested to his colleagues that they admit Derrida and Bouveresse at the same time: surely it would be a good idea to welcome to the Collège de France these two very different currents of contemporary philosophy? Only recently, after all, both Michel Foucault and Jules Vuillemin had been professors there. His efforts were in vain: while Bouveresse's candidacy succeeded without much difficulty, Derrida's then encountered such opposition that it was impossible to present him officially. According to Didier Eribon, 'It left Bourdieu feeling very bitter. He was actually pretty furious about this debacle ("I really let them walk all over me like a bloody fool," he kept telling me at that time). And he was saddened and dismayed that he hadn't managed to get Derrida elected.'[20]

Needless to say, Derrida was even more disappointed: he was cross with Bourdieu for luring him into this sticky situation, which brought back unhappy memories of Nanterre. This time, he finally realized that he could expect nothing from the French university system.

While this failure caused few ripples, another controversy hit the headlines soon afterwards. In March 1992, the announcement that Derrida was to receive an honorary doctorate from the University of Cambridge provoked an outcry. There had not been such a spectacular academic showdown since Margaret Thatcher had been refused an honorary doctorate by the rival university, Oxford, in 1985. The polemic was soon being splashed across the media.

On Saturday 9 May 1992, an open letter was published in *The Times*, under the heading 'A question of honour'. It was signed by a score of philosophers from various countries, including one of the major figures of American analytic philosophy, Willard Quine. Derrida's eternal enemy, Ruth Marcus, naturally played an active part in this campaign. But the signatories also included the famous mathematician René Thom. According to their letter – which cannot fail to evoke the novels of David Lodge – Derrida's 'nihilist' work posed formidable dangers. Its main effect was 'to stretch the normal form of academic scholarship beyond recognition':

> M. Derrida seems to have come clos[e] to making a career out of what we regard as translating into the academic sphere tricks and gimmicks similar to those of the Dadaists or of the concrete poets. Certainly he has shown considerable originality in this respect. But [. . .], we submit, such originality does not lend credence to the idea that he is a suitable candidate for an honorary degree.[21]

Over the following few weeks, the polemic was widely publicized, in Britain and elsewhere. In order to stigmatize Derrida's style and thought, a perfectly imaginary formula ('logical phalluses') was attributed to him. Howard Erskine-Hill, a professor of English literature, was one of the most virulent detractors of the author of *Glas*. In his view, Derrida's methods were so incompatible with the very concept of higher education and knowledge in general that to give him an honorary doctorate would be like appointing a pyromaniac to the post of chief fireman.[22] A university lecturer, Sarah Richmond, suggested in the German weekly *Der Spiegel* that Derrida's ideas could be poison for young people – a nicely ironic allusion to the charge laid against Socrates twenty-five centuries earlier. Meanwhile, *The Observer* described Derrida's work as a 'computer virus'. Everything was roped in to attack the French philosopher: in certain articles, it was even said that he had been arrested in Prague for 'drug trafficking', without any mention of the fact that it had been a set-up job.

On 16 May, Cambridge lecturers were asked to vote for or against Derrida's honorary doctorate: 'placet' or 'non placet'. It was the first time that such a vote had been called for thirty years. The opponents were obliged to admit they were beaten: the 'yes' vote won, 336 to 204. On 12 June 1992, in the neo-classical décor of the Senate House in the venerable shade of King's College, Jacques Derrida, in full academic fig, received his honorary degree from the hands of Prince Philip, Chancellor of the University. As the British monarchy was going through a rather rough patch that year, the Prince Consort murmured to Derrida that deconstruction had started to affect the Royal Family too.[23]

In October, *The Cambridge Review* devoted a detailed special issue to the affair, followed by a long interview with Derrida. He explained that he had deliberately held back from any intervention in the media before the story had come to a conclusion. But when he received other honorary doctorates, he did not fail to mention the 'war, both serious and comic', that had taken place in Cambridge. 'An event of that sort [. . .] gave me a sharper awareness of the fact that honorary degrees are sometimes more than purely conventional rituals.'[24]

Perhaps it was in response to the controversy across the Channel, or to try to draw a line under the lack of recognition that the French university system had shown him, but, on 14 July 1992, Derrida was made a *chevalier de la Légion d'Honneur*, following a proposal by the minister Jack Lang. The decoration was handed over to him at the Sorbonne by a close friend, Michèle Gendreau-Massaloux, who was then rector. The speech Derrida made that day, hitherto unpublished, goes beyond the usual protocols:

> Forgive me if I am still wondering: have I deserved it? [. . .]
> A malicious tradition, to which I may on occasion have granted a little credence, insistently insinuates that it is not enough to turn down the Légion d'Honneur. One needs, they say, not to have deserved it. This is to fail to register the irony inherent in every institution. [. . .]
> I think that I will have spent my life, especially in its academic aspects, which fortunately were not the whole story, wrestling with the laws and subterfuges of this institutional irony.[25]

The philosopher then pursued his meditation on the state, on honour, and on his own relation to institutions, especially those of academia. He described, with as much sincerity as the circumstances would allow, his constant ambivalence:

> Whether it was a matter of writing or thought, of teaching or research, of public life or private life, while I have never had anything against institutions, I have always liked counter-institutions, whether those of the state or those which were indeed not of the state or against the state. I also believe that one does not wage war on institutions except in their name, as if to pay them homage and in betraying, in every sense of the term [i.e. also making manifest] the love one bears them. [. . .] The irony is that the institution par excellence, the state, convinced that there is no absolute exteriority which can make any objection or form any opposition to it, always ends up recognizing counter-institutions and this is the moment when, ratified, chosen or confirmed, they turn back into order and legion.[26]

Cerisy was one of those parallel institutions of which Derrida was fond. From 11 to 21 July, a second *décade* was held on his work, called 'Le Passage des Frontières' ('Crossing Borders'). Two years before, when agreeing to the basic idea behind this conference, Derrida had expressed the wish that it should be dominated by the idea of renewal:

> Of course, the 1992 *décade* would be open to all those who took part in the 1980 one who wished to return to join in the discussions and refer to the memory of the previous conference. This would be a great boon in many ways. But should not a rule be imposed that *everything else be new*? I mainly have in mind the principal organizers and coordinators, then the general and less general themes, those responsible for the introductory presentations, etc. I am sure that one can (and so, in my view, one must) invite new French and foreign participants, mainly young people, in different fields or on other themes.[27]

Initially, the project was entrusted to a collective that included René Major, Charles Alluni, and Catherine Paoletti. But in actual fact, the heavy burden of getting the conference off the ground was taken on by Marie-Louise Mallet, whose 'smiling efficiency' worked miracles.[28] The programme was exceptionally rich: the mornings were filled by three simultaneous seminars – philosophy, literature, and politics – between which it was often difficult to choose; in the afternoons, there were two lectures; and even the evenings were mainly taken up with work. Even if this packed programme turned out to be a bit too much, the hundred and twenty participants would take away memories of a friendly and enthusiastic ambiance. It was a privilege to be invited: the chateau was filled to the rafters, and many people had not been able to get their proposals accepted. Derrida, in demand from all sides, demonstrated an extraordinary ability to listen and respond. As Geoffrey Bennington recalls: 'He paid close attention to all the papers and then managed to find the right thread to tug so as to find the interest in something that wasn't necessarily all that thrilling. He had the gift of responding in a generous and inventive way to banal questions and simplistic objections.'[29]

Derrida's own paper, given on 15 July, his sixty-second birthday, was called 'Aporias'. For many years 'this tired word' had 'often imposed itself' upon him, and recently it had 'done so even more often'.[30] An aporia is a way of 'thinking "the possibility of impossibility"': rejecting any binary logic, Derrida increasingly sets contradiction at the very heart of the object he is trying to think through. This was a principle to which he would constantly return, via themes such as pardon, hospitality, or auto-immunity. But the 1992 lecture focused mainly on the supreme frontier, the aporia of aporias: death. 'Is my death possible?' wondered Derrida, scrutinizing texts by Diderot, Seneca, and especially Heidegger, but also historians and anthropologists such as Philippe Ariès and Louis-Vincent Thomas.

For Derrida and most of the guests at Cerisy, these ten days were an 'incredible success', as well as an 'unprecedented festivity'. This made his return to everyday life all the more difficult, as he told Catherine Malabou: 'Nothing better [than this conference] could have happened to me, but, ipso facto, with a taste of love and death, and, more intense than ever, the spectrality that attends all my joys and enjoyments.'[31] Since his return home, he had suffered from the after-effects; and while he had settled back to work without a break, it was neither out of inclination or compulsion, but merely because he had promises to keep . . .

6

Of Deconstruction in America

The vogue for deconstruction may have peaked in the mid-eighties, just before the de Man affair, but interest in Derrida's work and person in the United States was still considerable at the start of the 1990s. The West Coast was just as enthralled by him as the East; however, the major universities of Northern California, Stanford and especially Berkeley – the fief of John R. Searle –, were still mainly hostile.

In July 1991, in the *Los Angeles Times*, Mitchell Stephens published a detailed portrait of the Irvine professor, after spending a whole day accompanying him on his various activities. Under the rather banal title 'Deconstructing Jacques Derrida', the article attempted to find a way into his work. The journalist was amazed that he could meet 'the world's most controversial living philosopher' on the terrace of a snack bar and listen to him defending his 'diabolically difficult theory'. Derrida's ideas had borne influence in the most varied fields, he explained, and everyone had been affected by them in one way or another.

> [Deconstruction] is becoming, like existentialism before it, a part of the language – to the point where a State Department official can speak of a plan for the 'deconstruction' of part of the American Embassy in Moscow, and where Mick Jagger can ask, 'Does anyone really know what deconstructivist means?' [. . .] But the main impact of Derrida's method has been felt on college campuses.[1]

On the evening of the interview, in the Hemingway restaurant in Newport Beach, Derrida started to divulge more personal details to the journalist. He, the prophet of complexity, who refused to accept hard-and-fast distinctions, confided in Mitchell Stephens that he sometimes dreamed of writing a naïve, straightforward book, a 'simple' book. Perhaps a novel, more probably an autobiographical narrative. Setting out the basis of what later became

Monolingualism of the Other, Derrida told him his life story: that of a Jewish boy from Algiers who felt neither French nor Jewish, then a penniless student endeavouring to force his way through the psychological and social barriers of the world of Parisian intellectuals.[2] 'I have the deep feeling of not having written what I would like to write and what I should have written,' said the philosopher. In one sense, everything that he had hitherto produced was, he said, a preliminary exercise for his one true project – which he feared he might never realize. 'I know it's not possible to write in an absolutely naïve fashion, but that's my dream.'[3]

A few weeks later, Derrida had the honour of appearing on the cover of the *London Review of Books*, which also provided a pen-portrait of him. This time, it was to the University of Chicago that the journalist had followed 'the great Jacques'. He was mainly struck by Derrida's physical appearance: 'Derrida is a short, compact, energetic man. [. . .] His eyes are a fine light blue, his short hair pure white. With glasses, he looks like an upper-level, not absolutely top-grade French bureaucrat, an administrator in a colonial territory [. . .]. Without glasses, he could pass for a French movie star, a mix of Jean Gabin and Alain Delon.' The journalist was impressed by the elegance and clarity of the lecture he attended, an extract from *Given Time*,[4] and admitted that he was surprised not to encounter the impenetrable and abstruse character that he associated with Derrida's writings. He was especially struck by Derrida's friendliness and kindness, and impressed to hear one of his female admirers say that he was also an excellent dancer.[5]

When he had started using the term 'deconstruction', Derrida had not in the slightest imagined that it would have such an impact – it even became, if we are to believe François Cusset, 'the most bankable product ever to emerge on the market of academic discourses'.[6] In Derrida's own eyes, it was a conceptual tool, but not in the slightest 'a master word'.[7] By 1984, he was already acknowledging this, in a somewhat negative way: 'Were I not so frequently associated with this adventure of deconstruction, I would risk, with a smile, the following hypothesis: America *is* deconstruction (l'Amérique, mais *c'est* la déconstruction). *In this hypothesis*, America would be the proper name of deconstruction in progress, its family name, its toponymy, its language and its place, its principal residence.'[8] Ten years later, the hypothesis was endorsed when it became the title of a conference at New York University: 'Deconstruction is/in America'.[9]

Jean-Joseph Goux – who had known Derrida well in France, but then lost sight of him for several years before running up against him in the United States (Goux had become professor at Rice University, Houston) – was struck by the contrast between the French Derrida and the American Derrida.

Even physically, the change was very evident. In the United States, Derrida always seemed to me more radiant and imposing. The way he had become a kind of star – which never happened in France – of course played a part in this. At the start of the 1980s, many departments had been won over by 'French Theory' and Derrida's thought. It had all started in French departments, then those of comparative literature. But architecture, aesthetics, anthropology, and law soon became receptive. The idea of deconstruction, which made it possible to create bridges between the disciplines, aroused immense enthusiasm. This was the period when 'cultural studies' really became important. Many professors demanded that their students position themselves vis-à-vis Derrida. This became a mandatory first stage, whatever the subject. These sudden crazes are a very American phenomenon . . . The only domain that remained really hostile to deconstruction was philosophy, a fact that lay behind a certain number of misunderstandings and false trails. For access to Derrida's work was often without the first-hand philosophical knowledge that was necessary. Many professors, and even more students, had no previous philosophical training and approached Plato, Kant, or Hegel through what Derrida said about them.[10]

This is also the opinion of Rodolphe Gasché, one of Derrida's first disciples, in his book *The Tain of the Mirror*.[11] In his view, Derrida's oeuvre is profoundly and self-evidently philosophical; if its literary angle is highlighted, it cannot fail to be distorted. But according to others, the main contribution of deconstruction is of a very different kind. This is the position ardently put forward by Avital Ronell in *Fighting Theory*, her book of interviews with Anne Dufourmantelle:

One can't imagine how whited-out the academic corridor was when Derrida arrived on the American scene. There was really no room for deviancy, not even for a quaint aberration or psychoanalysis. Besides offering up the luminous works that bore his signature, Derrida cleared spaces that looked like obstacle courses for anyone who did not fit the professorial profile at the time. He practiced, whether consciously or not, a politics of contamination. His political views, refined and, by our measure, distinctly leftist, knew few borders and bled into the most pastoral sites and hallowed grounds of higher learning. Suddenly color was added to the university – color and sassy women, something that would not easily be forgiven. [. . .] Derrida blew into our town-and-gown groves with protofeminist energy, often, and at great cost to the protocols of philosophical gravity, passing as a woman.[12]

This alliance with a new generation of 'supersexy, bold, bizarre women [who] showed up like surfers on the waves of "French Theory"' was, in Ronell's eyes, one of the keys to the movement's success: they found this theory was one they 'could live and breathe, whereas departments of philosophy – but not only these departments – are relatively unlivable for women and minorities'.[13] One of the first such women was Gayatri Spivak: having translated and prefaced *Of Grammatology*, she became the founding mother of postcolonial studies on minorities – black, Mexican, Asian or 'subaltern'. Her ideas – like those of Drucilla Cornell, Cythnia Chase, and Shoshana Felman – were of great importance for major theoreticians such as Eve Kosofsky Sedgwick and Judith Butler, who created gender studies and then queer studies, attempting to explore 'all the intermediary zones of sexual identity, any place where it became blurred'.[14]

Quite apart from any academic question, 'French Theory' seems first and foremost to have brought to America a hitherto unknown heterogeneity, an openness to racial and political minorities, to feminism and homosexuality, in a typically American form of appropriation. One of the most remarkable cases was indisputably the way in which Homi Bhabha took from Derrida the concept of dissemination, developed in the context of thinking about literature, and forged DissemiNation, a way of undoing the nation to deliver it over more effectively to its minorities. This was much more than a deformation: it was a real reinvention, a creative translation, perfectly Derridean in spirit.[15]

As his ideas spread, sometimes in unexpected ways, Derrida himself was a distinctly active presence on the American scene. Since he had started teaching at the École des Hautes Études, starting his seminars in November and ending at the end of March, trips abroad had been easier to organize. From the mid-1980s, he went to the United States at least twice a year: to the West Coast in spring, and the East Coast in autumn. As well as teaching in the major universities, he also took advantage of his travels to take part in conferences or give important lectures in many other cities. Even though he still had a slight accent, his mastery of English had become impressive. In discussions, he was now fully able to improvise. According to Andrzej Warminski, 'he was less confident in English than he should have been. His way of translating himself on the spot was impressive. His English became more and more idiomatic. He could have written directly in English, but he refused, since the question of language seemed so essential in his eyes.'[16]

At the University of California, Irvine, one post had been shared out between three professors: Jean-François Lyotard came in the autumn, Wolfgang Iser in the winter, and Derrida in the spring. In five packed weeks, Derrida crammed in the equivalent of ten traditional weeks: throughout the 1990s, he was paid around $30,000 per annum. Murray Krieger had had the right idea when he insisted on getting Derrida invited to Irvine. His mere presence had ensured that Irvine's department of Critical Theory had become the most famous in the whole United States, attracting students from more or less everywhere, as well as several significant personalities. These included Stephen Barker, a dancer and choreographer for ten years before becoming a philosopher: he asked for a post at Irvine because the author of *Glas* taught there too: 'The two most important men in my life were Nietzsche and Derrida. I was lucky enough to attend all the seminars right from the start. And I was far from being the only one. Many people arranged to be in Irvine for April.'[17]

Derrida was indeed something of a star, but he was first and foremost a full-time teacher, as attentive as he had always been. As David Carroll recalls:

He gave an open course to all students in social sciences and humanities. Many of those following his seminar were registered in history or anthropology. Only the people who ran the philosophy department tried to dissuade their students from going. Eventually, some of them did take the plunge, but those who stayed soon changed subject. Even at Irvine, it was impossible to do a philosophy thesis if you'd been labelled a Derridean . . . There was always a big audience; even his supposedly closed seminar was packed. But this didn't prevent Derrida from spending a great deal of time seeing students individually and discussing their papers, their theses, and their personal plans with them. He was supposed to be available in his office six hours a week, but he always spent longer than that so he could give each student as much time as possible.[18]

When he was on the campus, from Monday to Wednesday, Derrida was fully available. After his seminar, he invited close friends to dinner at the Koto, a Japanese restaurant that was a local high spot.[19] On Tuesdays, he had his ritual lunch with J. Hillis Miller; on other days, it was with friends and colleagues whom he liked. 'Derrida liked to pick up old habits and friends,' Ellen Burt recalls.

It was always Angie – Andrzej Warminski – and Hillis who came to collect him from the airport. Throughout his stay, it was always the same student who acted as his assistant. On the other days of the week, he often went on quick return trips to other universities, for lectures or conferences. But in the last years, he travelled less, preferring to save time so he could work in peace and quiet.[20]

David Carroll and his wife Suzanne Gearhart found Derrida a little house to rent, first in Laguna Beach, then at Victoria Beach, somewhat more off the beaten track. Derrida particularly enjoyed living by the sea for a few weeks, even though he could only occasionally go for a swim – the sea is pretty cold in spring on the Pacific Coast. Although he worked extremely hard, the pace of life was less exhausting than the rest of the year. He liked to stroll along the beach, observing the many local birds, and having dinner or seeing a film with his translator and close friend Peggy Kamuf.

Murray Krieger, who brought Derrida to Irvine at the same time as Hillis Miller, was one of the founders of the university, and a true innovator. In 1990, he suggested that Derrida entrust his personal archives to Langson Library, the main one in the university. Derrida was very touched: this was the first time anyone had shown any interest in his personal papers. The first agreement, making a gift to the Critical Theory Archive, was signed on 23 June 1990. 'It was all generous and quite informal,' says Peggy Kamuf.

> But right from the start, the university should have suggested that Derrida get help from a lawyer and draw up a more legal document; this would have helped avoid a great number of problems. What was always very clear was that Irvine would have no right to publish any of the material deposited. Consultation of the archives by scholars was completely free, but photocopies and quotation of extracts were subject to Derrida's personal approval. The reason why he didn't want to deposit his correspondence at Irvine was the difference between European law and American law: in the United States, the addressee is the only proprietor of the letter received, which put him in an awkward position vis-à-vis all those who had written to him.[21]

Given the huge number of manuscripts and documents of every nature preserved by Derrida, the concrete labour involved in selecting and copying them was, right from the start, considerable. Thomas Dutoit, one of Derrida's first Irvine students, had married a French woman and was at the time living in Germany. When he learned that the archives had been gifted to Irvine, he immediately offered his services. Between 1991 and 1998, he spent long periods in Ris-Orangis, classifying and photocopying papers. Most of the archives were quite carefully arranged – material for teaching was all gathered together, manuscripts and proofs assembled book by book, etc. – but boxes and folders had to be opened and a full inventory made.

'It had been agreed right from the start that Jacques Derrida would keep a copy of everything that could be of use to him,' remembers Tom Dutoit.

So I photocopied a huge number of things, but not everything, not the proofs, for example. As I worked, Derrida would often be there at home, but he kept only a distant eye on my work. He'd initially told me that I could interrupt him when I wanted to ask him about something: 'All interruption is the promise of a new start.' But when I asked him about some document, he soon started to get impatient. Sometimes, he told me, 'it's killing me', since it forced him to go back over his past too often . . . I had the key to the house, I could go anywhere I wanted, open all the drawers. I learned to decipher his handwriting quickly; I was never stumped by dates; for a few weeks, I was the person who knew his archives best . . . When the van came to pick up the documents, once a year, around September, Derrida was always troubled: 'Okay . . . It was my decision. I'm not going back on my word.' When he'd agreed to his donation, he wasn't really aware of what he was doing. Everything suggests that he had his regrets. One day, in the car, on the new road between Irvine and Laguna Beach, the light of the sunset was particularly beautiful and he said: 'After all, it's not such a bad idea that my papers will be here.'[22]

From 1992, New York became the main place where Derrida taught on the East Coast. The New York University buildings are in Washington Square, right in the middle of Greenwich Village. Ever since he had first discovered and marvelled at the city, in 1956, Derrida had been a real lover of New York, and his visits there every autumn were linked to a series of rituals.

I now land every year on a Saturday afternoon at JFK. The sweetness of this eternal return is like a blessed ecstasy for my soul, my effusion soothed, the first Sunday morning in Central Park. Then, almost out loud I speak to all the poets in Poets' Alley, cousins of my friends the birds of Laguna Beach. Not to be missed and something I wait all year for, this moment has to retain first of all the traits of a return, already. [. . .]

Another moment of autumnal euphoria, often the day before I leave: a promenade in Brooklyn Heights. In the interval, I retrace all my migrations, from Battery Park to Columbia, one end of Manhattan to the other. A city I venerate – that's the word – and know better, especially downtown (Gramercy Park, Union Square, Washington Square, Soho, South Street Seaport), I mean that I know it differently well than Paris, at whose altar I nevertheless worship unconditionally.[23]

In New York, Derrida taught very intensively for three weeks. To begin with, it was Tom Bishop, director of the Centre of French Civilization and Culture at NYU and a major figure in Franco-American relations, who invited him. Then, once he had started to teach in English, he was invited by the Poetic Institute of the department of English, whose director was Anselm Haverkamp. In his last years, it was Avital Ronell who asked him to come: now a Distinguished Global Professor, he was invited by the departments of English, French, and German. As Tom Bishop relates:

Derrida in New York was a whirlwind of activity: extraordinary. In spite of his huge fame, he didn't behave like a diva at all. In the Maison Française, the closed seminars were held round a big table, with thirty or so people. This enabled him to pursue a kind of dialogue that he loved; I can especially remember some extraordinary sessions devoted to readings of texts by Hugo and Camus on the death penalty. But NYU was only a minor part of his activities during his stay. He let people have their way, wore himself out, could never say no. He sometimes ended up taking a night train to give a lecture in Cornell or Princeton.[24]

'For a long time, October was synonymous with "Derrida's month" in New York,' confirms Avital Ronell.

One year, we'd planned at least one activity per day for him. We were afraid it might be too much, but he'd really liked it. So we fell back into the same pattern the following years. Symbolically, October was an important month, corresponding to Yom Kippur, to Nietzsche's birthday, and also to the anniversary of his father's death. Jacques was a sort of prodigy, he had so much energy. In addition to NYU and the New School for Social Research, he also taught at City University and the Cardozo Law School. He would sometimes speak on three different occasions in a single day. He was forever seeing people, giving seminars, lectures, interviews; he seemed able to lead ten lives at the same time. What was really incredible was the way he could adapt to every person he met and immediately enter the new problem that was submitted to him. During the times when he wasn't teaching, at NYU, his door was always open to any people who thought they had an idea to put to him. He greeted freebooters, the dissidents of every stripe, and those who might be called intellectual hobos, with openness and generosity.[25]

'It's easy to feel that you're a kind of Prussian general,' Jean-Luc Nancy once exclaimed to Derrida.[26] This was a dimension of Derrida's life that started to develop in the United States before being extended to the rest of the world. As far as the author of *Limited Inc* was concerned, there were friendly and hostile universities. He played hard to get over several years, for example, before agreeing to give a major conference in Stanford, 'The Future of the Humanities and Arts in Higher Education', which then became *The University without Condition.*[*] He was also often in Chicago, where he had several friends: at the university, he was always glad to see Thomas Mitchell and Arnold Davidson, the editors of *Critical Inquiry*; at the Catholic DePaul University, Michael Naas and Pascale-Anne Brault were faithful translators as well as friends. Other important places were Boston College, where John Sallis taught, and especially the University of Villanova, near Philadelphia. Here, in 1994, John D. Caputo created a department of continental philosophy that was particularly receptive to Derrida's work: Derrida kicked off the proceedings with a major debate for the opening session, later published as *Deconstruction in a Nutshell.*[27]

Of course, this cartography of academia was not written in stone. As Jean-Luc Nancy points out,

He always saw battles to be fought, fortresses to be taken and alliances to be made or consolidated. He very soon insisted that we too should go to America – Philippe, Sarah, and I – and suggested to Yves Mabin, head of the bureau of cultural missions at the Ministry of Foreign Affairs, that we be invited. It can't

---

* The first letter of invitation sent by Hans Ulrich Gumbrecht, head of the department of comparative literature at Stanford, was written on 23 January 1990. Derrida knew Gumbrecht, who had previously been professor at Siegen, in Germany. This did not make him any less reluctant to give a lecture in Stanford, even if Gumbrecht assured him that his work was no longer greeted with hostility there. It was only in 1995, after five years of repeated attempts that bordered on 'academic harrassment', in Gumbrecht's own words, that Derrida showed more enthusiasm and envisaged that a 'formula might be found' to come to Stanford. In the meantime, his friend Alexander García Düttmann had given a seminar on his work there, and reiterated that his visit would be 'a big gift for everyone, a real opportunity to be seized' (letter from Düttmann to Derrida, 24 April 1993). On 6 January 1998, Derrida agreed to give a big formal lecture, which he finally did on 15 and 16 April 1999, to an audience of around 1,700 people, after being warmly introduced by Richard Rorty. The packed day went off extremely well. Today, Stanford University Press is one of the houses that has published most works by Derrida in the United States.

be denied that he was trying to set up a network in the United States and Canada. In this context, it was important for him to maintain links with certain potential allies, even if they weren't intellectually all of the first order. He knew he needed a lot of people to pass on the torch for deconstruction.[28]

In a well-known article published just before the de Man affair broke out, 'How to become a dominant French philosopher: The case of Jacques Derrida', the sociologist Michèle Lamont tried to interpret Derrida's American career in terms of the methodical conquest of a cultural market.[29] This almost militaristic vision needs to be qualified. Admittedly, Derrida's behaviour in the United States showed much more practical cunning than it did in France, but he seems mainly to have benefited from a conjunction of favourable factors, as if deconstruction had arrived at just the right time. In particular, the extent of his success needs to be seen in relative terms. While the idea of deconstruction has passed into everyday language and Derrida's name has become extraordinarily famous in America, his work has never spread beyond academic circles. None of his books has become a real bestseller. Only after many years did sales of *Of Grammatology* finally pass the 100,000 mark. His other works in English, always published by academic houses, have sales of between 5,000 and 30,000 works – perfectly decent figures, and much more impressive than those in French, but far from bringing Derrida into the mass market. And while Derrida was able to count on several academic reviews in the United States – *Glyph*, *SubStance*, *Boundary 2*, *Critical Inquiry* –, it was hostility that prevailed in the main organs of the cultural press. The *Times Literary Supplement* has always been very hostile to him, the *New York Review of Books* even more so.[30]

However, certain folkloric aspects of the wave of Derrideanism cannot go unremarked. In *French Theory,* for instance, François Cusset relates that certain magazines on home décor were suggesting that their readers 'deconstruct the concept of the garden', while a comic book superhero had to confront 'Doctor Deconstructo'. As for the magazine *Crew*, it extolled the 'Derrida Jacket' and the 'Deconstruction Suit'.[31] In the middle of 'Monicagate', Bill Clinton himself used deconstruction in his own defence. Accused of lying when he had claimed not to have had sexual relations with the young intern, the President replied: 'It depends on what the meaning of the word "is" is' – a typically Derridean utterance.

The author of *The Post Card* was rather irritated by this superficial fall-out from his work. And he really did not like *Deconstructing Harry*, the Woody Allen film that hit the big screen in 1997. The allusion – which, symptomatically, disappeared in the French version, *Harry dans tous ses états* (*Harry's in a Real Stew*) – was in his view merely the pretext for a rather facile satire on the academic world. On a visit to Stanford, Derrida stated that he was very disappointed by the use to which deconstruction was put in the film. Raising his voice to defend the word, as if it were his child, he said: 'I felt it was an exploitation of the term. [. . .] At the end a graduate student uses the word deconstruction as a stereotype, to destroy it, to undermine it, to vulgarize it.'[32] Such, surely, is the price we pay for fame.

7

Specters of Marx

1993–1995

In February 1990, Jacques Derrida went to Moscow for the first time in his life. The Berlin Wall had fallen a few months earlier and the USSR was collapsing. In a typical act of provocation, while in Moscow Derrida talked about Marx, which caused something of a stir. A few weeks later, in Irvine, describing his trip and analysing the idiosyncratic literary genre of the 'return from the USSR', Derrida clearly explained what his position had always been:

> Even though I have never been either a Marxist or a Communist, *stricto sensu*, even though, in my youthful admiration for Gide, I read at fifteen (1945) his *Back from the USSR*, which left no doubt as to the tragic failure of the Soviet Revolution and today still seems to me a remarkable, solid and lucid work and even though, later, in Paris in the 1950s and 1960s, I had to resist – and it was not easy – a terrifying politico-theoretical intimidation of the Stalinist or neo-Stalinist type in my most immediate personal and intellectual environment, this never kept me from sharing, in the mode of both hope and nostalgia, something of Etiemble's disarmed passion or childish imaginary in this romantic relation with the Soviet Union. I am always bowled over when I hear the *Internationale*, I tremble with emotion and then I always want to 'go out into the streets' to fight against the Reaction. [. . .] I would not be able to describe what my trip to Moscow was, in full Perestroika, if I had not said at least something about this revolutionary pathos, about the history of this affect or this affection, which I cannot, and in truth do not want to, give up entirely.[1]

Two years later, Bernd Magus and Stephen Cullenberg asked Derrida to give the opening address at the international conference they were organizing in Riverside, a progressive campus at the University of California where his friend Michael Sprinker taught. The title 'Whither Marxism?' is a pun: where is Marxism going, but does it also risk withering away? Derrida, as was his wont, based much of what he said on this 'ambiguous title'.[2]

For nearly thirty years, friends of his – especially in France – had reproached him for having written nothing on Marx; there had been Althusser and his associates at the École Normale Supérieure, Sollers, Houdebine, and Scarpetta at the time of *Tel Quel* and *Promesse*, Gérard Granel, and, more recently, Bernard Stiegler and Catherine Malabou. And it was just when nobody was expecting it, on the West Coast of the United States, that Derrida suddenly decided to speak on this very subject. He explained his reasons in his interviews with Maurizio Ferraris:

> The conference on Marx might not have taken place, and in that case perhaps I would not have written that book on Marx; I hesitated, and I tried to ask myself whether responding on that occasion was strategically well calculated. There was a long period of deliberation, but at the end of the day, whatever the calculation might have been, there came a time when I said 'let's accept', and I accepted.[3]

Derrida had always been able to work fast. But never before had he completed such a demanding task to meet such a tight deadline. It was as if he had been bearing this book within him for a very long time, simply waiting for a favourable opportunity. As J. Hillis Miller recalls:

> One day in 1993, at Irvine, it must have been at the beginning of March, Jacques anxiously told me: 'I have to write a conference paper on Marx for the Riverside conference, but I've got nowhere with it.' He really had to get a move on, even if Peggy Kamuf translated the pages as he wrote them. Four or five weeks later, the first version of *Specters of Marx* was done. He'd managed to complete this long text, completely new, even though he'd still had to give his seminars, receive students, and probably speak on two or three occasions outside the university.

On 22 and 23 April, Derrida opened the Riverside conference with one of those exorbitant lectures which he had made his speciality. The opening was as mysterious as it was memorable:

> Someone, you or me, comes forward and says: *I would like to learn to live finally.*
>
> Finally but why?
>
> *To learn to live*: a strange watchword. Who would learn? From whom? To teach to live, but to whom? Will we ever

know? Will we ever know how to live and first of all what 'to learn to live' means? And why 'finally'?[4]

But he soon announced the tenor of his discourse: it was indeed Marx, his persistence and his pertinence, that Derrida was going to talk about. In Derrida's view, 'it will always be a fault' not to read him, reread him and discuss him, and now more than ever:

> When the dogma machine and the 'Marxist' ideological appara-tuses (States, parties, cells, unions, and other places of doctrinal production) are disappearing, we no longer have any excuse, only alibis, for turning away from this responsibility. There will be no future without this. Not without Marx, no future without Marx, without the memory and the inheritance of Marx: in any case of a certain Marx, of his genius, of at least one of his spirits. For this will be our hypothesis or rather our bias: *there is more than one of them, there must be more than one of them.*[5]

At the same time as wishing to give a rightful place to 'one at least' of Marx's spirits, Derrida brought out the spectral dimension running through several of his texts, right from the first sentence of the *The Communist Party Manifesto*: 'A spectre is haunting Europe – the spectre of communism.' He read Marx as a philosopher and a writer, as he had never been read before, echoing the many allu-sions to Shakespeare, especially Hamlet, that are found in his most theoretical works. While the theme of spectrality had preoccupied Derrida ever since the film *Ghost Dance*, and while the concept of *hauntology* looked like a new way of designating what he had long designated as *différance*, he was very far from having invented these themes: he revealed their presence within *The German Ideology* and other of Marx's works. As Derrida had announced twenty-two years earlier in a letter to Gérard Granel, before he could emerge from his silence about the author of *Capital*, he needed to 'do the work'. He had already sensed that this work would not lead to a 'conversion', 'but to oblique incisions, tangential displacements, following this or that unnoticed vein of the Marxist text'.[6]

Specters of Marx was not just a new reading, it was a thoroughly political intervention. In particular, it was a response to Francis Fukuyama, whose *The End of History and the Last Man* had been a great success the year before. Replying to the triumphalist discourses that had followed the fall of Communist regimes, Derrida numbered the gaping wounds of the 'New World Order': unemployment, the massive exclusion of the homeless, economic warfare, the aggrava-tion of foreign debt, the arms industry and arms trade, the spread of nuclear power, inter-ethnic wars and reactionary nationalisms, mafia and trafficking . . . No, history was not over.

A 'new international' is being sought through these crises of international law; it already denounces the limits of a discourse on human rights that will remain inadequate, sometimes hypocritical, and in any case formalistic and inconsistent with itself as long as the law of the market, the 'foreign debt', the inequality of techno-scientific, military, and economic development maintain an effective inequality as monstrous as that which prevails today; to a greater extent than in the history of humanity. For it must be cried out, at a time when some have the audacity to neo-evangelize in the name of the ideal of a liberal democracy that has finally realized itself as the ideal of human history: never have violence, inequality, exclusion, famine, and thus economic oppression affected as many human beings in the history of the earth and of humanity. Instead of singing the advent of the ideal of liberal democracy and the capitalist market in the euphoria of the end of history; instead of celebrating the 'end of ideologies' and the end of the great emancipatory discourses, let us never neglect this evident macroscopic fact, made up of innumerable singular sites of suffering: no degree of progress allows one to ignore that never before, in absolute figures, never have so many men, women, and children been subjugated, starved, or exterminated on the earth.[7]

Enlarged over the next few months, *Specters of Marx* was published almost immediately, as if with a feeling of urgency. This is how Derrida presented it in a letter to Françoise Dastur, in which he asked her to forgive him for his delay in replying: 'In the midst of my usual tiredness and overwork, I've been working on a little book on ghosts [. . .] in which, in my brusque and clumsy fashion, I try to imagine what "*Wir sterben um zu leben*" ["We die in order to live"] might mean without managing really to believe in it, and that's also my weakness.'[8]

The various digressions and the acute analyses do not stop the book as a whole from being sustained by a real lyrical *élan* and a great nobility of spirit. Marguerite remembers reading the proofs of *Specters of Marx* in Iceland; she had accompanied Jacques to Reykjavik before his departure that evening for the United States. At night, in her hotel bedroom, the text moved her so much that she wept.

The reception of the book would be completely different from that of Derrida's previous works. *Specters of Marx* came just at the right time. The title was intriguing and striking: it corresponded to hazy expectations. *Le Quotidien de Paris*, unsurprisingly, waxed ironical over 'Marx, a phantasm* of Derrida's', while Bernard-Henri Lévy,

---

* *Fantasme* also means ghost. – Tr.

in his column in *Le Point*, thought he was 'dreaming' when he heard of a 'return to Marx'.

In *Le Nouvel Observateur*, as the general tendency on the editorial board was one of hostility, Didier Eribon suggested a major interview in New York rather than a review. He started by referring to Derrida's success in the United States, emphasizing that this was no mere phenomenon of fashion, but 'a vast intellectual ebullition in scholarly circles'. With regard to *Specters of Marx*, Eribon noted that this 'peculiar book, which is simultaneously a political manifesto and a highly technical philosophical work', was actually very difficult to read. But he sensed that this would not stop it being a major event. According to Derrida himself, *Specters of Marx* was, first and foremost, 'a political act':

The most important thing is not scrutinizing Marx's texts. [. . .] The most urgent business, and what has impelled me to raise the tone by adopting a political position, is the growing impatience I feel – and I do not think I am alone – at the kind of consensus, both euphoric and grimacing, that is invading every discourse. [. . .] Any reference to Marx has become, as it were, cursed. I concluded that this showed a desire to exorcize it, to spirit it away, that deserved to be analysed and that also deserved to provoke insurrection. In some ways, my book is a book of insurrection. It is an apparently untimely gesture, that comes at the wrong time. But the idea of the 'wrong time' is at the very heart of the book. [. . .] What one always hopes when doing something 'at the wrong time' is that it will happen at the right time, at the moment when it is felt to be necessary.[9]

In *Libération*, *Specters of Marx* was hailed in a major article by Robert Maggiori. He emphasized that Derrida 'has never been a Marxist, even when everyone else was, and [. . .] has little intention of becoming one', and then went on to claim that his book 'will be one to mark with a white stone, as if it were an act of inauguration, if perchance the *spirit* of Marxism were again to blow across our lands'.[10] In *Le Monde*, Nicolas Weill also acknowledged the work's importance and its author's audacity, barely four years after the fall of the Berlin Wall, even though he felt that 'a debate with contemporary liberal thought should not be limited just to refuting Fukuyama'.[11] Like Gérard Guégan in *Sud-Ouest Dimanche*, many readers declared their conviction that *Specters of Marx* would restore confidence to those who no longer dared utter Marx's name, let alone study him: 'This is a book that is fully inhabited, and around it will gather the heirs. [. . .] It is more than the history of philosophy which demands as much; it is the fate of the world.'[12]

The French Communists could not ignore the opportunity

represented by such a work, written by such a prestigious figure. *L'Humanité*, which had already published extensive highlights from *Specters of Marx* on 23 September, provided a thoughtful review on 13 November. Derrida immediately thanked Arnaud Spire, and through him the whole editorial board, for the 'generous attention' they had shown him: 'I felt I must tell you how touched I am – as by a good sign, an encouraging sign, and not just for me – by the open-minded welcome that has just been shown, on two occasions, thanks to you, in *L'Humanité*. The future will doubtless have more to say about this than I can say here . . .'[13] A few weeks later, it was the turn of *L'Humanité Dimanche* to hail the work. And Robert Hue, the first secretary of the Communist Party, said he was touched by Derrida's latest move.[14]

But Derrida was not the man of any one party. *Le Nouveau Politis*, *Révolution*, and *Critique Communiste*, which all represented different tendencies of the radical left, also congratulated themselves on having found in him a significant new ally, at a time when revolutionary ideals were ebbing. Pierre Macherey, an alumnus of Normale Sup and co-author of *Reading Capital*, summarized the situation most eloquently:

Derrida took everyone by surprise, tripped them up, bowled them over, when, relatively late in the day, in 1993, he started speaking about Marx, speaking 'Marx', Marx's language, getting Marx to speak, *en différé* as it were. There was a reason for this anachronism, and even a sort of necessity: it was just at the moment when Marx had been shovelled into a hole, dead and buried, reduced to silence, treated like a dead dog, denied and almost cancelled out, [. . .] that the time seemed to have come to let him again have, if not 'his word' – a word that was properly his, his own word, fully integrated 'into the identity of his living presence – at least the spectral word of a 'ghost' [*revenant*] attributed to him by *Specters of Marx*.[15]

The reaction to this 'little book' – as Derrida would continue to call it, even if the French version is over three hundred pages long – was not, however, unanimous on the part of those who claimed to be followers of Marx. The debates around the work covered so many positions that Michael Sprinker, who ran the review *Thinking Marxism*, asked for the reactions of ten or so intellectuals, mainly English-speaking Marxists, and published them together with a reply by Derrida in *Ghostly Demarcations*.[16] Only Derrida's text was published in French, under the title 'Marx & Sons': he discussed the issues firmly but serenely with his critics, reserving his most virulent attacks for the article written by his former disciple Gayatri Spivak, which he found 'unbelievable from first to last'.[17]

A few months before *Specters of Marx*, the imposing collective work *La Misère du Monde* had been published, edited by Pierre Bourdieu, who again became the focus of intense media interest. This almost simultaneous reaffirmation of strong left-wing values helped to bring the two thinkers together again. Whatever critiques Derrida had made of Sartre, commitment was still in his view 'a fine word, still fresh and new'. As he stated on the occasion of the fiftieth anniversary of *Les Temps modernes*, it was crucial to 'keep or reactivate the forms of this "commitment" by changing its content and its strategies'.[18]

The idea of a 'Parliament of Culture' had been launched by Bourdieu in autumn 1991, at the Carrefour des Littératures Européennes in Strasbourg. In July 1993, after the assassination of the Algerian writer Tahar Djaout, some sixty writers, including Derrida and Bourdieu, called for the creation of an international structure to give concrete support to persecuted writers and intellectuals throughout the world. The inaugural meeting of the International Writers' Parliament was held in Strasbourg, from 4 to 8 November 1993. Jean-Luc Nancy and Philippe Lacoue-Labarthe involved themselves fully in the preparations, together with a member of the city council, Christian Salmon. Those invited included Susan Sontag and Édouard Glissant, as well as Toni Morrison, the recent Nobel laureate. But, on the evening of 7 November, the 'surprise' arrival of a heavily protected Salman Rushdie changed the whole tenor of the event: this was his third public appearance in France ever since the *fatwa* pronounced against him in February 1989. Derrida and Bourdieu joined him in a debate that was broadcast direct on Arte: they emerged from the experience feeling very ill at ease, as the chairperson had struck them as so dismal. This did not stop them following the venture of the International Writers' Parliament for several years, before preferring the creation of a series of 'refuge cities'.

It was also in July 1993 that Derrida lent his support to the 'Appeal for Vigilance' published in *Le Monde* on the initiative of Maurice Olender. In the view of the signatories, too many writers and intellectuals had collaborated recently on publications with links to the extreme right, such as *Krisis*, thereby helping to legitimize them or make them seem innocuous.[19] They thought it was essential to draw a line that could not be crossed. This appeal led Maurice Blanchot, for example, to break off relations with Bruno Roy and the Fata Morgana publishing house, after they had published a work by Alain de Benoist, an author with links to the far right.[20]

Derrida was particularly touched by the tragic situation of the Algerian people, caught between the attacks of the FIS – the Front Islamique du Salut (Islamic Salvation Front) – and the brutal clamp-down by the authorities. At the beginning of 1994, he signed an 'Appeal for Civil Peace in Algeria' and spoke in the main lecture hall of the Sorbonne on 7 February 1994 at a major meeting called to support Algerian intellectuals. He began by referring to his 'painful love for Algeria', 'which, though it is not the love of a citizen [. . .], and thus not any patriotic attachment to a nation state, is nonetheless something that makes it impossible for [him], here, to separate [his] heart, [his] mind, and a political stance'.[21] However difficult and entangled the situation, Derrida refused to soften his usual rigour. He methodically scrutinized the terms of the Appeal to try to shed light on what terms such as 'violence', 'civil peace', and 'democracy' actually meant within the Algerian context. He especially insisted that while *'voting* is of course not the whole of democracy [. . .], without it, and without this form and this counting of votes, there is no democracy'.[22]

Support for the Algerians had very definite implications in France. With Pierre Bourdieu and Sami Naïr, Derrida, who was usually so legalistic, did not hesitate to call for 'civic resistance' against laws on immigration and nationality as well as the recent decrees concerning Algerians. On 25 March 1995, during a demonstration in Nantes for the right to visas, he intervened for the first time in a directly militant way. 'I found myself there, pushed up onto – it wasn't a cask, but some kind of raised thing –, just like that, to harangue the crowds on behalf of Algerian emigrants,' he later recounted.[23] That day, without the least stylistic convolution, Derrida pointed out that in 1993, France had handed out 290,000 visas to Algerians, and three times fewer in 1994. He denounced 'the slamming shut of borders to Algerians who are living in a hell where there were at least 30,000 assassinations in 1994'.

The more people are killed in the world, the more France, whether its government be of the left or the right, simply stands by as a distant, disdainful observer while people are being massacred. The French Government is so aware of the intolerable nature of the situation that it has just banned the publication of the number of visas granted or turned down. Might it be ashamed of its policy?[24]

Derrida, who had so often reflected on writing and the materials on which language was inscribed, brought out the full resonance of the very word *'sans-papiers'*,* one of the issues that he constantly fought for during the 1990s, and one which gradually led him to move away from the French Socialist Party, which in his view was

---

* Illegal immigrants 'without papers'. – Tr.

much too timid on this question.[25]* When some people expressed surprise that he was intervening on such questions, even if it was in a less thunderous way than Bourdieu, Derrida replied that he did not feel there was any divorce between his writings and his commitments, 'only differences of rhythm, mode of discourse, context, and so on'.[26] In a long interview he gave to the *Cahiers de médiologie*, he explained, very convincingly, that 'law' and 'papers' were completely inseparable: 'The "paperless person" is an outlaw, a nonsubject legally, a noncitizen or the citizen of a foreign country refused the right conferred, *on paper*, by a temporary or permanent visa, a rubber stamp.'[27]

There were increasing bridges between his philosophical work and his political commitments. Hospitality, the topic of his seminar from 1995–7, became a recurrent theme, one of those to which his name would be most frequently attached. This was because the principle of hospitality concentrated within itself 'the most concrete urgencies, those most proper to articulate the ethical on the political'. Derrida stated this in a lecture whose title was a whole programme in itself: *Cosmopolites de tous les pays, encore un effort!*†

> Hospitality is culture itself and not simply one ethic among others. Insofar as it has to do with the *ethos*, that is, the residence, one's home, the familiar place of dwelling, inasmuch as it is a manner of being there, the manner in which we relate to ourselves and to others, to others as our own or foreigners, *ethics* is *hospitality*; ethics is so thoroughly coextensive with the experience of hospitality.[28]

Apart from politics, religion was the major field which preoccupied Derrida at this time. The Italian publisher Laterza planned an *Annuaire philosophique européen* that, year after year, would bring together European philosophers to discuss a particular theme. At the initial meeting, Derrida suggested they begin with a word, the word that was in his view 'the clearest and most obscure: *religion*'.[29]

At the end of February 1994, in a hotel on the isle of Capri, several philosophers sat round a table to exchange ideas in complete freedom. Together with Derrida, there were Gadamer, Vattimo, Ferraris, and others. 'We came rather unprepared,' Ferraris recalls,

---

* Derrida said of François Mitterrand, in a late interview with Franz-Olivier Giesbert: 'I met him several times. Even if he had rather limited views on literature or philosophy, he was a man of the book. I would have liked to admire him.' Derrida long continued, despite these reservations, to vote socialist and sometimes to call on others to do the same, as in the presidential election of 1995.

† Literally: 'Cosmopolitans of all lands – just one more effort!' – Tr.

'as if on a school trip for ageing schoolchildren. Except for Derrida, who turned up with an already full ring-bound notebook. He was the only one to have done his "homework" – a word he liked. His intervention was really thought-provoking and triggered the subsequent discussions.'[30]

The title may have seemed conventional – 'Faith and knowledge' – but was less so if we take into account its subtitle, with its echoes of Bergson and Kant, 'The two sources of "religion" at the limits of reason alone'. It is impressive in its scope and detail. As was his custom, Derrida drew on the most tangible aspect of the circumstances in which he found himself, insisting on the western and even European character of a meeting that was claiming, a little hastily, an international status.

We represent and speak four different languages, but our common 'culture', let's be frank, is more manifestly Christian, barely even Judaeo-Christian. No Muslim is among us, alas, even for this preliminary discussion, just at the moment when it is towards Islam, perhaps, that we ought to begin by turning our attention. No representative of other cults either. Not a single woman! We ought to take this into account: speaking on behalf of these mute witnesses without speaking for them, in place of them, and drawing from this all sorts of consequences.[31]

In 'Faith and knowledge', Derrida for the first time develops one of the key concepts of his late thinking, self-immunity, 'that strange behaviour where a living being, in quasi-*suicidal* fashion, "itself" works to destroy its own protection, to immunize itself *against* its "own" immunity'.[32] He also pondered the confrontation between different fundamentalisms and what he liked to designate – in one of those portmanteau words of which he was increasingly fond – as globalatinization, 'this strange alliance of Christianity, as the experience of the death of God, and tele-technoscientific capitalism'.[33]

A few months later, in Naples, not far from Capri, Derrida completed another important text, *Archive Fever*. This was the lecture he was due to deliver on 5 June 1994 at the Freud Museum in London, as the closing address in the conference 'Memory: The Question of Archives', organized by René Major and Élisabeth Roudinesco. In it, Derrida conducted a courteous but critical dialogue with a recent book by Yosef Hayim Yerushalmi: *Freud's Moses: Judaism Terminable and Interminable*. The questions raised by Yerushalmi were of the greatest significance to Derrida, probably because his own relation to Judaism was just as complicated as Freud's. He would return to the question in his dialogues with Élisabeth Roudinesco:

This celebration of a 'Jewish specificity' (having to do with memory, the future, the anticipation of psychoanalysis, etc.) seemed very debatable to me in its context [. . .]. I also wondered whether Yerushalmi did not risk giving sustenance, willingly or not, to a *political* use of the very serious theme of election (so difficult to interpret), and more precisely of the 'chosen people'.[34]

Yerushalmi attended the conference and had planned to be in the audience for Derrida's lecture. But things turned out otherwise: on that day, he was ill, and could not leave his hotel room. Only later, in New York, did the two men try to discuss the issue.

In 1994, Derrida was collapsing under the weight of all his plans. He wrote to Ferraris, shortly after his return from London: 'Personally, I'm more overwhelmed by work than ever (in particular because of *Politics of Friendship*, that wretched book that I promised to finish by the end of July). I don't know how I'm going to manage this summer with the rest, especially with [the text on] *Religion*!!'[35]

The 'wretched book' – which Derrida eventually presented as a long preface or foreword to a book he would like one day to write – was the huge expansion 'of what was merely the *first session* of a seminar given under that title, *Politics of Friendship*'.[36] This seminar had been given in 1988–89, just after the de Man affair and in its wake, even though there was no direct allusion to this. Each session had begun with the words of Montaigne, quoting a remark attributed to Aristotle: 'O my friends, there is no friend.' In this book, every chapter is based on this sentence, giving a new twist to its interpretation, as if 'the scenography could be set in motion around itself'. From Plato to Montaigne, from Aristotle to Kant, from Cicero to Hegel, Derrida reread the classical discussions of friendship to bring out their unstated presuppositions:

The principal question would rightly concern the hegemony of a philosophical canon in this domain: how has it prevailed? Whence derives its force? How has it been able to exclude the feminine or heterosexuality, friendship between women or friendship between men and women? Why can an inventory not be made of feminine or heterosexual experiences of friendship? Why this heterogeneity between *eros* and *philia*?[37]

One thing which he endeavoured to deconstruct was the '*familial, fraternalist*, and thus *androcentric*' configuration of the political that is almost inevitably produced by the traditional analyses of friendship:

Why should the friend be *like* a brother? Let us dream of a friendship which goes beyond this proximity of the congeric double, beyond kinship, the most as well as the least natural of parenthoods, when it leaves its signature, from the outset, on the name as on a double mirror of such a couple. Let's wonder what would then be the politics of such a 'beyond the principle of fraternity'.[38]

Over the years, Derrida had kept up his relations with Georges Canguilhem. Long retired from any official obligations, he sometimes called himself 'a superannuated cook of concepts'. Derrida still regularly sent him copies of his books, as he did to other old and new friends. In 1994, Canguilhem thanked him for his loyalty, though he felt he had not been very important in Derrida's career: 'I find *Politics of Friendship* really stimulating. It's a masterpiece. When you talk about Kant, or Nietzsche, I feel I'm in a position to judge. [. . .] What did surprise me was to come across Carl Schmitt [. . .]. I admire the cunning simplicity with which you enable Aristotle, Montaigne, and Blanchot to coexist.'[39]

On 15 December 1994, Catherine Malabou defended the thesis she had written under Derrida's supervision, later published as *The Future of Hegel: Plasticity, Temporality and Dialectic.* It was a brilliant, audacious piece of work, which did not hesitate to question several points in Derrida's reading of Hegel. During the thesis defence, as he often did, Derrida spoke for two hours, superbly, but the other members of the jury could not conceal their irritation, and several seemed on the point of walking out. Sylviane Agacinski, who was a friend of Catherine, was present in the audience. Even though Sylviane was still one of the authors published in the series 'La philosophie en effet', Jacques and she were no longer on speaking terms. 'But after the thesis defence,' recalls Catherine Malabou, 'he came over to us. He talked briefly with Sylviane, asking her how Daniel was, before adding: "I bless him every day." The two of us were left staring at one another, thunderstruck.'[40]

Six months earlier, Sylviane had married Lionel Jospin, with whom she had been living since 1990. He was very fond of Daniel and looked after him as if he had been his own son. Derrida had not seen the child again, apart from one completely chance encounter. One day, coming out of a plane in an airport in the south of France, he recognized Sophie Agacinski, Sylviane's sister, and her husband Jean-Marc Thibault. Jacques was about to greet them when a young boy ran up to hug them. No doubt about it: this had to be Daniel, who had come to spend a few days' holiday with his uncle and aunt. At the same moment, the three adults understood the situation:

without knowing it, Daniel and Jacques had just been travelling in the same plane. As if at a loss, Derrida turned away.

With the years, this story had assumed an increasingly painful significance. Derrida spoke so often in praise of secrets, but this was one he found hard to bear. It was one of the reasons why his relations with Sarah Kofman had cooled: she was an inveterate chatterbox, and had mentioned the previous liaison between Jacques and Sylviane in front of outsiders, and mentioned Daniel. This was, for Derrida, intolerable. He was probably most afraid that the story would reach the ears of his family in Nice. His two other sons had been in the know for a long time, but they had refrained from telling him so. One day, however, Pierre tried to broach the topic:

> As I had the impression that my father must feel guilty towards my brother and me, I took the initiative and arranged a face-to-face meeting with him. After talking about this and that, I told him that I knew about Daniel's existence, and that he wasn't to worry about it as far as I was concerned. He seemed very surprised that I knew, but he very quickly clammed up and told me he preferred not to talk about it. I know only that he didn't want to make any moves to see Daniel, but that if the child came to him, he'd be prepared to meet him. He thought this was highly unlikely: over the years, his view of Sylviane had become increasingly negative, and he worried about what she might have been saying about him . . . I realized there was no point returning to this subject. In my father's temperament, so open and audacious about most things, there were a few very archaic elements that brooked no discussion. This was particularly true of anything to do with the family, in the narrow sense and more broadly speaking.[41]

This period was painfully marked by three deaths, including two suicides.

Sarah Kofman killed herself on 15 October 1994, the anniversary of Nietzsche's birth: he had been one of the thinkers who had most influenced her. A few months earlier, she had published a short autobiographical narrative, *Rue Ordener, rue Labat*, in which for the first time she described her childhood under the Occupation, the deportation of her father, and her strained relations with her mother and the woman who had saved her life. In spite of various important publications, Kofman's academic career had been strewn with difficulties, and only in 1991 was she finally made a professor at the Sorbonne.

For Derrida, as for many others, Sarah had always been a

complicated friend. After a very lively exchange of letters about the Collège International de Philosophie, in 1983, they stopped writing to each other. But there then followed interminable phone calls which Derrida gradually forced himself to avoid, asking Marguerite or Jean-Luc to take over, pleading that he had neither the time nor the patience. Fragile, childish, terribly thin-skinned, Sarah tended to turn every incident into a crisis. She had a great liking for Derrida and his work, on which she wrote a fine book,[42] but she also demonstrated a powerful desire for independence from him. As the only woman in the quartet running 'La philosophie en effet', she felt she was not properly appreciated by the others.

Derrida was in New York when Sarah died and unable to attend her funeral. In the homage to her he wrote shortly afterwards, he made no attempt to conceal the complexity of their relationship – 'over twenty years of a tender, tense, and stormy friendship, an impossible friendship' – recognizing that, until the end, they had 'accused one another a great deal, and often'. 'Impossible: that is no doubt what we were for one another, Sarah and I. Perhaps more than others, or in some other way, in innumerable ways that I will not be able to recount here, considering all the scenes in which we found ourselves [. . .].'[43] Still, that did not prevent him from having as much affection for her as he had admiration for her work, which he encouraged everyone to read and reread.

But this homage was not enough to overcome a certain awkwardness: apparently, Jacques had not responded when she sent him her last, highly personal and emotionally charged book, *Rue Ordener, rue Labat*. Sarah's partner, Alexandre Kyritsos, found this posthumous text of Derrida's hard to swallow: it struck him as a belated attempt to make up.[44]

Deleuze had been ill for years: he committed suicide on 4 November 1995. While Derrida had frequently bumped into him, since their first encounters at the home of Maurice de Gandillac at the beginning of the 1950s, he had not really got to know him. Jean-Luc Nancy had dreamed of getting these two major philosophers into a discussion, but it never happened, and not just for contingent reasons. Deleuze's tragic death sharpened the feeling of loneliness that Derrida had long been suffering from. He increasingly perceived himself as a survivor, especially as he was the one who, each time, felt obliged to speak of the departed. In the eloquent homage that was published in *Libération*, he wrote: 'Each death is unique, of course, and therefore unusual. But what can be said about the unusual when, from Barthes to Althusser, from Foucault to Deleuze, it multiplies, as in a series, all these uncommon ends in the same "generation"?'[45]

The relationship between Derrida and Deleuze had not been easy, at the time of *Anti-Oedipus* and the Nietzsche conference at Cerisy, especially as Deleuze's long friendship with Foucault complicated things. Nevertheless, the two philosophers had a great mutual esteem and there were real philosophical affinities between them. Derrida recognized this:

> From the very beginning, all of his books (but first of all *Nietzsche and Philosophy, Difference and Repetition, The Logic of Sense*) have been for me not only, of course, strong provocations to think but each time the flustering, really flustering, experience of a closeness or of a nearly total affinity concerning the 'theses', if you will, across very obvious distances, in what I would call – lacking any better term – the 'gesture', the 'strategy', the 'manner' of writing, of speaking, of reading perhaps.[46]

Deleuze rarely referred to Derrida in his works, but he sometimes sent him signals of esteem and complicity – as, for example, when Derrida's commentary on *Drawings and Portraits of Antonin Artaud*, 'Maddening the subjectile', came out: Deleuze wrote to tell him of his admiration for this 'splendid' text, which 'goes further than anyone has been before in Artaud's work'.[47] For his part, in the seminars of his last years, Derrida returned on several occasions to Deleuze's works – including *A Thousand Plateaus*, which Deleuze wrote with Félix Guattari. It was as if the dialogue between them could take place only posthumously.

Emmanuel Levinas, now a great age, although he had been ill for years, died on 25 December 1995. His death came as no surprise, but it deeply affected Derrida. And yet again, on 27 December, in the cemetery at Pantin, he was the one who spoke:

> For a long time, for a very long time, I've feared having to say *Adieu* to Emmanuel Levinas.
> I knew that my voice would tremble at the moment of saying it, and especially saying it aloud, right here, before him, so close to him, pronouncing this word of *adieu*, this word *à-Dieu*, which, in a certain sense, I get from him, a word that he will have taught me to think or to pronounce otherwise. [. . .]
> Whom is one addressing at such a moment? And in whose name would one allow oneself to do so? Often those who come forward to speak, to speak publicly, thereby interrupting the animated whispering, the secret or intimate exchange that always links one, deep inside, to a dead friend or master, those who make themselves heard in a cemetery, end up addressing *directly, straight on*, the one who, as we say, is no longer, is no longer living, no longer there, who will no longer respond.[48]

His grief helped to bring him closer to Paul Ricoeur, who had first encouraged him to read *Totality and infinity*. A few days after the ceremony, Ricoeur wrote to his former *assistant* to tell him how touched he had been by his speech: 'Allow me to come and share my deep sadness with you. You said, standing before Levinas, named by his first name Emmanuel, the words that were needed, words which I endorse with all my thought. [. . .] May the uprightness which that master of justice taught us, continue to unite us.'[49]

A year later, in the amphithéâtre Richelieu in the Sorbonne, Derrida opened the proceedings in a conference on Levinas with a lecture called 'A word of welcome'. This was a powerful, vigilant homage to a philosophy that had been his constant companion but that seemed even more important now that Levinas had died. It was as if Derrida were essaying a 'beyond Levinas', continuing his work and taking it further. However great his loyal admiration and his respect, he did not want Levinas's death to deprive him of the right to dialogue and to argue with his texts.[50]

8

The Derrida International

1996–1999

Derrida's standing in the French media was gradually changing, especially now that his political commitments were providing
people with a more accessible image of him. On 1 February 1996,
Libération hailed his recent publications in a double-page spread:
these included *Resistances of Psychoanalysis, Aporias, Religion*, and
'Advances', his long preface to the first work by Serge Margel, *The
Tomb of the Artisan God*. 'Psychoanalysis, religion, the concept of
death: nothing escapes the thinking of Jacques Derrida, who can on
occasion show himself to be a demiurge,' announced the heading. A
few months later, in *Le Monde*, Christian Delacampagne devoted
a major article to the publication of *Monolingualism of the Other,
Echographies of Television*, and the proceedings of the conference
'Passions of Literature'. He first insisted on the sheer abundance
of Derrida's output, counting 'sixty-seven books in thirty-four
years, or an average of two a year'. 'There is something miraculous
in Derrida's productivity: an ability to renew himself ceaselessly,
a generosity which time seems unable to exhaust.' Delacampagne
expressed his surprise at the unfair reception given to Derrida, 'ill
loved in his own country, even though he is at present, together with
Paul Ricoeur, the most famous representative of French thought
in the whole world'. He emphasized what struck him as being the
two current tendencies of Derrida's work: 'a penchant for autobiography, as well as an increasingly marked political focus as the years
go by'.[1]

'Yes, my books are political,' Derrida acknowledged in his
interview with Didier Eribon.[2] He had long hesitated to intervene
directly in media debates, as the ground seemed to have been undermined by the champions of hand-me-down ideas. The trauma of the
nouveaux philosophes was still a sore point, as he explained in a late
interview:

> If you wanted to become a media figure very quickly, you had
> to simplify, talk in black-and-white terms, dump the whole

heritage without getting bogged down in concepts. [. . .] The ambiguity – and this is a complicating factor that I must take into account – is that those young people were often agitating on behalf of good causes, just causes: human rights, in particular. That generation was fighting for causes that were, in principle, often respectable, but they gave the impression that they were using them rather than being of use to them.[3]

And so, even when, fundamentally, his positions were not all that different from those of the *nouveaux philosophes*, Derrida found it extremely difficult to associate his name with theirs. He did belatedly recognize, however, that 'if this permeability between the intellectual and media fields is a very French phenomenon', this desire to speak out could become a good thing for the public space and for democracy, on condition that it did not become merely a matter of 'gesture' politics, or allow itself to be 'contaminated by little self-promoting narcissisms, facile demagogic ploys or the vulgar rapacity of publishers'.[4]

Derrida's attitude towards the press continued to be edged with wariness, except in relation to the few papers he considered to be 'friendly'. With *Libération*, in particular, especially with Robert Maggiori, his relations had become more cordial. As regards *Le Monde*, Derrida remained on the defensive, partly because of his complicated links with Roger-Pol Droit, and partly because the editor of the books section, Josyane Savigneau, was very close to Philippe Sollers. Even though the arrival of Dominique Dhombres, one of his former students at Normale Sup, helped to smooth over certain tensions, he was still mistrustful. 'Like Bourdieu, Derrida was a "tricky customer",' as Dhombres recalls. 'To begin with, he played along with interviews, and greatly enjoyed improvising. But he later wanted the result to resemble a real text, something that's difficult in the press. The need to observe word limits was something he completely rejected. The least little cut was, in his view, a form of censorship.'[5]

Derrida had eventually accepted photographs, recognizing belatedly that the ideological character of his earlier refusal also concealed a 'prudish flirtatiousness' and a 'tormented relation' with his own image.[6] For him, the problem had shifted its ground: it was now a question of whether or not to appear on television. He was never invited on *Apostrophes*, but he claimed he would have refused anyway. In February 1996, at a meeting with students from the University of Paris VIII, he stated his admiration for Patrick Modiano* in the programmes on which he was invited to appear:

---

* Modiano is a distinguished French novelist and a stammerer. – Tr.

'He's managed to get people to accept that they need to be patient when he can't find his words. [. . .] There's someone who has succeeded in transforming the public scene and forcing it to go at his own speed.'[7]

Two months later, a whole programme was devoted to Derrida, in Laure Adler's *Cercle de minuit*. Apart from his short and unhappy appearance on Arte, with Salman Rushdie and Pierre Bourdieu, this was the first time Derrida had spoken on French television since his return from Prague, on 2 January 1982. If he had said yes to Laure Adler, this was because he knew and admired her, and was able to discuss with her how the face-to-face discussion would go, in surroundings of the greatest sobriety. Françoise Giroud wrote appreciatively about the programme in her column in the *Nouvel Observateur*, while deploring its timing:

> Jacques Derrida at 1 a.m., what a waste! Laure Adler will allow us to say that much. Her *Cercle de minuit* is often interesting, but her audience is inevitably restricted. And so, offering then Derrida to watch . . . Someone we never see, someone who never speaks . . . So the most famous, outside France, of French philosophers had agreed to make an exception and put in an appearance. It was pure magic! A completely new freedom of expression, a fresh style of thinking, new paths boldly opened up . . . I've never seen anything like it before. Superb.[8]

However, it would be several years before the experience was repeated. In *Echographies of Television*, the transcription of filmed interviews made three years earlier with Bernard Stiegler, Derrida insisted on the modifications that television imposes structurally on the words of writers and intellectuals:

> As soon as someone says 'Roll tape!' a race begins, one starts not to speak, not to think in the same way anymore, almost not to think at all anymore . . . One's relation to words, to their way or coming or not coming, is different, you know this well. [. . .] Maybe intellectuals who appear on television all the time are better able to forget the effects of this artificiality which I, for one, am having such a hard time with here. I say this under the heading of process and of stasis, of the arrest, the halt. When the process of recording begins, I am inhibited, paralyzed, arrested, I 'don't get anywhere' [*je fais du 'sur-place'*] and I don't think, I don't speak in the way I do when I'm not in this situation.[9]

There was an interesting coincidence in the fact that, at the end of 1996, at the same time as *Echographies of Television*, Pierre

Bourdieu's *On Television* was published. The sociologist's analysis was quite close to Derrida's, but more radical and more militant in style.[10]

While he was open to new areas, Derrida stayed faithful to most of his old passions. This was why he was happy to agree to speak in the prestigious setting of the Museum of Modern Art in New York, on the occasion of the first major exhibition of paintings and drawings by Artaud: 'Antonin Artaud: Works on Paper'. In the lecture he gave on 16 October 1996, he tried once again to get closer to the man who nicknamed himself 'Artaud le Mômo' ('Artaud the Kiddy'). But he also pondered the 'strange event represented, in 1996, by the exhibition of Artaud's works in one of the greatest museum institutions in the city of New York – and the world'. The title chosen by Derrida, *Artaud le Moma*, was unfortunately not deemed 'presentable or decent' by the directors of MoMA. And so the talk was given without any real title: 'Jacques Derrida . . . will present a lecture about Artaud's drawings.'[11]

It was at this lecture that Derrida made the acquaintance of Serge Malausséna, Antonin Artaud's nephew, now his beneficiary. A serious legal dispute had embroiled them for years over the book that brought together the *Dessins et portraits*, published by Gallimard and Schirmer-Mosel in 1986. In 1991, Malausséna had also used a subpoena to block the publication of volume XXVI of Artaud's complete works by Gallimard. So relations were more than strained. However, the first contact with Malausséna was quite cordial. Derrida was struck by the astonishing physical resemblance between Artaud and his nephew, and by his evident passion for Artaud's work. Malausséna, for his part, greatly admired the lecture.

'Jacques Derrida struck me as being as charming as he was brilliant,' Malausséna recalls,

> but relations between us had been poisoned by Paule Thévenin. At this meeting in New York, and more particularly during a long meeting in Paris, I gave him my version of the story: the way Paule Thévenin had seized the papers, notebooks, and drawings on the very same day Artaud had died, and cleared out his room; the way she had concealed them for years with different people, fobbing off questions by alluding to mysterious collectors . . . Derrida was embarrassed by what I told him: 'I'd never seen things from that point of view,' he said. But he still insisted on his debt towards Paule Thévenin. Since she had passed away in 1993, he probably felt even more bound by loyalty.[12]

A few months before their second meeting, Derrida wrote to Malausséna saying that he wished to publish *Artaud le Moma* with reproductions, 'most in small format, and in colour',[13] which the beneficiary agreed to. But in 2002, when he saw the dummy of the book, Malausséna expressed his great shock on reading a note added in the definitive version, in which Derrida paid emphatic homage to Paule Thévenin. Malausséna wrote to tell him that, contrary to rumour, he had never opposed the publication of Artaud's works, but that he *had* wished to protest against the *'defective* edition' of the unpublished notebooks, which in his view had been 'massacred' by Thévenin. 'Retaining the manuscripts for half a century has allowed their possessor to act however she wanted, without any control, wielding absolute power over an oeuvre that Artaud *never entrusted her with.*' Looking forward to a new generation of scholars being able to work tranquilly 'without being subjected to the pressure of those men and women who had commandeered Artaud,' Malausséna concluded his letter by questioning Derrida's role in all this more explicitly: 'My brutal frankness in no way diminishes the esteem in which I hold you. I will simply note that you are setting yourself up as the high priest of a memory, conferring a sacred aura on someone who behaved, all her life long, as an autocrat.'[14]

The disagreement ran too deep to be resolved, and Derrida could merely acknowledge this. Regretting that the note he had added had offended Artaud's nephew, he agreed to alter it at proof stage.

> As for Paule Thévenin, without being either willing or able to engage in a fundamental debate (it would be too difficult in a letter), I can't deny what, like so many others, I personally owe to her work, what my reading of Artaud owes her, what I owe to the attentive friendship she showed towards me for a quarter of a century, especially in the (long) story of my little pieces on Artaud. You are well aware of this. So it was an impulse of respect and loyalty that I felt I had to obey each time I named Paule Thévenin in the final revisions of my text. I hope that, in spite of so many disagreements, you will understand what this gesture dictated.[15]

The difficulties that Derrida himself had experienced with Thévenin at the time he was writing *Glas* – and the problems Genet had related – could have led him to defend her in less unconditional terms. But, like de Man, Thévenin had become sacrosanct now that she was no longer there to defend herself.*

---

* The Artaud affair would take on a new lease of life during the last weeks of Derrida's life, when the big volume of Artaud's works came out in the 'Quarto' series. This anthology had been conceived, introduced, and annotated by Évelyne

Derrida, so vigilant in his relations with the media, sometimes fell into other traps. The great American jazz musician Ornette Coleman, a philosophy devotee, had long dreamed of meeting the father of deconstruction. When he came to Paris, at the end of June 1997, a meeting was organized and recorded by the magazine *Les Inrockuptibles*. The conversation was so cordial that Coleman invited Derrida to speak at a concert he was scheduled to give a few days later at the jazz festival in La Villette. Derrida, touched and attracted by the proposal, immediately agreed. Over the years, he had started to enjoy appearing in public. In spite of Marguerite's counsels of caution, he did not realize how different this context would be from those to which he was accustomed.

On the evening of 1 July, without having been introduced, Derrida suddenly appeared on stage, in front of a packed auditorium, and started reading, in jazzed-up rhythms, the text he had just written:

What's happening? What's happening? What's going to happen, Ornette, right now?
What's happening to me, here, now, with Ornette Coleman? With you? Who? Well, need to improvise, no? We need to

---

Grossman. She had been very close to Derrida over the previous years, had interviewed him several times and edited the issue of the review *Europe* devoted to him; they had even started to make plans for a 'Quarto' volume devoted to his work. But on 14 September 2004, already in hospital, Derrida sent Maurice Nadeau a fax for publication in *La Quinzaine littéraire*. Typed out by a third party, the document contains several corrections in his own hand:

'Dear Maurice Nadeau / When I dedicated *Artaud le Moma* to the memory of my friend Paule Thévenin, this was not merely to acknowledge a personal debt. It was also my way of saluting a woman who, as everyone knows, devoted almost her entire life to studying, deciphering, and publishing Artaud's works. M. Gallimard must be the first to know this./Now I have discovered, today, on a first stupefied reading, that the "Quarto" edition of Artaud's works does all it can (countless examples could be given) to *erase the name, the work and even the magnificent portraits of Paule Thévenin*. I suppose that this indescribable injustice has been perpetrated by Artaud's nephew whose hatred of Paule Thévenin is well known [. . .]. / I am convinced that I will not be the only one to ask M. Antoine Gallimard to do all he can to explain, and above all make reparation for, such a serious, flagrant, and saddening injustice.'

Deeply hurt by this attack on her work, Évelyne Grossman reacted in an interview that, with unfortunate timing, was published in *La Quinzaine* on 16 October 2004, a few days after Derrida's death. In it, she stated:

'Without in the least wishing to engage in a polemic (especially not with Jacques Derrida, whose friendship for and loyalty to Paule Thévenin I am aware of), I cannot fail to think that there is too much passion (in the sense of Christ's passion), too much sacrifice and sacredness in this story of Paule Thévenin's relations with Artaud's work. Not that I am denying the need for passion. [. . .] But to my mind, this does not in the least mean that the reader should be stuck in this immediate or epidermic adhesion to the oeuvre, in this blind identification with Artaud.'

improvise *well*. I knew Ornette was going to call me up here, this evening, he'd told me so when we met up to talk for a whole afternoon, last week. This stroke of luck scares me, I don't know what's going to happen. Well, I need to improvise, I need to improvise, but *well*, that – is already a *music lesson, your lesson*, Ornette, that disturbs our old idea of improvisation – I even think you've sometimes deemed it 'racist', this ancient, naïve idea of improvisation.[16]

The journalist from *Le Monde* wrote a rave review: 'The philosopher's intonations are naturally musical, as are his words. The saxophonist joins in with the words. Mellow!' But Derrida's text was, as usual, long. And people soon started protesting noisily. There were just a few dozen who resisted the charm of the thing, out of a thousand spectators, but this was enough to wreck the mood. They started yelling: 'That's enough!' 'Shut your face!' 'Off, off!' Some booed, others applauded. Mortified, Derrida was obliged to quit the stage long before he had finished his text. Sylvain Siclier's verdict: 'What was missing? It just needed the saxophonist to introduce the philosopher, a few words of explanation. [. . .] Ornette Coleman's idea was perhaps contrived [. . .], perhaps it clashed too much with the format of the concert.'[17]

Ten days later, however, at the château of Cerisy-la-Salle, Derrida found an audience that was ready to eat out of his hand. The idea of a third conference on his work had been mooted by Édith Heurgon and Jean Ricardou in 1993. Derrida was soon happy to go along, merely expressing the wish that the programme would be less packed, less 'inhumane', than in the two previous *décades*.[18] Marie-Louise Mallet would again be put in charge of organizing the event, and the conference would be called, in a way that was both open and enigmatic, 'The Autobiographical Animal'.

Derrida's paper, which he began giving on 15 July 1997, his birthday, went on for much of the following day. 'I inflicted a twelve-hour lecture on them!' he wrote, with some pride, to his friend Catherine Malabou.[19] But this time, there were no protests – quite the opposite. Since he had not had time to deal with Heidegger as he had wished, the participants even suggested that he improvise on the subject, on the last evening of the conference.[20]

The question of the animal had always been for him 'the most important and decisive question'. Rereading his work from this angle, he claimed that he had 'addressed it a thousand times, either directly or obliquely, by means of a reading of *all* the philosophers' in whom he had taken an interest.[21] But in his lecture at Cerisy, 'The animal that therefore I am', he started by treating it from a very concrete point of view, on the basis of a private experience:

I often ask myself, just to see, *who I am* – and who I am (follow-ing) at the moment when, caught naked, in silence, by the gaze of an animal, for example, the eyes of a cat, I have trouble, yes, a bad time overcoming my embarrassment.

Whence this malaise?

I have trouble repressing a reflex of shame. Trouble keeping silent within me a protest against the indecency. Against the impropriety [*malséance*] that can come of finding oneself naked, one's sex exposed, stark naked before a cat that looks at you without moving, just to see. The impropriety of a certain animal nude before the other animal, from that point on one might call it a kind of *animalséance*: the single, incomparable and original experience of the impropriety that would come from appearing in truth naked, in front of the insistent gaze of the animal, a benevolent or pitiless gaze, surprised or cogni-zant. The gaze of a seer, a visionary or extra-lucid blind one. It is as if I were ashamed, therefore, naked in front of this cat, but also ashamed for being ashamed. [. . .]

I must immediately make it clear, the cat I am talking about is a real cat, truly, believe me, *a little cat*. It isn't the *figure* of a cat. It doesn't silently enter the bedroom as an allegory for all the cats on the earth, the felines that traverse our myths and religions, our literature and our fables.[22]

A *décade* at Cerisy was never, for Derrida, just a matter of lec-tures and the subsequent discussions. There was 'something more affective, more tenacious, more inward, both inexpressible and unthinkable', residing in 'asides, in what might be nicknamed the comings and goings, the counter-comings and counter-goings of Cerisy, during meetings and discussions that are private, if not secret, and that are never collected or published'. It was mainly this which made it, in his view, an incomparable 'experience of thinking'.[23]

Yet again, the encounters at Cerisy had proved enriching, serene, and friendly. And Derrida again expressed all his gratitude to the woman in charge:

This *décade* was marvellous, a real 'marvel', yet again, and all thanks to you. I'm not saying this just on my own behalf. It was the feeling of all those present – they didn't want to leave, they had tears in their eyes . . . On a more personal level, you can imagine the strange stroke of luck, so wonderful and so troubling too, that has been given me – an anxious modesty prevents me from talking about it properly, but I'm sure you'll understand . . . The 'way home' is always melancholy, of course.[24]

In Michel Deguy's view, the way Derrida's work developed should be seen almost as a kind of enterprise: the 'Derrida International'.

> Over the last fifteen or twenty years of his life, there were thirty or so people working round him and contributing to spread the influence of deconstruction across the world: professors, heads of university departments, directors of reviews and publishers, conference organizers and editors of *Festschriften*. Their names varied somewhat over the years, but many of the faithful had been there for a long time. You just need to look at the lists of those who took part in the different conferences at Cerisy to realize this. Translators were among the most important mediators: Derrida's work was translated by associates of his, people who had come into translation because they were devotees of his work and could dialogue with him.[25]

Since the end of the 1960s, the United States had, of course, been Derrida's real stamping ground: the place where his presence had always been most evident, and from where most of its worldwide influence stemmed. From 1995, thanks to the three new works – *Specters of Marx*, *Force of Law*, and *Archive Fever* – that rapidly assumed classic status, there was a real upsurge of interest for his work in the United States. Even though Derrida registered a certain irritation when there was talk of a 'political turn' or 'ethical turn' in his work, there is no denying that new themes now occupied centre stage: justice, witness, hospitality, forgiveness, lying . . . There was no real break, as there was in Wittgenstein or Heidegger, but it is difficult not to see a series of inflections and slippages. The de Man affair had probably helped him to overcome his reserve.

> I am simply trying to pursue with some consistency a thinking that has been engaged around the same aporias for a long time. The question of ethics, law, or politics hasn't arisen unexpectedly, as when you come off a bend. And the way in which it is treated is not always reassuring for 'morale' – and perhaps because it asks too much of it.[26]

The triumph of 'French Theory' and deconstruction sometimes had its downsides. As if he were a victim of the effects of his own thinking, Derrida now found himself accused of being too conservative and insufficiently committed. Avital Ronell emphasizes this aspect: 'He was a male, a white, a seducer, a philosopher: all potential flaws that might lead to him being seen as on the side of traditional power. He was starting to become the victim of his own categories, his own war on phallogocentrism.' His alliance with several radical women seems, in this respect, to have been a valuable plus.[27]

At New York University, throughout the last years, Ronell and Derrida gave seminars together. She introduced the session, going back over the elements that had struck her at the previous session and adding a few references. After Jacques's paper, she took over and asked a few questions to get the discussion started.

Everywhere else, Derrida was the sole master of his seminar. But at NYU, he was, so to speak, my guest, and he accepted my way of doing things. The situation was very different at Irvine, where he carried on with the seminar he had started at the Hautes Études. At New York, he was presenting new material and his approach was still very open. One year, he'd chosen as his title the single word 'Forgiveness'; I didn't much like this, and I changed it to 'Violence and Forgiveness'. When we met just before the seminar, I told him I'd changed the title, since 'Forgiveness' by itself didn't work in English. He was really not very pleased: 'Look, Avital, how could you take a decision like that without consulting me? It's just not on.' But at the start of the session, he said completely the opposite, explaining that the word 'violence' was absolutely necessary. He said that *I* had tried to drop it, and that I was completely wrong to do so! You couldn't think of forgiveness without violence. There wasn't a trace of irony in his voice. And all I could do was explain to the audience why I'd wanted to drop the word. In the final analysis, each of us had committed a violent act on the other, but this had enabled us to move forward and produce thought . . . In the last years, he felt that I was overtaking him 'on his left' and this sometimes made him nervous. One day, he told me that my radicalism was starting to be dangerous for deconstruction. He claimed that *he* always took 'calculated' risks. I told him that this kind of calculation was impossible. But he sometimes had a really paranoid side to him. One day he told me that he didn't feel at ease having my book *Crack Wars* in his luggage when he crossed the border. He said he'd be arrested as a dealer – it's true that I was born in Prague! – and this kind of publication could wreck his American career. 'At all events,' he told me sometimes, 'they'll hold me responsible for this kind of language, saying that it all comes from me!'[28]

Derrida's travels had, like translations of his work, become more numerous – and extended across the world. And he could not conceal his annoyance when the French press placed a little too much emphasis on his American activities. As he wrote to Dominique Dhombres, from Cracow:

I travel a great deal, but I'm not just (or even essentially) 'American', as they often say (and always with two implications, the one provincial: 'you see, this lad of ours is really famous abroad', the other condescending: 'you see, only the Americans are interested in him, nobody knows what they see in him.' The two subtexts can perfectly well coexist).[29]

During the 1990s, Derrida held lectures and seminars in several countries which he had not hitherto visited, sometimes owing to a lack of people with whom he wished to discuss his ideas, but more often for political reasons:

Often I haven't visited a country until after the beginnings of 'democratization'. In this regard, I am thinking of all the Eastern European countries that I went to for the first time only after 1990 (except for Budapest in 1973 – but Hungary was already an exception, and Prague in 1981 – but that was in secret and I ended up in prison). Other 'first times' visiting 'brand-new' democracies: Greece, Spain, Portugal, Uruguay, Argentina, Chile, Brazil, South Africa.[30]

In the same way, he went to Moscow for the first time in 1990, when the USSR was collapsing. And he returned in 1994, when he also visited Saint Petersburg. In post-Soviet Russia, Derrida's work and person aroused considerable interest. As his translator Natalia Avtonomova relates:

Here, Derrida presents himself 'as what he is' as well as being the – sole living – representative of contemporary French philosophy. It creates a real stir. People wonder who he is, beyond the different images they have of him: someone who is overturning all values or someone who is affirming new ones, a pop star or a serious scholar? Journalists' fantasies – they sing his praises or decry him but are never indifferent – are the flipside of his popularity. For example, the magazine for men, *Medved*, entertains its readers with details of what ties he likes to wear, his favourite food – and the cheerleaders of post-Soviet literature boast of being on first-name terms with the 'master'. Derrida's resonant name echoes in student songs, and everyone has the word 'deconstruction' on their lips. [. . .]
   Derrida's two stays in Moscow have set the Muscovite public abuzz. Just imagine: they can see a 'classic' in flesh and blood, and not just any classic: one who defends Marx, when on all sides he is being kicked around like a wounded lion![31]

The fine book *Counterpath* enables us to follow in detail several of Derrida's travels during this period, thanks to the long letters he sent to Catherine Malabou.

In February 1997, Derrida went to India for the first time, giving lectures and interviews; in Calcutta, the 'guru of deconstruction' opened the Book Fair; in Bombay and New Delhi, he was given a triumphant reception. Over the next few months, he travelled to Dublin, Baltimore, Villanova, Montreal, Madrid, Istanbul, Tilburg, Turin, Pisa, London, Brighton, and Porto – not to mention his usual sojourns in Irvine and New York. From 9 to 14 December he was in Poland for the first time, receiving an honorary doctorate from Katowice and giving two lectures in Cracow and Warsaw. 'I went to Auschwitz but won't talk about that here,' he wrote.[32] He set off almost immediately for Athens, where he stayed from 18 to 21 December.

On 5 January 1998, he was at the Hebrew University of Jerusalem. It had been ten years since his last visit to Israel – the delay was mainly for political reasons. After his lecture in Tel Aviv and a 'relatively peaceful' debate, he had a long conversation with Shimon Peres. The following morning, loyal as ever to his Palestinian friends, he set off for Ramallah and spoke at Birzeit University.[33] The rest of the year was almost as busy. In summer 1998, for example, he took a long trip to South Africa, drawing huge audiences with his lecture 'Forgiving: the unforgivable and the imprescriptible'.[34] This was the first time he met Nelson Mandela, one of the politicians he had never ceased to admire, and declared that he was fascinated by the constitution of the new South Africa, which he deemed to be properly democratic and extremely modern.

This trip was also at the centre of the film his friend Safaa Fathy made about him in 1998 and 1999, *D'ailleurs Derrida* (*Moreover Derrida*), broadcast on Arte. She filmed him in France and the United States, as well as the south of Spain, amid landscapes reminiscent of those of his childhood. She also went to Algeria, but, for security reasons, Derrida could not join the team. The film is anything but didactic: it superimposes all these places without ever identifying them, to a soundtrack of Arabo-Andalusian music.

Derrida participated more or less graciously in the productions that were proposed to him. He often seemed ill at ease and a bit wooden. In *Shooting Words: On the Edge of a Film*, the book written to accompany the documentary, he pondered at length on 'the Actor' he had become, even if it was to play himself:

Never before have I played along to this extent. And yet never before has consent been so anxious, so under- and badly per- formed, painfully estranged from any complaisance, simply unable to say 'no', to draw on the store of the 'no' that I have always cultivated.

Never have I been so passive, basically, never have I let people do with me as they wished, direct me, to such an extent. How did I let myself be taken by surprise, *to this extent*, so unwisely? After all, right from the start, I have been or at least I think I have been, very wary, and I warn people that I am very wary, – of this situation of imprudence or improvidence (the photograph, the improvised interview, the impromptu remark, the movie camera, the microphone, the public space itself, etc.).[35]

Over the next few years, Safaa Fathy continued to film Derrida on several occasions, at conferences or public events, trying to compose an audiovisual memory to complement the archives at Irvine. She became a permanent presence, following the philosopher like a shadow, even though this irritated many of his friends. It was as if his relationship to the image had finally been reversed, as if, from a radical rejection of photography, Derrida had shifted to an almost uninterrupted video recording, a multiplicity of traces that was no doubt another form of effacement.

Travels, images . . . As these proliferated, so did his publications. What Derrida really liked about Galilée was the way it enabled him to publish as fast as he wanted. Big books, sometimes, but often smaller volumes containing just a lecture or two. He was happy with this kind of fragmentation. He had long been convinced that it was no longer possible to construct 'a big philosophical machine'; he preferred to proceed by a series of 'oblique little essays'. Faced with the philosophical concepts of the tradition, he felt 'like a fly who has sensed danger', he said one day during a debate with Jean-Luc Nancy. 'My instinct has always been to flee, as if, at first contact, just by *naming* these concepts, I was going to find myself, like the fly, with my legs trapped in glue: captive, paralysed, a hostage, trapped by a programme.'[36]

Derrida felt and saw himself more and more as a writer, and his thinking was less and less separable from its utterance. Though he was one of the most-translated French authors in the world, he was first and foremost a man who celebrated the genius of a language for which he confessed he had 'an anxious, jealous, tormented love'. Comparing his feeling with the more tranquil attitudes of Lévi-Strauss, Foucault, and Deleuze, he explained in his dialogues with Élisabeth Roudinesco that he felt that everything he tried to do involved 'a hand-to-hand struggle with the French language, a turbulent but *primal* hand-to-hand struggle'. 'I would dare to claim that between the French language and me [. . .], there will have been

[. . .] more love. More mad love, if you like. And more jealousy, reciprocal jealousy, if that doesn't seem too senseless and insane!'[37]

Derrida's love of the language and his passion for writing had brought him much closer to Hélène Cixous. In 1998, they collaborated on the book *Veils*: 'A silkworm of one's own', Derrida's text, took off from a few pages of 'Knowing', first written by Cixous. This was the first time she had brought out a book with Galilée, and it soon became her main publisher.

The same year, at the invitation of Mireille Calle-Gruber, Derrida delivered the immensely lengthy opening address at the conference 'Hélène Cixous, Crossroads of a Work' at Cérisy, with the inventive title *H.C. For Life, That is to Say . . .*, which he exploited in every possible way, celebrating thirty-five years of friendship, admiration, and mutual readings.

I will not be able to do much more than sketch out or anticipate, between the lines, the interminable conference paper or the interminable confidential remarks that I had dreamed of foisting on you. I would have liked to invent, for the occasion, for Hélène and in her honour, a new genre, and a new name for this genre, going beyond all the differences or rather playing on all the differences, from the whispers of confessional confidences and the authority of the lecture, whether philosophical or theoretical, or critical, or poïetic, a portmanteau or a mot-valise fort Cerisy, somewhere between the confidence, confidence, and the conference.[38]

Cixous refused to get left behind. She devoted two eloquent books to Derrida: *Portrait of Derrida as a Young Jewish Saint*, in 2001, and *Insister of Jacques Derrida*, in 2006.[39] During Derrida's last years, they were involved in many dialogues and common interventions. 'We had met at the start of our respective careers. Jacques sometimes wondered whether we could have had the same complicity if we had both been writers, or both philosophers. He tended to think not. I was convinced of the opposite. For me, at all events, he was a fully fledged writer.'[40]

'In the beginning is the word [*le mot*]', acknowledged Derrida in one of his last dialogues with Hélène Cixous. 'Both naming and word [*vocable*]. As if I could not think anything before writing: taken by surprise by some resource of the French language that I have not invented, I then make something of it that was not on the programme but was already rendered possible by a lexical and syntactic treasure.'[41] With Francis Ponge, whom he had admired since his teens, Derrida shared 'the religion of the *Littré* [dictionary], a secular and playful religion'.[42] Scrutinizing etymologies was not, for him, the quest of a pre-existing truth: keeping the language in a state of 'expansion', it was primarily invention.

Derrida could produce a whole text from French words such as *'pas'*, *'demeure'*, or *'voile'*, playing with them in different ways, celebrating all the resources they contained.

> I am always guided by untranslatability: when the phrase is forever indebted to the idiom, when the translation can only lose it. It is an apparent paradox that translators have taken much more interest in my texts than have the French, trying to reinvent in their own languages the experience that I have just described.[43]

Derrida loved the French language so much that he was always trying to enrich it. 'We owe him new words, active words (and in this respect his writing is violent, poetic),' Roland Barthes had noted back in 1972.[44] And Derrida himself liked telling the story of how, shortly after the word *'différance'* had made its entry in the Petit Robert dictionary, Avital Ronell had mentioned this fact in the presence of Jacques's mother as an event that deserved to be celebrated. Georgette Safar, with a frown of disapproval, had turned to her son and asked: 'But Jackie, have you *really* written "difference" with an "a"?'

Over the years, Derrida had coined more and more new words, despite the risk of shocking people other than his mother. In his little book *The Vocabulary of Jacques Derrida*, Charles Ramond listed and analysed scores of these neologisms and portmanteau words so avidly fabricated.[45] Some were ephemeral, others have become brand names: *adestination, archi-écriture, arrivance, clandestination, destinerrance, exappropriation, hantologie, médiagogique, mondialatinisation, restance, stricture* ... (*adestination, archi-writing* or *arche-writing, arrivance, clandestination, destinerrancy, exappropriation, hauntology, mediagogic, globalatinization, remnance, stricture* ...).*

Syntax was affected too: in Derrida's hands, it was forever freeing itself from the models of traditional philosophical writing. In this respect, his evolution is comparable to that of Francis Ponge, moving from the brevity and extreme density of *The Voice of Things* to the multiple variations of *The Notebook of the Pine Wood* or *Soap*. Derrida's texts were increasingly written for reading aloud. This gives them a highly individual rhythm in which 'writing always follows the voice. Whether or not this voice is internal, it always puts itself or finds itself on stage.'[46]

---

* Translations of these terms vary; these are just indicators. – Tr.

When reading his late works, one needs to let oneself be borne along by a quite particular breathing. A sentence by Derrida is closer to Henry James than to Proust: it seems to coil indefinitely round itself, before making a sudden leap forward.[47] A 1996 text, *Athens, Still Remains*, is highly revelatory in this regard. The whole work turns on a tirelessly repeated phrase: 'We owe ourselves to death' (*'Nous nous devons à la mort'*). As if it were this phrase and this phrase alone that Derrida was endlessly tracking, on the pretext of a discussion of a series of photos by Jean-François Bonhomme:

Surgie d'on ne sait où, ladite phrase ne m'appartenait plus. Elle n'avait d'ailleurs jamais été mienne, je ne m'en sentais pas encore responsable. Instantanément tombée dans le domaine public, elle m'avait traversé. Elle passait par moi, elle se disait en moi de passage. Devenu son otage, plutôt que son hôte, je devais lui offrir l'hospitalité, oui, la garder sauve, j'étais certes responsable d'une telle sauvegarde, et du salut de chacun de ses mots, comptable de l'immunité de chaque lettre alliée à chaque lettre. Mais la même dette, le même devoir me dictaient de ne pas la prendre, cette phrase tout entière, de ne m'en emparer en aucun cas comme d'une phrase par moi signée. Elle restait d'ailleurs imprenable.

Having surfaced from who knows where, the sentence in question no longer belonged to me. It had, in fact, never been mine, and I did not yet feel responsible for it. Having instantly fallen into the public domain, it had traversed me. It passed through me, saying from within me that it was just passing through. Having become its hostage rather than its host, I had to offer it hospitality, indeed to keep it safe: I was, to be sure, responsible for its safekeeping, for safeguarding each of its words, accountable for the immunity or indemnity of each letter joined to the next. But the same debt, the same obligation, dictated to me that I do not take this sentence, not take it as a whole, that I do not under any circumstances take hold of it like a sentence signed by me. And it did in fact remain impregnable.[48]

The reader initially has the sense of a single long melody, which could go on and on. In reality, the text is a series of short phrases, with a great deal of punctuation, though they follow one another in a series of tiny repetitions and displacements, repeating the same syllables (*-sable/-table/-nable*), playing on the same words (*otage/hôte/hospitalité*; *garder/sauve/sauvegarder*), even at the risk of seeming immobile. It could be read as a Mediterranean syntax with its discreet waves, its almost imperceptible ebb and flow. By a series of insidious transformations, less slow than they seem, an interplay of differences and repetitions, irritating or fascinating, Derrida gradually draws us into his meditative path. Poetry is there, very close, inseparable from philosophy.

> This acknowledgement of debt, this IOU, was like a thing, a simple thing lost in the world, but a thing already owed, already due, and I had to keep it without taking it. To hold on to it as if holding it in trust, as if on consignment, consigned to a photo-engraved safekeeping. What does this obligation, this first indebting, have to do with the verb of this declaration that can never be appropriated, 'we *owe* [devons] ourselves to death?' What does the obligation have to do with what the declaration seemed to mean? Not 'we owe ourselves to the death,' not 'we owe ourselves death,' but 'we owe ourselves *to* death.'
>
> But just who is death? (Where is it – or she – to be found? One says, curiously, in French, *trouver la mort*, to 'find death,' 'to meet with death' – and that means to die.)[49]

9

The Time of Dialogue

2000–2002

In January 2000, a new, important book came out under the Galilée imprint: Derrida's *On Touching: Jean-Luc Nancy*. It was, first and foremost, an imposing object: far from all the traditional norms of a philosophical work, it was 350 pages long, in square format, with several typographical variations; and the text was accompanied by a series of images by Simon Hantaï, described as 'works of reading' (*travaux de lecture*). As often when it came to a difficult book, Michel Delorme was also relying on bibliophiles, and the original edition of 129 copies was accompanied by an engraving.

A first, much shorter version of this text had appeared in the United States in 1992, in a special issue of the review *Paragraph*, on the initiative of Peggy Kamuf, but the main part of the work was composed between September 1998 and September 1999. It was during his trip to Oceania, in a hotel bedroom in Melbourne, that Derrida completed the final revisions.

The work's strange title might have put off some potential readers by implying that a good knowledge of Nancy's work would be necessary. Of course, Derrida had mainly wished to 'sketch out a first movement' to celebrate Jean-Luc Nancy, the man and, more especially, the 'major event' that his work represented.[1] But through the author of *L'Intrus*, Derrida was going back to a phenomenological approach that he had long since neglected, around a thread and a title, *On Touching*, that had constantly worried him even when they seemed inevitable. So there were in fact two books in one here. And probably more than that, as Derrida acknowledges in the insert.

> Firstly, a heterogeneous composition. Some will judge it, if they insist on using these categories, baroque or romantic (philosophy that never renounces anything + canonical history of philosophy + planned system + table of categories – but also fiction + phantasm + narration + biography + parentheses + digressions + confidences + private correspondence + unkept promises).[2]

Around the theme of touching, Derrida develops a series of 'tangents' in which he mentions Aristotle, Kant, Husserl, Heidegger, Merleau-Ponty, and Levinas, as well as authors to whom he had not previously referred, such as Maine de Biran, Ravaisson, Jean-Louis Chrétien, and various others, before returning to Nancy. Derrida, who had always drawn attention to the privilege granted to sight in much of the philosophical tradition, modified his position somewhat:

> *Intuition* means gaze; intuitionism is the thinking which grants to the gaze, to immediate vision, access to truth. [. . .] What I realized, in writing this book on touch and rereading all those texts, is that an even more powerful tradition, ever since Plato, subjected the gaze to the touch and that intuitionism became the experience of immediacy, of immediate contact, of the continuous, of plenitude and presence, the privilege of presence being granted even more to touch than to sight itself. I then talked in terms of a haptocentric intuitionism, which marked a change in the story of my little career, since the deconstruction of intuitionism had already been in progress since the beginning, but it was not addressed directly to touch but rather to sight. I was led to rearrange things in a different order.[3]

J. Hillis Miller was struck by the singularity of this work, which he viewed as one of the most important of Derrida's final years.

> Usually, Derrida waited until his friends were dead before he wrote an essay or a book on them. He did it at the time of their death, or very shortly thereafter. In almost all these homages, especially in the one on Levinas, you can see a double movement at work: he emphasizes their importance, but at the same time he places them or puts them in their place. So every time, structurally, he is the one to have the last word. The book *On Touching* is a quite particular case. Derrida had started to write a long article when Jean-Luc Nancy was waiting for a heart transplant and so was in danger of dying. But luckily, Nancy survived; we could almost say that he rose again. And, years later, Derrida took up his text again, greatly extending it. It's the only book of this type that he published while the author he was discussing was still alive. And so Nancy had an opportunity to reply to him, on the question of the deconstruction of Christianity, in a note in *Noli me tangere*. One might even say that *he* had the last word. Derrida had criticized him for being too Christian. And Nancy replied to Derrida that he was too rabbinic.[4]

But Nancy was mainly just moved by this homage. He gauged its value in terms both of friendship and of the extraordinary attention to his work that the book revealed.

It was a coup . . . I was thunderstruck to see the title, then the book itself. I think I then said to Jacques: I was speechless, it was too much. Of course, in matters of friendship there is no 'too much', and in this respect I was deeply moved. But there is in his analysis such a force of knowledge and problematization that I said to myself: I'm never going to be able to touch touch again [*je ne dois plus toucher au toucher*]. What you need to realize is that I'd never thematized touch as such, or hardly. In breathtaking fashion, Jacques had managed to read a number of texts in which this motif appeared from the sidelines. He had even tracked down the metaphorical uses of the word 'touch'. And he brought this extremely attentive reading into the huge set of other texts that he had read or reread to compose what was in every sense his book, his own book, on touch. Also, I'd clearly perceived the way he showed me the trap I'd only just avoided – let's call it 'haptocentrism', as he puts it. If I had avoided it, it was because I hadn't thematized it, and not out of any theoretical vigilance. And he also teaches me something of a lesson in this book. As you must know, it contains this phrase: 'I tell myself, in my heart of hearts [*à part moi*], Jean-Luc Nancy is the greatest philosopher of touch.' Jacques must have laughed over his amphibological *trouvaille*: 'I tell myself, in my heart of hearts [*à part moi*]' and 'I tell myself that, apart from me [*à part moi*] – who am in fact the greatest.' Finally, what I take away from this book is also the end: 'Just *salut*, greeting without salvation: just a *salut* on the way.' The word '*salut*'* becomes a concept in the form of an interjection of greeting or farewell: it's admirable, I often think of it.[5]

In the spring, Élisabeth Roudinesco and Jacques Derrida embarked on a book of dialogues that would take the title *For What Tomorrow* . . . The idea had been launched during a dinner, by Olivier Bétourné, the partner of Élisabeth Roudinesco, the then vice-president and manager of the publishing house Fayard. Struck by the way they were forever discussing current affairs, and ethical and political questions, he said he was convinced that such a work would be of the greatest interest and would attract new readers to Derrida.

---

* 'Salvation', but also 'hi!' or 'bye!' – Tr,

The interviews were recorded between 20 and 23 May 2000, at the height of the controversy around Renaud Camus.* 'On the second evening,' recalls Roudinesco,

> we were phoned by Claude Lanzmann who was launching a violent petition against Camus and asked Derrida to sign it. They had a frank exchange of views. Derrida was embarrassed at the labelling of such opinions as 'criminal', but he eventually agreed to sign. It was this current debate that led us to add a whole chapter on 'the anti-Semitism to come'.[6]

The death penalty was another theme by which Derrida was obsessed. He thought about it at length. Since the autumn of 1999, it had been the subject of his seminar. He read and reread a great number of philosophical texts on the subject, and started his seminar by expressing his amazement:

> To put it in a brief and economical way, I will proceed from what has long been for me the most significant and the most stupefying – also the most stupefied – fact about the history of Western philosophy: never, *to my knowledge*, has any philosopher *as a philosopher, in his or her own strictly and systematically philosophical discourse*, never has any philosophy *as such* contested the legitimacy of the death penalty. From Plato to Hegel, from Rousseau to Kant (who was undoubtedly the most rigorous of them all), they expressly, each in his own way, and sometimes not without much hand-wringing (Rousseau), took a stand *for* the death penalty.[7]

At the beginning of summer 2000, the Estates General of psychoanalysis, whose tireless organizer René Major had taken the initiative, offered Derrida an exceptional opportunity for developing these ethico-political questions. On the evening of 10 July, in

---

* In his Journal for 1984, published in spring 2000 by Fayard as *La Campagne de France*, Renaud Camus had written: 'The Jewish collaborators of Panorama on France-Culture are going a bit too far, all the same: for one thing, they comprise about four out of five on every broadcast, or four out of six or five out of seven, which, on a national or quasi-official station, comprises a definite over-representation of a given ethnic or religious group; and for another, they ensure that at least one programme per week is devoted to Jewish culture, to the Jewish religion, to Jewish writers, to the State of Israel and its politics, to the life of Jews in France and throughout the world, today or through the centuries.' This passage and several others – sometimes truncated or transformed – had triggered a widespread controversy, poisoned by publishers who were fighting for influence. Roudinesco and, to a lesser degree, Derrida played a significant part in the affair, which is discussed at several points in *For What Tomorrow* . . . .

the grand amphithéâtre of the Sorbonne, in front of over a thousand analysts from the whole world, he tackled this fundamental question: why is man the only being to enjoy evil for evil's sake? Extending Freud's reflections on the death drive, Derrida called psychoanalysis 'the only discourse which at present can claim the phenomenon of psychic cruelty as its own domain'.[8]

> Psychoanalysis would be the name of what, without any theological or other alibi, turns towards what is most *proper* to psychic cruelty [. . .]. Wherever a question of suffering *for* suffering, of doing evil or allowing it to be done *for the sake of* evil, in short, wherever the question of radical evil or of an evil worse than radical evil is no longer abandoned to religion or to metaphysics, no other discipline [*savoir*] is prepared to take an interest in something like cruelty – except for what is called psychoanalysis . . . .[9]

In Derrida's view, psychoanalysis 'has not yet tried, and so even less succeeded in, the task of thinking, penetrating, and changing the axioms of the ethical, the juridical, and the political'.[10] He would like to assign new roles to it, going beyond the treatment of individual suffering, if it wishes to preserve any theoretical relevance in a world that is no longer Freud's. Derrida is convinced: the 'Enlightenment to come' should take the logic of the unconscious into account. This involves, for example, answering a question that in his view is essential and yet rarely asked: 'Why does psychoanalysis never take root in the vast territory of Arabo-Islamic culture?'[11] All these questions would seem even more urgent in the wake of 11 September the following year.

A more personal question was now bothering him. Jacques had never much liked birthdays. But his seventieth birthday, on 15 July 2000, bugged him even more. He was prone to moments of depression and, contrary to his usual habits, took a great deal of Lexomil.[12*] On 1 September, he confided in Max Genève: 'I'm more than ever obsessed by age and the longing to "grow less old". [. . .] You'll see, being seventy is hell.'[13] Nonetheless, he still went swimming in the Mediterranean for hours on end.

This birthday rekindled Jacques's anxieties over his archives. Many of them had already been deposited in Irvine, but he sometimes regretted that he was leaving nothing in France. The IMEC – Institut Mémoires de l'Édition Contemporaine – is an association set up in 1988 on the initiative of scholars and members of the

---

* A sedative, also known as bromazepan. – Tr.

publishing industry to assemble archives. Among those already assembled (Céline, Duras, Barthes, Foucault . . .), two were of more particular interest to Derrida: Althusser and Genet. As related by Albert Dichy, the great Genet specialist and one of the people in charge of the IMEC: 'In 1991, there were some lively discussions between Althusser's friends about *The Future Lasts a Long Time*. Several, including Étienne Balibar, thought it was not the right time to publish it. Derrida was one of the few people to say that the text should indeed be published. In this delicate operation, he gave us his discreet support.'[14]

At the end of October 1997, following a conference at the Société des Gens de Lettres where they struck up a friendship, Olivier Corpet, the director of the IMEC, probed Derrida on the possibility of a partnership. Of course, there was no question of withdrawing anything from the Langson Library in Irvine. But new items could be entrusted to the IMEC. For scholars, the presence of several archives linked to his work would be a considerable draw. In Derrida's eyes, the IMEC also had the advantage of being independent: just like Cerisy, it was one of those 'counter-institutions' of which he was fond.

Corpet and Derrida met again at Ris-Orangis, at the end of 1997, and started to envisage in practical terms how a collaboration might work out. A few months later, Corpet wrote to tell him that he was fully prepared to go to Irvine to meet the people who ran the archives. 'A lot of things can "get sorted" on a face-to-face basis, and the IMEC is, as you know, very happy to engage in dialogue on the matter, since it is very anxious to establish a deep and trusting cooperation.'[15] He went to Irvine the following spring, and the partnership was in place by June 1999.

Derrida wished the originals of the letters he had received linked to France – far and away the most numerous – to be preserved in the IMEC, while letters linked to the United States and to other international developments of his work would be placed in Irvine, joining the manuscripts and documents that were already there. An exchange of photocopies was arranged between the two institutions to facilitate the work of scholars. So everything seemed to augur for the best.

The contract on the deposit of private archives was signed by Corpet and Derrida on 15 January 2002. But actually implementing it, when the time came to send off the letters, was another matter. As Albert Dichy remembers:

He'd open a folder, take out a letter, and tell me a bit about its context. He had long dreamed of rereading all his letters; he realized that he would now never do so . . . As the first boxes were loaded, with the oldest letters, he kept walking round the car. He took me by the arm: 'You have to realize it's my life you're taking away . . . If you were to have an accident . . .' I could see him in the rearview mirror, continuing to gaze after the vehicle as it headed off. There was a sense of twilight about him. His seventieth birthday had been really quite traumatic.[16]

As he grew older and the thought of death obsessed him more, Derrida seemed eager to come to a rapprochement with some of his former adversaries. In October 1999, in New York, he again met Jürgen Habermas at the home of their common friend Giovanna Barradori. At this unexpected encounter, Habermas had the 'smiling kindness' to propose that he and Derrida hold a discussion. Derrida accepted immediately: 'It's high time,' he said, 'let's not wait until it's too late.' The meeting took place in Paris shortly afterwards. During a friendly lunch, Habermas did all in his power to 'wipe out the traces of the previous polemic, with an exemplary probity' for which Derrida would always be grateful.[17]

The two men had not been on good terms for over twelve years, because of the two 'unfair and hasty' chapters that Habermas had written on Derrida in *The Philosophical Discourse of Modernity* and Derrida's stinging response in *Mémoires: For Paul de Man* and *Limited Inc.* Subsequently, though Derrida and Habermas themselves had remained silent, two rival camps had sprung up and waged what turned into a veritable war 'which doubtless gave people a lot to think about [. . .], but which also harmed a great number of students summarily required to choose their "camp" and sometimes being paralysed in their career'.[18] For Derrida, the quarrel with Habermas had had serious consequences: since the mid-1980s, access to the most important German publishers had been blocked, and his influence in the German-speaking world had been greatly hampered.

Their rapprochement was initially brought about on political terrain. Even during the years when they had been at odds, they had frequently been signing the same petitions and the same manifestoes. Derrida later acknowledged this in a fine homage that he wrote for the seventy-fifth birthday of his former enemy: 'I had always had more than just sympathy, but an admiring approval for the argued positions that Habermas had adopted in Germany itself, on problems in German history, on numerous occasions.'[19]

In 2000, Habermas and Derrida organized a seminar together in Frankfurt on problems in the philosophy of law, ethics, and politics. Alexander García Düttmann remembers the disquiet that this 'reconciliation' spread among the disciples of the two philosophers. 'This rapprochement irritated me. Philosophically, they had nothing to say to one another. But politically, okay, they agreed on several points. Also, we shouldn't underestimate tactical considerations. Derrida could be very trenchant, but he could also be a skilled negotiator when the occasion called for it. Depending on the context, he could be radical or almost consensual, courageous or calculating.'[20] Avital Ronell confirms that this episode caused their respective associates some heart-searching: 'One could write an entire history of great men or women [. . .] and their disciples, a history of associations or dissociations, of gravitational pull. [. . .] Small groups quarrel and suddenly their leader, Mafialike, perhaps, proposes a truce.'[21]

One thing is certain: making up with Habermas meant that Derrida quickly reassumed a position in Germany that he had lost. Several plans for translation and re-publication saw the light. But other factors also helped to thaw the situation. After many years spent in the United States, Werner Hamacher, a follower of Derrida, had returned to teach in Frankfurt in 1998; he soon invited Derrida there, to give the lecture 'The university without condition'. On this occasion, Derrida met up with Bernd Stiegler – not to be confused with Bernard Stiegler –, who had attended his seminar in Paris a few years earlier and now had an important position with the great publisher Suhrkamp. The Adorno Prize would soon seal Derrida's reconciliation with Germany.

From 3 to 5 December 2000, on the initiative of Joseph Cohen and Raphael Zagury-Orly, the international conference 'Judeities: Questions for Jacques Derrida' was held at the Centre communautaire de Paris. Habermas was one of the speakers: others included Hélène Cixous, Catherine Malabou, Jean-Luc Nancy, Gil Anidjar, and Gianni Vattimo.

Derrida's attitude to every form of communitarianism had always been ambivalent and somewhat distant. Nonetheless, ever since 'Circumfession', in 1991, and *Monolingualism of the Other*, in 1996, the question of Jewishness had moved centre stage in his work. But it had lost none of its complexity, as he acknowledged in the very first words of his lecture:

Early on, and for a long time I have trembled, I still tremble, before the title of this conference [. . .] and never has the privilege of a conference apparently addressed to me intimidated, worried, or flustered me this much, to the point of leaving me with the feeling that a grave misunderstanding threatened to make me forget how much I feel, and will always feel, out of place in speaking of it; out of place, misplaced, de-centred, very far from what could resemble the thing itself or the center of said questions, [. . .] Is it really to me, at the back of the class, in the last row, that such questions must be addressed or destined?[22]

'How to respond?' he wondered, before trying to explain the kind of silence, or at least reserve, that he had always kept. It was '[a]s if – a paradox that I will not stop unfolding and that summarizes all the torment of my life – I had to keep myself from Judaism [. . .] in order to retain within myself something that I provisionally call Jewishness'. Derrida insisted on his refusal to claim 'a communal, even national or especially state-national, solidarity and before speaking, before taking sides and taking a stand *as a Jew*'.[23]

> I do indeed have a hard time saying 'we', but there are occasions when I do say it. In spite of all the problems that torment me on this subject, beginning with the disastrous and suicidal politics of Israel and of a certain Zionism [. . .], well, in spite of all that and so many other problems I have with my 'Jewishness', I will never deny it. I will always say in certain situations, 'we Jews'. This so very tormented 'we' is at the heart of what is most worried in my thought, the thought of someone I once called, with just a bit of a smile, 'the last of the Jews'.[24]

Derrida had already indicated the complexity of his position in an interview with Élisabeth Weber, shortly after the publication of 'Circumfession': since he had both the impression of 'now being Jewish enough' and 'being too Jewish', it was important for him 'to try to think through, without being able to master it, this paradoxical logic'.[25] Although many people thought he had been influenced by the Talmud, even seeing him as a sort of crazed Talmudist, Derrida continually pointed out how scanty his Jewish culture actually was.

> It may be amusing to wonder how someone can be influenced by what he does not know. I don't rule it out. If I greatly regret not knowing the Talmud, for example, it's perhaps the case that it knows me, that it knows itself in me. A sort of unconscious, you see, and one can imagine some paradoxical trajectories. Unfortunately, I don't know Hebrew. The milieu of my childhood in Algiers was too colonized, too uprooted. No doubt by my own fault in part, I received there no true Jewish education.[26]

All this led Derrida to identify himself more and more with the figure of the Marrano. This term of contempt, a synonym of 'pig' in Spanish, was used in Spain and Portugal to designate the converted Jews and their descendants. Forced to abjure their religion, the Marranos continued to practise it in secret. But by keeping it secret, they sometimes forgot it completely. It was rather in this way that Derrida perceived his own Jewishness: 'Everything that I say can be interpreted as arising from the best Jewish tradition and at the same time as an absolute betrayal. I have to confess: this is exactly what I feel.'[27]

In 2001, Derrida travelled particularly widely, and this excessive activity sometimes made him melancholy. In April, he wrote to Catherine Malabou from Florida, from where he was due to set off the following day for Los Angeles. Soon, he told her, it would be a conference in the château at Castries, near Montpellier, then Beijing, Shanghai, Hong Kong, Frankfurt, then back to the United States. 'More than ever, I wonder where I am, where I'm going and why I'm doing all this.' Sometimes, he was overwhelmed by despair on all sides: it rose and fell within him 'like hemlock'.[28] But he worked intensely all summer, correcting the proofs of three books that were due to come out in the autumn – *For What Tomorrow . . .*, *The University without Condition*, and the major collection of essays, *Paper Machine* –, while writing his speech for the reception of the Adorno Prize and the lectures he was due to give in China in September.

This was a trip that had been planned at the end of the 1980s, but the events in Tiananmen Square had led to its being cancelled. Since that time, seven of Derrida's books had been translated into Chinese, but most of them had been translated from the English version, which created a series of misunderstandings. Derrida hoped to find *in situ* good conversation partners to relaunch things on a better basis. Before he left, his old friend Lucien Bianco gave him some practical advice and assured him that, at the Chinese University of Hong Kong, the students would appreciate it if he talked to them about the death penalty.[29] Derrida would like to have discussed it in other cities too, but so as to avoid an open breach with his hosts, he agreed not to make it the direct theme of his lectures. He referred to the issue every time he could, however.

His first lecture, delivered on 4 September at the University of Beijing, took the theme 'Forgiveness, the unforgivable and the inde-feasible'. Two other lectures, several seminars, and several interviews punctuated his journey, from Beijing to Nanjing, Shanghai, and Hong Kong. Derrida was fascinated by the power and modernity of China, the gigantic size of its hotels and the huge building sites to be seen in this rapidly developing country. His travelling condi-tions were excellent; he was greeted almost like a head of state and could not take a single step without being photographed. His hosts, in mandarin fashion, soon announced that 'all of Derrida' would be translated into Chinese.

Suddenly it happened, the unforeseeable event that would turn everything upside down. Derrida experienced 11 September as 'a personal blow'. In Shanghai, he spent practically the entire night in front of the television.

It was nighttime there, and the owner of the café I was in with a couple of friends came to tell us that an airplane had 'crashed' into the Twin Towers. I hurried back to my hotel, and from the first televised images, those of CNN, I note, it was easy to foresee that this was going to become, *in the eyes* of the world, what you called 'a major event.' [. . .] As far as I could tell, China tried during the first few days to circumscribe the importance of the event, as if it were a more or less local incident.[30]

The following day, Derrida began his lecture at the Fuda University by mentioning the gravity of the moment and the tragedy that had occurred overnight: it marked, he claimed, a new and unpredictable phase in world history.[31] The lecture he gave at Hong Kong a few days later on 'globalization and the death penalty' was considered to be the most brilliant and passionate for twenty years, but Derrida's heart and mind were now in New York, where he was expected a few days later and where he had so many friends. The catastrophe that had just struck the world, and would become a major spur to his ideas, had instantly driven away his melancholy. From Hong Kong, he wrote to Catherine Malabou:

This trip will have been extraordinary, because of what I have discovered on it, because of the 'malady' I was dragging around deep inside, that stopped me, much as ever, being where I was (that's what 'travelling' with myself means for me) – and above all because of what razed the World Trade Center, a place dear to my heart in many ways for twenty years and where I had hoped to take you to enjoy, with you, from the 130th floor, the most beautiful view of New York.[32]

Before he went to the United States, however, he had to stop in Frankfurt, where, on 22 September, he was awarded the Adorno Prize, probably the most important distinction he ever received. This prize, created by the City of Frankfurt in 1977 in memory of the philosopher, sociologist, and musicologist Theodor W. Adorno, was given every three years to an oeuvre which, in the spirit of the Frankfurt School, cut across the domains of philosophy, the social sciences, and the arts. Previous recipients had included Habermas, but also Pierre Boulez and Jean-Luc Godard.

It was in German that Derrida spoke the first and the last paragraph of a superb lecture called 'Fichus'. Even more than Adorno, Walter Benjamin was the object of his emphatic homage, recalling in passing one of the most tragic moments in his destiny.

As an epigraph to this modest and simple expression of gratitude, I would like to being by reading a sentence that Walter

Benjamin, one day, one night, himself dreamed *in French*. He told it *in French* to Gretel Adorno, in a letter he wrote her on October 12, 1939, from Nevers, where he was in an internment camp. In France at the time this was called a *camp de travailleurs volontaires* ('voluntary workers' camp'). In his dream, which, if we are to believe him, was euphoric, Benjamin says this to himself, in French: *Il s'agissait de changer en fichu une poésie* [It was about changing a poem into a *fichu*].[33]

As Benjamin, one of the authors most preoccupied by questions of translation, had liked to do, Derrida played with the resources of this word, turning it this way and that.

I won't pursue the derivations and uses of this extraordinary word, *fichu*. It means different things according to whether it is being used as a noun or an adjective. *The fichu* – and this is the most obvious meaning in Benjamin's sentence – designates a shawl, the piece of material that a woman may put on in a hurry, around her head or neck. But the adjective *fichu* denotes evil: that which is bad, lost, condemned. On day in September 1970, seeing his death approaching, my sick father said to me, 'I'm *fichu*.'[34]

But all thoughts were on 11 September, which explains the additions he made to the speech he had carefully composed a few weeks before. History was now accelerating, with the first political responses of George W. Bush.

My absolute compassion for all the victims of September 11 will not prevent me from saying: I do not believe in the political innocence of anyone in this crime. And if my compassion for all the innocent victims is limitless, it is because it does not stop with those who died on September 11 in the United States. That is my interpretation of what should be meant by what we have been calling since yesterday, in the White House's words, 'infinite justice': not to exonerate ourselves from our own wrongdoings and the mistakes of our own politics, even at the point of paying the most terrible price, out of all proportion.[35]

Derrida left almost immediately for New York. In this period dominated by anxiety and the fear of new catastrophes, although he had in the past suffered from a phobia of planes, he did not for an instant dream of cancelling his engagements. Like many of his other friends, Avital Ronell was very touched that he went to stand by them:

The Americans I know were profoundly grateful to Jacques. He came to see us straightaway, when most had cancelled their travel arrangements. The others were afraid, which is understandable. Another attack was feared, there was a real toxic atmosphere, people felt sick. But he came to console us, to talk to us and analyse us, so to speak. He went to Ground Zero. Though Jacques could be hard on American politics, he was loyal to Americans and especially to New Yorkers.[36]

When he landed on 26 September, Derrida was struck by an upsurge of patriotism of a kind he had never seen in his life. Everywhere, flags were flying, everyone was proudly affirming how proud they were to be American, rather as if the United States had just been founded anew. The conference at the University of Villanova was held from 27 to 29 September 2001, focusing on the *Confessions* of Saint Augustine and 'Circumfession', but, even with this theme, allusions to current events were unavoidable. Then Derrida went to a conference at Columbia, where he wanted – and needed – to weigh each of his words.

In New York, at the home of their mutual friend Richard Bernstein, Derrida was glad to see Habermas again. They both had the feeling of being very European, and knew they had to speak with considerable caution, even with American intellectuals, and this brought them even closer together.

In spite of what the cover might suggest, *Le 'concept' du 11 septembre* was not a book conceived by Derrida and Habermas, nor even a dialogue between them. Written by a friend of theirs, Giovanna Borradori, the work brings together, introduces, and discusses the long interviews she had had separately with the two philosophers. The book was first published by the University of Chicago Press as *Philosophy in a Time of Terror*. When it came out in France, Derrida suggested the new title, as he wished to 'draw attention, under the vigilant surveillance of the quotation marks, to the difficulties one encounters in trying to form the "concept" of a "thing" that is named by its date alone: "11 September".'[37]

The interview with Derrida was recorded in New York on 22 October 2001, three weeks after his arrival, at a time when it was impossible and practically forbidden 'to start speaking of anything, especially in public, without ceding to this obligation, without making an always somewhat blind reference to this date'.[38] In spite of the terrible pressures imposed by the event, Derrida insisted on holding to a nuanced position, at the risk of irritating some of his American readers. Giving up on complexity would in his view be 'an unacceptable obscenity',[39] as if he were being asked to bow down in servitude.

One can condemn unconditionally certain acts of terrorism (whether of the state or not) without having to ignore the situation that might have brought them about or even legitimated them [. . .] One can thus condemn *unconditionally*, as I do here, the attack of 11 September without having to ignore the real or alleged conditions that made it possible. Anyone in the world who either organized or tried to justify this attack saw it as a response to the state terrorism of the United States and its allies.[40]

But this desire not to disguise the contradictions and paradoxes did not stop Derrida from stating his commitments clearly:

[i]n this unleashing of violence without name, if I had to take one of the two sides and choose in a binary situation, well, I would. Despite my very strong reservations about the American, indeed the European, political posture, about the 'international antiterrorist' coalition, despite all the de facto betrayals, all the failures to live up to democracy, international law, and the very international institutions that the states of this 'coalition' themselves founded and supported up to a certain point, I would take the side of the camp that, in principle, by right of law, leaves a perspective open to perfectibility in the name of 'democracy,' international law, international institutions, and so on.[41]

The events of 11 September added particular weight to a notion that had obsessed Derrida for some years, that of auto-immunity. He had mentioned it for the first time in Capri, in 1994, at a conference on religion: 'that strange behaviour where a living being, in quasi-*suicidal* fashion, "itself" works to destroy its own protection, to immunize itself *against* its "own" immunity'.[42] To this logic of self-immunity, democracy must never yield. Even to respond to the worst, it could never lose sight of its own foundations.

After considerable rewriting on the part of its two authors, *For What Tomorrow . . .*, the book of dialogues with Élisabeth Roudinesco, came out in France in the immediate wake of 11 September 2001. Published jointly by Fayard and Galilée, it had a big print run, suggesting the high hopes its two publishers had in it. However, Claude Durand, the manager, accused Roudinesco and Derrida of trying to 'destabilize Fayard' with this book. The Paris publishers' polemics that had raged eighteen months earlier, during the Renaud Camus controversy, were far from over, and even political events were not enough for them to be forgotten.[43]

The press gave the book an excellent set of reviews. Christian

Delacampagne, in *Le Monde*, hailed it as 'the best introduction' to Derrida's thought. In the words of Philippe Petit, for *Marianne*: '[A]t last we have it: Derrida for dummies'; the philosopher, who was 'a continent in himself, a conscience, a memory, a Marrano of modern times' had agreed, this time, to 'make himself accessible to the public at large'. Only *L'Express*, in the person of François Busnel, thought the work was 'a botched encounter': 'a fireside chat between two old accomplices who don't give a damn about what their readers expect'. The best account was probably by Régis Debray, in a letter to Derrida: '*For What Tomorrow . . .* puts each and every reader in a position to realize his or her own contradictions, penchants or aversions. [. . .] Many people, thanks to this dialogue, will be able to join you, or break away, in knowledge of the facts.'[44]

While the book sold much better than Derrida's other works – around 18,000 copies in big format – it was not the success in France that it should have been. Fayard had hoped for better, but the promotion had been held up both by 11 September and by Derrida's long absence. Only in November was he able to accompany Élisabeth Roudinesco for a few radio and television programmes, and appearances in various bookshops. But, as for Derrida's other books, success came at the international level: *For What Tomorrow . . .* was translated into a score of languages.

The publication of the book, in which Derrida expressed at length his thoughts on political subjects, as well as the context of 11 September, rekindled another controversy. Derrida was viewed in some quarters as a 'bad Jew' because of his long-standing support for the Palestinian cause, ever since his friendship with Genet. His positions on the Israeli–Palestinian question had varied little across the years. As he had said, back in 1988, at a conference in Jerusalem, his attitude 'is not inspired not only by my concern for justice and by my friendship for both the Palestinians and the Israelis. It is meant also as an expression of respect for a certain image of Israel and as an expression of hope for its future.'[45]

It was perhaps in a long letter to Claude Lanzmann, the author of *Shoah* but also the editor of *Les Temps modernes*, that Derrida most clearly expressed his opinion on the subject. He had been profoundly taken aback by an article by Robert Redeker in the autumn 2001 issue, in which the author claimed that, ever since 11 September, 'there are more and more occasions on which we may witness the resurrection of left-wing Judeophobia. [. . .] The loss of inhibition in anti-Israel hatred has both made it possible to change the victims – the Americans – into the villains, and to lessen the responsibility of the real villains (Islamic terrorism fomented or supported by a certain number of Muslim states).'[46]

The letter Derrida sent Lanzmann is in some ways similar to that he had sent to Pierre Nora in 1961, on his book *Les Français en Algérie*. Derrida reiterated in full his friendship for Lanzmann. Without it, he would not have bothered to write to him, since he was not in the habit of protesting every time he read things that angered him. But this article had shocked him, both because of its place of publication and by the seriousness of some of the accusations formulated in it. Derrida refused to accept, for example, that anyone could say – as Redeker had done –, 'after all, in Sabra and Chatila, it was Arabs who had massacred other Arabs'. Eager to avoid any confusion, he took the opportunity to express his own convictions clearly:

> You mustn't think that my critical vigilance is unilateral. It is just as alert to anti-Semitism or a certain anti-Israeli feeling, just as alert to certain policies of various countries in the Middle East and even the Palestinian Authority [. . .], not to mention, of course, 'terrorism'. But I feel that is my responsibility to express it more to the side to which, by 'situation', I am deemed to belong: the 'French citizen' that I am will publicly demonstrate a greater critical attention to French policies than to others that are pursued on the other side of the world. The 'Jew', even if he is equally critical of the policies of Israel's enemies, will be more prepared to express his anxieties about an Israeli policy that endangers the safety [*salut*] and the image of those it is supposed to represent.[47]

If certain discourses were to be believed, Derrida continued, 'one should feel guilty or presumed guilty as soon as one murmurs the least reservation about Israeli policies, [. . .] or even about a certain alliance between a particular American policy and a certain Israeli policy.'

> Guilty under at least four headings: anti-Israelism, anti-Zionism, anti-Semitism, Judeophobia (a concept that has recently become, as you know, fashionable: it needs to be discussed at length) – not to mention what is known as visceral anti-Americanism . . .
>
> Well: no, no, no, and no! Four times no. That's exactly what I wanted to say to you, and that's why I've written to you. To tell you of my anxieties and to ask you, as a friend, that this will not become the 'position' of the 'strategy' of the *Temps modernes*. [. . .] If there are totalitarian procedures of intimidation, they lie there, precisely, in this attempt to silence any critical analysis of Israeli and American policies. [. . .] I want to be able to undertake this critical analysis, to make it more complex here, nuance it there, sometimes radicalize it, *without*

*the slightest Judeophobia, without the least anti-Americanism,
and, as if I needed to add it, without the least anti-Semitism.*

Dear Claude, I would have written this to you, as a matter
of conscience and the duty of friendship, at the risk of being
mistaken, *even if I were the only person to think it.* But I'm sure
you know this, I'm simply reminding you, I am not the only
one, doubtless even among your friends and admirers.[48]

At a conference a year after Derrida's death, Alain Badiou summarized perfectly what Derrida's line of conduct had been on the
political terrain. Faithful to his long-standing philosophical habits,
he explained, Derrida had constantly sought to undo opposi-
tions that had been fixed for too long, 'to unsort what had been
sorted': 'In the opposition Jew/Arab, in the Palestinian conflict,
Derrida adopted the position of deconstructing the duality.' More
fundamentally, in Badiou's view:

Derrida was, in all the questions on which he spoke out, what
I call a courageous man of peace. He was courageous because
you always need great courage not to get caught in the division
that has been set up. And a man of peace discovering what does
not fall within this opposition is, generally speaking, the path
of peace.[49]

In autumn 2001, politics caught up with Derrida on another level.
Though he had no hesitation about taking up difficult positions
on the public scene, the author of *Specters of Marx* had always
been extremely careful about his image, and taken pains to avoid
anything that might endanger it. For Derrida, the secret was a fundamental theme. He saw it as one of the foundations of democracy,
as he explained in an interview with Maurizio Ferraris. He had even
chosen the title *Il gusto del segreto* for this work (*The Taste for the
Secret* – unpublished in French).

I have a taste for the secret, it clearly has to do with not-belong-
ing; I have an impulse or fear or terror in the face of a political
space, for example, a public space that makes no room for the
secret. For me, the demand that everything be paraded in the
public square and that there be no internal forum is a glaring
sign of the totalitarianization of democracy. [. . .] if a right to
the secret is not maintained, we are in a totalitarian space.[50]

The French presidential election campaign in 2002 came as a
complete upheaval for Derrida, mixing the public and private
spheres in a way over which he had absolutely no control. Of course,

in 1995, Lionel Jospin had already been the candidate of the Left, and Derrida had even been on his supporting committee. But it had been a short campaign, and Sylviane Agacinski had remained in the background. Since 1997, Jospin had been Prime Minister, which had naturally focused attention on his wife. In autumn 2001, Derrida was particularly pained to see the story of his relationship with Sylviane exposed in two biographies of Jospin, long extracts from which were published in the press: one by Serge Raffy, the other by Claude Askolovitch.

Derrida could not stand his image starting to resemble the most conventional soap opera. In Raffy's book, he was presented as a 'star of French academia of the 1970s', 'the great rival of Jacques Lacan':

> Derrida, at that time, was a more Mediterranean version of Richard Gere, but with more diplomas. He was handsome and brilliant, but he was also married. Sylviane, however, embarked on a great love story that she knew could lead nowhere. She accepted this. She was a free woman, a modern woman. She gave birth in 1980 [*sic*] to Daniel, her son. As in the song by Jean-Jacques Goldmann, 'she had a baby all by herself'. Here too, she accepted the situation. Love is no respecter of common rules.[51]

The tale told by Claude Askolovitch was hardly less colourful. Agacinski was described as 'a philosophy *agrégée* who has been shaped by life as much as by her book studies', and Lionel Jospin as the 'Tarzan who repaired the injustice that life was to inflict on this woman who did not deserve it'. The author described the years of Sylviane's youth, when 'she orbited round the review *Tel Quel*, launched and directed by Philippe Sollers':

> Eventually, she started a relationship with Jacques Derrida. A great philosopher. A great thinker. A great man of the Left. But great men have their reasons too. Sylviane became pregnant. Derrida could not accept this. He did not want a secret family. It was her freedom. She wanted a child. It was her choice. To reject this pregnancy would mean saying no to life, being trapped in a world where she would be entirely dependent on the choices of others. Sylviane had a baby alone. Now she was a single mother, with a son, Daniel, whom she undertook to bring up alone.[52]

Derrida swung between fury and bitterness. He failed to understand why Sylviane had revealed in public that he was Daniel's father. In fact, she had not even needed to make this revelation.

Enough people were in the know for *Le Figaro* to mention the fact for the first time in its columns, when Jospin's candidacy was being discussed, without asking Sylviane the least question. She had neither denied nor commented on the statement. In any case, Derrida, always mistrustful of the media, could not accept the constraints that weighed on the wife of a Prime Minister, a man who was standing for President.

On 2 February 2002, the announcement that Jospin would indeed be a candidate arrived in press agencies by a fax sent from his home address. *Le Monde* highlighted the fact:

> It was Daniel, the son of Sylviane Agacinski – a student in *hypokhâgne* at the Lycée Condorcet in Paris –, who pressed the fax button [. . .] and thereby announced the candidacy of Lionel Jospin to AFP [Agence France Presse] and the French people. Just a detail, but a significant and meaningful image. Lionel Jospin, unlike Jacques Chirac, has a home, a kitchen (he poses in it, for the 7 March issue of *Paris-Match*), and a family. A lovely family, modern, reconstructed.[53]

Derrida could merely stand by, powerless and bitter, and watch as the two main candidates duly fought a battle of images with one another. Since the official start of the presidential campaign, Sylviane had been appearing a great deal in the media, far more than in 1995: an interview on TF1 on 20 March, and interviews with *Le Parisien* on 29 March, *Le Nouvel Observateur* on 4 April, *Elle* on 8 April, *Gala* on 11 April, and a photo reportage in *Paris-Match* on 18 April. Sylviane was much more discreet than her husband's biographers, and never mentioned Derrida's name. But the latter was hurt when he read: 'Daniel was five years old in 1989, and it was Lionel who raised him [. . .] I am more grateful than I can say to a man who was as tender and generous with me as he was with a young boy like that, who he treated like his own son – it moves me just to talk about it.'[54] 'It was Lionel who brought Daniel up. He made him his own son,'[55] says the legend of a photo of Sylviane in a double-page spread with the young man.*

Some enjoyed the chance to snigger, but Derrida's close friends could see how saddened he was. Avital Ronell remembers:

> For a long time, against all reason, Jacques must have told himself that nobody knew. It was like a reverse paranoia: he so

---

* In July 2004, Daniel Agacinski, barely twenty, passed the entrance exam to the École Normale Supérieure on the rue d'Ulm: Derrida certainly learned about this. Three years later, the young man came top in the philosophy *agrégation*. At the University of Toulouse-le-Mirail, he chose to write his thesis on the social and political conditions of the construction of heroic figures.

much wanted the secret to be kept that he was convinced this was the case. Hence his shock when things came out in public. During the 2002 campaign, he felt as if he were being punished for his affair with Sylviane. For him, it was even more of a drama because he was very vulnerable to rumours. He sometimes felt he was being persecuted by people in high places.[56]

Unlike in 1995, Derrida was not this time a member of the committee to elect Jospin. He was disappointed by several aspects of the policies Jospin was pursuing at the head of the government, especially in the matter of illegal immigrants. Derrida, who was tending to become increasingly radical, found the actions of the French Socialists too timid. He was extremely shocked by the 'partial and at least nominal preservation of the [harsh] "Pasqua–Debré laws" on immigration'.[57] Derrida was fully prepared to accept that 'unconditional hospitality' was impractical as such, and that if people tried to translate it immediately into a policy, it would always risk having untoward effects. But while remaining attentive to these risks, he felt that we could not and must not give up referring to unreserved hospitality.[58] Likewise, Derrida found it difficult to understand the change in Sylviane's intellectual positions. They had been so close to his own for twelve years: in contrast, in his view, her recent book *Politics of the Sexes* was imbued with biologism and conservatism.

The confrontation between them became public, and was highlighted by the dramatic turn of events taken by the election. On 21 April 2002, the evening of the first round, there was a huge shock, a real 'bolt from the blue': the current President, Jacques Chirac, came top, followed by Jean-Marie Le Pen, the candidate of the National Front. That same evening, Jospin announced that he was retiring from political life. On 5 May, Chirac was elected to a second term of office with 82.21% of the vote.

Two weeks later, in the feature on him published on the back page of *Libération*, Derrida confessed, among several other things, that for the first time in his life he had not voted in the first round of the presidential elections, 'since he was in a bad mood with all the candidates'.[59] The following day, Sylviane Agacinski commented on this declaration in her journal, which was published a few months later:

I read in *Libération* that Jacques Derrida did not vote in the first round as he was 'in a bad mood with all the candidates'. So it's a question of *mood*, yet again! It's always rearing its head in this journal. But I hadn't thought it could play a decisive role on election day. Let's hope at least that the philosopher will be in a better mood for the second round, when faced with the candidates Chirac and Le Pen.[60]

She then laid more aggressively into her ex-partner and his philosophy, which she felt was disconnected from the reality that she had just experienced:

> In any case, philosophy too can put you in a bad mood: the Derridean concept of 'unconditional hospitality', for example. It is not merely absurd (though this still needs to be said), it is provocative. While it seems praiseworthy to defend illegal immigrants, this certainly cannot be done in the name of *unconditional* hospitality, since there is nothing more *conditional* than hospitality. The unconditional, in general, answers the longing of beautiful souls for the absolute and the pure. It is Kantian in inspiration, in other words it sacrifices the understanding of empirical reality to the purity of the concept. But it gives up the attempt to think through reality as it is.[61]

In January 2003, in a long note to *Rogues*, Derrida replied almost vindictively:

> *Unconditional hospitality*, I emphasize. Several friends recently brought to my attention a certain publication ('a pathetic Parisian tabloid in the style of *Gala*,' as one of them put it) whose author pontificates, without verifying anything, on what I've written and taught for a number of years now under the name *unconditional hospitality*. Obviously understanding nothing, the author even gives me, as if still back in high school, a bad grade and explains peremptorily in the margins of my paper: 'Absurd'! Well, what can I say? . . .
> I have always, consistently and insistently, held *unconditional hospitality*, as *impossible*, to be *heterogeneous* to the *political*, the *juridical*, and even the *ethical*. But the impossible is not nothing. It is even that which happens, which comes, by definition. I admit that this remains rather difficult to think, but that's exactly what preoccupies thinking, if there is any and from the time there is any.[62]

Rather sadly, these seem to have been the last words exchanged between Jacques Derrida and Sylviane Agacinski.

In July 2002, there was a fourth *décade* at Cerisy on Derrida's work. Édith Heurgon had suggested this to him in April 1999, shortly after publication of *The Animal That Therefore I Am*. Derrida, very touched, asked to think it over first. 'Your suggestion (a "Derrida 4" for 2002) leaves me feeling dreamy. It would be a bit crazy, don't you think? . . . I won't say "no" but I need to think a bit more about it.'[63] By August, he had decided to go along with the project.

On reflection, and in spite of all sorts of sincere inner objections that you can imagine (wouldn't it be too much? do I deserve it, does my work deserve the honour of another *décade*? etc.), I feel I should accept, as I had intimated to you, the very generous invitation that has been extended to me yet again. I'm telling myself that after all, since it will be a matter of shared work and not of 'celebration', since past experiences will permit us to hope for another ten-day festival of friendship in so many languages, since the main thing is that we show that we are worthy of our hosts and the Cerisy tradition [. . .], being withdrawing or retiring, on pretext of modesty, is not appropriate. And then, life is too short, and we have no right to deprive some of our dearest friends of the opportunity these encounters provide.[64]

Derrida sent three requests in to the people at Cerisy. The first two were typical: that the theme was to be 'Politics of Friendship' – which struck him as both very political and very open –, and that Marie-Louise Mallet would once again be the organizer. The third seemed more unusual:

Finally, if possible, and say this out of a superstitious fixation on the past [*un passéisme superstitieux*], a *décade* again including the birthday date of 15 July would be both practical for many of the potential participants (those from abroad in particular) and soothing for my imagination. But this is a sort of 'whim'. Don't bother about it if it causes any inconvenience for the calendar of your programme.

I am fully aware of the unprecedented privilege of this gift and, without feeling that I really deserve it, I am drawing from it a great strength in these somewhat melancholy years of my life which the 'anniversaries' of Cerisy will have marked out and brightened.[65]

This wish was of course granted. As for the title, it developed somewhat, becoming 'The democracy to come', which in his view was not at all the same as 'future democracy'. For Derrida, democracy never exists in the present, 'but *there is the impossible*, whose promise democracy inscribes'.[66] At the opening address, whose proportions fully lived up to those of previous Cerisy conferences, he read what would be published a few months later by Galilée, as *Rogues*. This was a way of rereading his own work from a specific point of view, here political, as he had done with regard to the animal in 1997. Derrida had recently become much more radical. Following Chomsky's 'terrible indictment' of 'Rogue States',[67] he went so far as to state:

The first and most violent of rogue states are those that have
ignored and continue to violate the very international law they
claim to champion, the law in whose name they speak and in
whose name they go to war against so-called rogue states each
time their own interests so dictate. The name of these states?
The United States. [. . .]

Those states that are able or are in a state to denounce or
accuse some 'rogue state' of violating the law, of failing to live
up to the law, of being guilty of some perversion or deviation,
those United States that claim to uphold international law
and that take the initiative of war, of police or peacekeeping
operations because they have the force to do so, these states,
namely, the United States and its allied states in these actions,
are themselves, as sovereign, the first rogue states.[68]

But in Derrida's view, vigilance needed to be exercised on an
even more fundamental level, since 'every sovereign state is in fact
virtually and a priori able, that is, in a state [*en état*], to abuse its
power and, like a rogue state, transgress international law. There
is something of a rogue state in every state. The use of state power
is *originally* excessive and abusive.'[69] In spite of this, he continued
to place his trust in democracy, 'the only system, the only constitu-
tional paradigm, in which, in principle, one has or assumes the right
to criticize everything publicly, including the idea of democracy, its
concept, its history, and its name.[70]

In autumn 2002, Derrida was back in New York, where he attended
the première of the feature film *Derrida* by Kirby Dick and Amy
Ziering Kofman. Filming had taken several years, starting in 1997.
The approach was more American and aimed at a wider audience
than *D'ailleurs Derrida* by Safaa Fathy. Without any voiceover or
any real interview, the montage took biography as its central thread.
We follow Derrida in his life as a public figure, from the École des
Hautes Études en Sciences Sociales to New York via California and
South Africa, but also as a private man, at home, in his kitchen,
even at the barber's. He good-humouredly played along with all
this, despite his long-standing mistrust of images and the media,
as mentioned above. The music was by Ryuichi Sakamoto: he had
used certain of Derrida's texts in an opera a few years before.

Derrida was conceived for the big screen, and was presented as
an official selection at the Sundance Festival, and also at Locarno,
Venice, and Melbourne, and was unusually successful for this type
of film. The strapline, though cheesy, was an effective draw: 'What if
someone came along who changed not the way you think about everything, but everything about the way you think.' For the first time, at
least in New York, Derrida was frequently recognized in the street.

10

In Life and in Death

2003–2004

On 12 February 2003, at the sixth session of the second year of the seminar on 'The Beast & the Sovereign', Derrida finally tackled a subject that he had been promising to deal with for several weeks: the choice between burial and cremation. This was a theme that, curiously, had been little explored in philosophical discourses on death.

> One of the differences between burial and cremation is that the first pays due regard to the existence of a corpse, to its persistence and its territory, whereas the second spirits the corpse away. [. . .] if the dead person has passed away [*est un disparu*], the corpse of a person who has passed away does not pass away, it is not destroyed, as corpse, as it is by crema-tion. This not-passing away permits hope for the ghost, so to speak. Buried, I do not pass away [*je ne disparais pas*], and I can still cling to something, my ghost can still cling to my corpse, to the not-passing-away of my corpse after my own passing.[1]

Derrida then analysed at length what was at stake in the principle of cremation, described as a sort of 'irreversible murder' if it is decided on by the dead person's entourage and 'a sort of irreversible suicide' if it's the dying person who requests it.

> When the fire has done its work, and in the modernity of its gloomy theatre, one that is technically infallible, instantane-ously effective, invisible, almost inaudible, the corpse of the person who has passed away will, to all appearances, have passed away from its very passing away. [. . .] The dead person is at once everywhere and nowhere, nowhere because every-where, outside the world and everywhere in the world and in us. The pure interiorization, the pure idealization of the dead person, his spiritualization, his absolute idealization, his

dematerialization into the grieving survivor who can merely allow himself to be invaded by a dead person who now has no place outside of himself – this is both the greatest fidelity and the greatest treason, the best way of keeping the other while getting rid of him.[2]

These intimate reflections did not stop Derrida from being more preoccupied than ever by the political issues of the moment. In January 2003, he was one of the first signatories of the petition 'Not in our name' protesting against likely military intervention in Iraq. It was in this context that *Rogues*, the immense lecture he had given at Cerisy the previous summer, came out.

On 19 February, on the initiative of René Major, a debate entitled 'Why War?' – inspired by the celebrated exchange between Einstein and Freud in 1933 – allowed Baudrillard and Derrida to compare their views on the subject. There was nothing academic about the exercise. Five days earlier, Dominique de Villepin, the French Minister of Foreign Affairs, had given his celebrated speech to the UN, calling for Iraq to be disarmed rather than subjected to military intervention. It was in front of a packed auditorium that Derrida began with a profession of humility: 'Faced with such difficult and intimidating questions, I realize that it's the first time in my life, in spite of so many other experiences of political discussions, that I've taken part in a discussion on burning political issues.' Expressing his pleasure that, for two days, millions of people across the world had been demonstrating against the imminent war, he rejoiced at 'the German–French opposition to American enthusiasm', even if he did not feel 'any more *chiraquien* than *saddam-hussénien*'.[3] The debate was lively but courteous. There was some argument over the significance of 11 September. In Baudrillard's view, the forthcoming intervention was a direct effect of this. Without wishing to minimize the event, Derrida felt that 'the Iraq sequence is to some extent independent', and that the war on Iraq, long desired by George W. Bush and his entourage, would probably have happened anyway. He was later proved right.

The next day, 20 February, Derrida learned that Maurice Blanchot had died. This was a huge shock. His reflections on cremation formulated a few days previously at his seminar could not have been far from his thoughts as he attended, on 24 February, the cremation of this friend, so close and yet so distant. Apart from Jean-Luc Nancy, the other mourners were mainly Portuguese – friends and relatives of Cidalia Fernandez, Blanchot's adoptive daughter, who did not understood much French. In this really gloomy crematorium, Derrida did speak, as Blanchot had wished:

For several days and nights, I have been wondering in vain from whence I would derive the strength here, now, to raise my voice. I would like to think, I hope to be able to imagine again that I am receiving it, this strength that would otherwise fail me, from Maurice Blanchot himself. [. . .]

Maurice Blanchot, for as long as I can remember, throughout my adult life, since I started to read him (over fifty years ago), and especially since I met him, in May 1968, and he never ceased to honour me with his trust and his friendship, I had been used to hearing it, this name, differently from that of someone, a third party, the incomparable author who is quoted and from whom people draw inspiration: I heard it differently than as the great name of a man of whom I admire not just the power of exposition, in thought and existence, but also the power of withdrawal, the exemplary modesty, a discretion unique in our time [. . .].[4]

According to Avital Ronell, Derrida dated the symbolic origin of his final illness to this day:

He felt that everything was cracking up inside him. His seventieth birthday, 11 September and its consequences, the electoral campaign of 2002, and this really dispiriting ceremony at Blanchot's death, with this impression of talking into a vacuum: all these events, so different in level, helped to weaken him and bring back a deep layer of sadness that went back a long way.[5]

A few years before, Blanchot had asked Derrida to be his executor. Shortly after his friend's death, as he himself was starting to suffer from a mysterious 'bar in the stomach', Derrida went to Gallimard to speak up for a Pléiade edition of Blanchot's works. But Antoine Gallimard showed little enthusiasm: while Blanchot's name did rouse passions, sales of his fictional works had always remained extremely modest. Derrida would, in any case, not have time to bring this task to a conclusion. When Cidalia Fernandez asked him to come and examine a suitcase full of papers, he would no longer be in a condition to do so.[6]

In the first days of April, Derrida flew to Irvine. He was not in great form. As Marguerite remembers: 'He kept complaining of stomach aches, but the examinations he'd had didn't detect any problems. I didn't feel very well either, but I hadn't mentioned this to him as I didn't want to make him worry for no reason.'[7]

One of the events Derrida was very keen to attend, that spring, was the conference in honour of J. Hillis Miller organized by

Barbara Cohen and Dragan Kujundzic, a young professor he greatly liked. The lecture Derrida gave on 18 April 2003, in honour of one of his dearest American friends, was called, quite simply, 'Justices'. He also took the opportunity of his stay to talk about his archives with Jackie Dooley, who ran the Special Collection at the Langson Library. The situation had become more complicated since Derrida had decided to entrust the manuscripts of his recent works to the IMEC, but he confirmed that the originals of his American and international correspondence were meant for Irvine, as well as the copies of the other letters deposited at the IMEC. Dooley wished to clarify the rights of the University and access for consultation, especially in the long term. 'What will happen when you are no longer there – after your lifetime?' she asked him. Peggy Kamuf recalls that Derrida was struck by the English expression 'after your lifetime', and even discussed it at length in one of the last sessions of his seminar.[8]

In France, Marguerite's state of health was worsening. She was diagnosed with pneumonia, but refused to let Jacques be alerted. However, since her situation was giving cause for alarm – she had suffered from TB in her youth – Pierre and Jean asked their father to cut short his stay in California and return home as soon as possible. When he arrived in France, Marguerite was already feeling a bit better, but she was still very weak. Jacques took her to Dr Arago, their gastro-enterologist. After examining Marguerite, the doctor turned to her husband: 'And what about you – any better?' He admitted that his pains had not gone away. Still the same bar. An X-ray, a scan, and an echo-endoscopy were scheduled for 14 May, a few days later.

Generally, when Jacques had a medical test, he phoned Marguerite immediately afterwards, to reassure her. But that day, he did not phone.

> As soon as I managed to reach him, I could sense he was trying to keep something from me . . . And when I persisted, he told me: 'I've got a tumour on my pancreas.' That evening, he finally uttered the word 'cancer'. It was as if the roof had fallen in on me. I kept swinging from one feeling to another: I was terrified that it was his pancreas – one of the cancers with the worst survival rate – and at the same time convinced that he couldn't die. He concluded very quickly that he wouldn't recover.[9]

Dr Arago arranged for him to go to the Institut Curie. The doctors recommended starting chemotherapy straightaway, but Derrida was reluctant. He preferred to put off being hospitalized for ten days, so as not to have to cancel his trip to Israel and two other long-standing engagements. Even in these circumstances, he insisted on fulfilling his commitments. Though taken aback, the doctors agreed to the postponement.

On 22 May 2003, the first day of the conference on Hélène Cixous organized on the occasion of her gifting her archives to the Bibliothèque Nationale de France, Derrida told his friends about his illness. He had so often claimed to be 'marching towards death' (*il marche à la mort*: but also 'running on death' – in Derrida's words 'as an engine runs on petrol'); now he was showing, in spite of himself, how true this was. He had just received the terrible results of his analyses, but, overcoming his own turmoil, calmly delivered his long lecture 'Geneses, genealogies, genres and genius'.[10]

The next day, he flew to Jerusalem, where he was to be given an honorary doctorate. To limit the fatigue of this brief journey, he asked for a car to come and meet him on the tarmac of the airport and requested that he be spared the tiresome Israeli passport formalities, on arrival and departure. On 25 May, before Derrida gave a lecture on Paul Celan – probably a variation of *Béliers*, his homage to Gadamer –, Dominique de Villepin, still bathing in the afterglow of his speech against military intervention in Iraq, paid him a warm tribute at the Hebrew University of Jerusalem:

> Jacques Derrida, you give density back to the strongest and most simple words of Humanity [. . .]. You are in the forefront of those who have opened the path to a new thinking. [. . .] 'Deconstruction' is an attentive, scrupulous, activity, a thinking which takes shape as it tests out its object. An extremely creative, and liberating, activity. Undoing something, without destroying it, so as to go further.[11]

The minister also emphasized the continuity between this 'discourse on method' and Derrida's many public interventions: 'against the oppression of dissidents in the former Czechoslovakia, against racism in South Africa, or against the prison system in the United States'. He referred to Derrida's 'tireless vigilance' against injustice, and against anti-Semitism. And he concluded: 'You are in the tradition of intellectuals of honour, in love with the universal, on the path opened by Voltaire, Bernanos, Zola, and Sartre.'

On his return to France, Derrida also insisted on keeping another engagement. On the evening of 27 May, he and Mustapha Chérif chaired the closing session of the conference 'Algeria–France, a Homage to the Great Figures in the Dialogue between Civilizations', held at the Institut du Monde Arabe. The main lecture hall was packed; André Miquel, André Mandouze, and Jean-Pierre Chevènement were in the audience. On his arrival,

Derrida told Chérif that, if it had been any other meeting, he would have cancelled. But he was keen to speak, that evening, 'as an Algerian'. More than ever, it was important for him to link all the threads of his life: 'Among all the cultural riches that I have received, that I have inherited, my Algerian culture is among those that have sustained me most strongly.'[12]

Just after this meeting, Derrida began his treatment. He stopped writing for several weeks, as is shown by the few personal lines that accompany the 'Plea for a common foreign policy' for the whole of Europe, published on 31 May 2003 in *Libération* and several European newspapers.

> Jürgen Habermas and I wish to sign together this analysis which is also an appeal. We deem it necessary and urgent, today, for a German and a French philosopher, in spite of the differences that might have separated them in the past, to join their voices here. This text, as will easily be seen, is written by Jürgen Habermas. In spite of my wishes, personal circumstances have prevented me from writing such a text, so I suggested to Jürgen Habermas that I co-sign this appeal, whose premises and perspectives I essentially share.[13]

From the window of the room where he was receiving chemo at the Institut Curie, Derrida could see the rue d'Ulm and the entrance of the École where he had spent so many years of his life. He submitted docilely to the gruelling treatment, without altogether losing hope. After all, hadn't he been told of a patient who had been in remission for seventeen years . . . ? Hadn't Dr Jean-Marc Extra told him that enormous progress had recently been made in the treatment of pancreatic cancer . . . ? Marguerite Derrida relates that Jacques was determined not to lose weight and forced himself to eat even when he had no appetite: 'He lost some hair, but not much. Physically, he looked well and seemed to be in as good a shape as possible, given the circumstances. We all kept each other going with the idea that there would be a remission.'

The pernicious effects of chemotherapy turned out to be mainly psychological. The loss of energy and the terrible exhaustion plunged Derrida into a new attack of depression that made him feel distant from his projects and from the world. 'For the first time in decades, he was forced to press the pause button,' says Albert Dichy. 'While his capacity for work had always been huge, he had to give up a whole series of texts, lectures, and trips, and he found this really hard.'[14]

The other thing which Derrida found annoying was the pre-mortem compassion spreading across the intellectual world and the sudden solicitude that some were showing him 'before it was too late'. He even accused Jean-Luc Nancy of spreading the news of his illness. This was far from being the case, the latter assured him,

> but of course it is no coincidence if people are asking me whether what they have heard elsewhere is true. And since you told me: 'it's not a secret, but let it all be kept discreet' (in short), I've followed that rule. And above all, I haven't induced those morbid messages you're getting, and that revolt me as much as they do you.[15]

Throughout that difficult summer of 2003, Derrida was rarely left alone. When Marguerite was not there, his friends took it in turns to be at his side: Hélène Cixous on Mondays, Marie-Louise Mallet on Tuesdays, Safaa Fathy on Thursdays. More than ever, Derrida preferred to phone rather than write. He did not conceal the seriousness of his state from his friends. 'We had regular conversations,' relates J. Hillis Miller. 'He told me he could no longer write, just carry out simple tasks like correcting proofs.'[16]

However, Derrida was far from having stopped working completely. In a letter sent to David Wills on 5 July 2003, while still undergoing treatment, he made a series of highly specific remarks about the English translation of *La contre-allée* (i.e., *Counterpath*). He apologized for his handwriting, 'even more illegible than usual. It's one of the effects of chemotherapy that makes my hand tremble a bit.'[17] With this same trembling hand, which would soon become a source of reflection, he wrote on 10 July to the organizers of the 'Comité Radicalement Anti-Corrida', which was dedicated to the outlawing of bullfighting, that he agreed to become the honorary president of their movement: the animal cause was becoming ever dearer to his heart.

Throughout the summer, even though some people thought he was dying – he had been obliged to cancel the stay in New York scheduled for the autumn, as well as a conference –, Derrida continued to battle with cancer. After the first session of chemo and a new scan, the doctor told him that the tumour had shrunk. Derrida was still very weak, but he felt a little better. Towards the end of the summer, he even envisaged resuming his seminar in 2003–4, before finally giving up the idea.

But out of friendship for Elisabeth Weber, who was also suffering from cancer, he did not abandon a trip to Santa Barbara, on the West Coast, for the conference 'Irreconcilable Differences? Jacques Derrida and the Question of Religion' at the end of October. Weber remembers: 'Over the spring and summer of 2003, we spoke several times by phone to talk about this conference, but also about the chemotherapy that we were both undergoing.'[18] The title he chose for his lecture was like an echo of these conversations: 'Vivre "ensemble" – Living "together"'.

In November, Derrida went to Portugal to take part in three days of events based on his work, organized by Fernando Bernardo in the ancient university of Coimbra. 'All his friends felt a kind of relief on seeing him arrive,' says Michel Lisse, whom Derrida had reminded not to forget his gown for the honorary doctorate. 'He really rather enjoyed this very solemn ceremonial. And he was happy that it was the film director Manoel de Oliveira, almost a hundred years old, who was his partner for the ceremony.'[19] Crossing the old city in a snazzy black outfit, a mortar board perched on his head, Derrida did, however, confide in Marguerite: 'I feel that I'm going to my own funeral.' To which she retorted: 'If anyone goes to their funeral, it means they're still alive.' And Derrida was indeed very active: he gave the usual long lecture and took part in all the activities arranged for the three days, including the day devoted to 'Coimbra, city of refuge'. 'We all thought he was cured,' remembers Lisse.

Shortly after his return home, Derrida received a letter from Mireille Calle-Gruber, telling him how happy she was to have seen him 'in great shape, sparkling, speaking out, always taking the questions further'. 'We'd come to keep you company, give you some of the fire that you transmit inexhaustibly to us, and you were the most giving, the most generous.'[20]

Throughout the winter, the doctors, too, were flabbergasted by the number of Derrida's activities and his completely atypical energy. In fact, he was in pain only at night, but Lexomil was some relief, and in particular he brightened up in public and as soon as he received visits or was buoyed up by new projects. According to Peggy Kamuf, 'Jacques kept to many of his obligations and trips over this period. Giving up on that aspect of his life would have meant giving up on life itself.'[21]

If Derrida, as he had put it for a long time, 'was marching towards death', he also marched to the beat of friendship and loyalty. After the death of Louis Marin, in October 1992, he had written:

Why does one give and what can one give to a dead friend? [. . .]

Louis knew what I thought of him, he was aware of my admiration and my gratitude; he had countless indications of this in everything that was woven between our gestures, our various itineraries, our respective works as well, and in everything that went unspoken, which did not fail, as always, alas, to resound and resonate in this. But while he was aware of this admiration, I never really declared it to him to the extent that I am this evening. I am not saying this only, not only, to confess a mistake, a regret, or an inconsolable sadness. This situation is, in the end, rather common; it is what links me to more than one friend, no doubt to all those one calls 'best friends'.

But then why? Why wait for death? Tell me, why do we wait for death?[22]

This was a question that Derrida asked every time that a loved one died. He felt the same as at the death of his little brother Norbert, 'this indefatigable surprise before the fact of what I will never really understand or accept [. . .]: continuing or beginning once more to live after the death of someone close'.[23] Michael Naas and Pascale-Anne Brault, professors at DePaul University at Chicago, and translators of several of Derrida's works, took the initiative and collected and introduced a series of texts written or spoken by him on the occasion of the death of one his friends: Roland Barthes, Paul de Man, Michel Foucault, Louis Althusser, Edmond Jabès, Louis Marin, Sarah Kofman, Gilles Deleuze, Emmanuel Levinas, Jean-François Lyotard, Gérard Granel, and, just recently, Maurice Blanchot . . . Derrida sent to Naas and Brault a few homages which they did not know of, but insisted that it was their project. Many of these texts were unknown in the United States, and he was glad they would be published. But he was rather nervous about them appearing in France. He was afraid that some people would laugh at him, as if he were playing at being Bossuet or Malraux with his funeral orations. He liked the title chosen for the American edition, *The Work of Mourning*, but the ambiguity of the world 'work' – labour, but also work of art – could not be reproduced in French. The title *À la vie à la mort* (*In Life and in Death*) was going to be used, but then it appeared on the sleeve of a new CD by Johnny Halliday.[24] The book was eventually entitled *Chaque fois unique: la fin du monde* (*Each Time Unique: The End of the World*), which was a way of highlighting one of its fundamental ideas. Derrida had written it on the death of Althusser:

> What is coming to an end, what Louis is taking away with him, is not only something or other that we would have shared at some point or another, in one place or another, but the world itself, a certain origin of the world – his origin, no doubt, but also that of the world in which I lived, in which we lived a unique story. It is a story that is, in any case, irreplaceable, and it will have had one meaning or another for the two of us [. . .]. It is a world that is for us the whole world, the only world, and it sinks into an abyss from which no memory – even if we keep the memory, and we will keep it – can save it.[25]

This big book, with its light and shade, was well received in the press. In spite of their past divergences, Bernard-Henri Lévy hailed

Derrida in the 'Journal de la semaine', the column that *Libération* had asked him to write:

> It's an irresistible feeling of friendship that brings me back to my old master in *Comédie*. [. . .] You close your books. You close your eyes. They are the ones you can hear. [. . .] The whole spirit of the epoch is there. The bereavement of a generation. It is like a divine comedy whose bit parts have been reduced to the state, not of shades, but of voices, in a series of concentric regions in which Derrida plays the part of Virgil.[26]

Paul Ricoeur had been moved to tears on learning of Derrida's illness. The bonds between the two men had become stronger since the death of Levinas. In December 2002, they conducted a dialogue at the Maison de l'Amérique Latine on the theme: 'How can we talk about the other?' This question lay at the heart of their preoccupations, but also of the long story of their relationship. 'I have talent. Derrida has genius,' Ricoeur sometimes said to his friends. In a late letter to his former *assistant*, he admitted that he 'still regretted the unfortunate critique' of Derrida's work in *The Rule of Metaphor*, before adding: 'You deftly picked it out and brilliantly lifted it up.'[27] On learning of the seriousness of his state, Ricoeur wrote to Derrida how precious his life and thought were to him: 'I have kept my admiration for your work too silent, and, if you allow me, my friendship, which I have always thought found an echo in you. *Je vous embrasse.*'[28]

Just as generous was the way that, in December 2003, Derrida devoted one of his last texts to Ricoeur:

> Without even admitting, sincerely, to a sense of incompetence, I believe that my strength will never have failed me as much as it does when tackling, in the form of a study or a philosophical discussion, the immense work of Paul Ricoeur. [. . .] On rereading what I have just spontaneously written ('difficult, even impossible'), I smile. As I belatedly notice, these two words were, over the last two years, at the centre of a debate between Paul Ricoeur and myself, on evil and forgiveness.[29]

Derrida pondered the 'strange logic of this exchange without agreement or opposition', in which 'the encounter is sketched but also scotched' (*une rencontre 's'esquisse mais aussi s'esquive'*).

> We 'rubbed shoulders', he told me one day, when we were yet again trying to think *together* about what had happened, hadn't happened, a whole life long, between us. [. . .] Under or across an uncrossable abyss that we didn't manage to name, we can nonetheless speak to and hear one another.

To evoke 'an affection that has continued to grow', Derrida looked back on a few moments of their relationship. Ricoeur had written, during their old quarrel over metaphor: 'The masterly stroke, here, is to enter into metaphysics, not through the gate of birth, but, if I may say so, through the gate of death.' Derrida returned to this formula, twenty-eight years later, and gave his sincere response:

> Even if I doubt whether this is true of my text on metaphor, it hardly matters here today, I think that, over and above this debate, Ricoeur saw things aright, profoundly. In me and my philosophical gestures. I have always yielded to the affirmation and invincible reaffirmation of life, of the desire for life, by passing, alas, 'through the gate of death', my eyes fixed upon it, at every instant.[30]

At the beginning of 2004, Derrida started to feel in more pain again. Michel Lisse says: 'With the toxic effects of his oral chemotherapy, he was losing feeling in his fingers and toes, he had to spend a long time massaging them. His illness stopped him writing new texts. He still got up early, but he spent much of the afternoon resting. He was allowed to take only occasional phone calls.'[31]

He had not, however, ceased all activity – far from it. One of the projects dearest to him was the issue of the prestigious Cahiers de l'Herne that Marie-Louise Mallet and Ginette Michaud were putting together on him. With them he discussed whom to invite to contribute, trying not to forget anyone. He carefully chose the documents and the rich iconography: several photos, but also drawings and paintings by Camilla and Valerio Adami, Simon Hantaï and Gérard Titus-Carmel, as well as a musical score by Michaël Levinas. In particular, Derrida wrote a set of nine texts unpublished in French – a book inside the book, as it were.[32]

At the beginning of the year, Avital Ronell moved into Ris-Orangis for six months, so that Jacques would not be alone when Marguerite went back to Paris and her practice as an analyst. She discussed with him a potential conference that might be held in New York, in October 2004, to mark the publication of the Cahier de l'Herne. 'There was a particular weightiness, a rather scary solemnity, since we both sensed that this might be his last visit to the United States.' But most of the time, Avital concentrated on taking Jacques's mind off things and making him laugh, something for which she was very gifted. 'Jacques liked calling me "Avi", which sounded just like "*à vie*".* We did a little yoga together. Sometimes

---

* 'to or for life'. – Tr.

he let me give him a massage. But when I mentioned meditation to him, he said that the only meditations he knew were those of Descartes and Husserl.'[33]

Now that Derrida could no longer barely write, the spoken word, already such a significant feature in his life, became increasingly important. When Jean Birnbaum, who had done several interviews with him for France-Culture before moving to *Le Monde*, suggested they discuss his most recent works at the Musée d'Art et d'Histoire du Judaïsme, Derrida could not stop himself agreeing. But on the evening of 12 February, in front a packed audience, his fatigue was so obvious that he had to bring his illness out into the open. He was able to disguise it even less a few weeks later, in the very politically inflected interview he gave to *Les Inrockuptibles*: on 31 March, the weekly journal gave over eleven pages to him, as well as its cover, hailing in warm terms 'the commitments of a great intellectual'.[34] Shortly thereafter, at the request of Edwy Plenel, then in charge of the editorial board of *Le Monde*, Birnbaum went to Ris-Orangis to interview Derrida at length: it would occupy a double-page spread, something now quite exceptional. This was a matter of some importance and Derrida asked for a little time to review the text in detail.

While his relations with *Le Monde* had always been somewhat ambivalent, he was a great admirer of the monthly *Le Monde diplomatique*, a sister publication of the daily *Le Monde*, though one with a completely independent editorial set-up. On 8 May 2004, on that monthly's fiftieth anniversary, Derrida agreed to appear on stage at the Palais des Sports in Paris, to pay homage to what he called 'the most remarkable and ambitious journalistic venture of the past half-century, in other words [his] whole life as an adult and a citizen'. He used the opportunity to summarize his political convictions as they had stood since 11 September and the war in Iraq.

I'm not considered to be a Eurocentric philosopher. For the past forty years, I've probably more often been accused of the opposite. But I think that, without any Eurocentric illusions or pretensions, without the least European nationalism, and even without all that much confidence in Europe as it is, or seems to be evolving, we need to struggle on behalf of what this name represents today, with the memory of the Enlightenment, to be sure, but also with the guilty conscience, fully accepted, of the totalitarian, genocidal, and colonialist crimes of the past. Thus we need to struggle for the irreplaceable things that Europe must keep in the world to come, so that it will become more than a single market or currency, more than a neo-nationalist conglomerate, more than a new armed force, even though, on this point, I am tempted to think that it does need a military power and a foreign policy able to support a transformed United Nations, with its seat in Europe, and having the means to implement its resolutions without having to rely on the interests or the unilateral opportunism of the techno-economico-military might of the United States.[35]

The Europe he wished to promote should allow its free voice to be heard on the international scene, independent of any alignment:

A Europe in which one can criticize Israeli policy, especially that pursued by Sharon and Bush, without being accused of anti-Semitism or Judeophobia.

A Europe in which one can support the legitimate aspirations of the Palestinian people to recover its rights, its land and a state, without thereby approving of suicide attacks and the anti-Semitic propaganda that often – too often – tends, in the Arab world, to give renewed credit to the monstrous *Protocols of the Elders of Zion*. [. . .]

A Europe where, without anti-Americanism, without anti-Israelism, without anti-Palestinian Islamophobia, one can ally oneself with those who, whether American, Israeli, or Palestinian, criticize courageously, and sometimes more vigilantly that we ourselves, the governments or dominant forces of their own countries [. . .]

It was in this Europe of the future that, more than ever, he placed his hopes – the Europe that would 'sow the seeds of a new non-bipartisan policy', which in his view was now the only way forward.

Derrida repeated this message in Strasbourg, at the beginning of June, at the session of the Parliament of Philosophers dedicated to him. This city, one of those which he had most often visited, and one in which he had been given the warmest welcome, paid solemn homage to him. Here, on Monday, 7 June 2004, Derrida met secondary school teachers from the Lycée Fustel-de-Coulanges, and returned to one of the questions that had most preoccupied him for thirty years, the teaching of philosophy. The next day, under the title 'On friendship', he took part in an interview at the Kléber bookshop with Isabelle Baladine-Howald, before giving what would be his last lecture in France: 'On the "sovereign good" – Europe in need of sovereignty'. A teacher right to the end, on the Wednesday he participated in dialogue with four young doctoral candidates who had come to present their work. Then he met up again with Philippe Lacoue-Labarthe and Jean-Luc Nancy for a particularly emotional session. The tone of their conversation was more informal than ever, as if they had forgotten the presence of the audience. And death was present in everything Derrida said, in a way at once tragic and serene:

> In my anticipation of death, in my relation to the death to come, which I know will annihilate me and destroy me utterly, there is, beneath the surface, the desire to leave a testament, in other words the desire that something survive, be left behind, passed on – a heritage or something to which I do not aspire, which will not be mine [*qui ne me reviendra pas*], but which, perhaps, will remain . . . And this is a feeling that haunts me not only as regards what are called works or books, but for any daily or common gesture that will have been the witness of that and which will retain the memory of that when I am no longer there. Now, I have said that this was part, not of death, of the impossible experience of death, but of my anticipation of death. So for me, this has always assumed an obsessional character, which does not concern merely, to say it yet again, things which are in the public domain, writing, but even private things . . . [. . .] These kinds of thoughts, which I call 'testamentary' thoughts, and which I have tried to link to the structure of the trace – and every trace is essentially testamentary – have always haunted me. Even if it does not take place, if it is not accepted, there is a testamentary desire that is part of the experience of death.[36]

On 22 June 2004, past midnight, it was a relaxed Derrida, in rather good shape, who with Régis Debray took part in the last programme of the season of *Cultures et dépendances*, chaired by Franz-Olivier Giesbert. Introduced as 'the greatest living philosopher', Derrida launched into a challenging dialogue with Debray, on mainly political themes. Reassured by the calibre of his conversation partner and the benevolence of the chairperson, he expressed himself clearly and fluidly, without the least coquetry: 'I don't have anything against the media. I have a problem with my image as it is framed by the media.' And also: 'As always in politics, I'm a man of transaction.'

In spite of this, Derrida still maintained really radical political positions. Defending a new idea of the political, he again spoke in support of a deterritorialized Europe, at the cutting edge of *altermondialisation*. And when the journalist Élisabeth Lévy asked him, not without a hint of aggression, whether it was 'the same Derrida who had signed *Of Grammatology* and the petition for gay marriage', he was not in the least thrown off his stride, explaining that he had supported whole-heartedly the initiative of Noël Mamère but that, on a deeper level, he would like the word 'marriage' to disappear from the Civil Code, since the notion was in his view too tied to the religious sphere.*

In spite of the late hour of its broadcast, this very eloquent programme had, for the first time, a real impact on the sales of Derrida's books.

On 6 July, he went to Queen Mary College, London, for a new honorary doctorate. This was his first in Britain since Cambridge, in 1992; it was also to be his last. If Derrida undertook the journey, this was not to add yet another honour to an already long list, but to please Marian Hobson, a long-standing friend and the author of a book about him, and so as not to let down the principal and vice-principal of the university, who had been making preparations for the ceremony for a long time. It was also an opportunity to meet up with faithful friends such as Peggy Kamuf, Nicholas Royle, and Geoffrey Bennington. But the weather was very hot that day and Derrida was initially tired, something he blamed on the busy weeks he had just lived through. 'At first, I thought he had really aged,' says Alexander García Düttmann. 'But at the seminar and the questions-and-answers afterwards, as ever, he found his old form. There was even a certain gaiety about him. And then, at the dinner, fatigue got the upper hand and he asked to be driven back to his dear Russell Hotel.'[37]

All the same, he set off again almost immediately, for the Avignon Festival. On 9 August, with Gianni Vattimo and Heinz Wismann, he took part in a debate entitled 'The "old Europe" and ours', reading as a preamble a short letter with the title 'Double memory'. Several of his favourite themes came together in these three pages:

Old Europe,
I have never addressed you familiarly. I've spent many years saying what certain people interpreted as bad things about you. [. . .] Today, the situation has changed. I see in you what

---

* In his interview with Jean Birnbaum, Derrida went into more detail on this question: 'If I were a legislator, I would propose simply getting rid of the word and concept of "marriage" in our civil and secular code. "Marriage," as a religious, sacred, heterosexual value – with a vow to procreate, to be eternally faithful, and so on –, is a concession made by the secular state to the Christian church, and particularly with regard to monogamy, which is neither Jewish (it was imposed upon Jews by Europeans only in the nineteenth century and was not an obligation just a few generations ago in Jewish Maghreb), nor, as is well known, Muslim. By getting rid of the word and concept of "marriage," and thus this ambiguity or this hypocrisy with regard to the religious and the sacred – things that have no place in a secular constitution – one could put in their place a contractual "civil union," a sort of generalized *pacs*, one that has been improved, refined, and would remain flexible and adaptable to parties whose sex and number would not be prescribed.' (*Learning to Live Finally*, pp. 43–4.)

I would call, drawing inspiration from the name given to an old synagogue in Prague, the 'old new Europe', *Staronova synagoga*, a Europe that keeps its memory, its good and its bad memory, bright and dark. [. . .]

My hope is that, on the basis of your two memories, and especially the awakening of conscience and the repentance that followed your 'nocturnal memory', you, my new 'Old Europe', are starting down a path that you alone are able to follow today, between American hegemonism – which does not even respect the international law it claims to uphold –, fundamentalist theocracy, and China, which is already starting to become, if we take into consideration just the question of petrol, defining in the geopolitical lines of force of the present time.[38]

A few days later, Jacques and Marguerite Derrida set off for Meina, on the shores of Lake Maggiore, to the Drawing Academy founded by Valerio Adami. Now he could rest, in a region he had always loved, with very dear friends; it was here that he celebrated his seventy-fourth birthday. But there was also a conference on a theme chosen that summer by Édouard Glissant: 'How Not to Tremble'. In a more accessible language than ever, Derrida drew a comparison between his memory of trembling as a child, during the winter of 1942, as Algiers was being bombed, and the trembling of the hand from which he had been suffering for some time, and which now stopped him writing and even signing documents. This was the springboard to a meditation on the fault, the fault-line, and failure:

We should not pretend to *know* what trembling means, to know what it means really to tremble, since trembling will always remain heterogeneous to knowledge. [. . .] The thought of trembling is a singular experience of non-knowing. [. . .] The experience of trembling is always the experience of an absolute passivity, absolutely exposed, absolutely vulnerable, passive in the face of an irreversible past as well as in the face of an unpredictable future.

Shuddering can, to be sure, be a demonstration of fear, anxiety, the apprehension of death, when one shudders in advance at the idea of what is going to happen. But it can be light, on the surface of the skin, when shuddering announces pleasure or ecstasy. [. . .] Water, they tell us, shudders before it boils, which is what we called seduction.[39]

The conclusion was like a final salute to his friends Camilla and Valerio Adami: 'The artist is someone who becomes an artist only when his hand trembles, in other words when he basically does not know what is going to happen to him, when what is going to happen to him is dictated by the other.'[40] But had not Derrida himself finally realized the Nietzschean dream of the philosopher-artist?

Shortly after Jacques and Marguerite returned from Italy, their old friends David Carroll and Suzanne Gearhart came to dinner in Ris-Orangis. When they arrived, Derrida was still in his office, typing detailed reports on the papers of the Irvine students that continued to be sent to him, in spite of his illness, more than a year after his last seminar. As David Carroll told me, 'I don't know anyone else who would have taken the time, who would have made the effort, to correct and comment on students' essays in those conditions. He did so unhesitatingly – it's true he grumbled he bit – because it was his duty, because it was part of his commitments.'[41]

At dinner, one difficult subject was deliberately avoided: the Dragan Kujundzic affair, which for some months had been seriously affecting Derrida's relations with the University of California, Irvine. It had all begun in spring 2003, just after his last stay there. A short while before, Irvine had adopted new regulations that totally banned any intimate relations between professors and students, and even between members of the university staff. A woman student, whose final dissertation was being supervised by Dragan Kujundzic, had an affair with him, then laid a complaint of sexual harassment. The inquiry set up by the State of California concluded that there was no reason for pursuing the legal case, but the University had in spite of everything decided to terminate Kujundzic's contract.

J. Hillis Miller continues the story:

I had several phone conversations with Jacques on this business, which greatly preoccupied him. In the past, several professors, starting with Paul de Man, had married former women students of theirs, and the marriages had been happy ones. The rules had changed, in a way that struck us as excessive. Maybe Dragan had promised more to this young woman than he should have done, but Americans tend too often to confuse moralism and law. In this affair, Derrida defended not only a friend whom he felt was the victim of an injustice, but a worker mistreated by his employer.[42]

At all events, on 25 July 2004, Derrida wrote a long letter to the chancellor of the University of California, Irvine, Ralph J. Cicerone, to express his surprise, his anxiety, and his indignation.

I will begin by making it unequivocally clear that I fully approve the principles of all rules meant to prevent, or even to repress, the kinds of behaviour defined in the United States as 'sexual harassment.' In their principle, these laws seem to me just and useful. But everyone knows that, in practice, they can give rise to applications that are abusive, capricious, or even perverse and deceitful [. . .].

First, as concerns *probability*, I can testify on the basis of what I have been told by many colleagues (including Dragan, obviously). It would seem that the allegations of the plaintiff are unfair and in bad faith (I will not yet say perverse). When there has been neither any coercion or violence brought to bear on her, nor any attack (moreover very improbable!) on the presumed 'innocence' of a 27- or 28-year-old woman, where does she find the grounds, how can she claim to have the right to initiate such a serious procedure and to put in motion such a weighty juridico-academic bureaucracy against a respectable and universally respected professor? I have also heard said that all the legal procedures were not observed in the conduct of the inquiry, notably in the way in which the administration informed (in fact *failed to inform*) our colleagues of new aspects of the law.[43]

Hardening his tone, Derrida emphasized that it was because of the 'trusting friendship' that united him to the University of California, Irvine that he had donated all his archives to the library's Special Collection.

What I am preparing to say to you, I assure you with a solemn oath, constitutes in no way, in my mind, pressure brought to bear on anyone. But it is my duty to tell you the truth on this subject, without delay and in all strictness. The truth is this: if the scandalous procedure initiated against Dragan Kujundzic were not to be interrupted or cancelled, for all the reasons I have just laid out, if a sanction of whatever sort were allowed to sully both his honor and the honor of the university, I would sadly be obliged to put an end, immediately, to *all* my relations with UCI. [. . .]

Another consequence: since I never take back what I have *given*, my papers would of course remain the property of UCI and the Special Collections department of the library. However, it goes without saying that the spirit in which I contributed to the constitution of these archives (which is underway and growing every year) would have been seriously damaged. Without renouncing my commitments, I would regret having made them and would reduce their fulfillment to the barest minimum.

Several of Derrida's friends and colleagues at Irvine, however, regretted his position, feeling that he had yielded too quickly to pressure from his friends. 'It's a shame he didn't consult us,' deplores Stephen Barker. 'The university rules are clear, and Dragan Kujundzic had broken them. Derrida wrote his "J'accuse" in an excessive, rather naïve manner. In any case, the official proceedings had already gone too far forward, the chancellor no longer had any choice in the matter; he couldn't go back on the decision he had taken.'[44]*

Ever since April, Derrida had not had time to revise the interview he had given to Jean Birnbaum. All of a sudden, Edwy Plenel insisted on having it published as quickly as possible, before the end of summer. Derrida was irritated by this haste: he mistrusted *Le Monde*, which, he felt, had never liked him. It needed all of Birnbaum's insistence, with Marguerite's support, before Jacques would agree to take up the text again. Several working sessions were necessary before the final version was ready. As Birnbaum says: 'He revised everything in great detail, including my own interventions. He wanted to open the discussion by talking about his illness, but he really wanted me to raise the question. The twilit nature of these pages comes from him. He wanted to refine this testamentary text, and not allow anyone to have "the last word".'[45]

At the beginning of the interview, Derrida began by affirming, in the face of traditional wisdom:

'No, I never *learned-to-live*. In fact not at all! Learning to live should mean learning to die, learning to take into account, so as to accept, absolute mortality (that is, without salvation, resurrection, or redemption – neither for oneself nor for the other). That's been the old philosophical injunction since

---

* Relations with the staff of the Special Collection at the University of Irvine turned sour soon after Derrida's death. Jackie Dooley very quickly asked Marguerite when the archives would start to be forwarded again, as if Jacques's letter to the chancellor had never been written. And yet there was nothing private about it: translated by Peggy Kamuf, it circulated widely in the circles concerned before being posted on the Internet. So Marguerite reminded Dooley of Jacques's position vis-à-vis his archives: while there was no question of taking back what had been given, neither would there be any new contributions. A few months later, the judicial proceedings brought by the University of California, Irvine against the Derrida family came as a real shock: one morning, the postman brought Marguerite a registered letter from the Californian Court of Justice, demanding the payment of a fine of $500,000 for non-receipt of the 'rest' of the donation, in other words the recent manuscripts. This was probably a preventive strike: the university management was afraid that Marguerite, Pierre, and Jean Derrida would demand the return to France of the archives given to Irvine, something they had never dreamed of doing. At the beginning of 2007, several press articles picked up on this painful and in many respects indecent affair, both in France and the United States, until the University of Irvine withdrew its complaint and a *modus vivendi* was set up with the new staff at the Special Collection. The Derrida archives are currently divided between IMEC and Irvine, but, contrary to what had been originally envisaged, there was no exchange of photocopies between the two institutions.

Plato: to philosophize is to learn to die. I believe in this truth without being able to resign myself to it. And less and less so. I have never learned to accept it, to accept death, that is. We are all survivors who have been granted a temporary reprieve [*en sursis*]. [. . .] But I remain uneducable when it comes to any wisdom about knowing-how-to-die or, if you prefer, knowing-how-to-live. I still have not learned or picked up anything on this subject. In addition, since certain health problems have become, as we were saying, so urgent, the question of survival [*la survie*] or of reprieve [*le sursis*], a question that has always haunted me, literally *every instant* of my life, in a concrete and unrelenting fashion, has come to have a different resonance today. I have always been interested in this theme of survival, the meaning of which is *not to be added on* to living and dying. It is originary: life *is* living on, life *is* survival [*la vie* est *survie*].[46]

The full version of this long interview was turned into a short book, a year after Derrida's death. *Learning to Live Finally* is a superb, limpid text, perhaps the best introduction to his work. The last sentences are particularly emotional, allowing the free flow of a lyricism that had long been held in check:

I am never more haunted by the necessity of dying than in moments of happiness and joy. To feel joy and to weep over the death that awaits are for me the same thing. When I recall my life, I tend to think that I have had the good fortune to love even the unhappy moments in my life, and to bless them. Almost all of them, with just one exception. When I recall the happy moments, I bless them too, of course, at the same time as they propel me toward the thought of death, toward death, because all that has passed, come to an end . . . [47]

On the evening of 14 August 2004, just after a final read-through of the interview destined for *Le Monde*, Derrida flew to Rio de Janeiro for a conference on his work. The event, organized by the French and Brazilian governments, had been scheduled for over a year, and organized by Evando Nascimento, one of his former students at the École des Hautes Études who had become his major contact in Brazil. One month before the date arranged for his departure, Derrida had told Nascimento of his doubts: he was not feeling very well and was not sure he would be able to honour his engagements. Everyone put him at his ease, assuring him they would not mind if he had to cancel. But in the event he did decide to go to the city and the country of which he was very fond. When Nascimento met him at the airport, Derrida confided in him, affectionately: 'You know, this really is the most unlikely journey I've ever made.'

'He'd changed since Coimbra,' acknowledges Nascimento, 'but he still seemed in good shape. He was quite calm when he talked about his illness, and although I suggested several times that he rest in his hotel in Copacabana, he insisted on attending all the sessions in those three long days. He followed the simultaneous translation on headphones and intervened in the debates.'[48]

The conference was held in Rio in the auditorium of the Maison de France. People came from all over Brazil and other countries, especially the United States, and there simply was not enough room for everyone. It was in front of a huge, enthusiastic audience that, on 16 August 2004, Derrida gave the opening address, his last lecture, at his last conference: 'Pardon, reconciliation, truth: what genre?' He spoke for three full hours, superbly. 'Coming to Brazil was for him an affirmation of life,' says Evando Nascimento. 'Those who didn't know he was ill didn't realize, as he didn't show any sign of weakness. As he finished his lecture, he said with a smile: "There are many more things to be said, but I wouldn't want to tire you."'

Bernard Stiegler was chosen to give the final address. If he had taken the trouble to travel all this way, it was mainly to see, for one last time, the man who had played such an important role in his career. 'On arriving in the lecture hall,' he relates, 'I didn't recognize him at first. He had aged, was thinner, and seemed to have difficulty expressing himself. But right from the start of the lecture, he turned back into his old self. Politically, he had become much more radical; this is one of the things that most struck me.' Stiegler remembers a lunch at the French Embassy where Derrida, very indignant at Bush, defended Fidel Castro. 'On the last day of the conference,' he continues, 'just after my lecture, we had one of the few real arguments in our lives, the first since my thesis defence. He put up a real fight, wouldn't let go, but he did listen to my arguments. Perhaps the only real discussion in his view had to be public.'[49]

Jacques phoned Marguerite twice a day. He said he was very glad to be travelling and was feeling better. However, his timetable was as full as ever: he held a press conference, gave interviews to the television channel Globo, and to the *Folha de São Paulo*, and even agreed to an autograph session.

On his return from Brazil, he was handed the copy of *Le Monde* where his long interview with Jean Birnbaum had been published on 19 August, with the title 'I am at war with myself'. He seemed both pleased and upset: 'It's like an obituary,' he sighed. He was particularly bothered by the photo, which was big enough to bring out his illness. He said to Élisabeth Roudinesco: 'It's not enough for them to *know* that I'm ill, it's not enough for me to *say* it [. . .], they want to *see* the trace of illness on my face and they want the reader to see it.'[50]

By contrast, it was with unalloyed joy that he saw the issue of the Cahiers de l'Herne dedicated to him. 'With Marie-Louise Mallet, we worked on this huge issue a bit hastily,' remembers Ginette Michaud. 'We absolutely wanted him to see it. As he leafed through it, he was wonderstruck. He weighed the volume, 628 pages, large format, in his hands. He was as happy as a child.'[51]

But his condition soon started to deteriorate. He was eating less and less and his nights were increasingly difficult. At the beginning of September, in the middle of the weekend, Marguerite had to phone for an ambulance as he needed to be urgently hospitalized at Curie. 'That Sunday,' she relates, 'when the ambulance came for him, he turned round to look at the house, as if he sensed it was for the last time . . . "The illness can develop suddenly," the doctor told me the following day. "But none of us thought that his end was so near."'[52]

The medical personnel were very free and easy about visits, and Derrida had several. Pierre came with his partner Jeanne Balibar, Jean with his wife Emmanuelle. Jean-Luc Nancy, Marie-Louise Mallet, Hélène Cixous, and René Major also came frequently.

In the first days of October, rumours were flying around that Derrida was going to be awarded the Nobel Prize for Literature. His name had been mentioned the previous year, but this time the rumour was becoming more and more persistent. Several French newspapers were preparing major articles or special issues to greet the news. After a phone call from Safaa Fathy, Marguerite said to Jacques: 'It looks like you're going to get the Nobel.' Then she saw tears on his face. 'Why?' she asked him. 'They want to give it me because I'm dying.'

On 6 October, the prize was finally given to Elfriede Jelinek, depriving philosophy of a consecration it had not known since Henri Bergson (1927), Bertrand Russell (1950), and Jean-Paul Sartre (1964) – and also depriving Derrida of the fulfilment of his oldest and deepest dream:

> To leave traces in the history of the French language – that's what interests me. I live off this passion, that is, if not for France at least for something that the French language has incorporated for centuries. I think that if I love this language like I love my life, and sometimes more than certain native French do, it is because I love it as a foreigner who has been welcomed, and who has appropriated this language for himself as the only possible language for him.[53]

The skin patches used to suppress pain were now unable to provide relief, and Jacques needed treating with morphine, with a pump that he could operate as and when he wanted, but that he was afraid to use. One morning, he anxiously said to Marguerite: 'What's that music? Is there a cabaret nearby?' 'He thought he could hear Arabic music,' she says. 'Then he started to complain about strange cooking smells. A bit later, he told me that three men in black had got into his room and started to rummage about everywhere. It needed a bit of Aldol to stop these hallucinations.'

Derrida could now no longer feed himself at all. He was suffering from an intestinal blockage that needed an operation lasting over six hours. To Jean-Luc Nancy, who came to visit him just after he had come round, Derrida announced – in allusion to his friend's heart transplant – that he now had a scar just as big. 'He was joking – he always liked to laugh – but his fatigue was so great, and his anxiety too, that the tone wasn't all that cheerful.'[54] In the view of the medics, the operation had been a success and the treatment could resume. But the situation changed dramatically and Marguerite got a phone call the same night: 'Your husband is in a coma.' By the time she could reach the Hôpital Curie, it was already too late. In the ward, all the apparatus had already been disconnected. Jacques Derrida had died, on Saturday 9 October 2004, at the age of seventy-four.

In Ris-Orangis, Marguerite found, slipped into an envelope, a letter for her and her children that Jacques had written shortly before his hospitalization. In particular, he gave instructions for his funeral, with the wish that there not be many people and the greatest discretion possible. Contrary to Jewish tradition, and with a last wink to Jean-Luc Nancy, he asked not to be buried too quickly so as to give resurrection a chance.

On 12 October, despite there having been no announcement, a crowd gathered in the rue d'Ulm, blocking the pavements. But only members of the family and close friends attended the cortège from the Hôpital Curie, just a few yards away from the École Normale Supérieure.

Jacques Derrida, as one may easily imagine, wished to be buried rather than cremated. In the cemetery in Ris-Orangis, at the side of the open grave, there was grief and disarray. People had come from very far to pay a last homage, several had travelled all the way from California, but everything seemed to be going too fast for them. As Derrida had wished, there was nothing official about the ceremony, and if Jack Lang was there, this was in a private capacity. Pierre had secretly hoped, if not that Daniel would attend, at least that he would send some message. But nothing came, and no initiative was taken.

Though a few yarmulkes could be seen in the crowd, Jackie Élie Derrida had wished to be buried outside the Jewish section so as not to be separated from Marguerite when her time came. René, his older brother, wore his tallith. Nobody dared say a prayer, since Jacques hadn't wanted one. 'So,' confided René, 'I said the kaddish in my head.'

A heavy silence reigned, but only the people closest to the tomb could hear Pierre reading the few words prepared by his father. Derrida, reproducing his own father's gesture, thirty-four years earlier, had composed his epitaph himself:

> Jacques desired neither ritual nor prayer. He knows by experience what a trial it is for the friend who performs them. He asks me to thank you for coming, and to bless you, he begs you not to be sad, and to think just of the many happy times that you gave him the chance to share with him.
>
> Smile at me, he says, as I will have smiled at you until the end.
>
> Always prefer life and never stop affirming survival.
>
> I love you and I am smiling at you from wherever I am.[55]

Who is going to inherit, and how? Will there ever be any heirs?
   This question is more relevant today than ever before. It preoccupies me constantly. [. . .] When it comes to thought, the question of survival has taken on absolutely unforeseeable forms. At my age, I am ready to entertain the most contradictory hypotheses in this regard: I have simultaneously – I ask you to believe me on this – the *double feeling* that, on the one hand, to put it playfully and with a certain immodesty, one has not yet begun to read me, that even though there are, to be sure, many very good readers (a few dozen in the world, perhaps, people who are also writers-thinkers, poets), in the end it is later on that all this has a chance of appearing; but also, on the other hand, and thus simultaneously, I have the feeling that two weeks or a month after my death *there will be nothing left*. Nothing except what has been copyrighted and deposited in libraries. I swear to you, I believe sincerely and simultaneously in these two hypotheses.

                      Jacques Derrida, *Learning to Live Finally*

Notes

Introduction

1 'Thinking Lives: The Philosophy of Biography and the Biography of Philosophers', conference, New York University, 1996. Excerpts from Derrida's remarks can be seen in the film *Derrida* by Kirby Dick and Amy Ziering Kofman (DVD available from Blaq Out editions, 2007). Other fragments can be found on the Internet.

2 'Otobiographies: The teaching of Nietzsche and the politics of the proper name', tr. by Avital Ronell, in Jacques Derrida, *The Ear of the Other – Otobiography, Transference, Translation: Texts and Discussions with Jacques Derrida*, ed. by Christie McDonald; tr. by Peggy Kamuf (Lincoln: University of Nebraska Press, new edition, 1988), p. 5.

3 Jacques Derrida, 'Others are secret because they are other', interview with Antoine Spire, reprinted in *Paper Machine*, tr. by Rachel Bowlby (Stanford, Calif.: Stanford University Press, 2005), pp. 136–63; p. 145.

4 Jacques Derrida and Maurizio Ferraris, *A Taste for the Secret*, ed. by Giacomo Donis and David Webb; tr. by Giacomo Donis (Cambridge: Polity, 2001), p. 41.

5 Jacques Derrida, seminar of 1 February 1995, IMEC archives.

6 'Dialogue entre Jacques Derrida, Philippe Lacoue-Labarthe et Jean-Luc Nancy', *Rue Descartes* no. 52, 2006, p. 96.

7 Jacques Derrida, 'Entre le corps écrivant et l'écriture', interview with Daniel Ferrer, *Genesis* no. 17, December 2001, pp. 59–72.

8 'A life in philosophy', in Geoffrey Bennington, *Other Analyses: Reading Philosophy*, electronic text available on the site *http://bennington.zsoft.co.uk*.

Part I   Jackie *1930–1962*

Chapter 1   The Negus *1930–1942*

1 'Derrida l'insoumis', interview with Catherine David, *Le Nouvel Observateur*, 9 September 1983. Reprinted as 'Unsealing ("the old

new language")', in Jacques Derrida, *Points . . . Interviews, 1974–1994*, ed. by Elisabeth Weber, tr. by Peggy Kamuf et al. (Stanford, Calif.: Stanford University Press, 1995), pp. 119–20.

2 The interview with Didier Cahen, 'Le bon plaisir de Jacques Derrida', was published as 'Il n'y a pas *le* narcissisme'; English translation ('There is no *one* narcissism') in *Points . . .*, p. 203.

3 Geoffrey Bennington and Jacques Derrida, *Jacques Derrida*, tr. by Geoffrey Bennington (Chicago: University of Chicago Press, 1993), p. 322.

4 'À voix nue', radio interview with Catherine Paoletti, published in Jacques Derrida, *Sur parole: instantanés philosophiques* (La Tour d'Aigues: Éditions de l'Aube, 1999), p. 10.

5 Derrida, *Sur parole*, p. 11.

6 Benjamin Stora, *Les Trois Exils: Juifs d'Algérie* (Paris: Stock, 2006), p. 48. I am also drawing on another work by the same author: *Histoire de l'Algérie coloniale, 1830-1954* (Paris: La Découverte, collection 'Repères', 2004), p. 32.

7 Jacques Derrida, *Learning to Live Finally: The Last Interview. An Interview with Jean Birnbaum*, translated from the French (n.tr.) (Basingstoke: Palgrave Macmillan, 2007), p. 35.

8 'Circumfession', in Bennington and Derrida, *Jacques Derrida*, pp. 51–2. For several other details in this chapter, I am indebted to the 'Curriculum vitae' given on pp. 325–36 of this work.

9 Bennington and Derrida, *Jacques Derrida*, p. 130.

10 Ibid., pp. 119–20.

11 Derrida, *Sur parole*, pp. 11–12.

12 Derrida, 'Entre le corps écrivant et l'écriture'.

13 Jacques Derrida, 'L'école a été un enfer pour moi', interview with Bernard Defrance published in *Les Cahiers pédagogiques*, 270 and 272, January and March 1989. The text of this interview was not revised by Derrida.

14 Jacques Derrida, *Monolingualism of the Other, or, The Prosthesis of Origin*, tr. by Patrick Mensah (Stanford, Calif.: Stanford University Press, 1998), pp. 26 and 44–5.

15 Ibid., p. 26.

16 Jacques Derrida, in Frédéric Brenner, *Diaspora: Homelands in Exile*, 2 vols (London: Bloomsbury, 2004), vol. 2, *Voices*, pp. 67 and 21.

17 Jacques Derrida, *Memoirs of the Blind: The Self-Portrait and Other Ruins*, tr. by Pascale-Anne Brault and Michael Naas (Chicago; London: University of Chicago Press, 1993), p. 37.

18 Hélène Cixous and Jacques Derrida, *Veils*, tr. by Geoffrey Bennington (Stanford, Calif.: Stanford University Press, 2001), p. 43.

19 Conversations with Janine Meskel-Derrida, René Derrida, and Micheline Lévy.

20 Catherine Malabou and Jacques Derrida, *Counterpath: Travelling with Jacques Derrida*, tr. by David Willis (Stanford, Calif.: Stanford University Press, 2004), p. 23.

21 Quoted in Stora, *Les Trois Exils*, p. 78.

22 Ibid., p. 87. For further details on the situation in Algeria during the Second World War, see also the collective volume *Alger 1940–1962:*

une ville en guerres, ed. by Jean-Jacques Jordi and Guy Pervillé (Paris: Autrement, collection 'Mémoires' no. 56, 1999), pp. 34–5.

23 Derrida, *Sur parole*, p. 12.

24 Jacques Derrida, 'Abraham, the other', in Bettina Bergo, Joseph Cohen, and Raphale Zagury-Orly, eds, *Judeities: Questions for Jacques Derrida*, tr. by Bettina Bergo and Michael B. Smith (New York: Fordham University Press, 2007), p. 10.

25 Derrida, *Points . . .*, pp. 341–2.

Chapter 2   Under the Sun of Algiers *1942–1949*

1 Jacques Derrida, *The Post Card: From Socrates to Freud and Beyond*, tr., with an introduction and additional notes, by Alan Bass (Chicago: University of Chicago Press, 1987), p. 87.

2 For further details on these anti-Semitic measures, see the 'Curriculum vitae', in Bennington and Derrida, *Jacques Derrida*, pp. 325–6.

3 Derrida, *Sur parole*, p. 13.

4 Derrida, 'Circumfession', p. 58.

5 Jacques Derrida and Élisabeth Roudinesco, *For What Tomorrow . . . : A Dialogue*, tr. by Jeff Fort (Stanford, Calif.: Stanford University Press, 2004), p. 109.

6 Remarks by Derrida quoted by Hélène Cixous, 'Celle qui ne se ferme pas', in Mustapha Chérif, ed., *Derrida à Alger: un regard sur le monde. Essais* (Arles: Actes sud; [Alger]: Barzakh, 2008), pp. 48–9.

7 Jacques Derrida, 'Comment ne pas trembler', *Annali*, 2006/II, Bruno Mondadori, p. 91.

8 Derrida and Roudinesco, *For What Tomorrow . . .*, p. 111.

9 'The three ages of Jacques Derrida', interview with Kristine McKenna, *LA Weekly*, 8–14 November 2002.

10 'Le cinema et ses fantômes', interview reprinted in Antoine de Baecque, *Feu sur le quartier général*, Petite bibliothèque des Cahiers du Cinéma, 2008, pp. 54–5.

11 Stora, *Les Trois Exils*, p. 95.

12 Malabou and Derrida, *Counterpath*, p. 27.

13 Remarks by Derrida quoted by Hélène Cixous, 'Celle qui ne se ferme pas', p. 49.

14 Ibid., p. 49.

15 Derrida, *Sur parole*, p. 15.

16 Interview with Fernand Acharrok. I am very grateful to his son Jean-Philippe for helping me obtain this interview.

17 Albert Camus, 'Le minotaure', in *Essais*. Quoted by Pierre Mannoni, *Les Français d'Algérie: vie, moeurs, mentalité de la conquête des Territoires du Sud à l'indépendance* (Paris: L'Harmattan, 1993), p. 163. The Camus essay is translated as 'The Minotaur, or stopping in Oran', in Albert Camus, *Lyrical and Critical*, tr. by Philip Thody (London: Hamish Hamilton, 1968), p. 89.

18 Derrida, 'Le survivant, le sursis, le sursaut', *La Quinzaine littéraire* no. 882, 1–31 August 2004.

19 Derrida and Roudinesco, *For What Tomorrow . . .*, p. 107.

20 Ibid., pp. 107–8.

21 Malabou and Derrida, *Counterpath*, p. 32.

22 Interview with Micheline Lévy.

23 'Le cinéma et ses fantômes', p. 56.

24 Derrida, 'Entre le corps écrivant et l'écriture'.

25 Franz-Olivier Giesbert, 'Ce que disait Derrida . . .', *http://www. lepoint.fr/actualites-litterature/2007-01-17/philosophie-ce-que-disait-derrida/1038/0/31857.*

26 Derrida, *Sur parole*, p. 18.

27 Derrida, *Monolingualism of the Other*, p. 45.

28 Derrida, 'Les voix d'Artaud', interview with Évelyne Grossman, *Le Magazine littéraire* no. 434, September 2004.

29 For further details, see especially the article by Jacques Cantier, '1938–1945, une métropole en guerre', in Jordi and Pervillé, eds, *Alger 1940–1962*.

30 Derrida, *Glas*, tr. by John P. Leavey, Jr, and Richard Rand (Lincoln: University of Nebraska Press, 1986), p. 196.

31 Letter from Claude Bernady to Derrida, 21 March 1947.

32 Jean-Louis Jacquemin, 'Je suis un "Émile Félix Gautier"', *http:// esmma.free.fr/mde4/jacquemin.htm.*

33 Derrida, Personal Notebooks for 1976, Irvine archives. [This entry is grammatically somewhat confusing. – Tr.]

34 Bennington and Derrida, *Jacques Derrida*, pp. 327–8.

35 Derrida, *Sur parole*, p. 19.

36 Derrida, 'This strange institution called literature', in Derrida, *Acts of Literature*, ed. by Derek Attridge, tr. by Geoffrey Bennington and Rachel Bowlby (New York; London: Routledge, 1992), p. 34.

37 Interview with Jean-Claude Pariente. This is the only *hypokhâgne* classmate whom I have managed to trace. I am greatly indebted to him for the description of the year in question.

38 'Entretien avec Jacques Derrida', in Dominique Janicaud, *Heidegger en France*, vol. 2, *Entretiens* (Paris: Hachette-Littératures, coll. 'Pluriel', 2005), pp. 89–90.

39 Jacques Derrida, '"Dead man running": Salut, salut', in Derrida, *Negotiations: Interventions and Interviews, 1971–2001*, ed. and tr. by Elizabeth Rottenberg (Stanford, Calif.: Stanford University Press, 2002), p. 264.

40 Derrida, *Sur parole*, p. 82.

41 Derrida, 'L'une des pires oppressions: l'interdiction d'une langue', interview with Aïssa Khelladi, *Algérie Littérature action* no. 9, March 1997.

Chapter 3 The Walls of Louis-le-Grand *1949–1952*

1 This is the expression used by Hélène Cixous, who experienced the same 'small deportation' a few years later. See *So Close*, tr. by Peggy Kamuf (Cambridge: Polity, 2009), p. 28.

2 Giesbert, 'Ce que disait Derrida . . .'.

3 Derrida, *Monolingualism of the Other*, p. 44. [Baz'Grand = Grand Bazaar. – Tr.]

4 Letter from Fernand Acharrok to Derrida, 4 November 1949.

5 XXX [Pierre Nora], 'Khâgne 1950', *Le Débat* no. 3, July–August 1980. This description is also based on accounts by Jean Bellemin-Noël and Michel Monory.

6 Interview with Jean-Claude Pariente.

7 Ibid.

8 Interview with Robert Abirached.

9 Interview with Jean Bellemin-Noël.

10 Derrida, 'Le cinéma et ses fantômes', p. 57.

11 Derrida, 'Gérard Granel', in *Chaque fois unique: la fin du monde* (Paris: Galilée, 2003), pp. 314–15.

12 Interview with Michel Monory.

13 Bulletins 1949–50, archives of the Lycée Louis-le-Grand.

14 Letter from Derrida to Michel Monory, n.d. (summer 1950).

15 Letter from Derrida to Michel Monory, n.d. (summer 1950).

16 Letter from Derrida to Michel Monory, n.d (end of December 1950).

17 Letters from Derrida to Michel Monory, n.d. (January 1951).

18 Letter from Michel Monory to Derrida, n.d. (February 1951).

19 Letter from Derrida to Michel Monory, n.d. (February 1951).

20 Letter from Derrida to Michel Monory, n.d. (March 1951).

21 Letter from Derrida to Michel Monory, n.d. (March 1951).

22 Bulletins 1950–1, archives of the Lycée Louis-le-Grand.

23 Draft of letter from Derrida to Roger Pons, 10 September 1952.

24 Malabou and Derrida, *Counterpath*, p. 290.

25 Letter from Derrida to Michel Monory, 10 July 1951.

26 Letter from Derrida to Michel Monory, 16 July 1951.

27 Letter from Derrida to Michel Monory, n.d. (summer 1951).

28 Letter from Derrida to Michel Monory, n.d. (summer 1951).

29 Letter from Derrida to Michel Monory, 2 October 1951.

30 Letter from Derrida to Michel Monory, n.d. (summer 1951).

31 Interview with Michel Aucouturier.

32 Letters, n.d., from Michel Monory to Derrida. Interview with Michel Monory.

33 Interview with Pierre Foucher.

34 'The ends of man', 1968 lecture, reprinted in *Margins of Philosophy*, tr. with additional notes by Alan Bass (Brighton: Harvester Press, 1982), p. 115.

35 Draft of a letter from Derrida to Roger Pons, 10 September 1952.

36 Draft of a letter from Derrida to Claude Bonnefoy, n.d. (August 1952).

37 Letter from Derrida to Michel Monory, n.d. (August 1952).

38 Interview with Pierre Foucher.

39 Letter from Derrida to Michel Monory, 15 August 1952.

40 Letter from Derrida to Michel Monory, 26 August 1952.

Chapter 4   The École Normale Supérieure *1952–1956*

1 *http://fr.wikipedia.org/wiki/École_normale_supérieure_(rue_d'Ulm)*.

2 This was told me by Alain Pons.

3 'Le Pot', fragments of a motion, n.d., archives of Marguerite Derrida.

4 Interview with Jean Bellemin-Noël.

5 *Les Temps modernes* no. 82, August 1952.

6 *Les Temps modernes* no. 82, August 1952.
7 Derrida, '"Dead man running": Salut, salut', p. 282 (translation slightly modified).
8 Derrida, 'L'ami d'un ami de la Chine', in *Aux origines de la Chine contemporaine: en hommage à Lucien Bianco* (Paris: L'Harmattan, 2002), pp. viii–ix.
9 Much of this information comes from the first volume of Yann Moulier-Boutang, *Louis Althusser: une biographie* (Paris: Grasset, 1992).
10 Quoted in Didier Eribon, *Michel Foucault*, tr. by Betsy Wing (London: Faber and Faber, 1993), p. 50 (translation slightly modified). This memory is also mentioned in Derrida's penultimate seminar, *The Beast & the Sovereign*, vol. 2, ed. by Michel Lisse, Marie-Louise Mallet, and Ginette Michaud; tr. by Geoffrey Bennington (Chicago: University of Chicago Press, 2011), p. 415.
11 Letter from Derrida to Micheline Lévy, n.d. (Spring 1953).
12 Derrida, 'La parole – Donner, nommer, appeler', in Myriam Revault d'Allonnes and François Azouvi, eds, *Paul Ricoeur*, Cahier de l'Herne no. 81 (Paris: Éditions de l'Herne, 2004), pp. 19–25.
13 Letter from Derrida to Michel Serres, 11 September 1953.
14 Letter from Derrida to Michel Monory, 13 September 1953.
15 Derrida, 'Discours de réception de la Légion d'honneur', 1992, unpublished text in the archives of IMEC.
16 Letter from Derrida to Michel Monory, 13 November 1953.
17 Letter from Derrida to Micheline Lévy, 8 January 1954.
18 Interviews with Lucien Bianco and Alain Pons.
19 Interview with Rudolf Boehm.
20 The text Derrida eventually translated was published for the first time, complete, by Walter Biemel, in volume 6 of *Husserliana* (The Hague: Martinus Nijhoff, 1954).
21 Jacques Derrida, *The Problem of Genesis in Husserl's Philosophy*, tr. by Marion Hobson (Chicago: University of Chicago Press, 2003), p. 5.
22 Ibid., p. xv.
23 Letter from Jean-Luc Nancy to Derrida, 10 October 1990.
24 Letter from Derrida to Michel Monory, n.d. (1954).
25 Letter from Derrida to Michel Monory, n.d. (April 1954).
26 Letter from Michel Monory to Derrida, n.d. (1954).
27 Letter from Geneviève Bollème to Derrida, 4 October 1955.
28 Derrida, 'L'ami d'un ami de la Chine', p. ii.
29 Remark quoted in a letter from Lucine Bianco to Derrida, 1 October 1957.
30 Dissertation by Jacques Derrida and corrections by Althusser, November 1954, Irvine archives.
31 Derrida, 'Gérard Granel', pp. 296–7.
32 Derrida, *Sur parole*, p. 30.
33 Letter from Maurice de Gandillac to Derrida, 9 August 1955.
34 Interview with Marguerite Derrida.
35 Albert Camus, *Chroniques algériennes, 1939–1958* (Paris: Gallimard, coll. 'Folio-essais', 2002), pp. 139–42.
36 Ibid., pp. 12–13.
37 Interview with Lucien Bianco.

38 'Entretien avec Jacques Derrida', in Janicaud, *Heidegger en France*, vol. 2, pp. 94–5.
39 Interviews with Marguerite Derrida and Michel Aucouturier.
40 Letter from Derrida to Louis Althusser, 25 April 1956.
41 Letter from Derrida to Michel Monory, n.d. (May 1956).
42 Letter from Lucien Bianco to Derrida, 11 August 1956.
43 Letter from Derrida to Louis Althusser, 30 August 1956.
44 Letter from Louis Althusser to Derrida, 4 September 1956.
45 Letter from Derrida to Michel Monory, 22 August 1956.
46 Letter from Micheline Lévy to Derrida, n.d. (August 1956).

Chapter 5 A Year in America *1956–1957*

1 Letter from Lucien Bianco to Derrida, 11 August 1956.
2 Letter from Derrida to Michel Monory, 22 August 1956.
3 Letter from Derrida to Louis Althusser, 30 August 1956.
4 Jacques Vergès, *Pour Djamila Bouhired* (Paris: Éditions de Minuit, 1958).
5 Interview with Michel Aucouturier.
6 Letter from Georges Safar to Derrida, 30 October 1956.
7 Letter from Georges Safar to Derrida, 17 November 1956.
8 Letter from Micheline Lévy to Derrida, 20 October 1956.
9 Letter from Derrida to Louis Althusser, 11 February 1957.
10 Interview with Marguerite Derrida.
11 Letter from Derrida to Louis Althusser, 11 February 1957.
12 Derrida, 'The Villanova roundtable', in John D. Caputo, ed., *Deconstruction in a Nutshell: A Conversation with Jacques Derrida* (New York: Fordham University Press, 1997), p. 25.
13 Letter from Derrida to Lucien Bianco, 18 November 1956.
14 Letter from Derrida to Michel Monory, 27 February 1957.
15 Ibid.
16 Peggy Kamuf, 'The affect of America', in *Derrida's Legacies: Literature and Philosophy* (New York: Routledge, 2008), p. 144.
17 Letter from Derrida to Michel Monory, 27 February 1957.
18 Letter from Derrida to Louis Althusser, 11 February 1957.
19 Derrida 'Punctuations: The time of a thesis', in Derrida, *Eyes of the University. Right to Philosophy 2*, tr. by Jan Plug and others (Stanford, Calif.: Stanford University Press, 2004), p. 113–28; p. 114.
20 Derrida, *Sur parole*, p. 21.
21 Letter from Jean Hyppolite to Derrida, 4 December 1956.
22 Letter from Maurice de Gandillac to Derrida, 11 January 1957.
23 Letter from Michel Monory to Derrida, 28 April 1957.
24 Letter from Derrida to Michel Monory, 17 May 1957.

Chapter 6 The Soldier of Koléa *1957–1959*

1 Letter from Derrida to Michel Monory, 15 July 1957.
2 Interviews with Janine Meskel-Derrida and René Derrida.
3 Letter from Derrida to Michel Monory, n.d. (summer 1957).
4 Letter from Derrida to Michel Monory, n.d. (November 1957).

5 This was the basis for his first work, *Sociologie de l'Algérie* (Paris: PUF, 'Que sais-je?', 1958). For more information, see Marie-Anne Lescouret, *Bourdieu* (Paris: Flammarion, coll. 'Grandes biographies', 2008), as well as Bourdieu's posthumous text, *Esquisse pour une auto-analyse* (Paris: Raisons d'agir, 2004).

6 Henri Alleg, *The Question*, tr. by John Calder, preface by Jean-Paul Sartre (London: J. Calder, 1958). This work was first published in 1958 as *La Question* by the Éditions de Minuit, who would later publish some of Derrida's work; the same publisher, a few weeks after *La Question*, brought out Pierre Vidal-Naquet's *L'Affaire Audin*.

7 Letter from Lucien Bianco to Derrida, 27 April 1958.

8 Letter from Derrida to Lucien Bianco, 14–29 May 1958.

9 Guy Pervillé, 'Le temps des complots', in Jordi and Pervillé, eds, *Alger 1940–1962*, p. 158.

10 Charles de Gaulle, speech at the Forum d'Alger, 4 June 1958.

11 Letter from Lucien Bianco to Derrida, 21 June 1958.

12 Letter from Lucien Bianco to Derrida, 1 July 1958.

13 Letter from Lucien Bianco to Derrida, 10 September 1958.

14 Letter from Louis Althusser to Derrida, 17 November 1958.

15 Letter from Louis Althusser to Derrida, 13 December 1958.

16 Interviews with Marguerite Derrida and Lucien Bianco.

17 Letter from Derrida to Michel Monory, 15 December 1958.

18 Letter from Maurice de Gandillac to Derrida, 9 February 1959.

19 Derrida, 'Punctuations', p. 116.

20 Letter from Jean Hyppolite to Derrida, 13 May 1959.

21 Letters from Gérard Genette to Derrida, 12 and 16 April 1959.

22 Letter from Gérard Genette to Derrida, 11 May 1959.

23 Letter from Gérard Genette to Derrida, 25 June 1959.

24 Letters from Louis Althusser and Jean Hyppolite to Derrida, 15 July 1959.

25 Letter from Étienne Souriau to Derrida, 21 July 1959.

26 Derrida, 'Le modèle philosophique d'une "contre-institution"', in *Un siècle de rencontres intellectuelles: Pontigny, Cerisy*, IMEC, 2005, p. 257.

27 Ibid., p. 258.

28 Derrida, *Writing and Difference*, tr. with an introduction and additional notes by Alan Bass (London: Routledge and Kegan Paul, 1978), p. 202. This point is mentioned in the 'Derridex', an index of terms in Derrida's work available on the site *www.idixa.net/Pixa/pagixa-0509031313.html*.

29 Letter from Derrida to Louis Althusser, 4 September 1959.

30 Letter from Derrida to Michel Monory, 12 September 1959.

31 Letter from Louis Althusser to Derrida, 6 October 1959.

32 Charles de Gaulle, speech on Algerian self-determination, 16 September 1959.

Chapter 7   Melancholia in Le Mans *1959–1960*

1 Letter from Gérard Genette to Derrida, 12 November 1959.

2 Gérard Genette, *Codicille* (Paris: Le Seuil, coll. 'Fiction & Cie', 2009), p. 107.

3 Letter from Gérard Genette to Derrida, 14 September 1959.
4 Gérard Genette, *Bardadrac* (Paris: Le Seuil, coll. 'Fiction & Cie', 2006), p. 67.
5 Letter from Derrida to Micheline Lévy, 7 January 1960.
6 Interviews with Albert Daussin, Paul Cottin, and Njoh Mouellé.
7 Letter from Jean Hyppolite to Derrida, 11 March 1960.
8 Interview with Gérard Genette. The episode is also related in his book *Codicille*. Unfortunately, I have not managed to find the text of the speech given by Derrida.
9 Letter from Maurice de Gandillac to Derrida, 24 August 1960.

Chapter 8   Towards Independence *1960–1962*

1 Interview with Marguerite Derrida. These communities would completely disappear after independence and Leroi-Gourhan would soon be telling his student: 'But my dear girl, the field you are studying is slipping away beneath your feet.'
2 Letter from Michel Monory to Derrida, n.d. (September 1960).
3 Letter from Derrida to Jean Bellemin-Noël, n.d. (December 1960).
4 Derrida, 'Discours de réception de la Légion d'honneur', 1992, unpublished, IMEC archives.
5 Derrida, 'La parole', p. 21.
6 Interview with Françoise Dastur.
7 Interview with Jean Ristat.
8 Letter from Derrida to Pierre Nora, 27 April 1961.
9 Letter from Pierre Nora to Derrida, 22 June 1961.
10 Letter from Derrida to Pierre Nora, 30 June 1961.
11 Letter from Derrida to Pierre Nora, 4 August 1961.
12 Letter from Jean Hyppolite to Derrida, 23 October 1961.
13 Letter from Derrida to Paul Ricoeur, 24 November 1961.
14 Letter from Paul Ricoeur to Derrida, 27 December 1961.
15 Letter from Louis Althusser, 9 January 1962.
16 Letter from Derrida to Louis Althusser, 15 January 1962.
17 See Jordi and Pervillé, eds, *Alger 1940–1962*, pp. 250–7.
18 Interview with Martine Meskel.
19 Interviews with René and Évelyne Derrida.
20 Interviews with Janine Meskel-Derrida, Pierre Meskel, René and Évelyne Derrida.
21 Marcello Fabri, 'Nostalgérie', in *Alger 1860–1939* (Paris: Autrement, coll. 'Mémoires' no. 55, 2001), p. 94.
22 Derrida, 'Les mots autobiographiques – pourquoi pas Sartre', 23 March 1987, interview published in Japan, IMEC archives.
23 'Cultures et dépendances', France 3, 22 June 2004.
24 'Les voix d'Artaud'.

Part II Derrida *1963-1983*

Chapter 1   From Husserl to Artaud *1963-1964*

1 'A "madness" must watch over thinking', in Derrida, *Points* . . ., pp. 343-4.
2 Derrida, 'Introduction', in Husserl, *The Origin of Geometry*, tr. with a preface and afterword by John P. Leavey, Jr (Lincoln: University of Nebraska Press, 1989), p. 27.
3 Rudolf Bernet, 'La voie et le phénomène', in Marc Crépon and Frédéric Worms, eds, *Derrida, la tradition de la philosophie* (Paris: Galilée, 2008), p. 67. In spite of what its title might lead one to suppose, this text comprises a detailed and illuminating reading of the Introduction to *The Origin of Geometry*.
4 Derrida, 'Introduction', in Husserl, *The Origin of Geometry*, pp. 102-3.
5 Letter from Derrida and Michel Monory to Pierre Seghers, 2 November 1962.
6 Letter from Pierre Seghers to Derrida and Michel Monory, 15 November 1962.
7 Letter from Georges Canguilhem to Derrida, 1 January 1963.
8 Letter from Michel Foucault to Derrida, 27 January 1963, quoted in Marie-Louise Mallet and Ginette Michaud, eds, *Derrida*, Cahier de l'Herne no. 83 (Paris: Éditions de l'Herne, 2004), pp. 109-10.
9 Letter from Paul Ricoeur to Derrida, 5 March 1963.
10 Letter from Paul Ricoeur to Derrida, 7 April 2000.
11 Interview with Françoise Dastur.
12 Letter from Derrida to Michel Foucault, 3 February 1963. The *Journal métaphysique* is a work by Gabriel Marcel, first published by Gallimard in 1927.
13 Letter from Derrida to Michel Foucault, 2 February 1962.
14 Letter from Derrida to Michel Foucault, 3 February 1963.
15 Derrida, 'Cogito and the history of madness', in *Writing and Difference*, p. 37.
16 Letter from Michel Foucault to Derrida, 11 March 1963, quoted in Mallet and Michaud, eds, *Derrida*, pp. 115-16.
17 Letter from Michel Foucault to Derrida, 25 October 1963.
18 Letter from Michel Foucault to Derrida, 11 February 1964.
19 Editoral in the first issue, June 1946. For more details, see Sylvie Patron, *Critique, 1946-1996. Une Encyclopédie de l'esprit moderne* (Paris: Éditions de l'IMEC, 1999).
20 *Critique* no. 192, May 1963.
21 Letter from Michel Deguy to Derrida, 6 January 1963.
22 Derrida, *Paper Machine*, p. 20.
23 Derrida, 'Force and signification', first published as an essay in *Critique*, translated in *Writing and Difference*, p. 1.
24 Derrida, *Writing and Difference*, pp. 33 and 31.
25 Ibid., p. 91.
26 Ibid., p. 78.
27 Letter from Edmond Jabès to Derrida, 10 October 1963.
28 Letter from Edmond Jabès to Derrida, 13 February 1964.

29 Danielle Baglione and Albert Dichy, *Georges Schehadé: poète des deux rives* (Paris: IMEC, 1999), p. 47.
30 Letter from Derrida to Gabriel Bounoure, 25 January 1964.
31 Letter from Derrida to Gabriel Bounoure, 27 April 1964.
32 Letter from Derrida to Paul Ricoeur, 4 January 1996.
33 Letter from Derrida to Michel Deguy, n.d. (summer 1963).
34 Letter from Michel Deguy to Derrida, n.d. (September 1963).
35 Letter from Michel Deguy to Derrida, 6 December 1963.
36 Letter from Jean Piel to Derrida, 25 December 1963.
37 Letter from Derrida to Jean Piel, 30 January 1964.
38 Derrida, 'Violence and metaphysics: an essay on the thought of Emmanuel Levinas', in *Writing and Difference*, p. 98. [The 'that' which introduces each clause could also, and perhaps better, be rendered as 'whether' – Tr.]
39 Derrida, *Writing and Difference*, p. 103 and pp. 397–8, note 7.
40 Letter from Derrida to Emmanuel Levinas, 15 June 1964.
41 Letter from Derrida to Emmanuel Levinas, n.d. (October 1964).
42 Letter from Emmanuel Levinas to Derrida, 22 October 1964.
43 Letter from Maurice Blanchot to Derrida, n.d. (October or November 1964).
44 Letter from Philippe Sollers to Derrida, 10 February 1964. Interview with Philippe Sollers.
45 Interview with Gérard Genette. This episode is also related in his *Codicille*, p. 57.
46 Letter from Hélène Cixous to Derrida, 11 April 1964.
47 Letter from Hélène Cixous to Derrida, 19 May 1964.
48 Interview with Hélène Cixous.
49 Letter from Derrida to Gabriel Bounoure, 3 August 1964.
50 Letter from Derrida to Philippe Sollers, 16 August 1964.
51 Letter from Derrida to Philippe Sollers, 30 September 1964.
52 Letter from Derrida to Philippe Sollers, 1 December 1964.

Chapter 2   In the Shadow of Althusser *1963–1966*

1 Derrida and Roudinesco, *For What Tomorrow . . .*, p. 79.
2 Élisabeth Roudinesco, *Jacques Lacan & Co.: A History of Psychoanalysis in France, 1925–1985*, tr., with a foreword, by Jeffrey Mehlman (London: Free Association Books, 1990), II, p. 378.
3 Ibid., p. 362.
4 Letter from Jacques Lacan to Louis Althusser, 22 January 1964, in Althusser, *Writings on Psychoanalysis: Freud and Lacan*, ed. by Olivier Corpet and François Matheron, tr. and with a preface by Jeffrey Mehlman (New York, Chichester: Columbia University Press, 1996), p. 169.
5 Interviews with Régis Debray and Étienne Balibar.
6 Letter from Louis Althusser to Derrida, 3 April 1964.
7 Letter from Louis Althusser to Derrida, 14 May 1964.
8 Letter from Louis Althusser to Derrida, 3 August 1964.
9 Letter from Louis Althusser to Derrida, 24 August 1964.
10 Letter from Louis Althusser to Derrida, n.d.

11 Derrida, 'Politics and friendship', interview with Michael Sprinker, published in E. Ann Kaplan and Michael Sprinker, eds, *The Althusserian Legacy* (London: Verso, 1993), pp. 183–231. I quote after the original manuscript in French preserved at IMEC.
12 Letter from Derrida to Louis Althusser, 1 September 1964.
13 Letter from Jean Hyppolite to Derrida, 11 March 1964.
14 Derrida, 'Politics and friendship', interview quoted from manuscript.
15 Letter from Derrida to Paul Ricoeur, 28 September 1964.
16 Letter from Maurice de Gandillac to Derrida, 6 October 1964.
17 Letter from Maurice de Gandillac to Derrida, 23 October 1964.
18 Letter from Derrida to Jean Hyppolite, 24 October 1964.
19 Derrida, 'Politics and friendship', interview quoted from manuscript.
20 Ibid.
21 Interview with Étienne Balibar.
22 Letter from Derrida to Louis Althusser, 2 August 1965.
23 Letter from Derrida to Briec Bounoure, 26 December 1964. Interview with Marguerite Derrida.
24 Letter from Derrida to Gabriel Bounoure, 25 August 1965.
25 Remarks by Jeanine Verdès-Leroux quoted by Eribon, *Michel Foucault*, p. 166.
26 Interview with Dominique Dhombres.
27 Quoted by Eribon, *Michel Foucault*, p. 156.
28 There is an excellent description of the Marxist groups and *groupuscules* at the end of the 1960s in Roudinesco, *Jacques Lacan & Co.*, II, pp. 383–4.
29 François Dosse, *History of Structuralism*, tr. by Deborah Glassman (Minneapolis, London: University of Minnesota Press, 1997).
30 Interview with Bernard Pautrat.
31 Interview with Dominique Lecourt.
32 Letter from Bernard Pautrat to Derrida, 5 September 1966.

Chapter 3   Writing Itself *1965–1966*

1 Letter from Derrida to Gabriel Bounoure, 11 January 1965.
2 Letter from Derrida to Philippe Sollers, 28 February 1965.
3 Letter from Philippe Sollers to Derrida, 3 March 1965.
4 Derrida, 'La parole soufflée', in *Writing and Difference*, p. 245.
5 *Writing and Difference*, pp. 219–20.
6 Letter from Paule Thévenin to Derrida, 19 March 1965.
7 Everything to do with Paule Thévenin, the heritage of Antonin Artaud, and the publication of his *Oeuvres complètes* is still a matter of controversy. I will be returning to the subject later in this work. For more information, see Paule Thévenin, *Antonin Artaud: ce désespéré qui vous parle* (Paris: Le Seuil, Coll. 'Fiction & Cie', 1993). A very different point of view can be found in Florence de Mèredieu, *L'Affaire Artaud: journal ethnographique* (Paris: Fayard, 2009).
8 Interview with Albert Dichy. For more details on the relation between Jean Genet and Paule Thévenin, see Edmund White, *Genet*, with a chronology by Albert Dichy (London: Chatto & Windus, 1993).
9 Letter from Derrida to Paule Thévenin, n.d.

10 Letter from Jean Genet to Derrida, n.d.
11 Letter from Derrida to Louis Althusser, 2 August 1965.
12 Letter from Jean Piel to Derrida, 3 October 1965.
13 Derrida, *Of Grammatology*, tr. by Gayatri Chakravorty Spivak (Baltimore: Johns Hopkins University Press, 1976), p. 70.
14 Derrida, 'Letter to a Japanese friend', in *Psyche: Inventions of the Other*, vol. 2, ed. by Peggy Kamuf and Elizabeth Rottenberg (Stanford, Calif.: Stanford University Press, 2007), pp. 1–2. I feel it is important to note that in German the word '*Destruktion*' is not used in everyday life; it is exclusive to philosophy and does not have the nihilistic connotations that the word *destruction* would inevitably have in French [or English – Tr.].
15 Letter from Michel Foucault to Derrida, 21 December 1965.
16 Letter from Emmanuel Levinas to Derrida, 30 January 1966.
17 Letter from Derrida to Gabriel Bounoure, 21 January 1966.
18 Remarks by Roger Laporte quoted by Thierry Guichard in 'L'épreuve par neuf', *Le Matricule des Anges* no. 32, September–November 2000.
19 Letter from Derrida to Roger Laporte, 10 August 1965.
20 Letter from Derrida to Roger Laporte, 19 February 1966.
21 Letter from Derrida to Henry Bauchau, 24 July 1966.
22 Derrida and Roudinesco, *For What Tomorrow . . .*, p. 169.
23 Interview with Marguerite Derrida. It was thanks to Marguerite, but also probably through his friend Nicolas Abraham, whom he met in Cerisy in 1959, that Derrida discovered the work of Melanie Klein. He discusses one of her essays on psychoanalysis in *Of Grammatology*, p. 88.
24 *Writing and Difference*, p. 266.
25 Letter from Roland Barthes to Derrida, 8 August 1966.
26 Letter from Derrida to Roger Laporte, 29 December 1965.
27 Letter from Geneviève Bollème to Derrida, 16 June 1966.
28 Letter from Derrida to Michel Deguy, 20 August 1966.
29 Letter from Derrida to Philippe Sollers, n.d. (27 August 1966).
30 Letter from Philippe Sollers to Derrida, 27 August 1966.
31 Letter from Derrida to Roger Laporte, 24 September 1966.
32 Letter from Jean Piel to Derrida, 28 September 1966.
33 Letter from Derrida to Jean Piel, 30 October 1966.
34 Letter from Derrida to Jean Piel, 12 November 1966.
35 Derrida, 'For the love of Lacan', in *Resistances of Psychoanalysis*, tr. by Peggy Kamuf, Pascale-Anne Brault, and Michael Naas (Stanford, Calif.: Stanford University Press, 1998), p. 50.
36 Roudinesco, *Jacques Lacan & Co.*, II, p. 410. There is also an excellent discussion of the Baltimore conference in François Cusset, *French Theory: How Foucault, Derrida, Deleuze & Co. Transformed the Intellectual Life of the United States*, tr. by Jeff Fort with Josephine Berganza and Marlon Jones (Minneapolis: University of Minnesota Press, 2008), pp. 29–32.
37 Georges Poulet's words are quoted by Babette Genette in a letter to Marguerite and Jacques Derrida, 4 November 1966.
38 Interview with J. Hillis Miller.
39 Interview with David Carroll.
40 *Writing and Difference*, pp. 369–70.

41 Richard Macksey and Eugenio Donato, eds, *The Languages of Criticism and the Sciences of Man: The Structuralist Controversy* (the proceedings of the Baltimore conference) (Baltimore: Johns Hopkins University Press, 1970). (The debate was originally held in French.)

42 Letter from Derrida to Jacques Lacan, 2 December 1966.

43 Roudinesco, *Jacques Lacan & Co.*, II, pp. 410–11. Lacan's talk was republished in *Autres Écrits* (Paris: Seuil, 2001), p. 333. Derrida discusses the sequence in his paper 'For the love of Lacan', given in 1992 and reprinted in *Resistances of Psychoanalysis*.

Chapter 4   A Lucky Year *1967*

1 Letter from Derrida to Gabriel Bounoure, 12 January 1967. We need to remember that Pierre was at the time a mere four and a half years old.

2 Letter from Derrida to Gabriel Bounoure, 9 July 1967.

3 Letter from Gérard Granel to Derrida, 6 January 1967.

4 Letter from Gérard Granel to Derrida, 11 April 1967.

5 Letter from Derrida to Jean Piel, 26 February 1967. Badiou's article, 'Le (re)commencement du matérialisme dialectique', was eventually published in *Critique*, no. 240, May 1967.

6 Letter from Derrida to Philippe Sollers, 21 March 1967.

7 This is the oldest text in the volume, since the paper was given at Cerisy in 1959, but the proceedings were published only in 1965, by Éditions Mouton.

8 Letter from Jean-Claude Pariente to Derrida, 20 May 1967.

9 Letter from Jean Bellemin-Noël to Derrida, 13 May 1967.

10 Letter from Jean Bellemin-Noël to Derrida, 12 June 1967.

11 Letter from Michel Foucault to Derrida, 12 June 1967.

12 Letter from Emmanuel Levinas to Derrida, 16 May 1967.

13 Letter from Derrida to Emmanuel Levinas, 6 June 1967.

14 Letter from Paul Ricoeur to Derrida, 7 April 2000.

15 Letter from Maurice de Gandillac to Derrida, 14 February 1967.

16 Letter from Derrida to Michel Deguy, 10 July 1967.

17 Letter from Derrida to Gabriel Bounoure, 9 July 1967.

18 Derrida, 'Punctuations', p. 122.

19 Letter from Derrida to Michel Deguy, 10 July 1967.

20 Ibid.

21 Letter from Philippe Sollers to Derrida, 20 July 1967.

22 Letter from Derrida to Philippe Sollers, 25 July 1967.

23 'L'étrangère' ('The foreign woman', or 'The stranger') was the title of Roland Barthes's article on Julia Kristeva published on 1 June 1970 in *La Quinzaine littéraire* and reprinted in *The Rustle of Language*, tr. by Richard Howard as 'Kristeva's *Semeiotike*' (Oxford: Basil Blackwell, 1986), pp. 168–71.

24 Interview with Julia Kristeva.

25 Letter from Philippe Sollers to Derrida, 28 September 1967.

26 For further details on Kristeva's early years in France, see Philippe Forest, *Histoire de Tel Quel* (Paris: Le Seuil, Coll. 'Fiction & Cie', 1995), pp. 249–59.

27 Derrida, *Speech and Phenomena, and Other Essays on Husserl's Theory of Signs*, tr., with an introduction, by David B. Allison (Evanston, Ill.: Northwestern University Press, 1973), pp. 4–5.

28 Denis Kambouchner, 'Derrida: deconstruction et raison', paper given at Tongji University, Shanghai, 23 May 2007. (I am grateful to Denis Kambouchner for letting me have this paper, unpublished in French.) The reader can also usefully consult the article by Daniel Giovannangeli, 'La fidélité à la phénoménologie', *Le Magazine littéraire* no. 430, April 2004, p. 40.

29 Letter from Jean-Luc Nancy to the author.

30 Derrida and Ferraris, *A Taste for the Secret*, p. 29.

31 Derrida, *Of Grammatology*, p. 99.

32 Claude Lévi-Strauss, letter published in the *Cahiers pour l'analyse*, no. 8, 1967.

33 *Of Grammatology*, p. xlix.

34 *Le Monde*, 18 November 1967.

35 *La Tribune de Genève*, 15 November 1967.

36 Letter from Philippe Sollers to Derrida, 20 July 1967.

37 Letter from Julia Kristeva to Derrida, 31 October 1967.

38 This interview was later published in the review *Information sur les sciences sociales* VII in June 1968, before being reprinted in *Positions* in 1972.

39 Letter from Paul de Man to Derrida, 6 October 1967.

40 Derrida, *Mémoires: For Paul de Man*, tr. by Cecile Lindsay, Jonathan Culler, and Eduardo Cadava; translations edited by Avital Ronell and Eduardo Cadava (New York: Columbia University Press, 1986), p. 72.

41 Paul de Man, 'Rhetoric of blindness: Derrida reader of Rousseau'. This piece, published in French in *Poétique* no. 4, 1970, as 'Rhétorique de la cécité: Derrida lecteur de Rousseau', is one of the main chapters in *Blindness and Insight: Essays in the Rhetoric of Contemporary Criticism*, second edition, revised (London: Methuen, 1983). For Derrida, this article was a model of scrupulous generosity, unlike many of the occasionally violent critiques to which his work gave rise.

42 Interview with Samuel Weber.

43 David Carroll, 'Jacques Derrida ou le don d'écriture – quand quelque chose se passe', *Rue Descartes* no. 48, 2005: 'Salut à Jacques Derrida', p. 100.

44 Letter from Gérard Granel to Derrida, 8 September 1967.

45 Gérard Granel, 'Jacques Derrida et la rature de l'origine', *Critique* no. 246, November 1967.

46 Ibid.

47 Derrida, 'Gérard Granel', in *Chaque fois unique*, p. 319. In this text, Derrida states that Granel was never aware of the polemics that developed around the publication of his article in *Critique*. An analysis of the correspondence proves the contrary. On 20 October 1967, after softening a few formulations, Granel wrote to Derrida: 'Do you really think that "they" are going to howl here and there? We'll see . . . .'

48 Letter from Granel to Derrida, 4 February 1968.

49 'Implications', interview with Henri Ronse, *Les Lettres françaises*, no. 1211, December 1967. The interview was reprinted in *Positions*, p. 4.

50 'Entretien avec Jacques Derrida', in Janicaud, *Heidegger en France*, vol. 2, p. 103.
51 'Implications', p. 8.
52 Letter from Pierre Aubenque to Derrida, 6 December 1967.
53 Pierre Aubenque, *Faut-il déconstruire la métaphysique?* (Paris: Presses Universitaires de France, 2009), p. 60.
54 Letter from Michel Deguy to Derrida, 10 September 1968. See also Janicaud, *Heidegger en France*, vol. 1, pp. 240–60. [François Fédier was a pupil of Beaufret and an important translator of Heidegger – Tr.]

Chapter 5   A Period of Withdrawal *1968*

1 Letter from Henry Bauchau to Derrida, 16 January 1968.
2 Letter from Henry Bauchau to Derrida, 11 July 1968.
3 Letter from Derrida to Henry Bauchau, 30 January 1968.
4 Letter from Jean Hyppolite to Derrida, 13 February 1968.
5 Gérard Genette, *Bardadrac* (Paris: Le Seuil, Coll. 'Fiction & Cie', 2006), p. 78.
6 Derrida, 'Différance', in *Margins of Philosophy*, tr. with additional notes by Alan Bass (London: Harvester Press, 1982), p. 3.
7 *Bulletin de la société française de de philosophie* vol. LXIII, 1968, pp. 109–10. In a revealing piece of provocation, the original French text 'La différance' was published in autumn 1968 both in this austere *Bulletin* and in the collective *Théorie d'ensemble* published by Seuil by the 'Tel Quel' group. Two different sets of readers, but also two resolutely antagonistic worlds.
8 Derrida, 'Typewriter ribbon: Limited ink (2)', in *Without Alibi*, ed., tr., and with an intro. by Peggy Kamuf (Stanford, Calif.: Stanford University Press, 2002).
9 Letter from Derrida to Henry Bauchau, 30 January 1968.
10 Letter from Samuel Weber to Derrida, 28 February 1968.
11 Interview with Samuel Weber. The story has been told in several forms, including one version told by Heinz Wismann, in which the 'false Derrida' becomes a producer of pornographic films.
12 The character of Rudolf Kastner and the negotiations that enabled 1,684 Jews to leave Hungary for Switzerland have been the subject of violent polemics. For more details, see, for instance, Wikipedia: *http:// en.wikipedia.org/wiki/Rudolf_Kastner.*
13 Derrida, 'La langue n'appartient pas', interview with Évelyne Grossman, *Europe* nos 861–2, January–February 2001.
14 'Entretien avec Derrida', in Janicaud, *Heidegger en France*, vol. 2, p. 97.
15 Letter from Derrida to François Fédier, 27 November 1967.
16 'The Beaufret affair' is related in detail in Christophe Bident, *Maurice Blanchot: partenaire invisible* (Paris: Champ Vallon, 1998), pp. 463–67.
17 Letter from Maurice Blanchot and Jacques Derrida to the contributors to *L'Endurance de la pensée*, 2 April 1968.
18 Letter from Derrida to Gabriel Bounoure, 6 February 1968.

19 Derrida, 'Plato's pharmacy', in *Dissemination*, tr. with an introduction and additional notes by Barbara Johnson (London: Athlone Press, 1981), p. 63.

20 Ibid., p. 171.

21 Ibid., pp. 71–2.

22 Ibid., p. 126.

23 Letter from Derrida to Philippe Sollers, n.d. (December 1967 or January 1968).

24 Letter from Derrida to Philippe Sollers, 24 April 1968.

25 Letter from Jean-Pierre Faye to Derrida, n.d.

26 Letter from Jean-Pierre Faye to Derrida, 2 November 1967.

27 Letter from Jean-Pierre Faye to Derrida, 8 December 1967. For further details on Faye's break with *Tel Quel* and the creation of *Change*, see Forest, *Histoire de Tel Quel: 1962–1982* (Paris: Seuil, 1995), pp. 281–8 and pp. 342–6.

28 Letter from Jean-Pierre Faye to Derrida, 16 April 1968.

29 *La Nouvelle Critique*, November–December 1967, quoted in Dosse, *History of Structuralism*, vol. I, p. 280.

30 Forest, *Histoire de Tel Quel*, p. 291.

31 Vincent Descombes, *Modern French Philosophy*, tr. by L. Scott-Fox and J. M. Harding (Cambridge: Cambridge University Press, 1980), pp. 169–70.

32 Derrida, 'Contresignature', paper given at the Cerisy conference *Poétiques de Jean Genet: la traversée des genres*, August 2000, IMEC, Jean Genet collection.

33 Bident, *Maurice Blanchot*, p. 473. My account also draws on an interview with Éric Hoppenot.

34 Derrida, 'A "madness" must watch over thinking', in *Points . . .*, pp. 347–8 (trans. slightly modified).

35 Derrida and Ferraris, *A Taste for the Secret*, p. 50.

36 Letter from Derrida to Henry Bauchau, 27 July 1968.

37 Letter from Derrida to Philippe Sollers, n.d. (summer 1968).

38 Letter from Philippe Sollers to Derrida, 24 September 1968.

39 Interview with Julia Kristeva.

40 Letter from Philippe Sollers to Jacques Henric, 9 September 1968, quoted in Forest, *Histoire de Tel Quel*, p. 333.

41 Forest, *Histoire de Tel Quel*, p. 333.

42 Hélène Cixous, 'Pré-histoire', in Jean-Michel Djian, ed., *Vincennes: une aventure de la pensée critique* (Paris: Flammarion, 2009), p. 22.

43 Telegram from Hélène Cixous to Derrida, 7 August 1968.

44 Cixous, 'Pré-histoire', p. 22.

45 Interviews with Hélène Cixous and Gérard Genette. For further details on the creation of Vincennes, see also Genette's *Codicille*, pp. 310–12, as well as 'Bâtons rompus', the dialogue between Cixous and Derrida, in Thomas Dutoit and Philippe Romanski, eds, *Derrida d'ici, Derrida de là* (Paris: Galilée, 2009), p. 190.

46 Interviews with Dominique Dhombres and Bernard Pautrat.

47 Letter from Bernard Pautrat to Derrida, 29 August 1968.

48 *Counterpath*, p. 269.

49 Interview with J. Hillis Miller.
50 Letter from Derrida to Philippe Sollers, n.d. (October 1968).
51 Derrida, 'The ends of man', in *Margins of Philosophy*, p. 114.
52 Letter from Derrida to Henri Bauchau, 14 November 1968.
53 Letter from Gérard Genette to Derrida, 31 October 1970.
54 Letter from Gérard Genette to Derrida, 28 September 1968.
55 Letter from Maurice Blanchot to Derrida, 25 October 1968.
56 Letter from Bernard Pautrat to Derrida, 15 October 1968.
57 *Counterpath*, p. 275.
58 Interview with Marguerite Derrida.
59 Derrida, 'Punctuations', pp. 122–3.
60 Letter from Maurice de Gandillac to Derrida, 20 October 1968.
61 Letter from Maurice de Gandillac to Derrida, 21 January 1969.
62 Letter from Jean-Claude Pariente to Derrida, 30 December 1968.
63 Letter from Henry Bauchau to Derrida, 23 April 1969.
64 Letter from Derrida to Gabriel Bounoure, 14 January 1969.

Chapter 6   Uncomfortable Positions *1969–1971*

1 These articles were reprinted in the volume *Économie et symbolique* (Paris: Le Seuil, 1973).
2 Interview with Jean-Joseph Goux.
3 Interview with Philippe Sollers.
4 Interview with Jean-Joseph Goux. See also the excellent analysis of this 'social, political, and intellectual' chess game between Sollers, Kristeva and Derrida in Forest, *Histoire de Tel Quel*, p. 259.
5 Letter from Catherine Clément to Derrida, 4 May 1970.
6 *Dissemination*, pp. 245–6.
7 Ibid., pp. 252–3.
8 Giesbert, 'Ce que disait Derrida . . .', *http://www.lepoint.fr/actualites-litterature/2007-01-17/philosophie-ce-que-disait-derrida/1038/0/31857*.
9 Letter from Maurice Blanchot to Derrida, 13 May 1968.
10 Interview with Dominique Lecourt.
11 Interview with Dominique Dhombres.
12 Interview with Philippe Sollers. For further details on this affair, see Forest, *Histoire de Tel Quel*, pp. 361–3, and Roudinesco, *Jacques Lacan & Co.*, pp. 538–9.
13 Bernard-Henri Lévy, *Comédie* (Paris: Le Livre de poche, 2000), pp. 13–14.
14 Interview with Bernard-Henri Lévy.
15 Letter from Pierre Aubenque to Derrida, 21 July 1969.
16 Letter from Pierre Aubenque to Derrida, 13 January 1970.
17 Letter from Peter Szondi to Herbert Dieckmann, 20 November 1970, in Peter Szondi, *Briefe* (Frankfurt am Main: Suhrkamp Verlag, 1993).
18 This text was also published in *Tel Quel* 39, Autumn 1969, as 'Un pas sur la Lune'; it then served as an introduction to the Argentinian-Spanish translation of *Of Grammatology*.
19 Interview with Alan Montefiore.

20 'Des contradictions douloureuses', round table with Bernard Frederick, Antoine Casanova, Frédérique Mattonti, *Nouvelles Fondations* no. 3–4, 2006.

21 *L'Humanité*, 19 September 1969.

22 Letter from Jean-Pierre Faye to Derrida, 24 September 1969.

23 *La Gazette de Lausanne*, 10–11 October 1970.

24 Letter from Jean-Louis Houdebine to Derrida, 17 March 1970.

25 Interview with Élisabeth Roudinesco. See also her *Jacques Lacan & Co.*, pp. 540–1 and Forest, *Histoire de Tel Quel*, pp. 350–4.

26 Letter from Derrida to Jean-Luc Nancy, 22 April 1969.

27 Interview with Jean-Luc Nancy.

28 Letter from Derrida to Jean-Luc Nancy, 21 April 1970.

29 Philippe Lacoue-Labarthe, 'Hommage', *Rue Descartes* no. 48, 2005: 'Salut à Jacques Derrida', p. 75.

30 Jean-Luc Nancy and Philippe Lacoue-Labarthe, 'Derrida à Strasbourg', in Jacques Derrida et al., *Penser à Strasbourg* (Paris: Galilée, 2004), pp. 14–15.

31 Letter from Derrida to Jean-Luc Nancy, 13 September 1970.

32 Letter from Derrida to Roger Laporte, n.d. (October 1970).

33 Interview with Marguerite Derrida.

34 Letter from Derrida to Philippe Lacoue-Labarthe, 5 November 1970.

35 For further details on the events of this period, see Robert Flacelière, *Normale en peril* (Paris: Presses Universitaires de France, 1971), as well as the articles by Christian Hottin, '80 ans de la vie d'un monument aux morts: le monument aux morts de l'École normale supérieure' (*http://labyrinthe.revues.org/index262.html*) and Pierre Petitmengin, 'Georges Pompidou vu de l'École' (*http://www.georges-pompidou.org/Actualites/2004_04_Petitmengin.html*).

36 Letter from Derrida to Roger Laporte, 21 April 1971.

37 Letter from Derrida to Pierre Foucher, 14 June 1974.

38 Letter from Derrida to Pierre Foucher, 2 March 1975.

39 Letter from Gérard Granel to Derrida, 28 January 1971.

40 Letter from Derrida to Gérard Granel, 4 February 1971.

41 The press cuttings relating to these various petitions are in the Derrida archives at IMEC.

42 Letter from Derrida to Jean Genet, 20 August 1971. The complete version of this text was first published in English translation in *Negotiations: Interventions and Interviews, 1971–2001*, texts by Derrida collected and introduced by Elizabeth Rottenberg (Stanford, Calif.: Stanford University Press, 2002), then reprinted in Mallet and Michaud, eds, *Derrida*, pp. 318–20.

43 Letter from Jean-Louis Houdebine to Derrida, 20 December 1970.

44 And not 17 June, as stated in *Positions*.

45 Derrida, *Positions*, pp. 62–3.

46 Ibid., p. 54.

47 Fragment of a letter quoted in Forest, *Histoire de Tel Quel*, p. 368.

48 *Positions*, p. 107 n. 44.

49 Ibid., pp. 108–9 n. 44.

50 Letters from Jean-Louis Houdebine to Derrida, 30 July and 7 August 1971.

51 Derrida, 'L'ami d'un ami de la Chine', in *Aux origines de la Chine contemporaine: En hommage à Lucien Bianco*, pp. ii–iii.

52 Interview with Martine Meskel.

53 The papers by Ricoeur and Derrida, and their debate, were published in *La Communication, Actes du XVe Congrès de l'Association des sociétés de philosophie de language française* (Montréal: Université de Montréal, Éditions Montmorency, 1973). Ricoeur's text was reprinted in *La Métaphore vive*, a book he sent to Derrida with the following dedication: 'For Jacques Derrida, this beginning of an explanation, looking forward to new *intersections*, a homage of faithful thought.' What has sometimes been called the *querelle de la métaphore* was further pursued in several of Derrida's texts: 'White mythology', in *Margins of Philosophy*, pp. 207–71 (first published as 'La mythologie blanche' in *Poétique* 5, 1971) and, more directly, 'The *retrait* of metaphor', in *Psyche*, vol. 1, pp. 48–80 (first published as 'Le retrait de la métaphore', *Po&sie* 7, 1978). For further details, see François Dosse, *Paul Ricoeur, les sens d'une vie (1913–2005)*, enlarged edition (Paris: La Découverte/Poche, 2008), pp. 359–63.

54 Letter from Derrida to Michel Deguy, n.d. (September or October 1971).

55 Interview with Alan Bass.

56 Derrida, *Speech and Phenomena and Other Essays on Husserl's Theory of Signs*, tr. by David B. Allison (Evanston, Ill.: Northwestern University Press, 1973. ['Form and meaning: A note on the phenomenology of language' appears on pp. 107–28 and 'Differance' appears on pp. 129–60. – Tr.]

57 Letter from Paul de Man to Derrida, 13 October 1971.

58 Letter from Bernard Pautrat to Derrida, 16 October 1971.

59 Letter from Louis Althusser to Derrida, 29 October 1971.

60 Letter from Pautrat to Derrida, 16 October 1971.

61 For further details on these tragicomic ups and downs, see Forest, *Histoire de Tel Quel*, pp. 384–441.

62 Letter from Louis Althusser to Derrida, 29 October 1971.

63 Letter from Jean-Louis Houdebine to Derrida, 2 November 1971.

64 This passage is quoted in a letter from Jean-Louis Houdebine to Derrida, 12 March 1972, by which time the argument between the two men had grown more rancorous.

65 Letter from Derrida to Rodolphe Gasché, 21 December 1971.

Chapter 7 Severed Ties *1972–1973*

1 Letter from Derrida to Henry Bauchau, 7 January 1972.

2 Letter from Derrida to Philippe Sollers, 14 January 1972.

3 Letter from Derrida to Jean-Louis Houdebine, 18 January 1972.

4 Forest, *Histoire de Tel Quel*, p. 402.

5 Letter from Derrida to Édith Heurgon, 19 January 1972.

6 Letter from Philippe Sollers to Derrida, 23 January 1972.

7 The novel by Morgan Sportes, *Ils ont tué Pierre Overney* (Paris: Grasset, 2008), mentions this episode.

8 'Curriculum vitae', in Bennington and Derrida, *Jacques Derrida*, p. 333.

9 Interview with Éric Clémens.
10 Letter from Derrida to Éric Clémens, 18 March 1972.
11 Ibid.
12 'Politics and friendship', p. 210.
13 Interview with Jean Ristat. Derrida thanked Louis Aragon following the publication of the special issue on him in *Les Lettres françaises*. On 30 March 1972, he wrote to say that he was finishing the 'enjoyable' reading of his book *Henri Matisse, roman* just down the road from the building in Cimiez where Matisse lived.
14 *Les Lettres françaises* no. 1429, 29 March 1972.
15 Ibid.
16 Letter from Derrida to Roland Barthes, 30 March 1972.
17 Originally published in *Poétique* no. 47 (Le Seuil, September 1981), 'The deaths of Roland Barthes' was reprinted in *Psyche*, vol. 1, then in *The Work of Mourning*, ed. by Pascale-Anne Brault and Michael Naas (Chicago; London: University of Chicago Press, 2003).
18 *Tel Quel – mouvement de juin 71 – Informations* no. 2–3, IMEC Archives.
19 Ibid.
20 Interview with Bernard Pautrat.
21 'Reply to Derrida', in Michel Foucault, *History of Madness*, ed. by Jean Khalfa (London; New York: Routledge, 2009), pp. 575–90; pp. 574–5.
22 Foucault, 'My body, this paper, this fire', in *History of Madness*, pp. 550–74; p. 573.
23 Ibid.
24 Derrida's personal library.
25 Michel Foucault, 'Prisons et asiles dans le mécanisme du pouvoir', in *Dits et écrits I, 1954–1975*, p. 1389.
26 Interview with Jean-Luc Nancy.
27 Gilles Deleuze and Félix Guattari, *Anti-Oedipus*, tr. by Helen R. Lane, Robert Hurley, and Mark Seem (London: Continuum, 2004), p. 1. Descombes, *Modern French Philosophy*, p. 173.
28 This stormy dinner was recalled after another quarrel, in a letter from Gérard Granel to Derrida, 8 April 1975.
29 Letter from Derrida to Roger Laporte, 24 June 1972.
30 Letter from Derrida to Roger Laporte, 4 June 1972.
31 *Nietzsche aujourd'hui? 1 – Intensités*, 10/18, 1973, p. 186.
32 Derrida, 'Le modèle philosophique d'une "contre-institution"', pp. 258–9.
33 Derrida, *Spurs = Éperons. Nietzsche's Styles = Les Styles de Nietzsche*, intro. by Stefano Agostini, tr. by Barbara Harlow, ill. by François Loubrieu (Chicago; London: University of Chicago Press, 1979), pp. 101–3.
34 Ibid., p. 107.
35 *Nietzsche aujourd'hui? 1 – Intensités*, p. 117.
36 Derrida, unpublished seminar, IMEC.
37 Interview with Maurice Olender. Although Derrida did not go so far as to cancel his participation at a day-long conference organized by Olender, who ran 'La Librairie du XXIe siècle', the series in which this

volume was published, he did in the end decide not to attend. Olender had, however, told him that these other correspondences with Celan would be published at a later date.

38 Derrida, *Spurs*, p. 35.
39 *http://www.ccic-cerisy.asso.fr/temoignages.html#JeanLuc_Nancy.*
40 Sylviane Agacinski, *Journal interrompu* (Paris: Le Seuil, 2002), p. 85.
41 Letter from Derrida to Philippe Lacoue-Labarthe, 4 August 1972.
42 Letter from Derrida to Laporte, 18 September 1972.
43 Letter from Derrida to Michel Deguy, 20 August 1972.
44 Derrida, 'Entretien avec Lucette Finas', *La Quinzaine littéraire*, 16–30 November 1972. Reprinted in Lucette Finas, ed., *Écarts: quatre essais à propos de Jacques Derrida* (Paris: Fayard, 1973).
45 Jacqueline Demornez, 'Le nouveau savoir-vivre snob', *Elle*, February 1972.
46 *Le Journal de Genève*, 2 December 1972.
47 Lucien Braun, 'À mi-chemin entre Heidegger et Derrida', *Penser à Strasbourg* (Paris: Galilée, 2004), pp. 24–5.
48 Jacques Taminiaux, homage to Jacques Derrida delivered at the Théâtre-Poème de Bruxelles on 7 November 1998: many thanks to Jacques Taminiaux for having passed on this unpublished text to me.
49 Letter from Philippe Lacoue-Labarthe to Derrida, 7 October 1973.
50 Letter from Derrida to Jean-Luc Nancy, 2 October 1972.
51 Jacques Lacan, *Encore* (Paris: Le Seuil, 1975), p. 62.
52 Interview with Jean-Luc Nancy.
53 Letter from Derrida to Jean Piel, 4 August 1973.
54 Letter from Derrida to Jean Piel, 15 August 1973.
55 *Le Monde*, 15 June 1973.
56 Letter from Derrida to Catherine Clément, 17 May 1973. Interview with Catherine Clément.
57 Derrida, ' "There is no *one* narcissism" (autobiophotographies)', in *Points . . .*, pp. 196–7.
58 Catherine Clément, 'Le Sauvage', *L'Arc* 54, 1973, 'Jacques Derrida', p. 1.
59 Emmanuel Levinas, 'Tout autrement', *L'Arc* 54, pp. 33–4.
60 *L'Arc* 54, p. 37.
61 Letter from Derrida to Levinas, 9 October 1973.

Chapter 8   *Glas 1973–1975*

1 Letter from Derrida to Roger Laporte, 30 June 1973.
2 Letter from Derrida to Michel Deguy, 4 August 1973.
3 Interview broadcast on the France-Culture programme 'Le bon plaisir de Jacques Derrida', 22 March 1986; the transcript is preserved in the Derrida archives at IMEC. Derrida had already described the genesis of *Glas* in a radio interview with Maurice Olender, on RTB, 21 February 1973.
4 Letter from Derrida to Roger Laporte, 26 September 1973.
5 Publisher's blurb included in the work.
6 Derrida, 'A "madness" must watch over thinking', in *Points . . .*, p. 350.

7 Derrida, *Glas*, p. 29.
8 *Le Monde*, 3 January 1975.
9 Letter from Louis Althusser to Derrida, n.d.
10 Letter from Pierre Bourdieu to Derrida, n.d.
11 Geoffrey Hartman, *A Scholar's Tale* (New York: Fordham University Press, 2007).
12 Letter from Paule Thévenin to Derrida, 20 October 1974.
13 Letter from Paule Thévenin to Derrida, 22 December 1974.
14 Albert Dichy and Michel Dumoulin, interview with Derrida for the film *Jean Genet l'écrivain*, 1992, IMEC, fonds Jean Genet.
15 Derrida, *Glas*, pp. 36–7.
16 Letter from Derrida to Antoine Bourseiller, 9 November 1975.
17 Letter from Bourseiller to Derrida, 9 November 1975.
18 *Cinders* and 'Circumfession', in their original French versions (*Feu la cendre* and 'Circonfession'), were published as audio recordings by Éditions des Femmes, in 1987 and 1993.
19 Interview with Derrida and Adami, in *Valerio Adami: couleurs et mots* (Paris: Le Cherche Midi, 2000), p. 27.
20 Ibid., p. 31.
21 Ibid.
22 *Derrière le miroir* no. 214, May 1975. This text, with three others, was reprinted in *The Truth in Painting*, tr. by Geoff Bennington and Ian McLeod (Chicago: University of Chicago Press, 1987).
23 *Valerio Adami: couleurs et mots*, p. 24. Interviews with Valerio and Camilla Adami.
24 Interview with Camilla Adami. Nearly thirty years after writing on Valerio Adami's work, Derrida devoted one of his last texts to the paintings of Camilla Adami, 'Tête-à-Tête', in *Camilla Adami* (La Seyne-sur-Mer: Villa Tamaris centre d'art, 2004).

Chapter 9   In Support of Philosophy *1973–1976*

1 Letter from Derrida to Philippe Lacoue-Labarthe, 22 August 1973.
2 Letter from Derrida to Jean-Luc Nancy, n.d. (summer 1973).
3 Jean-Luc Nancy and Philippe Lacoue-Labarthe, *The Literary Absolute: The Theory of Literature in German Romanticism*, tr. and with an introduction and additional notes by Philip Barnard and Cheryl Lester (Albany: State University of New York Press, 1988).
4 Jean-Luc Nancy, 'Philippe Lacoue-Labarthe à Strasbourg', *Europe* no. 973, May 2010, pp. 12–14.
5 Derrida, 'Le lieu dit: Strasbourg', in Derrida et al., *Penser à Strasbourg*, p. 46.
6 *Mimesis* (Paris: Aubier-Flammarion, 1975), cover blurb.
7 Interview with Jean-Luc Nancy.
8 Letter from Derrida to Jean-Luc Nancy, n.d. (November 1974). Sylviane Agacinski's first book, *Aparté: conceptions et morts de Sören Kierkegaard*, was published in the series 'La philosophie en effet' in March 1977. (Published in English as *Aparté: Conceptions and Death of Søren Kierkegaard*, tr. by Kevin Newmark, Gainesville: University of Florida Press, 1988.)

9 Letter from Derrida to Philippe Lacoue-Labarthe, 4 September 1974.
10 Letter from Derrida to Lacoue-Labarthe, 24 August 1974.
11 Letter from Lacoue-Labarthe to Derrida, 27 August 1974.
12 Derrida, in *The Post Card*, p. 425.
13 *The Post Card*, p. 414.
14 Derrida, 'Entretien avec Lucette Finas', in Finas, ed., *Écarts*, p. 311.
15 Letter from Derrida to Elias L. Rivers, 8 October 1973.
16 Letter from Derrida to Paul de Man, 22 January 1974.
17 Letter from Paul de Man to Derrida, 28 April 1974.
18 Letter from Paul de Man to Derrida, 7 January 1975.
19 Letter from Derrida to Paul de Man, 12 October 1975.
20 Letter from Paul de Man to Derrida, 17 October 1975.
21 Derrida, 'La langue de l'autre', interview with Tetsuya Takahashi, IMEC archives.
22 This document was published in the collective volume *Qui a peur de la philosophie?* (Paris: Champs-Flammarion, 1977), pp. 433–7. Relevant documents are translated in Jacques Derrida, *Who's Afraid of Philosophy? Right to Philosophy 1*, tr. by Jan Plug (Stanford, Calif.: Stanford University Press, 2002).
23 Derrida, 'Philosophy and its classes', in *Who's Afraid of Philosophy?*, pp. 158–63; p. 159.
24 Ibid., pp. 232–3.
25 Ibid., pp. 235–6.
26 Interview with Marie-Louise Mallet. See also the interview between Mallet and Derrida, 'Du Greph aux états généraux de la philosophie et au-delà', in Mallet and Michaud, eds, *Derrida*, pp. 221–3.
27 *Qui a peur de la philosophie?*, pp. 469–70.
28 Denis Kambouchner, note on Jackie Derrida in the Annuaire des anciens élèves de l'ENS, 2005.
29 Denis Kambouchner, 'Jupiter parmi nous', *Rue Descartes* no. 48, 2005, pp. 95–8.
30 Interview with Souleymane Bachir Diagne.
31 Letter from Derrida to Roger Laporte, 2 March 1975.
32 Derrida, *Signéponge = Signsponge*, tr. by Richard Rand (New York: Columbia University Press, 1984), p. 2. Fragments of the original French text had been published in *Digraphe* no 8, in 1978, then the following year in the conference *Francis Ponge*, published by 10/18.
33 Letter from Derrida to Roger Laporte, 4 September 1975.
34 Postcard from Derrida to Philippe Lacoue-Labarthe, n.d. (autumn 1975).
35 *La Quinzaine littéraire* no. 231, 16–30 April 1976.
36 'Six auteurs, une voix anonyme', *Le Monde*, 30 April 1976.
37 Letter from Derrida to Paul de Man, 8 April 1976.
38 Interview with Richard Rand. There is also an excellent portrait of Paul de Man in Geoffrey Hartman's autobiographical *A Scholar's Tale*.
39 Michèle Lamont, 'How to become a French dominant philosopher: The case of Jacques Derrida', *The American Journal of Sociology* vol. 93, no. 3, November 1983, pp. 584–622.

40 Interview with Ellen Burt.
41 *Yale Daily News*, 11 October 2004.
42 For further details on this translation, which had a decisive impact on the reception of Derrida, see Gayatri Chakravorty Spivak, 'Touched by deconstruction', *Grey Room* no. 20, 2005, pp. 95–104.
43 Cusset, *French Theory*, pp. 109–11.
44 Letter from Derrida to Paul de Man, 10 October 1976.
45 Jacques Derrida, 'Me – psychoanalysis', in *Psyche*, vol. 1, p. 132.
46 Further details on Nicolas Abraham and Maria Torok (or Mária Török) can be found at: *http://www.abraham-torok.org/*.
47 During her training analysis, Marguerite Derrida – partly for financial reasons – translated several works by Melanie Klein: *Mourning and Depression, Child Psychoanalysis*, and part of *Envy and Gratitude and Other Essays*. Over the same period, she also translated Vladimir Propp's *Morphology of the Folktale* into French.
48 Interview with Marguerite Derrida.
49 Letter from Jacques Derrida to Sarah Kofman, 6 August 1976.
50 Roudinesco, *Jacques Lacan & Co.*, II, p. 599.
51 Jacques Lacan, *L'insu que sait de l'une-bévue s'aile à mourre*, Seminar XXIV, 1976–7, p. 48. I am here quoting from an internal document of the International Freudian Association available online (*http://emc.psycho.free.fr/lacan*). The official version published in *Ornicar* no. 17–18, 1978, was greatly abbreviated: the references to Derrida – suggesting that he was then in analysis – were eliminated.
52 Lacan, *L'insu*, pp. 52–3.
53 'For the love of Lacan', in *Resistances of Psychoanalysis*, p. 47.
54 Lacan, *L'insu*, p. 52.
55 Interview with René Major. See also his *Lacan avec Derrida* (Paris: Champs-Flammarion, 2001).
56 Letter from René Major to Derrida, 26 November 1976.
57 Roudinesco, *Jacques Lacan & Co.*, II, p. 604.
58 Derrida, 'Du tout', in *The Post Card*, pp. 497–521.

Chapter 10   Another Life *1976–1977*

 1 Interview with Pierre Alféri.
 2 Interview with Jean Derrida.
 3 Interview with Camilla Adami.
 4 Interviews with Martine Meskel, Marie-Louise Mallet, and Michel Deguy.
 5 Interview with Pierre Alféri.
 6 Letter from Derrida to Roger Laporte, 16 March 1976.
 7 Letter from Derrida to Laporte, 24 December 1976.
 8 Derrida, *Sur parole*, pp. 18–19.
 9 Derrida and Bennington, *Jacques Derrida*, p. 89.
10 Derrida, personal notebooks, note of 24 December 1976, Irvine archives. This text was published in a slightly different form in 'Circumfession', in Derrida and Bennington, *Jacques Derrida*, pp. 115–16. The fragments of notebooks quoted in 'Circumfession' were significantly rewritten.

11 Derrida, personal notebooks, note of 28–9 December 1976 (night), Irvine archives.

12 Personal notebooks, note n.d. (December 1976), Irvine archives.

13 Personal notebooks, 30 December 1976, Irvine archives.

14 Personal notebooks, 24 December 1976, Irvine archives.

15 Personal notebooks, note of 31 December 1976, Irvine archives. This fragment is published in slightly modified form in 'Circumfession', pp. 169–70.

16 Letter from Derrida to Paul de Man, 21 February 1977.

17 It was probably at this time that Derrida wrote 'Limited Inc a b c ...', his reply to John R. Searle, one of his most violent texts. I will be discussing this in chapter 12.

18 Derrida, *The Post Card*, p. 7.

19 Ibid., p. 8.

20 Ibid., pp. 9–10.

21 Letter from Derrida to Sarah Kofman, n.d. (August 1977).

22 Derrida, *The Post Card*, p. 82.

23 Letter from Derrida to Philippe Lacoue-Labarthe, 1 September 1977.

24 Letter from Paul de Man to Derrida, 14 May 1977.

25 Derrida, personal notebooks, note of 12 October 1977, Irvine archives. This fragment is published in slightly modified form in 'Circumfession', p. 202.

26 Personal notebooks, 12 October 1977, Irvine archives. 'Circumfession', pp. 207–8.

27 Personal notebooks, 14 October 1977, Irvine archives. Derrida provides a few further details on the attic and his way of working in 'Je n'écris pas sans lumière artificielle', an interview with André Rollin, published in 1982 in the review *Le fou parle* and republished at: *http://www.jacquesderrida.com.ar/frances/artificielle.htm*.

28 Avital Ronell, *Fighting Theory: In Conversation with Anne Dufourmantelle*, tr. by Catherine Porter (Urbana: University of Illinois Press, 2010), p. 155.

29 Agacinski, *Aparté*, pp. 112–14.

30 Derrida, 'Living on', p. 62. This text, published in French in *Parages*, first came out in English in the collective volume *Deconstruction and Criticism* together with contributions from Paul de Man, J. Hillis Miller, Geoffrey Hartman, and Harold Bloom (New York: Continuum, 1979). It was viewed as a sort of manifesto for the Yale School. The interminable footnote in the form of a diary running under the text became especially famous.

31 Derrida, 'Cartouches', in *The Truth in Painting*, pp. 183–253; pp. 239–40.

Chapter 11 From the *Nouveaux Philosophes* to the Estates General *1977–1979*

1 For further details on these changes in the publishing and media scenes in France, see Olivier Bessard-Banquy, *La Vie du livre contemporain: étude sur l'édition littéraire, 1975–2000* (Bordeaux: Presses

Universitaires de Bordeaux & du Lérot, éditeur) and *Les Intellocrates* by Hervé Hamon and Patrick Rotman (Paris: Ramsay, 1981).

2 Gilles Deleuze, *À propos des nouveaux philosophes et d'un problème plus général*, free supplement to no. 24 of the review *Minuit*, May 1977.

3 Letter from Jean Piel to Derrida, 29 August 1977.

4 Letter from Derrida to Philippe Lacoue-Labarthe, 1 September 1977.

5 Letter from Derrida to Jean Piel, 9 September 1977.

6 Interview with Daniel Giovannangeli. A revised version of this thesis was published in 1979 in the 10/18 series as *Écriture et répétition: approche de Derrida*.

7 Derrida, 'Ja, ou le faux-bond', interview with Denis Kambouchner, Jean Ristat, and Danièle Sallenave published in *Digraphe* no. 11, March 1977. Reprinted in *Points . . .* and translated in the English version of the same volume as '*Ja*, or the *faux-bond* II', pp. 71–2.

8 Letter from Derrida to Madeleine Aubier-Gabail, 4 April 1978.

9 Letter from Derrida to Sarah Kofman, 8 August 1978.

10 Letter from Jean-Luc Nancy to Derrida, 22 April 1979.

11 Letter from Derrida to Jean-Luc Nancy, n.d. (April 1979).

12 Ibid.

13 Vladimir Jankélévitch, 'Pour la philosophie', in *États généraux de la philosophie* (Paris: Champs-Flammarion, 1979), pp. 23–6.

14 Derrida, 'Philosophie des états généraux', in *États généraux de la philosophie*, p. 37.

15 Interview with Bernard-Henri Lévy.

16 Ibid.

17 *États généraux de la philosophie*, pp. 205–6.

18 *Who's Afraid of Philosophy?*, p. 192.

19 Letter from Catherine Clément to Derrida, 22 June 1979. Many thanks to Catherine Clément for agreeing, after her initial reluctance, to the publication of this extremely revealing letter.

20 For a more detailed analysis of this phenomenon, see Geoffrey de Lagasnerie, *L'Empire de l'Université: sur Bourdieu, les intellectuels et le journalisme* (Paris: Éditions Amsterdam, 2007).

21 *http://www.mediapart.fr/club/edition/les-invites-de-mediapart/article/050210/defense-de-philosopher*.

Chapter 12   Postcards and Proofs *1979–1981*

1 Derrida, 'Envois', in *The Post Card*, p. 197. 'Me – psychoanalysis' was first published in English in *Diacritics*, spring 1977; it was published in French in *Psyché*, and the English version later appeared in *Psyche*, vol. 1.

2 Interview with Avital Ronell.

3 Soon after receiving the work, Derrida fully expressed his gratitude to Alan Bass for this work 'of an intelligence, a rigour and a proximity, a probity too and a generosity that are all exemplary. [. . .] The translation of a book in the United States is a sort of rebirth [. . .] and this is due to you' (letter from Derrida to Bass, 23 November 1978). Even though he had by now become a psychoanalyst, Alan Bass went on to

translate several of Derrida's other major works at the beginning of the 1980s: *Positions*, *Margins of Philosophy*, and *The Post Card*.

4 Interview with Pierre Alféri.

5 Letter from Derrida to Paul de Man, n.d. (end of December 1979). This meeting is referred to in *Mémoires: For Paul de Man*.

6 The conference paper and the discussions following it were published as *The Ear of the Other*.

7 Interview with Pierre Alféri.

8 Interview with Avital Ronell.

9 Derrida, 'Unsealing ("the old new language")', in *Points . . .*, p. 118.

10 Derrida, *The Post Card*, p. 3.

11 Ibid., p. 232.

12 Ibid., p. 177.

13 Letter from Jean-Luc Nancy to Derrida, 22 July 1979.

14 Cover blurb to the original French version of *The Post Card*.

15 Interview with Alan Bass.

16 Letter from Derrida to Hans-Joachim Metzger, 13 September 1981.

17 Letter from Élisabeth de Fontenay to Derrida, 10 June 1980.

18 Interview with Pierre Alféri.

19 Max Genève, *Qui a peur de Derrida?* (Paris: Anabet, 2008), p. 103.

20 *Libération*, 6 June 1980.

21 Marcel Gauchet, 'Les droits de l'homme ne sont pas une politique', *Le Débat* no. 3, July–August 1980, quoted in Didier Eribon, *D'une révolution conservatrice et de ses effets sur la gauche française* (Paris: Léo Scheer, 2007), p. 102.

22 The episode is related in detail in Dosse, *Paul Ricoeur*, pp. 405–18.

23 Interview with Françoise Dastur.

24 Letter from Derrida to Paul Ricoeur, 1 July 1979.

25 Letter from Paul Ricoeur to Derrida, 17 July 1979.

26 François Dosse, *Paul Ricoeur: le sens d'une vie (1913–2005)*, 1st edn (Paris: La Découverte, 2001). This chapter was omitted from the definitive version, but is freely available online: *d05431_chapitres.pdf*, p. 99.

27 Interview with François Angelier.

28 Derrida, 'Punctuations', p. 127.

29 Remarks quoted in Alain David, 'Fidélité (la voie de l'animal)', in Mallet and Michaud, eds, *Derrida*, p. 155.

30 I quote this intervention from Levinas's manuscript notes preserved in the Derrida archives at IMEC.

31 E-mail from Jean-Luc Nancy to the author, 29 January 2009.

32 Letter from Derrida to Philippe Lacoue-Labarthe and Jean-Luc Nancy, 25 August 1980.

33 Postcard from Derrida to Philippe Lacoue-Labarthe and Jean-Luc Nancy, n.d. (September 1980).

34 *Les Fins de l'Homme*, focusing on the work of Derrida (Paris: Galilée, 1981).

35 Dominique Dhombres, 'Louis Althusser, le coup de folie du philosophe', *Le Monde*, 30 July 2006. A detailed account of Hélène's murder – from the point of view of Louis Althusser – is given in his posthumous work, *The Future Lasts a Long Time; and, The Facts*, ed.

by Olivier Corpet and Yann Moulier Boutang, tr. by Richard Veasey (London: Chatto & Windus, 1993).

36 Interview with Dominique Lecourt.

37 Interview with Étienne Balibar.

38 Interview with Régis Debray.

39 *Le Quotidien de Paris*, 17 November 1980.

40 *Le Quotidien de Paris*, 18 November 1980.

41 *Le Monde*, 19 November 1980.

42 Letter to an unidentified lawyer, 18 November 1980; this letter was signed by Daniel Bennequin (tutor in mathematics), Jacques Derrida (*maître assistant* in philosophy), Jean-Pierre Lefebvre (*maître assistant* in German), and Bernard Pautrat (*maître assistant* in philosophy).

43 Letter from Jos Joliet to Derrida, 28 November 1980.

44 This is article 122-1 of the Code Pénal (previously article 64). For further details, see the article by Jean-Paul Doucet that explicitly refers to the Althusser affair: *http://ledroitcriminel.free.fr/dictionnaire/lettre_a/lettre_a_as.htm*.

45 *Le Monde*, 25–6 January 1981.

46 Interview with Dominique Lecourt.

47 'Note relative à la situation de M. Louis Althusser', document, n.d., signed by Jacques Derrida, Étienne Balibar, and Dominique Lecourt.

48 Interview with Étienne Balibar.

49 Interview with Dominique Lecourt.

50 Dosse, *Paul Ricoeur* (*d05431_chapitres.pdf*), p. 99.

51 In the 'Curriculum vitae' in Geoffrey Bennington's book, the episode is related in the following terms: '[A]fter 1980, and although he had been urged to defend his thesis to be a candidate for a chair, succeeding Paul Ricoeur, this post is immediately suppressed by A. Saulnier-Seité, then minister of education, and when another post is given in replacement and on certain conditions, the university colleagues who had "invited" J.D. to apply, and those of the national body, vote against him' (p. 331). This passage, like many others in the 'Curriculum vitae', was obviously written by Derrida himself.

52 Letter from Dominique Janicaud to Derrida, 20 March 1981.

53 Letter from Derrida to Paul de Man, 8 May 1981.

54 Jacques Derrida, 'Comme il avait raison! Mon Cicérone Hans-Georg Gadamer', *Frankfurter Allgemeine Zeitung*, 23 March 2002. The speeches by Derrida and Gadamer on 25 April 1981 were published in the *Revue internationale de philosophie* no. 151, 1984, pp. 333–47.

55 Letter from Derrida to Roger Laporte, 28 June 1981.

56 Letter from Derrida to Paul de Man, 14 May 1981.

57 Letter from Paul de Man to Derrida, 8 July 1977.

58 Letter from Derrida to Paul de Man, 14 May 1981.

59 Written in homage to J. Hillis Miller, 'Le parjure, peut-être ("brusques sauts de syntaxe")' was first published by Ginette Michaud and Georges Leroux in *Derrida lecteur: études françaises* 38, 1–2 (Montréal, Les Presses de l'Université de Montréal, 2002). It was reprinted in Mallet and Michaud, eds, *Derrida*. This long, eloquent article can also be read as a postscript to *Mémoires: For Paul de Man*.

60 Letter from Derrida to Jean-Luc Nancy, 23 July 1981.

61 Letter from Derrida to Paul de Man, 13 October 1981.
62 Letter from Geoffrey Hartman to Derrida, 1 September 1981.
63 Interview with Bernard Pautrat.
64 Derrida, 'L'avenir de l'école littéraire: quelques propositions pour un avant-projet', November 1981, IMEC archives.
65 Pamphlet by Emmanuel Martineau, December 1981, IMEC archives.
66 'Bâtons rompus', dialogue between Hélène Cixous and Jacques Derrida, in Dutoit and Romanski, eds, *Derrida d'ici, Derrida de là*, p. 197.

Chapter 13   Night in Prague *1981–1982*

1   Interviews with Catherine Audard and Alan Montefiore.
2   Seminar of Wednesday 6 January 1982, IMEC archives.
3   I am partly relying on the account given by Barbara Day in *The Velvet Philosophers* (London: Claridge Press, 1999).
4   Interview given by Derrida to the 8 p.m. news programme on the TV channel Antenne 2, on 2 January 1982: *http://www.ina.fr/video/CAB91050888/liberation-de-jacques-derrida.fr.html*.
5   Interview given by Derrida to the 12.45 p.m. news programme on Antenne 2, on 2 January: *http://www.ina.fr/video/CAB91050879/recit-derrida.fr.html*.
6   Derrida, interview with Catherine David published as 'Derrida l'insoumis' in *Le Nouvel Observateur*, 9–15 September 1983; English translation in *Points . . .*, 'Unsealing ("the old new language")', p. 128.
7   'Unsealing ("the old new language")', in *Points . . .*, pp. 128–9.
8   Interview with Marguerite Derrida.
9   Interview with Denis Belbourg.
10 'Unsealing ("the old new language")', p. 128.
11 Interview with Marguerite Derrida.
12 All the Antenne 2 sequences devoted to Derrida's return can be seen on the INA website: *http://www.ina.fr*.
13 Interviews with Jean Derrida and Avital Ronell.
14 Ministry of Foreign Affairs, diplomatic archives of la Courneuve. Dossier EU 1981–1985, TCH 13-2.
15 Letter from Philippe Sollers to Derrida, 2 January 1982.
16 Letter from Derrida to Philippe Sollers, n.d. (January 1982).
17 '"To do justice to Freud": The history of madness in the age of psychoanalysis', in Derrida, *Resistances of Psychoanalysis*, p. 81.
18 This was told me by Étienne Balibar.
19 Derrida, 'Circumfession', p. 71 and p. 300.
20 Malabou and Derrida, *Counterpath*, p. 32 n. 9.

Chapter 14   A New Hand of Cards *1982–1983*

1   *Libération*, 21 and 22 November 1981. This interview was reprinted in *Eyes of the University*.
2   Interview with Dominique Lecourt.
3   Letter quoted in *Le Rapport bleu: les sources historiques et théoriques du Collège international de philosophie*, co-authored by François

Châtelet, Jacques Derrida, Jean-Pierre Faye, and Dominique Lecourt (Paris: Presses Universitaires de France, 1998), p. 2.

4 Letter from Derrida to Paul de Man, 15 July 1982.

5 Letter from Derrida to Jack Lang, 5 August 1982.

6 Letter from Derrida to Paul de Man, 15 July 1982.

7 Interview with Pierre Alféri.

8 Letter from Paul de Man to Derrida, 24 August 1982. This letter fragment is quoted by Derrida in *Mémoires: For Paul de Man*, p. xix.

9 The sequence can be seen on the Internet, e.g. at *http://www.youtube.com/user/kenmcmullenweb/featured*.

10 Jacques Derrida and Bernard Stiegler, *Echographies of Television: Filmed Interviews*, tr. by Jennifer Bajorek (Cambridge: Polity, 2002), pp. 119–20.

11 Letter from Derrida to Pierre Foucher, 25 January 1984.

12 Letter from Jean-Pierre Faye to Derrida, 6 September 1982.

13 Interview with Dominique Lecourt. For all details concerning the establishment of the Collège International de Philosophie, I also draw on interviews with Marie-Louise Mallet and Jean-Pierre Faye.

14 Derrida, 'Of a certain Collège International de Philosophie still to come', in *Points . . .*, p. 110; original interview with Jean-Loup Thiébaut in *Libération*, 11 August 1983.

15 Letter from Jean-Pierre Faye to Derrida, 28 September 1983.

16 Letter from Derrida to Sarah Kofman, 23 September 1983. This letter drew a brutal response from Sarah's partner, Alexandre Kyritsos, to which Derrida in turn reacted harshly.

17 Interview with Avital Ronell. Letter from Ronell to Derrida, 8 October 1983.

18 'Unsealing ("the old new language")', p. 466.

19 Letter from Derrida to Rodolphe Gasché, 22 August 1983.

20 Letter from Lucien Bianco to Derrida, 20 September 1983.

21 Letter from Derrida to Lucien Bianco, n.d. (November 1983).

22 Letter from Lucien Bianco to Derrida, 27 November 1983.

23 Letter from Derrida to Gérard Genette, 29 November 1983.

24 Letter from Derrida to Paul de Man, 12 December 1983.

Part III Jacques Derrida 1984–2004

Chapter 1   The Territories of Deconstruction *1984–1986*

1 Hélène Cixous and Jacques Derrida, 'Bâtons rompus', in Dutoit and Romanski, eds, *Derrida d'ici, Derrida de là*, p. 218.

2 On this precise and highly personal sequence of memories, Sylviane Agacinski agreed to provide me with details. I am deeply grateful to her.

3 Interviews with Élisabeth Roudinesco, René Major, and Jean-Luc Nancy.

4 Interview with Pierre Alféri.

5 Derrida and Roudinesco, *For What Tomorrow . . .*, p. 43.

6 Sylviane Agacinski, *Drame des sexes: Ibsen, Strindberg, Bergman* (Paris: Le Seuil, coll. 'Librairie du XXIe siècle', 2008).

7 Sylviane Agacinski, *Corps en miettes* (Flammarion: coll. 'Café Voltaire', 2009).

8 Sylviane Agacinski, *Parity of the Sexes*, tr. by Lisa Walsh (New York: Columbia University Press), pp. 44–5.

9 Derrida, 'In memoriam: Of the soul', in *The Work of Mourning*, p. 72.

10 Derrida, *Mémoires: For Paul de Man*, p. 3.

11 Ibid., p. 49.

12 Jonathan Culler, *On Deconstruction: Theory and Criticism after Structuralism* (Ithaca, NY: Cornell University Press, 1982), p. 85.

13 *Mémoires: For Paul de Man*, p. 41 n. 5.

14 Letter from Ruth Barcan Marcus to Laurent Fabius, 12 March 1984. This letter was quoted by Derrida in his book *Limited Inc*, p. 158. The expression 'terrorist obscurantism', attributed to Michel Foucault, was relentlessly repeated by John R. Searle in his attacks on Derrida.

15 Letter from Derrida to the members of the Council of Administration, the Haut Conseil de Réflexion, and the Collège Provisoire of the CIPh, 12 January 1984, in the IMEC archives.

16 Interview with René Major.

17 Jacques Derrida and Jean-Luc Nancy, 'Ouverture', *Rue Descartes* no. 45, 2004: 'Les 20 ans du Collège international de philosophie', p. 28.

18 Ibid., p. 46.

19 From the early 1980s onwards, Derrida's travels became so numerous that it is impossible to mention them all in the present work. There is a good description of them in the book he wrote jointly with Catherine Malabou, *Counterpath.*

20 Derrida, 'Psyche: invention of the other', in *Psyche*, vol. 1, p. 1. Many of his interventions from the early 1980s are brought together in this bulky work (650 pages in the original French, split across two volumes in English). In her article 'Venir aux débuts', Peggy Kamuf gave a fine analysis of the opening lines of works by Derrida (Mallet and Michaud, eds, *Derrida*, pp. 329–34).

21 Maurizio Ferraris, *Jackie Derrida: Rittrato a memoria* (Turin: Bollati Borighiri, 2006), p. 36.

22 Postcard from Derrida to Sarah Kofman, n.d. (summer 1984).

23 Letter from Derrida to David and Suzanne Carroll, 5 January 1985.

24 Letter from Derrida to Michel Deguy, n.d. (February or March 1985).

25 Letter from Michel Deguy to Derrida, 14 March 1985.

26 Michel Deguy, *Le Comité: Confessions d'un lecteur de grande maison* (Paris: Champ Vallon, 1988), pp. 75–7. Derrida started publishing with Gallimard only indirectly, with the *Dessins et portaits d'Antonin Artaud*, co-authored with Paule Thévenin and originally brought out by the German publisher Schirmer-Mosel. Gallimard also published the collective work *Pour Nelson Mandela* in 1986; Derrida was one of the main contributors.

27 Luc Ferry has himself acknowledged this, in the portrait of him published in *Libération*, 3 March 1997.

28 This is taken from the cover blurb of the original French text of the book by Luc Ferry and Alain Renaut, *Le Pensée 68: essai sur l'anti-humanisme contemporain* (Paris: Gallimard, 1985).

29 Luc Ferry and Alain Renaut, *French Philosophy of the Sixties: An Essay on Antihumanism*, tr. by Mary H.S. Cattani (Cambridge: University of Massachusetts Press, 1990), p. 123.

30 Ibid., p. 140.

31 The book by Ferry and Renaut is mentioned several times in the first chapter, 'Choosing one's heritage', of *For What Tomorrow . . . .* It was republished in 2003 in the Champs-Flammarion series.

32 Interview with Élisabeth Roudinesco.

33 Letter from Élisabeth Roudinesco to Derrida, 6 June 1985.

34 Interview with Étienne Balibar.

35 Derrida, 'Politics and friendship', pp. 189–90.

36 Letter from Derrida to Jean-Luc Nancy, 15 March 1985.

37 Letter from Charles-Henri Flammarion to the four directors of the series 'La philosophie en effet', 15 July 1985.

38 *Parages*, ed. by John P. Leavey, tr. by Tom Conley, James Hulbert, John P. Leavey, and Avital Ronell (Stanford, Calif.: Stanford University Press, 2011), p. 3. The original French, with the same title (Paris: Galilée, 1986), was brought out in a new edition in 2003, with an additional text, 'Maurice Blanchot est mort' ('Maurice Blanchot is dead').

39 'Grâce (soit) rendue à Jacques Derrida' is the title of Maurice Blanchot's text written for an issue of the *Revue philosophique de la France et de l'étranger* (no. 2, April–June 1990) and republished in Mallet and Michaud, eds, *Derrida*.

40 Letter from Maurice Blanchot to Derrida, 21 August 1985.

41 Letter from Maurice Blanchot to Derrida, 10 March 1986. Quoted in Mallet and Michaud, eds, *Derrida*.

42 Derrida, 'Shibboleth: For Paul Celan', tr. by Joshua Wilner, in Arios Fioretos, ed., *Word Traces: Readings of Paul Celan* (Baltimore; London: Johns Hopkins University Press, 1994), pp. 24–5.

43 'I had decided at that time to put before you the question of competence, of legitimacy, and of the Joycean institution. Who has a recognized right to speak of Joyce, to write on Joyce, and who does this well? What do competence and performance consist of here?' ('Hear say yes in Joyce', in *Acts of Literature*, p. 279).

44 Interview with Jean Bollack.

45 *L'Autre Journal*, 22–7 May 1986.

46 Colin Campbell, 'The tyranny of the Yale critics', *The New York Times Magazine*, 9 February 1986.

47 Interview with J. Hillis Miller. Letter from J. Hillis Miller to Derrida, 26 August 1985.

48 Interview with Samuel Weber.

49 Derrida, 'Désistance', in *Psyche*, vol. 2, p. 201.

50 Letter from Philippe Lacoue-Labarthe to Derrida, 5 November 1986.

51 Interview with Bernard Stiegler. *Passer à l'acte*, which discusses this period, was published in 2003 (Paris: Galilée).

52 Letter from Bernard Stiegler to Derrida, 16 December 1982.

53 Interview with Catherine Malabou.

54 Evando Nascimento, 'Entretien avec Jacques Derrida', *Folha de São Paulo*, 15 August 2004.

55 Derrida, 'The laws of reflection: Nelson Mandela, in admiration', in *Psyche*, vol. 2, pp. 63 and 64.
56 Ibid., p. 73.
57 'How to avoid speaking: Denials', in *Psyche*, vol. 2, pp. 151–2.
58 Ibid., p. 309 n. 13.
59 Marie-Françoise Plissart, *Right of Inspection*, with an essay by Derrida, tr. by David Wills (New York: Monacelli Press, 1998). J. Hillis Miller devotes most of his preface to Michael O'Rourke, ed., *Derrida and Queer Theory* (London: Palgrave Macmillan, forthcoming) to this work.
60 Paule Thévenin and Jacques Derrida, *Antonin Artaud: dessins et portraits* (Paris: Gallimard, 1986). This work, co-published with the German company Schirmer-Mostel, involved its authors in a lawsuit with the holders of Artaud's copyright. I discuss this in more detail below.
61 Derrida, 'Aphorism countertime', in *Psyche*, vol. 2, pp. 127–42.
62 Derrida, 'This strange institution', interview with Derek Attridge, in Dutoit and Romanski, eds, *Derrida d'ici, Derrida de là*, p. 285.
63 Derrida, 'Entre le corps écrivant et l'écriture'.
64 Interview with Bernard Tschumi. There are two texts by Derrida concerning the plans for the park at La Villette: 'No (point of) madness – maintaining architecture', in *Psyche*, vol. 2, pp. 87–103 (first published in Bernard Tschumi, *La Case vide*, box including essays and illustrations, published in London in 1986) and 'Why Peter Eisenman writes such good books', in *Psyche*, vol. 2, pp. 104–16 (first published in the Japanese review *Architecture and Urbanism*, Tokyo, 1987).
65 *Khôra* was first published in 1987 in *Poikilia: études offertes à Jean-Pierre Vernant*, then in book form (Paris: Galilée, 1993).
66 The seven working sessions in which Derrida took part were transcribed in the book co-authored by Derrida and Eisenman, *Chora L Works* (New York: Monacelli Press, 1997).
67 Remarks quoted in François Chaslin, 'Derrida: déconstruction et architectures', *L'Humanité*, 26 October 2004. The relations between Derrida and the deconstructivist school have been studied at book length: Mark Wigley, *The Architecture of Deconstruction: Derrida's Haunt* (Cambridge, Mass.: MIT Press, 1993).

Chapter 2 From the Heidegger Affair to the de Man Affair
1987–1988

1 Derrida, 'Kant, le Juif, l'Allemand', unpublished seminar, Irvine archives.
2 Derrida, 'Heidegger: l'enfer des philosophes', interview with Didier Eribon, *Le Nouvel Observateur*, 6 November 1987, tr. in *Points . . .*, 'Heidegger, the philosophers' hell', p. 185.
3 Jean-Pierre Faye's *Langages totalitaires* (preceded by *Théorie du récit*) came out in 1972 (Éditions Hermann).
4 Christian Jambet, 'Préface', in Victor Farías, *Heidegger et la nazisme* (Paris: Verdier, 1987), pp. 13–14. [This preface isn't contained in the English edition: *Heidegger and Nazism*, ed., with a foreword by Joseph Margolis and Tom Rockmore; French materials tr. by Paul Burrell

with the advice of Dominic Di Bernardi; German materials tr. by Gabriel R. Ricci (Philadelphia: Temple University Press, 1989). – Tr.]

5 Derrida, 'Heidegger, the philosophers' hell', p. 181.

6 Ibid., p. 182.

7 Victor Farías, '13 faits pour J. Derrida', *El País*, 17 December 1987. Interestingly, in a recent text, 'Heidegger, la politique et l'intelligentsia française' (reprinted in *Essais IV: Pourquoi pas de philosophes?* Paris: Agone, 2004, pp. 129–61), Jacques Bouveresse continues this polemic while referring more to Derrida than to Heidegger himself.

8 Robert Maggiori, 'Derrida tient Heidegger en respect', *Libération*, 27 November 1987.

9 Interview with Maggiori.

10 Roger-Pol Droit, 'Jacques Derrida et les troubles du labyrinthe', *Le Monde*, 4 December 1987.

11 Interviews with Mireille Calle-Gruber and Michel Lisse.

12 Unpublished transcript of the Heidelberg meeting of 5 February 1988, IMEC archives. It was Maurice Blanchot to whom Derrida was here implicitly replying. In *Le Nouvel Observateur* of 22 January 1988, Blanchot had just restated his position: '[I]t is Heidegger's silence on the Extermination that constitutes his irreparable wrong' (quoted by Christophe Bident in *Maurice Blanchot: partenaire invisible*, pp. 58–69).

13 The question of the possibility or impossibility of dialogue would crop up again in *Béliers. Le dialogue ininterrompu: entre deux infinis, le poème*, a lecture given by Derrida at Heidelberg on 5 February 2003, shortly after Gadamer's death, and published by Galilée the following year.

14 Interview with Philippe Beck.

15 Pierre Bourdieu, *Distinction: A Social Critique of the Judgement of Taste*, tr. by Richard Nice (Cambridge, Mass.: Harvard University Press), p. 494.

16 Ibid., p. 495.

17 Ibid., p. 496.

18 Derrida, 'Privilege: Justificatory title and introductory remarks', in *Who's Afraid of Philosophy?* p. 104.

19 *http://www.didiereribon.blogspot.com.*

20 Robert Maggiori, 'Heidegger: le krach de la philosophie', interview with Pierre Bourdieu, *Libération*, 10 March 1988.

21 Interview with Geoffrey Bennington.

22 '*Derrida–Bourdieu. Débat*', *Libération*, 19 March 1988.

23 Pierre Bourdieu, *Sketch for a Self-Analysis*, tr. by Richard Nice (Cambridge: Polity, 2007), pp. 4–5, 72.

24 Interview with Ortwin de Graef.

25 Derrida, 'Like the sound of the sea deep within a shell: Paul de Man's war', in *Mémoires: For Paul de Man*, p. 219.

26 Ibid.

27 Interview with Alan Bass.

28 Interview with Richard Rand.

29 Paul de Man's wartime articles were published as *Wartime Journalism, 1939–1943*, tr. by Werner Hamacher, Neil Hertz, and Thomas Keenan (Lincoln, Nebraska: University of Nebraska Press, 1988).

30 Interview with Jean-Marie Apostolidès. For further details on the situation of Belgium under the Occupation, see Apostolidès, *The Metamorphoses of Tintin*, tr. by Jocelyn Hoy (Stanford, Calif.: Stanford University Press, 2010). Perhaps I can also refer the reader to my own book, *Hergé, Son of Tintin*, tr. by Tina A. Kover (Baltimore: Johns Hopkins University Press, 2012), which discusses at length *Le Soir volé* and its collaborators.

31 Entry on Henri de Man in the *Biographie nationale publiée par l'Académie royale des sciences, des lettres et des beaux-arts de Balgique*, vol. XXXVIII, fasc. 2, pp. 535–554 (Brussels: Éditions Émile Bruylant, 1974).

32 Zeev Sternhel, *Neither Right Nor Left: Fascist Ideology in France*, tr. by David Maisel (Princeton: Princeton University Press, 1986), p. 141. The first edition of this work was published in 1983, by Le Seuil.

33 Hartman, *A Scholar's Tale*, p. 82.

34 Quoted by David Lehman in 'Deconstructing de Man's life', *Newsweek*, 15 February 1988, p. 63. According to Jeffrey Mehlman, this sentence had been truncated and distorted by the journalist, as he explains in his book *Adventures in the French Trade. Fragments Toward a Life* (Stanford, Calif.: Stanford University Press, 2010), pp. 78–9. (In an analysis of the texts published by Maurice Blanchot in his youth, Jeffrey Mehlman had already attacked Derrida in 1986 in his article '*Writing and Deference*: The politics of literary adulation' (*Representations* no. 15, summer 1986 – this article was published in French translation in *L'Infini*, no. 22, 1988).

35 'Like the sound of the sea' was first published in her translation in *Critical Inquiry*, vol. 14, no. 3, Spring 1988.

36 Ibid., p. 172.

37 Ibid., p. 201.

38 Ibid., pp. 206–7.

39 Ibid., pp. 165–6.

40 Ibid., p. 259 n. 44.

41 Ibid., p. 257 n. 44.

42 David Carroll, 'The sorrow and the pity of friendship and politics: An open letter to Jacques Derrida', unpublished, Irvine Archives. Another version of this text would eventually be published as 'The temptation of fascism and the question of literature: Justice, sorrow, and political error (an open letter to Jacques Derrida)', *Cultural Critique* no. 15, Spring 1990.

43 Interview with Avital Ronell.

44 Letter from Arnold I. Davidson to Derrida, 26 January 1989.

45 Jacques Derrida, 'Biodegradables: Seven diary fragments', *Critical Inquiry* vol. 15, no. 4, summer 1989, pp. 812–73.

46 'Papers' of the CIPh no. 11: 'Autour de Paul de Man'. All the documents relating to this very complex debate are freely available online: *http://www.ciph.org/fichiers_papiers/papiers11.pdf*.

47 Jürgen Habermas, *The Philosophical Discourse of Modernity. Twelve Lectures*, tr. by Frederick Lawrence (Cambridge, Mass.: MIT Press, 1987), p. 193.

48 Ibid., p. 161.

49 Ibid., p. 210.
50 *Frankfurter Rundschau*, 5 March 1988. Alexander García Düttmann drew Derrida's attention to this article, which led to him cancelling an engagement to speak at the University of Tübingen, where Manfred Frank was at that time teaching.
51 *Mémoires: For Paul de Man*, p. 259 n. 44.
52 Derrida, *Limited Inc*, p. 112.
53 Derrida, 'La vérité blessante ou le corps à corps des langues', interview with Évelyne Grossman, *Europe* no. 901, *Jacques Derrida*, May 2004, p. 21.

Chapter 3   Living Memory *1988–1990*

1 Ronell, *Fighting Theory*, p. 155.
2 Interview with Elisabeth Weber.
3 Interview with Geoffrey Bennington.
4 Derrida, 'La machine à traitement de texte', *La Quinzaine littéraire*, August 1996; tr. in *Paper Machine* as 'The word processor' (pp. 19–32).
5 Derrida, 'Circumfession', p. 27.
6 Note of 4 September 1981, in ibid., p. 274.
7 Letter from Derrida to Gérard Granel, 9 November 1989.
8 'Circumfession', pp. 22–3.
9 Letter from Derrida to Michel Monory, 4 January 1992.
10 *Memoirs of the Blind: The Self-Portrait and Other Ruins*, tr. by Pascale-Anne Brault and Michael Naas (Chicago: University of Chicago Press, 1993), p. 32. The exhibition itself was held from 26 October 1990 to 21 January 1991, in the Hall Napoléon.
11 Interview with Pierre Alféri.
12 Interview with Marguerite Derrida.
13 Derrida and Ferraris, *A Taste for the Secret*, p. 29.
14 Derrida, *Passions* (Paris: Galilée, 1993), pp. 31–2.
15 Letter from Jacques Derrida to Michel Monory, 4 January 1992.
16 In 2010, Jean Derrida published his first book with Galilée: *La Naissance du corps (Plotin, Proclus, Damascius)*.
17 Interview with Pierre Alféri.
18 Derrida, note, n.d., IMEC archives.
19 Interview with Catherine Malabou.
20 Summary of the Report of the Commission on the Teaching of Philosophy, 1990. *http://www.acireph.org/cote_philo_1_chomienne_reforme_programmes_422.htm*.
21 Interview with Catherine Malabou.
22 Jacques Bouveresse, 'Défendre la vérité désarmée', remarks quoted in Évelyne Rognon and Régine Tassi, *Nouveaux Regards: Revue de l'Institut de recherches de la FSU* no. 34, July–September 2006, pp. 71–4.
23 This letter, together with the other documents relating to the controversy, is published in the appendices to the proceedings of the conference *Lacan avec les philosophes* (Paris: Albin Michel, 1992), p. 425.
24 Derrida, *Resistances of Psychoanalysis*, p. 42.
25 Ibid., p. 46.

26 Julia Kristeva, *The Samurai: A Novel*, tr. by Barbara Bray (New York: Columbia University Press, 1992), p. 109. Derrida mentions this work in *Resistances of Psychology* (see note on p. 121 of that work). Derrida never forgot this attack and turned a cold shoulder to Kristeva's attempts at a rapprochement in 1997.
27 Interview with Philippe Beck.
28 Interviews with Avital Ronell and Jean-Luc Nancy.
29 'Papers' of the CIPh, 'Autour de Paul de Man'.
30 Interview with Jean-Luc Nancy.
31 Interview with Samuel Weber.
32 Interview with Philippe Beck.
33 Postcard from Derrida to Jean-Luc Nancy, n.d. (1989).
34 Letter from Derrida to Jean-Luc Nancy, 9 July 1990.
35 Interview with Jean-Luc Nancy. See also his 'The intruder', in *Corpus*, tr. by Richard A. Rand (New York: Fordham University Press, 2008), a superb reflection on his heart transplant.
36 Interview with Alexander García Düttmann.
37 Derrida, *On Touching: Jean-Luc Nancy*, tr. by Christine Irizarry (Stanford: Stanford University Press, 2005), p. 337.
38 Derrida, 'Louis Althusser', in *The Work of Mourning*, p. 117.
39 Althusser, *The Future Lasts a Long Time*, p. 19.

Chapter 4   Portrait of the Philosopher at Sixty

1 Derrida, unpublished interview, IMEC archives.
 2 Interview with Pierre Alféri.
 3 Michel Deguy, 'Pour Jacques Derrida', in Mallet and Michaud, eds, *Derrida*, p. 78.
 4 Interview with Jean Derrida.
 5 Interview with Claire Nancy.
 6 Interview with Samuel Weber.
 7 Élisabeth Roudinesco, 'Jacques Derrida: l'exercice des médias lui a été profitable', *L'Humanité dimanche*, 16 January 2005.
 8 Interview with Jean-Luc Nancy.
 9 Kambouchner, 'Jupiter parmi nous', pp. 95–8.
10 Kristine McKenna, 'The three ages of Jacques Derrida: An interview with the father of Deconstructionism', *LA Weekly*, 6 November 2002.
11 Michel Lisse, *Jacques Derrida* (Paris: ADPF/Ministère des Affaires étrangères, 2005), p. 32.
12 Letter from Max Genève to Derrida, 10 December 1991.
13 *Points . . .*, p. 197.
14 Interview with Maurice Olender.
15 Interview with Marie-Claire Boons.
16 Interview with Hélène Cixous.
17 Interview with Avital Ronell.
18 Interview with Marguerite Derrida.
19 Interview with Alexander García Düttmann. Some of these memories are related in Düttmann, *Derrida und ich: Das Problem der Dekonstruktion* (Bielefeld: Reihe Edition Moderne Postmoderne, 2008).
20 Interview with Marguerite Derrida.

21 Malabou and Derrida, *Counterpath*, p. 104.
22 'Dialogue avec Jacques Derrida, Jean-Luc Nancy et Philippe Lacoue-Labarthe', *Rue Descartes* no. 52, 2006.
23 *Points . . .*, p. 152 (translation slightly modified).
24 *Derrida*, feature film by Amy Ziering Kofman and Dick Kirby, Jane Doe films, 2002.
25 Derrida, *Paper Machine*, p. 20.
26 Derrida, 'Entre le corps écrivant et l'écriture'.
27 Interview with Alexander García Düttmann.
28 Malabou and Derrida, *Counterpath*, p. 29.
29 Derrida and Stiegler, *Echographies of Television*, pp. 137–8.
30 Ibid.
31 Peggy Kamuf, 'Effect of America', in *Derrida's Legacies: Literature and Philosophy* (New York: Routledge, 2008), p. 145. Interview with Peggy Kamuf.
32 Interview with Avital Ronell.
33 Letter to Éric Clémens, 12 August 1986.
34 Interview with René Major.
35 Interview with Élisabeth Roudinesco.
36 *Rue Descartes* no. 45, 2004, p. 109.
37 Derrida, *Points . . .*, p. 141.
38 Derrida, 'Entre le corps écrivant et l'écriture'.
39 Ibid.
40 Derrida, 'Heidegger's hand', in *Psyche*, vol. 2, p. 35.
41 Interview with J. Hillis Miller.
42 Derrida, 'Je n'écris pas sans lumière artificielle'.
43 Derrida, 'Entre le corps écrivant et l'écriture'.
44 Patrick Mauriès, 'Jacques Derrida, la déconstruction du monde', *Libération*, 8 August 1985.
45 Derrida and Ferraris, *A Taste for the Secret*, p. 14.
46 Derrida, 'Marx & Sons', in Michael Sprinker, ed., *Ghostly Demarcations: A Symposium on Jacques Derrida's 'Specters of Marx'* (London: Verso, 1999), p. 224.
47 Malabou and Derrida, *Counterpath*, p. 34.
48 Ibid., p. 290.
49 Ibid., pp. 34 and 36.
50 Ibid., p. 145.
51 Ferraris, *Jackie Derrida*.
52 Malabou and Derrida, *Counterpath*, p. 54.
53 Ibid., p. 5.
54 Quoted in Catherine Malabou, 'Prières', in Mallet and Michaud, eds, *Derrida*, p. 105.
55 Malabou and Derrida, *Counterpath*, p. 15.
56 Antoine de Baecque, *Feu sur le quartier général* (Paris: Petite bibliothèque des Cahiers du cinéma, 2008), p. 71. In this work, the author reprints an interview published in *Les Cahiers du cinéma* no. 534, April 1999, as 'Le cinéma et ses fantômes'.
57 De Baecque, *Feu sur le quartier général*, p. 72.
58 Carole Desbarats and Jean-Paul Gorce, *L'Effet Godard* (Toulouse: Milan, 1989), p. 110.

59 For further details, see 'The spatial arts: An interview with Jacques Derrida', conducted by Peter Brunette and David Wills, in *Deconstruction and the Visual Arts* (Cambridge: Cambridge University Press, 1994).
60 Interview with Bernard Stiegler.
61 Letter from Marie-Claire Boons to Derrida, 30 August 1982.
62 Letter from Derrida to Pierre Foucher, 5 February 1988.
63 Interview with Alexander García Düttmann.
64 Interview with Avital Ronell.
65 'Le bon plaisir de Jacques Derrida', broadcast by Didier Cahen, France Culture, March 1986. This fragment of the interview was not published in *Points de suspension* or its English translation *Points . . .* ; I am quoting from the transcription preserved in IMEC.
66 Derrida, personal notebooks, 30 December 1976, Irvine archives.
67 Derrida, 'Circumfession', p. 161.
68 Interview with Micheline Lévy.
69 Interviews with Janine and Pierrot Meskel, René and Évelyne Derrida.
70 Malabou and Derrida, *Counterpath*, p. 269.
71 'Télépathie' was initially published in the review *Furor* in 1981.
72 Interview with Avital Ronell.
73 Derrida, *Points . . .*, pp. 139–40.

Chapter 5   At the Frontiers of the Institution *1991–1992*

1 Interview with Geoffrey Bennington.
2 'Acts', in Bennington and Derrida, *Jacques Derrida*, pp. 320 and 322.
3 Letter from Jean Bellemin-Noël to Derrida, 1 March 1991.
4 *Le Nouvel Observateur*, 14 March 1991.
5 *Le Monde*, 12 July 1991.
6 'Circumfession' inspired, in an almost Talmudic way, several other works: Hélène Cixous, *Portrait of Jacques Derrida as a Young Jewish Saint*, tr. by Beverley Bie Brahic (New York: Columbia University Press, 2004); Bruno Clément, *L'Invention du commentaire: Augustin, Jacques Derrida* (Paris: Presses Universitaires de France, coll. 'Écriture', 2000); and the conference organized by the University of Villanova in September 2001, the French version of which was published by Stock, in the series 'L'autre pensée', 2007.
7 Derrida, *The Other Heading: Reflections on Today's Europe*, tr. by Pascale-Anne Brault and Michael B. Naas; intro. by Michael B. Naas (Bloomington: Indiana University Press, 1992), p. 9.
8 Ibid., p. 82.
9 *Le Magazine littéraire* no. 286, March 1991, p. 16.
10 Interview with Carlos Freire. Four of the images are reproduced in the present biography.
11 Interview with Bernard Pautrat.
12 Derrida, 'Aimer-manger-l'autre' ('Loving-eating-the-other'), unpublished seminar, session of 7 November, 1990, Irvine archives.
13 Ibid.
14 Yves Charnet, 'Un jour pour parler', homage to Derrida delivered in 2004 and published online: *http://remue.net/cont/derrida_charnet.html*.
15 Interview with Françoise Dastur.

16 Interview with Avital Ronell.
17 Letter from Yves Bonnefoy to Derrida, 14 July 1990.
18 Letter from Yves Bonnefoy to Derrida, 12 December 1990.
19 Letter from Yves Bonnefoy to Derrida, 19 January 1991.
20 *http://didiereribon.blogspot.co.uk/2008/03/la-biographie-de-bourdieu-et-la-mienne_14.html.*
21 *The Times*, 9 May 1992.
22 Quoted by Marc Roche in *Le Point* no. 1029, 6 June 1992.
23 Interviews with Alan Montefiore, Catherine Audard, and Geoffrey Bennington.
24 'La chance et l'hospitalité', speech delivered at Queen's University, Ontario, on 28 October 1995, IMEC archives.
25 Speech on receiving the Légion d'honneur, July 1992, IMEC archives.
26 Ibid.
27 Letter from Derrida to Édith Heurgon, 5 August 1990.
28 Letter from Derrida to Édith Heurgon, 20 March 1992.
29 Interview with Geoffrey Bennington.
30 This text was first published in the huge volume that brought together the proceedings of the conference 'Le Passage des frontières' (Paris: Galilée, 1994). It was then republished in book form: *Apories* (Paris: Galilée, 1996); in English as *Aporias*, tr. by Thomas Dutoit (Stanford, Calif.: Stanford University Press, 1993), pp. 12–13.
31 Letter from Derrida to Catherine Malabou, 27 July 1992.

Chapter 6   Of Deconstruction in America

1 Mitchell Stephens, 'Deconstructing Jacques Derrida', *Los Angeles Times*, 21 July 1991.
2 The first version of this very fine text was presented in April 1992, at the University of Baton Rouge, Louisiana, at the conference 'Echoes from Elsewhere/Renvois d'ailleurs' on the initiative of Édouard Glissant and David Wills. *Le monolinguisme de l'autre* was published by Galilée in 1996; it was translated as *Monolingualism of the Other, or, The Prosthesis of Origin.*
3 Mitchell Stephens, 'Deconstructing Derrida'.
4 Based on a seminar given at the École Normale Supérieure in 1976–7, *Donner le temps* was written during this period. Published by Galilée in 1991 as *Donner le temps 1: la fausse monnaie*, it was translated as *Given Time. 1. Counterfeit money*, tr. by Peggy Kamuf (Chicago: University of Chicago Press, 1992). The second volume was never published.
5 Richard Stern, 'Derridiary', *London Review of Books*, 15 August 1991.
6 Cusset, *French Theory*, p. 107.
7 Derrida, *Points . . .*, p. 211.
8 Derrida, *Mémoires: For Paul de Man*, p. 18.
9 This conference, organized by Anselm Haverkamp, was held in 1993; Tom Bishop and Anselm Haverkamp chose the title, which Derrida claimed had come as a surprise to him, but on which he commented at length in his lecture 'The time is out of joint'. The conference proceedings were published in New York, by New York University Press, in 1995.

10 Interview with Jean-Joseph Goux.
11 Rodolphe Gasché, *The Tain of the Mirror* (Lincoln: University of Nebraska Press, 1986).
12 Ronell, *Fighting Theory*, p. 161.
13 Ibid., pp. 114–15.
14 Cusset, *French Theory*, p. 152.
15 Homi K. Bhabha, 'DissemiNation (Time, narrative and the margins of the modern nation)', reprinted in Bhabha, *The Location of Culture* (London: Routledge, 1994), p. 140.
16 Interview with Andrzej Warminski. On the Derridean conception of language, see *Monolingualism of the Other* and 'Qu'est-ce qu'une traduction "relevante"', a lecture given at Arles, in 1998, during the 'Quinzièmes Assises de la traduction littéraire'; this text was reprinted in Mallet and Michaud, eds, *Derrida*, pp. 561–6.
17 Interview with Stephen Barker.
18 Interview with David Carroll. For further details on Derrida's teaching at Irvine, see the homage given by Karen Lawrence and Andrzej Warminski shortly after his death: *http://www.humanities.uci.edu/remembering_jd/lawrence_warminski.htm*.
19 Peggy Kamuf, 'Effect of America', p. 145.
20 Interview with Ellen Burt.
21 Interview with Peggy Kamuf.
22 Interview with Thomas Dutoit.
23 Malabou and Derrida, *Counterpath*, pp. 101–2.
24 Interview with Tom Bishop.
25 Interview with Avital Ronell.
26 'Dialogue entre Jacques Derrida et Jean-Luc Nancy', *Rue Descartes* no. 45, 2004: 'Les 20 ans du Collège international de philosophie'.
27 'The Villanova Round Table: A conversation with Jacques Derrida', in *Deconstruction in a Nutshell* (New York: Fordham University Press, 1997).
28 Interview with Jean-Luc Nancy.
29 *The American Journal of Sociology* vol. 93, no. 3, November 1987, pp. 584–622.
30 Interview with Michael Naas and Pascale-Anne Brault.
31 Cusset, *French Theory*, p. 121.
32 *http://prelectur.stanford.edu/lecturers/derrida/nytderrida.html*.

Chapter 7 *Specters of Marx 1993–1995*

1 Derrida, 'Back from Moscow, in the USSR', tr. by Mary Quantaire and Peggy Kamuf, in Mark Poster, ed., *Politics, Theory and Contemporary Culture* (New York: Columbia University Press, 1993), pp. 211–12.
2 Derrida, *Specters of Marx: The State of the Debt, the Work of Mourning, and the New International*. tr. by Peggy Kamuf, with an intro. by Bernd Magnus and Stephen Cullenberg (New York; London: Routledge, 1994), p. xiii.
3 Derrida and Ferraris, *A Taste for the Secret*, pp. 60–1.
4 Derrida, *Specters of Marx*, p. xvii.
5 Ibid., p. 13.

6 Letter from Derrida to Gérard Granel, 4 February 1971.
7 Derrida, *Specters of Marx*, p. 85.
8 Letter from Derrida to Françoise Dastur, 20 August 1993: '*Wir sterben um zu leben*' is a quotation from Hölderlin in *Hyperion*, a work mentioned by Dastur in the letter she had sent Derrida.
9 *Le Nouvel Observateur*, 21 October 1993.
10 *Libération*, 4 November 1993.
11 *Le Monde*, 3 December 1993.
12 *Sud-Ouest Dimanche*, 7 November 1993.
13 Letter from Derrida to Arnaud Spire, 14 November 1993.
14 Derrida's close links with *L'Humanité* lasted for the whole of the following decade. In particular, Derrida published in it a very fine text, 'Mes "humanités" du dimanche', expressing his best wishes for the new version of the daily paper (*L'Humanité*, 4 March 1999). Like most of his interventions in this period, the article was reprinted in *Paper Machine* ('My Sunday "humanities"', pp. 100–8).
15 Pierre Macherey, 'Le Marx intempestif de Derrida', in Crépon and Worms, eds, *Derrida: la tradition de la philosophie*, pp. 135–6.
16 Sprinker, ed., *Ghostly Demarcations: A Symposium on Jacques Derrida's 'Specters of Marx'* (London: Verso, 1999).
17 Derrida, 'Marx & Sons', in ibid., p. 222. The text was written in 1998 and the English version came out the following year.
18 Derrida, ' "Dead man running": Salut, salut', p. 282.
19 Published in *Le Monde* on 13 July 1993, this appeal was reprinted and discussed in Maurice Olender, *Race sans histoire* (Paris: Le Seuil, coll. 'Points', 2009), pp. 244–8.
20 This polemic became a fully fledged 'affair' after the publication of an open letter from Maurice Blanchot to Bruno Roy in *La Quinzaine littéraire* no. 703, 1–15 November 1996, p. 5. For further details, see Bident, *Maurice Blanchot*, p. 573. In July 1995, at the conference in Louvain-la-Neuve, 'Passions of Literature', Derrida discussed *The Instant of My Death*, quoting the entire text within his own paper. Blanchot thanked him warmly for this when Derrida published his book *Athens, Still Remains*: 'How grateful I am to you for saving, with your peerless commentary, my last book from the hateful publisher whom I have left and condemned, as you probably know' (letter from Blanchot to Derrida, 15 January 1998).
21 Derrida, 'Parti pris pour l'Algérie'. This text was published in *Les Temps modernes* no. 580, January–February 1995; it was later reprinted in *Papier Machine* (Paris: Galilée, 2001), p. 222. [This is not in the English edition. – Tr.]
22 Ibid., pp. 224–5.
23 Meeting on 16 May 2001 with Étienne Balibar and Thierry Briault, published in *Philosophie, philosophie* no. 9, a review of the philosophy students at the University of Paris VIII Vincennes at Saint-Denis, 2007.
24 Speech given at Nantes, 25 March 1995, IMEC archives.
25 'Manquements – du droit à la justice (mais que manque-t-il donc aux sans-papiers?)', improvised intervention of 21 December 1996 at the Théâtre des Amandiers, in Jacques Derrida and Marc Guillaume, *Marx en jeu* (Paris: Descartes et Cie, 1997), pp. 73–91.

26 Derrida, *Paper Machine*, p. 153.
27 Ibid., p. 60.
28 Derrida, *On Cosmopolitanism and Forgiveness*, no tr. (London: Routledge, 2001), pp. 16–17.
29 Derrida, 'Faith and knowledge: The two sources of "religion" at the limits of reason alone', in Jacques Derrida and Gianni Vattimo, eds, *Religion* (Cambridge: Polity, 1998), p. 3.
30 Interview with Maurizio Ferraris.
31 Derrida, 'Faith and knowledge', p. 5.
32 See *Philosophy in a Time of Terror: Dialogues with Jürgen Habermas and Jacques Derrida*, interviewed by Giovanna Borradori (Chicago: University of Chicago Press, 2003), p. 94.
33 Derrida, 'Faith and knowledge', p. 13.
34 Derrida and Roudinesco, *For What Tomorrow . . .*, p. 189.
35 Letter from Derrida to Maurizio Ferraris, 26 June 1994.
36 Derrida, *Politics of Friendship*, tr. by George Collins (London: Verso, 1997), p. viii.
37 Ibid., p. 277.
38 Ibid., p. viii.
39 Letter from Georges Canguilhem to Derrida, n.d. (autumn 1994).
40 Interview with Catherine Malabou.
41 Interview with Pierre Alféri.
42 Sarah Kofman, *Lectures de Derrida* (Paris: Galilée, 1984).
43 Derrida, 'Sarah Kofman', in *The Work of Mourning*, p. 171.
44 Interviews with Marguerite Derrida, Adelaide Russo, Françoise Dastur, Claire Nancy, and Jean-Luc Nancy.
45 Derrida, 'Gilles Deleuze', in *The Work of Mourning*, p. 193.
46 Ibid., p. 192.
47 Letter from Gilles Deleuze to Derrida, 3 February 1987. This letter is reproduced in Mallet and Michaud, eds, *Derrida*, p. 328.
48 Derrida, *Adieu – to Emmanuel Levinas*, tr. by Pascale-Anne Brault and Michael Naas (Stanford, Calif.: Stanford University Press, 1999), pp. 1–2.
49 Letter from Paul Ricoeur to Derrida, 31 December 1995. Ricoeur was even more moved by the letter Derrida wrote him in 1998 on the death of his wife Simone.
50 Derrida, *Adieu*, p. 15.

Chapter 8   The Derrida International *1996–1999*

1 *Le Monde*, 15 November 1996.
2 *Le Nouvel Observateur*, 21 February 1996.
3 Derrida, 'Si je peux faire plus qu'une phrase . . .', interview with Sylvain Bourmeau, Jean-Max Colard, and Jade Lindgaard, *Les Inrockuptibles* no. 435, 31 March 2004, pp. 27–8.
4 Ibid., p. 27.
5 Interview with Dominique Dhombres. An interesting analysis of this phenomenon can be found in Geoffrey de Lagasnerie, *L'Empire de l'Université*.
6 Derrida, 'Si je peux faire plus qu'une phrase . . .', p. 28.

7 'Portrait d'un philosophe, Jacques Derrida', transcript of a meeting with students from the University of Paris VIII in the Théâtre de l'Odéon, 26 February 1996, *Philosophie, philosophie* no. 9, 1997, p. 27.

8 *Le Nouvel Observateur*, 23 April 1996.

9 Derrida and Stiegler, *Echographies of Television*, pp. 70–1.

10 Pierre Bourdieu, *On Television*, tr. by Priscilla Parkhurst Ferguson (Cambridge: Polity, 2011).

11 Derrida, *Artaud le Moma* (Paris: Galilée, 2002), pp. 11–12.

12 Interview with Serge Malausséna. On this whole particularly vexed affair, see also Florence de Mèredieu, *L'Affaire Artaud: Journal ethnographique* (Paris: Fayard, 2009).

13 Letter from Derrida to Serge Malausséna, 14 March 1998.

14 Letter from Serge Malausséna to Derrida, 8 February 2002.

15 Letter from Derrida to Serge Malausséna, 16 February 2002.

16 Derrida, 'Joue – le prénom', *Les Inrockuptibles* no. 115, 20 August 1997, p. 41. This issue also contains a transcript of the dialogue between Ornette Coleman and Jacques Derrida, as well as an article by Thierry Jousse relating the incident at La Villette.

17 Article by Sylvain Siclier, *Le Monde*, 3 July 1997.

18 Letter from Derrida to Édith Heurgon, 9 May 1993.

19 Letter from Derrida to Catherine Malabou, 18 August 1997.

20 Interview with Marie-Louise Mallet.

21 Derrida, *The Animal That Therefore I Am*, ed. by Marie-Louise Mallet; tr. by David Wills (New York: Fordham University Press, 2008), p. 34.

22 Ibid., pp. 3–4, 6.

23 Derrida, 'Le modèle philosophique d'une "contre-institution"', p. 251.

24 Postcard from Derrida to Édith Heurgon, 1 August 1997.

25 Interview with Michel Deguy.

26 Derrida, *Paper Machine*, p. 89.

27 See, for example, Nancy J. Holland, ed., *Feminist Interpretations of Jacques Derrida* (University Park, Pa: Pennsylvania State University Press, 1997).

28 Interview with Avital Ronell.

29 Letter from Derrida to Dominique Dhombres, 10 December 1997.

30 Malabou and Derrida, *Counterpath*, p. 237.

31 Natalia Avtonomova, 'Paradoxes de la réception de Derrida en Russie', in Mallet and Michaud, eds, *Derrida*, pp. 400–1.

32 Malabou and Derrida, *Counterpath*, p. 237.

33 Ibid., p. 263.

34 The text of this lecture – one of those which Derrida delivered most frequently over this period, adapting it each time to the context of the country in which he happened to be – was published in *Derrida*, Cahier de l'Herne, 2004, pp. 541–60. On the same subject, see also '*Versöhnung, ubuntu*, pardon: quel genre?', in *Vérité, réconciliation, réparation* (Paris: Le Seuil, coll. 'Le genre humain', 2004), pp. 111–59.

35 Jacques Derrida and Safaa Fathy, *Tourner les mots: Au bord d'un film* (Paris: Galilée/Arte éditions, 2000), p. 73.

36 'Responsabilité d'un sens à venir', debate between Derrida and Nancy, in *Sens en tous sens, autour des travaux de Jean-Luc Nancy* (Paris: Galilée, 2004).

37 Derrida and Roudinesco, *For What Tomorrow . . .*, p. 14.
38 Derrida, *H.C. pour la vie, c'est à dire . . .* (Paris: Galilée, 2002), p. 20.
39 The two works were published by Galilée. See also *L'Événement comme écriture: Cixous et Derrida se lisant*, proceedings of a 2005 conference organized by Marta Segarra (Paris: Éditions Campagne-Première, 2001).
40 Interview with Hélène Cixous.
41 'Du mot à la vie: un dialogue entre Jacques Derrida et Hélène Cixous', *Le Magazine littéraire* no. 430, April 2004, p. 26.
42 Derrida, *Déplier Ponge*, interview with Gérard Frasse (Presses Universitaires du Septentrion, 2005), p. 15.
43 'Du mot à la vie', pp. 26–7.
44 *Les Lettres françaises*, no. 1429, 29 March 1972.
45 Charles Ramond, *Le vocabulaire de Jacques Derrida* (Paris: Ellipses, 2001). Jean-Pierre Moussaron has written a very good article on Derrida's neologisms, 'L'esprit de la lettre', in Mallet and Michaud, eds, *Derrida*, pp. 363–71.
46 'Du mot à la vie', p. 22.
47 My analysis overlaps to some degree those of Cornelius Crowley, in his interesting article, 'Un rapport sur le mode du non-rapport: James and Derrida', in Dutoit and Romanski, eds, *Derrida d'ici, Derrida de là*, pp. 87–108, and J. Hillis Miller, 'The late Derrida', in his book *For Derrida* (New York: Fordham University Press, 2009).
48 Derrida, *Athens, Still Remains: The Photographs of Jean-François Bonhomme*, tr. by Pascale-Anne Brault and Michael Naas (New York: Fordham University Press, 2010), pp. 4–5.
49 Ibid., p. 5.

Chapter 9   The Time of Dialogue *2000–2002*

1 Insert in French edition: Derrida, *Le toucher: Jean-Luc Nancy* (Paris: Galilée, 2000).
2 Ibid.
3 'La decision, la fiction, la présence', *Revue ah! Oui de la philosophie* (Brussels: Éditions de l'Université de Bruxelles, 2005), p. 173.
4 Interview with J. Hillis Miller.
5 Interview with Jean-Luc Nancy.
6 Interview with Élisabeth Roudinesco.
7 Derrida and Roudinesco, *For What Tomorrow . . .*, pp. 145–6.
8 Derrida, *États d'âme de la psychanalyse* (Paris: Galilée, 2000), p. 12.
9 Ibid., p. 13.
10 Ibid., p. 21.
11 Ibid., pp. 41–2.
12 Interviews with Marguerite Derrida and Avital Ronell.
13 Letter from Derrida to Max Genève, 1 September 2000.
14 Interview with Albert Dichy.
15 Letter from Olivier Corpet to Derrida, 20 March 1998.
16 Interview with Albert Dichy.
17 Derrida 'Unsere Redlichkeit', *Frankfurter Rundschau*, 18 June 2004.
18 Ibid.

19 Ibid.
20 Interview with Alexander Garcia Düttmann.
21 Ronell, *Fighting Theory*, p. 111.
22 Derrida, 'Abraham, the other', in *Judeities: Questions for Jacques Derrida*, ed. by Bettina Bergo, Joseph Cohen, and Raphael Zagury-Orly, tr. by Bettina Bergo and Michael B. Smith (New York: Fordham University Press, 2007), p. 4.
23 Ibid., pp. 4, 6–7.
24 Derrida, *Learning to Live Finally*, pp. 38–9.
25 'Un témoignage donné', in *Questions au judéisme: entretiens avec Élisabeth Weber* (Paris: Desclée de Brouwer, 1996), p. 77.
26 *Points . . .*, p. 80.
27 'Confession et *Circumfession*', debate with Richard Kearney, in *Des confessions* (Paris: Stock, 2007), p. 83.
28 Letter from Derrida to Catherine Malabou, 14 April 2001.
29 Letter from Lucien Bianco to Derrida, n.d. (summer 2001).
30 Habermas and Derrida, *Philosophy in a Time of Terror*, pp. 109–10.
31 Ning Zhang, 'Jacques Derrida's First Visit to China: A Summary of His Lectures and Seminars', *Dao: A Journal of Comparative Philosophy*, December 2002, vol. 2, no. 1, p. 145.
32 Letter from Jacques Derrida to Catherine Malabou, 17 September 2001.
33 Derrida, '*Fichus*', in *Paper Machine*, p. 165.
34 Ibid., p. 173.
35 Ibid., p. 179.
36 Interview with Avital Ronell.
37 Cover of French edition: Derrida and Habermas, *Le 'concept' du 11 septembre* (Paris: Galilée, 2004).
38 Habermas and Derrida, *Philosophy in a Time of Terror*, p. 87.
39 Derrida, *Learning to Live Finally*, p. 30.
40 Habermas, *Philosophy in a Time of Terror*, pp. 107.
41 Ibid., pp. 113–14.
42 Ibid., p. 94.
43 Interview with Élisabeth Roudinesco.
44 Letter from Régis Debray to Derrida, n.d. (Autumn 2001).
45 Derrida, 'Interpretations at war: Kant the Jew, the German', in *Psyche*, vol. 2, p. 243.
46 Robert Redeker, 'De New York à Gaillac: trajet d'une épidémie logo-toxique', *Les Temps modernes* no. 615–16, September–November 2001. On 19 September 2006, Robert Redeker, a professor of philosophy, published in *Le Figaro* a piece with the title 'Face aux intimidations islamistes, que doit faire le monde libre?' As a result of this text, which triggered a major controversy, he was subjected to death threats. For further details: *http://en.wikipedia.org/wiki/Robert_Redeker*.
47 Letter from Derrida to Claude Lanzmann, 30 January 2002.
48 Ibid.
49 Alain Badiou, 'Derrida, ou l'inscription de l'inexistant', in Crépon and Worms, eds, *Derrida, la tradition de la philosophie*, p. 179.
50 Derrida and Ferraris, *A Taste for the Secret*, p. 59.
51 Serge Raffy, *Jospin, secrets de famille* (Paris: Fayard, 2001), pp. 307–8.

52 Claude Askolovitch, *Lionel* (Paris: Grasset, 2001), p. 307.
53 Ariane Chemin, 'Comment M. Chirac et M. Jospin mènent leur bataille d'images. Le meeting du Premier ministre à Marseille sera "familial"', *Le Monde*, 22 March 2002.
54 *Le Nouvel Observateur*, 4 April 2002.
55 *Gala*, 11 April 2002.
56 Interview with Avital Ronell. These remarks have been confirmed to me by Élisabeth Roudinesco, Micheline Lévy, Pierre Lévy, and Jean Derrida.
57 Derrida, 'Non pas l'utopie, l'im-possible', interview published in *Die Zeit* on 5 March 1998 and reprinted in *Paper Machine* ('Not utopia, the impossible', p. 123).
58 Ibid., p. [tbc].
59 Luc le Vaillant, 'Jacques Derrida: Le bel et différent', *Libération*, 22 May 2002.
60 Agacinski, *Journal interrompu*, p. 152.
61 Ibid., p. 153.
62 Derrida, *Rogues: Two Essays on Reason*, tr. by Pascale-Anne Brault and Michael Naas (Stanford, Calif.: Stanford University Press, 2005), p. 172 n. 12.
63 Letter from Derrida to Édith Heurgon, 29 June 1999.
64 Letter from Derrida to Édith Heurgon, 24 August 1999.
65 Ibid.
66 Habermas and Derrida, *Philosophy in a Time of Terror*, p. 120.
67 Noam Chomsky, *Rogue States: The Rule of Force in World Affairs* (London: Pluto Press, 2000).
68 Derrida, *Rogues*, pp. 96 and 102.
69 Ibid., p. 156.
70 Ibid., p. 87.

Chapter 10 In Life and in Death *2003–2004*

1 Derrida, *The Beast & the Sovereign*, vol. 2, p. 161 (translation modified).
2 Ibid., p. 169 (translation modified).
3 I am grateful to René Major for allowing me to see the transcript of this unpublished debate.
4 Derrida, 'À Maurice Blanchot', in *Chaque fois unique*, p. 323. On 26 February, in his seminar, Derrida mentioned, 'without having the heart' really to talk about it, this cremation that took place 'in conditions, in a landscape, and in a provincial crematorium among the most *unheimlich* one could imagine in the twenty-first century' (*The Beast & the Sovereign*, vol. 2, p. 175).
5 Interview with Avital Ronell.
6 Interview with Éric Hoppenot.
7 Interview with Marguerite Derrida.
8 Interview with Peggy Kamuf.
9 Interviews with Marguerite Derrida, Jean Derrida, and Pierre Alféri.
10 Edited by Mireille Calle-Gruber, the conference 'Hélène Cixous: Genèse Généalogies Genres', took place at the Bibliothèque Nationale

de France from 22 to 24 May 2003. Derrida's text *Genèses, généalogies, genres et le génie* was published by Galilée in 2003.

11 Speech by Dominique de Villepin to the Hebrew University of Jerusalem, 25 May 2003.

12 Mustapha Chérif, *L'Islam et l'Occident: Rencontre avec Jacques Derrida* (Paris: Odile Jacob, 2006), pp. 53–4.

13 Derrida, 'Pourquoi je signe cet appel', and 'Europe: plaidoyer pour une politique extérieure commune', *Libération*, 31 May 2003. Like Habermas, Derrida viewed the 'enormous demonstrations' that took place on 15 February 2003 – when millions of citizens took to the streets against the war – as signalling the birth of a European public space.

14 Interview with Albert Dichy.

15 Letter from Jean-Luc Nancy to Derrida, n.d. (summer 2003).

16 Interview with J. Hillis Miller.

17 Letter from Derrida to David Wills, 5 July 2003.

18 Interview with Elisabeth Weber.

19 Interview with Michel Lisse.

20 Letter from Mireille Calle-Gruber to Jacques Derrida, 26 November 2003.

21 Interview with Peggy Kamuf.

22 Derrida, 'Louis Marin', in *The Work of Mourning*, p. 164.

23 Malabou and Derrida, *Counterpath*, p. 23.

24 Interview with Michael Naas and Pascale-Anne Brault.

25 Derrida, 'Louis Althusser', in *The Work of Mourning*, p. 115.

26 Bernard-Henri Lévy, 'Journal de la semaine', *Libération*, 20–1 December 2003.

27 Late letter from Paul Ricoeur to Derrida, n.d.

28 Letter from Paul Ricoeur to Derrida, 5 November 2003.

29 Derrida, 'La parole – Donner, nommer, appeler', in d'Allones and Azouvi, eds, *Paul Ricoeur*, p. 19.

30 Ibid., p. 24.

31 Interview with Michel Lisse.

32 Ginette Michaud discusses the compilation of this iconographic volume and analyses some of the photographs in her *Veilleuses: Autour de trois images de Jacques Derrida* (Paris: Nota Bene, 2009).

33 Interview with Avital Ronell.

34 Derrida, 'Si je peux faire plus qu'une phrase . . .'.

35 Derrida, speech given on 8 May 2004 on the occasion of the fiftieth anniversary of *Le Monde diplomatique*. The full text of this speech is available online: *http://www.monde-diplomatique.fr/2004/11/DERRIDA/11677*. A video version is available at: *http://www.dailymotion.com/video/xws9r_jacques-derrida_events*.

36 'Dialogue entre Jacques Derrida, Philippe Lacoue-Labarthe et Jean-Luc Nancy', p. 93. The small collective volume *Penser à Strasbourg* was published jointly by Galilée and the Ville de Strasbourg in June 2004. It contains an important text by Derrida, 'Le lieu dit: Strasbourg'.

37 Interview with Alexander García Düttmann.

38 Derrida, 'Double mémoire', in *Le théâtre des idées: 50 penseurs pour comprendre le XXIe siècle* (Paris: Flammarion, 2008), pp. 15–16.

39 Derrida, 'Comment ne pas trembler', *Annali*, 2006-II, Bruno Mondadori, pp. 97–8.
40 Ibid., p. 97.
41 Carroll, 'Jacques Derrida ou le don d'écriture – quand quelque chose se passe', p. 106.
42 Interview with J. Hillis Miller.
43 Letter from Derrida to Ralph J. Cicerone, 25 July 2004. The full text is available online at: *http://jacques-derrida.org/Cicerone.html.*
44 Interview with Stephen Barker.
45 Interview with Jean Birnbaum.
46 Derrida, *Learning to Live Finally*, pp. 24–6.
47 Ibid., p. 52.
48 Interview with Evando Nascimento.
49 Interview with Bernard Stiegler.
50 Élisabeth Roudinesco, 'Jacques Derrida: l'exercice des medias lui a éte profitable', *L'Humanité Dimanche*, 16 January 2005.
51 Interview with Ginette Michaud.
52 Interview with Marguerite Derrida.
53 Derrida, *Learning to Live Finally*, p. 37.
54 Jean-Luc Nancy, 'Trois phrases de Jacques Derrida', *Rue Descartes* no. 48: 'Salut à Jacques Derrida', p. 69.
55 Ibid., p. 6.

Sources

DERRIDA'S ARCHIVES

Most of Jacques Derrida's personal archives are assembled in two collections, which I have explored in great detail:

The Derrida collection in the 'Special Collections' of the University of California, Irvine

This includes in particular:

> his student work: *lycée, hypokhâgne*, and *khâgne*, 1946–1952;
>   École Normale Supérieure, 1952–1956;
> manuscripts of classes and seminars, 1959–1995;
> manuscripts of books, articles, and lectures, 1959–1995;
> personal notebooks;
> documents relating to the Paul de Man affair;
> press articles, 1969–2002.

The Derrida collection at the Institut Memoires de l'Édition Contemporaine (IMEC) near Caen, in France

This includes in particular:

> manuscripts of classes and seminars, 1995–2004;
> manuscripts of books, articles, and lectures, 1995–2004;
> press articles, 1963–2004;
> all letters received, 1949–2004;
> many books, issues of reviews, and articles by and about
>   Derrida;
> sound and audiovisual archives.

List of the main correspondents whose letters I have consulted at IMEC:

Robert Abirached, Suzanne Allen, Louis Althusser, Pierre Aubenque, Madeleine Aubier-Gabail, Michel Aucouturier, Étienne Balibar, Roland Barthes, Henry Bauchau, Jean Bellemin-Noël, Jean-Marie Benoist, Lucien Bianco, Maurice Blanchot, Lisa Block de Behar, Jean Bollack, Geneviève Bollème, Claude Bonnefoy, Yves Bonnefoy, Marie-Claire Boons, Pierre Bourdieu, Antoine Bourseiller, Mireille Calle-Gruber, Georges Canguilhem, John D. Caputo, Hélène Cixous, Éric Clémens, Catherine Clément, Olivier Corpet, Catherine David, Régis Debray, Michel Deguy, Jean Domerc, Didier Eribon, Jean-Pierre Faye, Maurizio Ferraris, Charles-Henri Flammarion, Élisabeth de Fontenay, Michel Foucault, Pierre Foucher, Maurice de Gandillac, Rodolphe Gasché, Jean Genet, Gérard Genette, Max Genève, Hans-Dieter Gondek, Jean-Joseph Goux, Gérard Granel, Hans Ulrich Gumbrecht, Karin Gundersen, Geoffrey Hartman, Édith Heurgon, Jean-Louis Houdebine, Jean Hyppolite, Edmond Jabès, Jos Joliet, Peggy Kamuf, Sarah Kofman, Julia Kristeva, Philippe Lacoue-Labarthe, Jack Lang, Claude Lanzmann, Roger Laporte, Emmanuel Levinas, Micheline Lévy, Jérôme Lindon, Michel Lisse, Robert Maggiori, René Major, Catherine Malabou, Serge Malausséna, Paul de Man, J. Hillis Miller, Michel Monory, Alan Montefiore, Jean-Luc Nancy, Pierre Nora, Jean-Claude Pariente, Bernard Pautrat, Jean Piel, Jean Ricardou, Paul Ricoeur, Jean Ristat, Avital Ronell, Élisabeth Roudinesco, Michel Serres, Philippe Sollers, Bernard Stiegler, Paule Thévenin, Elisabeth Weber, Samuel Weber, David Wills, Heinz Wismann.

Documents relating to Jacques Derrida are also kept at IMEC in the following collections: Louis Althusser, Roland Barthes, Centre Culturel International de Cerisy-la-Salle, Collège International de Philosophie, Michel Deguy, Jean Genet, Sarah Kofman, Emmanuel Levinas, Parlement International des Écrivains, the reviews *Critique* and *Tel Quel*.

OTHER ARCHIVES CONSULTED

Archives of Gérard Granel
Archives of the Lycée Louis-le-Grand
Archives of Roger Laporte
French diplomatic archives, La Courneuve
Henry Bauchau collection, Louvain-la-Neuve
Jacques Derrida's working library in Ris-Orangis
Paul Ricoeur collection, Paris

While he kept all the letters he received, including postcards and even the shortest notes, Derrida only rarely made copies of his own letters. So a significant amount of research has been necessary to track down and consult the most important letters he sent, for example to Louis Althusser, Henry Bauchau, Maurice Blanchot, Gabriel Bounoure, Michel Foucault, Sarah Kofman, Philippe Lacoue-Labarthe, Roger Laporte, Emmanuel Levinas, Catherine Malabou, Paul de Man, Jean-Luc Nancy, Paul Ricoeur, Avital Ronell, Philippe Sollers, et al. Of even more interest, sometimes, are the letters sent by Derrida to a few of the friends from his youth, during his formative years, especially Michel Monory and Lucien Bianco.

INTERVIEWS

A list of the people I have interviewed, in alphabetical order:

Robert Abirached, Fernand Acharrok, Camilla Adami, Valerio Adami, Pierre Alféri, François Angelier, Jean-Marie Apostolidès, Michel Aucouturier, Catherine Audard, Étienne Balibar, Denis Baril, Stephen Barker, Alan Bass, Philippe Beck, Jean Bellemin-Noël, Geoffrey Bennington, Lucien Bianco, Jean Birnbaum, Tom Bishop, Rudolf Boehm, Jean Bollack, Marie-Claire Boons, Pascale-Anne Brault, Christine Buci-Glucksmann, Ellen Burt, Mireille Calle-Gruber, David Carroll, Hélène Cixous, Éric Clémens, Catherine Clément, Chantal Colliot, Olivier Corpet, Paul Cottin, Marc Crépon, Françoise Dastur, Albert Daussin, Régis Debray, Michel Deguy, Denis Delbourg, Évelyne Derrida, Janine Derrida-Meskel, Jean Derrida, Marguerite Derrida, René Derrida, Dominique Dhombres, Souleymane Bachir Diagne, Albert Dichy, Thomas Dutoit, Alexander García Düttmann, Didier Eribon, Jean-Pierre Faye, Maurizio Ferraris, Jean-Jacques Forté, Pierre Foucher, Carlos Freire, Gérard Genette, Max Genève, Daniel Giovannangeli, Jean-Joseph Goux, Ortwin de Graef, Évelyne Grossman, Karin Gundersen, Werner Hamacher, Geoffrey Hartman, Robert Harvey, Éric Hoppenot, Jean-Louis Houdebine, Denis Kambouchner, Peggy Kamuf, Julia Kristeva, Jack Lang, Hadrien Laroche, Dominique Lecourt, Bernard-Henri Lévy, Micheline Lévy, Michel Lisse, Robert Maggiori, René Major, Catherine Malabou, Serge Malausséna, Marie-Louise Mallet, Martine Meskel, Pierrot Meskel, Ginette Michaud, J. Hillis Miller, Michel Monory, Alan Montefiore, Jean-Paul Morel, Njoh Mouellé, Michael Naas, Claire Nancy, Jean-Luc Nancy, Evando Nascimento, Monique Nemer, Maurice Olender, Jean-Claude Pariente, Bernard Pautrat, Alain Pons, Richard Rand, Jean Ristat, Élisabeth Roudinesco, Adelaïde Russo, Philippe Sollers, Bernard Stiegler, Bernard Tschumi, Andrzej Warminski, Elisabeth Weber, Samuel Weber, David Wills, Heinz Wismann.

Bibliography

This is a list of Derrida's main books and texts arranged in chrono-logical order of publication in French, followed by details of English translations.*

1962

Edmund Husserl, *L'origine de la géométrie*, tr. and intro. by Jacques Derrida (Paris: Presses Universitaires de France); *Edmund Husserl's 'Origin of Geometry': An Introduction*, ed. by David B. Allison, tr. and with a preface by John P. Leavey, Jr (New York: N. Hays; Hassocks: Harvester Press, 1978).

1967

De la grammatologie (Paris: Minuit); *Of Grammatology*, tr. by Gayatri Chakravorty Spivak (Baltimore; London: Johns Hopkins University Press, 1976).

L'écriture et la différence (Paris: Seuil); *Writing and Difference*, tr. with an intro. and additional notes by Alan Bass (London: Routledge and Kegan Paul, 1978).

La voix et le phénomène: Introduction au problème du signe dans la phénoménologie de Husserl (Paris: Presses Universitaires de France); *Speech and Phenomena, and Other Essays on Husserl's Theory of Signs*, tr., with an intro., by David B. Allison (Evanston, Ill.: Northwestern University Press, 1973).

---

* The texts and books used in writing this bibliography have been quoted in the notes. Complete bibliographies of Derrida's articles and interviews, as well as works on him, can be found in Marie-Louise Mallet and Ginette Michaud, eds, *Derrida*, Cahiers de l'Herne no. 83 (Paris: Éditions de l'Herne, 2004) as well as in Geoffrey Bennington and Jacques Derrida, *Jacques Derrida*, tr. by Geoffrey Bennington (Chicago: University of Chicago Press, 1993).

1972

La dissémination (Paris: Seuil); *Dissemination*, tr., with intro. and additional notes, by Barbara Johnson (London: Athlone Press, 1981).

Marges – de la philosophie (Paris: Minuit); *Margins of Philosophy*, tr. with additional notes by Alan Bass (Brighton: Harvester Press, 1982).

Positions (Paris: Minuit); *Positions*, tr. and annotated by Alan Bass, revised edn (London: Continuum, 2002).

1973

'L'archéologie du frivole' (introduction to *L'essai sur l'origine des connaissances humaines de Condillac*) (Paris: Galilée); *The Archeology of the Frivolous: Reading Condillac*, tr. by John P. Leavey, Jr (Pittsburgh: Duquesne University Press, 1980).

1974

Glas (Paris: Galilée); *Glas*, tr. by John P. Leavey, Jr, and Richard Rand (Lincoln: University of Nebraska Press, 1986).

1975

'Economimesis', in Sylviane Agacinski et al., *Mimésis (des articulations)* (Paris: Aubier-Flammarion); 'Economimesis', tr. by Richard Klein, in *Diacritics* 11, no. 2 (1981), pp. 3–25.

1976

'Fors', preface to *Le Verbier de l'Homme aux Loups* by Nicolas Abraham and Maria Torok (Paris: Auber-Flammarion); 'Fors: The Anglish words of Nicolas Abraham and Maria Torok', tr. by Barbara Johnson, preface to *The Wolf Man's Magic Word: A Cryptonymy*, tr. by Nicholas Rand (Minneapolis: University of Minnesota Press, 1986).

1978

Éperons: Les styles de Nietzsche (Paris: Flammarion); *Spurs = Éperons: Nietzsche's Styles = Les styles de Nietzsche*, tr. by Barbara Harlow, with an intro. by Stefano Agosti (Chicago; London: University of Chicago Press, 1979).

La vérité en peinture (Paris: Flammarion); *The Truth in Painting*, tr. by Geoff Bennington and Ian McLeod (Chicago: University of Chicago Press, 1987).

'Scribble', preface to the *Essai sur les hiéroglyphes* [i.e. *Essay on Hieroglyphics*] by William Warburton (Partis Aubier-Flammarion); 'Scribble (Writing Power)', tr. by Cory Plotkin, *Yale French Studies* 58 (1979), pp. 17–147.

1980

La Carte postale: De Socrate à Freud et au-delà (Paris: Flammarion); *The Post Card: From Socrates to Freud and Beyond*, tr., with an introduction and additional notes, by Alan Bass (Chicago: University of Chicago Press, 1987).

1982

L'oreille de l'autre: otobiographies, transferts, traductions. Textes et débats avec Jacques Derrida, ed. by Claude Levesque and Christie McDonald (Montréal: VLB éditeur); *The Ear of the Other – Otobiography, Transference, Translation. Texts and Discussion with Jacques Derrida*, ed. by Christie McDonald; tr. by Peggy Kamuf (Lincoln: University of Nebraska Press, new edn, 1988).

1983

D'un ton apocalyptique naguère adopté en philosophie (Paris: Galilée); 'Of an apocalyptic tone recently adopted in philosophy', tr. by John P. Leavey, Jr, in Peter David Fenves, *Raising the Tone of Philosophy: Late Essays by Immanuel Kant, Transformative Critique by Emmanuel Derrida* (Baltimore; London: Johns Hopkins University Press, 1993).

1984

Otobiographies: L'enseignement de Nietzsche et la politique du nom propre (Paris: Galilée); English translation in *The Ear of the Other* (see **1982** above).

1985

'Lecture' in Marie-Françoise Plissart, *Droit de regards* (Paris: Minuit); *Right of Inspection*, tr. by David Wills (New York: Monacelli Press, 1998).

'Préjugés: devant la loi', in *La faculté de juger: Colloque de Cerisy* (Paris: Minuit); 'Before the law', in *Acts of Literature*, ed. by Derek Attridge (New York; London: Routledge, 1992). [This translation is a revised version of Derrida's original paper, which was more focused on the work of Lyotard.]

1986

'Forcener le subjectile', in *Dessins et portraits d'Antonin Artaud* (Paris: Gallimard); 'Maddening the subjectile', *Yale French Studies* 84 (1994), pp. 154–71.

Parages (Paris: Galilée); new French edition 2003; *Parages*, ed. by John P. Leavey, tr. by Tom Conley, James Hulbert, John P. Leavey, and Avital Ronell (Stanford, Calif.: Stanford University Press, 2011).

Schibboleth, pour Paul Celan (Paris: Galilée); 'Shibboleth: For Paul Celan', tr. by Joshua Wilner, in Arios Fioretos, ed., *Word Traces: Readings of Paul Celan* (Baltimore; London: Johns Hopkins University Press, 1994).

1987

De l'esprit: Heidegger et la question (Paris: Galilée); *Of Spirit: Heidegger and the Question*, tr. by Geoffrey Bennington and Rachel Bowlby (Chicago: University of Chicago Press, 1989).

Feu la cendre (Paris: Des Femmes); *Cinders*, tr. By Ned Lukacher (Lincoln: University of Nebraska Press, 1991).

Psyché: Inventions de l'autre (Paris: Galilée); *Psyche: Inventions of the Other*, 2 vols, ed. by Peggy Kamuf and Elizabeth Rottenberg (Stanford, Calif.: Stanford University Press, 2007).

Ulysse gramophone: Deux mots pour Joyce (Paris: Galilée); 'Ulysses gramophone: Hear say yes in Joyce', in *Acts of Literature* (see **1985** above).

1988

Mémoires – pour Paul de Man (Paris: Galilée); *Mémoires: For Paul de Man*, tr. by Cecile Lindsay, Jonathan Culler, and Eduardo Cadava (New York: Columbia University Press, 1986).

1990

Du droit à la philosophie (Paris: Galilée); *Who's Afraid of Philosophy? Right to Philosophy I*, tr. By Jan Plug (Stanford, Calif.: Stanford University Press, 2002).

Mémoires d'aveugle: L'autoportrait et autres ruines (Paris: Louvre, Réunion des musées nationaux); *Memoirs of the Blind: The Self-Portrait and Other Ruins*, tr. by Pascale-Anne Brault and Michael Naas (Chicago; London: University of Chicago Press, 1993).

Le Problème de la genèse dans la philosophie de Husserl (Paris: Presses Universitaires de France); *The Problem of Genesis in Husserl's Philosophy*, tr. by Marian Hobson (Chicago: University of Chicago Press, 2003).

1991

L'autre cap (Paris: Galilée); *The Other Heading: Reflections on Today's Europe*, tr. by Pascale-Anne Brault and Michael B. Naas with an intro. by Michael Naas (Bloomington: Indiana University Press, 1992).

Circonfession, in Geoffrey Bennington and Jacques Derrida, *Jacques Derrida* (Paris: Seuil); 'Circumfession' in Geoffrey Bennington and Jacques Derrida, *Jacques Derrida*, tr. by Geoffrey Bennington (Chicago: University of Chicago Press, 1993).

Donner le temps. 1. La fausse monnaie (Paris: Galilée); *Given Time: Counterfeit Money*, tr. by Peggy Kamuf (Chicago: University of Chicago Press, 1992).

1992

Points de suspension (Paris: Galilée); *Points ... Interviews, 1974–1994*, ed. by Elisabeth Weber, tr. by Peggy Kamuf et al. (Stanford, Calif.: Stanford University Press, 1995).

1993

Khôra (Paris: Galilée); 'Khôra', in *On the Name*, ed. by Thomas Dutoit; tr. by David Wood, John P. Leavey, Jr, and Ian McLeod (Stanford, Calif.: Stanford University Press, 1995).
Passions (Paris: Galilée); 'Passions: "An oblique offering"', in *On the Name*.
Sauf le nom (Paris: Galilée); 'Sauf le nom: Post-scriptum', in *On the Name*.
Spectres de Marx (Paris: Galilée); *Specters of Marx: The State of the Debt, the Work of Mourning, and the New International*, tr. by Peggy Kamuf, with an intro. by Bernd Magnus and Stephen Cullenberg (New York; London: Routledge, 1994).

1994

Force de loi: Le fondement mystique de l'autorité (Paris: Galilée); 'Force of law: The "mystical foundations of authority"', tr. by Mary Quaintance, *Cardozo Law Review* vol. 11 (1992), pp. 919–1045.
Politiques de l'amitié (Paris: Galilée).

1995

'Avances', preface to Serge Margel, *Tombeau du dieu artisan* (Paris: Minuit).
Mal d'archive (Paris: Galilée); *Archive Fever: A Freudian Impression*, tr. by Eric Prenowitz (Chicago; London: University of Chicago Press, 1996).
Moscou aller-retour (Paris: Éditions de l'Aube).

1996

Apories (Paris: Galilée); *Aporias: Dying – Awaiting (One Another at) the 'Limits of Truth' = (mourir – s'attendre aux 'limites de la vérité')*, tr. by Thomas Dutoit (Stanford, Calif.: Stanford University Press, 1993).
'Foi et savoir: Les deux sources de la "religion" aux limites de la simple raison', in Jacques Derrida and Gianni Vattimo, eds, *La Religion: Séminaire de Capri* (Paris: Seuil, 1996); 'Faith and knowledge: The two sources of "religion" at the limits of reason

alone', in Jacques Derrida and Gianni Vattimo, eds, *Religion* (Cambridge: Polity, 1998).

Le monolingualisme de l'autre (Paris: Galilée); *Monolingualism of the Other, or, The prosthesis of origin*, tr. by Patrick Mensah (Stanford, Calif.: Stanford University Press, 1998).

Résistances – de la psychanalyse (Paris: Galilée); *Resistances of Psychoanalysis*, tr. by Peggy Kamuf, Pascale-Anne Brault, and Michael Naas (Stanford, Calif.: Stanford University Press, 1998).

Échographies – de la télévision, interviews filmed with Bernard Stiegler (Paris: Galilée); Derrida and Stiegler, *Echographies of Television: Filmed Interviews*, tr. by Jennifer Bajorek (Cambridge: Polity, 2002).

1997

Adieu – à Emmanuel Levinas (Paris: Galilée); *Adieu – to Emmanuel Levinas*, tr. by Pascale-Anne Brault and Michael Naas (Stanford, Calif.: Stanford University Press, 1999).

Cosmopolites de tous les pays, encore un effort! (Paris: Galilée); *On Cosmopolitanism and Forgiveness*, no tr. (London: Routledge, 2001).

Le droit à la philosophie du point de vue cosmopolitique (Paris: Verdier).

De l'hospitalité, with Anne Dufourmantelle (Paris: Calmann-Lévy); *Of Hospitality: Anne Dufourmantelle Invites Jacques Derrida to Respond*; tr. by Rachel Bowlby (Stanford, Calif.: Stanford University Press, 2000).

Demeure – Maurice Blanchot (Paris: Galilée); 'Demeure: fiction and testimony', included with Maurice Blanchot, *The Instant of My Death*, tr. by Elizabeth Rottenberg (Stanford, Calif.: Stanford University Press, 2000).

Voiles, with Hélène Cixous (Paris: Galilée); Cixous and Derrida, *Veils*, tr. by Geoffrey Bennington; with drawings by Ernest Pignon-Ernest (Stanford, Calif.: Stanford University Press, 2001).

1999

Donner la mort (Paris: Galilée); *The Gift of Death; and Literature in Secret*, tr. by David Wills (Chicago; London: University of Chicago Press, 2008).

Sur parole: Instantanés philosophiques (Paris: Éditions de l'Aube/ France-Culture).

La contre-allée: Voyager avec Jacques Derrida, by Catherine Malabou and Jacques Derrida (Paris: La Quinzaine littéraire/ Louis Vuitton); Malabou and Derrida, *Counterpath: Travelling with Jacques Derrida*, tr. by David Wills (Stanford, Calif.: Stanford University Press, 2004).

2000

États d'âme de le psychanalyse (Paris: Galilée)

Foi et savoir (Paris: Seuil)

Le toucher: Jean-Luc Nancy (Paris: Galilée); *On Touching: Jean-Luc Nancy*, tr. by Christine Irizarry (Stanford, Calif.: Stanford University Press, 2005).

Tourner les mots: Au bord d'un film, with Safaa Fathy (Paris: Galilée/Arte editions).

2001

'Une certaine possibilité impossible', in *Dire l'événement, est-ce possible?*, seminar in Montréal (Paris: L'Harmattan); 'A certain impossible possibility of saying the event', tr. by Gila Walker, *Critical Inquiry* vol. 33 (2007), pp. 441–61.

'De la couleur à la lettre', in *Atlan grand format* (Paris: Gallimard).

'La forme et la façon', preface to Alain David, *Racisme et antisémitisme* (Paris: Ellipses).

Papier Machine (Paris: Galilée); *Paper Machine*, tr. by Rachel Bowlby (Stanford, Calif.: Stanford University Press, 2005).

L'Université sans condition (Paris: Galilée); 'The future of the humanities or the university without condition (thanks to the "Humanities", what *could take place* tomorrow)', in Tom Cohen, ed., *Jacques Derrida and the Humanities: A Critical Reader* (Cambridge University Press, 2002).

'La veilleuse', preface to Jacques Trilling, *James Joyce ou l'Écriture matricide* (Paris: Circé).

La connaissance des textes: Lecture d'un manuscript illisible, with Simon Hantaï and Jean-Luc Nancy (Paris: Galilée).

De quoi demain . . ., dialogue with Élisabeth Roudinesco (Paris: Fayard/Galilée); Derrida and Roudinesco, *For What Tomorrow . . .: A Dialogue*, tr. by Jeff Fort (Stanford, Calif.: Stanford University Press, 2004).

'Tête-à-tête', in *Camilla Adami* (Edizioni Gabriele Mazzotta).

2002

Artaud le Moma (Paris: Galilée).

Fichus (Paris: Galilée). '*Fichus*: Frankfurt Address', in *Paper Machine* (see **2001**).

H.C. pour la vie, c'est à dire (Paris: Galilée); *H.C. for Life, That is to Say*, tr. with additional notes by Laurent Milesi and Stefan Herbrechter (Sanford, Calif.: Stanford University Press, 2006).

Marx & Sons (Presses Universitaires de France/Galilée); 'Marx & Sons', in Michael Spinker, ed., *Ghostly Demarcations: A Symposium on Jacques Derrida's 'Specters of Marx'* (London: Verso, 1999).

Au-delà des apparences, interview with Antoine Spire (Paris: Le Bord de l'eau).

2003

Béliers. Le dialogue ininterrompu: entre deux infinis, le poème (Paris: Galilée); 'Rams: Uninterrupted dialogue: Between two infinities, the poem', in Derrida, *Sovereignties in Question: The Poetics of Paul Celan*, ed. by Thomas Dutoit and Outi Pasanen (New York: Fordham University Press, 2005).

Chaque fois unique: La fin du monde (Paris: Galilée); *The Work of Mourning*, ed. by Pascale-Anne Brault and Michael Naas (Chicago; London: University of Chicago Press, 2003).

Genèses, genealogies, genres et le génie (Paris: Galilée); *Geneses, Genealogies, Genres, and Genius*, tr. by Beverley Bie Brahic (New York: Columbia University Press, 2006).

Voyous (Paris: Galilée); *Rogues: Two Essays on Reason*, tr. by Pascale-Anne Brault and Michael Naas (Stanford, Calif.: Stanford University Press, 2005).

2004

Le 'concept' du 11 septembre, with Jürgen Habermas (Paris: Galilée); *Philosophy in a Time of Terror: Dialogues with Jürgen Habermas and Jacques Derrida*, interviewed by Giovanna Borradori (Chicago; London: University of Chicago Press, 2003).

'Le lieu-dit: Strasbourg', in *Penser à Strasbourg* (Paris: Galilée).

Prégnances. Lavis de Colette Deblé. Peintures (Paris: L'Atelier des brisants).

2005

Apprendre à vivre enfin, with Jean Birnbaum (Paris: Galilée); *Learning to Live Finally: The Last Interview. An Interview with Jean Birnbaum* (Basingstoke: Palgrave Macmillan, 2007).

Déplier Ponge: Entretien avec Gérard Farasse (Presses Universitaires du Septentrion).

2006

L'animal que donc je suis (Paris: Galilée); *The Animal That Therefore I Am*, ed. by Marie-Louise Mallet; tr. by David Wills (New York: Fordham University Press, 2008).

'Le sacrifice', postface to Daniel Mesguich, *L'Éternel Éphémère* (Paris: Verdier).

'En composant "Circonfession"', in *Des Confessions: Jacques Derrida et Saint Augustin* (Paris: Stock).

2008

Séminaire La bête et le souverain, vol. 1 (Paris: Galilée); *The Beast & the Sovereign*, vol. 1, ed. by Michel Lisse, Marie-Louise Mallet, and Ginette Michaud; tr. by Geoffrey Bennington (Chicago: University of Chicago Press, 2009).

2009
Demeure, Athènes, with photographs by Jean-François Bonhomme (Paris: Galilée); *Athens, Still Remains: The Photographs of Jean-François Bonhomme,* tr. by Pascale-Anne Brault and Michael Naas (New York: Fordham University Press, 2010).

2010
Séminaire La bête et le souverain, vol. 2 (Paris: Galilée); *The Beast & the Sovereign,* vol. 2, ed. by Michel Lisse, Marie-Louise Mallet, and Ginette Michaud; tr. by Geoffrey Bennington (Chicago: University of Chicago Press, 2011).

Index